Programming with Microsoft®

Visual Basic® .NET
Second Edition

Diane Zak

THOMSON

COURSE TECHNOLOGY

Australia • Canada • Mexico • Singapore • Spain • United Kingdom • United States

THOMSON

COURSE TECHNOLOGY

Programming with Microsoft Visual Basic .NET, Second Edition

by Diane Zak

Executive Editor:
Mac Mendelsohn

Associate Product Manager:
Sarah Santoro

Cover Designer:
Abby Scholz

Managing Editor:
William Pitkin III

Marketing Manager:
Brian Berkeley

Compositor:
Gex Publishing Services

Senior Acquisitions Editor:
Drew Strawbridge

Editorial Assistant:
Jennifer Smith

Manufacturing Coordinator:
Laura Burns

Senior Product Manager:
Tricia Boyle

Production Editor:
Daphne Barbas

Disclaimer
Course Technology reserves the right to revise this publication and make changes from time to time in its content without notice.

ISBN 0-619-21718-9 [Student Edition]

ISBN 0-619-21729-4 [Instructor Edition]

Preface

Programming with Microsoft Visual Basic .NET, Second Edition is designed for a beginning programming course. This book uses Visual Basic .NET (version 2003), an object-oriented language, to teach programming concepts. This book capitalizes on the energy and enthusiasm students naturally have for Windows-based applications and clearly teaches students how to take full advantage of the power of Visual Basic .NET. It assumes students have learned basic Windows skills and file management from one of Course Technology's other books covering the Microsoft Windows operating system.

Organization and Coverage

Programming with Microsoft Visual Basic .NET, Second Edition contains an Overview and twelve chapters that present hands-on instruction, as well as three appendices. In the chapters, students with no previous programming experience learn how to plan and create their own interactive Windows applications. Using this book, students will be able to master more advanced tasks sooner than they would using other introductory texts; a perusal of the Table of Contents affirms this. By the end of the book, students will have learned how to work with controls and write If...Then...Else, Select Case, Do...Loop, and For...Next statements, as well as how to create and manipulate variables, constants, sequential access files, structures, and arrays. Students also will learn how to manipulate strings and include multiple forms in a project. GUI design skills are emphasized and advanced skills such as creating and printing reports, creating classes, and accessing information in a database using a Windows form and a Web form are taught. The text also introduces students to object-oriented programming concepts and terminology.

Approach

Programming with Microsoft Visual Basic .NET, Second Edition distinguishes itself from other Windows textbooks because of its unique two-pronged approach. First, it motivates students by demonstrating why they need to learn the concepts and skills. This book teaches programming concepts using a task-driven rather than a command-driven approach. By working through the chapters—which are each motivated by a realistic case—students learn how to use programming applications they are likely to encounter in the workplace. This is much more effective than memorizing a list of commands out of context. Second, the content, organization, and pedagogy of this book exploit the Windows environment. The material presented in the chapters capitalizes on the power of Visual Basic .NET to perform complex programming tasks earlier and more easily than was possible under DOS.

Features

Programming with Microsoft Visual Basic .NET, Second Edition is an exceptional textbook because it also includes the following features:

- **"Read This Before You Begin" Section** This section is consistent with Course Technology's unequaled commitment to helping instructors introduce technology into the classroom. Technical considerations and assumptions about hardware, software, and default settings are listed in one place to help instructors save time and eliminate unnecessary aggravation.

New!

- **Naming Conventions** For many years, most Visual Basic programmers used a form of Hungarian Notation when naming objects and variables. With the introduction of .NET, however, a new naming convention for objects and variables has emerged. Form names now begin with the form's purpose followed by the word "Form" and are entered using Pascal case, as in CopyrightForm. Control names are now made up of the control's purpose followed by its type. Additionally, it is recommended that control names begin with the lowercase letters "ui", which stand for "user interface." Beginning all control names with "ui" assures that the names are listed together when using the IntelliSense feature in the Code Editor window, making coding easier. The convention is to enter control names using camel case—for example, uiExitButton. The names of variables also should be entered using camel case. Microsoft recommends that the variable's name indicate only the variable's purpose, rather than its data type and purpose, as in previous versions of Visual Basic. This is because the data types used in the various .NET languages are simply aliases for the data types in the .NET Framework. For example, the Integer data type in Visual Basic .NET is an alias for the Int32 data type in the .NET Framework. Using the new naming convention, a variable that stores a sales amount might be named `sales` or `salesAmount`. To ascertain a variable's data type, you need to simply hover your mouse pointer over the variable's name in the Code Editor window.

New!

- **.NET Methods** The book focuses on .NET methods rather than on Visual Basic functions. This is because the .NET methods can be used in any .NET language, whereas the Visual Basic functions can be used only in Visual Basic .NET. The only exception to this is the Val and Format functions, which are introduced in Chapter 2. These functions are covered in the book simply because it is likely that students will encounter them in existing Visual Basic programs. However, in Chapter 3, the student is taught to use the .NET Parse method and the .NET Convert class methods rather than the Val function. In Chapter 4, the Format function is replaced with the .NET ToString method.

New!

- **Option Statements** All programs now include the `Option Explicit On` and `Option Strict On` statements.

New!

- **Error Trapping** In Chapter 4, students are taught how to use a Try/Catch block to trap program errors.

New!

- **Figures** Figures that introduce new statements, functions, or methods now contain the syntax as well as examples of using the syntax. Including the syntax in the figures makes the examples more meaningful.

New!

- **Comments** Projects now contain comments that indicate the project's name and purpose, as well as the programmer's name and the date the project was either created or modified.

- **Chapter Cases** Each chapter begins with a programming-related problem that students could reasonably expect to encounter in business, followed by a demonstration of an application that could be used to solve the problem. Showing the students the completed application before they learn how to create it is motivational and instructionally sound. By allowing the students to see the type of application they will be able to create after completing the chapter, the students will be more motivated to learn because they can see how the programming concepts they are about to learn can be used and, therefore, why the concepts are important.

- **Lessons** Each chapter is divided into three lessons—A, B, and C. Lesson A introduces the programming concepts that will be used in the completed application. In Lessons B and C, the student creates the application required to solve the problem specified in the Chapter Case.

New!
- **Lesson A** The tutorial-style steps have been removed from Lesson A in all chapters except Chapter 1, which introduces the Visual Studio .NET 2003 IDE. Lesson A now contains only programming concepts, which are illustrated with code examples. In many lessons, a sample run of the application associated with the code is provided. Removing the tutorial-style steps from the lesson allows professors and students to concentrate on the programming concepts being taught.

New!
- **Chapters 11 and 12** *Programming with Microsoft Visual Basic .NET, Second Edition* contains two new chapters.
    - Chapter 11 shows students how to create classes and then instantiate objects from those classes.
    - Chapter 12 teaches how to use ADO.NET to access the information contained in a database, and use ASP.NET to create a Web page.

New!
- **Appendices B and C** *Programming with Microsoft Visual Basic .NET, Second Edition* contains two new appendices.
    - Appendix B summarizes the GUI design tips taught in the chapters, making it easier for the student to follow the guidelines when designing an application's interface.
    - Appendix C shows how to create a report using Crystal Reports.

- **Random Access Files Chapter** A chapter on Random Access Files is available online in PDF format. You can access this chapter on the Course Technology Web site by going to **http://www.course.com**, and then searching for this book by title or ISBN. The chapter is password protected.

HELP?
- **Help?** These notes anticipate the problems students are likely to encounter and help them resolve these problems on their own. This feature facilitates independent learning and frees the instructor to focus on substantive conceptual issues rather than on common procedural errors.

- **Tip** These notes provide additional information about a procedure—for example, an alternative method of performing the procedure. They also relate the OOP terminology learned in the Overview to applications created in Visual Basic .NET.

- **GUI Design Tips** GUI Design Tips contain guidelines and recommendations for designing applications that follow Windows standards. Appendix B provides a summary of the GUI design guidelines covered in the chapters.

- **Summary** Following each lesson is a Summary, which recaps the programming concepts, commands, and objects covered in the lesson.

- **Questions and Exercises** Each lesson concludes with meaningful, conceptual Questions that test students' understanding of what they learned in the lesson. The Questions are followed by Exercises, which provide students with additional practice of the skills and concepts they learned in the lesson.

discovery ▶ • Discovery Exercises The Windows environment allows students to learn by exploring and discovering what they can do. The Discovery Exercises are designated by the word "discovery" in the margin. They encourage students to challenge and independently develop their own programming skills while exploring the capabilities of Visual Basic .NET.

debugging • Debugging Exercises One of the most important programming skills a student can learn is the ability to find and fix problems in an existing application. The Debugging Exercises are designated by the word "debugging" in the margin and provide an opportunity for students to detect and correct errors in an existing application.

Teaching Tools

The following supplemental materials are available when this book is used in a classroom setting. All of the teaching tools available with this book are provided to the instructor on a single CD-ROM. Most are also available (password protected) at the Course Technology Web site—**www.course.com.**

Electronic Instructor's Manual The Instructor's Manual that accompanies this textbook includes additional instructional material to assist in class preparation, including items such as Sample Syllabi, Chapter Outlines, Technical Notes, Lecture Notes, Quick Quizzes, Teaching Tips, Discussion Topics, and Key Terms.

ExamView® This textbook is accompanied by ExamView, a powerful testing software package that allows instructors to create and administer printed, computer (LAN-based), and Internet exams. ExamView includes hundreds of questions that correspond to the topics covered in this text, enabling students to generate detailed study guides that include page references for further review. The computer-based and Internet testing components allow students to take exams at their computers, and also save the instructor time by grading each exam automatically.

PowerPoint Presentations This book offers Microsoft PowerPoint slides for each chapter. These are included as a teaching aid for classroom presentation, to make available to students on the network for chapter review, or to be printed for classroom distribution. Instructors can add their own slides for additional topics they introduce to the class.

Data Files Data Files to accompany this text contain all of the data necessary for steps within the chapters and the end-of-lesson Exercises. Both students and instructors should have access to these, so they are not password protected.

Solution Files Solutions to end-of-lesson Questions and Exercises are also provided. The solutions are password protected.

Distance Learning Course Technology is proud to present online courses in WebCT and Blackboard, to provide the most complete and dynamic learning experience possible. When you add online content to one of your courses, you're adding a lot: self tests, links, glossaries, and, most of all, a gateway to the 21st century's most important information resource. We hope you will make the most of your course, both online and offline. For more information on how to bring distance learning to your course, contact your local Course Technology sales representative.

Acknowledgments

Writing a book is a team effort rather than an individual one. I would like to take this opportunity to thank my team, especially Tricia Boyle (Senior Product Manager) and Daphne Barbas (Production Editor). Thank you for your support, enthusiasm, patience, and hard work. I could not have completed this project without the two of you. I also want to thank Serge Palladino (Quality Assurance) for his thoroughness. Last, but certainly not least, I want to thank the following reviewers for their invaluable ideas and comments: James Ball, Indiana State University, and Michael Danchak, Rensselaer Polytechnic Institute.

Diane Zak

Brief Contents

Contents

chapter 2

DESIGNING APPLICATIONS 77

c h a p t e r 3

USING VARIABLES AND CONSTANTS 145

c h a p t e r   4

THE SELECTION STRUCTURE *209*

chapter 8

MANIPULATING STRINGS 461

chapter 11

CLASSES AND OBJECTS 631

Please visit www.course.com for a chapter covering Random Access Files.

FOR MORE INFORMATION ON HOW TO ACCESS THIS CHAPTER, GO TO FEATURES IN THE PREFACE OF THIS BOOK.

Read This Before You Begin

To the User

Data Files

To complete the steps and exercises, you will need data files that have been created for this book. Your instructor may provide the data files to you. You also can obtain the files electronically from the Course Technology Web site by going to **http://www.course.com**, and then searching for this book by title or ISBN.

Each chapter in this book has its own set of data files, which are stored in a separate folder within the VBNET folder. For example, the files for Chapter 1 are stored in the VBNET\Chap01 folder. Similarly, the files for Chapter 2 are stored in the VBNET\Chap02 folder. Throughout this book, you will be instructed to open files from or save files to these folders.

You can use a computer in your school lab or your own computer to complete the material in this book.

Using Your Own Computer

To use your own computer to complete the material in this book, you will need the following:

- **A 486-level or higher personal computer running Microsoft Windows.** This book was written and Quality Assurance tested using Microsoft Windows XP.

- **Microsoft Visual Studio .NET 2003 Professional Edition or Enterprise Edition, or Microsoft Visual Basic .NET 2003 Standard Edition must be installed on your computer.** This book was written using Microsoft Visual Studio .NET 2003 Professional Edition and Quality Assurance tested using Microsoft Visual Basic .NET 2003 Standard Edition. If you purchased a copy of the text, then you also received Microsoft Visual Basic .NET 2003 Standard Edition contained on a set of 6 CD-ROMs.

- **Data files.** You will not be able to complete the material in this book using your own computer unless you have the data files. You may get the data files from your instructor, or you may obtain the data files from the Course Technology Web site by going to **http://www.course.com**, and then searching for this book by title or ISBN.

Figures

Many of the figures in this book reflect how your screen will look if you are using a Microsoft Windows XP system. Your screen may appear slightly different in some instances if you are using another version of Microsoft Windows.

Visit Our World Wide Web Site

Additional materials might be available for your course on the Web. Visit the Course Technology Web site—**www.course.com**—and periodically search this site for more details.

To the Instructor

To complete the materials, your students must use a set of data files. These files are included on the Teaching Tools CD. They also may be obtained electronically through the Course Technology Web site at **http://www.course.com**. Follow the instructions in the Help file to copy the data files to your server or standalone computer. You can view the Help file using a text editor such as WordPad or Notepad. Once the files are copied, you should instruct your students how to copy the files to their own computers or workstations.

The material in this book was Quality Assurance tested using Microsoft Visual Basic .NET 2003 Standard Edition on a Microsoft Windows XP system.

Course Technology Data Files

You are granted a license to copy the data files to any computer or computer network used by individuals who have purchased this book.

An Overview of Programming

A History and a Demonstration of Visual Basic .NET

Programmers

Although computers appear to be amazingly intelligent machines, they cannot yet think on their own. Computers still rely on human beings to give them directions. These directions are called **programs**, and the people who write the programs are called **programmers**. Programmers make it possible for us to communicate with our personal computers; without them, we wouldn't be able to use the computer to write a letter or play a game.

Typical tasks performed by a computer programmer include analyzing a problem statement or project specification, planning an appropriate solution, and converting the solution to a language that the computer can understand. According to the career Web site *WetFeet.com*, successful programmers are analytical thinkers; they are able to approach a problem in many different ways and identify the strengths and weaknesses of each approach. Patience, strong writing and communication skills, and the ability to work well in a team are also important characteristics of successful programmers. "The most successful programmers are not only competent code writers, but well liked among their peers."

The U.S. Department of Labor's Bureau of Labor Statistics ranks computer programming as the fastest growing occupation between the years 2000 and 2010: the number of jobs is expected to increase from 380,000 to 760,000. Depending on geographical location, the median salary of programmers ranges from $46,000 to $81,000.

A Brief History of Programming Languages

Just as human beings communicate with each other through the use of languages such as English, Spanish, Hindi, and Chinese, programmers use a variety of special languages, called **programming languages**, to communicate with the computer. Some popular programming languages are Visual Basic .NET, Visual C# .NET, C++, Visual C++ .NET, Java, Perl (Practical Extraction and Report Language), C, and COBOL (Common Business Oriented Language). In the next sections, you follow the progression of programming languages from machine languages to assembly languages, and then to high-level languages.

Machine Languages

Within a computer, all data is represented by microscopic electronic switches that can be either off or on. The off switch is designated by a 0, and the on switch is designated by a 1. Because computers can understand only these on and off switches, the first programmers had to write the program instructions using nothing but combinations of 0s and 1s; for example, a program might contain the instruction 00101 10001 10000. Instructions written in 0s and 1s are called **machine language** or **machine code**. The machine languages (each type of machine has its own language) represent the only way to communicate directly with the computer. As you can imagine, programming in machine language is very tedious and error-prone and requires highly trained programmers.

Assembly Languages

Slightly more advanced programming languages are called **assembly languages**. The assembly languages simplify the programmer's job by allowing the programmer to use mnemonics in place of the 0s and 1s in the program. **Mnemonics** are memory aids—in this case, alphabetic abbreviations for instructions. For example, most assembly languages use the mnemonic ADD to represent an add operation and the mnemonic MUL to represent a multiply operation. An example of an instruction written in an assembly language is MUL b1, ax.

Programs written in an assembly language require an **assembler**, which also is a program, to convert the assembly instructions into machine code—the 0s and 1s the computer can understand. Although it is much easier to write programs in assembly language than in machine language, programming in assembly language still is tedious and requires highly trained programmers.

High-Level Languages

Because high-level languages are more machine-independent than are machine and assembly languages, programs written in a high-level language can be used on many different types of computers.

High-level languages represent the next major development in programming languages. High-level languages are a vast improvement over machine and assembly languages, because they allow the programmer to use instructions that more closely resemble the English language. An example of an instruction written in a high-level language is `grossPay = hours * rate`.

Programs written in a high-level language require either an interpreter or a compiler to convert the English-like instructions into the 0s and 1s the computer can understand. Like assemblers, both interpreters and compilers are separate programs. An **interpreter** translates the high-level instructions into machine code, line by line, as the program is running, whereas a **compiler** translates the entire program into machine code before running the program.

Like their predecessors, the first high-level languages were used to create procedure-oriented programs. When writing a **procedure-oriented program**, the programmer concentrates on the major tasks that the program needs to perform. A payroll program, for example, typically performs several major tasks, such as inputting the employee data, calculating the gross pay, calculating the taxes, calculating the net pay, and outputting a paycheck. The programmer must instruct the computer every step of the way, from the start of the task to its completion. In a procedure-oriented program, the programmer determines and controls the order in which the computer processes the instructions. In other words, the programmer must determine not only the proper instructions to give the computer, but the correct sequence of those instructions as well. Examples of high-level languages used to create procedure-oriented programs include COBOL, BASIC (Beginner's All-Purpose Symbolic Instruction Code), and C.

Recently, more advanced high-level languages have emerged; these languages are used to create object-oriented programs. Different from a procedure-oriented program, which focuses on the individual tasks the program must perform, an **object-oriented program** requires the programmer to focus on the objects that the program can use to accomplish its goal. The objects can take on many different forms. For example, programs written for the Windows environment typically use objects such as check boxes, list boxes, and buttons. A payroll program, on the other hand, might utilize objects found in the real world, such as a time card object, an employee object, and a check object. Because each object is viewed as an independent unit, an object can be used in more than one program, usually with little or no modification. A check object used in a payroll program, for example, also can be used in a sales revenue program (which receives checks from customers) and an accounts payable program (which issues checks to creditors). The ability to use an object for more than one purpose saves programming time and money—an advantage that contributes to the popularity of object-oriented programming. Examples of high-level languages used to create object-oriented programs include Visual Basic .NET, Java, C++, Visual C++ .NET, and Visual C# .NET.

In this book, you learn how to create object-oriented programs using the Visual Basic .NET language. Although you may have either heard or read that object-oriented programs are difficult to write, do not be intimidated. Admittedly, creating object-oriented programs does take some practice. However, you already are familiar with many of the concepts upon which object-oriented programming is based. Much of the anxiety of object-oriented programming stems from the terminology used when discussing it. Many of the terms are unfamiliar, because they typically are not used in everyday conversations. The next section will help to familiarize you with the terms used in discussions about object-oriented programming. Do not be concerned if you do not understand everything right away; you will see further explanations and examples of these terms throughout this book.

OOP Terminology

When discussing object-oriented programs, you will hear programmers use the terms OOP (pronounced like *loop*) and OOD (pronounced like *mood*). **OOP** is an acronym for object-oriented programming and simply means that you are using an object-oriented language to create a program that contains one or more objects. OOD, on the other hand, is an acronym for object-oriented design. Like top-down design, which is used to plan procedure-oriented programs, **OOD** also is a design methodology, but it is used to plan object-oriented programs. Unlike top-down design, which breaks up a problem into one or more tasks, OOD divides a problem into one or more objects.

An **object** is anything that can be seen, touched, or used; in other words, an object is nearly any *thing*. As mentioned earlier, the objects used in an object-oriented program can take on many different forms. The menus, check boxes, and buttons included in most Windows programs are objects. An object also can represent something encountered in real life—such as a wristwatch, a car, a credit card receipt, and an employee.

Every object has attributes and behaviors. The **attributes**, also called **properties**, are the characteristics that describe the object. When you tell someone that your wristwatch is a Farentino Model 35A, you are describing the watch (an object) in terms of some of its attributes—in this case, its maker and model number. A watch also has many other attributes, such as a crown, dial, hour hand, minute hand, and movement.

An object's **behaviors**, also called **methods**, are the operations (actions) that the object is capable of performing. A watch, for example, can keep track of the time. Some watches also can keep track of the date. Still others can illuminate their dials when a button on the watch is pushed.

You also will hear the term "class" in OOP discussions. A **class** is a pattern or blueprint used to create an object. Every object used in an object-oriented program comes from a class. A class contains—or, in OOP terms, it **encapsulates**—all of the attributes and behaviors that describe the object the class creates. The blueprint for the Farentino Model 35A watch, for example, encapsulates all of the watch's attributes and behaviors. Objects created from a class are referred to as **instances** of the class, and are said to be "instantiated" from the class. All Farentino Model 35A watches are instances of the Farentino Model 35A class.

"Abstraction" is another term used in OOP discussions. **Abstraction** refers to the hiding of the internal details of an object from the user; hiding the internal details helps prevent the user from making inadvertent changes to the object. The internal mechanism of a watch, for example, is enclosed (hidden) in a case to protect the mechanism from damage. Attributes and behaviors that are not **hidden** are said to be **exposed** to the user. Exposed on a Farentino Model 35A watch are the crown used to set the hour and minute hands, and the button used to illuminate the dial. The idea behind abstraction is to expose to the user only those attributes and behaviors that are necessary to use the object, and to hide everything else.

Another OOP term, **inheritance**, refers to the fact that you can create one class from another class. The new class, called the **derived class**, inherits the attributes and behaviors of the original class, called the **base class**. For example, the Farentino company might create a blueprint of the Model 35B watch from the blueprint of the Model 35A watch. The Model 35B blueprint (the derived class) will inherit all of the attributes and behaviors of the Model 35A blueprint (the base class), but it then can be modified to include an additional feature, such as an alarm.

The class itself is not an object; only an instance of the class is an object.

The term "encapsulate" means "to enclose in a capsule." In the context of OOP, the "capsule" is a class.

▶ You can use the acronym A PIE (Abstraction, Polymorphism, Inheritance, and Encapsulation) to remember some of the OOP terms.

Finally, you also will hear the term "polymorphism" in OOP discussions. **Polymorphism** is the object-oriented feature that allows the same instruction to be carried out differently depending on the object. For example, you open a door, but you also open an envelope, a jar, and your eyes. You can set the time, date, and alarm on a Farentino watch. Although the meaning of the verbs "open" and "set" are different in each case, you can understand each instruction because the combination of the verb and the object makes the instruction clear. Figure 1 uses the wristwatch example to illustrate most of the OOP terms discussed in this section.

Base class

A watch's attributes and behaviors are encapsulated into the blueprint. Some attributes and behaviors are hidden; some are exposed

Derived class inherits properties of base class

Objects—instances of a class

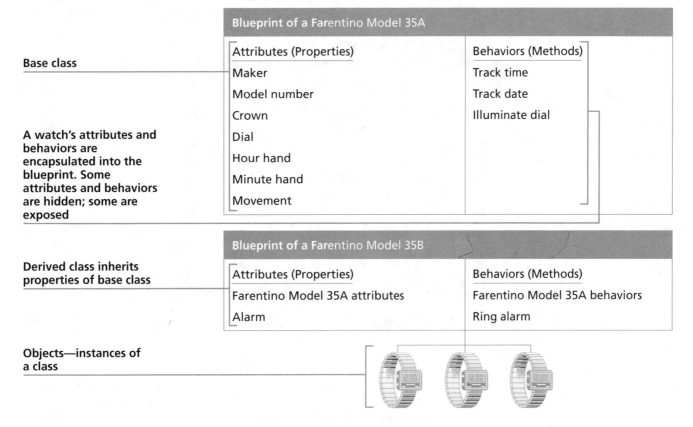

Figure 1: Illustration of OOP terms

In the next section, you run a Visual Basic .NET application that gives you a quick look at some of the objects you learn how to create in the following chapters.

A Visual Basic .NET Demonstration

The Visual Basic .NET application you are about to run shows you only some of the objects you learn how to create in the chapters. For now, it is not important for you to understand how these objects were created or why the objects perform the way they do. Those questions will be answered in the chapters.

To run the Visual Basic .NET application:

1   Click the **Start** button on the Windows taskbar, and then click **Run** on the Start menu to open the Run dialog box. Click the **Browse** button in the Run dialog box. The Browse dialog box opens.

2   Locate and then open the VBNET\Overview folder on your computer's hard disk. Click **MonthPay** (MonthPay.exe) in the list of filenames, and then click the **Open** button. The Browse dialog box closes and the Run dialog box appears again. Click the **OK** button. After a few moments, the Monthly Payment Calculator application shown in Figure 2 appears on the screen.

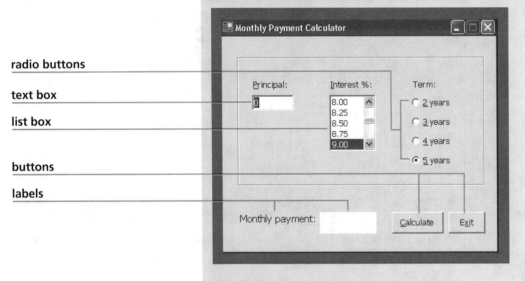

Figure 2: Monthly Payment Calculator application

Figure 2 identifies some of the different objects appearing in the application's interface. Notice that the interface contains a text box, a list box, buttons, radio buttons, and labels. You can use this application to calculate the monthly payment for a car loan. For example, determine the monthly payment for a $30,000 loan at 8% interest for five years.

To compute a monthly car payment:

1   Type **30000** in the Principal text box, and then click **8.00** in the Interest % list box. The radio button corresponding to the five-year term is already selected, so you just need to click the **Calculate** button to compute the monthly payment. The Monthly Payment Calculator application indicates that your monthly payment would be $608.29, as shown in Figure 3.

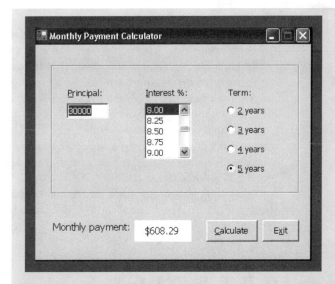

Figure 3: Computed monthly payment

Now determine what your monthly payment would be if you borrowed $10,000 at 7.25% interest for four years.

2 Type **10000** in the Principal text box.

3 Scroll up the Interest % list box until the 7.25 rate is visible, and then click **7.25**.

4 Click the **4 years** radio button, and then click the **Calculate** button to compute the monthly payment. The Monthly Payment Calculator application computes and displays the monthly payment of $240.62.

5 Click the **Exit** button to close the Monthly Payment Calculator application.

Using the Chapters Effectively

The chapters in this book will help you learn about Microsoft Visual Basic .NET. The chapters are designed to be used at your computer. Begin by reading the text that explains the concepts. Then when you come to the numbered steps, follow the steps on your computer. Read each step carefully and completely before you try it.

As you work, compare your screen with the figures to verify your results. Don't worry if your screen display differs slightly from the figures. The important parts of the screen display are labeled in each figure. Just be sure you have these parts on your screen. (The figures in this book reflect how your screen will look if you are using a Microsoft Windows XP system. Your screen may appear slightly different in some instances if you are using another version of Microsoft Windows.)

Do not worry about making mistakes; that's part of the learning process. Help? notes identify common problems and explain how to get back on track. You should complete the steps in the Help? notes only if you are having the problem described. Tip notes provide additional information about a procedure—for example, an alternative method of performing the procedure.

Each chapter is divided into three lessons. You might want to take a break between lessons. Following each lesson is a Summary section that lists the important elements of the lesson. After the Summary section are questions and exercises designed to review and reinforce that lesson's concepts. You should complete all of the end-of-lesson questions and exercises before going on to the next lesson. You cannot learn Visual Basic .NET without a lot of practice, and future chapters assume that you have mastered the information found in the previous chapters. Some of the end-of-lesson exercises are Discovery exercises, which allow you to both "discover" the solutions to problems on your own and experiment with material that is not covered in the chapter.

In each chapter you will find one or more Debugging exercises. In programming, the term **debugging** refers to the process of finding and fixing any errors in a program. Debugging exercises provide debugging tips and allow you to practice debugging applications.

Throughout the book you will find GUI (Graphical User Interface) design tips. These tips contain guidelines and recommendations for designing applications. You should follow these guidelines and recommendations so that your applications follow the Windows standard.

This book is designed for a beginning programming course; however, it assumes students have learned basic Windows skills and file management from one of Course Technology's other books that covers the Microsoft Windows operating system.

QUESTIONS

1. The set of directions given to a computer is called _____.
   a. computerese
   b. commands
   c. instructions
   d. a program
   e. rules

2. Instructions written in 0s and 1s are called _____.
   a. assembly language
   b. booleans
   c. computerese
   d. machine code
   e. mnemonics

3. _____ languages allow the programmer to use mnemonics, which are alphabetic abbreviations for instructions.
   a. Assembly
   b. High-level
   c. Machine
   d. Object
   e. Procedure

4. _____ languages allow the programmer to use instructions that more closely resemble the English language.
   a. Assembly
   b. High-level
   c. Machine
   d. Object
   e. Procedure

5. A(n) _____ translates high-level instructions into machine code, line by line, as the program is running.
   a. assembler
   b. compiler
   c. interpreter
   d. program
   e. translator

6. A(n) _____ translates the entire high-level program into machine code before running the program.
   a. assembler
   b. compiler
   c. interpreter
   d. program
   e. translator

7. A(n) _____ converts assembly instructions into machine code.
   a. assembler
   b. compiler
   c. interpreter
   d. program
   e. translator

8. In procedure-oriented programs, the emphasis is on the major tasks needed to accomplish the program's goal.
   a. True
   b. False

9. In object-oriented programs, the emphasis is on the objects needed to accomplish the program's goal.
   a. True
   b. False

10. A(n) _____ is a pattern or blueprint.
    a. attribute
    b. behavior
    c. class
    d. instance
    e. object

11. Which of the following is not an attribute that can be used to describe a human being?
    a. brown eyes
    b. female
    c. red hair
    d. talk
    e. thin

12. The object that you create from a class is called a(n) _____.
    a. abstraction
    b. attribute
    c. instance
    d. procedure
    e. subclass

13. In the context of OOP, the combining of an object's attributes and behaviors into one package is called _____.
    a. abstraction
    b. combining
    c. encapsulation
    d. inheritance
    e. polymorphism

14. In the context of OOP, the hiding of the internal details of an object from the user is called _____.
    a. abstraction
    b. combining
    c. encapsulation
    d. inheritance
    e. polymorphism

15. _____ is the OOP feature that allows the same instruction to be carried out differently depending on the object.
    a. Abstraction
    b. Combining
    c. Encapsulation
    d. Inheritance
    e. Polymorphism

16. Alcon Toys manufactures several versions of a basic doll. Assume that the basic doll is called Model A and the versions are called Models B, C, and D. In the context of OOP, the Model A doll is called the _____ class; the other dolls are called the _____ class.
    a. base, derived
    b. base, inherited
    c. derived, base
    d. exposed, hidden
    e. inherited, derived

17. In the context of OOP, _____ refers to the fact that you can create one class from another class.
    a. abstraction
    b. combining
    c. encapsulation
    d. exposition
    e. inheritance

18. Use Figure 4 to answer the following questions:

Dog class	
Head	Eat
Body	Run
Legs	Play
Heart	Walk
Lungs	Bark

Figure 4

    a. What are the attributes (data or properties) associated with a dog class?
    b. What are the behaviors associated with a dog class?
    c. How many instances (objects) of the dog class are shown in Figure 4?

An Introduction to Visual Basic .NET

Creating a Copyright Screen

case ▶ Interlocking Software Company, a small firm specializing in custom programs, hires you as a programmer trainee. In that capacity, you learn to write applications using Visual Basic .NET, Microsoft's newest version of the Visual Basic programming language.

On your second day of work, Chris Statton, the senior programmer at Interlocking Software, assigns you your first task: create a copyright screen. The copyright screen will serve as a splash screen for each custom application created by Interlocking Software. A **splash screen** is the first image that appears when an application is run. It is used to introduce the application and to hold the user's attention while the application is being read into the computer's memory. The copyright screen you create will identify the application's author and copyright year and include the Interlocking Software Company logo. Although this first task is small, creating the copyright screen will give you an opportunity to learn the fundamentals of Visual Basic .NET without having to worry about the design issues and programming concepts necessary for larger applications.

Previewing the Copyright Screen

Before starting the first lesson in this chapter, you preview a completed copyright screen. The copyright screen is stored in the VBNET\Chap01\Copy.exe file on your computer's hard disk.

To preview a completed copyright screen:

1. Click the **Start** button on the Windows taskbar, and then click **Run** on the Start menu. When the Run dialog box opens, click the **Browse** button. The Browse dialog box opens. Locate and then open the **VBNET\Chap01** folder.

2. Click **Copy** (Copy.exe) in the list of filenames. (Depending on how Windows is set up on your computer, you may see the .exe extension on the filename. If you do, click the Copy.exe filename.) Click the **Open** button. The Browse dialog box closes and the Run dialog box appears again.

3. Click the **OK** button in the Run dialog box. The copyright screen appears. The author's name and the copyright year appear on the copyright screen, as shown in Figure 1-1. Shortly thereafter, the copyright screen closes.

Figure 1-1: Copyright screen

In this chapter, you learn how to create your own copyright screen.

Chapter 1 is designed to help you get comfortable with the Visual Studio .NET integrated development environment. You also learn about the Visual Basic .NET language. Remember that each chapter contains three lessons. You should complete a lesson in full and do the end-of-lesson questions and exercises before moving on to the next lesson.

After completing this lesson, you will be able to:

- Start and customize Visual Studio.NET
- Create a Visual Studio .NET solution
- Add a Visual Basic .NET project to a solution
- Set the properties of an object
- Restore a property to its default setting
- Save a solution, project, and form
- Close a solution
- Open an existing solution

Creating a Windows-Based Application in Visual Basic .NET

Starting and Customizing Visual Studio .NET

Before you can use Visual Basic .NET to create your copyright screen, you must start Visual Studio .NET, which is Microsoft's newest integrated development environment. An **integrated development environment (IDE)** is an environment that contains all of the tools and features you need to create, run, and test your programs. For example, an IDE contains an editor for entering your program instructions, and a compiler for running and testing the program.

Included in Visual Studio .NET are the Visual Basic .NET, Visual C++ .NET, Visual C# .NET, and Visual J# .NET programming languages. You can use the languages available in Visual Studio .NET to create Windows-based or Web-based programs, referred to as **applications**. A **Windows-based application** has a Windows user interface and runs on a desktop computer. A **user interface** is what you see and interact with when using an application. Graphics programs, data-entry systems, and games are examples of Windows-based applications. A **Web-based application**, on the other hand, has a Web user interface and runs on a server. You access a Web-based application using your computer's browser. Examples of Web-based applications include e-commerce applications available on the Internet and employee handbook applications accessible on a company's intranet.

To start Visual Studio .NET 2003, which is the version of Visual Studio .NET used in this book:

1 Click the **Start** button on the Windows taskbar to open the Start menu.

2 Point to **All Programs**, then point to **Microsoft Visual Studio .NET 2003**, and then click **Microsoft Visual Studio .NET 2003**. The Microsoft Visual Studio .NET copyright screen appears momentarily, and then the Microsoft Development Environment window opens.

3 If the Start Page window is not open, click **Help** on the menu bar, and then click **Show Start Page**.

Notice that the Start Page window contains three tabs, which are labeled Projects, Online Resources, and My Profile. The Projects tab allows you to open a new or existing project, and also lists the names and dates of projects on which you have recently worked. The Online Resources tab provides online access to information about Visual Studio .NET. For example, you can use the Online Resources tab to search the MSDN (Microsoft Developer's Network) Online library, or to download the latest product updates and sample code. The My Profile tab allows you to customize various program settings in the IDE, such as the keyboard scheme, window layout, and help filter. A collection of customized preferences is called a profile. Visual Studio .NET provides a set of predefined profiles for your convenience. The steps and figures in this book assume you are using the Visual Studio Developer profile.

4 Click the **My Profile** tab on the Start Page window. The My Profile pane appears in the Start Page window, as shown in Figure 1-2. (Your screen might not look identical to Figure 1-2.)

My Profile tab

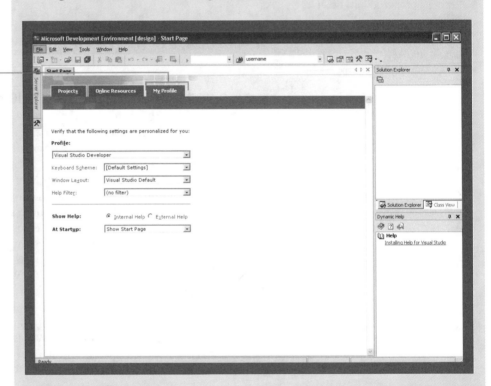

Figure 1-2: My Profile pane in the Start Page window

5 If necessary, click the **Profile** list arrow, and then click **Visual Studio Developer** in the list.

6 If necessary, change the Keyboard Scheme, Window Layout, Help Filter, and At Startup list box selections on your screen to match those shown in Figure 1-2.

7 If necessary, click the **Internal Help** radio button to select it. If the "Changes will not take effect until Visual Studio is restarted" message appears in a dialog box, click the **OK** button to close the dialog box.

8 Click the **Projects** tab on the Start Page window. The Projects pane appears in the Start Page window, as shown in Figure 1-3. (Do not be concerned if your Projects pane shows project names and dates.)

Solution Explorer window

Server Explorer window

Toolbox window

your Projects pane may show
project names and dates

Class View window

Dynamic Help window

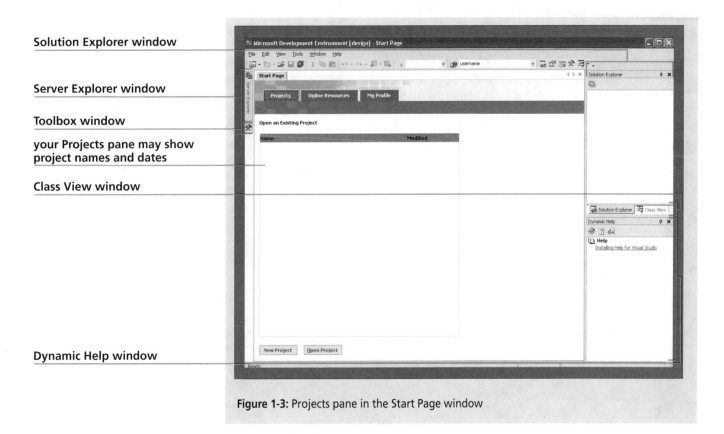

Figure 1-3: Projects pane in the Start Page window

As Figure 1-3 indicates, the Visual Studio .NET IDE contains five windows in addition to the Start Page window: Solution Explorer, Server Explorer, Toolbox, Class View, and Dynamic Help. Figure 1-4 briefly describes the purpose of each window in the IDE.

Window	Purpose
Class View	display the classes, methods, and properties included in a solution
Dynamic Help	display links to context-sensitive help
Server Explorer	display data connections and servers
Solution Explorer	display the names of projects and files included in a solution
Start Page	display the Projects, Online Resources, and My Profile panes
Toolbox	display items that you can use when creating a project

Figure 1-4: Purpose of the windows included in the IDE

You learn more about the Solution Explorer and Dynamic Help windows later in this lesson, and about the Toolbox window in Lesson B.

Recall that your task in this chapter is to create a simple application: a copyright screen. The copyright screen will be a Windows-based application, which means it will have a Windows user interface and run on a desktop computer.

Creating the Copyright Screen Application

Applications created in Visual Studio .NET are composed of solutions, projects, and files. You create an application by first creating a blank Visual Studio .NET solution, and then you add one or more projects to the solution. A **solution** is a container that stores the projects and files for an entire application. A **project** also is a container, but it stores files associated with only a specific piece of the solution. Although the idea of solutions, projects, and files may sound confusing, the concept of placing things in containers is nothing new to you. Think of a solution as being similar to a drawer in a filing cabinet. A project then is similar to a file folder that you store in the drawer, and a file is similar to a document that you store in the file folder. You can place many file folders in a filing cabinet drawer, just as you can place many projects in a solution. You also can store many documents in a file folder, similar to the way you can store many files in a project. Figure 1-5 illustrates this analogy.

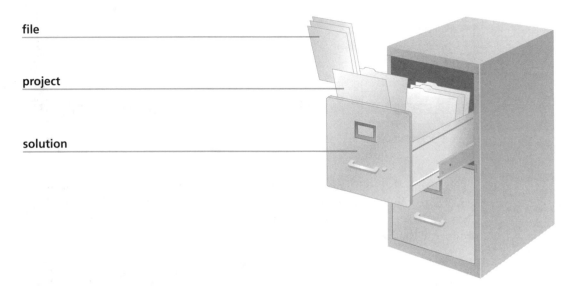

file

project

solution

Figure 1-5: Illustration of a solution, project, and file

You can create a blank Visual Studio .NET solution by clicking File on the menu bar, pointing to New, and then clicking Blank Solution.

To create a blank Visual Studio .NET solution:

1   Click **File** on the menu bar, point to **New**, and then click **Blank Solution**. The New Project dialog box opens with Visual Studio Solutions selected in the Project Types list box, and Blank Solution selected in the Templates list box. The message located below the Project Types list box indicates that the Blank Solution template creates an empty solution containing no projects.

A **template** is simply a pattern that Visual Studio .NET uses to create solutions and projects. Each template listed in the Templates list box includes a set of standard folders and files appropriate for the solution or project. The Blank Solution template, for example, contains one folder and two files. The folder and files are automatically created on your computer's hard disk when you click the OK button in the New Project dialog box.

2   Change the name entered in the Name text box to **Copyright Solution**. If necessary, use the Browse button, which appears to the right of the Location text box, to open the **VBNET\Chap01** folder on your computer's hard disk. Figure 1-6 shows the completed New Project dialog box.

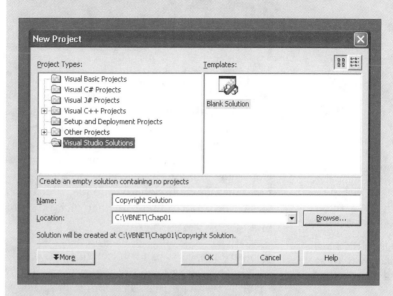

Figure 1-6: New Project dialog box used to create a blank solution

HELP?   If the More button is not displayed, click the Less button.

Notice that the message "Solution will be created at C:\VBNET\Chap01\Copyright Solution." appears above the More button in the dialog box.

3   Click the **OK** button to close the New Project dialog box. Visual Studio .NET creates a blank solution on your computer's hard disk. It also records in the Solution Explorer window the solution's name (Copyright Solution) and the number of projects contained in the solution (0 projects). See Figure 1-7.

Figure 1-7: Solution Explorer window showing the name of a blank solution

HELP?   If the Solution Explorer window does not appear in the IDE, click View on the menu bar, and then click Solution Explorer.

When a solution's name appears in the Solution Explorer window, it indicates that the solution is open and ready for you to add information to it. (You also can delete information from a solution.)

tip

> To view the names of hidden files, open the My Computer window, then click Tools on the menu bar, and then click Folder Options. When the Folder Options dialog box appears, click the View tab, then click the Show hidden files and folders radio button to select it, and then click the OK button.

Recall that when you use the Blank Solution template to create a solution, Visual Studio .NET automatically creates one folder and two files on your computer's hard disk. The folder has the same name as the solution; in this case, the folder is named Copyright Solution. The two files, which are stored in the folder, also bear the solution's name. However, one file has .sln (which stands for "solution") as its filename extension, and the other has .suo (which stands for "solution user options"). The Copyright Solution.sln file keeps track of the projects and files included in the solution. The Copyright Solution.suo file, which is a hidden file, records the options associated with your solution so that each time you open the solution, it includes any customizations you made.

After you create a blank solution, you then add one or more projects to it. The number of projects in a solution depends on the application you are creating. Most simple applications require one project only, while complex applications usually involve several projects. The copyright screen you are working on is a simple application and requires just one project, which you will create using Visual Basic .NET.

You can add a new project to the current solution by clicking File on the menu bar, pointing to Add Project, and then clicking New Project. You also can right-click the solution's name in the Solution Explorer window, point to Add, and then click New Project. Additionally, you can click the New Project button on the Projects pane in the Start Page window.

To add a new Visual Basic .NET project to the current solution:

1 Right-click **Solution 'Copyright Solution' (0 projects)** in the Solution Explorer window. Point to **Add** and then click **New Project**. The Add New Project dialog box opens.

The Project Types list box lists the various types of projects you can add to a solution.

2 If necessary, click **Visual Basic Projects** in the Project Types list box.

The Templates list box lists the project templates available in Visual Basic .NET.

3 If necessary, click **Windows Application** in the Templates list box. This is the appropriate template to use for the copyright screen application, because you want the application to have a Windows user interface.

4 Change the name in the Name text box to **Copyright Project**.

5 Verify that the Location text box contains the location of the Copyright Solution folder. The completed Add New Project dialog box is shown in Figure 1-8. Notice that the message "Project will be created at C:\VBNET\Chap01\Copyright Solution\Copyright Project." appears below the Location text box in the dialog box.

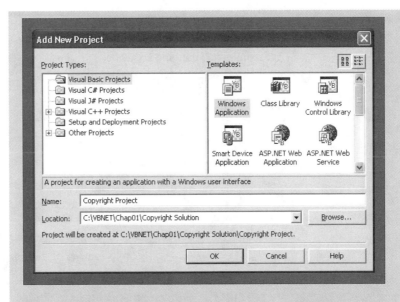

Figure 1-8: Completed Add New Project dialog box

As you learned earlier, a template contains a set of standard folders and files. The folders and files included in the Windows Application template are automatically created on your computer's hard disk when you click the OK button in the Add New Project dialog box.

6   Click the **OK** button to close the Add New Project dialog box. Visual Studio .NET adds a new Visual Basic .NET Windows Application project to the current solution. It also records the project's name (Copyright Project), as well as other information pertaining to the project, in the Solution Explorer window. See Figure 1-9.

project name

Auto Hide button

project information

Properties window

Windows Form Designer window

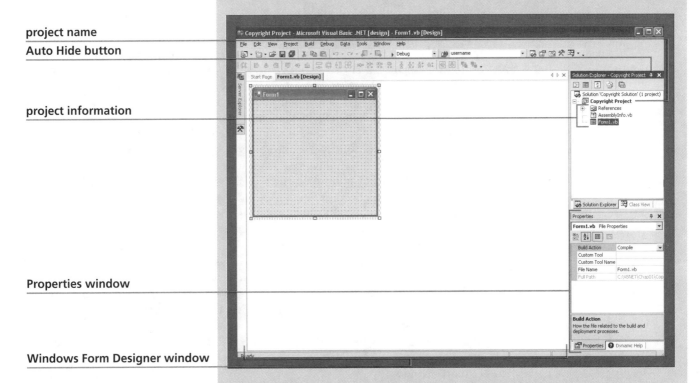

Figure 1-9: New Visual Basic .NET project added to the solution

HELP? If the Windows Form Designer window does not appear in the IDE, click Form1.vb in the Solution Explorer window, if necessary. Then click View on the menu bar, and then click Designer.

HELP? If the Output window appears in the IDE, click the Close button on its title bar.

HELP? If the Properties window does not appear in the IDE, click View on the menu bar, and then click Properties Window.

HELP? If a plus box appears next to the project name in the Solution Explorer window, click the plus box.

HELP? If a minus box appears next to the References folder in the Solution Explorer window, click the minus box.

HELP? If the Solution Explorer window displays more folders and files than are shown in Figure 1-9, click the Show All Files button on the Solution Explorer window's toolbar.

HELP? If a Misc row appears in the Properties window, click the Alphabetic button on the Properties window's toolbar.

Notice that, in addition to the six windows mentioned earlier, two new windows appear in the development environment: the Windows Form Designer window and the Properties window. Having eight windows open at the same time can be confusing, especially when you are first learning the IDE. In most cases, you will find it easier to work in the IDE if you either close or auto-hide the windows you are not currently using. In the next section, you learn how to manage the windows in the IDE.

Managing the Windows in the IDE

The easiest way to close an open window in the IDE is to click the Close button on the window's title bar. In most cases, the View menu provides an appropriate option for opening a closed window. To open the Toolbox window, for instance, you click View on the menu bar, and then click Toolbox on the menu. The options for opening the Start Page and Dynamic Help windows, however, are located on the Help menu rather than on the View menu.

You can use the Auto Hide button (see Figure 1-9) on a window's title bar to auto-hide a window. When you auto-hide a window and then move the mouse pointer away from the window, the window is minimized and appears as a tab on the edge of the IDE. Additionally, the vertical pushpin on the Auto Hide button is replaced by a horizontal pushpin, which indicates that the window is auto-hidden. The Server Explorer and Toolbox windows shown in Figure 1-9 are examples of auto-hidden windows.

To temporarily display a window that has been auto-hidden, you simply place your mouse pointer on the window's tab; doing so slides the window into view. You can permanently display an auto-hidden window by clicking the Auto Hide button on the window's title bar. When you do so, the horizontal pushpin on the button is replaced by a vertical pushpin, which indicates that the window is not auto-hidden.

In the next set of steps, you close the Server Explorer, Start Page, Class View, and Dynamic Help windows, because you will not need these windows to create the copyright screen. You also practice auto-hiding and displaying the Solution Explorer window.

To close some of the windows in the IDE, and then auto-hide and display the Solution Explorer window:

1 Place your mouse pointer on the **Server Explorer** tab. (The Server Explorer tab is usually located on the left edge of the IDE.) When the Server Explorer window slides into view, which may take several moments, click the **Close** button ☒ on its title bar.

Now close the Start Page and Class View windows.

2 Click the **Start Page** tab to make the Start Page window the active window, then click the **Close** button on its title bar.

3 Click the **Class View** tab to make the Class View window the active window, then click the **Close** button on its title bar.

You close the Dynamic Help window next. The **Dynamic Help window** is a context-sensitive system. As you are working in the IDE, the window is constantly being updated with links pertaining to whatever is appropriate for what you are doing at the time. An advantage of keeping the Dynamic Help window open is that it allows you to conveniently access help as you are working in the IDE. A disadvantage is that an open Dynamic Help window consumes computer memory and processor time, both of which are required to keep the window updated. In most instances, it is better to close the Dynamic Help window while you are working in the IDE.

4 Click the **Dynamic Help** tab to make the Dynamic Help window the active window, then click the **Close** button on its title bar.

Next, auto-hide the Solution Explorer window.

5 Click the **Auto Hide** button (the vertical pushpin) on the Solution Explorer window's title bar, then move the mouse pointer away from the window. The Solution Explorer window is minimized and appears as a tab on the right edge of the IDE.

HELP? If the Solution Explorer window remains on the screen when you move your mouse pointer away from the window, click another window's title bar.

Now temporarily display the Solution Explorer window.

6 Place your mouse pointer on the **Solution Explorer** tab. The Solution Explorer window slides into view. Notice that a horizontal pushpin now appears on the Auto Hide button.

7 Move your mouse pointer away from the Solution Explorer window. The window is minimized and appears as a tab again.

Next, use the Auto Hide button to permanently display the Solution Explorer window on the screen.

8 Place your mouse pointer on the **Solution Explorer** tab. When the Solution Explorer window slides into view, click the **Auto Hide** button (the horizontal pushpin) on its title bar. Notice that the horizontal pushpin on the button is replaced by a vertical pushpin.

9 Move your mouse pointer away from the Solution Explorer window. The window remains displayed on the screen. Figure 1-10 shows the current status of the windows in the development environment.

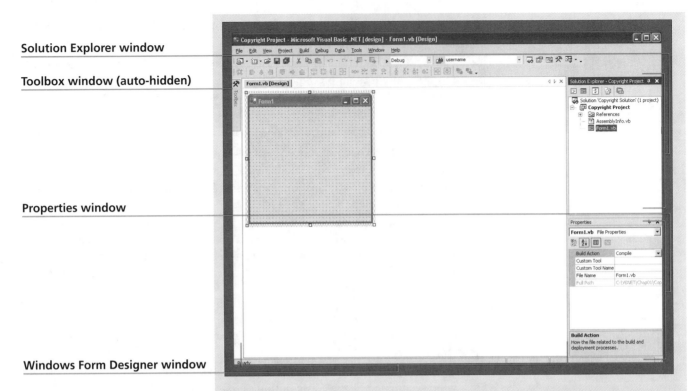

Solution Explorer window

Toolbox window (auto-hidden)

Properties window

Windows Form Designer window

Figure 1-10: Current status of the windows in the development environment

Notice that only four (rather than eight) windows are open: the Toolbox window (which is auto-hidden), the Windows Form Designer window, the Solution Explorer window, and the Properties window.

In the next several sections, you take a closer look at the Windows Form Designer, Solution Explorer, and Properties windows. (Recall that the Toolbox window is covered in Lesson B.)

The Windows Form Designer Window

Figure 1-11 shows the **Windows Form Designer window,** where you create (or design) the graphical user interface, referred to as a **GUI,** for your project. Recall that a user interface is what you see and interact with when using an application.

name of the disk file that contains the Windows Form object

title bar

Windows Form object

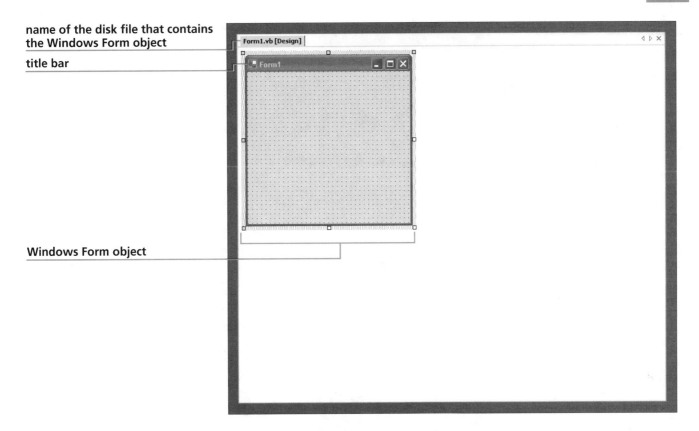

Figure 1-11: Windows Form Designer window

Currently, only a Windows Form object appears in the designer window. A **Windows Form object**, or **form**, is the foundation for the user interface in a Windows-based application. You create the user interface by adding other objects, such as buttons and text boxes, to the form. Dots are displayed in the form to assist you in aligning the objects. The dots will not be visible when you run the application.

Notice that a title bar appears at the top of the Windows Form object. The title bar contains a default caption—in this case, Form1—as well as Minimize, Maximize, and Close buttons.

At the top of the designer window is a tab labeled Form1.vb [Design]. [Design] simply identifies the window as the designer window. Form1.vb is the name of the file (on your computer's hard disk) that contains the Visual Basic .NET instructions required to create a Windows Form object. As you learned in the Overview, all objects in an object-oriented program come from—or, in OOP terms, are instances of—a class. The Windows Form object, for example, is an instance of the Windows Form class. The form object is automatically instantiated for you when you create a Windows-based application.

Next, take a closer look at the Solution Explorer window.

The Solution Explorer Window

The **Solution Explorer window** displays a list of the projects contained in the current solution, and the items contained in each project. Figure 1-12 shows the Solution Explorer window for the Copyright Solution.

tip

In addition to appearing on a tab in the designer window, the Form1.vb filename also appears in the Solution Explorer window and in the Properties window.

Figure 1-12: Solution Explorer window

The Solution Explorer window indicates that the Copyright Solution contains one project named Copyright Project. Within the Copyright Project is a References folder, which contains information needed by the project, and two files named AssemblyInfo.vb and Form1.vb. View the contents of the References folder.

To view the contents of the References folder:

1 Click the **plus box** next to the References folder. The contents of the References folder appear. See Figure 1-13.

Figure 1-13: Contents of the References folder

The References folder contains **references**, which are simply addresses of memory cells within the computer's internal memory; each reference points to a namespace. You can picture a namespace as a block of internal memory cells. A **namespace** contains the instructions that define a group of related classes. The System.Windows.Forms namespace, for instance, contains the definition of the Windows Form class, which is the class used to create—or, using OOP terminology, instantiate—a Windows Form object. When a project contains a reference to a namespace, it can use the classes that are defined in the namespace to create objects.

Recall that the Copyright Project also contains two files named AssemblyInfo.vb and Form1.vb. The .vb on both filenames indicates that the files are "Visual Basic" source files. A **source file** is a file that contains program instructions, called **code**. The AssemblyInfo.vb source file stores the code needed to deploy (install and configure) the project. Currently, the Form1.vb file contains the code that creates (instantiates) the Windows Form object displayed in the designer window. As you add objects (such as buttons and text boxes) to the form, the code to instantiate those objects is automatically added to the Form1.vb file. The file also will contain the Visual Basic .NET instructions you enter to tell the objects how to respond when they are clicked, double-clicked, scrolled, and so on. You enter the instructions in the Code Editor window, which you view in Lesson B.

In addition to the References folder and two source files, the Copyright Project contains other folders and files as well. Currently, the names of the additional folders and files are not displayed in the Solution Explorer window. You can display the names using the Show All Files button on the Solution Explorer window's toolbar.

To view the names of the additional folders and files contained in the current project:

1 Click the **Auto Hide** button on the Properties window's title bar, then move the mouse pointer away from the window. Auto-hiding the Properties window allows you to view more of the Solution Explorer window.

2 Click the **Show All Files** button on the Solution Explorer window's toolbar, then click any **plus boxes** in the window. See Figure 1-14.

Show All Files button

Figure 1-14: Additional folders and files displayed in the Solution Explorer window

The Show All Files button acts like a toggle switch: clicking it once turns the folder and file display on, and clicking it again turns the display off.

3 Click the **Show All Files** button to hide the names of the additional folders and files.

4 Click the **minus box** next to the References folder to hide the reference names.

5 Place your mouse pointer on the **Properties** tab. When the Properties window slides into view, click the **Auto Hide** button to display the window.

As you learned earlier, the code to create a Windows Form object is stored in a source file on your computer's hard disk. The source file is referred to as a **form file**, because it contains the code associated with the form. The code associated with the first Windows Form object included in a project is automatically stored in a form file named Form1.vb. The code associated with the second Windows Form object in the same project is stored in a form file named Form2.vb, and so on. Because a project can contain many Windows Form objects and, therefore, many form files, it is a good practice to give each form file a more meaningful name; this will help you keep track of the various form files in the project. You can use the Properties window to change the filename.

The Properties Window

As is everything in an object-oriented language, a form file is an object. Each object has a set of attributes that determine its appearance and behavior. The attributes, called **properties**, are listed in the **Properties window**. In the context of OOP, the Properties window exposes the object's properties to the programmer.

When an object is created, a default value is assigned to each of its properties. The Properties window shown in Figure 1-15, for example, lists the default values assigned to the properties of the Form1.vb file contained in the Copyright Project.

Object box

Properties list

Settings box

Description pane

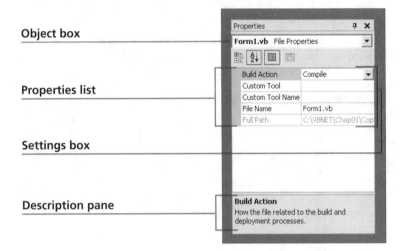

Figure 1-15: Properties window showing the properties of the Form1.vb file object

As indicated in Figure 1-15, the Properties window includes an Object box and a Properties list. The Object box is located immediately below the Properties window's title bar. The **Object box** contains the name of the selected object; in this case, it contains Form1.vb, which is the name of the form file object selected in the Solution Explorer window. When an object is selected, its properties appear in the Properties window.

The **Properties list** has two columns. The left column displays the names of the properties associated with the selected object. You can use the Alphabetic or Categorized buttons, which are located below the Object box, to display the property names either alphabetically or by category. The right column in the Properties list is called the **Settings box** and displays the current value, or setting, of each of the properties. For example, the current value of the Build Action property shown in Figure 1-15 is Compile. Notice that a brief description of the selected property appears in the Description pane located at the bottom of the Properties window.

Depending on the property, you can change the default value by selecting the property in the Properties list, and then either typing a new value in the Settings box or selecting a predefined value from a list or dialog box. For example, to change the value of the File Name property, you click File Name in the Properties list and then type the new filename in the Settings box. However, to change the value of the Build Action property, you click Build Action in the Properties list, then click the list arrow button in the Settings box, and then click one of the predefined settings that appears in a drop-down list.

tip

You also can change the File Name property by right-clicking Form1.vb in the Solution Explorer window, and then clicking Rename on the context menu.

Use the Properties window to change the name of the form file object from Form1.vb to Copyright Form.vb.

It is easy to confuse the Windows Form object with the form file object. The Windows Form object is the form itself. A Windows Form object can be viewed in the designer window and appears on the screen when the application is running. The form file object, on the other hand, is the disk file that contains the code to create the Windows Form object.

To change the name of the form file object:

1 Verify that Form1.vb File Properties appears in the Object box in the Properties window.

   HELP? If Form1.vb File Properties does not appear in the Object box, click Form1.vb in the Solution Explorer window.

2 Click **File Name** in the Properties list. The Description pane indicates that the File Name property is used to set the name of the file or folder.

   HELP? If the Description pane is not displayed in the Properties window, right-click anywhere on the Properties window (except on the title bar), and then click Description on the context menu.

3 Type **Copyright Form.vb** and press **Enter**. (Be sure to include the .vb extension on the filename; otherwise, Visual Basic .NET will not recognize the file as a source file.) Copyright Form.vb appears in the Solution Explorer and Properties windows and on the designer window's tab, as shown in Figure 1-16.

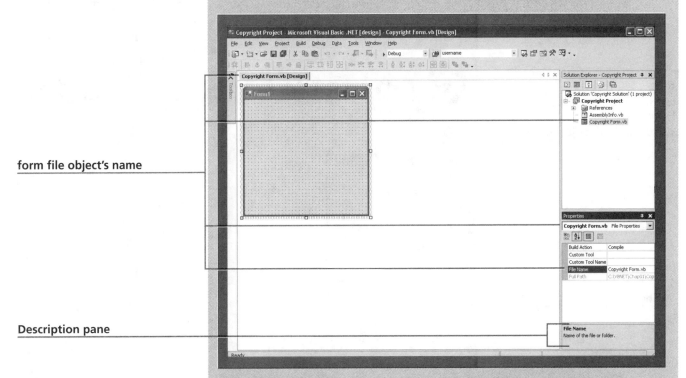

form file object's name

Description pane

Figure 1-16: Form file object's name displayed in the designer, Solution Explorer, and Properties windows

Notice that you do not have to erase the old text in the Settings box before entering the new text. You need simply to select the appropriate property and then type the new value; the new value replaces the old value for the selected property.

Next, view the properties of the Windows Form object.

Properties of the Windows Form Object

Like the form file object, the Windows Form object also has a set of properties. The properties will appear in the Properties window when you select the Windows Form object in the designer window.

To view the properties of the Windows Form object:

1 Click the **Windows Form** object in the designer window. The properties of the Windows Form object appear in the Properties window.

2 Click the **Auto Hide** button on the Solution Explorer window's title bar, then move the mouse pointer away from the window. Auto-hiding the Solution Explorer window allows you to view more of the Properties window.

The names of the properties can be listed either alphabetically or by category.

3 If the properties in your Properties window are listed by category, click the **Alphabetic** button. If the properties are listed alphabetically, click the **Categorized** button to view the category display, then click the **Alphabetic** button. The Properties window in Figure 1-17 shows a partial listing of the properties of a Windows Form object. The vertical scroll bar on the Properties window indicates that there are more properties to view.

class

location of the Windows
Form object class

Windows Form object name

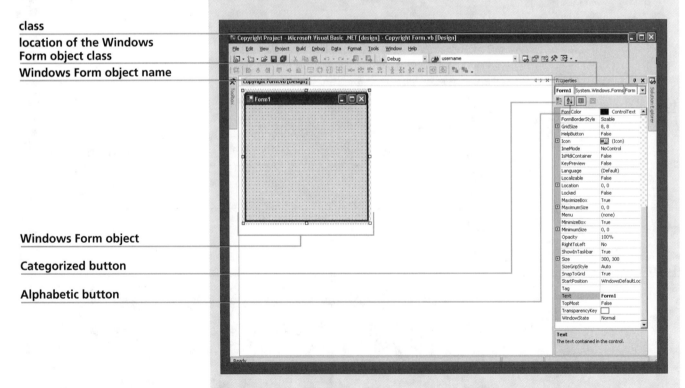

Windows Form object

Categorized button

Alphabetic button

Figure 1-17: Windows Form object properties listed alphabetically in the Properties window

Notice that Form1 System.Windows.Forms.Form appears in the Object box. Form1 is the name of the Windows Form object. The name is automatically assigned to the form when the form is created—or, in OOP terms, instantiated. System.Windows.Forms.Form is the name (Form) and location (System.Windows.Forms) of the class used to instantiate the Windows Form object. The period that separates each word in the name is called the **dot member access operator**. Similar to the backslash (\) in a folder path, the dot member access operator indicates a hierarchy, but of namespaces rather than folders. In other words, the backslash in the path C:\VBNET\Chap01\Copyright Solution\Copyright Project\Copyright Form.vb indicates that the Copyright Form.vb file is contained in (or is a member of) the Copyright Project folder, which is a member of the Copyright Solution folder, which is a member of the Chap01 folder, which is a member of the VBNET folder, which is a member of the C: drive. Likewise, the name System.Windows.Forms.Form indicates that the Form class is a member of the Forms namespace, which is a member of the Windows namespace, which is a member of the System namespace. The dot member access operator allows the computer to locate the Form class in the computer's internal memory, similar to the way the backslash (\) allows the computer to locate the Copyright Form.vb file on your computer's hard disk.

4 Drag the scroll box in the Properties window to the top of the vertical scroll bar. As you scroll, notice the various properties associated with a Windows Form object.

As you did with the form file object, you should assign a more meaningful name to the Windows Form object; this will help you keep track of the various forms in a project. Keep in mind that the names of the forms within the same project must be unique.

The Name Property

Unlike a form file object, the Windows Form object has a Name property rather than a File Name property. You use the name entered in an object's **Name property** to refer to the object in code. The name must begin with a letter and contain only letters, numbers, and the underscore character. You cannot use punctuation characters or spaces in the name. For many years, most Visual Basic programmers used Hungarian notation when naming objects. **Hungarian notation** is a naming convention that uses the first three characters in the name to represent the object's type (form, button, and so on), and the remainder of the name to represent the object's purpose. Using Hungarian notation, you would name the current form frmCopyright. The "frm" identifies the object as a form, and "Copyright" reminds you of the form's purpose.

Recently, a new naming convention for forms has emerged. In the new naming convention, the three-character ID ("frm") is omitted from the form's name. The name now begins with the form's purpose, followed by the word "Form". Additionally, the name is entered using **Pascal case**, which means that the first letter in the name and the first letter of each subsequent word in the name are capitalized. Using this naming convention, you would name the current form CopyrightForm. You will use the new naming convention in this book.

You also can scroll the Properties window using the ↑, ↓, Home, End, Page Down, and Page Up keys on your keyboard, but you first must make the Properties window the active window.

Visit *www.irritatedVowel. com* **for an interesting article on why Hungarian notation has fallen out of favor with .NET programmers.**

Although Microsoft recommends the new naming convention for forms, your company (or instructor) may have a different naming convention you are expected to use. Your company's (or instructor's) naming convention supersedes the one recommended by Microsoft.

Pascal is a programming language that was created by Niklaus Wirth in the late 1960s. It was named in honor of the seventeenth-century French mathematician Blaise Pascal, and is used to develop scientific applications.

The Name property is used by the programmer, whereas the Text property is read by the user.

To change the name of the Windows Form object:

1   Click (**Name**) in the Properties list.

2   Type **CopyrightForm** and press **Enter**. Notice that the designer window's tab now includes an asterisk (*) after [Design]. The asterisk indicates that you have made a change to the form, and the change has not yet been saved to the form file. You learn how to save the form file later in this lesson.

You set the Text property of the Windows Form object next.

The Text Property

Programmers who create applications for the Windows environment need to be aware of the conventions used in Windows applications. One such convention is that the name of the application (for example, Microsoft Visual Basic .NET or Microsoft Word) usually appears in the application window's title bar. Because the Windows Form object in the designer window will become your application's window when the application is run, its title bar should display an appropriate name.

A form's **Text property** controls the caption displayed in the form's title bar. The content of the Text property also is displayed on the application's button on the taskbar while the application is running. The default caption, Form1, is automatically assigned to the first form in a project. A better, more descriptive caption would be "Interlocking Software Company"—the name of the company responsible for the copyright screen application.

To set the Text property of the Windows Form object:

1   Scroll the Properties window until you see the Text property in the Properties list, then click **Text** in the Properties list.

2   Type **Interlocking Software Company** and press **Enter**. The new text appears in the Settings box to the right of the Text property, and also in the form's title bar.

Next, you set the StartPosition property of the Windows Form object.

The StartPosition Property

You use the **StartPosition property** to determine where the Windows Form object is positioned when the application is run and the form first appears on the screen. A form that represents a splash screen should be positioned in the middle of the screen.

For some properties—such as the BackColor property—a color palette rather than a list appears when you click the list arrow button in the Settings box.

To center a Windows Form object on the screen:

1   Click **StartPosition** in the Properties list. The list arrow button in the Settings box indicates that the StartPosition property has predefined settings. When you click the list arrow button, a list appears containing the valid settings for the StartPosition property. You then select the setting you want from the list.

2   Click the **list arrow** button in the Settings box, then click **CenterScreen** in the list.

Next you set the Size property of the Windows Form object.

The Size Property

As you can with any Windows object, you can size a Windows Form object by selecting it and then dragging the sizing handles that appear around it. You also can set its **Size property**.

> You also can size a form by selecting it and then pressing and holding down the Shift key as you press the ↑, ↓, →, or ← key on your keyboard.

To set the Size property of the Windows Form object:

1   Click **Size** in the Properties list. Notice that the Size property contains two numbers separated by a comma and a space. The first number represents the width of the form, measured in pixels; the second number represents the height, also measured in pixels.

A **pixel**, which is short for "picture element", is one spot in a grid of thousands of such spots that form an image produced on the screen by a computer or printed on a page by a printer. You can click the plus box that appears next to the Size property to verify that the first number listed in the property represents the width and the second number represents the height.

2   Click the **plus box** that appears next to the Size property. The Width and Height properties appear below the Size property in the Properties window.

Assume you want to change the Width property to 370 pixels and the Height property to 315 pixels. You can do so by entering 370 in the Width property's Settings box and 315 in the Height property's Settings box; or, you can simply enter 370, 315 in the Size property's Settings box.

3   Type **370, 315** in the Size property's Settings box and press **Enter**. Figure 1-18 shows the current status of the copyright screen application.

the asterisk indicates that changes to the form have not been saved to the form file

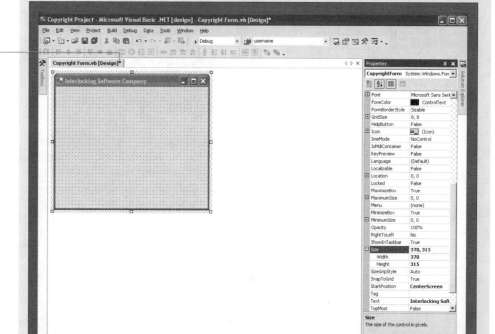

Figure 1-18: Current status of the copyright screen application

Before learning how to save the form file, you practice setting and then restoring the value of a property.

Setting and Restoring the Value of a Property

In the next set of steps, you set and then restore the value of the BackgroundImage property. You can use the **BackgroundImage property** to display a graphic as the background of a form.

To set and then restore the BackgroundImage property:

1   Click **BackgroundImage** in the Properties list. When you click the ellipsis (...) button in the Settings box, a dialog box opens. You use the dialog box to select the file that contains the graphic you want to display.

2   Click the **...** (ellipsis) button in the Settings box. The Open dialog box opens.

Visual Studio .NET comes with a variety of graphics files, which typically are located in the Program Files\Microsoft Visual Studio .NET 2003\Common7\Graphics folder on either the local hard drive or the network drive.

3   Locate and then open the **Program Files\Microsoft Visual Studio .NET 2003\Common7\Graphics** folder.

The various graphics files are grouped by type. You will use an icon file.

4   Open the **icons** folder. The icon you will use is located in the Misc folder. Open the **Misc** folder. Click **FACE05.ICO** in the list of filenames, and then click the **Open** button. A smiling face icon fills the background of the form.

You can restore the BackgroundImage property to its default setting, which is (none), by right-clicking the property and then clicking Reset on the context menu.

5   Right-click **BackgroundImage** in the Properties list, and then click **Reset** on the context menu. The graphic is removed from the form, and the BackgroundImage property is returned to its default setting.

Next, you learn how to save the work you have done so far.

Saving a Solution

It is a good practice to save the current solution every 10 or 15 minutes so that you will not lose a lot of work if the computer loses power. One way to save the solution is to click File on the menu bar, and then click Save All. Doing so saves any changes made to the files included in the solution. You also can click the Save All button on the Standard toolbar.

To save your work:

1   Click **File** on the menu bar, and then click **Save All**.

You also can use the Save button on the Standard toolbar to save the solution, but you first must select the solution's name in the Solution Explorer window, because the Save button saves only the changes made to the selected item. For example, if the form file is selected, then the Save button saves only the changes made to the form file. Similarly, if the project name is selected, then only changes made to the files included in the project will be saved. The tooltip box that appears when you rest your mouse pointer on the Save button indicates which files will be saved. In this case, the tooltip box will say Save Copyright Form.vb if the form file's name is selected in the Solution Explorer window, Save Copyright Project if the project name is selected, and Save Copyright Solution.sln if the solution name is selected.

Next, you learn how to close the current solution, and how to open an existing solution. Both of these skills will help you complete the end-of-lesson exercises.

Closing the Current Solution

You close a solution using the Close Solution option on the File menu. When you close a solution, all projects and files contained in the solution also are closed. If unsaved changes were made to the solution, project, or form, a dialog box opens and prompts you to save the appropriate files. The dialog box contains Yes, No, Cancel, and Help buttons. You click the Yes button to save the files before the solution is closed. You click the No button to close the solution without saving the files. You click the Cancel button to leave the solution open, and you click the Help button to display Help pertaining to the dialog box. Use the File menu to close the Copyright Solution.

To close the Copyright Solution:

1   Click **File** on the menu bar, and then click **Close Solution**.

2   Temporarily display the Solution Explorer window to verify that the entire Copyright Solution is closed.

Now you learn how to open a solution that was saved previously.

Opening an Existing Solution

You can open an existing solution by clicking File on the menu bar and then clicking Open Solution. You then select the appropriate solution file in the Open Solution dialog box. (Recall that names of solution files have an .sln filename extension.) If a solution is already open in the IDE, it is closed before another solution is opened. In other words, only one solution can be open in the IDE at any one time. Use the File menu to open the Copyright Solution.

To open the Copyright Solution:

1   Click **File** on the menu bar, and then click **Open Solution**. The Open Solution dialog box opens.

2   Locate and then open the **VBNET\Chap01\Copyright Solution** folder on your computer's hard disk.

3   Copyright Solution (Copyright Solution.sln) should be selected in the list of filenames. Click the **Open** button.

4   If the Windows Form Designer window is not displayed, click **View** on the menu bar, and then click **Designer**.

5   Temporarily display the Solution Explorer window to verify that the entire solution is open.

You will complete the copyright screen in the remaining two lessons. Lastly, you learn how to exit Visual Studio .NET.

Exiting Visual Studio .NET

As in most Windows applications, you exit an application using either the Close button on the application window's title bar, or the Exit option on the File menu.

> To exit Visual Studio .NET:
> **1** Click the **Close** button on the IDE title bar.

You have now completed Lesson A. You can either take a break or complete the end-of-lesson questions and exercises before moving on to the next lesson.

S U M M A R Y

To start Visual Studio .NET:

- Click the Start button on the Windows taskbar. Point to All Programs, then point to Microsoft Visual Studio .NET 2003, and then click Microsoft Visual Studio .NET 2003.

To customize the IDE:

- Use the My Profile pane in the Start Page window.

To create a blank solution:

- Click File on the menu bar, point to New, and then click Blank Solution.

To add a new project to the current solution:

- Click File on the menu bar, point to Add Project, and then click New Project. You also can right-click the solution's name in the Solution Explorer window, point to Add, and then click New Project. Additionally, you can click the New Project button on the Projects pane in the Start Page window.

To close a window in the IDE:

- Click the window's Close button.

To open a closed window in the IDE:

- Use the Help menu for the Start Page and Dynamic Help windows. Use the View menu for all other windows.

To auto-hide a window in the IDE:

- Click the Auto Hide (vertical pushpin) button on the window's title bar.

To permanently display an auto-hidden window in the IDE:

- Click the Auto Hide (horizontal pushpin) button on the window's title bar.

To set the value of a property:

- Select the object whose property you want to set, then select the appropriate property in the Properties list. Type the new property value in the selected property's Settings box, or choose the value from the list, color palette, or dialog box.

To give a more meaningful name to an object:

- Set the object's Name property.

To control the text appearing in the form's title bar, and on the application's button on the Windows taskbar when the application is running:

- Set the Windows Form object's Text property.

To control the starting location of the Windows Form object:

- Set the Windows Form object's StartPosition property.

To size a Windows Form object:

- Drag the form's sizing handles. You also can set the form's Size, Height, and Width properties in the Properties window. Additionally, you can select the form and then press and hold down the Shift key as you press the ↑, ↓, →, or ← key on your keyboard.

To display a graphic as the background of a Windows Form object:

- Set the Windows Form object's BackgroundImage property. Visual Studio .NET comes with a variety of graphics files, which typically are located in the Program Files\Microsoft Visual Studio .NET 2003\Common7\Graphics folder on either the local hard drive or the network drive.

To restore a property to its default setting:

- Right-click the property in the Properties list, and then click Reset.

To save a solution:

- Click File on the menu bar, and then click Save All. You also can click the Save All button 🖫 on the Standard toolbar.

To open an existing solution:

- Click File on the menu bar, and then click Open Solution.

To exit Visual Studio .NET:

- Click the Close button on the IDE title bar. You also can click File on the IDE menu bar, and then click Exit.

QUESTIONS

1. A _____ is a pattern that Visual Studio .NET uses to create solutions and projects.
   a. design
   b. profile
   c. solution
   d. template
   e. user interface

2. A _____ is a container that stores the projects and files for an entire application.
   a. form file
   b. profile
   c. solution
   d. template
   e. None of the above.

3. You use the _____ window to set the characteristics that control an object's appearance and behavior.
   a. Characteristics
   b. Object
   c. Properties
   d. Toolbox
   e. Windows Form Designer

4. The _____ window lists the projects and files included in a solution.
   a. Object
   b. Project
   c. Properties
   d. Solution Explorer
   e. Windows Form Designer

5. Solution files in Visual Studio .NET have a(n) _____ extension on their filenames.
   a. .frm
   b. .prg
   c. .sln
   d. .src
   e. .vb

6. Which of the following statements is false?
   a. You can auto-hide a window by clicking the Auto-Hide (vertical pushpin) button on its title bar.
   b. An auto-hidden window appears as a tab on the edge of the IDE.
   c. You temporarily display an auto-hidden window by placing your mouse pointer on its tab.
   d. You permanently display an auto-hidden window by clicking the Auto-Hide (horizontal pushpin) button on its title bar.
   e. None of the above.

7. Visual Basic .NET source files have a(n) _____ extension on their filenames.
    a. .frm
    b. .prg
    c. .sln
    d. .src
    e. .vb

8. The code that creates a Windows Form object is stored in a file whose filename extension is _____.
    a. .frm
    b. .prg
    c. .sln
    d. .src
    e. .vb

9. The _____ property controls the text appearing in the title bar on a Windows Form object.
    a. Caption
    b. FormCaption
    c. Text
    d. Title
    e. TitleBar

10. You give an object a more meaningful name by setting the object's _____ property.
    a. Application
    b. Caption
    c. Form
    d. Name
    e. Text

11. You can size a Windows Form object by _____.
    a. dragging its sizing handles
    b. setting its Height property
    c. setting its Size property
    d. setting its Width property
    e. All of the above.

12. The _____ property determines the position of a form when the application is run and the form first appears on the screen.
    a. InitialLocation
    b. Location
    c. Start
    d. StartLocation
    e. StartPosition

13. The _____ property allows you to display a graphic as the background of a Windows Form object.
    a. BackgroundImage
    b. BackgroundPicture
    c. GraphicBackground
    d. IconBackground
    e. Image

14. When you close a solution, all projects and files included in the solution also are closed.
    a. True
    b. False

15. A project can contain one or more Windows Form objects.
    a. True
    b. False

16. Explain the difference between a Windows-based application and a Web-based application.

17. Explain the difference between a Windows Form object's Text property and its Name property.

18. Explain the difference between a form file object and a Windows Form object.

19. Define the terms "reference" and "namespace".

20. What does the dot member access operator indicate in the text System.Windows.Forms.Label?

E X E R C I S E S

1. In this exercise, you change the properties of an existing Windows Form object.
    a. If necessary, start Visual Studio .NET and permanently display the Solution Explorer window.
    b. Click File on the menu bar, and then click Open Solution. Open the Charities Solution (Charities Solution.sln) file, which is contained in the VBNET\Chap01\Charities Solution folder. If necessary, use the View menu to open the designer window.
    c. Change the following properties of the Windows Form object:

Name:	CharityForm
BackColor:	Select a light blue square on the Custom tab (This property determines the background color of the form.)
Size:	300, 350
StartPosition:	CenterScreen
Text:	Charities Unlimited

    d. Click File on the menu bar, and then click Save All to save the solution.
    e. Click File on the menu bar, and then click Close Solution to close the solution.

2. In this exercise, you create a Visual Basic .NET Windows-based application.
    a. If necessary, start Visual Studio .NET and permanently display the Solution Explorer window.
    b. Create a blank solution named Photo Solution. Save the solution in the VBNET\Chap01 folder.
    c. Add a Visual Basic .NET Windows Application project to the solution. Name the project Photo Project.
    d. Assign the filename Photo Form.vb to the form file object.
    e. Assign the name MyPhotoForm to the Windows Form object.
    f. The Windows Form object's title bar should say Photos Incorporated. Set the appropriate property.
    g. The Windows Form object should be centered on the screen when it first appears. Set the appropriate property.
    h. Include a background image on the form.
    i. Save and then close the solution.

3. In this exercise, you create a Visual Basic .NET Windows-based application.

 a. If necessary, start Visual Studio .NET and permanently display the Solution Explorer window.

 b. Create a blank solution named Yorktown Solution. Save the solution in the VBNET\Chap01 folder.

 c. Add a Visual Basic .NET Windows Application project to the solution. Name the project Yorktown Project.

 d. Assign the filename Yorktown Form.vb to the form file object.

 e. Assign the name ShoppingForm to the Windows Form object.

 f. Include a background image on the form.

 g. The Windows Form object's title bar should say Yorktown Shopping Center. Set the appropriate property.

 h. The Windows Form object should be centered on the screen when it first appears. Set the appropriate property.

 i. Remove the background image from the form. (You included the background image in Step f.)

 j. Save and then close the solution.

discovery ▶ **4.** In this exercise, you learn about the ControlBox, MaximizeBox, and MinimizeBox properties of a Windows Form object.

 a. If necessary, start Visual Studio .NET and permanently display the Solution Explorer window.

 b. Open the Greenwood Solution (Greenwood Solution.sln) file, which is contained in the VBNET\Chap01\Greenwood Solution folder. If necessary, use the View menu to open the designer window.

 c. View the properties of the Windows Form object.

 d. Click the ControlBox property. What is the purpose of this property? (Refer to the Description pane in the Properties window.)

 e. Set the ControlBox property to False. How does this setting affect the Windows Form object?

 f. Set the ControlBox property to True.

 g. Click the MaximizeBox property. What is the purpose of this property?

 h. Set the MaximizeBox property to False. How does this setting affect the Windows Form object?

 i. Set the MaximizeBox property to True.

 j. Click the MinimizeBox property. What is the purpose of this property?

 k. Set the MinimizeBox property to False. How does this setting affect the Windows Form object?

 l. Set the MinimizeBox property to True.

 m. Close the solution without saving it.

discovery ▶ **5.** In this exercise, you use the Description pane in the Properties window to research two properties of a Windows Form object.

 a. If necessary, start Visual Studio .NET and permanently display the Solution Explorer window.

 b. Open the Greenwood Solution (Greenwood Solution.sln) file, which is contained in the VBNET\Chap01\Greenwood Solution folder. If necessary, use the View menu to open the designer window.

 c. View the properties of the Windows Form object.

 d. What property allows you to remove the dots (referred to as the positioning grid) from the form?

 e. What property determines whether the value stored in the form's Text property appears on the Windows taskbar when the application is running?

 f. Close the solution without saving it.

After completing this lesson, you will be able to:

- Add a control to a form
- Set the properties of a label, picture box, and button control
- Select multiple controls
- Center controls on the form
- Set the properties of a project
- Start and end an application
- Enter code in the Code Editor window
- Terminate an application using the Me.Close method

Working with Controls

The Toolbox Window

In Lesson A, you learned about the Windows Form Designer, Solution Explorer, and Properties windows. In this lesson, you learn about the Toolbox window. First, however, you open the Copyright Solution you created in Lesson A.

To open the Copyright Solution:

1 If necessary, start Visual Studio .NET.

You will not need the Start Page window, so you can close it.

2 Close the Start Page window.

3 Click **File** on the menu bar, and then click **Open Solution**. The Open Solution dialog box opens. Open the **Copyright Solution** (Copyright Solution.sln) file, which is contained in the VBNET\Chap01\Copyright Solution folder.

4 If necessary, use the View menu to open the designer window.

5 If necessary, permanently display the Properties window and auto-hide the Solution Explorer window.

6 Permanently display the Toolbox window. If necessary, size the Toolbox window so that the entire form appears in the designer window. See Figure 1-19.

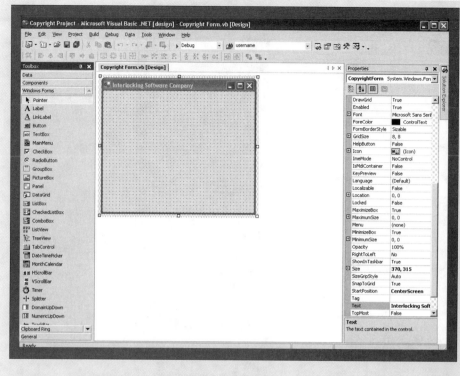

Figure 1-19: Copyright Solution opened in the IDE

The **Toolbox window,** or **toolbox,** contains the tools and other components you use when creating your application. The contents of the toolbox vary depending on the designer in use. The toolbox shown in Figure 1-20 appears when you are using the Windows Form Designer.

up arrow button

Windows Forms tab

down arrow button

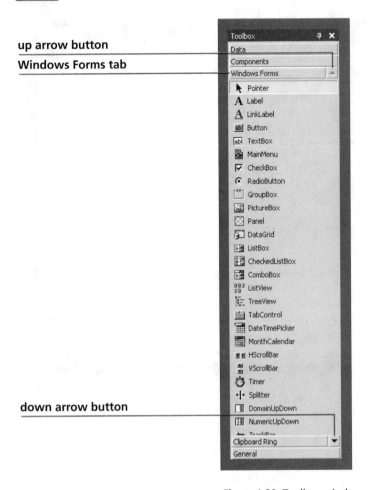

Figure 1-20: Toolbox window

The Windows Forms tab on the toolbox contains 47 basic tools that you can use when designing your application's user interface. Each tool is identified by both an icon and a name. The up and down arrow buttons on the tab allow you to scroll the list of tools. (Appendix A lists the names of the basic tools and provides a brief description of each tool.)

In the context of OOP, each tool in the toolbox represents a class—a pattern from which one or more objects are instantiated. The object's attributes (properties) and behaviors (methods) are encapsulated (combined) in the tool. The tools allow you to instantiate objects such as text boxes, list boxes, and radio buttons. These objects, called **controls**, are displayed on the form.

The first tool you learn about is the Label tool.

Using the Label Tool

You use the **Label tool** to instantiate (create) a label control. The purpose of a **label control** is to display text that the user is not allowed to edit while the application is running. In this application, for example, you do not want the user to change the author name and copyright year on the copyright screen. Therefore, you will display the information using two label controls: one for the name of the application's author and the other for the copyright year.

tip

You also can add a control to the form by clicking the control's tool in the toolbox and then clicking the form. Additionally, you can click the control's tool in the toolbox, then place the mouse pointer on the form, and then press the left mouse button and drag the mouse pointer until the control is the desired size.

class used to instantiate
the label control

name of the label control

sizing handle

Text property value

To use the Label tool to create two label controls:

1. Click the **Label** tool in the toolbox, but do not release the mouse button. Hold down the mouse button as you drag the mouse pointer to the center of the form. (You do not need to worry about the exact size or location of the control.) As you drag the mouse pointer, both an outline of a rectangle and a plus box follow the mouse pointer.

2. Release the mouse button. A label control appears on the form. Notice that sizing handles appear around the label control. You can use the sizing handles to size the control. Also notice that Label1 System.Windows.Forms.Label appears in the Object box in the Properties window. Label1 is the default name assigned to the label control. System.Windows.Forms.Label indicates that the control is an instance of the Label class, which is defined in the System.Windows.Forms namespace. See Figure 1-21. (Do not be concerned if your label control is in a different location than the one shown in the figure.)

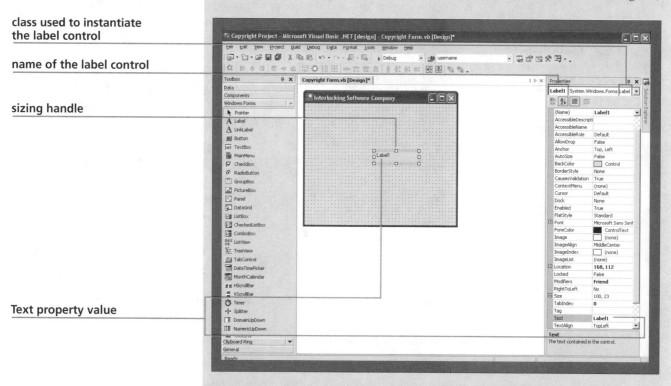

Figure 1-21: Label control added to the form

HELP? If the wrong control appears on the form, press Delete to remove the control, then repeat steps 1 and 2.

Recall from Lesson A that a default value is assigned to each of an object's properties when the object is created. Label1, for example, is the default value assigned to the Text and Name properties of the first label control added to a form. The value of the Text property appears inside the label control, as indicated in Figure 1-21. (You can verify that the Name property also contains Label1 by scrolling to the top of the Properties window.)

3. Click the **Label** tool in the toolbox, and then drag another label control onto the form. Position the new label control below the existing one. (Do not worry about the exact location.) Notice that Label2 is assigned to the Text property of the second label control added to the same form. Label2 also is assigned to the control's Name property.

In the next set of steps, you assign a more meaningful name to each label control. Assigning meaningful names to the controls on a form will help you keep track of the various controls in the user interface. As you learned earlier, for many years most Visual Basic programmers used Hungarian notation when naming objects. For example, they typically would name the label control that displays the author's name lblAuthor. The "lbl" identifies the object as a label control, and "Author" indicates the control's purpose. However, the new naming convention for controls omits the three-character ID from the name. Similar to form names, control names now should be made up of the control's purpose followed by the control's type. Although not required, it is recommended that you begin a control's name with the lowercase letters "ui", which stand for "user interface." Beginning all controls with "ui" will assure that the control names are listed together when using the IntelliSense feature in the Code Editor window. You learn about the Code Editor window in Lesson B.

Control names should be entered using **camel case**, which means that you lowercase the letters "ui" and then uppercase the first letter of each word in the name. Using this naming convention, you would name the label control that displays the author's name uiAuthorLabel. You will use the new naming convention in this book.

To assign a more meaningful name to the label controls:

1 Click the **Label1** control to select it. Sizing handles appear around the control to indicate that the control is selected.

2 Scroll to the top of the Properties list, and then click (**Name**).

The Label1 control will display the application author's name, so you will name it uiAuthorLabel.

3 Type **uiAuthorLabel** in the Settings box and press **Enter**.

The Label2 control will display the copyright year, so you will name it uiYearLabel.

4 Click the **Label2** control to select it. Click (**Name**) in the Properties list, then type **uiYearLabel** in the Settings box and press **Enter**.

Next, set the Text and AutoSize properties of both label controls.

Setting the Text and AutoSize Properties

As you learned earlier, a label control's Text property determines the value that appears inside the control. In this application, you want the words "Written by" and your name to appear in the uiAuthorLabel control, and the words "Copyright Year" and the year 2006 to appear in the uiYearLabel control. Therefore, you will need to set the Text property of both controls.

To set the Text property of the two label controls:

1 Currently, the uiYearLabel control is selected on the form. Scroll down the Properties window until you locate the control's Text property. Click **Text** in the Properties list, then type **Copyright Year 2006** and press **Enter**. The new text appears in the Text property's Settings box and in the uiYearLabel control.

Because the text is longer than the width of the label control, some of the information wraps around to the next line. You can use the control's sizing handles to adjust the size of the control. You also can use the control's AutoSize property. The **AutoSize property** does just what its name implies: it automatically sizes the control to fit its current contents.

2 Click **AutoSize** in the Properties list, then click the **list arrow** button in the Settings box.

Notice that the AutoSize property can be set to either True or False. Many of the other properties shown in the Properties list also have only these two settings. The settings are called **Boolean** values, named after the English mathematician George Boole. The True setting turns the property on, and the False setting turns the property off. You use the True setting to automatically size a control.

3 Click **True** in the list. The uiYearLabel control stretches automatically to fit the contents of its Text property. Notice that a thin line, rather than sizing handles, surrounds the control. The thin line indicates that the control's AutoSize property is set to True.

4 Click the **uiAuthorLabel** control on the form. Sizing handles appear around the control to indicate that it is selected, and that its AutoSize property is currently set to False. Notice that the thin line that surrounded the uiYearLabel control in the previous step disappears when you click another control. This is because the thin line appears only when an auto-sized control is selected.

5 Set the uiAuthorLabel control's AutoSize property to **True**. A thin line replaces the sizing handles around the control.

6 Click **Text** in the Properties list. Type **Written By** and press the **spacebar**, then type your name and press **Enter**. The uiAuthorLabel control stretches automatically to fit the contents of its Text property.

Now specify the placement of the two label controls on the form.

Setting the Location Property

You can move a control to a different location on the form by placing your mouse pointer ▯ on the control until ▯ becomes ✛, and then dragging the control to the desired location. You also can set the control's Location property, because the property specifies the position of the upper-left corner of the control.

To set the Location property of the two label controls:

1 Click the **uiYearLabel** control to select it.

2 Click **Location** in the Properties list, then click the **plus box** next to the property's name. Two additional properties, X and Y, appear below the Location property in the Properties list.

The **X property** specifies the number of pixels from the left border of the form to the left border of the control. The **Y property** specifies the number of pixels between the top border of the form and the top border of the control. Change the X value to 175, and change the Y value to 250.

3 Type **175, 250** in the **Location** property and press **Enter**. The uiYearLabel control moves to its new location.

4 Click the **minus box** next to the Location property's name.

Now select the uiAuthorLabel control and then set its Location property. In addition to selecting a control by clicking it on the form, you also can select a control by clicking its entry (name and class) in the Object box in the Properties window. Try this now.

5   Click the **list arrow** button in the Properties window's Object box, and then click **uiAuthorLabel System.Windows.Forms.Label** in the list. Set the control's Location property to **175, 225**. The uiAuthorLabel control moves to its new location.

6   Click **File** on the menu bar, and then click **Save All** to save the solution.

Now set the Font property of the two label controls. As you will see in the next section, you can set the Font property for both controls at the same time.

Changing the Property for More Than One Control at a Time

You can use the Font property to change the appearance of many of the objects in your user interface. The **Font property** allows you to change the type of font used to display the text in the object, as well as the style and size of the font. A **font** is the general shape of the characters in the text. Courier, Tahoma, and Microsoft Sans Serif are examples of font types; font styles include regular, bold, and italic. The numbers 8, 10, and 18 are examples of font sizes, which typically are measured in points, with one **point** equaling 1/72 of an inch.

One reason for changing a font is to bring attention to a specific part of the screen. In the copyright screen, for example, you can make the text in the two label controls more noticeable by increasing the size of the font used to display the text. You can change the font size for both controls at the same time by clicking one control and then pressing and holding down the Control key as you click the other control in the form. You can use the Control+click method to select as many controls as you want. To cancel the selection of one of the selected controls, press and hold down the Control key as you click the control. To cancel the selection of all of the selected controls, release the Control key, then click the form or an unselected control on the form.

tip

You also can select a group of controls on the form by placing the mouse pointer slightly above and to the left of the first control you want to select, then pressing the left mouse button and dragging. A dotted rectangle appears as you drag. When all of the controls you want to select are within (or at least touched by) the dotted rectangle, release the mouse button. All of the controls surrounded or touched by the dotted rectangle will be selected.

To select both label controls, and then set their Font property:

1   Verify that the uiAuthorLabel control is selected.

2   Press and hold down the **Ctrl** (or Control) key as you click the **uiYearLabel** control, then release the Ctrl key. The thin line that surrounds each label control indicates that both controls are selected. (Recall that the thin line appears only when an auto-sized control is selected, and both label controls are auto-sized. If the label controls were not auto-sized—in other words, if their AutoSize property was set to False—sizing handles rather than a thin line would appear around each control to indicate that each is selected.) See Figure 1-22.

both label controls are selected

Figure 1-22: Label controls selected on the form

3 Click **Font** in the Properties list, then click the **...** (ellipsis) button in the Settings box. The Font dialog box opens.

Typically, the default font is the regular style of the Microsoft Sans Serif font, and the default font size is approximately 8 points, or 1/9 of an inch. (Recall that one point is 1/72 of an inch.) For applications that will run on systems running Windows 2000 or Windows XP, it is recommended that you use the Tahoma font, because it offers improved readability and globalization support. You will change the font type to Tahoma, and increase the font size to 12 points (1/6 of an inch).

4 Scroll the Font list box and click **Tahoma**, then click **12** in the Size list box. See Figure 1-23.

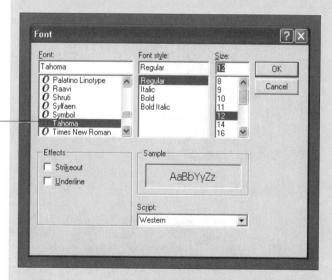

font type recommended for Windows 2000 and Windows XP applications

Figure 1-23: Completed Font dialog box

5 Click the **OK** button. The Font dialog box closes, and the text in the two label controls appears in the new font and font size. Depending on the number of characters in your name, the uiAuthorLabel control might extend beyond the right border of the form. You fix that problem in the next section.

Next, you learn how to use the Format menu to center the label controls, horizontally, on the form.

Using the Format Menu

The Format menu provides options that allow you to manipulate the controls in the user interface. The Align option, for example, allows you to align two or more controls by their left, right, top, or bottom borders. You can use the Make Same Size option to make two or more controls the same width and/or height. The Format menu also has a Center in Form option that centers one or more controls either horizontally or vertically on the form. Use the Center in Form option to center the two label controls on the form. (You practice with the Align and Make Same Size options in Discovery Exercise 4 at the end of this lesson.)

To center the uiAuthorLabel and uiYearLabel controls horizontally on the form:

1 Click the **Copyright Form.vb [Design]*** tab to make the designer window the active window. The two label controls should still be selected.

2 Click **Format** on the menu bar. Point to **Center in Form**, then click **Horizontally**. The two label controls are centered horizontally on the form.

3 Click the **form** to deselect the label controls.

4 Click **File** on the menu bar, and then click **Save All** to save the solution.

Next, you use the PictureBox tool to add a picture box control to the form.

Using the PictureBox Tool

According to the application you previewed at the beginning of this chapter, you need to include the Interlocking Software Company logo on your copyright screen. You can do so by displaying the logo in a **picture box control**, which you create using the **PictureBox tool**.

To add a picture box control to the form:

1 Click the **PictureBox** tool in the toolbox, then drag a picture box control to the form. (You do not need to worry about the exact location.) An empty rectangular box with sizing handles appears on the form, and PictureBox1 System.Windows.Forms.PictureBox appears in the Object box in the Properties window. PictureBox1 is the default name assigned to the first picture box control added to a form. System.Windows.Forms.PictureBox indicates that the control is an instance of the PictureBox class, which is defined in the System.Windows.Forms namespace.

2 Set the picture box control's Name property to **uiLogoPictureBox**.

3 Set the picture box control's Location property to **8, 10**.

You use the picture box control's **Image property** to specify the image you want displayed inside the control.

4 Click **Image** in the Properties list, then click the **...** (ellipsis) button in the Settings box. The Open dialog box opens.

The Interlocking Software Company logo is stored in the Logo file, which is contained in the VBNET\Chap01 folder.

5 Open the **VBNET\Chap01** folder. Click **Logo** (Logo.bmp) in the list of filenames, and then click the **Open** button. Only a small portion of the logo appears in the picture box control.

You can make the picture box control larger by dragging its sizing handles; or you can simply set its **SizeMode property**.

6 Set the picture box control's SizeMode property to **AutoSize**. The picture box control automatically sizes to fit its current contents.

7 Click the **form's title bar** to deselect the picture box control. See Figure 1-24.

Figure 1-24: Picture box control added to the form

The last tool you learn about in this lesson is the Button tool.

Using the Button Tool

Every Windows application should give the user a way to exit the program. Most Windows applications provide either an Exit option on a File menu or an Exit button for this purpose. When the user clicks the menu option or button, the application ends and the user interface is removed from the screen.

Recall that the copyright screen will serve as a splash screen for each custom application created by Interlocking Software. Splash screens typically do not contain an Exit button; rather, they use a Timer control to automatically remove the splash screen after a set period of time. You learn how to include a Timer control in a splash screen in Lesson C. In this lesson, the copyright screen will provide an Exit button.

In Windows applications, a **button control** performs an immediate action when clicked. Examples of button controls used in most Windows applications include the OK and Cancel buttons, as well as the Open and Save buttons. You create a button using the **Button tool** in the toolbox.

To add a button control to the form:

1   Click the **Button** tool in the toolbox, then drag a button control to the form. Position the button control to the immediate right of the label controls. (You do not need to worry about the exact location.) Notice that Button1 System.Windows.Forms.Button appears in the Object box in the Properties window. Button1 is the default name assigned to the first button control added to a form. System.Windows.Forms.Button tells you that the control is an instance of the Button class, which is defined in the System.Windows.Forms namespace.

First, assign a more meaningful name to the button control. Then change the button control's font and location.

2   Set the button control's Name property to **uiExitButton**.

Next, change the button control's font and location.

3   Set the button control's Font property to **Tahoma, 12 pt.**

4   Set the button control's Location property to **270, 240**.

The button control's Text property determines the caption that appears on the button. Change the Text property from Button1 to Exit.

5   Set the button control's Text property to **Exit**. Figure 1-25 shows the button control added to the form.

Figure 1-25: Button control added to the form

You will not need the Toolbox and Properties windows, so you can auto-hide them.

6   Auto-hide the Toolbox and Properties windows.

7   Click **File** on the menu bar, and then click **Save All** to save the solution.

Now that the user interface is complete, you can start the copyright screen application to see how it will look to the user.

Starting and Ending an Application

Before you start an application for the first time, you need to specify the name of the **startup form,** which is the form that the computer automatically displays. You select the name from the Startup object list box in the Property Pages dialog box.

To specify the startup form:

1   Right-click **Copyright Project** in the Solution Explorer window, and then click **Properties**. The Copyright Project Property Pages dialog box opens. If necessary, click the **Common Properties** folder to open it, then click **General**.

2   Click the **Startup object** list arrow, and then click **CopyrightForm** in the list.

You can start an application by clicking Debug on the menu bar, and then clicking Start; or you can simply press the F5 key on your keyboard. When you start an application, Visual Studio .NET automatically creates a file that can be run outside the Visual Studio .NET IDE. The file, referred to as an **executable file**, has the same name as the project, but with an .exe filename extension. If you want to change the name of the executable file, you can use the Property Pages dialog box to do so.

To change the name of the executable file, then save the solution and start and end the application:

1   The Copyright Project Property Pages dialog box should still be open. Change the filename in the Assembly name text box to **Copyright**. Notice that the Output name in the Information section of the dialog box now says Copyright.exe. See Figure 1-26.

name of the executable file

name of the startup form

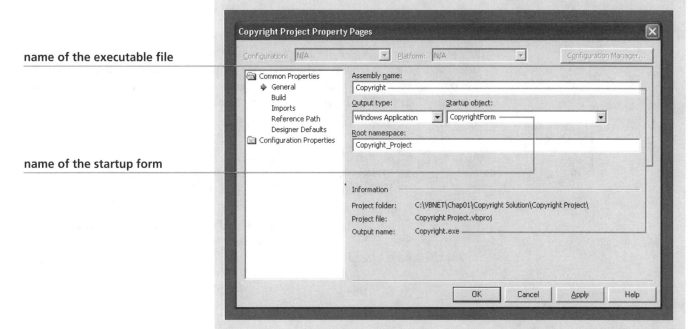

Figure 1-26: Completed Copyright Project Property Pages dialog box

2   Click the **OK** button to close the Copyright Project Property Pages dialog box.

Now save the solution and then start the application.

3   Click **File** on the menu bar, and then click **Save All** to save the solution.

4   Click **Debug** on the menu bar, and then click **Start** to start the application. See Figure 1-27. (Do not be concerned about the windows that appear at the bottom of the screen.)

form's Close button

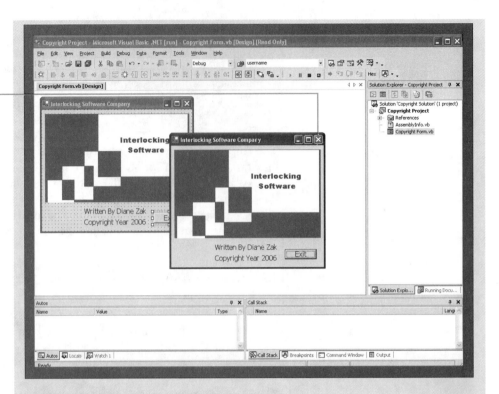

Figure 1-27: Result of starting the copyright screen application

Recall that the purpose of the Exit button is to allow the user to end the application. Currently, the button will not work as intended, because you have not yet entered the instructions that tell the button how to respond when clicked. You can verify that the Exit button does not work by clicking it.

5 Click the **Exit** button on the copyright screen. Notice that it does not end the application.

At this point, you can stop the application by clicking the Close button on the form's title bar. You also can click the designer window to make it the active window, then click Debug on the menu bar, and then click Stop Debugging; another option is to press Shift+F5.

6 Click the **Close** button on the form's title bar. When the application ends, you are returned to the IDE, and an Output window appears at the bottom of the screen. See Figure 1-28.

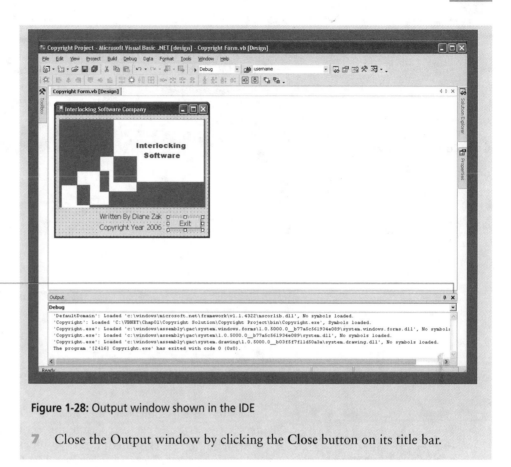

Output window's Close button

Figure 1-28: Output window shown in the IDE

7   Close the Output window by clicking the **Close** button on its title bar.

Next, you learn how to instruct the Exit button to stop the copyright screen application when the button is clicked.

Writing Visual Basic .NET Code

Think about the Windows environment for a moment. Did you ever wonder why the OK and Cancel buttons respond the way they do when you click them, or how the Exit option on the File menu knows to close the application? The answer to these questions is very simple: a programmer gave the buttons and menu option explicit instructions on how to respond to the actions of the user. Those actions—such as clicking, double-clicking, and scrolling—are called **events**. The set of Visual Basic .NET instructions, or code, that tells an object how to respond to an event is called an **event procedure**.

At this point, the Exit button in the copyright screen does not know what it is supposed to do. You tell the button what to do by writing an event procedure for it. You enter the event procedure in the Code Editor window, which is a window you have not yet seen. You can use various methods to open the Code Editor window. For example, you can right-click anywhere on the form (except the form's title bar), and then click View Code on the context menu. You also can click View on the menu bar, and then click Code; or you can press the F7 key on your keyboard. (To use the View menu or the F7 key, the designer window should be the active window.)

tip

You also can open the Code Editor window by double-clicking the form or a control on the form. Doing so displays (in the Code Editor window) a default event procedure for the object you double-clicked.

To open the Code Editor window:

1 Right-click the **form**, and then click **View Code** on the context menu. The Code Editor window opens in the IDE, as shown in Figure 1-29. Notice that the Code Editor window already contains some Visual Basic .NET code (instructions).

Code Editor window's tab

designer window's tab

class definition

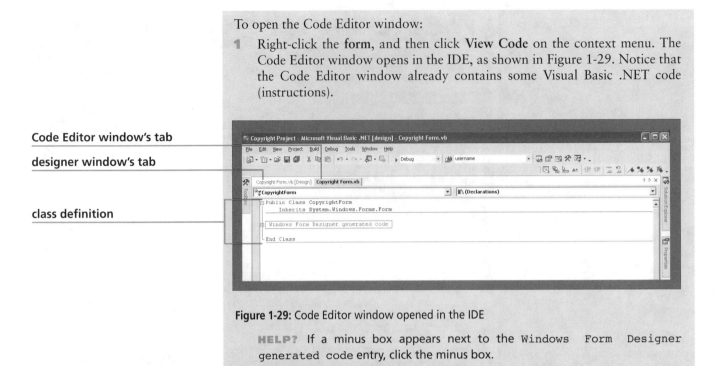

Figure 1-29: Code Editor window opened in the IDE

HELP? If a minus box appears next to the `Windows Form Designer generated code` entry, click the minus box.

tip

The `Public` keyword in the class definition indicates that the class can be used by code defined outside the class.

As Figure 1-29 indicates, the block of code that begins with the `Public Class CopyrightForm` instruction and ends with the `End Class` instruction is a class definition. A **class definition** is a block of code that specifies (or defines) the attributes and behaviors of an object. The CopyrightForm class definition, for example, specifies the attributes and behaviors of a CopyrightForm object. When you start the application, Visual Basic .NET uses the class definition to create (instantiate) the object.

Notice the `Inherits System.Windows.Forms.Form` instruction included in the CopyrightForm class definition. As you learned in the Overview, you can create one class (called the derived class) from another class (called the base class). The derived class inherits all of the attributes and behaviors of the base class, but then can be modified to, for instance, include an additional feature. The `Inherits System.Windows.Forms.Form` instruction allows the CopyrightForm class (the derived class) to inherit the attributes and behaviors of the Form class (the base class), which is provided by Visual Studio .NET and defined in the System.Windows.Forms namespace. In other words, rather than you having to write all of the code necessary to create a Windows Form object, Visual Studio .NET provides the basic code in the Form class. As you add controls to your Windows Form object, the Windows Form Designer makes the appropriate modifications to the derived class. You can view the additional code generated by the designer by clicking the plus box next to the `Windows Form Designer generated code` entry in the Code Editor window.

To view the code generated by the designer:

1 Click the **plus box** next to the `Windows Form Designer generated code` entry in the Code Editor window. Do not be overwhelmed by the code generated by the designer. In most cases, you do not need to concern yourself with this code.

2   Scroll the Code Editor window as shown in Figure 1-30.

Method Name list box

Class Name list box

instantiates the
uiAuthorLabel control

assigns the True value to the
uiAuthorLabel control's
AutoSize property

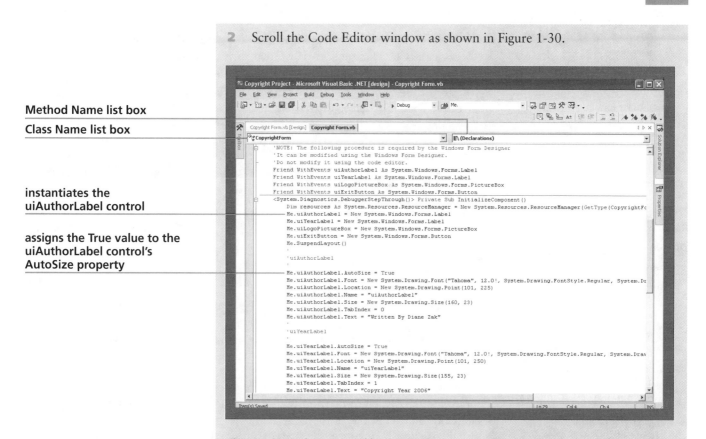

Figure 1-30: Code generated by the Windows Form Designer

Each time you added a control to the CopyrightForm form and then set the control's properties, the designer entered the appropriate code in the CopyrightForm class definition. For example, when you used the toolbox to add the uiAuthorLabel control to the form, the designer entered the instruction `Me.uiAuthorLabel = New System.Windows.Forms.Label` in the CopyrightForm class definition. The `Me` in the instruction refers to the current form, which, in this case, is the CopyrightForm. Similarly, when you set the uiAuthorLabel's AutoSize property to True in the Properties window, the designer recorded the instruction `Me.uiAuthorLabel.AutoSize = True` in the CopyrightForm class definition. The instruction, called an **assignment statement**, assigns the value True to the AutoSize property of the uiAuthorLabel control on the CopyrightForm form.

3   Scroll to the top of the Code Editor window, then click the **minus box** next to the `#Region " Windows Form Designer generated code "` entry. This collapses to one line the code generated by the designer.

As Figure 1-30 indicates, the Code Editor window also contains a Class Name list box and a Method Name list box. The **Class Name list box** lists the names of the objects included in the user interface, and the **Method Name list box** lists the events to which the selected object is capable of responding. In OOP, the events are considered behaviors, because they represent actions that the object can have performed on it. The Code Editor window exposes the object's behaviors to the programmer.

You use the Class Name and Method Name list boxes to select the object and event, respectively, that you want to code. In this case, you want the Exit button to end the application when the button is clicked, so you will select uiExitButton in the Class Name list box and select Click in the Method Name list box.

To select the uiExitButton object's Click event:

1 Click the **Class Name** list arrow, then click **uiExitButton** in the list.

2 Click the **Method Name** list arrow, then click **Click** in the list. See Figure 1-31. (Do not be concerned if you cannot view all of the uiExitButton control's code. The font used to display the text in the Code Editor window shown in Figure 1-31 was changed to 13-point Microsoft Sans Serif so that you could view all of the code in the figure. It is not necessary for you to change the font.)

procedure header

procedure footer

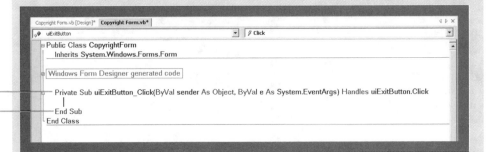

Figure 1-31: uiExitButton's Click event procedure shown in the Code Editor window

tip

You can use the Options dialog box to change the font used to display text in the Code Editor window. To open the Options dialog box, click Tools on the menu bar, and then click Options. When the Options dialog box appears, open the Environment folder, then click Fonts and Colors. Select Text Editor from the Show settings for list box, and Text from the Display items list box.

Notice that, when you select an object and event, additional code automatically appears in the Code Editor window. The additional code is called a **code template**. The Code Editor provides the code template to help you follow the rules of the Visual Basic .NET language; the rules of a programming language are called **syntax**. The first line in the code template is called the **procedure header**, and the last line is called the **procedure footer**.

The procedure header begins with the two keywords `Private Sub`. A **keyword** is a word that has a special meaning in a programming language. The `Sub` keyword is an abbreviation of the term **sub procedure**, which, in programming terminology, refers to a block of code that performs a specific task. The `Private` keyword indicates that the procedure can be used only within the class in which it is defined—in this case, only within the CopyrightForm class.

Following the `Sub` keyword is the name of the object (`uiExitButton`), an underscore (_), the name of the event (`Click`), and parentheses containing `ByVal sender as Object, ByVal e As System.EventArgs`. The items within the parentheses are called parameters and represent information that is passed to the procedure when it is invoked. For now, you do not need to worry about the parameters; you learn more about parameters later in this book.

Following the items in parentheses in the procedure header is `Handles uiExitButton.Click`. This part of the procedure header indicates that the procedure handles (or is associated with) the uiExitButton's Click event. In other words, the procedure will be processed when the uiExitButton object is clicked. As you learn later in this book, you can associate the same procedure with more than one event by listing each event, separated by commas, in the `Handles` section of the procedure header.

The code template ends with the procedure footer, which contains the keywords `End Sub`. You enter your Visual Basic .NET instructions between the `Private Sub` and `End Sub` lines. In this case, the instructions you enter will tell the uiExitButton control how to respond to the Click event.

Notice that the keywords in the code appear in a different color from the rest of the code. The Code Editor window displays keywords in a different color to help you quickly identify these elements. In this case, the color-coding helps you easily locate the procedure header and footer.

The insertion point located in the event procedure indicates where you enter your code for the uiExitButton_Click procedure. The Code Editor automatically indents the line between the procedure header and footer (as shown in Figure 1-31). Indenting the lines within a procedure makes the instructions easier to read and is a common programming practice.

When the user clicks the Exit button on the copyright screen, it indicates that he or she wants to end the application. You stop an application by entering the Me.Close method in the button's Click event procedure.

The Me.Close Method

If you forget to enter the parentheses after a method's name, the Code Editor will enter them for you when you move the insertion point to another line in the Code Editor window.

You use the **Me.Close method** to instruct the computer to terminate the current application. A **method** is a predefined Visual Basic .NET procedure that you can call (or invoke) when needed. You call the Me.Close method by entering the instruction `Me.Close()` in a procedure. Notice the empty set of parentheses after the method's name in the instruction. The parentheses are required when calling any of Visual Basic .NET's methods; however, depending on the method, the parentheses may or may not be empty.

To code the uiExitButton's Click event procedure, then save and start the application:

1 Type **me.close()** in the Code Editor window, and then press **Enter**. See Figure 1-32.

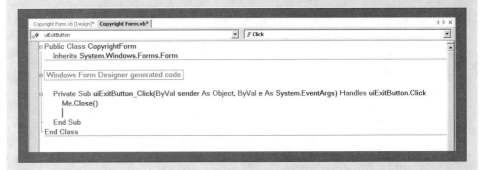

Figure 1-32: Me.Close method entered in the uiExitButton's Click event procedure

When the user clicks the Exit button on the copyright screen, the computer processes the instructions entered in the uiExitButton's Click event procedure. It is probably no surprise to you that the instructions are processed, one after another, in the order in which they appear in the procedure. In programming, this is referred to as **sequential processing** or as the **sequence structure**. (You learn about two other programming structures [selection and repetition] in future chapters.) You are finished with the Code Editor window, so you can close it.

2 Click the **Close** button on the Code Editor window's title bar.

3 Click **File** on the menu bar, and then click **Save All**.

Now start the application to verify that the Exit button ends the application.

4   Click **Debug** on the menu bar, and then click **Start**. The copyright screen appears.

5   Click the **Exit** button to end the application. The application ends and you are returned to the designer window.

6   Close the Output window, then use the File menu to close the solution.

7   Permanently display the Toolbox and Solution Explorer windows.

You have now completed Lesson B. You can either take a break or complete the end-of-lesson questions and exercises before moving on to the next lesson.

SUMMARY

To add a control to a form:

■   Click the appropriate tool in the toolbox, but do not release the mouse button. Drag the mouse pointer to the form. As you drag, both an outline of a rectangle and a plus box follow the mouse pointer. When you release the mouse button, the control appears on the form.

■   You also can add a control to a form by clicking the appropriate tool in the toolbox and then clicking the form. Additionally, you can click the control's tool in the toolbox, then place the mouse pointer on the form, and then press the left mouse button and drag the mouse pointer until the control is the desired size.

To display text that the user cannot edit while the application is running:

■   Use the Label tool to create a label control; then set the label control's Text property.

To automatically size a label control to fit its current contents:

■   Set the label control's AutoSize property to True.

To move a control to a different location on the form:

■   Drag the control to the desired location. You also can set the control's Location property. Additionally, you can select the control and then press and hold down the Control key as you press the ↑, ↓, →, or ← key on your keyboard.

To size a control:

■   Drag the control's sizing handles. You also can set the control's Size, Height, and Width properties. Additionally, you can select the control and then press and hold down the Shift key as you press the ↑, ↓, →, or ← key on your keyboard.

To control the type, style, and size of the font used to display text in a control:

■   Set the control's Font property.

To select multiple controls:

■ Click the first control you want to select, then Control+click each of the other controls you want to select.

■ You also can select a group of controls on the form by placing the mouse pointer slightly above and to the left of the first control you want to select, then pressing the left mouse button and dragging. A dotted rectangle appears as you drag. When all of the controls you want to select are within (or at least touched by) the dotted rectangle, release the mouse button. All of the controls surrounded or touched by the dotted rectangle will be selected.

To cancel the selection of one or more controls:

■ You cancel the selection of one of the selected controls by pressing and holding down the Control key as you click the control.

■ You cancel the selection of all of the selected controls by releasing the Control key and then clicking the form or an unselected control on the form.

To center one or more controls on the form:

■ Select any controls you want to center. Click Format on the menu bar, point to Center in Form, and then click either Horizontally or Vertically.

To align the borders of two or more controls on the form:

■ Select the controls you want to align. The last control selected is the reference control (refer to Discovery Exercise 4). Click Format on the menu bar, point to Align, and then click the appropriate option.

To make two or more controls on the form the same size:

■ Select the controls you want to size. The last control selected is the reference control (refer to Discovery Exercise 4). Click Format on the menu bar, point to Make Same Size, and then click the appropriate option.

To display a graphic in a control in the user interface:

■ Use the PictureBox tool to create a picture box control; then set the control's Image and SizeMode properties.

To display a standard button that performs an action when clicked:

■ Use the Button tool to create a button control.

To change a project's properties:

■ Right-click the project's name in the Solution Explorer window, then click Properties.

To start and stop an application:

■ Click Debug on the menu bar, and then click Start to start the application. You also can press the F5 key on your keyboard.

■ Click Debug on the menu bar, and then click Stop Debugging to stop the application. You also can press Shift+F5.

To open the Code Editor window:

■ Right-click anywhere on the form (except the form's title bar), and then click View Code on the context menu. You also can click View on the menu bar, and then click Code; or you can press the F7 key on your keyboard. (To use the View menu or the F7 key, the designer window should be the active window.) You also can open the Code Editor window by double-clicking the form or a control on the form. Doing so brings up a default event procedure for the object you double-clicked.

To display an object's event procedure in the Code Editor window:

■ Open the Code Editor window. Use the Class Name list box to select the desired object, and then use the Method Name list box to select the desired event.

To allow the user to end a running application:

■ One way of allowing the user to end a running application is to include the Me.Close method in the Click event procedure of a button control.

Q U E S T I O N S

1. The tools you use when designing your user interface are found on the _____ tab on the Toolbox window.
    a. Clipboard Ring
    b. Components
    c. Data
    d. General
    e. Windows Forms

2. The purpose of the _____ control is to display text that the user is not allowed to edit while the application is running.
    a. Button
    b. DisplayBox
    c. Label
    d. PictureBox
    e. TextBox

3. Which of the following properties automatically adjusts the size of a label control to fit the control's current contents?
    a. AutoSize
    b. AutoSizeControl
    c. AutoSizeLabel
    d. Size
    e. SizeAuto

4. The text displayed in a label control is stored in the control's _____ property.
    a. Caption
    b. Display
    c. Label
    d. Name
    e. Text

5. How can you tell when a button control is selected in the designer window?
   a. A thin line surrounds the control.
   b. Sizing handles appear around the control.
   c. The Object box in the Properties window contains the control's name and class.
   d. Both a and c.
   e. Both b and c.

6. How can you tell when an auto-sized label control is selected in the designer window?
   a. A thin line surrounds the control.
   b. Sizing handles appear around the control.
   c. The Object box in the Properties window contains the control's name and class.
   d. Both a and c.
   e. Both b and c.

7. The first value stored in the Location property specifies the number of _____.
   a. pixels from the left border of the form to the left border of the control
   b. pixels from the right border of the form to the right border of the control
   c. pixels between the top border of the form and the top border of the control
   d. pixels between the bottom border of the form and the bottom border of the control

8. The Font property allows you to change the _____ of the font used to display text in an object.
   a. type
   b. style
   c. size
   d. All of the above.

9. The Format menu contains options that allow you to _____.
   a. align two or more controls
   b. center one or more controls horizontally within the form
   c. center one or more controls vertically within the form
   d. make two or more controls the same size
   e. All of the above.

10. The _____ property determines the graphic to display in a picture box control.
    a. DisplayImage
    b. Graphic
    c. Image
    d. Picture
    e. PictureBox

11. You can size a picture box control to fit its current contents by setting the control's _____ property.
    a. AutoSize
    b. ImageSize
    c. PictureSize
    d. Size
    e. SizeMode

12. The Button class is defined in the _____ namespace.
    a. System.Forms
    b. System.Windows.Forms
    c. System.Windows.Forms.Button
    d. Windows.Button
    e. Windows.Forms

13. The caption that appears on a button is stored in the button control's
_____ property.
- a. Caption
- b. Command
- c. Control
- d. Label
- e. Text

14. Which of the following statements is false?
- a. You can start an application by clicking Debug on the menu bar, and then clicking Start.
- b. The executable file that Visual Studio .NET automatically creates when you start an application has the same name as the solution, but with an .exe extension.
- c. You can use the Project Properties dialog box to change the executable file's name.
- d. You can use the Project Properties dialog box to select the startup form.
- e. None of the above.

15. The _____ method terminates the application.
- a. Me.Close
- b. Me.Done
- c. Me.Finish
- d. Me.Stop
- e. None of the above.

16. Actions such as clicking, double-clicking, and scrolling are called _____.
- a. actionEvents
- b. events
- c. happenings
- d. procedures
- e. None of the above.

17. Define the term "syntax".

18. Explain the purpose of the Class Name and Method Name list boxes in the Code Editor window.

19. Define the term "keyword".

20. What is a class definition?

EXERCISES

1. In this exercise, you add controls to a Windows Form. You also change the properties of the form and its controls.
- a. If necessary, start Visual Studio .NET and permanently display the Solution Explorer window.
- b. Click File on the menu bar, and then click Open Solution. Open the Mechanics Solution (Mechanics Solution.sln) file, which is contained in the VBNET\Chap01\Mechanics Solution folder. If the designer window is not open, click the form file's name in the Solution Explorer window, then use the View menu to open the designer window.
- c. Assign the filename Mechanics Form.vb to the form file object.
- d. Assign the name MechForm to the Windows Form object.

e. The Windows Form object's title bar should say IMA. Set the appropriate property.

f. The Windows Form object should be centered on the screen when it first appears. Set the appropriate property.

g. Add a label control to the form. Change the label control's name to uiCompanyLabel.

h. The label control should stretch to fit its current contents. Set the appropriate property.

i. The label control should display the text "International Mechanics Association" (without the quotation marks). Set the appropriate property.

j. Display the label control's text in italics using the Tahoma font. Change the size of the text to 12 points.

k. The label control should be located 16 pixels from the top of the form.

l. Center the label control horizontally on the form.

m. Add a button control to the form. Change the button control's name to uiExitButton.

n. The button control should display the text "Exit" (without the quotation marks). Set the appropriate property.

o. Display the button control's text using the Tahoma font. Change the size of the text to 12 points.

p. The button control should be located 200 pixels from the left border of the form, and 240 pixels from the top of the form.

q. Open the Code Editor window. Enter the Me.Close method in the uiExitButton's Click event procedure.

r. Display the Mechanics Project Properties Pages dialog box. Open the Common Properties folder, then click General. Use the Assembly name text box to change the executable file's name to IMA. Change the startup form to MechForm.

s. Save the solution. Start the application, then use the Exit button to stop the application.

t. Close the Output window, then close the solution.

2. In this exercise, you create the user interface shown in Figure 1-33.

a. If necessary, start Visual Studio .NET and permanently display the Solution Explorer window.

b. Create a blank solution named Costello Solution. Save the solution in the VBNET\Chap01 folder.

c. Add a Visual Basic .NET Windows Application project to the solution. Name the project Costello Project.

d. Assign the filename Costello Form.vb to the form file object.

e. Create the interface shown in Figure 1-33. Name the Windows Form object and controls appropriately. You can use any font type, style, and size for the label controls.

Figure 1-33

    f. Code the Exit button so that it terminates the application when it is clicked.

    g. Change the executable file's name to Costello Motors. Change the startup form to the name of your Windows Form object.

    h. Save the solution. Start the application, then use the Exit button to stop the application.

    i. Close the Output window, then close the solution.

3. In this exercise, you create the user interface shown in Figure 1-34.

    a. If necessary, start Visual Studio .NET and permanently display the Solution Explorer window.

    b. Create a blank solution named Tabatha Solution. Save the solution in the VBNET\Chap01 folder.

    c. Add a Visual Basic .NET Windows Application project to the solution. Name the project Tabatha Project.

    d. Assign the filename Tabatha Form.vb to the form file object.

    e. Create the interface shown in Figure 1-34. Name the Windows Form object and controls appropriately. You can use any font type, style, and size for the label controls.

Figure 1-34

    f. Code the Exit button so that it terminates the application when it is clicked.

    g. Change the executable file's name to Tabatha. Change the startup form to the name of your Windows Form object.

    h. Save the solution. Start the application, then use the Exit button to stop the application.

    i. Close the Output window, then close the solution.

discovery ▶ **4.** In this exercise, you learn about the Format menu's Align and Make Same Size options.

    a. If necessary, start Visual Studio .NET and permanently display the Solution Explorer window.

    b. Open the Jerrods Solution (Jerrods Solution.sln) file, which is contained in the VBNET\Chap01\Jerrods Solution folder. If the designer window is not open, click the form file's name in the Solution Explorer window, then use the View menu to open the designer window.

    c. Click one of the button controls on the form, then press and hold down the Ctrl (or Control) key as you click the remaining two button controls.

Notice that the sizing handles on the last button selected are black, whereas the sizing handles on the other two button controls are white. The Align and Make Same Size options on the Format menu use the control with the black sizing handles as the reference control when aligning and sizing the selected controls. First, practice with the Align option by aligning the three button controls by their left borders.

d. Click Format, point to Align, and then click Lefts. The left borders of the first two controls you selected are aligned with the left border of the last control you selected.

The Make Same Size option makes the selected objects the same height, width, or both. Here again, the last object you select determines the size.

e. Click the form to deselect the three buttons. Click Button2, then Ctrl+click Button3, and then Ctrl+click Button1. Click Format, point to Make Same Size, and then click Both. The height and width of the first two controls you selected now match the height and width of the last control you selected. Click the form to deselect the button controls.

f. Save and then close the solution.

discovery ▶ 5. In this exercise, you learn how to change the display of the tools on the Windows Forms tab in the toolbox.

a. If necessary, start Visual Studio .NET and permanently display the Solution Explorer window.

b. Open the Jerrods Solution (Jerrods Solution.sln) file, which is contained in the VBNET\Chap01\Jerrods Solution folder. If the designer window is not open, click the form file's name in the Solution Explorer window, then use the View menu to open the designer window.

By default, the tools on the Windows Forms tab in the toolbox are listed in order by their estimated frequency of use, with the most used tools listed first. If you prefer, you can list the tools alphabetically by name.

c. If necessary, permanently display the Toolbox window. Right-click the Windows Forms tab, and then click Sort Items Alphabetically on the context menu. The tools appear in alphabetical order by name, with one exception: the Pointer tool appears first in the list.

You also can choose to view the tool icons only, rather than the icons and names; this creates a more compact display of the tools and allows you to view all of the tools at the same time.

d. Right-click the Windows Forms tab. A checkmark appears next to the List View option, which indicates that the option is selected. When the List View option is selected, the Windows Form tab displays both the tool icons and names.

e. Click List View to deselect the option; this will remove the checkmark. Now only the tool icons appear on the tab. You can display a tool's name by resting the mouse pointer on the tool's icon.

f. Place your mouse pointer on the CheckBox tool icon. The tool name, CheckBox, appears in a tooltip box.

You can use the Customize Toolbox dialog box to restore the Windows Forms tab to its original state.

g. Click Tools on the menu bar, and then click Add/Remove Toolbox Items. The Customize Toolbox dialog box opens. (It may take several moments for the dialog box to open.)

h. Click the Reset button on the .NET Framework Components tab. A Microsoft Development Environment dialog box opens and informs you that the Toolbox default settings will be restored and all custom Toolbox items will be removed. The message in the dialog box asks if you want to continue.

i. Click the Yes button. (It will take the computer several moments to restore the default settings.)

j. Click the OK button to close the Customize Toolbox dialog box, then click the Windows Forms tab in the toolbox. The Windows Forms tab appears in its original state, with the tools listed in order by their frequency of use.

k. Close the solution.

After completing this lesson, you will be able to:

- Set the properties of a timer control
- Delete a control from the form
- Delete code from the Code Editor window
- Code the timer control's Tick event
- Remove and/or disable the Minimize, Maximize, and Close buttons
- Prevent the user from sizing a form
- Print the project's code

Completing the Copyright Screen

Using the Timer Tool

Recall that the copyright screen will serve as a splash screen for each custom application created by Interlocking Software. Splash screens typically do not contain an Exit button; rather, they use a timer control to automatically remove the splash screen after a set period of time. You create a timer control using the **Timer tool** in the toolbox. In this lesson, you remove the Exit button from the copyright screen and replace it with a timer control. First, open the Copyright Solution.

To open the Copyright Solution:

1. If necessary, start Visual Studio .NET and close the Start Page window.

2. Click **File** on the menu bar, and then click **Open Solution**. The Open Solution dialog box opens. Open the **Copyright Solution** (Copyright Solution.sln) file, which is contained in the VBNET\Chap01\Copyright Solution folder.

3. If necessary, permanently display the Toolbox and Properties windows, and auto-hide the Solution Explorer window.

4. If necessary, open the designer window to view the copyright screen.

tip

A millisecond is 1/1000 of a second.

You can use a **timer control** to process code at regular time intervals. You simply set the control's **Interval property** to the length of the desired time interval, in milliseconds. You also set its Enabled property to True. The **Enabled property** determines whether an object can respond to an event—in this case, whether it can respond to the Tick event. In the timer control's Tick event, you enter the code you want processed. The Tick event procedure tells the computer what to do after each time interval has elapsed. Use the Timer tool to add a timer control to the copyright screen.

To add a timer control to the copyright screen, and then change its properties:

1. Click the **Timer** tool in the toolbox, then drag a timer control to the form. (Do not worry about the exact location.) When you release the mouse button, a timer control appears in the component tray, as shown in Figure 1-35.

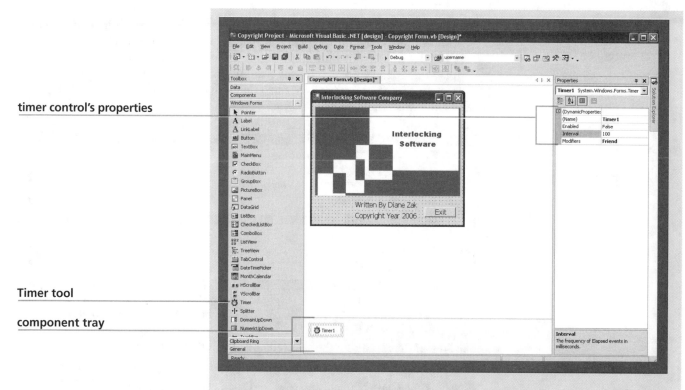

timer control's properties

Timer tool

component tray

Figure 1-35: Timer control placed in the component tray

Unlike the label, picture box, and button controls, the timer control does not appear in the user interface when the application is run. Controls that do not appear in the interface are placed in the **component tray** pane of the designer window.

2 Set the timer control's Name property to **uiExitTimer**.

3 Set the timer control's Enabled property to **True**.

You will have the timer control end the application after eight seconds, which is 8000 milliseconds.

4 Set the timer control's Interval property to **8000**.

5 Auto-hide the Toolbox and Properties windows.

Now that you have a timer control on the form, you no longer need the Exit button, so you can delete it and its associated code. You then will enter the Me.Close method in the timer control's Tick event procedure.

To delete the uiExitButton and its code, then code the uiExitTimer control:

1 Click the **uiExitButton** to select it, then press **Delete** to delete the control from the Windows form.

Note that deleting a control from the form does not delete the control's code, which remains in the Code Editor window.

2 Right-click the **form**, and then click **View Code**. Select the entire Click event procedure for the uiExitButton, as shown in Figure 1-36. (Do not be concerned if you cannot view all of the uiExitButton's code. The font used to display the text in the Code Editor window shown in Figure 1-36 was changed to 13-point Microsoft Sans Serif so that you could view all of the code in the figure. It is not necessary for you to change the font.)

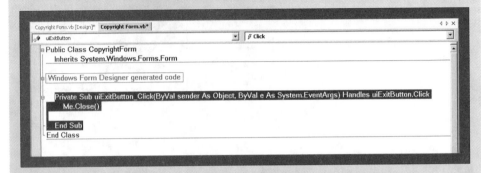

Figure 1-36: uiExitButton's Click event procedure selected in the Code Editor window

3 Press **Delete** to delete the selected code from the Code Editor window.

Now enter the Me.Close method in the uiExitTimer's Tick event procedure.

4 Click the **Class Name** list arrow, and then click **uiExitTimer** in the list. Click the **Method Name** list arrow, and then click **Tick** in the list. The uiExitTimer's Tick event procedure appears in the Code Editor window.

5 Type **me.close()** and press **Enter**. See Figure 1-37. (Recall that the font used to display the text shown in the Code Editor was changed to 13-point Microsoft Sans Serif.)

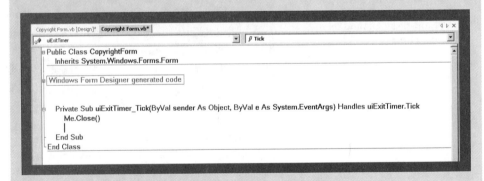

Figure 1-37: uiExitTimer's Tick event procedure

Now save the solution and then start the application.

6 Click **File** on the menu bar, and then click **Save All**.

7 Click **Debug** on the menu bar, and then click **Start**. The CopyrightForm appears on the screen. Place your mouse pointer ⊾ on the right border of the form until ⊾ becomes ↔, then drag the form's border to the left. Notice that you can size the form while the application is running. As a general rule, the user typically is not allowed to change the size of a splash screen. You can prevent the user from sizing the form by changing the form's FormBorderStyle property.

After eight seconds elapse, the application ends and the copyright screen is removed from view.

8   Close the Output window. Click the **Copyright Form.vb [Design]** tab to make the designer window the active window.

Now learn about the FormBorderStyle property of a Windows Form object.

Setting the FormBorderStyle Property

The **FormBorderStyle property** determines the border style of a Windows Form object. Figure 1-38 lists the valid settings for the FormBorderStyle property and provides a brief description of the border provided by each setting.

FormBorderStyle setting	Description of the border
Fixed3D	fixed, three-dimensional
FixedDialog	fixed, thick dialog-style
FixedSingle	fixed, thin line
FixedToolWindow	fixed, tool window style
None	no border
Sizable	sizable, normal style (default setting)
SizableToolWindow	sizable, tool window style

Figure 1-38: FormBorderStyle settings

For most applications, you will want to leave the FormBorderStyle setting at its default value, Sizable. When the FormBorderStyle property is set to Sizable, the user can drag the form's borders to change the form's size while the application is running. If you want to prevent the user from sizing the form, you can set the FormBorderStyle property to any of the fixed settings shown in Figure 1-38; splash screens typically use either the None setting or the FixedSingle setting. When the FormBorderStyle property is set to None, no border is drawn around the form. Setting the FormBorderStyle property to FixedSingle, on the other hand, draws a fixed, thin line around the form. You will set the copyright screen's FormBorderStyle property to FixedSingle.

To change the FormBorderStyle property, then save and start the application:

1   Click the **form's title bar** to select the form.

2   Set the FormBorderStyle property to **FixedSingle**.

3   Click **File** on the menu bar, and then click **Save All**.

4   Click **Debug** on the menu bar, and then click **Start**. Try to size the form by dragging one of its borders. You will notice that you cannot size the form using its border.

5   When the application ends, click **Debug** on the menu bar, and then click **Start** to display the splash screen again. Notice that the copyright screen's title bar contains a Minimize button, a Maximize button, and a Close button. As a general rule, most splash screens do not contain these elements. You learn how to remove the elements, as well as the title bar itself, in the next section.

6   If necessary, click the **Close** button on the splash screen's title bar.

7   When the application ends, close the Output window.

Now learn about a Windows Form object's MinimizeBox, MaximizeBox, and ControlBox properties.

The MinimizeBox, MaximizeBox, and ControlBox Properties

You can use a Windows Form object's MinimizeBox property to disable the Minimize button that appears on the form's title bar. Similarly, you can use the MaximizeBox property to disable the Maximize button. You experiment with both properties in the next set of steps.

To experiment with the MinimizeBox and MaximizeBox properties:

1   If necessary, click the **form's title bar** to select the form.

First, disable the Minimize button.

2   Set the MinimizeBox property to **False**. Notice that the Minimize button appears dimmed (grayed-out) on the title bar. This indicates that the button is not available for use.

Now enable the Minimize button and disable the Maximize button.

3   Set the MinimizeBox property to **True**, then set the MaximizeBox property to **False**. Now the Maximize button appears dimmed (grayed-out) on the title bar.

Now observe what happens if both the MinimizeBox and MaximizeBox properties are set to False.

4   Set the MinimizeBox property to **False**. (The MaximizeBox property is already set to False.) Notice that when both properties are set to False, the buttons are not disabled; rather, they are removed from the title bar.

Now return the buttons to their original state.

5   Set the MinimizeBox and MaximizeBox properties to **True**.

Unlike most applications, splash screens typically do not contain a title bar. You can remove the title bar by setting the Windows Form object's ControlBox property to False, and then removing the text from its Text property. You try this next.

To remove the title bar from the copyright screen:

1   If necessary, click the **form's title bar** to select the form.

2   Set the ControlBox property to **False**. Notice that setting this property to False removes the title bar elements (icon and buttons) from the form; however, it does not remove the title bar itself. To remove the title bar, you must delete the contents of the form's Text property.

3   Delete the contents of the form's Text property.

4   Click **File** on the menu bar, and then click **Save All**.

5   Click **Debug** on the menu bar, and then click **Start**. The copyright screen appears without a title bar. See Figure 1-39.

Figure 1-39: Completed copyright screen

6   When the application ends, close the Output window.

Before ending this lesson you learn how to print the application.

Printing Your Code

You always should print a copy of the code entered in the Code Editor window, because the printout will help you understand and maintain the application in the future. To print the code, the Code Editor window must be the active, or current, window.

To print the copyright screen's code:

1   Click the **Copyright Form.vb** tab to make the Code Editor window the active window.

Only the code that is not collapsed will be sent to the printer for printing.

2   Verify that the only plus box in the Code Editor window appears next to the `Windows Form Designer generated code` entry. If a plus box appears anywhere else in the Code Editor window, click the plus box. (You typically do not need to print the code generated by the designer.)

3   Click **File** on the menu bar, then click **Print**. The Print dialog box opens.

4   If your computer is connected to a printer, click the **OK** button to begin printing; otherwise, click the **Cancel** button. If you clicked the OK button, your printer prints the code.

5   Close the Code Editor window by clicking the **Close** button on its title bar.

6   Click **File** on the menu bar, and then click **Close Solution**.

7   Click **File** on the menu bar, and then click **Exit** to exit Visual Studio .NET.

You have now completed Chapter 1. You can either take a break or complete the end-of lesson questions and exercises.

SUMMARY

To perform code at specified intervals of time:

■ Use the Timer tool to add a timer control to the form. Set the timer control's Interval property to the number of milliseconds for each interval. Set the timer control's Enabled property to True to turn the timer control on. Enter the code in the timer control's Tick event procedure.

To delete a control:

■ Select the control you want to delete, then press Delete. If the control contains code, open the Code Editor window and delete the control's event procedures.

To enable/disable the Minimize button on the form's title bar:

■ Set the form's MinimizeBox property.

To enable/disable the Maximize button on the form's title bar:

■ Set the form's MaximizeBox property.

To control whether the icon, as well as the Minimize, Maximize, and Close buttons, appear in the form's title bar:

■ Set the form's ControlBox property.

To control the border style of the form:

■ Set the form's FormBorderStyle property.

To print the Visual Basic .NET code:

■ Open the Code Editor window. Click File on the menu bar, and then click Print. Click the OK button in the Print dialog box.

QUESTIONS

1. You can use a _____ control to process code at regular time intervals.
   a. clock
   b. stopwatch
   c. timer
   d. watch
   e. None of the above.

2. The _____ property determines whether an object can respond to an event.
    a. Enabled
    b. Event
    c. PermitResponse
    d. Respond
    e. Response

3. After each time interval has elapsed, the code in a timer control's _____ is processed.
    a. Interval property
    b. Interval event procedure
    c. Tick property
    d. Tick event procedure
    e. Timer event procedure

4. Ten seconds equals _____ milliseconds.
    a. 100
    b. 1000
    c. 10,000
    d. 100,000
    e. 1,000,000

5. Which of the following is false?
    a. When you add a timer control to a form, the control appears in the component tray.
    b. The user can see a timer control while the application is running.
    c. You can delete a control from the component tray by right-clicking it and then clicking Delete.
    d. The number entered in a timer control's Interval property represents the number of milliseconds for each interval.
    e. None of the above.

6. To disable the Minimize button on a form's title bar, set the form's _____ property to False.
    a. ButtonMin
    b. ButtonMinimize
    c. Minimize
    d. MinimizeBox
    e. MinimizeButton

7. The _____ property determines whether the user can drag a form's borders while the application is running.
    a. BorderStyle
    b. Drag
    c. FormBorder
    d. StyleBorder
    e. None of the above.

8. You can remove the Minimize, Maximize, and Close buttons from a form's title bar by setting the form's _____ property to False.
    a. ControlBox
    b. ControlButton
    c. Elements
    d. TitleBar
    e. TitleBarElements

9. Explain how you print a project's code.

10. Explain how you delete a control that contains code.

EXERCISES

1. In this exercise, you modify an existing form by replacing its button control with a timer control.
   a. If necessary, start Visual Studio .NET and permanently display the Solution Explorer window.
   b. Click File on the menu bar, and then click Open Solution. Open the Jefferson Solution (Jefferson Solution.sln) file, which is contained in the VBNET\Chap01\Jefferson Solution folder. If the designer window is not open, click the form file's name in the Solution Explorer window, then use the View menu to open the designer window.
   c. Delete the uiExitButton from the form, then delete the uiExitButton's code from the Code Editor window.
   d. Return to the designer window. Add a timer control to the form. Change the timer control's name to uiExitTimer.
   e. Set the timer control's Enabled property to True.
   f. The timer control should end the application after 10 seconds have elapsed. Set the appropriate property. Then, enter the Me.Close method in the appropriate event procedure in the Code Editor window.
   g. Save the solution. Start the application. After 10 seconds, the application should end.
   h. Remove the elements (icon and buttons) from the form's title bar.
   i. Delete the text that appears in the form's title bar.
   j. Set the form's FormBorderStyle property to FixedSingle.
   k. Save the solution. Start the application. After 10 seconds, the application should end.
   l. Close the Output window, then close the solution.

2. In this exercise, you design your own user interface.
   a. If necessary, start Visual Studio .NET and permanently display the Solution Explorer window.
   b. Create a blank solution named My Interface Solution. Save the solution in the VBNET\Chap01 folder.
   c. Add a Visual Basic .NET Windows Application project to the solution. Name the project My Interface Project.
   d. Assign the filename My Interface Form.vb to the form file object.
   e. Use one or more label and picture box controls in your interface. Include a button that the user can click to end the application. You can use any font type, style, and size for the label control(s). You also can use any graphic for the picture box.
   f. Be sure to name the Windows Form object and controls appropriately.
   g. Change the executable file's name to My Interface. Change the startup form to the name of your Windows Form object.
   h. Disable the Minimize and Maximize buttons on the form.
   i. Save the solution. Start the application, then use the Exit button to stop the application.
   j. Close the Output window, then close the solution.

discovery ▶ 3. In this exercise, you learn how to enter an assignment statement in an event procedure.

    a. If necessary, start Visual Studio .NET and permanently display the Solution Explorer window.

    b. Create a blank solution named Icon Solution. Save the solution in the VBNET\Chap01 folder.

    c. Add a Visual Basic .NET Windows Application project to the solution. Name the project Icon Project.

    d. Assign the filename Icon Form.vb to the form file object.

    e. Add a picture box control and three buttons to the form. (The location and size of the controls are not important.) Name the controls uiIconPictureBox, uiOnButton, uiOffButton, and uiExitButton.

    f. Include any graphic in the picture box control.

    g. The captions for the three buttons should be On, Off, and Exit. Change the appropriate property for each button.

    h. The Exit button should end the application when clicked. Enter the appropriate code in the Code Editor window.

    i. Display the uiOffButton's Click event procedure in the Code Editor window. In the procedure, enter the instruction `Me.uiIconPictureBox.Visible = False`. This instruction is called an assignment statement, because it assigns a value to a container; in this case, the container is the Visible property of the uiIconPictureBox control. When you click the uiOffButton, the `Me.uiIconPictureBox.Visible = False` instruction will hide the picture box from view.

    j. Display the uiOnButton's Click event procedure in the Code Editor window. In the procedure, enter an instruction that will display the picture box.

    k. Save the solution, then start the application. Use the uiOffButton to hide the picture box, then use the uiOnButton to display the picture box. Finally, use the uiExitButton to end the application.

    l. Close the Output window, then close the solution.

discovery ▶ 4. In this exercise, you learn how to display a graphic on the face of a button control. (This exercise assumes that you have completed Discovery Exercise 3.)

    a. If necessary, start Visual Studio .NET and permanently display the Solution Explorer window.

    b. Click File on the menu bar, and then click Open Solution. Open the Icon Solution (Icon Solution.sln) file, which is contained in the VBNET\Chap01\Icon Solution folder. If the designer window is not open, click the form file's name in the Solution Explorer window, then use the View menu to open the designer window.

    You use a button's Image property to specify the graphic you want displayed on the face of the button. You use a button's ImageAlign property to specify the graphic's alignment on the button.

    c. Click the uiOnButton. Set the Image property using any of the Visual Studio .NET icons. The icons are usually stored in the Program Files\Microsoft Visual Studio .NET 2003\Common7\Graphics\icons folder on either the local hard drive or the network drive.

    d. Set the uiOnButton's ImageAlign property to TopLeft. (*Hint*: When you click the ImageAlign property's list arrow, nine buttons will appear in the list. Select the button in the top left.)

    e. Set the Image and ImageAlign properties of the uiOffButton and uiExitButton.

    f. Close the solution.

discovery ▶   5.   In this exercise, you learn how to display a tooltip.

a. If necessary, start Visual Studio .NET and permanently display the Solution Explorer window.

b. Click File on the menu bar, and then click Open Solution. Open the Tooltip Solution (Tooltip Solution.sln) file, which is contained in the VBNET\Chap01\ Tooltip Solution folder. If the designer window is not open, click the form file's name in the Solution Explorer window, then use the View menu to open the designer window.

c. Locate the ToolTip tool in the toolbox. Drag a tooltip control to the form. Notice that the control appears in the component tray rather than on the form. Name the tooltip control uiToolTip1.

d. Click the uiExitButton to select it. Set the button's ToolTip on uiToolTip1 property to "Ends the application." (without the quotation marks).

e. Save the solution, then start the application. Hover your mouse pointer over the Exit button. The tooltip "Ends the application." appears in a tooltip box.

f. Click the Exit button to end the application.

g. Close the Output window, then close the solution.

debugging   6.   In this exercise, you debug an existing application.

a. If necessary, start Visual Studio .NET and permanently display the Solution Explorer window.

b. Click File on the menu bar, and then click Open Solution. Open the Debug Solution (Debug Solution.sln) file, which is contained in the VBNET\Chap01\ Debug Solution folder. If the designer window is not open, click the form file's name in the Solution Explorer window, then use the View menu to open the designer window.

c. Start the application. Click the Exit button. Notice that the Exit button does not end the application.

d. Click the Close button on the form's title bar to end the application.

e. Locate and then correct the error.

f. Start the application. Click the Exit button, which should end the application.

g. Close the Output window, then close the solution.

Designing Applications

Creating an Order Screen

case ▶ During your second week at Interlocking Software, you and Chris Statton, the senior programmer, meet with the sales manager of Skate-Away Sales. The sales manager, Jacques Cousard, tells you that his company sells skateboards by phone. The skateboards are priced at $100 each and are available in two colors—yellow and blue. He further explains that Skate-Away Sales employs 20 salespeople to answer the phones. The salespeople record each order on a form that contains the customer's name, address, and the number of blue and yellow skateboards ordered. They then calculate the total number of skateboards ordered and the total price of the skateboards, including a 5% sales tax.

Mr. Cousard feels that having the salespeople manually perform the necessary calculations is much too time-consuming and prone to errors. He wants Interlocking to create a computerized application that will solve the problems of the current order-taking system.

Solving the Problem Using a Procedure-Oriented Approach

As you learned in the Overview, the first high-level languages were used to create procedure-oriented programs. When writing a procedure-oriented program, the programmer concentrates on the major tasks that the program needs to perform. The programmer must instruct the computer every step of the way, from the start of each task to its completion. The procedure-oriented approach to problem solving requires a programmer to think in a step-by-step, top-to-bottom fashion. Planning tools such as flowcharts and pseudocode make this approach easier. A **flowchart** uses standardized symbols to show the steps needed to solve a problem. **Pseudocode** uses English phrases to describe the required steps. Some programmers prefer to use flowcharts, while others prefer pseudocode. (You learn more about pseudocode in Lesson C of this chapter, and about flowcharts in Chapter 4, as these planning tools also are useful in object-oriented programming.) Take a look at a procedure-oriented approach to solving Skate-Away's problem. Figure 2-1 shows the solution written in pseudocode.

1. get customer name, street address, city, state, ZIP, number of blue skateboards, number of yellow skateboards

2. calculate total skateboards = number of blue skateboards + number of yellow skateboards

3. calculate total price = total skateboards * $100 * 105%

4. print customer name, street address, city, state, ZIP, number of blue skateboards, number of yellow skateboards, total skateboards, total price

5. end

Figure 2-1: Pseudocode for the procedure-oriented solution

Notice that the pseudocode indicates the sequence of steps the computer must take to process an order. Using the pseudocode as a guide, the programmer then translates the solution into a language that the computer can understand. Figure 2-2 shows the pseudocode translated into Microsoft's QuickBASIC language. QuickBASIC is a predecessor of the Visual Basic programming language and is used to create procedure-oriented programs.

```
Ans$ = "Y"
While Ans$ = "Y" or Ans$ = "y"
        Input "Enter the customer's name", Names$
        Input "Enter the street address:", Address$
        Input "Enter the city:", City$
        Input "Enter the state:", State$
        Input "Enter the zip code:", Zip$
        Input "Enter the number of blue skateboards:", Blue
        Input "Enter the number of yellow skateboards:", Yellow
        Totboards = Blue + Yellow
        Totprice = Totboards * 100 * 1.05
        Print "Customer name:", Names$
        Print "Address:", Address$
        Print "City:", City$
        Print "State:", State$
        Print "Zip:", Zip$
        Print "Blue skateboards:", Blue
        Print "Yellow skateboards:", Yellow
        Print "Total skateboards:", Totboards
        Print "Total price: $", Totprice
        Input "Do you want to enter another order? Enter Y if you
        do, or N if you don't.", Ans$
Wend
End
```

Figure 2-2: Procedure-oriented program written in QuickBASIC

Practice entering an order using this procedure-oriented program.

To use the procedure-oriented program to enter an order:

1 Use the Run command on the Windows Start menu to run the **Procedure** (**Procedure.exe**) file, which is contained in the VBNET\Chap02 folder on your computer's hard disk. A prompt requesting the customer's name appears on the screen.

Assume that Sport Warehouse wants to place an order for 10 blue skateboards and 20 yellow skateboards.

2 Type **Sport Warehouse** and press **Enter**. A prompt requesting the street address appears on the screen.

3 Type **123 Main** and press **Enter**, then type **Glendale** for the city and press **Enter**, then type **IL** for the state and press **Enter**, and then type **60134** for the ZIP code and press **Enter**. The program now prompts you to enter the number of blue skateboards ordered.

4   Type **10** as the number of blue skateboards ordered, then press **Enter**. A prompt requesting the number of yellow skateboards ordered appears next.

5   Type **20** as the number of yellow skateboards ordered, then press **Enter**. The program computes and displays the total skateboards ordered (30) and the total price of the order ($3,150.00). (Recall that skateboards are $100 each and there is a 5% sales tax.) See Figure 2-3.

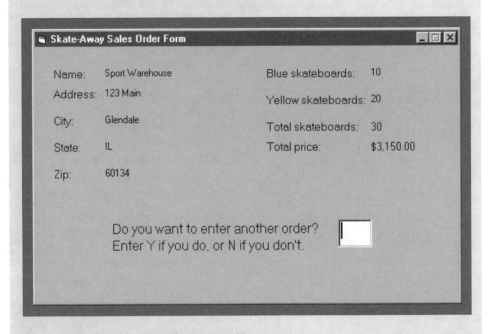

Figure 2-3: Results of the procedure-oriented program

Notice that the screen also contains a prompt that asks if you want to enter another order.

6   Type **n** and press **Enter** to end the program.

Although Skate-Away Sales could use this procedure-oriented program to record its phone orders, the program has one very important limitation that is inherent in all procedure-oriented programs: the user has little, if any, control over the processing of the program. Recall, for example, that you could not control the sequence in which the order information was entered. What if the customer wants to order the yellow skateboards before the blue skateboards? Also recall that you could not change the information once you entered it. What if the customer changes his or her mind about how many blue skateboards to order? And, finally, recall that you had no control over when the program calculated the total order and the total price. What if the customer wants to know the total price of the blue skateboards before placing the yellow skateboard order?

Now look at an object-oriented approach to programming.

Solving the Problem Using an Object-Oriented (OO) Approach

In object-oriented languages, the emphasis of a program is on the **objects** included in the user interface (such as scroll bars or buttons) and the **events** that occur on those objects (such as scrolling or clicking). Unlike the procedure-oriented approach to problem solving, the object-oriented (OO) approach does not view the solution as a step-by-step, top-to-bottom process. Instead, the OO programmer's goal is to give the user as much control over the program as possible.

When using the OO approach to problem solving, the programmer begins by identifying the tasks the application needs to perform. Then the programmer decides on the appropriate objects to which those tasks will be assigned and on any events necessary to trigger those objects to perform their assigned task(s). For example, the copyright screen you created in Chapter 1 had to provide the user with a way to end the application. Recall that you assigned that task to the Exit button in Lesson B. The event that triggered the Exit button to perform its assigned task was the Click event. In this book, you will use a **TOE** (Task, Object, Event) **chart** to assist you in planning your object-oriented programs.

Before learning how to plan an OO application, run an OO application written in Visual Basic .NET and designed to solve Skate-Away's problem.

To run the OO application:

1   Use the Run command on the Start menu to run the **OO** (OO.exe) file, which is contained in the VBNET\Chap02 folder on your computer's hard disk. The order screen shown in Figure 2-4 appears.

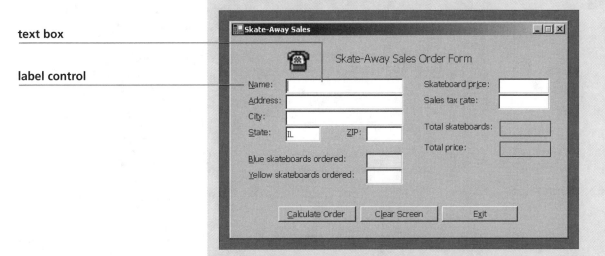

Figure 2-4: Order screen created by the OO application

The order screen contains a new control: a text box. You use a **text box** to provide areas in the form where the user can enter information.

Notice that Visual Basic .NET displays an insertion point in the first text box. The label control to the left of the text box identifies the information the user should enter; in this case, the user should enter the customer's name. Enter Sport Warehouse's information.

2   Type **Sport Warehouse** as the customer's name, then press **Tab** twice. The insertion point appears in the City text box.

3   Type **Glendale** as the city, then press **Shift+Tab** (press and hold down the Shift key as you press the Tab key) to move the insertion point to the Address text box.

Notice that the OO application allows you to enter the order information in any order.

4   Type **123 Main** as the address, then press **Tab** twice. Because most of Skate-Away's customers reside in Illinois, the OO application already contains IL in the State box.

5   Press **Tab**, then type **60134** as the ZIP code, and then press **Tab**. The insertion point appears in the Blue skateboards ordered text box.

6   Type **10** as the number of blue skateboards ordered and press **Tab** twice. Type **100** as the skateboard price and press **Tab**, then type **.05** as the sales tax rate and press **Tab**. Click the **Calculate Order** button. The Calculate Order button calculates the total skateboards (10) and the total price ($1,050.00). Notice that the OO application allows you to tell the customer the cost of the blue skateboards before the yellow skateboard order is placed.

7   Click the **Yellow skateboards ordered** text box, type **20**, and then click the **Calculate Order** button. The application recalculates the total skateboards (30) and the total price ($3,150.00).

Now assume that Sport Warehouse wants to change the number of blue skateboards ordered to 20.

8   Change the number of blue skateboards ordered from 10 to **20**, then click the **Calculate Order** button. The application recalculates the total skateboards (40) and the total price ($4,200.00). See Figure 2-5.

tip

· · · · · · · · · · · · · · · ·

▶ You also can click inside a text box to place the insertion point in the text box.

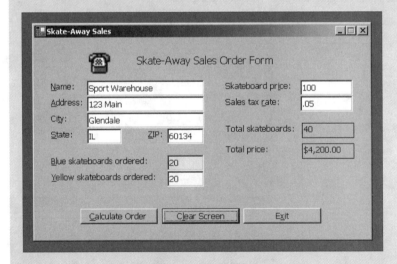

Figure 2-5: Completed order using the OO program

Notice that the captions that identify each button and text box in the interface have an underlined letter, which is called an access key. An **access key** allows the user to select a control using the Alt key in combination with a character, such as a letter or number. For example, when the salesperson is finished with an order, he or she can clear the screen either by clicking the Clear Screen button or by pressing the Alt key along with the letter l—the Clear Screen button's access key.

9   Press **Alt+l** (the letter "l") to clear the screen for the next order. The previous customer's information (except the state, skateboard price, and sales tax rate) disappears, and the insertion point appears in the Name text box.

   HELP? Pressing Alt+l means to press and hold down the Alt key as you type the letter l. Be sure to type the letter l, and not the number 1.

You learn more about access keys in Lesson B.

10 Press **Alt + x** (or click the **Exit** button) to end the application.

Unlike the procedure-oriented program, the OO program gives users a great deal of control. Users can enter information in any order, change what they entered at any time, and calculate a subtotal whenever they like.

In Lesson A, you learn how a Visual Basic .NET programmer plans an OO application. Then, in Lessons B and C, you create the OO application that you just viewed.

LESSON A

objectives

After completing this lesson, you will be able to:

- **Plan an OO application in Visual Basic .NET**
- **Complete a TOE (Task, Object, Event) chart**
- **Follow the Windows standards regarding the layout and labeling of controls**

Planning an Object-Oriented (OO) Application in Visual Basic .NET

Creating an OO Application

The process a programmer follows when creating an OO application is similar to the process a builder follows when building a home. Both processes are shown in Figure 2-6.

A builder's process	A programmer's process
1. Meet with the client	1. Meet with the client
2. Plan the home (blueprint)	2. Plan the application (TOE chart)
3. Build the frame	3. Build the user interface
4. Complete the home	4. Code the application
5. Inspect the home and fix any problems	5. Test and debug the application
6. Assemble the documentation	6. Assemble the documentation

Figure 2-6: Processes used by a builder and a programmer

As Figure 2-6 shows, both the builder and the programmer first meet with the client to discuss the client's wants and needs. They then create a plan (blueprint) for the project. After the client approves the plan, the builder builds the home's frame; likewise, the programmer builds the user interface, which is the application's frame. Once the frame is built, the builder completes the home by adding the electrical wiring, walls, and so on. Similarly, the programmer completes the application by adding the necessary code (instructions) to the user interface. When the home is complete, the builder makes a final inspection and corrects any problems before the customer moves in. Likewise, the programmer tests the completed application, and any problems, called **bugs**, are fixed before the application is given to the user. The final step in both processes is to assemble the project's documentation (paperwork), which then is given to the customer/user.

You learn how to plan an OO application in this lesson. Steps three through six of the process are covered in Lessons B and C.

Planning an OO Application

As any builder will tell you, the most important aspect of a home is not its beauty; rather, it is how closely the home matches the buyer's wants and needs. For example, a large dining room may be appropriate for someone who frequently entertains; for someone who does not, it may be a waste of space. The same is true for an OO application. Therefore, for an application to meet the user's needs, it is essential for the programmer to plan the application jointly with the user. It cannot be stressed enough that the only way to guarantee the success of an application is to actively involve the user in the planning phase. Planning an OO application requires the following four steps:

1. Identify the tasks the application needs to perform.
2. Identify the objects to which you will assign those tasks.
3. Identify the events required to trigger an object into performing its assigned tasks.
4. Draw a sketch of the user interface.

You can use a TOE (Task, Object, Event) chart to record the application's tasks, objects, and events. In the next section, you begin completing a TOE chart for the Skate-Away Sales application. The first step is to identify the application's tasks.

Identifying the Application's Tasks

Realizing that it is essential to involve the user when planning the application, you meet with the sales manager of Skate-Away Sales, Mr. Cousard, to determine his requirements. You ask Mr. Cousard to bring the form the salespeople currently use to record the orders. Viewing the current forms and procedures will help you gain a better understanding of the application. You also can use the current form as a guide when designing the user interface. Figure 2-7 shows the current order form used by Skate-Away Sales.

Figure 2-7: Current order form used by Skate-Away Sales

When identifying the tasks an application needs to perform, it is helpful to ask the following questions:

- What information, if any, will the application need to display on the screen and/or print on the printer?
- What information, if any, will the user need to enter into the user interface to display and/or print the desired information?
- What information, if any, will the application need to calculate to display and/or print the desired information?
- How will the user end the application?
- Will previous information need to be cleared from the screen before new information is entered?

The answers to these questions will help you identify the application's major tasks. The answers for each question for the Skate-Away Sales application are as follows.

What information, if any, will the application need to display on the screen and/or print on the printer? (Notice that "display" refers to the screen, and "print" refers to the printer.) The Skate-Away Sales application should display the customer's name, street address, city, state, ZIP code, skateboard price, sales tax rate, the number of blue skateboards ordered, the number of yellow skateboards ordered, the total number of skateboards ordered, and the total price of the order. In this case, the application does not need to print anything on the printer.

What information, if any, will the user need to enter into the user interface to display and/or print the desired information? In the Skate-Away Sales application, the salesperson (the user) must enter the customer's name, street address, city, state, ZIP code, skateboard price, sales tax rate, and the number of blue and yellow skateboards ordered.

What information, if any, will the application need to calculate to display and/or print the desired information? The Skate-Away Sales application needs to calculate the total number of skateboards ordered and the total price of the order.

How will the user end the application? In Chapter 1, you learned that all applications should give the user a way to exit the program. The Skate-Away Sales application needs to provide a way to end the application.

Will previous information need to be cleared from the screen before new information is entered? After Skate-Away's salesperson enters and calculates an order, he or she will need to clear the customer's information from the screen before entering the next order.

Figure 2-8 shows the Skate-Away Sales application's tasks listed in a TOE chart. Unlike procedure-oriented planning, OO planning does not require the TOE chart tasks to be listed in any particular order. In this case, the data entry tasks are listed first, followed by the calculation tasks, display tasks, application ending task, and screen clearing task.

Task	Object	Event

Get the following order information from the user:
  Customer's name
  Street address
  City
  State
  ZIP code
  Price of a skateboard
  Sales tax rate
  Number of blue skateboards ordered
  Number of yellow skateboards ordered		

Calculate the total skateboards ordered and the total price		

Display the following information:
  Customer's name
  Street address
  City
  State
  ZIP code
  Price of a skateboard
  Sales tax rate
  Number of blue skateboards ordered
  Number of yellow skateboards ordered
  Total skateboards ordered
  Total price		

End the application		
Clear the screen for the next order		

Figure 2-8: Tasks entered in a TOE chart

tip

You can draw a TOE chart by hand, or you can draw one using the table feature in a word processor (such as Microsoft Word).

Next, identify the objects that will perform the tasks listed in the TOE chart.

Identifying the Objects

After completing the Task column of the TOE chart, you then assign each task to an object in the user interface. For this application, the only objects you will use, besides the Windows form itself, are the button, label, and text box controls. As you learned in Chapter 1, you use a label control to display information that you do not want the user to change while your application is running, and you use a button control to perform an action immediately after the user clicks it. As you learned earlier, you use a text box to give the user an area in which to enter data. Now assign each of the tasks in the TOE chart to an object.

The first task listed in Figure 2-8 is to get the order information from the user. The order information includes the customer's name, address, city, state, and ZIP code, as well as the skateboard price, sales tax rate, and the number of blue and yellow skateboards ordered. Because you need to provide the salesperson with areas in which to enter the information, you assign the first task to nine text boxes—one for each item of information. The names of the text boxes will be uiNameTextBox, uiAddressTextBox, uiCityTextBox, uiStateTextBox, uiZipTextBox, uiPriceTextBox, uiRateTextBox, uiBlueTextBox, and uiYellowTextBox.

The second task listed in the TOE chart is to calculate both the total number of skateboards ordered and the total price. So that the salesperson can calculate these amounts at any time, you assign the task to a button named uiCalcButton.

The third task listed in the TOE chart is to display the order information, the total number of skateboards ordered, and the total price. The order information will be displayed automatically when the user enters that information in the nine text boxes. The total skateboards ordered and the total price, however, are not entered by the user; rather, those amounts are calculated by the uiCalcButton. Because the user should not be allowed to change the calculated results, you will have the uiCalcButton display the total skateboards ordered and the total price in two label controls named uiTotalBoardsLabel and uiTotalPriceLabel. Recall from Chapter 1 that a user cannot access the contents of a label control while the application is running. Notice that the task of displaying the total skateboards ordered involves two objects (uiCalcButton and uiTotalBoardsLabel). The task of displaying the total price also involves two objects (uiCalcButton and uiTotalPriceLabel).

The last two tasks listed in the TOE chart are "End the application" and "Clear the screen for the next order." You assign these tasks to buttons so that the user has control over when the tasks are performed. You name the buttons uiExitButton and uiClearButton. Figure 2-9 shows the TOE chart with the Task and Object columns completed.

Task	Object	Event
Get the following order information from the user: 　Customer's name 　Street address 　City 　State 　ZIP code 　Price of a skateboard 　Sales tax rate 　Number of blue skateboards ordered 　Number of yellow skateboards ordered	 uiNameTextBox uiAddressTextBox uiCityTextBox uiStateTextBox uiZipTextBox uiPriceTextBox uiRateTextBox uiBlueTextBox uiYellowTextBox	
Calculate the total skateboards ordered and the total price	uiCalcButton	
Display the following information: 　Customer's name 　Street address 　City 　State 　ZIP code 　Price of a skateboard 　Sales tax rate 　Number of blue skateboards ordered 　Number of yellow skateboards ordered 　Total skateboards ordered 　Total price	 uiNameTextBox uiAddressTextBox uiCityTextBox uiStateTextBox uiZipTextBox uiPriceTextBox uiRateTextBox uiBlueTextBox uiYellowTextBox uiCalcButton, uiTotalBoardsLabel uiCalcButton, uiTotalPriceLabel	
End the application	uiExitButton	
Clear the screen for the next order	uiClearButton	

Figure 2-9: Tasks and objects entered in a TOE chart

tip

Not all objects in a user interface will need an event to occur in order for the object to perform its assigned tasks.

After defining the application's tasks and assigning those tasks to objects in the user interface, you then determine which objects need an event (such as clicking or double-clicking) to occur for the object to do its assigned task. Identify the events required by the objects listed in Figure 2-9's TOE chart.

Identifying the Events

The nine text boxes listed in the TOE chart in Figure 2-9 are assigned the task of getting and displaying the order information. Text boxes accept and display information automatically, so no special event is necessary for them to do their assigned task.

The two label controls listed in the TOE chart are assigned the task of displaying the total number of skateboards ordered and the total price of the order. Label controls automatically display their contents so, here again, no special event needs to occur. (Recall that the two label controls will get their values from the uiCalcButton.)

The remaining objects listed in the TOE chart are the three buttons: uiCalcButton, uiClearButton, and uiExitButton. You will have the buttons perform their assigned tasks when the user clicks them. Figure 2-10 shows the TOE chart with the tasks, objects, and events necessary for the Skate-Away Sales application.

Task	Object	Event
Get the following order information from the user:		
Customer's name	uiNameTextBox	None
Street address	uiAddressTextBox	None
City	uiCityTextBox	None
State	uiStateTextBox	None
ZIP code	uiZipTextBox	None
Price of a skateboard	uiPriceTextBox	None
Sales tax rate	uiRateTextBox	None
Number of blue skateboards ordered	uiBlueTextBox	None
Number of yellow skateboards ordered	uiYellowTextBox	None
Calculate the total skateboards ordered and the total price	uiCalcButton	Click
Display the following information:		
Customer's name	uiNameTextBox	None
Street address	uiAddressTextBox	None
City	uiCityTextBox	None
State	uiStateTextBox	None
ZIP code	uiZipTextBox	None
Price of a skateboard	uiPriceTextBox	None
Sales tax rate	uiRateTextBox	None
Number of blue skateboards ordered	uiBlueTextBox	None
Number of yellow skateboards ordered	uiYellowTextBox	None
Total skateboards ordered	uiCalcButton, uiTotalBoardsLabel	Click, None
Total price	uiCalcButton, uiTotalPriceLabel	Click, None
End the application	uiExitButton	Click
Clear the screen for the next order	uiClearButton	Click

Figure 2-10: Completed TOE chart ordered by task

If the application you are creating is small, as is the Skate-Away Sales application, you can use the TOE chart in its current form to help you write the code. When the application you are creating is large, however, it is helpful to rearrange the TOE chart so that it is ordered by object instead of by task. To do so, you simply list all of the objects in the Object column, being sure to list each object only once. Then list the tasks you have assigned to each object in the Task column, and list the event in the Event column. Figure 2-11 shows the rearranged TOE chart, ordered by object rather than by task.

Task	Object	Event
1. Calculate the total skateboards ordered and the total price 2. Display the total skateboards ordered and the total price in the uiTotalBoardsLabel and uiTotalPriceLabel	uiCalcButton	Click
Clear the screen for the next order	uiClearButton	Click
End the application	uiExitButton	Click
Display the total skateboards ordered (from uiCalcButton)	uiTotalBoardsLabel	None
Display the total price (from uiCalcButton)	uiTotalPriceLabel	None
Get and display the order information	uiNameTextBox, uiAddressTextBox, uiCityTextBox, uiStateTextBox, uiZipTextBox, uiPriceTextBox, uiRateTextBox, uiBlueTextBox, uiYellowTextBox	None

Figure 2-11: Completed TOE chart ordered by object

After completing the TOE chart, the next step is to draw a rough sketch of the user interface.

Drawing a Sketch of the User Interface

Although the TOE chart lists the objects you need to include in the application's user interface, it does not tell you *where* to place those objects in the interface. While the design of an interface is open to creativity, there are some guidelines to which you should adhere so that your application is consistent with the Windows standards. This consistency will make your application easier to both learn and use, because the user interface will have a familiar look to it.

In Western countries, you should organize the user interface so that the information flows either vertically or horizontally, with the most important information always located in the upper-left corner of the screen. In a vertical arrangement the information flows from top to bottom; the essential information is located in the first column of the screen, while secondary information is placed in subsequent columns. In a horizontal arrangement, on the other hand, the information flows from left to right; the essential information is placed in the first row of the screen, with secondary information placed in subsequent rows. You can use white (empty) space, a group box control, or a panel control to group related controls together.

If buttons appear in the interface, they typically are positioned either in a row along the bottom of the screen, or stacked in either the upper-right or lower-right corner. You should limit to six the number of buttons in the interface, and place the most commonly used button first—either on the left when the buttons are along the bottom of the screen, or on the top when the buttons are stacked in either the upper-right or lower-right corner.

Figures 2-12 and 2-13 show two different sketches of the Skate-Away Sales interface. In Figure 2-12, the information is arranged vertically; white space is used to group the related controls together and the buttons are positioned along the bottom of the screen. In Figure 2-13, the information is arranged horizontally; a group box control is used to group the related controls together, and the buttons are stacked in the upper-right corner of the screen.

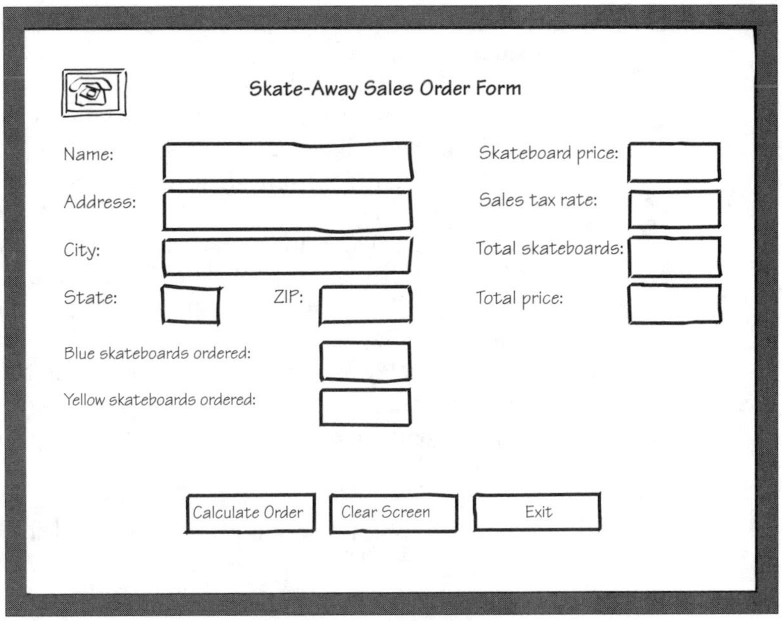

Figure 2-12: Vertical arrangement of the Skate-Away Sales interface

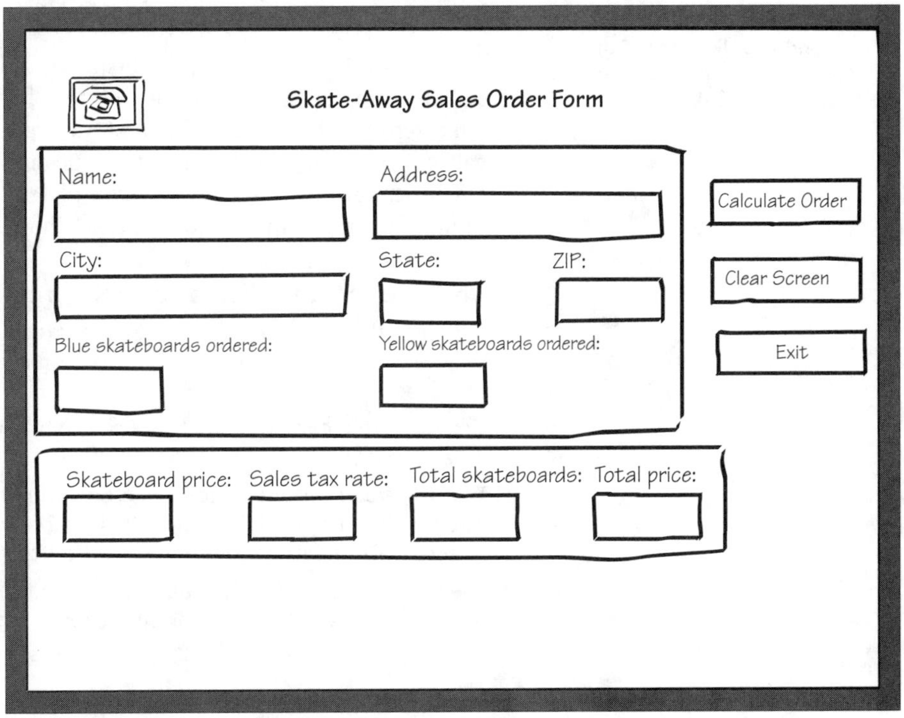

Figure 2-13: Horizontal arrangement of the Skate-Away Sales interface

Notice that each text box and button control in the interface is labeled so the user knows the control's purpose. Labels that identify other controls (such as text boxes) should be left-aligned and positioned either above or to the left of the control they identify. As you learned in Chapter 1, buttons are identified by a caption that appears on the button itself. Identifying labels and captions should be from one to three words only, and each should appear on one line. Labels and captions should be meaningful. The label identifying a text box, for example, should tell the user the type of information to enter. A button's caption, on the other hand, should indicate the action the button will perform when it is clicked.

Notice that each text box's identifying label ends with a colon (:). The colon distinguishes an identifying label from other text in the user interface, such as the heading text "Skate-Away Sales Order Form". The Windows standard is to use sentence capitalization for identifying labels. **Sentence capitalization** means you capitalize only the first letter in the first word and in any words that are customarily capitalized. The Windows standard for button captions is to use book title capitalization. When using **book title capitalization**, you capitalize the first letter in each word, except for articles, conjunctions, and prepositions that do not occur at either the beginning or the end of the caption.

When laying out the controls in the interface, try to minimize the number of different margins so that the user can more easily scan the information. You can do so by aligning the borders of the controls wherever possible, as shown in Figures 2-12 and 2-13.

In this section you learned some basic guidelines to follow when sketching a GUI (Graphical User Interface). You will learn more GUI guidelines as you progress through this book. For now, however, you have completed the second of the six steps involved in creating an OO application: plan the application. Recall that the planning step requires you to:

1. Identify the tasks the application needs to perform.
2. Identify the objects to which you will assign those tasks.
3. Identify the events required to trigger an object into performing its assigned tasks.
4. Draw a sketch of the user interface.

In Lesson B you use the sketch shown in Figure 2-12 as a guide when building the Skate-Away Sales interface. Recall that building the user interface is the third of the six steps involved in creating an OO application. For now, you can either take a break or complete the end-of-lesson questions and exercises before moving on to the next lesson. In Lesson C, you complete the fourth (code the application), fifth (test and debug the application), and sixth (assemble the documentation) steps.

Appendix B lists the GUI design guidelines that you learn in this book.

Layout and Organization of the User Interface

- Organize the user interface so that the information flows either vertically or horizontally, with the most important information always located in the upper-left corner of the screen.

- Group related controls together using white (empty) space, a group box control, or a panel control.

- Typically, you position buttons in a row along the bottom of the screen, or stack them in either the upper-right or lower-right corner. Use no more than six buttons on a screen. Place the most commonly used button first (either on the left or on the top).

- Use meaningful captions in buttons. Place the caption on one line and use from one to three words only. Use book title capitalization for button captions.

Some companies have their own standards for user interfaces. A company's standards supersede the Windows standards.

- Use a label to identify each text box in the user interface. The label text should be from one to three words only, and entered on one line. Left-justify the label text, and position the label either above or to the left of the control. Follow the label text with a colon (:) and use sentence capitalization.
- Align the borders of the controls in the user interface to minimize the number of different margins.

SUMMARY

To create an OO application:

- Follow these six steps:
    1. Meet with the client.
    2. Plan the application.
    3. Build the user interface.
    4. Code the application.
    5. Test and debug the application.
    6. Assemble the documentation.

To plan an OO application in Visual Basic .NET:

- Follow these four steps:
    1. Identify the tasks the application needs to perform.
    2. Identify the objects to which you will assign those tasks.
    3. Identify the events required to trigger an object into performing its assigned tasks.
    4. Draw a sketch of the user interface.

To assist you in identifying the tasks an application needs to perform, ask the following questions:

- What information, if any, will the application need to display on the screen and/or print on the printer?
- What information, if any, will the user need to enter into the user interface to display and/or print the desired information?
- What information, if any, will the application need to calculate to display and/or print the desired information?
- How will the user end the application?
- Will prior information need to be cleared from the screen before new information is entered?

QUESTIONS

1. You use a _____ control to display information you do not want the user to change.
    a. button
    b. form
    c. label
    d. text box
    e. user

2. You use a _____ control to accept or display information you will allow the user to change.
   a. button
   b. changeable
   c. form
   d. label
   e. text box

3. You use a _____ control to perform an immediate action when the user clicks it.
   a. button
   b. form
   c. label
   d. text box

4. You can use a(n) _____ chart to plan your OO applications.
   a. EOT
   b. ETO
   c. OET
   d. OTE
   e. TOE

5. When designing a user interface, you should organize the information _____.
   a. either horizontally or vertically
   b. horizontally only
   c. vertically only

6. When designing a user interface, the most important information should be placed in the _____ of the screen.
   a. center
   b. lower-left corner
   c. lower-right corner
   d. upper-left corner
   e. upper-right corner

7. You can use _____ to group related controls together in an interface.
   a. a group box control
   b. a panel control
   c. white space
   d. All of the above.
   e. None of the above.

8. Buttons in an interface are typically _____.
   a. positioned in a row along the bottom of the screen
   b. stacked in either the upper-left or lower-left corner of the screen
   c. stacked in either the upper-right or lower-right corner of the screen
   d. either a or b
   e. either a or c

9. Use no more than _____ buttons on a screen.
   a. five
   b. four
   c. seven
   d. six
   e. two

10. If more than one button appears in an interface, the most commonly used button should be placed _____.

    a. first

    b. in the middle

    c. last

    d. either a or c

11. Which of the following statements is false?

    a. A button's caption should appear on one line.

    b. A button's caption should be from one to three words only.

    c. A button's caption should be entered using book title capitalization.

    d. A button's caption should end with a colon (:).

12. The labels that identify text boxes should be entered using _____.

    a. book title capitalization

    b. sentence capitalization

    c. either a or b

13. Which of the following statements is false?

    a. Labels that identify text boxes should be aligned on the left.

    b. An identifying label should be positioned either above or to the left of the control it identifies.

    c. Labels that identify text boxes should be entered using book title capitalization.

    d. Labels that identify text boxes should end with a colon (:).

14. _____ means you capitalize only the first letter in the first word and any words that are customarily capitalized.

    a. Book title capitalization

    b. Sentence capitalization

15. Button captions should be entered using _____, which means you capitalize the first letter in each word, except for articles, conjunctions, and prepositions that do not occur at either the beginning or the end of the caption.

    a. book title capitalization

    b. sentence capitalization

16. Listed below are the four steps you should follow when planning an OO application. Put them in the proper order by placing a number (1 through 4) on the line to the left of the step.

    _____ Identify the objects to which you will assign those tasks.

    _____ Draw a sketch of the user interface.

    _____ Identify the tasks the application needs to perform.

    _____ Identify the events required to trigger an object into performing its assigned tasks.

17. Listed below are the six steps you should follow when creating an OO application. Put them in the proper order by placing a number (1 through 6) on the line to the left of the step.

    _____ Test and debug the application.

    _____ Build the user interface.

    _____ Code the application.

    _____ Assemble the documentation.

    _____ Plan the application.

    _____ Meet with the client.

EXERCISES

1. In this exercise, you prepare a TOE chart and create two sketches of the application's user interface. Use the GUI design guidelines listed in Appendix B to verify that the interface you create adheres to the GUI standards outlined in this book.

   Scenario: Sarah Brimley is the accountant at Paper Products. The salespeople at Paper Products are paid a commission, which is a percentage of the sales they make. The current commission rate is 10%. (In other words, if you have sales totaling $2,000, your commission is $200.) Sarah wants you to create an application that will compute the commission after she enters the salesperson's name, territory number, and sales.

   a. Prepare a TOE chart ordered by task.

   b. Rearrange the TOE chart created in Step a so that it is ordered by object.

   c. Draw two sketches of the user interface—one using a horizontal arrangement and the other using a vertical arrangement.

2. In this exercise, you prepare a TOE chart and create two sketches of the application's user interface. Use the GUI design guidelines listed in Appendix B to verify that the interface you create adheres to the GUI standards outlined in this book.

   Scenario: RM Sales divides its sales territory into four regions: North, South, East, and West. Robert Gonzales, the sales manager, wants an application in which he can enter the current year's sales for each region and the projected increase (expressed as a percentage) in sales for each region. He then wants the application to compute the following year's projected sales for each region. (For example, if Robert enters 10000 as the current sales for the South region, and then enters a 10% projected increase, the application should display 11000 as next year's projected sales.)

   a. Prepare a TOE chart ordered by task.

   b. Rearrange the TOE chart created in Step a so that it is ordered by object.

   c. Draw two sketches of the user interface—one using a horizontal arrangement and the other using a vertical arrangement.

3. In this exercise, you modify an existing application's user interface so that the interface follows the GUI design guidelines you have learned so far.

   a. If necessary, start Visual Studio .NET. Open the Time Solution (Time Solution.sln) file, which is contained in the VBNET\Chap02\Time Solution folder. If the designer window is not open, right-click the form file's name in the Solution Explorer window, then click View Designer.

   b. Lay out and organize the interface so it follows all of the GUI design guidelines you have learned so far. (Refer to Appendix B for a listing of the guidelines.)

   c. Save and start the application, then click the Exit button to end the application. (The Exit button contains the code to end the application.)

After completing this lesson, you
will be able to:

■ Build the user interface using your
TOE chart and sketch

■ Follow the Windows standards
regarding the use of graphics, color,
and fonts

■ Set the BorderStyle property

■ Add a text box to a form

■ Lock the controls on the form

■ Assign access keys to controls

■ Use the TabIndex property

Building the User Interface

Preparing to Create the User Interface

In Lesson A, you completed the second of the six steps involved in creating an OO application: plan the application. You now are ready to tackle the third step, which is to build the user interface. You use the TOE chart and sketch you created in the planning step as guides when building the interface, which involves placing the appropriate controls on the form and setting the applicable properties of those controls. Recall that a property controls the appearance and behavior of an object, such as the object's font, size, and so on. Some programmers create the entire interface before setting the properties of each object. Other programmers change the properties of each object as it is added to the form. Either way will work, so it's really just a matter of personal preference.

To save you time, your computer's hard disk contains a partially completed application for Skate-Away Sales. When you open the application, you will notice that most of the user interface has been created and most of the properties have been set. Only one control—a text box—is missing from the form. You add the missing control and set its properties later in this lesson.

To open the partially completed application:

1 Start Microsoft Visual Studio .NET, if necessary. Close the Start Page window.

2 Click **File** on the menu bar, then click **Open Solution**. Open the **Order Solution** (Order Solution.sln) file, which is contained in the VBNET\Chap02\ Order Solution folder on your computer's hard disk.

3 If the designer window is not open, right-click **Order Form.vb** in the Solution Explorer window, then click **View Designer**.

Figure 2-14 identifies the controls already included in the application. (You won't see the names of the controls on your screen. The names are included in Figure 2-14 for your reference only.)

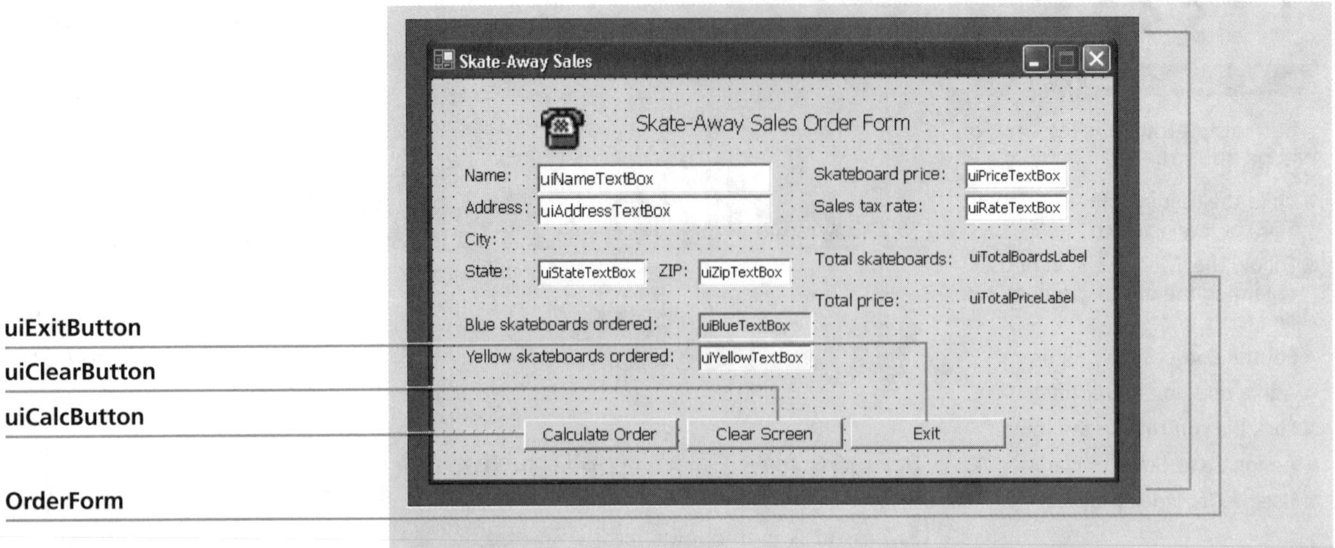

uiExitButton

uiClearButton

uiCalcButton

OrderForm

Figure 2-14: Partially completed Skate-Away Sales application

The user interface shown in Figure 2-14 resembles the sketch shown in Lesson A's Figure 2-12. Recall that the sketch was created using the guidelines you learned in Lesson A. For example, the information is arranged vertically, with the most important information located in the upper-left corner of the screen. The buttons are positioned along the bottom of the screen, with the most commonly used button placed first. The buttons contain meaningful captions, which are entered using book title capitalization. Each caption appears on one line, and no caption exceeds the three-word limit. The labels that identify text boxes are left-aligned and positioned to the left of their respective control; each uses sentence capitalization and each ends with a colon.

Notice that the controls are aligned wherever possible to minimize the number of different margins appearing in the user interface. You can use the dots that the Windows Form Designer displays on the form during design time to help you align the various controls in the interface. As you learned in Chapter 1, you also can use the Align option on the Format menu.

When positioning the controls, be sure to maintain a consistent margin from the edge of the form; two or three dots is recommended. For example, notice in Figure 2-14 that three dots separate the bottom border of the three buttons from the bottom edge of the form. Also notice that three dots appear between the left edge of the form and the left border of the six labels located in the first column.

As illustrated in Figure 2-14, related controls typically are placed on succeeding dots. For example, notice that the top of the uiAddressTextBox control is placed on the horizontal line of dots found immediately below the uiNameTextBox control. Also notice that the left edge of the Clear Screen button is placed on the vertical line of dots found to the immediate right of the Calculate Order button. Controls that are not part of any logical grouping may be positioned from two to four dots away from other controls.

Always size the buttons in the interface relative to each other. When the buttons are positioned on the bottom of the screen, as they are in Figure 2-14, all the buttons should be the same height; their widths, however, may vary if necessary. If the buttons are stacked in either the upper-right or lower-right corner of the screen, on the other hand, all the buttons should be the same height and the same width.

When building the user interface, keep in mind that you want to create a screen that no one notices. Snazzy interfaces may get "oohs" and "aahs" during their initial use, but they become tiresome after a while. The most important point to remember is that the interface should not distract the user from doing his or her work. Unfortunately, it is difficult for some application developers to refrain from using the many different colors, fonts, and graphics available in Visual Basic .NET; actually, using these elements is not the problem—overusing them is. So that you do not overload your user interfaces with too much color, too many fonts, and too many graphics, the next three sections provide some guidelines to follow regarding these elements. Consider the graphics first.

Placing and Sizing Design Elements

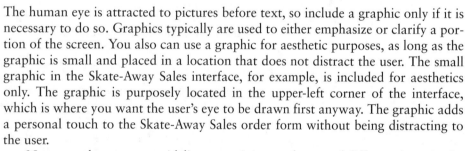

- When positioning the controls on a form, you should maintain a consistent margin from the edge of the form; two or three dots is recommended.
- Related controls typically are placed on succeeding dots. Controls that are not part of any logical grouping may be positioned from two to four dots away from other controls.
- When buttons are positioned horizontally on the screen, all the buttons should be the same height; their widths, however, may vary if necessary. When buttons are stacked vertically on the screen, all the buttons should be the same height and the same width.
- Try to create a user interface that no one notices.

Including Graphics in the User Interface

The human eye is attracted to pictures before text, so include a graphic only if it is necessary to do so. Graphics typically are used to either emphasize or clarify a portion of the screen. You also can use a graphic for aesthetic purposes, as long as the graphic is small and placed in a location that does not distract the user. The small graphic in the Skate-Away Sales interface, for example, is included for aesthetics only. The graphic is purposely located in the upper-left corner of the interface, which is where you want the user's eye to be drawn first anyway. The graphic adds a personal touch to the Skate-Away Sales order form without being distracting to the user.

Next, you learn some guidelines pertaining to the use of different fonts in the interface.

Adding Graphics

- Include a graphic only if it is necessary to do so. If the graphic is used solely for aesthetics, use a small graphic and place it in a location that will not distract the user.

Including Different Fonts in the User Interface

As you learned in Chapter 1, you can change the type, style, and size of the font used to display the text in an object. Recall that Tahoma, Microsoft Sans Serif, and Courier are examples of font types. Regular, bold, and italic are examples of font styles; and 8, 10, and 18 points are examples of font sizes.

Some fonts are serif, and some are sans serif. A **serif** is a light cross stroke that appears at the top or bottom of a character. The characters in a serif font have the light strokes, whereas the characters in a sans serif font do not. ("Sans" is a French word meaning "without.") Books use serif fonts, because those fonts are easier to read on the printed page. Sans serif fonts, on the other hand, are easier to read on the screen, so you should use a sans serif font for the text in a user interface. The default font type used for interface elements in Windows is Microsoft Sans Serif. However, for applications that will run on systems running Windows 2000 or Windows XP, it is recommended that you use the Tahoma font, because it offers improved readability and globalization support. You should use only one font type

As you learned in Chapter 1, a point is 1/72 of an inch.

GUI Design Tips

for all of the text in the interface. The Skate-Away Sales interface, for example, uses only the Tahoma font.

You can use 8-, 9-, 10-, 11-, or 12-point fonts for the elements in the user interface, but be sure to limit the number of font sizes used to either one or two. The Skate-Away Sales application uses two font sizes: 12 point for the heading at the top of the interface, and 10 point for everything else.

Avoid using italics and underlining in an interface, because both make text difficult to read. Additionally, limit the use of bold text to titles, headings, and key items that you want to emphasize.

Selecting Appropriate Font Types, Styles, and Sizes

- Use only one font type for all of the text in the interface. Use a sans serif font—preferably the Tahoma font. If the Tahoma font is not available, use either Microsoft Sans Serif or Arial.
- Use 8-, 9-, 10-, 11-, or 12-point fonts for the text in an interface.
- Limit the number of font sizes used to either one or two.
- Avoid using italics and underlining, because both make text difficult to read.
- Limit the use of bold text to titles, headings, and key items that you want to emphasize.

In addition to overusing graphics and fonts, many application developers make the mistake of using either too much color or too many different colors in the user interface. In the next section you learn some guidelines pertaining to the use of color.

Including Color in the User Interface

Just as the human eye is attracted to graphics before text, it also is attracted to color before black and white, so use color sparingly. It is a good practice to build the interface using black, white, and gray first, then add color only if you have a good reason to do so. Keep the following four points in mind when deciding whether to include color in an interface:

1. Many people have some form of either color-blindness or color confusion, so they will have trouble distinguishing colors.
2. Color is very subjective; a pretty color to you may be hideous to someone else.
3. A color may have a different meaning in a different culture.
4. Although rare, some users may be working on monochrome monitors.

Usually, it is best to use black text on a white, off-white, or light gray background. The Skate-Away Sales interface, for example, displays black text on a light gray background. Because dark text on a light background is the easiest to read, never use a dark color for the background or a light color for the text; a dark background is hard on the eyes, and light-colored text can appear blurry.

If you are going to include color in the interface, limit the number of colors to three, not including white, black, and gray. Be sure that the colors you choose complement each other.

Although color can be used to identify an important element in the interface, you should never use it as the only means of identification. In the Skate-Away Sales application, for example, the colors blue and yellow help the salesperson quickly identify where to enter the order for blue and yellow skateboards, respectively. Notice, however, that color is not the only means of identifying those areas in the interface; the labels to the left of the controls also tell the user where to enter the orders for blue and yellow skateboards.

Selecting Appropriate Colors

- Build the interface using black, white, and gray first, then add color only if you have a good reason to do so.
- Use white, off-white, or light gray for an application's background, and black for the text.
- Never use a dark color for the background or a light color for the text. A dark background is hard on the eyes, and light-colored text can appear blurry.
- Limit the number of colors in an interface to three, not including white, black, and gray. The colors you choose should complement each other.
- Never use color as the only means of identification for an element in the user interface.

Now you can begin completing the Skate-Away Sales user interface. First, observe how the interface looks with a white background instead of a gray one.

To change the background color of the form:

1   Click the **form** to select it. Click **BackColor** in the Properties list, then click the **Settings box list arrow**. Click the **Custom** tab, then click a **white color square**. The background color of the form changes to white. Notice that the background color of most of the controls on the form also changes to white.

If you do not explicitly set the BackColor property of a control in Visual Basic .NET, the control inherits the color setting of its parent. In this case, the form is the parent of each control in the Skate-Away Sales interface. Therefore, when the form's BackColor property is set to white, the BackColor property of the uiNameTextBox, uiAddressTextBox, and so on is also set to white. Notice, however, that the color of the uiBlueTextBox and uiYellowTextBox controls did not change; this is because the BackColor properties of those controls were explicitly set to blue and yellow, respectively.

Now explicitly set the background color of the Calculate Order button.

2   Click the **Calculate Order** button. Click **BackColor** in the Properties list, then click the **Settings box list arrow**. Click the **System** tab, then click **Control**. The background color of the Calculate Order button changes to gray.

Assume you prefer the way the interface originally looked. You can use the Undo option to cancel the changes you just made.

3   Click **Edit** on the menu bar, then click **Undo** to change the background color of the Calculate Order button to white, which is the color of its parent form.

4   Click **Edit** on the menu bar, then click **Undo** to change the background color of the form to its original color, gray.

Next, you learn about the BorderStyle property.

The BorderStyle Property

The **BorderStyle property** determines the style of a control's border and can be set to None, FixedSingle, or Fixed3D. Controls with a BorderStyle property set to None have no border. Setting the BorderStyle property to FixedSingle surrounds the control with a thin line, and setting it to Fixed3D gives the control a three-dimensional appearance. Currently, the BorderStyle property of each label control on the Skate-Away Sales form is set to None, which is the default for a label control. The BorderStyle property of each text box is set to Fixed3D—the default for a text box.

Text boxes should have their BorderStyle property left at the default of Fixed3D. Label controls that identify other controls (such as those that identify text boxes) should have their BorderStyle property left at the default of None. However, you typically set to FixedSingle the BorderStyle property of label controls that display program output, such as those that display the result of a calculation. In the Skate-Away Sales application, you will set the BorderStyle property of the uiTotalBoardsLabel and uiTotalPriceLabel controls to FixedSingle, because both controls display calculated results.

GUI Design Tips

Setting the BorderStyle Property of a Text Box and Label

- Leave the BorderStyle property of text boxes at the default value, Fixed3D.
- Leave the BorderStyle property of labels that identify other controls at the default value, None.
- Set to FixedSingle the BorderStyle property of labels that display program output, such as those that display the result of a calculation.
- In Windows applications, a control that contains data that the user is not allowed to edit does not usually appear three-dimensional. Therefore, you should avoid setting a label control's BorderStyle property to Fixed3D.

To change the BorderStyle property of the uiTotalBoardsLabel and uiTotalPriceLabel controls:

1   Select the **uiTotalBoardsLabel** and **uiTotalPriceLabel** controls.

HELP? To select both controls, click the uiTotalBoardsLabel control, then Ctr+click the uiTotalPriceLabel control. If necessary, refer back to Figure 2-14 for the location of these two controls.

2   Set the selected controls' BorderStyle property to **FixedSingle**, then click the **form** to deselect the controls. Notice that both label controls appear as flat boxes on the screen.

Next you learn about the Text property.

Setting the Text Property

Recall that most of Skate-Away's customers are in Illinois. Instead of having the salesperson enter IL in the uiStateTextBox control for each order, it would be more efficient to have IL appear automatically in the State text box when the application is run. If the user needs to change the state entry while the application is running, he or she can simply click the State text box, then delete the current entry and retype the new one. You can display IL in the uiStateTextBox control by setting the control's Text property to IL.

To set the uiStateTextBox control's Text property:

1   Click the **uiStateTextBox** control.

2   Click **Text** in the Properties list, then type **IL** and press **Enter**. IL appears in the uiStateTextBox control.

Notice that the text box control in which the user enters the city is missing from the interface. You add the control next.

Adding a Text Box Control to the Form

A **text box control** provides an area in the form where the user can enter data. Add the missing text box control to the form and then set its properties.

tip

Recall that, in the context of OOP, each tool in the toolbox is a class—a pattern from which one or more objects, called controls, are created. Each control you create is an instance of the class. The TextBox1 text box, for example, is an instance of the TextBox class.

tip

Be sure to use either the Delete key or the Backspace key to delete the highlighted text in the Properties list. Do not use the Spacebar to delete the highlighted text. Pressing the Spacebar does not clear the property's contents; rather, it replaces the highlighted text with a space.

To add a text box control to the form, and then set its properties:

1   Click the **TextBox tool** in the toolbox, then drag a text box control to the form. Position the text box control to the right of the City: label, immediately below the uiAddressTextBox control.

The TextBox1 text that appears inside the text box is the current setting of the control's Text property. You should delete the contents of the Text property so that it does not appear in the interface when the application is run.

2   Double-click **Text** in the Properties list. This highlights the TextBox1 text in the Settings box.

   HELP? If the TextBox1 text is not highlighted in the Settings box, double-click the Text property again until the TextBox1 text is highlighted. You also can drag in the Settings box to highlight the TextBox1 text.

3   Press **Delete**, then press **Enter** to remove the highlighted text. The text box is now empty.

Now change the text box's default name (TextBox1) to uiCityTextBox. Also change the font size to 10 points.

4   Set the following two properties for the text box control:

   Name: **uiCityTextBox**

   Font: **10** points

   HELP? Recall that the Name property is listed third when the properties are listed alphabetically in the Properties list. It is listed in the Design category when the properties are listed by category.

Now use the Align option on the Format menu to align the left border of the uiCityTextBox control with the left border of the uiAddressTextBox control.

5   Press and hold down the **Control** (or Ctrl) key as you click the **uiAddressTextBox control**. The uiCityTextBox and uiAddressTextBox controls should now be selected.

6   Click **Format** on the menu bar, point to **Align**, and then click **Lefts** to align the left border of both controls.

Next, use the Make Same Size option on the Format menu to size the uiCityTextBox control appropriately.

7   Click **Format** on the menu bar, point to **Make Same Size**, and then click **Both** to make the uiCityTextBox control's height and width the same as the uiAddressTextBox control's height and width.

8   Click the **form** to deselect the controls. See Figure 2-15.

Figure 2-15: Form showing additional text box

text box added to the form

Before saving the solution, you learn how to lock the controls on the form.

Locking the Controls on a Form

Once you have placed all of the controls in the desired locations on the form, it is a good idea to lock the controls in their current positions so you do not inadvertently move them. Once the controls are locked, you will not be able to move them until you unlock them; you can, however, delete them.

To lock the controls on the form, and then save the solution:

1   Right-click the **form** (or any control on the form), then click **Lock Controls** on the context menu.

2   Try dragging one of the controls to a different location on the form. You will not be able to do so.

If you need to move a control after you have locked the controls in place, you can either change the control's Location property setting in the Properties list or unlock the controls by selecting the Lock Controls option again. The Lock Controls option is a toggle option: selecting it once activates it, and selecting it again deactivates it.

3   Click **File** on the menu bar, and then click **Save All** to save the solution.

Next you learn how to assign access keys to the controls that can accept user input.

Assigning Access Keys

An **access key** allows the user to select an object using the Alt key in combination with a letter or number. For example, you can select Visual Basic .NET's File menu by pressing Alt+F, because the letter "F" is the File menu's access key. Access keys are not case sensitive—in other words, you can select the File menu by pressing either Alt+F or Alt+f.

GUI Design Tips

Locking the Controls

• Lock the controls in place on the form.

You also can use the Lock Controls option on the Format menu to lock and unlock the controls on a form.

You also can save the solution by clicking the Save All button 🔲 on the Standard toolbar.

You should assign access keys to each of the controls (in the interface) that can accept user input. Examples of such controls include text boxes and buttons, because the user can enter information in a text box and he or she can click a button. It is important to assign access keys to these controls for the following three reasons:

1. Access keys allow a user to work with the application even if the mouse becomes inoperative.
2. Access keys allow users who are fast typists to keep their hands on the keyboard.
3. Access keys allow people with disabilities, which may prevent them from working with a mouse, to use the application.

You assign an access key by including an ampersand (&) in the control's caption or identifying label. For example, to assign an access key to a button, you include the ampersand in the button's Text property, which is where a button's caption is stored. To assign an access key to a text box, on the other hand, you include the ampersand in the Text property of the label control that identifies the text box. (As you learn later in this lesson, you also must set the identifying label's TabIndex property to a value that is one number less than the value stored in the text box's TabIndex property.) You enter the ampersand to the immediate left of the character you want to designate as the access key. For example, to assign the letter C as the access key for the Calculate Order button, you enter &Calculate Order in the button's Text property. To assign the letter N as the access key for the uiNameTextBox control, you enter &Name: in the Text property of its identifying label control.

Each access key appearing in the interface should be unique. The first choice for an access key is the first letter of the caption or identifying label, unless another letter provides a more meaningful association. For example, the letter X typically is the access key for an Exit button, because the letter X provides a more meaningful association than does the letter E. If you can't use the first letter (perhaps because it already is used as the access key for another control) and no other letter provides a more meaningful association, then use a distinctive consonant in the caption or label. The last choices for an access key are a vowel or a number. Assign an access key to each button and text box in the Skate-Away Sales interface.

tip

············

The ampersand in a label control's Text property designates an access key only if the label control's UseMnemonic property is set to True, which is the default for that property. In the rare cases where you do not want the ampersand to designate an access key—for example, you want the label control's Text property to say, literally, J & M Sales—then you need to set the label control's UseMnemonic property to False.

To assign an access key to each button and text box in the interface:

1   Click the **Calculate Order** button, then click **Text** in the Properties list. Use the letter C as the access key for the Calculate Order button.

2   Place the mouse pointer in the Text property's Settings box. The mouse pointer becomes an I-bar $\bar{\text{I}}$.

3   Place the $\bar{\text{I}}$ to the left of the C in Calculate, then click at that location. The insertion point appears before the word Calculate.

4   Type & (ampersand), then press **Enter**. The Text property should now say &Calculate Order, and the interface should show the letter C underlined in the button's caption.

     HELP?   If you are using Windows XP and the letter C does not appear underlined in the button's caption, you will need to open the Display Properties dialog box. To open the dialog box, click Start on the Windows taskbar, click Control Panel, click Appearance and Themes, and then click Display. Click the Appearance tab on the dialog box, and then click the Effects button. Click the Hide underlined letters for keyboard navigation until I press the Alt key check box to remove the checkmark. Click the OK button twice, then close the Appearance and Themes window.

Now assign the letter "l" as the access key for the Clear Screen button. (In this case, you cannot use the letter "C" for the Clear Screen button, because the letter "C" is the access key for the Calculate Order button and access keys should be unique.)

5   Click the **Clear Screen** button, then change its Text property to **C&lear Screen**.

As mentioned earlier, the letter "X" is customarily the access key for an Exit button.

6   Click the **Exit** button, then change its Text property to **E&xit**.

7   Use the information in Figure 2-16 to include an access key in the label controls that identify text boxes in the interface.

Control name	Text	Access key
uiIdNameLabel	Name:	N
uiIdAddressLabel	Address:	A
uiIdCityLabel	City:	T
uiIdStateLabel	State:	S
uiIdZipLabel	ZIP:	Z
uiIdBlueLabel	Blue skateboards ordered:	B
uiIdYellowLabel	Yellow skateboards ordered:	Y
uiIdPriceLabel	Skateboard price:	I
uiIdRateLabel	Sales tax rate	R

Figure 2-16: Access keys included in the label controls that identify text boxes

Notice that you do not include an access key in the Text property of the Total skateboards: and Total price: labels. This is because these labels do not identify text boxes; rather they identify other label controls. Recall that users cannot access label controls while an application is running, so it is inappropriate to assign an access key to them.

The last step in completing an interface is to set the TabIndex property of the controls.

Setting the TabIndex Property

The **TabIndex property** determines the order in which a control receives the focus when the user presses either the Tab key or an access key while the application is running. A control having a TabIndex of 2, for instance, will receive the focus immediately after the control whose TabIndex is 1. Likewise, a control with a TabIndex of 18 will receive the focus immediately after the control whose TabIndex is 17. When a control has the **focus**, it can accept user input.

When you add to a form a control that has a TabIndex property, Visual Basic .NET sets the control's TabIndex property to a number that represents the order in which the control was added to the form. The TabIndex property for the first control added to a form is 0 (zero), the TabIndex property for the second control is 1, and so on. In most cases, you will need to change the TabIndex values, because the order in which the controls were added to the form rarely represents the order in which each should receive the focus.

Not all controls have a TabIndex property. Examples of controls that do not have a TabIndex property include PictureBox, MainMenu, and Timer controls.

To determine the appropriate TabIndex settings for an application, you first make a list of the controls (in the interface) that can accept user input. The list should reflect the order in which the user will want to access the controls. For example, in the Skate-Away Sales application, the user typically will want to access the uiNameTextBox control first, then the uiAddressTextBox control, the uiCityTextBox control, and so on. If a control that accepts user input is identified by a label control, you also include the label control in the list. (A text box is an example of a control that accepts user input and is identified by a label control.) You place the name of the label control immediately above the name of the control it identifies. For example, in the Skate-Away Sales application, the uiIdNameLabel control (which contains Name:) identifies the uiNameTextBox control; therefore, uiIdNameLabel should appear immediately above uiNameTextBox in the list. The names of controls that do not accept user input, and those that are not identifying controls, should be listed at the bottom of the list; these names do not need to appear in any specific order.

After listing the controls, you then assign each control in the list a TabIndex value, beginning with the number 0. Figure 2-17 shows the list of controls for the Skate-Away Sales interface, along with the appropriate TabIndex values. Rows pertaining to controls that accept user input are shaded in the figure.

Controls that accept user input, along with their identifying label controls	TabIndex setting
uiIdNameLabel (Name:)	0
uiNameTextBox	1
uiIdAddressLabel (Address:)	2
uiAddressTextBox	3
uiIdCityLabel (City:)	4
uiCityTextBox	5
uiIdStateLabel (State:)	6
uiStateTextBox	7
uiIdZipLabel (ZIP:)	8
uiZipTextBox	9
uiIdBlueLabel (Blue skateboards ordered:)	10
uiBlueTextBox	11
uiIdYellowLabel (Yellow skateboards ordered:)	12
uiYellowTextBox	13
uiIdPriceLabel (Skateboard price:)	14
uiPriceTextBox	15
uiIdRateLabel (Sales tax rate:)	16
uiRateTextBox	17
uiCalcButton	18
uiClearButton	19
uiExitButton	20

identifying label — uiIdNameLabel (Name:)

text box — uiNameTextBox

Figure 2-17: List of controls and TabIndex settings

Other controls	TabIndex setting
uiIdHeadingLabel (Skate-Away Sales Order Form)	21
uiIdTotalBoardsLabel (Total skateboards:)	22
uiIdTotalPriceLabel (Total price:)	23
uiTotalBoardsLabel	24
uiTotalPriceLabel	25
uiPhonePictureBox	This control does not have a TabIndex property.

Figure 2-17: List of controls and TabIndex settings (continued)

As Figure 2-17 indicates, 12 controls in the Skate-Away Sales interface—nine text boxes and three buttons—can accept user input. Notice that each text box in the list is associated with an identifying label control, whose name appears immediately above the text box name in the list. Also notice that the TabIndex value assigned to each text box's identifying label control is one number less than the value assigned to the text box itself. For example, the uiIdNameLabel control has a TabIndex value of 0, and its corresponding text box (uiNameTextBox) has a TabIndex value of 1. Likewise, the uiIdAddressLabel control and its corresponding text box have TabIndex values of 2 and 3, respectively. For a text box's access key (which is defined in the identifying label) to work appropriately, you must be sure to set the identifying label control's TabIndex property to a value that is one number less than the value stored in the text box's TabIndex property.

You can use the Properties list to set the TabIndex property of each control; or, you can use the Tab Order option on the View menu. You already know how to set a property using the Properties list. In the next set of steps, you learn how to use the Tab Order option on the View menu.

To set the TabIndex values:

1   Click **View** on the menu bar, then click **Tab Order**. The current TabIndex value for each control except the PictureBox control appears in blue boxes on the form. (PictureBox controls do not have a TabIndex property.) The TabIndex values reflect the order in which each control was added to the form.

    HELP? If the Tab Order option does not appear on the View menu, click the form, then repeat Step 1.

According to Figure 2-17, the first control in the tab order should be the uiIdNameLabel control, which contains the text Name:. Currently, this control has a TabIndex value of 2, which indicates that it was the third control added to the form.

2   Place the mouse pointer on the Name: label. (You cannot see the entire label, because the box containing the number 2 covers the letters Na.) A rectangle surrounds the label and the mouse pointer becomes a crosshair, as shown in Figure 2-18.

crosshair

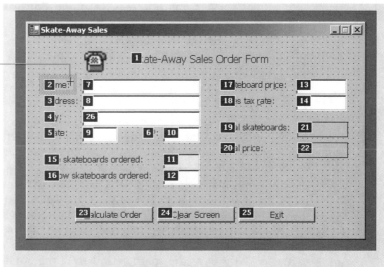

Figure 2-18: Crosshair positioned on the Name: label

3   Click the Name: label (or click the box containing the number 2). The number 0 replaces the number 2 in the box, and the color of the box changes from blue to white to indicate that you have set the TabIndex value.

4   Click the uiNameTextBox control, which appears to the immediate right of the Name: label. The number 1 replaces the number 7 in the box, and the color of the box changes from blue to white.

5   Use the information in Figure 2-19 to set the TabIndex values for the remaining controls—the controls with TabIndex values of 2 through 25. Be sure to set the values in numerical order. If you make a mistake, press the Esc key to remove the TabIndex boxes from the form, then repeat Steps 1 through 5. When you have finished setting all of the TabIndex values, the color of the boxes will automatically change from white to blue, as shown in Figure 2-19.

tip

· · · · · · · · · · · · · · · · · · · ·

You also can remove the TabIndex boxes by clicking View, and then clicking Tab Order.

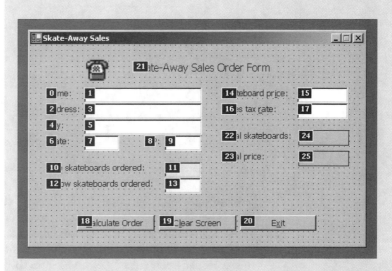

Figure 2-19: Correct TabIndex values shown in the form

6   Verify that the TabIndex values shown on your screen agree with those shown in Figure 2-19, then press **Esc** to remove the TabIndex boxes from the form.

GUI Design Tips

Rules for Assigning Access Keys and Controlling the Focus

- Assign a unique access key to each control (in the interface) that can receive user input (for example, text boxes, buttons, and so on).
- When assigning an access key to a control, use the first letter of the caption or identifying label, unless another letter provides a more meaningful association. If you can't use the first letter and no other letter provides a more meaningful association, then use a distinctive consonant. Lastly, use a vowel or a number.
- Assign a TabIndex value to each control in the interface, except for controls that do not have a TabIndex property (begin with 0). The TabIndex values should reflect the order in which the user will want to access the controls.
- To give users keyboard access to text boxes, assign an access key to the text box control's identifying label. Set the TabIndex property of the label control so that its value is one number less than the value in the TabIndex property of the corresponding text box. (In other words, the TabIndex value of the text box should be one number greater than the TabIndex value of its identifying label control.)

Now save the solution and start the application to verify that it is working correctly.

tip

. . . .

You also can start the application by pressing the F5 key.

To save the solution and then start the application:

1   Click the **Save All** button 🖫 on the Standard toolbar to save the solution. Click **Debug** on the menu bar, and then click **Start** to start the application. See Figure 2-20.

insertion point

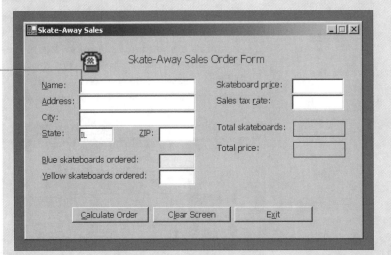

Figure 2-20: Completed user interface for the Skate-Away Sales application

When you start an application, Visual Basic .NET sends the focus to the control whose TabIndex value is 0—in this case, that control is the uiIdNameLabel (Name:) control. However, because label controls cannot receive the focus, Visual Basic .NET sends the focus to the next control in the tab order sequence—in this case, that control is the uiNameTextBox. Notice that an insertion point appears in the uiNameTextBox control. The insertion point indicates that the text box has the focus and is ready to receive input from you.

2   Type **Sport Warehouse** in the uiNameTextBox. Notice that a text box displays the information it receives from you. The information is recorded in the text box's Text property. In this case, for example, the information is recorded in the Text property of the uiNameTextBox.

In Windows applications, the Tab key moves the focus forward, and the Shift + Tab key combination moves the focus backward.

3   Press **Tab** to move the focus to the uiAddressTextBox, then press **Shift + Tab** to move the focus back to the uiNameTextBox.

Use the Tab key to verify the tab order of the controls in the interface.

4   Press **Tab**, slowly, nine times. The focus moves to the following controls: uiAddressTextBox, uiCityTextBox, uiStateTextBox, uiZipTextBox, uiBlueTextBox, uiYellowTextBox, uiPriceTextBox, uiRateTextBox, and uiCalcButton.

Notice that, when the focus moves to the Calculate Order button, the button's border is highlighted and a dotted rectangle appears around its caption. Pressing the Enter key when a button has the focus invokes the button's Click event and causes the computer to process any code contained in the event procedure.

5   Press **Tab** three times. The focus moves to the uiClearButton, then to the uiExitButton, and finally back to the uiNameTextBox.

You also can move the focus using a text box's access key.

6   Press **Alt+b** to move the focus to the uiBlueTextBox, then press **Alt+n** to move the focus to the uiNameTextBox.

7   On your own, try the access keys for the remaining text boxes in the interface.

Unlike pressing a text box's access key, which moves the focus, pressing a button's access key invokes the button's Click event procedure; any code contained in the event procedure will be processed by the computer.

8   Press **Alt+x** to invoke the Exit button's Click event procedure, which contains the `Me.Close()` instruction. The application ends, and you are returned to the designer window.

9   Close the Output window, then use the File menu to close the solution.

You now have finished planning the application and building the user interface. For now, you can either take a break or complete the end-of-lesson questions and exercises before moving on to Lesson C, where you complete the remaining steps involved in creating an OO application.

SUMMARY

To control the border around a label control:

■   Set the label control's BorderStyle property.

To lock/unlock the controls on the form:

■   Right-click the form or any control on the form, then select Lock Controls on the context menu. To unlock the controls, simply select the Lock Controls option again. You also can lock/unlock controls by using the Lock Controls option on the Format menu.

To assign an access key to a control:

■ Type an ampersand (&) in the Text property of the control's caption or identifying label. The ampersand should appear to the immediate left of the letter or number that you want to designate as the access key. (The ampersand in a label control's Text property designates an access key only if the label control's UseMnemonic property is set to True, which is the default for that property.)

To give users keyboard access to a text box:

■ Assign an access key to the text box control's identifying label control. Set the label control's TabIndex property so that its value is one number less than the TabIndex value of the text box.

To access a control that has an access key:

■ Press and hold down the Alt key as you press the control's access key.

To set the tab order:

■ Set each control's TabIndex property to a number that represents the order in which you want the control to receive the focus. Remember to begin with 0 (zero). You can use the Properties list to set the TabIndex values. Or, you can use the Tab Order option on the View menu.

QUESTIONS

1. The _____ property determines the order in which a control receives the focus when the user presses the Tab key or an access key.
   a. OrderTab
   b. SetOrder
   c. TabIndex
   d. TabOrder
   e. TabStop

2. When placing controls on a form, you should maintain a consistent margin of _____ dots from the edge of the form.
   a. one or two
   b. two or three
   c. two to five
   d. three to 10
   e. 10 to 20

3. If the buttons are positioned horizontally on the screen, then each button should be _____ .
   a. the same height
   b. the same width
   c. the same height and the same width

4. If the buttons are positioned vertically on the screen, then each button should be
    _____.
    a. the same height
    b. the same width
    c. the same height and the same width

5. The human eye is attracted to _____.
    a. black and white before color
    b. color before black and white
    c. graphics before text
    d. text before graphics
    e. both b and c

6. When building an interface, always use _____.
    a. dark text on a dark background
    b. dark text on a light background
    c. light text on a dark background
    d. light text on a light background
    e. either b or c

7. Use _____ fonts for the elements in the user interface.
    a. 6-, 8-, or 10-point
    b. 8-, 9-, 10-, 11-, or 12-point
    c. 10-, 12-, or 14-point
    d. 12-, 14-, or 16-point

8. Limit the number of font sizes used in an interface to _____.
    a. one or two
    b. two or three
    c. three or four

9. Use a _____ font for the text in the user interface.
    a. sans serif
    b. serif

10. Limit the number of font types used in an interface to _____.
    a. one
    b. two
    c. three
    d. four

11. To put a border around a label control, you set the label control's _____
    property to FixedSingle.
    a. Appearance
    b. BackStyle
    c. Border
    d. BorderStyle
    e. Text

12. You use the _____ character to assign an access key to a control.
    a. &
    b. *
    c. @
    d. $
    e. ^

13. You assign an access key using a control's _____ property.
   a. Access
   b. Caption
   c. Key
   d. KeyAccess
   e. Text

14. Explain the procedure for choosing a control's access key.

15. Explain how you give users keyboard access to a text box.

EXERCISES

1. In this exercise, you finish building a user interface.
   a. If necessary, start Visual Studio .NET. Open the Paper Solution (Paper Solution.sln) file, which is contained in the VBNET\Chap02\Paper Solution folder. If the designer window is not open, right-click the form file's name in the Solution Explorer window, then click View Designer.
   b. Finish building the user interface shown in Figure 2-21 by adding a text box named uiNameTextBox. Assign access keys to the text boxes and buttons, as shown in the figure. Also, adjust the TabIndex values appropriately. (The user will enter the name, then the territory number, and then the sales.)

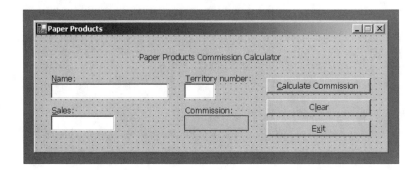

Figure 2-21

   c. Lock the controls on the form.
   d. Change the background color of the form to pale yellow. Change the background color of the buttons to gray (use the Control setting on the System tab).
   e. Save the solution, then start the application. Verify that the tab order is correct, and that the access keys work appropriately. Click the Exit button to end the application. (The Exit button has already been coded for you. You will code the Calculate Commission and Clear buttons in Lesson C's Exercise 1.)

2. In this exercise, you finish building a user interface.
   a. If necessary, start Visual Studio .NET. Open the RMSales Solution (RMSales Solution.sln) file, which is contained in the VBNET\Chap02\RMSales Solution folder. If the designer window is not open, right-click the form file's name in the Solution Explorer window, then click View Designer.

b. Finish building the user interface shown in Figure 2-22 by adding a text box named uiNsalesTextBox. Adjust the TabIndex values appropriately. (The user will enter the North region's sales and increase percentage before entering the South region's sales and increase percentage.)

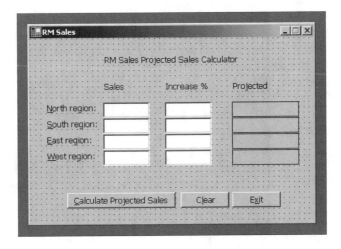

Figure 2-22

c. Lock the controls on the form.

d. Change the BorderStyle property of the label controls appropriately.

e. Save the solution, then start the application. Verify that the tab order is correct, and that the access keys work appropriately. Click the Exit button to end the application. (The Exit button has already been coded for you. You will code the Calculate Projected Sales and Clear buttons in Lesson C's Exercise 2.)

3. In this exercise, you modify the application that you saved in Lesson A's Exercise 3.

a. If necessary, start Visual Studio .NET. Open the Time Solution (Time Solution.sln) file, which is contained in the VBNET\Chap02\Time Solution folder. If the designer window is not open, right-click the form file's name in the Solution Explorer window, then click View Designer.

b. Lock the controls on the form.

c. Assign access keys to the controls that can accept user input.

d. Set each control's TabIndex property appropriately.

e. Save the solution, then start the application. Verify that the tab order is correct, and that the access keys work appropriately. Click the Exit button to end the application.

LESSON C

objectives

After completing this lesson, you will be able to:

- Use the TOE chart to code the application
- Use pseudocode to plan an object's code
- Write an assignment statement
- Use the Focus method
- Include internal documentation in the code
- Write arithmetic expressions
- Use the Val and Format functions

Coding, Testing, Debugging, and Documenting the Application

Coding the Application

After meeting with the client, planning the application, and building the user interface, you then write the Visual Basic .NET instructions to tell the objects in the interface how to respond to events. The instructions are called **code**, and the process of writing the instructions is called **coding**. You will need to write code for each object that has an event listed in the third column of the TOE chart you created in Lesson A. For your reference while coding, the TOE chart is shown in Figure 2-23.

Task	Object	Event
1. Calculate the total skateboards ordered and the total price 2. Display the total skateboards ordered and the total price in the uiTotalBoardsLabel and uiTotalPriceLabel	uiCalcButton	Click
Clear the screen for the next order	uiClearButton	Click
End the application	uiExitButton	Click
Display the total skateboards ordered (from uiCalcButton)	uiTotalBoardsLabel	None
Display the total price (from uiCalcButton)	uiTotalPriceLabel	None
Get and display the order information	uiNameTextBox, uiAddressTextBox, uiCityTextBox, uiStateTextBox, uiZipTextBox, uiPriceTextBox, uiRateTextBox, uiBlueTextBox, uiYellowTextBox	None

Figure 2-23: Completed TOE chart ordered by object

According to the TOE chart, only the three buttons require coding, as they are the only objects with an event listed in the third column of the chart. The Exit button has already been coded for you, so you need to write the code for only the Clear Screen and Calculate Order buttons. First, however, open the Order application from Lesson B.

To open the Order application:

1 Start Microsoft Visual Studio .NET, if necessary. Close the Start Page window.

2 Click **File** on the menu bar, then click **Open Solution**. Open the **Order Solution** (Order Solution.sln) file, which is contained in the VBNET\ Chap02\Order Solution folder on your computer's hard disk.

3 If the designer window is not open, right-click **Order Form.vb** in the Solution Explorer window, then click **View Designer**.

Figure 2-24 identifies the objects included in the user interface. Recall that the controls are locked on the form. (You won't see the names of the controls on your screen. The names are included in Figure 2-24 for your reference only.)

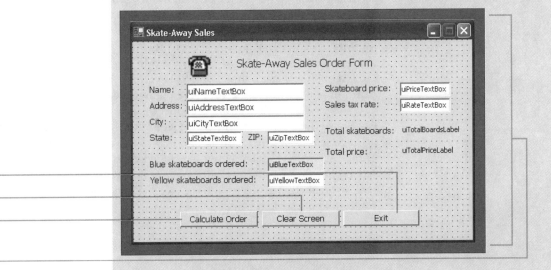

Figure 2-24: Skate-Away Sales user interface

You code the Clear Screen button first.

Coding the Clear Screen Button

According to the TOE chart, the Clear Screen button is assigned the task of clearing the screen for the next order. Clearing the screen involves assigning a zero-length string to the Text property of the uiNameTextBox, uiAddressTextBox, uiCityTextBox, uiZipTextBox, uiBlueTextBox, uiYellowTextBox, uiTotalBoardsLabel, and uiTotalPriceLabel controls, and assigning the string "IL" to the Text property of the uiStateTextBox control. A **string** is simply a group of characters enclosed in quotation marks. The word "Jones", for example, is a string. Likewise, "45" is a string, but 45 is not; 45 is a number. "Jones" is a string with a length of five, because there are five characters between the quotation marks. "45" is a string with a length of two, because there are two characters between the quotation marks. Following this logic, a **zero-length string**, also called an **empty string**, is a set of quotation marks with nothing between them, like this: "". Assigning a zero-length string to the Text property of a control removes the contents of the control. Figure 2-25 lists what you want the Clear Screen button to do when the user clicks the button.

Clear Screen button

1. assign a zero-length string to the Text property of the uiNameTextBox, uiAddressTextBox, uiCityTextBox, uiZipTextBox, uiBlueTextBox, and uiYellowTextBox

2. assign "IL" to the uiStateTextBox's Text property

3. assign a zero-length string to the Text property of the uiTotalBoardsLabel and uiTotalPriceLabel

4. send the focus to the uiNameTextBox

Figure 2-25: Steps for the Clear Screen button

Notice that the list shown in Figure 2-25 is composed of short statements in English. The statements represent the steps the Clear Screen button must follow to prepare the screen for the next order. In programming terms, the list of steps shown in Figure 2-25 is called pseudocode. As you learned in Lesson A, pseudocode is a tool programmers use to help them plan the steps that an object must take to perform its assigned task. Even though the word *pseudocode* might be unfamiliar to you, you already have written pseudocode without even realizing it. Think about the last time you gave directions to someone. You wrote each direction down on paper, in your own words; your directions were a form of pseudocode.

The programmer uses the pseudocode as a guide when coding the application. For example, you will use the pseudocode shown in Figure 2-25 to write the appropriate Visual Basic .NET instructions for the Clear Screen button. The first three steps in the pseudocode assign either a zero-length string or the string "IL" to the Text property of various controls in the interface. You use an **assignment statement**, which is one of many types of Visual Basic .NET instructions, to set the value of a property while an application is running.

Assigning a Value to a Property During Run Time

You use the syntax [**Me.**]*object.property* = *expression* to set the value of an object's property while an application is running. In the syntax, **Me** refers to the current form. Notice that **Me.** is optional, as indicated by the square brackets ([]) in the syntax. *Object* and *property* are the names of the object and property, respectively, to which you want the value of the *expression* assigned. You use a period to separate the form reference (Me) from the object name, and the object name from the property name. You use an equal sign (=) to separate the [**Me.**]*object.property* information from the *expression*. When it appears in an assignment statement, the equal sign (=) is often referred to as the **assignment operator**.

When an assignment statement is encountered in a program, the computer assigns the value of the expression appearing on the right side of the assignment operator (=) to the object and property that appears on the left side of the assignment operator. For example, the assignment statement `Me.uiNameTextBox.Text = ""` assigns a zero-length string to the Text property of the uiNameTextBox control. (Because the `Me.` is optional, you also could use the instruction `uiNameTextBox.Text = ""`.) Similarly, the assignment statement `Me.uiStateTextBox.Text = "IL"` assigns the string "IL" to the Text property of the uiStateTextBox control. As you learn later in this lesson, the assignment statement `Me.uiSumTextBox.Text = 3 + 5` assigns the value 8 to the Text property of the uiSumTextBox control. You will use assignment statements to code the Clear Screen button.

tip

The period that appears in an assignment statement is called the dot member access operator. It tells the computer that what appears to the right of the dot is a member of what appears to the left of the dot. For example, the assignment statement `Me.uiNameTextBox.Text` indicates that the Text property is a member of the uiNameTextBox control, which is a member of the current form.

You also can open the Code Editor window by pressing the F7 key, or by clicking View on the menu bar, and then clicking Code.

To begin coding the Clear Screen button:

1   Right-click the **form** (or a control on the form), and then click **View Code** to open the Code Editor window.

2   Click the **Class Name** list arrow in the Code Editor window, and then click **uiClearButton** in the list. Click the **Method Name** list arrow, and then click **Click** in the list. The code template for the uiClearButton object's Click event procedure appears in the Code Editor window.

Step 1 in the pseudocode shown in Figure 2-25 is to assign a zero-length string to the Text property of six of the text boxes. You can do so using either the instruction `Me.`*textbox*`.Text = ""` or the instruction *textbox*`.Text = ""`, where *textbox* is the name of the appropriate text box. (Recall that the `Me.` part of an assignment statement is optional.) You can type the assignment statement on your own; or you can use the IntelliSense feature that is built into Visual Basic .NET. In the next set of steps, you learn how to use the IntelliSense feature.

To practice using the IntelliSense feature:

1   Type **me.** (but don't press Enter). When you type the period, the IntelliSense feature displays a list of choices from which you can select. See Figure 2-26. (The font used to display the text in the Code Editor window shown in Figure 2-26 was changed to 11-point Courier New so that you could view all of the code in the figure. It is not necessary for you to change the font.)

Figure 2-26: IntelliSense feature displays a list of choices

HELP?   If the list of choices does not appear, the IntelliSense feature on your computer may have been turned off. To turn it on, click Tools on the menu bar, and then click Options. Open the Text Editor folder in the Options dialog box, and then open the Basic folder. Click General in the Basic folder, then select the Auto list members check box. Click the OK button to close the Options dialog box.

2   Type **uin** (but don't press Enter). The IntelliSense feature highlights the uiNameTextBox choice in the list, as shown in Figure 2-27.

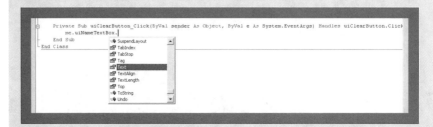

Figure 2-27: uiNameTextBox choice highlighted in the list

3   Press the **Tab** key on your keyboard to select the uiNameTextBox choice, then type . (a period). The IntelliSense feature highlights the Text property in the list, as shown in Figure 2-28.

```
        Private Sub uiClearButton_Click(ByVal sender As Object, ByVal e As System.EventArgs) Handles uiClearButton.Click
            me.uiNameTextBox.
    End Sub                    SuspendLayout
End Class                      TabIndex
                               TabStop
                               Tag
                               Text
                               TextAlign
                               TextLength
                               Top
                               ToString
                               Undo
```

Figure 2-28: Text property highlighted in the list

4   Press **Tab** to select the Text property, then type = " " (be sure you do not type any spaces between the quotation marks) and press **Enter**. The completed assignment statement is shown in Figure 2-29.

two quotation marks ————

```
        Private Sub uiClearButton_Click(ByVal sender As Object, ByVal e As System.EventArgs) Handles uiClearButton.Click
            Me.uiNameTextBox.Text = ""

    End Sub
End Class
```

Figure 2-29: Assignment statement entered in the Click event procedure

When entering code, you can type the names of commands, objects, and properties in lowercase letters. When you move to the next line, the Code Editor automatically changes your code to reflect the proper capitalization of those elements. This provides a quick way of verifying that you entered an object's name and property correctly, and that you entered the code using the correct syntax. If the capitalization does not change, then the Code Editor does not recognize the object, command, or property.

Rather than typing `Me.` to activate the IntelliSense feature, you also can use the Control key along with the spacebar. You will use this method to enter the instruction `uiAddressTextBox.Text = ""`.

5   Press and hold down the **Ctrl** (or Control) key on your keyboard as you press the **spacebar,** then release the Ctrl key. The IntelliSense feature displays the list of choices shown in Figure 2-30.

Figure 2-30: Choices displayed when you use Ctrl+spacebar

6 Type **ui** (but don't press Enter). The IntelliSense feature highlights the uiAddressTextBox choice in the list.

7 Press **Tab** to select the uiAddressTextBox choice, then type **.** (a period). The IntelliSense feature highlights the Text property in the list.

8 Press **Tab** to select the Text property, then type **= ""** (be sure you do not type any spaces between the quotation marks) and press **Enter**. The completed assignment statement, `uiAddressTextBox.Text = ""`, appears in the Click event procedure.

Some programmers include the `Me.` in their code so that the code agrees with the code automatically generated by the Windows Form Designer. (Refer to Figure 1-30 in Chapter 1 for a sample of the code generated by the designer.) Other programmers feel that including the `Me.` in their code makes the code longer and more difficult to read. In this book, you will always be instructed to enter the `Me.` in your instructions. Additionally, you will always be given the complete instruction; however, keep in mind that you can use the IntelliSense feature to enter the instruction.

To continue coding the Clear Screen button:

1 Position the insertion point at the beginning of the `uiAddressTextBox.Text = ""` assignment statement. Type **me.** (but don't press Enter). When the IntelliSense feature displays the list of choices, press the **Esc** key on your keyboard to close the list, then click the line below the assignment statement. The statement changes to `Me.uiAddressTextBox.Text = ""`.

2 Use the IntelliSense feature to enter the following four instructions:

   Me.uiCityTextBox.Text = " "

   Me.uiZipTextBox.Text = " "

   Me.uiBlueTextBox.Text = " "

   Me.uiYellowTextBox.Text = " "

The second step in the pseudocode shown earlier in Figure 2-25 is to assign the string "IL" to the Text property of the uiStateTextBox.

3 Type **me.uistatetextbox.text = "IL"** and press **Enter**.

Step 3 in the pseudocode is to assign a zero-length string to the uiTotalBoardsLabel and uiTotalPriceLabel controls.

4 Type the additional assignment statements shown in Figure 2-31, and then position the insertion point as shown in the figure.

tip

You are assigning "IL" to the uiStateTextBox control in case the user changed the state when he or she entered an order. Remember that most, but not all, of Skate-Away's customers are in Illinois.

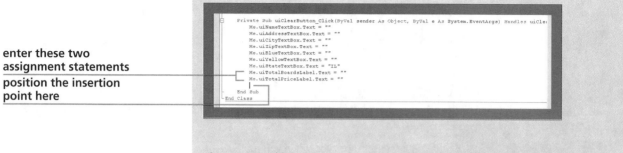

enter these two
assignment statements

position the insertion
point here

Figure 2-31: Additional assignment statements entered in the Click event procedure

The last step in the pseudocode shown earlier in Figure 2-25 is to send the focus to the uiNameTextBox. You can accomplish this using the Focus method. As you learned in Chapter 1, a method is a predefined Visual Basic .NET procedure that you can call (or invoke) when needed.

Using the Focus Method

The **Focus method** allows you to move the focus to a specified control while the application is running. The syntax of the Focus method is [**Me.**]*object*.**Focus()**, where *object* is the name of the object to which you want the focus sent.

To enter the Focus method in the Clear Screen button's Click event procedure, then save the solution:

1   Type **me.uinametextbox.focus()** and press **Enter**.
2   Click **File** on the menu bar, and then click **Save All**.

It is a good practice to leave yourself some comments as reminders in the Code Editor window. Programmers refer to this as **internal documentation**.

Internally Documenting the Program Code

Visual Basic .NET provides an easy way to document a program internally. You simply place an apostrophe (') before the statement you want treated as a comment. Visual Basic .NET ignores everything that appears after the apostrophe on that line. Add some comments to the Clear Screen button's code.

To internally document the Clear Screen button's code, then test the code to verify that it is working correctly:

1   Position the insertion point at the beginning of the `Me.uiNameTextBox.Text = ""` statement in the uiClearButton object's Click event procedure.
2   Press **Enter** to insert a blank line above the statement.
3   Press the **up arrow** key on your keyboard to position the insertion point in the blank line. Press **Tab** twice to indent the code you are about to type, then type '**prepare screen for next order** (be sure to type the apostrophe).

Notice that the internal documentation appears in a different color from the rest of the code. Recall from Chapter 1 that the Code Editor displays keywords and key symbols in a different color to help you quickly identify these elements in your code. In this case, the color coding helps you easily locate the comments.

4   Position the insertion point after the `Me.uiTotalPriceLabel.Text = ""` statement. Press **Enter** to insert a blank line below the statement, then type '**send focus to the Name text box**. Figure 2-32 shows the completed Click event procedure for the Clear Screen button.

comment ──────────────────────────────┐
comment ──────────────────────┐   │

```
Private Sub uiClearButton_Click(ByVal sender As Object, ByVal e As System.EventArgs) Handles uiClea
    'prepare screen for next order
    Me.uiNameTextBox.Text = ""
    Me.uiAddressTextBox.Text = ""
    Me.uiCityTextBox.Text = ""
    Me.uiZipTextBox.Text = ""
    Me.uiBlueTextBox.Text = ""
    Me.uiYellowTextBox.Text = ""
    Me.uiStateTextBox.Text = "IL"
    Me.uiTotalBoardsLabel.Text = ""
    Me.uiTotalPriceLabel.Text = ""
    'send focus to the Name text box
    Me.uiNameTextBox.Focus()

End Sub
End Class
```

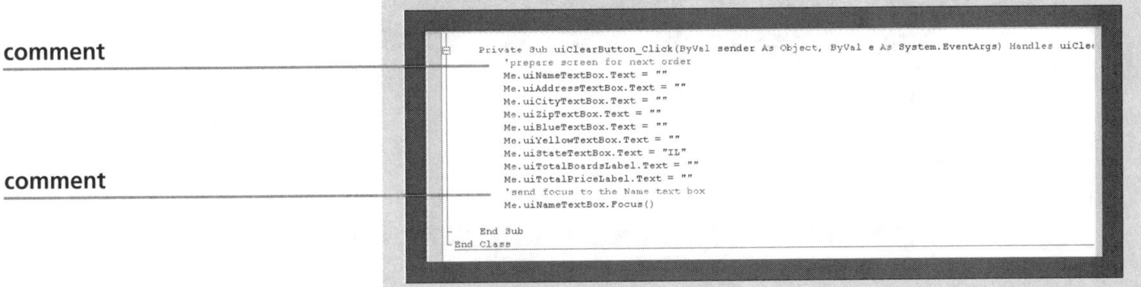

Figure 2-32: Completed Click event procedure for the Clear Screen button

It is a good programming practice to write the code for one object at a time, and then test and debug that object's code before coding the next object. This way, if something is wrong with the program, you know exactly where to look for the error.

5   Save the solution, then start the application.

6   Enter your name and address information (including the city, state, and ZIP) in the appropriate text boxes, then enter **10** for the number of blue skateboards ordered and **10** for the number of yellow skateboards ordered. Enter **100** for the skateboard price and **.05** for the sales tax rate.

7   Click the **Clear Screen** button. Following the instructions you entered in the Clear Screen button's Click event procedure, the computer removes the contents of the uiNameTextBox, uiAddressTextBox, uiCityTextBox, uiZipTextBox, uiBlueTextBox, uiYellowTextBox, uiTotalBoardsLabel, and uiTotalPriceLabel controls. It also places the string "IL" in the uiStateTextBox control, and sends the focus to the Name text box. Notice that the uiPriceTextBox control still contains 100, and the uiRateTextBox control still contains .05. Recall that you did not instruct the Clear Screen button to clear the contents of those controls.

8   Click the **Exit** button to end the application. You are returned to the Code Editor window.

9   Close the Output window.

Many programmers also use comments to document the project's name and purpose, as well as the programmer's name and the date the code was either created or modified. Typically, such comments are placed at the beginning of the application's code, above the `Public Class` statement. The area above the `Public Class` statement in the Code Editor window is called the General Declarations section.

To include comments in the General Declarations section:

1   Position the insertion point at the beginning of the `Public Class OrderForm` instruction. Press **Enter** to insert a blank line above the instruction.

2   Press the **up arrow** key on your keyboard to position the insertion point in the blank line.

3   Type the comments shown in Figure 2-33. Replace the `<enter your name here>` and `<enter the date here>` text with your name and the current date.

General Declarations section

enter these three comments

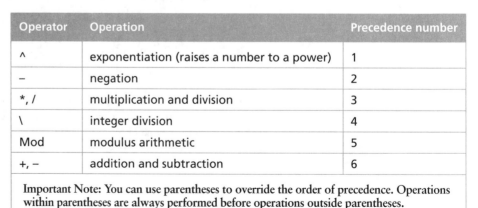

```
OrderForm.vb [Design]   Order Form.vb
(General)                                                          (Declarations)
'Project name:      Order Project
'Project purpose:   The project calculates the total number of skateboards ordered and the total price.
'Created/revised by: <enter your name here> on <enter the date here>

Public Class OrderForm
    Inherits System.Windows.Forms.Form

    Windows Form Designer generated code
```

Figure 2-33: Comments entered in the General Declarations section

4   Save the solution.

The Calculate Order button is the only object that still needs to be coded. However, before coding the button, you learn how to write arithmetic expressions in Visual Basic .NET.

Writing Arithmetic Expressions

Most applications require the computer to perform one or more calculations. You instruct the computer to perform a calculation by writing an arithmetic expression that contains one or more arithmetic operators. Figure 2-34 lists the arithmetic operators available in Visual Basic .NET, along with their precedence numbers. The **precedence numbers** indicate the order in which the computer performs the operation in an expression. Operations with a precedence number of 1 are performed before operations with a precedence number of 2, which are performed before operations with a precedence number of 3, and so on. However, you can use parentheses to override the order of precedence, because operations within parentheses always are performed before operations outside parentheses.

tip

. . . .

The difference between the negation and subtraction operators shown in Figure 2-34 is that the negation operator is unary, whereas the subtraction operator is binary. *Unary* and *binary* refer to the number of operands required by the operator. Unary operators require one operand; binary operators require two operands.

Operator	Operation	Precedence number
^	exponentiation (raises a number to a power)	1
−	negation	2
*, /	multiplication and division	3
\	integer division	4
Mod	modulus arithmetic	5
+, −	addition and subtraction	6
Important Note: You can use parentheses to override the order of precedence. Operations within parentheses are always performed before operations outside parentheses.		

Figure 2-34: Arithmetic operators and their order of precedence

Notice that some operators shown in Figure 2-34 have the same precedence number. For example, both the addition and subtraction operators have a precedence number of 6. If an expression contains more than one operator having the same priority, those operators are evaluated from left to right. In the expression 3 + 12 / 3 - 1, for instance, the division (/) is performed first, then the addition (+), and then the subtraction (-). In other words, the computer first divides 12 by 3, then adds the result of the division (4) to 3, and then subtracts 1 from the result of the addition (7). The expression evaluates to 6.

You can use parentheses to change the order in which the operators in an expression are evaluated. For example, the expression 3 + 12 / (3 - 1) evaluates to 9, not 6. This is because the parentheses tell the computer to subtract 1 from 3 first, then divide the result of the subtraction (2) into 12, and then add the result of the division (6) to 3.

Two of the arithmetic operators listed in Figure 2-34 might be less familiar to you; these are the integer division operator (\) and the modulus arithmetic operator (Mod). You use the **integer division operator** (\) to divide two integers (whole numbers), and then return the result as an integer. For example, the expression 211\4 results in 52—the integer result of dividing 211 by 4. (If you use the standard division operator [/] to divide 211 by 4, the result is 52.75 rather than simply 52.)

The modulus arithmetic operator also is used to divide two numbers, but the numbers do not have to be integers. After dividing the numbers, the **modulus arithmetic operator** returns the remainder of the division. For example, 211 Mod 4 equals 3, which is the remainder of 211 divided by 4. One use for the modulus arithmetic operator is to determine whether a year is a leap year—one that has 366 days rather than 365 days. As you may know, if a year is a leap year, then its year number is evenly divisible by the number 4. In other words, if you divide the year number by 4 and the remainder is 0 (zero), then the year is a leap year. You can determine whether the year 2004 is a leap year by using the expression 2004 Mod 4. This expression evaluates to 0 (the remainder of 2004 divided by 4), so the year 2004 is a leap year. Similarly, you can determine whether the year 2005 is a leap year by using the expression 2005 Mod 4. This expression evaluates to 1 (the remainder of 2005 divided by 4), so the year 2005 is not a leap year.

When entering an arithmetic expression in code, you do not enter the dollar sign ($) or the percent sign (%). If you want to enter a percentage in an arithmetic expression, you first must change the percentage to its decimal equivalent; for example, you would change 5% to .05.

In addition to the arithmetic operators, Visual Basic .NET also allows you to use comparison operators and logical operators in an expression. You learn about comparison and logical operators in Chapter 4. To code the Calculate Order button in the Skate-Away Sales application, you need to know only the arithmetic operators.

Coding the Calculate Order Button

According to the TOE chart for the Skate-Away Sales application (shown earlier in Figure 2-23), the Calculate Order button is responsible for calculating both the total number of skateboards ordered and the total price of the order, and then displaying the calculated amounts in the uiTotalBoardsLabel and uiTotalPriceLabel controls. The instructions to accomplish the Calculate Order button's tasks should be placed in the button's Click event procedure, because you want the instructions processed when the user clicks the button. Figure 2-35 shows the pseudocode for the Calculate Order button's Click event procedure. The pseudocode lists the steps the button must take to accomplish its tasks.

Calculate Order button
1. calculate total skateboards = blue skateboards + yellow skateboards
2. calculate total price = total skateboards * skateboard price * (1 + sales tax rate)
3. display total skateboards and total price in uiTotalBoardsLabel and uiTotalPriceLabel controls
4. send the focus to the Clear Screen button

Figure 2-35: Pseudocode for the Calculate Order button

The first step listed in the pseudocode shown in Figure 2-35 is to calculate the total number of skateboards ordered. This is accomplished by adding the number of blue skateboards ordered to the number of yellow skateboards ordered. Recall that the number of blue skateboards ordered is recorded in the uiBlueTextBox control's Text property as the user enters that information in the interface. Likewise, the number of yellow skateboards ordered is recorded in the uiYellowTextBox control's Text property. You can use an assignment statement to add together the Text property of the two text boxes, and then assign the sum to the Text property of the uiTotalBoardsLabel control, which is where the TOE chart indicates the sum should be displayed. The total skateboards calculation is illustrated in Figure 2-36.

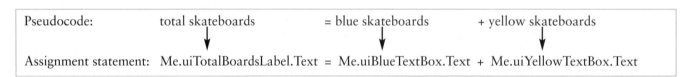

Pseudocode: total skateboards   = blue skateboards   + yellow skateboards

Assignment statement: Me.uiTotalBoardsLabel.Text = Me.uiBlueTextBox.Text + Me.uiYellowTextBox.Text

Figure 2-36: Illustration of the total skateboards calculation

The next step shown in the pseudocode is to compute the total price of the order. This is accomplished by multiplying the total number of skateboards ordered by the skateboard price ($100), and then adding a 5% sales tax to the result. The total number of skateboards ordered is recorded in the uiTotalBoardsLabel control, the price is entered in the uiPriceTextBox control, and the sales tax rate is entered in the uiRateTextBox control. The TOE chart indicates that the total price should be displayed in the uiTotalPriceLabel control. The total price calculation is illustrated in Figure 2-37.

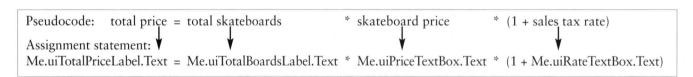

Pseudocode: total price = total skateboards   * skateboard price   * (1 + sales tax rate)

Assignment statement:
Me.uiTotalPriceLabel.Text = Me.uiTotalBoardsLabel.Text * Me.uiPriceTextBox.Text * (1 + Me.uiRateTextBox.Text)

Figure 2-37: Illustration of the total price calculation

Step 3 in the pseudocode is to display the total skateboards and total price in the uiTotalBoardsLabel and uiTotalPriceLabel controls. This step was accomplished in the assignment statements shown in Figures 2-36 and 2-37.

The last step in the Calculate Order button's pseudocode is to send the focus to the Clear Screen button. After calculating an order, the salesperson typically will want to clear the screen for the next order. Sending the focus to the Clear Screen button after a calculation is made allows the user to select the button simply by pressing the Enter key. Begin coding the Calculate Order button's Click event procedure.

To begin coding the Calculate Order button's Click event procedure:

1   Click the **Class Name** list arrow in the Code Editor window, and then click **uiCalcButton** in the list. Click the **Method Name** list arrow, and then click **Click** in the list. The code template for the uiCalcButton's Click event procedure appears in the Code Editor window.

2   Type '**calculate total number of skateboards and total price** and press **Enter**.

3   Type **me.uitotalboardslabel.text = me.uibluetextbox.text + me.uiyellowtextbox.text** and press **Enter**. Recall that this instruction calculates the total number of skateboards ordered.

The instruction that calculates the total price of the order is quite long. You can use the **line continuation character**, which is a space followed by an underscore, to break up a long instruction into two or more physical lines in the Code Editor window; this makes the instruction easier to read and understand.

4   Type **me.uitotalpricelabel.text = me.uitotalboardslabel.text * me.uiprice-textbox.text _** (be sure to include a space before the underscore) and press **Enter**.

5   Press **Tab** to indent the line, then type *** (1 + me.uiratetextbox.text)** and press **Enter**.

Finally, enter the instruction to send the focus to the Clear Screen button.

6   Enter the additional comment and instruction indicated in Figure 2-38.

enter this comment and instruction

```
Private Sub uiCalcButton_Click(ByVal sender As Object, ByVal e As System.EventArgs) Handles uiCalcE
    'calculate total number of skateboards and total price
    Me.uiTotalBoardsLabel.Text = Me.uiBlueTextBox.Text + Me.uiYellowTextBox.Text
    Me.uiTotalPriceLabel.Text = Me.uiTotalBoardsLabel.Text * Me.uiPriceTextBox.Text _
        * (1 + Me.uiRateTextBox.Text)
    'send the focus to the Clear Screen button
    Me.uiClearButton.Focus()

End Sub
End Class
```

Figure 2-38: Code entered in the Calculate Order button's Click event procedure

7   Save the solution, then start the application.

8   Press **Tab** five times to move the focus to the uiBlueTextBox control. Type **5** as the number of blue skateboards ordered, then press **Tab**. Type **10** as the number of yellow skateboards ordered, then press **Tab**. Type **100** as the skateboard price, then press **Tab**. Type **.05** as the sales tax rate, then click the **Calculate Order** button. The Calculate Order button calculates, incorrectly, the total skateboards and the total price, then moves the focus to the Clear Screen button, as shown in Figure 2-39.

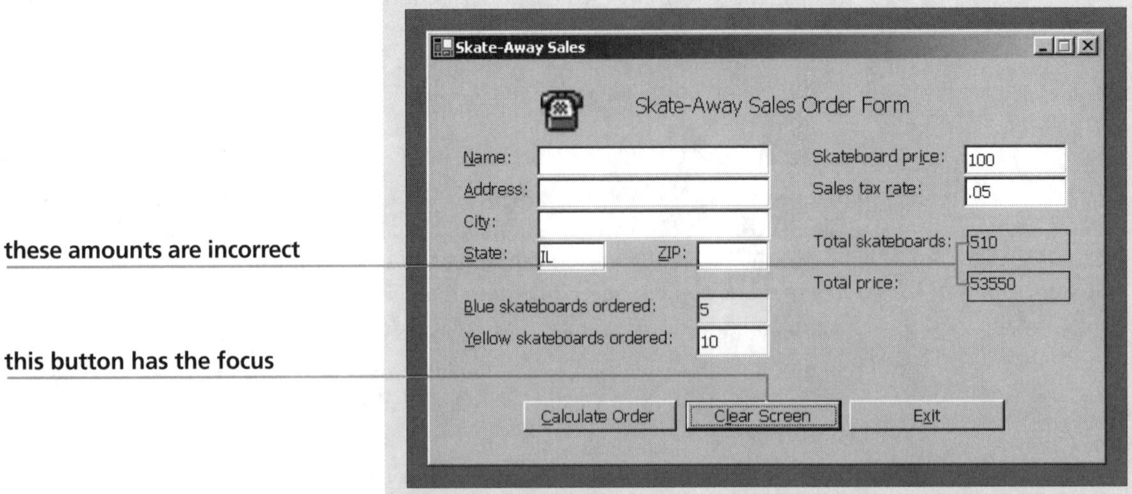

these amounts are incorrect

this button has the focus

Figure 2-39: Screen showing the incorrect amounts calculated by the Calculate Order button

Notice that the screen shows 510 as the total number of skateboards ordered. Rather than mathematically adding the two order quantities together, which should have resulted in a total of 15, the computer appended the second order quantity to the end of the first order quantity, giving 510. When the total skateboards ordered figure is incorrect, it follows that the total price figure also will be incorrect, as the total skateboards ordered figure is used in the total price calculation.

9 Click the **Exit** button to end the application. You are returned to the Code Editor window.

10 Close the Output window.

The `Me.uiTotalBoardsLabel.Text = Me.uiBlueTextBox.Text + Me.uiYellowTextBox.Text` equation you entered in the Calculate Order button's Click event procedure is supposed to calculate the total skateboards ordered, but the equation is not working correctly. Instead of the plus sign (+) adding the blue skateboard quantity to the yellow skateboard quantity, the plus sign appends the latter quantity to the end of the first one. This occurs because the plus sign in Visual Basic .NET performs two roles: it adds numbers together and it concatenates (links together) strings. You learn about string concatenation in Chapter 3. (Recall that strings are groups of characters enclosed in quotation marks.)

In Visual Basic .NET, a value stored in the Text property of an object is treated as a string rather than as a number, even though you do not see the quotation marks around the value. Adding strings together does not give you the same result as adding numbers together. As you observed in the Skate-Away Sales application, adding the string "5" to the string "10" results in the string "510," whereas adding the number 5 to the number 10 results in the number 15. To fix the problem, you need to instruct the computer to treat the entries in the Text property of both the uiBlueTextBox and uiYellowTextBox controls as numbers rather than as strings; you can use the Val function to do so.

The Val Function

Like a method, a **function** is a predefined procedure that performs a specific task. However, unlike a method, a function always returns a value after performing its task. The **Val function**, for instance, temporarily converts a string to a number, and then returns the number. (The number is stored in the computer's memory only while the function is processing.)

The syntax of the Val function is **Val**(*string*), where *string* is the string you want treated as a number. Because the computer must be able to interpret the *string* as a numeric value, the *string* cannot include a letter or a special character, such as the dollar sign, the comma, or the percent sign (%); it can, however, include a period and a space. When the computer encounters an invalid character in the Val function's *string*, it stops converting the *string* to a number at that point. Figure 2-40 shows some examples of how the Val function converts various strings. Notice that the Val function converts the "$56.88", the "Abc", and the "" (zero-length string) to the number 0.

This Val function:	Would be converted to:
Val("456")	456
Val("24,500")	24
Val("123X")	123
Val("$56.88")	0
Val("Abc")	0
Val("")	0
Val("25%")	25
Val("24 500")	24500

Figure 2-40: Examples of the Val function

You will use the Val function in the Calculate Order button's Click event procedure to temporarily convert to numbers the Text property of the controls included in calculations.

If you are thinking that the instructions in the Code Editor window are getting a bit unwieldy, you are correct. In Chapter 3 you learn how to write more compact assignment statements.

To include the Val function in the Calculate Order button's code:

1   Change the `Me.uiTotalBoardsLabel.Text = Me.uiBlueTextBox.Text + Me.uiYellowTextBox.Text` statement to **Me.uiTotalBoardsLabel.Text = Val(Me.uiBlueTextBox.Text) + Val(Me.uiYellowTextBox.Text)**. Be sure to watch the placement of the parentheses.

2   Change the instruction that calculates the total price as shown in Figure 2-41. Be sure to watch the placement of the parentheses in the instruction. Also, notice that there are two parentheses at the end of the instruction. (Do not be concerned if you cannot view all of the uiCalcButton's code. The font used to display the text in the Code Editor window shown in Figure 2-41 was changed to 11-point Microsoft Sans Serif so that you could view all of the total price equation in the figure. It is not necessary for you to change the font.)

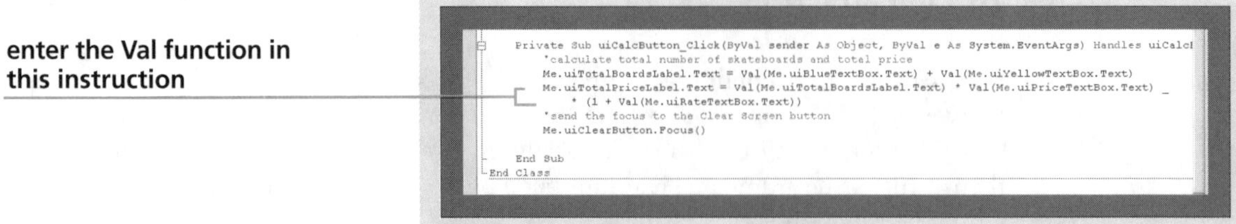

```
Private Sub uiCalcButton_Click(ByVal sender As Object, ByVal e As System.EventArgs) Handles uiCalc
    'calculate total number of skateboards and total price
    Me.uiTotalBoardsLabel.Text = Val(Me.uiBlueTextBox.Text) + Val(Me.uiYellowTextBox.Text)
    Me.uiTotalPriceLabel.Text = Val(Me.uiTotalBoardsLabel.Text) * Val(Me.uiPriceTextBox.Text) _
        * (1 + Val(Me.uiRateTextBox.Text))
    'send the focus to the Clear Screen button
    Me.uiClearButton.Focus()

End Sub
End Class
```

Figure 2-41: Val function entered in the Calculate Order button's code

3 Save the solution, then start the application.

4 Click the **uiBlueTextBox** control, type **5** as the number of blue skateboards ordered, then press **Tab.** Type **10** as the number of yellow skateboards ordered, **100** as the skateboard price, and **.05** as the sales tax rate. Click the **Calculate Order** button. The application correctly calculates the total skateboards (15) and the total price (1575), then sends the focus to the Clear Screen button.

In the next section, you improve the appearance of the interface by including a dollar sign, a comma thousand separator, and two decimal places in the total price amount.

5 Press **Enter** to clear the screen, then click the **Exit** button. You are returned to the Code Editor window.

6 Close the Output window.

Next, learn about the Format function.

Using the Format Function

You can use the **Format function** to improve the appearance of the numbers displayed in an interface. The syntax of the Format function is **Format(**_expression_, _style_**)**. _Expression_ specifies the number, date, time, or string whose appearance you want to format. _Style_ is either the name of a predefined Visual Basic .NET format style or, if you want more control over the appearance of the _expression_, a string containing special symbols that indicate how you want the _expression_ displayed. (You can display the Help screen for the Format function to learn more about these special symbols.) In this case, you will use one of the predefined Visual Basic .NET format styles, some of which are explained in Figure 2-42.

tip

You could have included the Format function in the equation that calculates the total price, but then the equation would be so long that it would be difficult to understand.

Format style	Description
Currency	Displays a number with a dollar sign and two decimal places; if appropriate, displays a number with a thousand separator; negative numbers are enclosed in parentheses
Fixed	Displays a number with at least one digit to the left and two digits to the right of the decimal point
Standard	Displays a number with at least one digit to the left and two digits to the right of the decimal point; if appropriate, displays a number with a thousand separator
Percent	Multiplies a number by 100 and displays the number with a percent sign (%); displays two digits to the right of the decimal point

Figure 2-42: Some of the predefined format styles in Visual Basic .NET

You will use the Currency format style to display the total price amount with a dollar sign, a comma thousand separator, and two decimal places.

To format the total price amount:

1 Insert a blank line below the total price equation, then enter the additional line of code shown in Figure 2-43.

enter this line of code

```
Private Sub uiCalcButton_Click(ByVal sender As Object, ByVal e As System.EventArgs) Handles uiCalcl
    'calculate total number of skateboards and total price
    Me.uiTotalBoardsLabel.Text = Val(Me.uiBlueTextBox.Text) + Val(Me.uiYellowTextBox.Text)
    Me.uiTotalPriceLabel.Text = Val(Me.uiTotalBoardsLabel.Text) * Val(Me.uiPriceTextBox.Text) _
        * (1 + Val(Me.uiRateTextBox.Text))
    Me.uiTotalPriceLabel.Text = Format(Me.uiTotalPriceLabel.Text, "currency")
    'send the focus to the Clear Screen button
    Me.uiClearButton.Focus()

    End Sub
End Class
```

Figure 2-43: Format function entered in the Calculate Order button's Click event procedure

2 Save the solution, start the application, then enter the following order:

Sport Warehouse, 123 Main, Glendale, IL, 60134, 10 blue skateboards, 15 yellow skateboards

3 Enter **100** as the skateboard price and **.05** as the sales tax rate.

4 Click the **Calculate Order** button. The application calculates the total skateboards and total price. The total price appears formatted, as shown in Figure 2-44.

total price appears with
a $, a comma thousand
separator, and
two decimal places

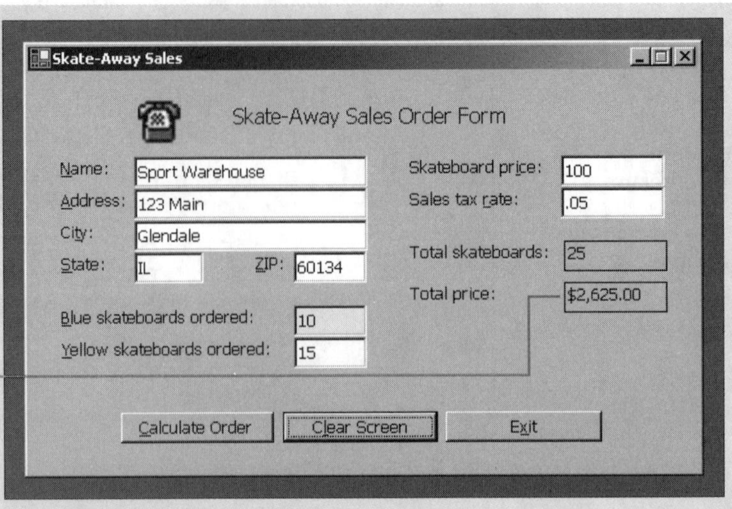

Figure 2-44: Total price displayed using the Format function

5   Click the **Exit** button. You are returned to the Code Editor window.

6   Close the Output window.

You have now completed the first four of the six steps involved in creating an OO application: meeting with the client, planning the application, building the user interface, and coding the application. The fifth step is to test and debug the application.

Testing and Debugging the Application

You test an application by starting it and entering some sample data. You should use both valid and invalid test data. **Valid data** is data that the application is expecting. For example, the Skate-Away Sales application is expecting the user to enter a numeric value as the skateboard price. **Invalid data**, on the other hand, is data that the application is not expecting. The Skate-Away Sales application, for example, is not expecting the user to enter a letter for the number of either blue or yellow skateboards ordered. You should test the application as thoroughly as possible, because you don't want to give the user an application that ends abruptly when invalid data is entered.

Debugging refers to the process of locating errors in the program. Program errors can be either syntax errors or logic errors. Most **syntax errors** are simply typing errors that occur when entering instructions; for example, typing `Me.Clse()` instead of `Me.Close()` results in a syntax error. The Code Editor detects most syntax errors as you enter the instructions. An example of a much more difficult type of error to find, and one that the Code Editor cannot detect, is a logic error. You create a **logic error** when you enter an instruction that does not give you the expected results. An example of a logic error is the instruction `Me.uiAverageLabel.Text = Val(Me.uiNum1TextBox.Text) + Val(Me.uiNum2TextBox.Text) / 2`, which is supposed to calculate the average of two numbers. Although the instruction is syntactically correct, it is logically incorrect. The instruction to calculate the average of two numbers, written

correctly, is `Me.uiAverageLabel.Text = (Val(Me.uiNum1TextBox.Text)`
`+ Val(Me.uiNum2TextBox.Text)) / 2`. Because division has a higher precedence number than does addition, you must place parentheses around the
`Val(Me.uiNum1TextBox.Text) + Val(Me.uiNum2TextBox.Text)` part of
the equation.

To test and debug the Skate-Away Sales application with both valid and
invalid data:

1   Start the application. First, test the application by clicking the **Calculate
Order** button without entering any data. The application displays 0 as the
total number of skateboards ordered, and $0.00 as the total price.

2   Next, enter the letter **r** for the number of blue skateboards ordered and the letter **p** for the number of yellow skateboards ordered. Enter **100** for the skateboard price and **.05** for the sales tax rate. Click the **Calculate Order** button.
The application displays 0 as the total number of skateboards ordered, and
$0.00 as the total price. (Recall that the Val function converts letters to the
number 0.)

3   Click the **Clear Screen** button. Enter **10** as the number of blue skateboards
ordered, and **10** as the number of yellow skateboards ordered. Now replace
the 100 in the uiPriceTextBox control with the letters **xyz**. Click the
Calculate Order button. The application displays 20 as the total number of
skateboards ordered, and $0.00 as the total price.

4   Click the **Clear Screen** button, then enter an order that is correct. Click the
Calculate Order button.

5   Click the **Clear Screen** button, then practice with other entries to see how the
application responds.

6   When you are finished, click the **Exit** button to end the application.

7   When you are returned to the Code Editor window, close the Output window.

After you have tested the application to verify that it is working correctly, you
can move to the last step involved in creating an OO application, which is to assemble the documentation.

Assembling the Documentation

Assembling the documentation refers to putting your planning tools and a printout
of the application's interface and code in a safe place, so you can refer to them if
you need to change the application in the future. Your planning tools include the
TOE chart, sketch of the user interface, and either the flowcharts or pseudocode.

To print the application's code and interface:

1   While viewing the Code Editor window, click **File** on the menu bar, then click
Print. When the Print dialog box appears, click the **OK** button to print the
code. The application's code is shown in Figure 2-45.

```
'Project name:        Order Project
'Project purpose:     The project calculates the total number of skateboards ordered and the total price.
'Created/revised by: <enter your name here> on <enter the date here>

Public Class OrderForm
    Inherits System.Windows.Forms.Form

[Windows Form Designer generated code]

    Private Sub uiExitButton_Click(ByVal sender As Object, ByVal e As System.EventArgs) Handles uiExitButton.Click
        Me.Close()
    End Sub

    Private Sub uiClearButton_Click(ByVal sender As Object, ByVal e As System.EventArgs) Handles uiClearButton.Click
        'prepare screen for next order
        Me.uiNameTextBox.Text = ""
        Me.uiAddressTextBox.Text = ""
        Me.uiCityTextBox.Text = ""
        Me.uiZipTextBox.Text = ""
        Me.uiBlueTextBox.Text = ""
        Me.uiYellowTextBox.Text = ""
        Me.uiStateTextBox.Text = "IL"
        Me.uiTotalBoardsLabel.Text = ""
        Me.uiTotalPriceLabel.Text = ""
        'send focus to the Name text box
        Me.uiNameTextBox.Focus()
    End Sub

    Private Sub uiCalcButton_Click(ByVal sender As Object, ByVal e As System.EventArgs) Handles uiCalcButton.Click
        'calculate total number of skateboards and total price
        Me.uiTotalBoardsLabel.Text = Val(Me.uiBlueTextBox.Text) + Val(Me.uiYellowTextBox.Text)
        Me.uiTotalPriceLabel.Text = Val(Me.uiTotalBoardsLabel.Text) * Val(Me.uiPriceTextBox.Text) _
            * (1 + Val(Me.uiRateTextBox.Text))
        Me.uiTotalPriceLabel.Text = Format(Me.uiTotalPriceLabel.Text, "currency")
        'send the focus to the Clear Screen button
        Me.uiClearButton.Focus()

    End Sub
End Class
```

Figure 2-45: Order application's code

Now print the interface.

2   Start the application. The Skate-Away Sales interface appears on the screen.

3   Press **Alt + Print Screen** (or Prt Sc) to place a picture of the interface on the clipboard.

4   Click the **Exit** button to end the application.

5   When you are returned to the Code Editor window, close the Output window, then close the Code Editor window.

6   Start Microsoft Word (or any application that can display a picture) and open a new document. Click **Edit** on the Word menu bar, then click **Paste** to paste the contents of the clipboard in the document. (You also can press Ctrl + v.)

7 Click **File** on the Word menu bar, and then click **Print**. When the Print dialog box appears, click the **OK** button to print the document.

8 Click **File** on the Word menu bar, and then click **Exit**. When you are asked if you want to save the changes made to the document, click the **No** button.

9 Click **File** on the Visual Basic .NET menu bar, and then click **Close Solution**.

You now have completed the six steps involved in creating an application:
1. Meet with the client.
2. Plan the application.
3. Build the user interface.
4. Code the application.
5. Test and debug the application.
6. Assemble the documentation.

You have now completed Chapter 2. You can either take a break or complete the end-of-lesson questions and exercises.

S U M M A R Y

To assign a value to the property of an object while an application is running:

■ Use an assignment statement that follows the syntax [**Me.**]*object.property* = *expression*.

To move the focus to an object while the program is running:

■ Use the Focus method. The method's syntax is [**Me.**]*object*.**Focus**().

To document Visual Basic code with comments:

■ Begin the comment with an apostrophe (').

To divide two integers, and then return the result as an integer:

■ Use the integer division operator (\).

To divide two numbers, and then return the remainder as an integer:

■ Use the modulus arithmetic operator (Mod).

To temporarily convert a string to a number:

■ Use the Val function. The function's syntax is **Val**(*string*).

To improve the appearance of numbers in the user interface:

■ Use the Format function. The function's syntax is **Format**(*expression*, *style*).

QUESTIONS

1. Which of the following is a valid assignment statement?
   a. `Me.uiNameTextBox = 'Jones'`
   b. `Me.uiNameTextBox.Caption = "Jones"`
   c. `Me.uiNameTextBox.Text = 'Jones'`
   d. `Me.uiNameTextBox.Text = "Jones"`
   e. None of the above is valid.

2. Which of the following assignment statements will not calculate correctly?
   a. `Me.uiTotalLabel.Text = Val(Me.uiSales1TextBox.Text) + Val(Me.uiSales2TextBox.Text)`
   b. `Me.uiTotalLabel.Text = Val(Me.uiSales1Label.Text) + Val(Me.uiSales2Label.Text)`
   c. `Me.uiTotalLabel.Text = Val(Me.uiRedTextBox.Text) * 2`
   d. `Me.uiTotalLabel.Text = Val(Me.uiBlueLabel.Text) * 1.1`
   e. All of the above are correct.

3. You use the _____ function to display a dollar sign and a thousand separator in numbers.
   a. Display
   b. Focus
   c. Format
   d. Style
   e. Val

4. The _____ function temporarily converts a string to a number.
   a. Convert
   b. Format
   c. String
   d. StringToNum
   e. Val

5. Listed below are the six steps you should follow when creating an OO application. Put them in the proper order by placing a number (1 to 6) on the line to the left of the step.
   _____ Assemble the documentation.
   _____ Plan the application.
   _____ Code the application.
   _____ Build the user interface.
   _____ Test and debug the application.
   _____ Meet with the client.

6. The instruction `Me.uiTotalLabel.Text = Val(Me.uiNumTextbox.Text) / 2`, which should multiply the contents of the uiNumTextbox by 2 and then assign the result to the uiTotalLabel, is an example of _____.
   a. a logic error
   b. a syntax error
   c. a correct instruction

7. The instruction `Me.uiSalesLabel.Text = Format(Me.uiSalesLabel.Text, "curency")` is an example of _____.
   a. a logic error
   b. a syntax error
   c. a correct instruction

8. What value is assigned to the uiNumLabel control when the `Me.uiNumLabel.Text = 73 / 25` instruction is processed?

9. What value is assigned to the uiNumLabel control when the `Me.uiNumLabel.Text = 73 \ 25` instruction is processed?

10. What value is assigned to the uiNumLabel control when the `Me.uiNumLabel.Text = 73 Mod 25` instruction is processed?

E X E R C I S E S

NOTE: In Exercises 4 through 11, and in Exercises 13 through 19, you perform the second through sixth steps involved in creating an OO application. Recall that the six steps are:

1. Meet with the client.

2. Plan the application. (Prepare a TOE chart that is ordered by object, and draw a sketch of the user interface.)

3. Build the user interface. (To help you remember the names of the controls as you are coding, print the application's interface and then write the names next to each object.)

4. Code the application. (Be sure to write pseudocode for each of the objects that will be coded.)

5. Test and debug the application. (Use the sample data provided in each of the exercises.)

6. Assemble the documentation (your planning tools and a printout of the interface and code).

1. In this exercise, you complete the application that you saved in Lesson B's Exercise 1.
   a. If necessary, start Visual Studio .NET. Open the Paper Solution (Paper Solution.sln) file, which is contained in the VBNET\Chap02\Paper Solution folder. If the designer window is not open, right-click the form file's name in the Solution Explorer window, then click View Designer.
   b. Code the Calculate Commission button appropriately. Recall that the commission rate is 10%. Be sure to use the Val function. Use the Format function to display the commission with a dollar sign, a comma thousand separator, and two decimal places. Use the Focus method to send the focus to the Clear button.
   c. Code the Clear button appropriately. Send the focus to the Name text box.
   d. Save the solution, then start the application. Test the application with both valid and invalid data. Use the following information for the valid data:
Name:	Pat Brown
Territory number:	10
Sales:	2500

2. In this exercise, you complete the application that you saved in Lesson B's Exercise 2.
   a. If necessary, start Visual Studio .NET. Open the RMSales Solution (RMSales Solution.sln) file, which is contained in the VBNET\Chap02\RMSales Solution folder. If the designer window is not open, right-click the form file's name in the Solution Explorer window, then click View Designer.
   b. Code the Calculate Projected Sales button appropriately. Be sure to use the Val function. Use the Format function to display the projected sales using the Standard format. Send the focus to the Clear button.

   c. Code the Clear button appropriately. Send the focus to the uiNsalesTextBox control.

   d. Save the solution, then start the application. Test the application with both valid and invalid data. Use the following information for the valid data:

North sales and percentage:	25000, .05
South sales and percentage:	30000, .07
East sales and percentage:	10000, .04
West sales and percentage:	15000, .11

3. In this exercise, you complete the application that you saved in Lesson B's Exercise 3.

   a. If necessary, start Visual Studio .NET. Open the Time Solution (Time Solution.sln) file, which is contained in the VBNET\Chap02\Time Solution folder. If the designer window is not open, right-click the form file's name in the Solution Explorer window, then click View Designer.

   b. Code the Calculate button appropriately. Be sure to use the Val function. Send the focus to the Monday text box.

   c. Save the solution, then start the application. Test the application with both valid and invalid data. Use the following information for the valid data:

Monday hours:	7
Tuesday hours:	8
Wednesday hours:	6
Thursday hours:	5
Friday hours:	4
Saturday hours:	2
Sunday hours:	0

4. Scenario: In previous versions of Visual Basic, the location of a control on a form was measured in twips. A twip is 1/1440 of an inch; in other words, 1440 twips equal one inch. Create an application that allows you to enter the number of twips, and then converts the twips to inches.

   a. If necessary, start Visual Studio .NET. Create a blank solution named Twips Solution. Save the solution in the VBNET\Chap02 folder.

   b. Add a Visual Basic .NET Windows Application project to the solution. Name the project Twips Project.

   c. Perform the steps involved in creating an OO application. (See the NOTE at the beginning of the Exercises section. Use the GUI design guidelines listed in Appendix B to verify that the interface you create adheres to the GUI standards outlined in this book.)

   d. Test the application two times, using the following data.

      Twips: 2880   Twips: abc

5. Scenario: John Lee wants an application in which he can enter the following three pieces of information: his cash balance at the beginning of the month, the amount of money he earned during the month, and the amount of money he spent during the month. He wants the application to compute his ending balance.

   a. If necessary, start Visual Studio .NET. Create a blank solution named JohnLee Solution. Save the solution in the VBNET\Chap02 folder.

   b. Add a Visual Basic .NET Windows Application project to the solution. Name the project JohnLee Project.

   c. Perform the steps involved in creating an OO application. (See the NOTE at the beginning of the Exercises section. Use the GUI design guidelines listed in Appendix B to verify that the interface you create adheres to the GUI standards outlined in this book.)

   d. Test the application twice using the following data.

Beginning cash balance: 5000	Earnings: 2500	Expenses: 3000
Beginning cash balance: xyz	Earnings: xyz	Expenses: xyz

6. Scenario: Lana Jones wants an application that will compute the average of any three numbers she enters.

   a. If necessary, start Visual Studio .NET. Create a blank solution named LanaJones Solution. Save the solution in the VBNET\Chap02 folder.

   b. Add a Visual Basic .NET Windows Application project to the solution. Name the project LanaJones Project.

   c. Perform the steps involved in creating an OO application. (See the NOTE at the beginning of the Exercises section. Use the GUI design guidelines listed in Appendix B to verify that the interface you create adheres to the GUI standards outlined in this book.)

   d. Test the application twice, using the following data.

First Number: 27	Second Number: 9	Third Number: 18
First Number: A	Second Number: B	Third Number: C

7. Scenario: Martha Arenso, manager of Bookworms Inc., needs an inventory application. Martha will enter the title of a book, the number of paperback versions of the book currently in inventory, the number of hardcover versions of the book currently in inventory, the cost of the paperback version, and the cost of the hardcover version. Martha wants the application to compute the value of the paperback versions of the book, the value of the hardcover versions of the book, the total number of paperback and hardcover versions, and the total value of the paperback and hardcover versions.

   a. If necessary, start Visual Studio .NET. Create a blank solution named Bookworms Solution. Save the solution in the VBNET\Chap02 folder.

   b. Add a Visual Basic .NET Windows Application project to the solution. Name the project Bookworms Project.

   c. Perform the steps involved in creating an OO application. (See the NOTE at the beginning of the Exercises section. Use the GUI design guidelines listed in Appendix B to verify that the interface you create adheres to the GUI standards outlined in this book.) Format the dollar amounts to show a dollar sign, comma thousand separator, and two decimal places.

   d. Test the application twice, using the following data.

   Book Title: An Introduction to Visual Basic .NET

Paperback versions: 100	Paperback cost: 40
Hardcover versions: 50	Hardcover cost: 75

   Book Title: Advanced Visual Basic .NET

Paperback versions: A	Paperback cost: B
Hardcover versions: C	Hardcover cost: D

8. Scenario: Jackets Unlimited is having a 25% off sale on all its merchandise. The store manager asks you to create an application that requires the clerk simply to enter the original price of a jacket. The application should then compute the discount and new price.

   a. If necessary, start Visual Studio .NET. Create a blank solution named Jackets Solution. Save the solution in the VBNET\Chap02 folder.

   b. Add a Visual Basic .NET Windows Application project to the solution. Name the project Jackets Project.

   c. Perform the steps involved in creating an OO application. (See the NOTE at the beginning of the Exercises section. Use the GUI design guidelines listed in Appendix B to verify that the interface you create adheres to the GUI standards outlined in this book.) Format the discount and new price using the Standard format style.

   d. Test the application twice, using the following data.

   Jacket's original price: 50

   Jacket's original price: ***

9. Scenario: Typing Salon charges $.10 per typed envelope and $.25 per typed page. The company accountant wants an application to help her prepare bills. She will enter the customer's name, the number of typed envelopes, and the number of typed pages. The application should compute the total bill.

   a. If necessary, start Visual Studio .NET. Create a blank solution named TypingSalon Solution. Save the solution in the VBNET\Chap02 folder.

   b. Add a Visual Basic .NET Windows Application project to the solution. Name the project TypingSalon Project.

   c. Perform the steps involved in creating an OO application. (See the NOTE at the beginning of the Exercises section. Use the GUI design guidelines listed in Appendix B to verify that the interface you create adheres to the GUI standards outlined in this book.) Format the total bill using the Currency format style.

   d. Test the application twice, using the following data.
   Customer's name: Alice Wong

   | Number of typed envelopes: 250 | Number of typed pages: 200 |

   Customer's name: Alice Wong

   | Number of typed envelopes: $4 | Number of typed pages: AB |

10. Scenario: Management USA, a small training center, plans to run two full-day seminars on December 1. The seminars are called "How to Be an Effective Manager" and "How to Run a Small Business." Each seminar costs $200. Registration for the seminars will be done by phone. When a company calls to register its employees, the phone representative will ask for the following information: the company's name, address (including city, state, and ZIP), the number of employees registering for the "How to Be an Effective Manager" seminar, and the number of employees registering for the "How to Run a Small Business" seminar. Claire Jenkowski, the owner of Management USA, wants the application to calculate the total number of employees the company is registering and the total cost.

   a. If necessary, start Visual Studio .NET. Create a blank solution named Management Solution. Save the solution in the VBNET\Chap02 folder.

   b. Add a Visual Basic .NET Windows Application project to the solution. Name the project Management Project.

   c. Perform the steps involved in creating an OO application. (See the NOTE at the beginning of the Exercises section. Use the GUI design guidelines listed in Appendix B to verify that the interface you create adheres to the GUI standards outlined in this book.) Format the total cost using the Currency format style.

   d. Test the application twice, using the following data.
   Company Name: ABC Company
   Address: 345 Main St.
   City, State, ZIP: Glen, TX 70122
   Registrants for "How to Be an Effective Manager": 10
   Registrants for "How to Run a Small Business": 5

   Company Name: 1
   Address: 2
   City, State, ZIP: 3
   Registrants for "How to Be an Effective Manager": A
   Registrants for "How to Run a Small Business": B

11. Scenario: Suman Gadhari, the payroll clerk at Sun Projects, wants an application that will compute the net pay for each of the company's employees. Suman will enter the employee's name, hours worked, and rate of pay. For this application, you do not have to worry about overtime, as this company does not allow anyone to work more than

40 hours. Suman wants the application to compute the gross pay, the federal withholding tax (FWT), the Social Security tax (FICA), the state income tax, and the net pay. Use the following information when computing the three taxes:

FWT: 20% of gross pay

FICA: 8% of gross pay

state income tax: 2% of gross pay

a. If necessary, start Visual Studio .NET. Create a blank solution named SunProjects Solution. Save the solution in the VBNET\Chap02 folder.

b. Add a Visual Basic .NET Windows Application project to the solution. Name the project SunProjects Project.

c. Perform the steps involved in creating an OO application. (See the NOTE at the beginning of the Exercises section. Use the GUI design guidelines listed in Appendix B to verify that the interface you create adheres to the GUI standards outlined in this book.) Format the dollar amounts to the Standard format style.

d. Test the application twice, using the following data.

Employee's name: Susan Reha

Hours worked: 40

Rate of pay: 12

Employee's name: Susan Reha

Hours worked: X

Rate of pay: Y

discovery ▶ 12. In this exercise, you learn about the TabStop property.

a. Open the Order Solution (Order Solution.sln) file that you completed in Lesson C. The file is located in the VBNET\Chap02\Order Solution folder. The TabStop property allows you to bypass a control in the tab order when the user is tabbing. You can use the TabStop property in the Skate-Away Sales application to bypass the uiStateTextBox control. Because most of Skate-Away's customers are located in Illinois, there is no need for the user to tab into the uiStateTextBox control when entering data. Should the user want to change the State value, he or she needs simply to click the control or use the control's access key.

b. Change the uiStateTextBox control's TabStop property to False, then save the solution and start the application. Verify that the uiStateTextBox control is bypassed when you tab through the controls in the interface.

discovery ▶ 13. Scenario: Colfax Industries needs an application that allows the shipping clerk to enter the quantity of an item in inventory and the number of the items that can be packed in a box for shipping. When the shipping clerk clicks a button, the application should compute and display the number of full boxes that can be packed and how many of the item are left over.

a. If necessary, start Visual Studio .NET. Create a blank solution named Colfax Solution. Save the solution in the VBNET\Chap02 folder.

b. Add a Visual Basic .NET Windows Application project to the solution. Name the project Colfax Project.

c. Perform the steps involved in creating an OO application. (See the NOTE at the beginning of the Exercises section. Use the GUI design guidelines listed in Appendix B to verify that the interface you create adheres to the GUI standards outlined in this book.)

d. Test the application using the following information. Colfax has 45 skateboards in inventory. If six skateboards can fit into a box for shipping, how many full boxes could the company ship, and how many skateboards will remain in inventory?

discovery ▶ **14.** Scenario: Perry Brown needs an application that will allow him to enter the length of four sides of a polygon. The application should compute and display the perimeter of the polygon.

    a. If necessary, start Visual Studio .NET. Create a blank solution named PerryBrown Solution. Save the solution in the VBNET\Chap02 folder.

    b. Add a Visual Basic .NET Windows Application project to the solution. Name the project PerryBrown Project.

    c. Perform the steps involved in creating an OO application. (See the NOTE at the beginning of the Exercises section. Use the GUI design guidelines listed in Appendix B to verify that the interface you create adheres to the GUI standards outlined in this book.)

    d. Test the application using the following information. Each day Perry rides his bike around a park that has side lengths of 1/2 mile, 1 mile, 1/2 mile, and 1 mile. How far does Perry ride his bike each day?

discovery ▶ **15.** Scenario: Builders Inc. needs an application that will allow its salesclerks to enter both the diameter of a circle and the price of railing material per foot. The application should compute and display the circumference of the circle and the total price of the railing material. (Use 3.14 as the value of pi.)

    a. If necessary, start Visual Studio .NET. Create a blank solution named Builders Solution. Save the solution in the VBNET\Chap02 folder.

    b. Add a Visual Basic .NET Windows Application project to the solution. Name the project Builders Project.

    c. Perform the steps involved in creating an OO application. (See the NOTE at the beginning of the Exercises section. Use the GUI design guidelines listed in Appendix B to verify that the interface you create adheres to the GUI standards outlined in this book.) Display the total price with a dollar sign, a comma thousand separator, and two decimal places.

    d. Test the application using the following information. Jack Jones, one of Builders Inc.'s customers, is building a railing around a circular deck having a diameter of 36 feet. The railing material costs $2 per foot. What is the circumference of the deck and the total price of the railing material?

discovery ▶ **16.** Scenario: Temp Employers wants an application that will allow its employees to enter the number of hours worked. The application should compute and display the number of weeks (assume a 40-hour week), days (assume an eight-hour day), and hours worked. For example, if the user enters the number 70, the application should display 1 week, 3 days, and 6 hours.

    a. If necessary, start Visual Studio .NET. Create a blank solution named Temp Solution. Save the solution in the VBNET\Chap02 folder.

    b. Add a Visual Basic .NET Windows Application project to the solution. Name the project Temp Project.

    c. Perform the steps involved in creating an OO application. (See the NOTE at the beginning of the Exercises section. Use the GUI design guidelines listed in Appendix B to verify that the interface you create adheres to the GUI standards outlined in this book.)

    d. Test the application three times, using the following data.

    Hours worked: 88

    Hours worked: 111

    Hours worked: 12

discovery ▶ **17.** Scenario: Tile Limited wants an application that will allow its salesclerks to enter the length and width (in feet) of a rectangle, and the price of a square foot of tile. The application should compute and display the area of the rectangle and the total price of the tile.

    a. If necessary, start Visual Studio .NET. Create a blank solution named Tile Solution. Save the solution in the VBNET\Chap02 folder.

    b. Add a Visual Basic .NET Windows Application project to the solution. Name the project Tile Project.

    c. Perform the steps involved in creating an OO application. (See the NOTE at the beginning of the Exercises section. Use the GUI design guidelines listed in Appendix B to verify that the interface you create adheres to the GUI standards outlined in this book.) Display the total price with a dollar sign, comma thousand separator, and two decimal places.

    d. Test the application using the following data. Susan Caper, one of Tile Limited's customers, is tiling a floor in her home. The floor is 12 feet long and 14 feet wide. The price of a square foot of tile is $1.59. What is the area of the floor and how much will the tile cost?

discovery ▶ 18. Scenario: Willow Pools wants an application that will allow its salespeople to enter the length, width, and height of a rectangular pool. The application should compute and display the volume of the pool.

    a. If necessary, start Visual Studio .NET. Create a blank solution named Willow Solution. Save the solution in the VBNET\Chap02 folder.

    b. Add a Visual Basic .NET Windows Application project to the solution. Name the project Willow Project.

    c. Perform the steps involved in creating an OO application. (See the NOTE at the beginning of the Exercises section. Use the GUI design guidelines listed in Appendix B to verify that the interface you create adheres to the GUI standards outlined in this book.)

    d. Test the application using the following data. The swimming pool at a health club is 100 feet long, 30 feet wide, and 4 feet deep. How many cubic feet of water will the pool contain?

discovery ▶ 19. Scenario: Quick Loans wants an application that will allow its clerks to enter the amount of a loan, the interest rate, and the term of the loan (in years). The application should compute and display the total amount of interest and the total amount to be repaid. Use the Pmt function. (*Hint*: Use the Help menu to display the Pmt function's Help window.)

    a. If necessary, start Visual Studio .NET. Create a blank solution named Loan Solution. Save the solution in the VBNET\Chap02 folder.

    b. Add a Visual Basic .NET Windows Application project to the solution. Name the project Loan Project.

    c. Perform the steps involved in creating an OO application. (See the NOTE at the beginning of the Exercises section. Use the GUI design guidelines listed in Appendix B to verify that the interface you create adheres to the GUI standards outlined in this book.) Format the total interest and total repaid using the Standard format style.

    d. Test the application using the following data. You visit Quick Loans because you want to borrow $9000 to buy a new car. The loan is for three years at an annual interest rate of 12%. How much will you pay in interest over the three years, and what is the total amount you will repay?

debugging 20. In this exercise, you debug an existing application. The purpose of the exercise is to demonstrate the importance of using the Val function in calculations that include the Text property.

    a. If necessary, start Visual Studio .NET. Open the Debug Solution (Debug Solution.sln) file, which is contained in the VBNET\Chap02\Debug Solution folder. If the designer window is not open, right-click the form file's name in the Solution Explorer window, then click View Designer. The application allows you to enter a number. It then multiplies the number by 3 and displays the result.

    b. Open the Code Editor window. Enter your name and the current date in the General Declarations section.

    c. Start the application. When the interface appears, type the number 4 in the Enter a number text box, then click the Triple Number button. The number 12 appears in the Number tripled label control.

    d. Delete the number 4 from the Enter a number text box, then type the letter R in the text box. Click the Triple Number button. An error message appears in a dialog box, and the instruction causing the error appears highlighted in the Code Editor window. See Figure 2-46.

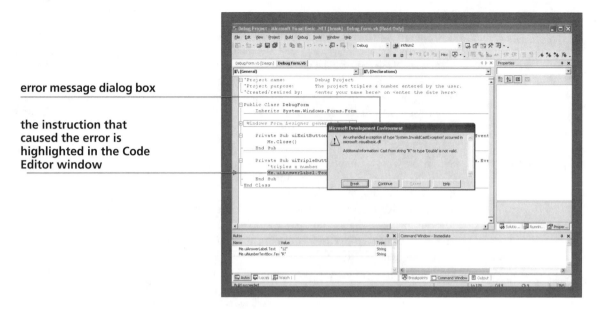

error message dialog box

the instruction that caused the error is highlighted in the Code Editor window

Figure 2-46

The error message first informs you that an unhandled exception occurred. It then gives you some additional information about the error; in this case, it displays the message *Cast from String "R" to type 'Double' is not valid.* The message means that the computer is unable to convert the letter R to a number. (*Double* is a numeric data type; you learn about data types in Chapter 3.)

e. Click the Break button in the dialog box. The dialog box closes. Highlighted in the Code Editor window is the `Me.uiAnswerLabel.Text = Me.uiNumberTextBox.Text * 3` instruction, which is causing the error. See Figure 2-47.

you use the Val function to correct this instruction

Figure 2-47

f. Click Debug on the menu bar, then click Stop Debugging.

g. Use the Val function to tell the computer to treat the contents of the uiNumberTextBox control's Text property as a number rather than as a string.

h. Save the solution, then start the application. Type the letter R in the Enter a number text box, then click the Triple Number button. Rather than displaying an error message, the application displays the number 0 in the Number tripled control.

i. Click the Exit button to end the application.

j. Close the Output window and the Code Editor window, then close the solution.

Using Variables and Constants

Revising the Skate-Away Sales Application

case ▶ Mr. Cousard, the manager of Skate-Away Sales, informs you that he wants to make a change to the Skate-Away Sales application that you created in Chapter 2. He now wants to include a message on the order form. The message should say "The sales tax was", followed by the sales tax amount and the name of the salesperson who recorded the order. In this chapter, you modify the application's code to accommodate this change.

Previewing the Completed Application

Before you begin modifying the Skate-Away Sales application, you first preview the completed application.

To preview the completed application:

1   Use the Run command on the Start menu to run the **Skate** (Skate.exe) file, which is contained in the VBNET\Chap03 folder on your computer's hard disk. An order form similar to the one that you created in Chapter 2 appears on the screen.

2   Enter the following customer information on the order form: **Skaters Inc., 34 Plum Drive, Chicago, IL, 60654.**

3   Click the **Skateboard price** text box, then type **100** and press **Tab**. Type **.05** for the sales tax rate.

4   Click the **Blue skateboards ordered** text box, then type **25** as the number of blue skateboards ordered.

5   Press **Tab**, then type **5** as the number of yellow skateboards ordered.

Although the Calculate Order button does not have the focus, you still can select it by pressing the Enter key, because the Calculate Order button is the default button in the user interface. You learn how to designate a default button in Lesson B.

6   Press **Enter** to calculate the order. A Name Entry dialog box appears and requests the salesperson's name, as shown in Figure 3-1.

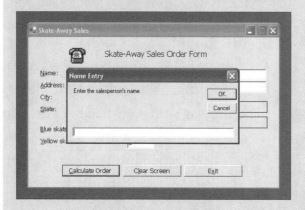

Figure 3-1: Name Entry dialog box

7   Type your name in the dialog box's text box and press **Enter**. The application calculates the order. The completed order form is shown in Figure 3-2.

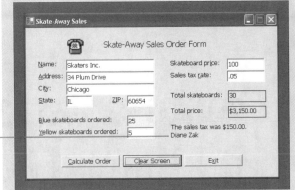

your name will appear here

Figure 3-2: Completed order form

Notice that the sales tax amount and the salesperson's name (your name) appear on the order form. The application uses string concatenation, which you learn about in Lesson B, to display the information.

8 Click the **Yellow skateboards ordered** text box, then type **10**. The application clears the contents of the label controls that display the total skateboards ordered, total price, and message. In Lesson C, you learn how to clear the contents of a control when the value stored in a different control changes.

9 Click the **Calculate Order** button to calculate the order. The Name Entry dialog box appears and displays your name in a text box. Press **Enter**. The application recalculates the total skateboards ordered, total price, and sales tax amount.

10 Click the **Exit** button to end the application.

In Lesson A, you learn how to store information, temporarily, in memory locations inside the computer. You modify the Skate-Away Sales application in Lessons B and C.

After completing this lesson, you will be able to:

- Create a procedure-level and module-level variable
- Select an appropriate data type for a variable
- Select an appropriate name for a variable
- Assign data to an existing variable
- Explain the scope and lifetime of a variable
- Create a named constant

Creating Variables and Named Constants

Using Variables to Store Information

Recall that all of the skateboard information in the Skate-Away Sales application is temporarily stored in the properties of various controls on the order form. For example, the number of blue skateboards ordered is stored in the Text property of the uiBlueTextBox control, and the number of yellow skateboards ordered is stored in the Text property of the uiYellowTextBox control. Also recall that the assignment statement `Me.uiTotalBoardsLabel.Text = Val(Me.uiBlueTextBox.Text) + Val(Me.uiYellowTextBox.Text)` calculates the total skateboards ordered by adding the value stored in the uiBlueTextBox control's Text property to the value stored in the uiYellowTextBox control's Text property, and then assigns the sum to the Text property of the uiTotalBoardsLabel control. Similarly, the total price equation, `Me.uiTotalPriceLabel.Text = Val(Me.uiTotalBoardsLabel.Text) * Val(Me.uiPriceTextBox.Text) * (1 + Val(Me.uiRateTextBox.Text))`, calculates the total price of the order and assigns the result to the uiTotalPriceLabel control.

Besides storing data in the properties of controls, a programmer also can store data, temporarily, in memory locations inside the computer. The memory locations are called **variables**, because the contents of the locations can change as the application is running. It may be helpful to picture a variable as a small box inside the computer. You can enter and store data in the box, but you cannot actually see the box.

One use for a variable is to hold information that is not stored in a control on the user interface. For example, if you did not need to display the total number of skateboards ordered on the Skate-Away Sales order form, you could eliminate the uiTotalBoardsLabel control from the form and store the total number of skateboards ordered in a variable instead. You then would use the value stored in the variable, rather than the value stored in the Text property of the uiTotalBoardsLabel control, in the total price equation.

You also can store the data contained in a control's property in a variable. For example, you can store the data contained in the Text property of a text box or label control in a variable. Programmers typically do so when the data is a numeric amount that will be used in a calculation. As you will learn in the next section, assigning numeric data to a variable allows you to control the preciseness of the data. It also makes your code run more efficiently, because the computer can process data stored in a variable much faster than it can process data stored in the property of a control.

Before learning how to create a variable in a Visual Basic .NET application, you learn how to select an appropriate data type and name for the variable.

Selecting a Data Type for a Variable

The programmer must assign a data type to each variable used in an application. The **data type** determines the type of data the variable can store. Figure 3-3 describes the basic data types available in Visual Basic .NET. Each data type is a class, which means that each data type is a pattern from which one or more objects—in this case, variables—are created (instantiated).

tip

Unicode is the universal character-encoding scheme for characters and text. It assigns a unique numeric value and name to each character used in the written languages of the world. For more information, see The Unicode Standard at *www.unicode.org*.

Type	Stores	Memory required
Boolean	logical value (True or False)	2 bytes
Byte	binary number (0 to 255)	1 byte
Char	one Unicode character	2 bytes
Date	date and time information	8 bytes
Decimal	fixed-point number	16 bytes
Double	floating-point number, 14 digits of accuracy +/-4.9E-324 to 1.7E308	8 bytes
Integer	integer (-2,147,483,648 to 2,147,483,647)	4 bytes
Long	very large integers	8 bytes
Object	object reference	4 bytes
Short	integer (-32,768 to 32,767)	2 bytes
Single	floating-point number, six digits of accuracy +/-1.4E-45 to 3.4E38	4 bytes
String	text	varies

Figure 3-3: Basic data types in Visual Basic .NET

As Figure 3-3 indicates, variables assigned the Integer, Long, or Short data type can store **integers**, which are whole numbers—numbers without any decimal places. The differences among these three data types are in the range of integers each type can store and the amount of memory each type needs to store the integer. The memory requirement of a data type is an important consideration when coding an application. If you want to reduce the amount of internal memory that an application consumes, thereby improving the application's efficiency, you should use variables with smaller memory requirements wherever possible. For example, although an Integer variable can store numbers in the Short range of -32,768 to 32,767, the Integer data type takes twice as much memory as the Short data type to do so. Therefore, you can conserve internal memory by storing a person's age in a Short variable.

Keep in mind, however, that memory usage is not the only important factor in determining an application's efficiency; the speed at which the application executes also is important. Although a Short variable uses less internal memory than does an Integer variable, a calculation containing Integer variables takes less time to process than the equivalent calculation containing Short variables. This is because the computer must convert the contents of a Short variable to the Integer data type before the calculation is performed.

Figure 3-3 indicates that Single and Double variables can store a **floating-point number**, which is a number that is expressed as a multiple of some power of 10. Floating-point numbers are written in E (exponential) notation, which is similar to scientific notation. For example, the number 3,200,000 written in E (exponential) notation is 3.2E6; written in scientific notation it is 3.2×10^6. Notice that exponential notation simply replaces "$\times 10^6$" with the letter E followed by the power number—in this case, 6.

Another way of viewing 3.2E6 is that the positive number after the E indicates how many places to the right to move the decimal point. In this case, E6 means to move the decimal point six places to the right; so 3.2E6 becomes 3,200,000. Moving the decimal point six places to the right is the same as multiplying the number by 10 to the sixth power.

Floating-point numbers also can have a negative number after the E. For example, 3.2E-6 means 3.2 divided by 10 to the sixth power, or .0000032. The negative number after the E tells you how many places to the left to move the decimal point. In this case, E-6 means to move the decimal point six places to the left.

Floating-point numbers, which can be stored in either Single or Double variables, are used to represent both extremely small and extremely large numbers. The differences between the Single and Double types are in the range of numbers each type can store and the amount of memory each type needs to store the numbers. Although a Double variable can store numbers in a Single variable's range, a Double variable takes twice as much memory to do so.

Variables declared using the Decimal data type store numbers with a fixed decimal point. Unlike floating-point numbers, fixed-point numbers are not expressed as a multiple of some power of 10. For example, the number 32000 expressed as a floating-point number is 3.2E4, but that same number expressed as a fixed-point number is simply 32000. Calculations involving fixed-point numbers are not subject to the small rounding errors that may occur when floating-point numbers are used. In most cases, these small rounding errors do not create any problems in an application. One exception, however, is when the application contains complex equations dealing with money, where you need accuracy to the penny. In those cases, the Decimal data type is the best type to use.

Also listed in Figure 3-3 are the Char data type, which can store one character, and the String data type, which can store from zero to approximately two billion characters. As you learned in Chapter 2, a string is a group of characters enclosed in quotation marks. "Desk" and "AB345" are two examples of strings.

You use a Boolean variable to store the Boolean values True and False, and a Date variable to store date and time information. The Byte data type is used to store binary numbers.

If you do not assign a specific data type to a variable, Visual Basic .NET assigns the Object type to it. Unlike other variables, an Object variable can store many different types of data, and it also can freely change the type of stored data while the application is running. For example, you can store the number 40 in an Object variable at the beginning of the application and then, later on in the application, store the string "John Smith" in that same variable. Although the Object data type is the most flexible data type, it is less efficient than the other data types. At times it uses more memory than necessary to store a value and, because the computer must determine which type of data is currently stored in the variable, your application will run more slowly.

In addition to assigning a data type to the variables used in an application, the programmer also must assign a name to each variable.

Selecting a Name for a Variable

You should assign a descriptive name to each variable used in an application. The name, also called the **identifier**, should help you remember the purpose of the variable—in other words, the meaning of the value stored therein. The names `length` and `width`, for example, are much more meaningful than are the names `x` and `y`, because `length` and `width` remind you that the amounts stored in the variables represent a length and width measurement, respectively.

One popular naming convention is to include a three-character ID at the beginning of a variable's name to indicate the variable's data type. Using this naming convention, a Single variable that stores a sales amount would be named `sngSales`. The "sng" identifies the variable as a Single variable, and "Sales" reminds the programmer of the variable's purpose—in this case, to store a sales amount. This naming convention, which has been used for years by Visual Basic programmers, is referred to as Hungarian notation.

More recently, a new naming convention for variables has emerged. In the new naming convention, the three-character ID that designates the variable's type is omitted from the variable's name. The name now indicates only the variable's purpose and is entered using lowercase letters. However, if a variable's name contains two or more words, you capitalize the first letter in the second and subsequent words. Using this naming convention, a variable that stores a sales amount would be named `sales` or `salesAmount`. The practice of capitalizing the first letter in the second and subsequent words in the name is referred to as **camel casing**, because the uppercase letters, which are taller than the lowercase letters, appear as "humps" in the name. You will use the new naming convention in this book.

In addition to being descriptive, the name that a programmer assigns to a variable must follow several specific rules, which are listed in Figure 3-4. Also included in the figure are examples of valid and invalid variable names.

Visit *www.irritatedVowel. com* for an interesting article on why Hungarian notation has fallen out of favor with .NET programmers.

Although Microsoft recommends the new naming convention for variables, your company (or instructor) may have a different naming convention you are expected to use. Your company's (or instructor's) naming convention supersedes the ones recommended by Microsoft.

Rules for naming variables
1. The name must begin with a letter or the underscore.
2. The name must contain only letters, numbers, and the underscore character. No punctuation characters or spaces are allowed in the name.
3. Although the name can contain thousands of characters, the recommended maximum number of characters to use is thirty-two.
4. The name cannot be a reserved word, such as Val or Print.

Valid variable names	Invalid variable names	
printMargin	print	(the name cannot be a reserved word)
sales2006	2006Sales	(the name must begin with a letter or the underscore)
westSales	west Sales	(the name cannot contain a space)
firstName	first.Name	(the name cannot contain punctuation)

Figure 3-4: Rules for variable names along with examples of valid and invalid names

Now that you know how to select an appropriate data type and name for a variable, you can learn how to declare a variable in code. Declaring a variable tells the computer to set aside a small section of its internal memory.

Declaring a Variable

You use a declaration statement to declare, or create, a variable. Figure 3-5 shows the syntax of a declaration statement and includes several examples of declaring variables. As the examples show, you can declare more than one variable in the same `Dim` statement.

Declaring a variable
<u>Syntax</u> **{Dim	Private	Static}** *variablename* **[As** *datatype*]**[=** *initialvalue*]

<u>Examples</u>
`Dim hoursWorked As Integer`
 	
declares an Integer variable named `hoursWorked`; the variable is automatically initialized to 0
 	
`Dim itemPrice, discount As Decimal`
 	
declares two Decimal variables named `itemPrice` and `discount`; the variables are automatically initialized to 0
 	
`Dim itemPrice As Decimal`
`Dim discount As Decimal`
 	
same as the previous example
 	
`Dim dataOk As Boolean = True`
 	
declares a Boolean variable named `dataOK` and initializes it using the keyword `True`
 	
`Dim name As String, age As Integer`
 	
declares a String variable named `name` and an Integer variable named `age`; the String variable is automatically initialized to `Nothing`, and the Integer variable is automatically initialized to 0
 	
`Dim name As String`
`Dim age As Integer`
 	
same as the previous example

Figure 3-5: Syntax and examples of variable declaration statements

"Dim" comes from the word "dimension", which is how programmers in the 1960s referred to the process of allocating the computer's memory.

A declaration statement also can begin with a keyword other than the ones shown in Figure 3-5. The other keywords are beyond the scope of this book.

The **{Dim | Private | Static}** portion of the syntax shown in Figure 3-5 indicates that you can select only one of the keywords appearing within the braces. In this case, you can select `Dim`, `Private`, or `Static`. In most instances, you declare a variable using the keyword `Dim`. (You learn about the `Private` keyword later in this lesson. The `Static` keyword is covered in Lesson C.)

Variablename in the syntax is the variable's name, and *datatype* is the variable's data type. As mentioned earlier, a variable is considered an object in Visual Basic .NET and is an instance of the class specified in the *datatype* information. The `Dim hoursWorked as Integer` statement, for example, creates an object named `hoursWorked`. The `hoursWorked` object is an instance of the Integer class.

Although the "**As** *datatype*" part of a declaration statement is optional, as indicated by the square brackets in the syntax, you always should assign a specific data type to each variable you declare. If you do not assign a data type to a variable, Visual Basic .NET assigns the Object type, which is not the most efficient data type.

Initialvalue in the syntax is the value you want stored in the variable when it is created in the computer's internal memory. Notice that the "= *initialvalue*" part of a declaration statement also is optional. If you do not assign an initial value to a variable when it is declared, Visual Basic .NET stores a default value in the variable; the default value depends on the variable's data type. A variable declared using one of the numeric data types is automatically initialized to—in other words, given a beginning value of—the number 0. Visual Basic .NET automatically initializes a Boolean variable using the keyword `False`, and a Date variable to 12:00 AM January 1, 0001. Object and String variables are automatically initialized using the keyword `Nothing`. Variables initialized to `Nothing` do not actually contain the word "Nothing"; rather, they contain no data at all.

After a variable is created, you can use an assignment statement to store other data in the variable.

Assigning Data to an Existing Variable

In Chapter 2, you learned how to use an assignment statement to set the value of a property while an application is running. You also can use an assignment statement to assign a value to a variable while an application is running. Figure 3-6 shows the syntax and several examples of assignment statements that assign values to variables.

Recall from Chapter 2 that the = symbol appearing in an assignment statement is referred to as the assignment operator.

Assigning a value to a variable
<u>Syntax</u>
variablename = *value*
<u>Examples</u>
`Dim quantityOrdered As Integer` `quantityOrdered = 500`
assigns the integer 500 to an Integer variable named `quantityOrdered`
`Dim firstName As String` `firstName = "Mary"`
assigns the string "Mary" to a String variable named `firstName`
`Dim state As String` `state = Me.uiStateTextBox.Text`
assigns the string contained in the uiStateTextBox control's Text property to a String variable named `state`
`Dim discountRate As Double` `discountRate = .03`
assigns the Double number .03 to a Double variable named `discountRate`
`Dim taxRate As Decimal` `taxRate = .05D`
converts the number .05 from Double to Decimal, and then assigns the result to a Decimal variable named `taxRate`

Figure 3-6: Syntax and examples of assignment statements that assign values to variables

When the computer processes an assignment statement, it assigns the value that appears on the right side of the assignment operator (=) to the variable whose name appears on the left side of the assignment operator. The data type of the value should be the same data type as the variable. For example, the `quantityOrdered = 500` assignment statement shown in Figure 3-6 stores the number 500, which is an integer, in an Integer variable named `quantityOrdered`. Similarly, the `firstName = "Mary"` assignment statement stores the string "Mary" in a String variable named `firstName`. The number 500 and the string "Mary" are called literal constants. A **literal constant** is an item of data whose value does not change while the application is running. The number 500 is a numeric literal constant, and the string "Mary" is a string literal constant. Notice that you can store literal constants in variables. Also notice that string literal constants are enclosed in quotation marks, but numeric literal constants and variable names are not. The quotation marks differentiate a string from both a number and a variable name. In other words, "500" is a string, but 500 is a number. Similarly, "Mary" is a string, but Mary (without the quotation marks) would be interpreted by Visual Basic .NET as the name of a variable.

As you learned in Chapter 2, a value stored in the Text property of an object is treated as a string rather than as a number. Therefore, the `state = Me.uiStateTextBox.Text` assignment statement shown in Figure 3-6 assigns the string contained in the uiStateTextBox control's Text property to a String variable named `state`.

In Visual Basic .NET, a numeric literal constant that has a decimal place is automatically treated as a Double number. As a result, the `discountRate = .03` statement shown in Figure 3-6 assigns the Double number .03 to a Double variable named `discountRate`. The next assignment statement in the figure, `taxRate = .05D`, shows how you convert a numeric literal constant of the Double data type to the Decimal data type, and then assign the result to a Decimal variable. The D that follows the number .05 in the statement is one of the literal type characters in Visual Basic .NET. A **literal type character** forces a literal constant to assume a data type other than the one its form indicates. In this case, the D forces the Double number .05 to assume the Decimal data type.

Figure 3-7 lists the literal type characters in Visual Basic .NET and includes an example of using each character. Notice that you append the literal type character to the end of the literal constant. (The I in the `hours = 40I` example in Figure 3.7 is not necessary, because Visual Basic .NET treats a numeric literal constant that does not have a decimal place as an Integer number, unless the number is large enough to be a Long number.)

Literal type character	Data type	Example
S	Short	age = 35S
I	Integer	hours = 40I
L	Long	population = 20500L
D	Decimal	rate = .03D
F	Single	rate = .03F
R	Double	sales = 2356R
C	Char	initial = "A"C

Figure 3-7: Literal type characters

Many times, the data type of the value you need to assign to a variable is different than the data type of the variable itself. As you just learned, if the value is a literal constant, you can use a literal type character to change the literal constant's data type to match the variable's data type. If the value is not a literal constant, however, you use either the Parse method or one of the methods contained in the Convert class. You learn about the Parse method first, and then you learn about the Convert class.

The Parse Method

Recall that each data type in Visual Basic .NET is a class, which is a group of instructions used to create an object; in this case, the object is a variable. Most classes have methods. A method is a specific portion of the class instructions, and its purpose is to perform a task for the class. Every numeric data type in Visual Basic .NET, for example, has a **Parse method** that can be used to convert a string to that numeric data type. Figure 3-8 shows the syntax and examples of the Parse method.

Using the Parse method

<u>Syntax</u>

numericDataType.**Parse**(*string*)

<u>Examples</u>

```
Dim sales As Decimal
sales = Decimal.Parse(Me.uiSalesTextBox.Text)
```

converts the contents of the uiSalesTextBox control's Text property to Decimal, and then assigns the result to a Decimal variable named sales

```
Dim age As Integer
Dim studentAge As String = "25"
age = Integer.Parse(studentAge)
```

converts the contents of a String variable named studentAge to Integer, and then assigns the result to an Integer variable named age

```
Dim discountRate As Single
discountRate = Single.Parse(Me.uiRateLabel.Text)
```

converts the contents of the uiRateLabel control's Text property to Single, and then assigns the result to a Single variable named discountRate

```
Dim amountDue As Double, inputAmount As String = "7.68"
amountDue = Double.Parse(inputAmount)
```

converts the contents of a String variable named inputAmount to Double, and then assigns the result to a Double variable named amountDue

Figure 3-8: Syntax and examples of the Parse method

tip

Unlike the Val function, the Parse methods cannot convert either the empty string or a non-numeric character (such as a letter) to a numeric value. If the *string* argument in a Parse method does not contain a value that can be converted to a number, an error occurs in the program.

In the syntax, *numericDataType* is one of the numeric data types available in Visual Basic .NET, and *string* is the string you want converted to the numeric data type. In the first example shown in Figure 3-8, the Decimal.Parse method converts the string stored in the uiSalesTextBox control's Text property to the Decimal data type; the statement assigns the converted value to a Decimal variable named sales. In the second example, the Integer.Parse method converts the contents of a String variable named studentAge to the Integer data type; the statement assigns the converted value to an Integer variable named `age`. When processing the `discountRate = Single.Parse(Me.uiRateLabel.Text)` statement in the third example, the computer converts the string stored in the uiRateLabel control's Text property to the Single data type, and then assigns the result to a Single variable named `discountRate`. The `amountDue = Double.Parse(inputAmount)` statement shown in the last example converts the contents of a String variable named `inputAmount` to the Double data type before assigning it to a Double variable named `amountDue`.

Next, you learn about the Convert class.

The Convert Class

The **Convert class** contains methods that you can use to convert a numeric value to a specified data type. Figure 3-9 lists the most commonly used methods contained in the Convert class. Notice that you use a period to separate the class name (`Convert`) from the method name (`ToDecimal`, `ToDouble`, `ToInt32`, `ToSingle`, and `ToString`). As you learned in Chapter 1, the period is called the dot member access operator, and it indicates that what appears to the right of the operator is a member of what appears to the left of the operator. In this case, the dot member access operator indicates that the `ToDecimal`, `ToDouble`, `ToInt32`, `ToSingle`, and `ToString` methods are members of the Convert class.

Convert class methods	
Method	Use to convert a value to the
ToDecimal	Decimal data type
ToDouble	Double data type
ToInt32	Integer data type
ToSingle	Single data type
ToString	String data type

Figure 3-9: Most commonly used methods contained in the Convert class

Figure 3-10 shows the syntax and examples of the Convert class methods listed in Figure 3-9.

Using the Convert class methods

Syntax

Convert.*method*(*value*)

Examples

```
Dim sales As Integer = 1000
Dim bonus As Double
bonus = Convert.ToDouble(sales) * .05
```

converts the contents of an Integer variable named `sales` to Double, then multiplies the converted value by the Double number .05, and then assigns the result to a Double variable named `bonus`

```
Dim purchase As Double = 500
Dim tax As Decimal
tax = Convert.ToDecimal(purchase) * .03D
```

converts both the contents of a Double variable named `purchase` and the Double number .03 to Decimal before multiplying both amounts, and then assigns the result to a Decimal variable named `tax`

```
Dim test1 As Integer
Dim test2 As Integer
Me.uiTotalLabel.Text = Convert.ToString(test1 + test2)
```

adds together the contents of two Integer variables named test1 and test2, then converts the sum to String, and then assigns the result to the uiTotalLabel control's Text property

Figure 3-10: Syntax and examples of methods contained in the Convert class

In the Convert method's syntax, *method* is one of the methods listed in Figure 3-9, and *value* is the value you want to convert. In the first example shown in Figure 3-10, the `bonus = Convert.ToDouble(sales) * .05` statement first converts the contents of the `sales` variable to Double. It then multiplies the converted value by the Double number .05, and then assigns the result to a Double variable named `bonus`. In the second example, the `tax = Convert.ToDecimal (purchase) * .03D` statement converts the contents of the `purchase` variable to Decimal and also converts the Double number .03 to Decimal. The statement then multiplies both converted values and assigns the result to a Decimal variable named `tax`. The last assignment statement shown in the figure, `Me.uiTotalLabel. Text = Convert.ToString(test1 + test2)`, first adds together the contents of two Integer variables named `test1` and `test2`. It then uses the Convert.ToString method to convert the sum to a String before assigning it to the uiTotalLabel control's Text property.

It is important to remember that a variable can store only one item of data at any one time. When you use an assignment statement to assign another item to the variable, the new data replaces the existing data. To illustrate this point, assume that a button's Click event procedure contains the following three lines of code:

```
Dim number As Integer
number = 500
number = number * 2
```

When you run the application and click the button, the three lines of code are processed as follows:

■ The Dim statement creates the number variable in memory and automatically initializes it to the number zero.

■ The number = 500 assignment statement removes the zero from the number variable and stores the number 500 there instead. The number variable now contains the number 500 only.

■ The number = number * 2 assignment statement first multiplies the contents of the number variable (500) by the number two, giving 1000. The assignment statement then replaces the current contents of the number variable (500) with 1000. Notice that the calculation appearing on the right side of the assignment operator (=) is performed first, and then the result is assigned to the variable whose name appears on the left side of the assignment operator.

As you can see, after data is stored in a variable, you can use the data in calculations, just as you can with the data stored in the properties of controls. When a statement contains the name of a variable, the computer uses the value stored inside the variable to process the statement.

You now know how to use a variable declaration statement to declare a variable. Recall that the statement allows you to assign a name, data type, and initial value to the variable you are declaring. You also know how to use an assignment statement to store literal constants and the result of arithmetic expressions in an existing variable. There are just two more things about variables that you need to learn to complete this chapter's application: in addition to a name and a data type, every variable also has both a scope and a lifetime.

The Scope and Lifetime of a Variable

A variable's **scope** indicates where in the application's code the variable can be used, and its **lifetime** indicates how long the variable remains in the computer's internal memory. Most of the variables used in an application will have procedure scope; however, some may have module scope or block scope. The scope is determined by where you declare the variable—in other words, where you enter the variable's declaration statement. Typically, you enter the declaration statement either in a procedure, such as an event procedure, or in the Declarations section of a form.

When you declare a variable in a procedure, the variable is called a **procedure-level variable** and is said to have **procedure scope**, because only that procedure can use the variable. For example, if you enter the Dim number As Integer statement in the uiCalcButton's Click event procedure, only the uiCalcButton's Click event procedure can use the number variable. No other procedures in the application are allowed to use the number variable. As a matter of fact, no other procedures in the application will even know that the number variable exists. Procedure-level variables remain in the computer's internal memory only while the procedure in which they are declared is running; they are removed from memory when the procedure ends. In other words, a procedure-level variable has the same lifetime as the procedure that declares it. As mentioned earlier, most of the variables in your applications will be procedure-level variables.

Figure 3-11 shows two procedures that declare procedure-level variables. It is customary to enter the variable declaration statements at the beginning of the procedure, as shown in the figure.

procedure-level
variables declared in the
uiCalcTax2Button's Click
event procedure

procedure-level
variables declared in the
uiCalcTax5Button's Click
event procedure

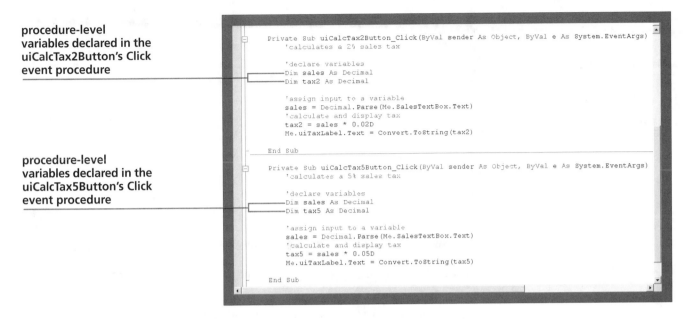

```
Private Sub uiCalcTax2Button_Click(ByVal sender As Object, ByVal e As System.EventArgs)
    'calculates a 2% sales tax

    'declare variables
    Dim sales As Decimal
    Dim tax2 As Decimal

    'assign input to a variable
    sales = Decimal.Parse(Me.SalesTextBox.Text)
    'calculate and display tax
    tax2 = sales * 0.02D
    Me.uiTaxLabel.Text = Convert.ToString(tax2)

End Sub

Private Sub uiCalcTax5Button_Click(ByVal sender As Object, ByVal e As System.EventArgs)
    'calculates a 5% sales tax

    'declare variables
    Dim sales As Decimal
    Dim tax5 As Decimal

    'assign input to a variable
    sales = Decimal.Parse(Me.SalesTextBox.Text)
    'calculate and display tax
    tax5 = sales * 0.05D
    Me.uiTaxLabel.Text = Convert.ToString(tax5)

End Sub
```

Figure 3-11: Procedure-level variables declared in two procedures

As you will learn in Lesson C, you can use the `Static` keyword to declare a procedure-level variable that remains in the computer's memory, and therefore retains its value, when the procedure in which it is declared ends.

Module-level variables also are referred to as form-level variables.

Although you also can use the `Dim` keyword to declare a module-level variable, most Visual Basic programmers use the `Private` keyword.

Both procedures shown in Figure 3-11 declare two procedure-level Decimal variables. In the uiCalcTax2Button's Click event procedure, the variables are named `sales` and `tax2`; only the uiCalcTax2Button's Click event procedure can use these variables. The variables in the uiCalcTax5Button's Click event procedure are named `sales` and `tax5` and can be used only by the uiCalcTax5Button's Click event procedure. Notice that both procedures declare a variable named `sales`. When you use the same name to declare a variable in more than one procedure, each procedure creates its own variable when the procedure is invoked. Each procedure also destroys its own variable when the procedure ends. In other words, although the `sales` variables in the two procedures have the same name, they are not the same variable; rather, each is created and destroyed independently from the other.

In addition to declaring a variable in a procedure, you also can declare a variable in the form's Declarations section, which begins with the `Public Class` statement and ends with the `End Class` statement. When you declare a variable in the form's Declarations section, the variable is called a **module-level variable** and is said to have **module scope**. You typically use a module-level variable when you need more than one procedure in the *same* form to use the *same* variable, because a module-level variable can be used by all of the procedures in the form, including the procedures associated with the controls contained on the form. Unlike a procedure-level variable, which you declare using the `Dim` keyword, you declare a module-level variable using the `Private` keyword. For example, when entered in the form's Declarations section, the statement `Private number As Integer` creates a module-level variable named `number`. Because it is a module-level variable, the `number` variable can be used by every procedure in the form. Module-level variables retain their values and remain in the computer's internal memory until the application ends. In other words, a module-level variable has the same lifetime as the application itself. Figure 3-12 shows a module-level variable declared in the form's Declarations section. Notice that you place the declaration statement after the `[Windows Form Designer generated code]` entry in the section, but before the first `Private Sub` statement.

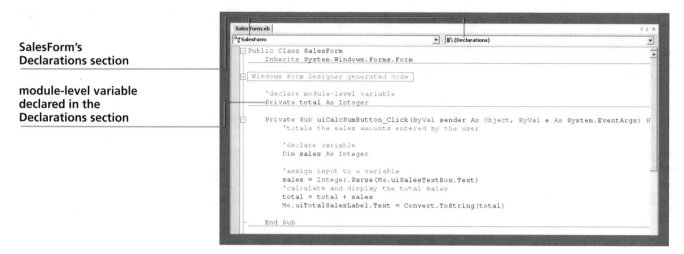

SalesForm's
Declarations section

module-level variable
declared in the
Declarations section

Figure 3-12: Module-level variable declared in the form's Declarations section

As mentioned earlier, variables also can have **block scope**; such variables are called **block-level variables**. Block-level variables are declared within specific blocks of code, such as within If...Then...Else statements or For...Next statements. A block-level variable can be used only by the block of code in which it is declared. You learn more about block-level variables in Chapter 4.

In addition to literal constants and variables, you also can use named constants in your code.

Named Constants

Like a variable, a **named constant** is a memory location inside the computer. However, unlike a variable, the contents of a named constant cannot be changed while the application is running. You create a named constant using the **Const statement**. Figure 3-13 shows the syntax and examples of the Const statement.

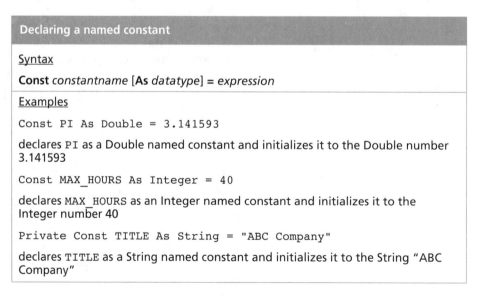

Declaring a named constant
<u>Syntax</u>
Const constantname [**As** datatype] = expression
<u>Examples</u>
Const PI As Double = 3.141593
declares PI as a Double named constant and initializes it to the Double number 3.141593
Const MAX_HOURS As Integer = 40
declares MAX_HOURS as an Integer named constant and initializes it to the Integer number 40
Private Const TITLE As String = "ABC Company"
declares TITLE as a String named constant and initializes it to the String "ABC Company"

Figure 3-13: Syntax and examples of the Const statement

In the Const statement's syntax, *constantname* and *datatype* are the constant's name and data type, respectively, and *expression* is the value you want assigned to the named constant. The *expression* can be a literal constant or another named constant; it also can contain arithmetic and logical operators. (You learn about logical operators in Chapter 4.) The *expression* cannot, however, contain variables.

The square brackets in the Const statement's syntax indicate that the "**As** *datatype*" portion is optional. If you do not assign a data type to a named constant, Visual Basic .NET assigns a data type based on the *expression*. For example, if you create a named constant for the number 45.6 and do not assign a data type to the constant, Visual Basic .NET assigns the Double data type to it, because a numeric literal constant having a decimal place is assumed to be a Double number. It is a good programming practice to include the "**As** *datatype*" portion in a constant declaration statement, because doing so gives you control over the constant's data type.

The rules for naming a named constant are the same as for naming a variable. However, the customary practice is to use uppercase letters in the name, as in the `PI`, `MAX_HOURS`, and `TITLE` names shown in the examples in Figure 3-13. This naming convention helps to distinguish the named constants from the variables used in an application.

Similar to creating variables, you create a procedure-level constant by entering the Const statement in the appropriate procedure, and you create a module-level constant by entering the Const statement, preceded by the keyword `Private`, in the form's Declarations section.

Named constants make code more self-documenting and, therefore, easier to modify, because they allow you to use meaningful words in place of values that are less clear. The named constant `PI`, for example, is much more meaningful than is the number 3.141593, which is the value of pi rounded to six decimal places. Once you create a named constant, you then can use the constant's name rather than its value in the code. Unlike variables, named constants cannot be inadvertently changed while your application is running. Figure 3-14 shows a named constant declared and used in a procedure.

named constant

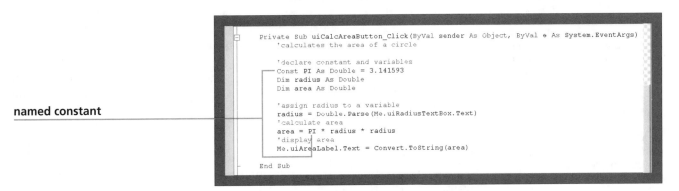

```
Private Sub uiCalcAreaButton_Click(ByVal sender As Object, ByVal e As System.EventArgs)
    'calculates the area of a circle

    'declare constant and variables
    Const PI As Double = 3.141593
    Dim radius As Double
    Dim area As Double

    'assign radius to a variable
    radius = Double.Parse(Me.uiRadiusTextBox.Text)
    'calculate area
    area = PI * radius * radius
    'display area
    Me.uiAreaLabel.Text = Convert.ToString(area)

End Sub
```

Figure 3-14: Named constant declared and used in a procedure

In Chapter 2, you learned that many programmers use comments to document the project's name and purpose, as well as the programmer's name and the date the code was either created or modified. Recall that such comments typically are placed in the General Declarations section in the Code Editor window. In addition to the comments, you also should enter two Option statements in the General Declarations section.

Option Explicit and Option Strict

Earlier in this chapter you learned that it is important to declare the variables and named constants used in an application; by doing so you have control over their data type. Unfortunately, in Visual Basic .NET you can create variables "on the fly," which means that if your code contains the name of an undeclared variable— a variable that does not appear in either a Dim or a Private statement—Visual Basic .NET creates one for you and assigns the Object data type to it. Recall that the Object type is not a very efficient data type. Because it is so easy to forget to declare a variable—and so easy to misspell a variable's name while coding, thereby inadvertently creating an undeclared variable—Visual Basic .NET provides a way that will prevent you from using undeclared variables in your code. You simply enter the statement `Option Explicit On` in the General Declarations section of the Code Editor window. Then if your code contains the name of an undeclared variable, the Visual Basic .NET compiler informs you of the error.

In this chapter you also learned that the data type of the value that appears on the right side of the assignment operator in an assignment statement should be the same as the data type of the variable that appears on the left side of the assignment operator. If the value's data type does not match the memory location's data type, the computer uses a process called **implicit type conversion** to convert the value to fit the memory location. For example, if you assign the integer 9 to a Decimal memory location, which stores fixed-point numbers, the computer converts the integer to a fixed-point number before storing the value in the memory location; it does so by appending a decimal point and the number 0 to the end of the integer. In this case, for example, the integer 9 is converted to the fixed-point number 9.0, and it is the fixed-point number 9.0 that is assigned to the Decimal memory location. When a value is converted from one data type to another data type that can store larger numbers, the value is said to be **promoted**. If the Decimal memory location is used subsequently in a calculation, the results of the calculation will not be adversely affected by the implicit promotion of the number 9 to the number 9.0.

However, if you inadvertently assign a Double number—such as 3.2—to a memory location that can store only integers, the computer converts the Double number to an integer before storing the value in the memory location. It does so by rounding the number to the nearest whole number and then truncating (dropping off) the decimal portion of the number. In this case, the computer converts the Double number 3.2 to the integer 3. As a result, the number 3, rather than the number 3.2, is assigned to the memory location. When a value is converted from one data type to another data type that can store only smaller numbers, the value is said to be **demoted**. If the memory location is used subsequently in a calculation, the results of the calculation probably will be adversely affected by the implicit demotion of the number 3.2 to the number 3; more than likely, the conversion will cause the calculated results to be incorrect.

With implicit type conversions, data loss can occur when the value of one data type (for example, Double) is converted to a data type with less precision or smaller capacity (for example, Integer). You can eliminate the problems that occur as a result of implicit type conversions by entering the `Option Strict On` statement in the General Declarations section of the Code Editor window. When the `Option Strict On` statement appears in an application's code, Visual Basic .NET uses the following type conversion rules:

- Strings will not be implicitly converted to numbers, and numbers will not be implicitly converted to strings.
- Lower-ranking data types will be implicitly promoted to higher-ranking types. A data type ranks higher than another data type if it can store larger numbers.

tip

Rather than entering the `Option Explicit On` and `Option Strict On` statements in the General Declarations section, you also can turn on both options for the current project by right-clicking the project name in the Solution Explorer window, and then clicking Properties. Open the Common Properties folder, and then click Build. Use the list boxes in the Compiler Defaults section to turn on both options. To turn on both options for all projects you create, click Tools on the menu bar, and then click Options. Open the Projects folder, and then click VB Defaults. Use the list boxes in the Default Project Settings section to turn on both options.

For example, a Short will be implicitly promoted to an Integer or Long, and a Single will be implicitly converted to a Double.

■   Higher-ranking data types will not be implicitly demoted to lower-ranking data types; rather, a syntax error will occur. For example, a Double will not be implicitly demoted to a Single. Similarly, a Long will not be implicitly demoted to an Integer or Short.

Figure 3-15 shows both Option statements entered in the General Declarations section. The statements typically are entered below the comments that document the project's name, the project's purpose, the programmer's name, and the date the code was either created or modified.

General Declarations section

comments

Option statements

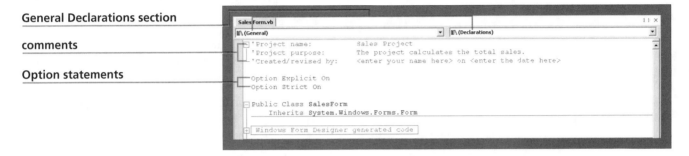

Figure 3-15: Option statements entered in the General Declarations section

You now have completed Lesson A. You will use procedure-level and module-level variables in the Skate-Away Sales application, which you modify in Lessons B and C. Now you can either take a break or complete the end-of-lesson questions and exercises before moving on to the next lesson.

SUMMARY

To create a variable:

■   The syntax of a variable declaration statement is {**Dim** | **Private** | **Static**} *variablename* [**As** *datatype*][= *initialvalue*].

■   To create a procedure-level variable, enter the variable declaration statement in a procedure. To create a module-level variable, enter the variable declaration statement in a form's Declarations section.

■   Use the `Dim` keyword to create a procedure-level variable. Use the `Private` keyword to create a module-level variable.

To use an assignment statement to assign data to a variable:

■   Use the syntax *variablename = value*.

To force a literal constant to assume a different data type:

■   Use one of the literal type characters listed in Figure 3-7.

To convert a string to a numeric data type:

▨ Use the Parse method. The method's syntax is *numericDataType*.**Parse**(*string*).

To convert a numeric value to a different data type:

▨ Use one of the Convert methods listed in Figure 3-9. The method's syntax is **Convert**.*method*(*value*).

To create a named constant:

▨ Use the Const statement, whose syntax is **Const** *constantname* [**As** *datatype*] = *expression*.
▨ The rules for naming constants are the same as for naming variables, except you capitalize the letters in the name.
▨ To create a procedure-level named constant, enter the Const statement in a procedure. To create a module-level named constant, enter the Const statement, preceded by the keyword `Private`, in a form's Declarations section.

To prevent the computer from creating an undeclared variable:

▨ Enter the `Option Explicit` On statement in the Declarations section of a form.

To prevent the computer from making implicit type conversions that may result in a loss of data:

▨ Enter the `Option Strict` On statement in the Declarations section of a form.

QUESTIONS

1. _____ are computer memory locations in which you store information, temporarily.
   a. Boxes
   b. Literal constants
   c. Named constants
   d. Variables
   e. Both c and d.

2. Which of the following is the correct data type to use for a variable that will always contain a whole number less than 50,000?
   a. Decimal
   b. Integer
   c. Long
   d. Single
   e. Object

3. A variable known only to the procedure in which it is declared is called _____.
   a. a current variable
   b. an event variable
   c. a module-level variable
   d. a procedure-level variable
   e. None of the above.

4. A _____ is a data item whose value does not change while the application is running.
   a. literal constant
   b. literal variable
   c. named constant
   d. symbolic variable
   e. variable

5. A _____ is a memory location whose value cannot change while the application is running.
   a. literal constant
   b. literal variable
   c. named constant
   d. symbolic variable
   e. variable

6. If you do not provide a data type in a variable declaration statement, Visual Basic .NET assigns the _____ data type to the variable.
   a. Decimal
   b. Integer
   c. Object
   d. String
   e. None of the above.

7. You use the _____ keyword to declare a module-level variable.
   a. `Dimension`
   b. `Global`
   c. `Module`
   d. `Private`
   e. `Public`

8. Data stored in a variable can be processed much faster than data stored in the property of a control.
   a. True
   b. False

9. Which of the following declares a procedure-level String variable?
   a. `Dim String city`
   b. `Dim city As String`
   c. `Private String city`
   d. `Private city As String`

10. Which of the following assigns the number 2.89 to a Decimal variable named `price`? (Assume that the application contains the `Option Strict On` statement.)
    a. `price = 2.89`
    b. `price = 2.89D`
    c. `price = D2.89`
    d. None of the above.

11. Which of the following assigns the contents of the uiSalesTextBox control to a Single variable named `sales`? (Assume that the application contains the `Option Strict On` statement.)
    a. `sales = Me.uiSalesTextBox.Text`
    b. `sales = Me.uiSalesTextBox.Convert.ToSingle`
    c. `sales = Parse.Single(Me.uiSalesTextBox)`
    d. `sales = Single.Parse(Me.uiSalesTextBox.Text)`

12. Which of the following declares a Double named constant?
   a. `Const RATE As Double = .09`
   b. `Const RATE As Double = .09D`
   c. `Constant RATE = .09`
   d. both a and b

13. Which of the following assigns the sum of two Integer variables to the Text property of the TotalLabel control? (Assume that the application contains the `Option Strict On` statement.)
   a. `Me.uiTotalLabel.Text = Convert.ToInteger(num1 + num2)`
   b. `Me.uiTotalLabel.Text = Convert.ToInt32(num1 + num2)`
   c. `Me.uiTotalLabel.Text = Convert.ToString(num1) + Convert.ToString(num2)`
   d. None of the above.

14. Most of the variables used in an application are _____.
   a. block-level
   b. module-level
   c. procedure-level
   d. variable-level

15. The _____ statement prevents data loss due to implicit type conversions.
   a. `Option Explicit On`
   b. `Option Strict On`
   c. `Option Implicit Off`
   d. `Option Convert Off`

EXERCISES

1. Assume a procedure needs to store an item's name and its price. The price may have a decimal place. Write the appropriate Dim statement(s) to create the necessary procedure-level variables.

2. Assume a procedure needs to store the name of an item in inventory and its height and weight. The height may have decimal places; the weight will be whole numbers only. Write the appropriate Dim statement(s) to create the necessary procedure-level variables.

3. Assume a procedure needs to store the name of an inventory item, the number of units in stock at the beginning of the current month, the number of units purchased during the current month, the number of units sold during the current month, and the number of units in stock at the end of the current month. (The number of units is always a whole number.) Write the appropriate Dim statement(s) to create the necessary procedure-level variables.

4. Assume a procedure needs to store the name and the population of a city. Write the appropriate Dim statement(s) to create the necessary procedure-level variables.

5. Assume your application needs to store the part number of an item and its cost. (An example of a part number for this application is A103.) Write the appropriate Private statement(s) to create the necessary module-level variables.

6. Write an assignment statement that assigns Miami to a String variable named `cityName`.

7. Write an assignment statement that assigns the part number AB103 to a String variable named `partNumber`.

8. Write an assignment statement that assigns the word Desk to a String variable named `itemName`. Also write an assignment statement that assigns the number 40 to an Integer variable named `quantityInStock`, and an assignment statement that assigns the number 20 to an Integer variable named `quantityOnOrder`.

9. Write an assignment statement that adds together the contents of two Double variables (`northSales` and `southSales`), and then assigns the sum to a Double variable named `totalSales`.

10. Write an assignment statement that multiplies the contents of a Decimal variable named `salary` by the number 1.5, and then assigns the result to the `salary` variable.

11. Assume a form contains two buttons named uiSalaryButton and uiBonusButton. Both buttons' Click event procedures need to use the `employeeName` variable. Write the appropriate statement to declare the `employeeName` variable. Also specify where you will need to enter the statement and whether the variable is a procedure-level or module-level variable.

12. Assume a form contains two buttons named uiWestButton and uiSouthButton. The Click event procedure for the uiWestButton needs to use a variable named `westSales`. The Click event procedure for the uiSouthButton needs to use a variable named `southSales`. Both buttons' Click event procedures need to use the `companySales` variable. Write the appropriate statements to declare the `westSales`, `southSales`, and `companySales` variables. Also specify where you will need to enter each statement and whether each variable is a procedure-level or module-level variable.

13. Write the statement to declare a procedure-level named constant named `TAX_RATE`. The constant's data type is Double and its value is .05.

14. Assume two procedures in a form need to use the `AGE` named constant, whose data type is Integer and value is 21. Write the statement to declare the constant. Also specify where you will need to enter the statement and whether the constant is a procedure-level or module-level constant.

discovery ▶ 15. In this exercise, you experiment with procedure-level and module-level variables.

a. If necessary, start Visual Studio .NET. Open the Scope Solution (Scope Solution.sln) file, which is contained in the VBNET\Chap03\Scope Solution folder. The Scope application allows the user to calculate either a 2% or a 5% commission on a sales amount. It displays the sales and commission amounts in the uiSalesLabel and uiCommissionLabel controls, respectively.

b. Open the Code Editor window. Code the uiSalesButton's Click event procedure so that it declares a procedure-level, Integer variable named `sales`. The procedure also should use an assignment statement to assign the number 500 to the `sales` variable. Additionally, the procedure should display the contents of the `sales` variable in the uiSalesLabel control on the form.

c. Save the solution, then start the application. Click the Display Sales button. What does the uiSalesButton's Click event procedure display in the uiSalesLabel control? When the Click event procedure ends, what happens to the procedure-level `sales` variable?

d. Click the Exit button to end the application, then close the Output window.

e. In the uiComm2Button's Click event procedure, enter an assignment statement that multiplies a variable named `sales` by .02, and then assigns the result to the uiCommissionLabel on the form. Notice the jagged line that appears below the variable's name (`sales`) in the instruction. The jagged line indicates that there is something wrong with the code. To determine the problem, you need simply to rest your mouse pointer somewhere on the word (or words) immediately above the jagged line. In this case, for example, you need to rest your mouse pointer on the variable name, sales. The message in the box indicates that the sales variable is not declared. In other words, the uiComm2Button's Click event procedure cannot locate the variable's declaration statement, which you previously entered in the uiSalesButton's Click event procedure. As you learned in Lesson A, only the procedure in which a variable is declared can use the variable. No other procedure even knows that the variable exists.

f. Now observe what happens if you use the same name to declare a variable in more than one procedure. Insert a blank line above the assignment statement in the uiComm2Button's Click event procedure. In the blank line, type a statement that declares a procedure-level, Integer variable named sales, then click the assignment statement to move the insertion point away from the current line. Notice that the jagged line disappears from the assignment statement.

g. Save the solution, and then start the application. Click the Display Sales button. The contents of the sales variable declared in the uiSalesButton's Click event procedure (500) appears in the uiSalesLabel control.

h. Click the 2% Commission button. Why does the number 0 appear in the uiCommissionLabel control? What happens to the sales variable declared in the uiComm2Button's Click event procedure when the procedure ends?

i. Click the Exit button to end the application. As this example shows, when you use the same name to declare a variable in more than one procedure, each procedure creates its own procedure-level variable. Although the variables have the same name, each refers to a different location in memory.

j. Next, you use a module-level variable in the application. Position the insertion point above the uiExitButton's Click event procedure. ScopeForm appears in the Class Name list box, and (Declarations) appears in the Method Name list box. Press Enter to insert a blank line. In the blank line, type a statement that declares a module-level Integer variable named sales.

k. Delete the Dim statement from the uiSalesButton's Click event procedure. Also delete the Dim statement from the uiComm2Button's Click event procedure.

l. In the uiComm5Button's Click event procedure, enter an assignment statement that multiplies the sales variable by .05, and then assigns the result to the uiCommissionLabel on the form.

m. Save the solution, and then start the application. The variable declaration statement in the form's Declarations section creates and initializes (to the number 0) an Integer variable named sales.

n. Click the Display Sales button. The uiSalesButton's Click event procedure stores the number 500 in the sales variable, and then displays the contents of the sales variable (500) in the uiSalesLabel.

o. Click the 2% Commission button. The uiComm2Button's Click event procedure multiplies the contents of the sales variable (500) by .02, and then displays the result (10) in the uiCommissionLabel.

p. Click the 5% Commission button. The uiComm5Button's Click event procedure multiplies the contents of the sales variable (500) by .05, and then displays the result (25) in the uiCommissionLabel. As this example shows, any procedure in the form can use a module-level variable.

q. Click the Exit button to end the application. What happens to the sales variable when the application ends?

r. Close the Output window, then close the solution.

discovery ▶ 16. In this exercise, you experiment with a named constant.

a. If necessary, start Visual Studio .NET. Open the Constant Solution (Constant Solution.sln) file, which is contained in the VBNET\Chap03\Constant Solution folder. The Constant application allows the user to calculate and display the area of a circle, using the radius entered in the uiRadiusTextBox.

b. Open the Code Editor window. The formula for calculating the area of a circle is Area = πr^2. In the uiCalcButton's Click event procedure, enter a statement that declares a Single named constant. The constant should be named PI and have a value of 3.141593. Also enter the statement to calculate the area of a circle.

c. Save the solution, then start the application.

d. What is the area of a circle whose radius is 5?

e. Click the Exit button to end the application. Close the Output window, then close the solution.

After completing this lesson, you will be able to:

- Include a procedure-level and module-level variable in an application
- Concatenate strings
- Get user input using the InputBox function
- Include the `ControlChars. NewLine` constant in code
- Designate the default button for a form

Modifying the Skate-Away Sales Application

Storing Information Using Variables

Recall that Mr. Cousard, the manager of Skate-Away Sales, has asked you to modify the order form that you created in Chapter 2. The order form should now display the message "The sales tax was" followed by the sales tax amount and the name of the salesperson who recorded the order. Before making modifications to an application's existing code, you should review the application's documentation and revise the necessary documents. In this case, you need to revise the Skate-Away Sales application's TOE chart and also the pseudocode for the Calculate Order button, which is responsible for making the application's calculations. The revised TOE chart is shown in Figure 3-16. Changes made to the original TOE chart, which is shown in Chapter 2's Figure 2-11, are shaded in the figure. (You will view the revised pseudocode for the Calculate Order button later in this lesson.)

Task	Object	Event
1. Calculate the total skateboards ordered and the total price	uiCalcButton	Click
2. Display the total skateboards ordered and the total price in the uiTotalBoardsLabel and uiTotalPriceLabel		
3. Calculate the sales tax		
4. Display the message, sales tax, and salesperson's name in the uiMessageLabel		
Clear the screen for the next order	uiClearButton	Click
End the application	uiExitButton	Click
Display the total skateboards ordered (from uiCalcButton)	uiTotalBoardsLabel	None
Display the total price (from uiCalcButton)	uiTotalPriceLabel	None
Get and display the order information	uiNameTextBox, uiAddressTextBox, uiCityTextBox, uiStateTextBox, uiZipTextBox, uiPriceTextBox, uiRateTextBox, uiBlueTextBox, uiYellowTextBox	None
Get the salesperson's name	OrderForm	Load
Display the message, sales tax, and salesperson's name (from uiCalcButton)	uiMessageLabel	None

Figure 3-16: Revised TOE chart for the Skate-Away Sales application

Notice that the uiCalcButton control's Click event procedure now has two more tasks to perform: it must calculate the sales tax and also display the message, sales tax, and salesperson's name in the uiMessageLabel control. Two additional objects (OrderForm and uiMessageLabel) also are included in the revised TOE chart. The OrderForm's Load event procedure, which occurs before the OrderForm is displayed the first time, is responsible for getting the salesperson's name when the application is started. The uiMessageLabel control will display the message, sales tax, and salesperson's name. As the revised TOE chart indicates, you need to change the code in the uiCalcButton's Click event procedure, and you also need to code the form's Load event procedure. The uiMessageLabel control, however, does not need to be coded.

Before you can begin modifying its code, you need to open the Skate-Away Sales application.

To open the Skate-Away Sales application:

1 Start Microsoft Visual Studio .NET, if necessary.

2 If necessary, close the Start Page window.

3 Open the **Order Solution** (Order Solution.sln) file, which is contained in the VBNET\Chap03\Order Solution folder.

4 Auto-hide the Toolbox, Solution Explorer, and Properties windows, if necessary. The Skate-Away Sales order form is shown in Figure 3-17.

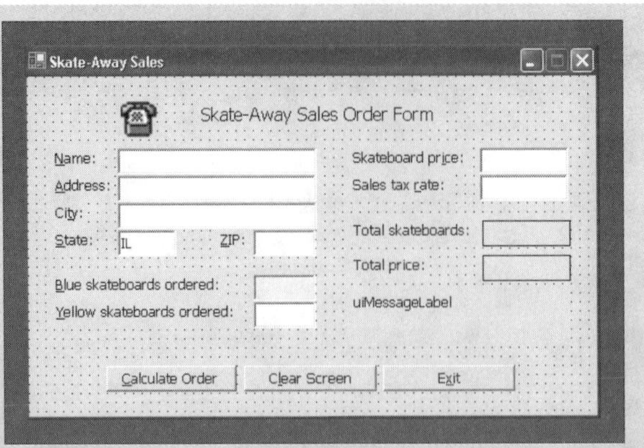

Figure 3-17: Skate-Away Sales order form

Two minor modifications were made to the order form that you created in Chapter 2. First, the order form now contains a label control named uiMessageLabel. You will use the uiMessageLabel control to display the message that contains both the sales tax amount and the name of the salesperson. Second, the instruction `Me.uiMessageLabel.Text = ""` was added to the Clear Screen button's Click event procedure. The instruction will remove the message from the uiMessageLabel control when the user clicks the Clear Screen button.

5 Click the **uiMessageLabel** control to select it.

The uiMessageLabel control should be empty when the order form first appears on the screen.

6 Delete the contents of the uiMessageLabel control's Text property.

> **HELP?** To delete the contents of the Text property, double-click Text in the Properties list; this will highlight the contents of the Text property in the Settings box. Press the Delete key to delete the highlighted text, then press Enter.

7 Click the **form's title bar** to select the form.

Before you begin modifying the Calculate Order button's code, you will record your name and the current date at the top of the program. You also will enter the `Option Explicit On` and `Option Strict On` statements. As you learned in Lesson A, the `Option Explicit On` statement prevents the computer from creating an undeclared variable. The `Option Strict On` statement prevents the computer from making implicit type conversions that may result in a loss of data.

To enter your name, the current date, and the two Option statements:

1 Open the Code Editor window. Replace the `<enter your name here>` and `<enter the date here>` text in the third comment with your name and the current date, respectively.

2 Position the insertion point in the line below the third comment, then press the **Enter** key to insert a blank line.

3 Type **option explicit on** and press **Enter**, then type **option strict on** and press **Enter**.

Now begin modifying the Skate-Away Sales application so that it displays the sales tax amount on the order form.

Modifying the Calculate Order Button's Code

Currently, the Calculate Order button calculates the amount of sales tax as part of the total price equation. Recall that the total price equation from Chapter 2 is `Me.uiTotalPriceLabel.Text = Val(Me.uiTotalBoardsLabel.Text) * Val(Me.uiPriceTextBox.Text) * (1 + Val(Me.uiRateTextBox.Text))`. Now that Mr. Cousard wants the sales tax amount to appear on the order form, you need to include a separate equation for the sales tax amount in the Calculate Order button's code. In this lesson, you first remove the existing code from the Calculate Order button's Click event procedure. You then recode the procedure using variables (rather than control properties) in the equations. Figure 3-18 shows the revised pseudocode for the Calculate Order button's Click event procedure. Changes made to the original pseudocode, which is shown in Chapter 2's Figure 2-35, are shaded in the figure.

Calculate Order button

1. declare variables

2. assign values to variables

3. calculate total skateboards = blue skateboards + yellow skateboards

4. calculate subtotal = total skateboards * skateboard price

5. calculate sales tax = subtotal * sales tax rate

6. calculate total price = subtotal + sales tax

7. display total skateboards and total price in uiTotalBoardsLabel and uiTotalPriceLabel controls

8. display "The sales tax was" message, sales tax, and salesperson's name in the uiMessageLabel control

9. send the focus to the Clear Screen button

Figure 3-18: Revised pseudocode for the Calculate Order button's Click event procedure

Notice that, in addition to using variables, the Click event procedure now includes two additional calculations—one for a subtotal and the other for the sales tax. The subtotal amount is computed by multiplying the total skateboards ordered by the skateboard price. The sales tax amount is computed by multiplying the subtotal amount by the sales tax rate. Also notice that the total price equation has changed; it now simply adds the subtotal amount to the sales tax amount. Before sending the focus to the Clear Screen button, the Click event procedure displays a message, the sales tax amount, and the salesperson's name in the uiMessageLabel control.

In the next set of steps, you review the code contained in the Calculate Order button's Click event procedure.

To review the code in the Calculate Order button's Click event procedure:

1 Scroll down the Code Editor window until the entire uiCalcButton Click event procedure is visible. See Figure 3-19. (The font used to display the text in the Code Editor window shown in Figure 3-19 was changed to 11-point Courier New so that you could view more of the code in the figure. It is not necessary for you to change the font.)

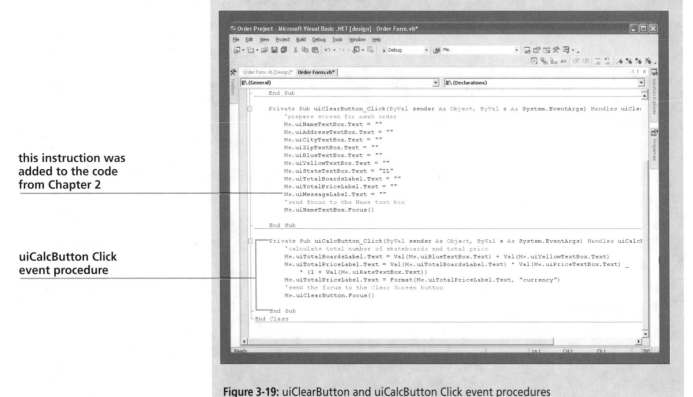

this instruction was added to the code from Chapter 2

uiCalcButton Click event procedure

Figure 3-19: uiClearButton and uiCalcButton Click event procedures

The equations that calculate the total skateboards ordered and the total price use the Text property of various controls included on the interface. The Val function in the equations is necessary because the Text property of a control is treated as a string rather than as a number. As you learned in Chapter 2, the Val function returns the numeric equivalent of a string. What you did not learn in Chapter 2, however, is that the Val function returns a number whose data type is Double. Therefore, when the computer processes the total skateboard equation, it first converts the contents of both the uiBlueTextBox.Text and uiYellowTextBox.Text properties to Double type numbers, then adds the Double numbers together and assigns the sum to the uiTotalBoardsLabel. As you may remember, the Double data type consumes 8 bytes of the computer's internal memory. In this case, because a customer can order only a whole number of blue and yellow skateboards, and the number of skateboards ordered is typically under 1,000 for each color, it would be more efficient to store the blue and yellow skateboard information in either Short (2 bytes of memory) or Integer (4 bytes of memory) variables. You will use Integer variables, because a calculation containing Integer variables takes less time to

tip

. . . .

You are using Single (4 bytes of memory) rather than Decimal (16 bytes of memory) variables for the price, subtotal, sales tax, and total price amounts because these variables will not need to store large money values. Also, the equations that use these variables are not complex, so rounding errors will not be a problem. Recall that it is best to use a smaller data type whenever possible.

process than the equivalent calculation containing Short variables. Assigning the Text property of the uiBlueTextBox and uiYellowTextBox controls to Integer variables allows you to control the data type of the numbers used in the total skateboards equation. You will assign the result of the total skateboards equation to an Integer variable named totalBoards. Figure 3-20 lists the names and data types of the variables you will use in the Calculate Order button's Click event procedure, as well as the values that you will assign to each variable.

Variable	Data type	Assign to variable
blueBoards	Integer	contents of uiBlueTextBox.Text
yellowBoards	Integer	contents of uiYellowTextBox.Text
totalBoards	Integer	sum of blueBoards + yellowBoards
boardPrice	Single	contents of uiPriceTextBox.Text
salesTaxRate	Single	contents of uiRateTextBox.Text
subtotal	Single	product of totalBoards * boardPrice
salesTax	Single	product of subtotal * salesTaxRate
totalPrice	Single	sum of subtotal + salesTax

Figure 3-20: List of variables and what you will assign to each

Now remove the existing code from the uiCalcButton's Click event procedure.

To remove the code from the uiCalcButton's Click event procedure:

1   Highlight the six lines of code below the comment, as shown in Figure 3-21.

```
Private Sub uiCalcButton_Click(ByVal sender As Object, ByVal e As System.EventArgs) Handles uiCalc
    'calculate total number of skateboards and total price
    Me.uiTotalBoardsLabel.Text = Val(Me.uiBlueTextBox.Text) + Val(Me.uiYellowTextBox.Text)
    Me.uiTotalPriceLabel.Text = Val(Me.uiTotalBoardsLabel.Text) * Val(Me.uiPriceTextBox.Text)
        * (1 + Val(Me.uiRateTextBox.Text))
    Me.uiTotalPriceLabel.Text = Format(Me.uiTotalPriceLabel.Text, "currency")
    'send the focus to the Clear Screen button
    Me.uiClearButton.Focus()

End Sub
```

Figure 3-21: Instructions highlighted in the uiCalcButton Click event procedure

2   Press **Delete** to remove the highlighted code.

    HELP? If you inadvertently deleted the `Private Sub` and `End Sub` instructions, click the Class Name list arrow, then click uiCalcButton in the list. Click the Method Name list arrow, and then click Click in the list.

The first step listed in the pseudocode shown in Figure 3-18 is to declare the variables. Because only the Calculate Order button's Click event procedure will need to use the eight variables listed in Figure 3-20, you will declare the variables as procedure-level variables.

To begin coding the Calculate Order button's Click event procedure:

1   Press **Enter** to insert a blank line below the existing comment, then enter the two Dim statements shown in Figure 3-22. Position the insertion point as shown in the figure.

enter these Dim statements

position the insertion point here

```
Private Sub uiCalcButton_Click(ByVal sender As Object, ByVal e As System.EventArgs) Handles uiCalcI
    'calculate total number of skateboards and total price

    Dim blueBoards, yellowBoards, totalBoards As Integer
    Dim boardPrice, salesTaxRate, subtotal, salesTax, totalPrice As Single

    |

End Sub
```

Figure 3-22: Dim statements entered in the procedure

tip

Type the variable names in the Dim statement using the exact capitalization you want. Then, any time you want to refer to the variables in the code, you can enter their names using any case and the Code Editor will adjust the name to match the case used in the Dim statement.

The next step in the pseudocode is to assign values to the variables. The blueBoards, yellowBoards, boardPrice, and salesTaxRate variables will get their values from the uiBlueTextBox, uiYellowTextBox, uiPriceTextBox, and uiRateTextBox controls, respectively. The remaining variables will get their values from the equations that calculate the total skateboards, subtotal, sales tax, and total price amounts. Rather than using the Val function, which converts a string to a Double number, you will use the `Integer.Parse` method to convert the contents of the uiBlueTextBox and uiYellowTextBox controls to the Integer data type. You will use the Single.Parse method to convert the contents of the uiPriceTextBox and uiRateTextBox controls to the Single data type.

2   Enter the comment and four assignment statements shown in Figure 3-23, then position the insertion point as shown in the figure.

enter this comment and lines of code

position the insertion point here

```
Private Sub uiCalcButton_Click(ByVal sender As Object, ByVal e As System.EventArgs) Handles uiCalcI
    'calculate total number of skateboards and total price

    Dim blueBoards, yellowBoards, totalBoards As Integer
    Dim boardPrice, salesTaxRate, subtotal, salesTax, totalPrice As Single

    'assign values to variables
    blueBoards = Integer.Parse(Me.uiBlueTextBox.Text)
    yellowBoards = Integer.Parse(Me.uiYellowTextBox.Text)
    boardPrice = Single.Parse(Me.uiPriceTextBox.Text)
    salesTaxRate = Single.Parse(Me.uiRateTextBox.Text)

    |

End Sub
```

Figure 3-23: Comment and assignment statements entered in the procedure

The first two assignment statements shown in Figure 3-23 convert the contents of the uiBlueTextBox and uiYellowTextBox controls to Integer type numbers before storing them in the `blueBoards` and `yellowBoards` variables. Similarly, the next two assignment statements convert the values in the Text properties of the uiPriceTextBox and uiRateTextBox controls to Single type numbers. The statements assign the numbers to the `boardPrice` and `salesTaxRate` variables.

The next step in the pseudocode is to calculate the total number of skateboards ordered by adding the number of blue skateboards ordered to the number of yellow skateboards ordered. When entering the total skateboards equation, you will use the variables that you declared in the procedure, rather than the control properties that you used in Chapter 2's equation. In other words, you will enter `totalBoards` `=` `blueBoards` `+` `yellowBoards` instead of `Me.uiTotalBoardsLabel.Text` `=` `Val(Me.uiBlueTextBox.Text)` `+` `Val(Me.uiYellowTextBox.Text)`. Notice how, in addition to making your application run more efficiently and allowing you to control the preciseness of the numbers used in the calculations, variables also make the lines of code much shorter and easier to understand.

To continue coding the uiCalcButton Click event procedure:

1   Type '**perform calculations** and press **Enter**, then type **totalboards = blueboards + yellowboards** and press **Enter**.

The next steps in the pseudocode are to calculate the subtotal, sales tax, and total price amounts. You calculate the subtotal amount by multiplying the number of skateboards ordered (which is stored in the `totalBoards` variable) by the skateboard price (which is stored in the `boardPrice` variable).

2   Type **subtotal = totalboards * boardprice** and press **Enter**.

You calculate the sales tax amount by multiplying the subtotal amount (which is stored in the `subtotal` variable) by the sales tax rate (which is stored in the `salesTaxRate` variable).

3   Type **salestax = subtotal * salestaxrate** and press **Enter**.

To calculate the total price amount, you simply add the sales tax amount to the subtotal amount. The subtotal amount is stored in the `subtotal` variable, and the sales tax amount is stored in the `salesTax` variable.

4   Type **totalprice = subtotal + salestax** and press **Enter** twice.

The next step in the pseudocode is to display the total skateboards and the total price in the uiTotalBoardsLabel and uiTotalPriceLabel controls on the form. As you did in Chapter 2, you will use the Format function to format the total price as currency, which will display a dollar sign ($), a comma thousand separator, and two decimal places. (In Chapter 4, you will learn another way to format numeric output.)

5   Type '**display total amounts in controls** and press **Enter**.

6   Type **me.uitotalboardslabel.text = convert.tostring(totalboards)** and press **Enter**, then type **me.uitotalpricelabel.text = format(totalprice, "currency")** and press **Enter** twice.

The next step in the pseudocode is to display a message, the sales tax, and the salesperson's name in the uiMessageLabel control. For now, just display the sales tax so you can verify that the sales tax equation is working correctly. Use the Format function to display the sales tax in the currency format.

7   Type '**display message, tax, and name** and press **Enter**, then type **me.uimessagelabel.text = format(salestax, "currency")** and press **Enter** twice.

The last step in the pseudocode is to send the focus to the Clear Screen button. As you learned in Chapter 2, you can use the Focus method to send the focus to a control.

8   Type '**send focus to Clear Screen button** and press **Enter**, then type **me.uiclearbutton.focus()**.

9   Compare your code to the code shown in Figure 3-24. Make any necessary corrections before continuing.

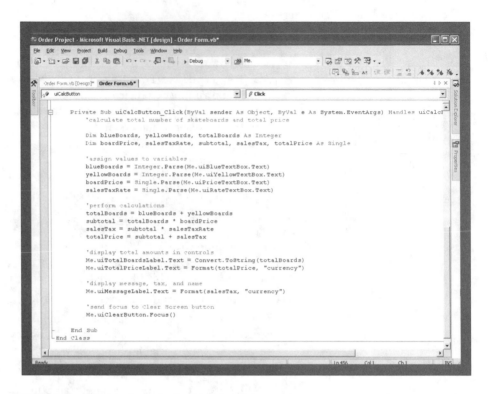

Figure 3-24: Calculate Order button's Click event procedure

Now test the code entered in the uiCalcButton's Click event procedure.

To test the uiCalcButton's Click event procedure:

1　Click **File** on the menu bar, and then click **Save All**. Click **Debug** on the menu bar, and then click **Start**.

2　Enter the following order:

blue skateboards ordered:	10
yellow skateboards ordered:	10
skateboard price:	100
sales tax rate:	.05

3　Click the **Calculate Order** button. The application displays the total number of skateboards ordered in the uiTotalBoardsLabel control, the total price in the uiTotalPriceLabel control, and the sales tax in the uiMessageLabel control, then sends the focus to the Clear Screen button, as shown in Figure 3-25.

sales tax amount

this button has the focus

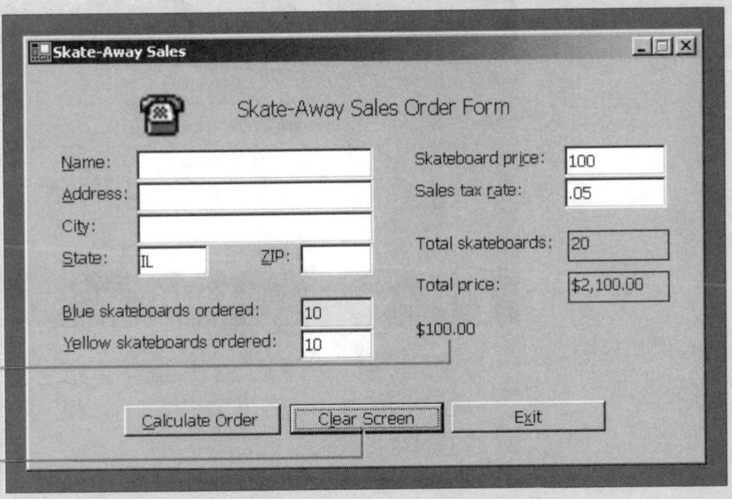

Figure 3-25: Order form showing sales tax amount

4   Click the **Exit** button. When you return to the Code Editor window, close the Output window.

In addition to displaying the sales tax, the uiMessageLabel control also must display the message "The sales tax was" and the name of the salesperson recording the order. Before you can accomplish this task, you need to learn how to concatenate (link together) strings.

Concatenating Strings

You also can use the plus sign (+) to concatenate strings. To avoid confusion, however, you should use the plus sign for addition and the ampersand for concatenation.

You use the **concatenation operator**, which is the ampersand (&), to concatenate (connect or link) strings together. When concatenating strings, you must be sure to include a space before and after the ampersand; otherwise, Visual Basic .NET will not recognize the ampersand as the concatenation operator. Figure 3-26 shows some examples of string concatenation. As the last example shows, you do not need to use the `Convert.ToString` method when concatenating a numeric value to a string. This is because Visual Basic .NET automatically converts, to a string, a numeric value preceded by the concatenation operator.

Concatenating strings		
Assume you have the following variables:		

Variables	Data type	Contents
firstName	String	Sue
lastName	String	Chen
age	Integer	21

Using the above variables, this concatenated string:	Would result in:
firstName & lastName	SueChen
firstName & " " & lastName	Sue Chen
lastName & ", " & firstName	Chen, Sue
"She is " & Convert.ToString(age) & "!"	She is 21!
"She is " & age & "!"	She is 21!

Figure 3-26: Examples of string concatenation

You will use the concatenation operator to link the string "The sales tax was" to the sales tax stored in the salesTax variable, and then concatenate the sales tax to a period, which will mark the end of the sentence. Using the examples shown in Figure 3-26 as a guide, the correct syntax for the uiMessageLabel control's assignment statement would be `Me.uiMessageLabel.Text = "The sales tax was " & Format(salesTax, "currency") & "."`.

To concatenate a message, the sales tax amount, and a period, and then save the solution and start the application:

1   Change the `Me.uiMessageLabel.Text = Format(salesTax, "currency")` assignment statement as shown in Figure 3-27.

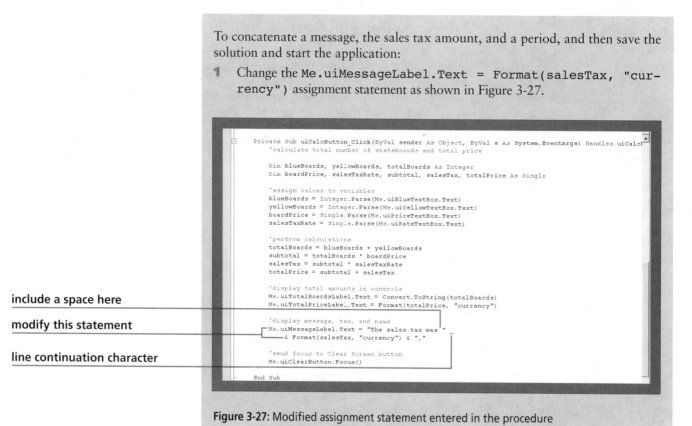

```
Private Sub uiCalcButton_Click(ByVal sender As Object, ByVal e As System.EventArgs) Handles uiCalcr
    'calculate total number of skateboards and total price

    Dim blueBoards, yellowBoards, totalBoards As Integer
    Dim boardPrice, salesTaxRate, subtotal, salesTax, totalPrice As Single

    'assign values to variables
    blueBoards = Integer.Parse(Me.uiBlueTextBox.Text)
    yellowBoards = Integer.Parse(Me.uiYellowTextBox.Text)
    boardPrice = Single.Parse(Me.uiPriceTextBox.Text)
    salesTaxRate = Single.Parse(Me.uiRateTextBox.Text)

    'perform calculations
    totalBoards = blueBoards + yellowBoards
    subtotal = totalBoards * boardPrice
    salesTax = subtotal * salesTaxRate
    totalPrice = subtotal + salesTax

    'display total amounts in controls
    Me.uiTotalBoardsLabel.Text = Convert.ToString(totalBoards)
    Me.uiTotalPriceLabel.Text = Format(totalPrice, "currency")

    'display message, tax, and name
    Me.uiMessageLabel.Text = "The sales tax was "
        & Format(salesTax, "currency") & "."

    'send focus to Clear Screen button
    Me.uiClearButton.Focus()

End Sub
```

include a space here

modify this statement

line continuation character

Figure 3-27: Modified assignment statement entered in the procedure

2   Save the solution, and then start the application.

3   Enter the following order:

blue skateboards ordered	10
yellow skateboards ordered	10
skateboard price	100
sales tax rate	.05

4   Click the **Calculate Order** button. The application displays the total number of skateboards ordered, the total price, and the message, including the sales tax, as shown in Figure 3-28.

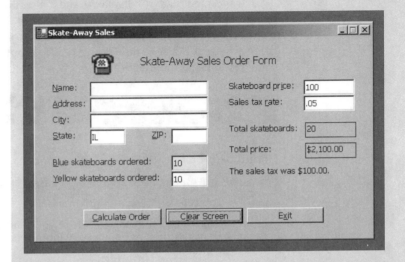

Figure 3-28: Order form showing the message and sales tax amount

5   Click the **Exit button.** When you return to the Code Editor window, close the Output window.

Now that you have the message and sales tax amount displaying correctly in the uiMessageLabel control, you just need to get the salesperson's name and then concatenate it to the end of the message. You can use the InputBox function to obtain the name from the user.

The InputBox Function

The **InputBox function** displays one of Visual Basic .NET's predefined dialog boxes. The dialog box contains a message, along with an OK button, a Cancel button, and an input area in which the user can enter information. Figure 3-29 shows an example of a dialog box created by the InputBox function.

title
prompt
input area
defaultResponse

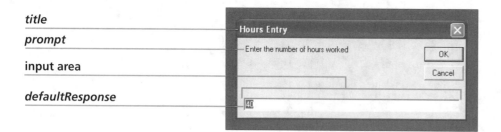

Figure 3-29: Example of a dialog box created by the InputBox function

The message that you display in the dialog box should prompt the user to enter the appropriate information in the input area of the dialog box. The user then needs to click either the OK button or the Cancel button to continue working in the application. Figure 3-30 shows the syntax of the InputBox function and includes several examples of using the function.

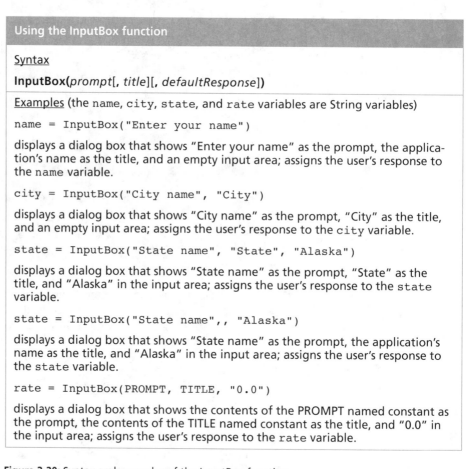

Using the InputBox function

Syntax

InputBox(*prompt*[, *title*][, *defaultResponse*]**)**

Examples (the `name`, `city`, `state`, and `rate` variables are String variables)

`name = InputBox("Enter your name")`

displays a dialog box that shows "Enter your name" as the prompt, the application's name as the title, and an empty input area; assigns the user's response to the `name` variable.

`city = InputBox("City name", "City")`

displays a dialog box that shows "City name" as the prompt, "City" as the title, and an empty input area; assigns the user's response to the `city` variable.

`state = InputBox("State name", "State", "Alaska")`

displays a dialog box that shows "State name" as the prompt, "State" as the title, and "Alaska" in the input area; assigns the user's response to the `state` variable.

`state = InputBox("State name",, "Alaska")`

displays a dialog box that shows "State name" as the prompt, the application's name as the title, and "Alaska" in the input area; assigns the user's response to the `state` variable.

`rate = InputBox(PROMPT, TITLE, "0.0")`

displays a dialog box that shows the contents of the PROMPT named constant as the prompt, the contents of the TITLE named constant as the title, and "0.0" in the input area; assigns the user's response to the `rate` variable.

Figure 3-30: Syntax and examples of the InputBox function

tip

The InputBox function's syntax also includes *XPos* and *YPos* arguments, which allow you to specify the horizontal and vertical position of the dialog box on the screen. Both arguments are optional; if omitted, the dialog box appears centered on the screen.

In the syntax for the InputBox function, *prompt* is the message you want displayed inside the dialog box, *title* is the text you want displayed in the dialog box's title bar, and *defaultResponse* is the text you want displayed in the input area of the dialog box. In Figure 3-29, "Enter the number of hours worked" is the *prompt*, "Hours Entry" is the *title*, and "40" is the *defaultResponse*.

tip

You learned about both sentence and book title capitalization in Chapter 2.

When entering the InputBox function in the Code Editor window, the *prompt*, *title*, and *defaultResponse* arguments must be enclosed in quotation marks, unless that information is stored in a named constant or variable. The Windows standard is to use sentence capitalization for the *prompt*, but book title capitalization for the *title*. The capitalization (if any) you use for the *defaultResponse* depends on the text itself.

Notice that the *title* and *defaultResponse* arguments are optional, as indicated by the square brackets in the syntax. If you omit the *title*, the project name appears in the title bar. If you omit the *defaultResponse* argument, a blank input area appears when the dialog box opens.

As you learned in Chapter 2, a function is a predefined procedure that performs a specific task and then returns a value after completing the task. The task performed by the InputBox function is to display a dialog box. The value returned by the InputBox function depends on whether the user clicks the dialog box's OK button, Cancel button, or Close button. If the user clicks the OK button, the InputBox function returns the value contained in the input area of the dialog box; this value is always treated as a string. However, if the user clicks either the Cancel button in the dialog box or the Close button on the dialog box's title bar, the InputBox function returns a zero-length (or empty) string.

Design Tips — GUI

InputBox Function's Prompt and Title Capitalization

- In the InputBox function, use sentence capitalization for the *prompt*, and book title capitalization for the *title*.

You will use the InputBox function in the Skate-Away Sales application to prompt the salesperson to enter his or her name. You will create named constants for the *prompt* and *title* arguments, and store the function's return value in a String variable. The InputBox function will be entered in the OrderForm's Load event procedure because, according to the revised TOE chart (shown earlier in Figure 3-16), that is the procedure responsible for getting the salesperson's name. Recall that a form's Load event occurs before the form is displayed the first time. After the Load event procedure obtains the salesperson's name, you then can have the uiCalcButton's Click event procedure concatenate the name to the message displayed in the uiMessageLabel control. Figure 3-31 shows the pseudocode for the form's Load event procedure.

Order Form

1. declare named constants
2. get the salesperson's name and assign the name to a String variable

Figure 3-31: Pseudocode for the OrderForm's Load event procedure

Before entering the InputBox function in the Load event procedure, you must decide where to declare the String variable that will store the function's return value. In other words, should the variable be a procedure-level or module-level variable? When deciding, consider the fact that the form's Load event procedure needs to assign to the variable the value returned by the InputBox function. The Calculate Order button's Click event procedure also needs to use the variable, because the procedure must concatenate the variable to the message displayed in the uiMessageLabel control. Recall from Lesson A that when two procedures in the *same* form need to use the *same* variable, you declare the variable as a module-level variable by entering the variable declaration statement in the form's Declarations section.

To continue coding the Skate-Away Sales application, then save the solution and start the application:

1   Scroll to the top of the Code Editor window. Position the mouse pointer in the blank line immediately above the uiExitButton Click event procedure, then click at that location. When you do so, the Class Name list box will say OrderForm and the Method Name list box will say (Declarations).

First, declare a module-level String variable named `salesPerson`.

2   Press **Enter** to insert a blank line, then type '**declare module-level variable** and press **Enter**. Type **private salesPerson as string** and press **Enter**. See Figure 3-32.

OrderForm's Declarations section

Option statements

module-level variable declaration statement

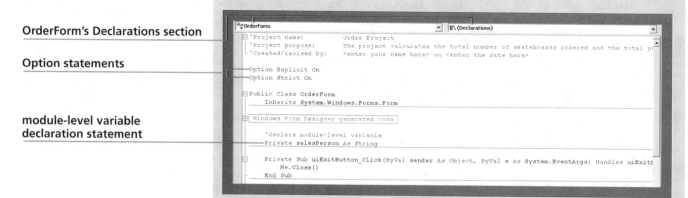

Figure 3-32: Module-level variable declared in the form's Declarations section

Now enter the InputBox function in the form's Load event procedure, so the function will be processed as soon as the salesperson starts the application. You access the form's procedures by selecting (OrderForm Events) in the Class Name list box.

3   Click the **Class Name** list arrow, and then click (**OrderForm Events**) in the list.

4   Click the **Method Name** list arrow to view a list of the form's procedures. Scroll down the list until you see Load, then click **Load** in the list. The OrderForm's Load event procedure appears in the Code Editor window.

To make the assignment statement that contains the InputBox function shorter and easier to understand, you will create named constants for the function's *prompt* ("Enter the salesperson's name") and *title* ("Name Entry") arguments, and then use the named constants rather than the longer strings in the function. You are using named constants rather than variables because the *prompt* and *title* will not change as the application is running.

5   Type the comments and code shown in Figure 3-33.

enter these comments and lines of code

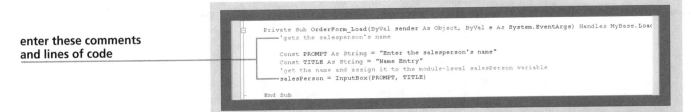

```
Private Sub OrderForm_Load(ByVal sender As Object, ByVal e As System.EventArgs) Handles MyBase.Load
    'gets the salesperson's name

    Const PROMPT As String = "Enter the salesperson's name"
    Const TITLE As String = "Name Entry"
    'get the name and assign it to the module-level salesPerson variable
    salesPerson = InputBox(PROMPT, TITLE)

End Sub
```

Figure 3-33: Form's Load event procedure

The InputBox function will prompt the user to enter the salesperson's name, and then store the response in the module-level `salesPerson` variable. Recall that module-level variables remain in memory until the application ends.

Now modify the Calculate Order button's Click event procedure by concatenating the `salesPerson` variable to the message assigned to the uiMessageLabel control.

6 Locate the uiCalcButton's Click event procedure in the Code Editor window, then modify the uiMessageLabel control's assignment statement as shown in Figure 3-34.

```
Private Sub uiCalcButton_Click(ByVal sender As Object, ByVal e As System.EventArgs) Handles uiCalc
    'calculate total number of skateboards and total price

    Dim blueBoards, yellowBoards, totalBoards As Integer
    Dim boardPrice, salesTaxRate, subtotal, salesTax, totalPrice As Single

    'assign values to variables
    blueBoards = Integer.Parse(Me.uiBlueTextBox.Text)
    yellowBoards = Integer.Parse(Me.uiYellowTextBox.Text)
    boardPrice = Single.Parse(Me.uiPriceTextBox.Text)
    salesTaxRate = Single.Parse(Me.uiRateTextBox.Text)

    'perform calculations
    totalBoards = blueBoards + yellowBoards
    subtotal = totalBoards * boardPrice
    salesTax = subtotal * salesTaxRate
    totalPrice = subtotal + salesTax

    'display total amounts in controls
    Me.uiTotalBoardsLabel.Text = Convert.ToString(totalBoards)
    Me.uiTotalPriceLabel.Text = Format(totalPrice, "currency")

    'display message, tax, and name
    Me.uiMessageLabel.Text = "The sales tax was " _
        & Format(salesTax, "currency") & "." & salesPerson

    'send focus to Clear Screen button
    Me.uiClearButton.Focus()

End Sub
```

add this to the assignment statement

Figure 3-34: Modified assignment statement

Next, save the solution and start the application to test the code in the form's Load event procedure and in the Calculate Order button's Click event procedure.

7 Save the solution and then start the application. The Name Entry dialog box created by the InputBox function appears first. See Figure 3-35.

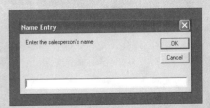

Figure 3-35: Dialog box created by the InputBox function

8   Type your name in the input area of the dialog box, then click the **OK** button. The order form appears.

9   Enter the following order:

blue skateboards ordered	**10**
yellow skateboards ordered	**10**
skateboard price	**100**
sales tax rate	**.05**

10   Click the **Calculate Order** button. Your name appears in the uiMessageLabel control; however, it appears much too close to the period.

At this point you could replace the period ("."") in the uiMessageLabel control's assignment statement with a period and two spaces (". "). Or, you could display the salesperson's name on the next line in the uiMessageLabel control. You will use the NewLine character, which you learn about in the next section, to place the name on a separate line.

11   Click the **Exit** button. When you return to the Code Editor window, close the Output window.

The NewLine Character

The NewLine character, which is `Chr(13) & Chr(10)`, instructs the computer to issue a carriage return followed by a line feed. The combination of the carriage return followed by a line feed will advance the insertion point to the next line in the uiMessageLabel control. Whenever you want to start a new line, you simply type the NewLine character at that location in your code. In this case, for example, you want to advance to a new line after displaying the period—in other words, before displaying the salesperson's name.

tip

Chr, which stands for "character," is a function.

You could include the NewLine character in the uiMessageLabel control's assignment statement, like this: `Me.uiMessageLabel.Text = "The sales tax was " & Format (salesTax, "currency") & "." & Chr(13) & Chr(10) & salesPerson`. The disadvantage of using `Chr(13) & Chr(10)` in your code is that it forces you and the next programmer looking at your code to remember that this combination of the Chr function displays a new line. A better way of displaying a new line is to use the `ControlChars.NewLine` constant, like this: `Me.uiMessageLabel.Text = "The sales tax was " & Format (salesTax, "currency") & "." & ControlChars.NewLine & salesPerson`. The `ControlChars.NewLine` constant is an intrinsic constant, which is a named constant built into Visual Basic .NET. The **ControlChars.NewLine** constant advances the insertion point to the next line on the screen.

To use the `ControlChars.NewLine` constant to display the salesperson's name on a separate line:

1   Modify the uiMessageLabel control's assignment statement as indicated in Figure 3-36. This will complete the uiCalcButton Click event procedure.

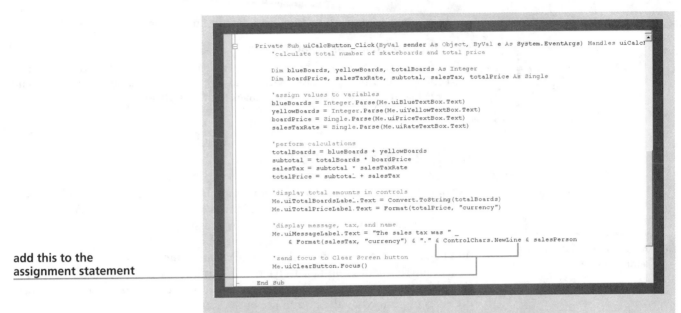

```
Private Sub uiCalcButton_Click(ByVal sender As Object, ByVal e As System.EventArgs) Handles uiCalcl
    'calculate total number of skateboards and total price

    Dim blueBoards, yellowBoards, totalBoards As Integer
    Dim boardPrice, salesTaxRate, subtotal, salesTax, totalPrice As Single

    'assign values to variables
    blueBoards = Integer.Parse(Me.uiBlueTextBox.Text)
    yellowBoards = Integer.Parse(Me.uiYellowTextBox.Text)
    boardPrice = Single.Parse(Me.uiPriceTextBox.Text)
    salesTaxRate = Single.Parse(Me.uiRateTextBox.Text)

    'perform calculations
    totalBoards = blueBoards + yellowBoards
    subtotal = totalBoards * boardPrice
    salesTax = subtotal * salesTaxRate
    totalPrice = subtotal + salesTax

    'display total amounts in controls
    Me.uiTotalBoardsLabel.Text = Convert.ToString(totalBoards)
    Me.uiTotalPriceLabel.Text = Format(totalPrice, "currency")

    'display message, tax, and name
    Me.uiMessageLabel.Text = "The sales tax was " _
        & Format(salesTax, "currency") & "." & ControlChars.NewLine & salesPerson

    'send focus to Clear Screen button
    Me.uiClearButton.Focus()

End Sub
```

add this to the
assignment statement

Figure 3-36: Completed uiCalcButton Click event procedure

2   Save the solution and then start the application. The Name Entry dialog box created by the InputBox function appears first. See Figure 3-37.

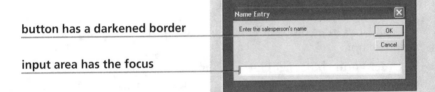

button has a darkened border

input area has the focus

Figure 3-37: Focus and default button shown in the dialog box

Notice that the OK button in the dialog box has a darkened border, even though it does not have the focus; the input area has the focus, as indicated by the position of the insertion point. In Windows terminology, a button that has a darkened border when it does not have the focus is called the default button. You can select a default button by pressing Enter at any time. You try this next.

3   Type your name in the input area of the dialog box. Then, instead of clicking the OK button, simply press **Enter**. The order form appears.

4   Enter the following order:

blue skateboards ordered	10
yellow skateboards ordered	10
skateboard price	100
sales tax rate	.05

5   Click the **Calculate Order** button. Your name now appears on a separate line in the uiMessageLabel control.

6   Click the **Exit** button to end the application. When you return to the Code Editor window, close the Output window.

In the next section, you designate a default button for the order form.

Design Tips

Rules for Assigning the Default Button

- The default button should be the button that is most often selected by the user, except in cases where the tasks performed by the button are both destructive and irreversible. The default button typically is the first button.

Designating a Default Button

A form can have only one default button.

As you already know from using Windows applications, you can select a button by clicking it or by pressing Enter when the button has the focus. If you make a button the **default button**, you also can select it by pressing the Enter key even when the button does not have the focus. When a button is selected, the computer processes the code contained in the button's Click event procedure.

An interface does not have to have a default button. However, if one is used, it should be the button that is most often selected by the user, except in cases where the tasks performed by the button are both destructive and irreversible. For example, a button that deletes information should not be designated as the default button. If you assign a default button in an interface, it typically is the first button, which means that it is on the left when the buttons are positioned horizontally, and on the top when the buttons are stacked vertically. You specify the default button (if any) by setting the form's **AcceptButton property** to the name of the button.

A Windows form also has a CancelButton property, which determines which button's Click event procedure is processed when the user presses the Esc key. A form can have only one cancel button.

To make the Calculate Order button the default button, then save the solution and start the application:

1 Click the **Order Form.vb [Design]** tab to return to the designer window.

2 Click the **form's title bar**, if necessary, to select the form, then set the form's AcceptButton property to **uiCalcButton**. A darkened border appears around the Calculate Order button, as shown in Figure 3-38.

default button has a
darkened border

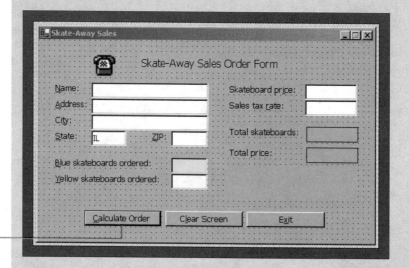

Figure 3-38: Darkened border shown around the Calculate Order button

3   Save the solution, and then start the application. When prompted for the salesperson's name, type your name and press **Enter**.

4   When the order form appears, type **10** as the number of blue skateboards ordered, **10** as the number of yellow skateboards ordered, **100** as the skateboard price, and **.1** as the sales tax rate. Press **Enter** to calculate the order. "The sales tax was $200.00." and your name appears in the uiMessageLabel control.

5   Click the **Exit** button. When you return to the Code Editor window, close the Output window, then close the Code Editor window.

6   Click **File** on the menu bar, then click **Close Solution**.

You now have completed Lesson B. In Lesson C you modify the Skate-Away Sales application so that it requests the salesperson's name before each order is calculated. Now you can either take a break or complete the end-of-lesson questions and exercises before moving on to the next lesson.

SUMMARY

To concatenate strings:

■   Use the concatenation operator—the ampersand (&). Be sure to put a space before and after the ampersand.

To display a dialog box containing a prompt, an input area, an OK button, and a Cancel button:

■   Use the InputBox function, whose syntax is **InputBox**(*prompt*[, *title*][, *defaultResponse*]). The *prompt*, *title*, and *defaultResponse* arguments must be enclosed in quotation marks, unless the information is stored in a variable or named constant. Use sentence capitalization for the *prompt*, but book title capitalization for the *title*.

■   If the user clicks the OK button, the InputBox function returns the value contained in the input area of the dialog box; the value is treated as a string. If the user clicks either the Cancel button or the Close button, the InputBox function returns a zero-length (or empty) string.

To advance the insertion point to the next line:

■   Use the ControlChars.NewLine constant in code.

To make a button the default button:

■   Set the form's AcceptButton property to the name of the button.

QUESTIONS

1. The InputBox function displays a dialog box containing which of the following?
   a. Cancel button
   b. input area
   c. OK button
   d. prompt
   e. All of the above.

2. Which of the following is the concatenation operator?
   a. @
   b. #
   c. $
   d. &
   e. *

3. Assume the `region1` variable contains the string "North" and the `region2` variable contains the string "West". Which of the following will display the string "NorthWest" (one word) in the uiRegionLabel control?
   a. `Me.uiRegionLabel.Text = region1 & region2`
   b. `Me.uiRegionLabel.Text = "region1" & "region2"`
   c. `Me.uiRegionLabel.Text = region1 $ region2`
   d. `Me.uiRegionLabel.Text = region1 # region2`
   e. `Me.uiRegionLabel.Text = region1 @ region2`

4. Assume the `cityName` variable contains the string "Boston" and the `stateName` variable contains the string "MA". Which of the following will display the string "Boston, MA" (the city, a comma, a space, and the state) in the uiAddressLabel control?
   a. `Me.uiAddressLabel.Text = cityName #, & stateName`
   b. `Me.uiAddressLabel.Text = "cityName" & ", " & "stateName"`
   c. `Me.uiAddressLabel.Text = cityName $ ", " $ stateName`
   d. `Me.uiAddressLabel.Text = cityName & ", " & stateName`
   e. `Me.uiAddressLabel.Text = "cityName," & "stateName"`

5. Which of the following intrinsic constants advances the insertion point to the next line?
   a. `Advance`
   b. `ControlChars.Advance`
   c. `ControlChars.NewLine`
   d. `ControlChars.NextLine`
   e. None of the above.

6. If you want to give the user the ability to select a specific button when the button does not have the focus, set the form's _____ property to the name of the button.
   a. AcceptButton
   b. DefaultButton
   c. EnterButton
   d. FocusButton
   e. None of the above.

7. Which of the following statements prompts the user for a number, and then correctly assigns the user's response to a Double variable named `number`?
   a. `InputBox("Enter a number:", "Number") = number`
   b. `number = Double.Parse(InputBox("Enter a number:", "Number"))`
   c. `number = InputBox("Enter a number:", "Number")`
   d. `number = Parse.Double(InputBox("Enter a number:", "Number"))`
   e. `number = Double(InputBox("Enter a number:", "Number"))`

8. Which of the following statements prompts the user for the name of a city, and then correctly assigns the user's response to a String variable named `cityName`?
   a. `InputBox("Enter the city:", "City") = cityName`
   b. `cityName = Chr(InputBox("Enter the city:", "City"))`
   c. `cityName = InputBox("Enter the city:", "City")`
   d. `cityName = String(InputBox("Enter the city:", "City")`
   e. `cityName = Val(InputBox("Enter the city:", "City"))`

9. The InputBox function's *prompt* argument should be entered using _____.
   a. book title capitalization
   b. sentence capitalization

10. The InputBox function's *title* argument should be entered using _____.
    a. book title capitalization
    b. sentence capitalization

EXERCISES

1. In this exercise, you modify the code in an existing application so that it uses variables rather than control properties. The application calculates the commission earned on a salesperson's sales using a commission rate of 10%.
   a. If necessary, start Visual Studio .NET. Open the Commission Solution (Commission Solution.sln) file, which is contained in the VBNET\Chap03\Commission Solution folder.
   b. Make the Calculate Commission button the default button.
   c. Review the code in the Calculate Commission button's Click event procedure. Recode the procedure so that it uses variables rather than control properties in the equation that calculates the commission. Be sure to enter the `Option Explicit On` and `Option Strict On` statements.
   d. Save the solution, then start the application. Test the application by calculating the commission for Mary Smith, whose sales are 7500.
   e. Click the Exit button to end the application.
   f. Close the Output window, then close the solution.

2. In this exercise, you code an application that calculates the square root of a number.
   a. If necessary, start Visual Studio .NET. Open the Square Root Solution (Square Root Solution.sln) file, which is contained in the VBNET\Chap03\Square Root Solution folder.
   b. Make the Calculate Square Root button the default button.
   c. Code the Calculate Square Root button so that it calculates and displays the square root of a whole number. Be sure to assign the numeric equivalent of the uiNumberTextBox.Text property to an Integer variable. Assign the square root of the number to a Single variable. You can use the Math.Sqrt function, whose syntax is **Math.Sqrt**(*number*), to calculate the square root.
   d. Save the solution, then start the application. Test the application by calculating the square root of 144.
   e. Click the Exit button to end the application.
   f. Close the Output window, then close the solution.

3. In this exercise, you code an application for Mingo Sales. The application allows the sales manager to enter the sales made in three states. It should calculate both the total sales made and the total commission earned in the three states.
   a. If necessary, start Visual Studio .NET. Open the Mingo Solution (Mingo Solution.sln) file, which is contained in the VBNET\Chap03\Mingo Solution folder.
   b. Make the Commission button the default button.

c. Code the Exit button so that it ends the application when it is clicked.

d. Use the pseudocode shown in Figure 3-39 to code the Commission button's Click event procedure. (Be sure to use variables.) Format the total sales and the commission using the Standard format style.

Commission button

1. declare variables for the three state sales, the total sales, and the commission

2. assign values to variables

3. calculate total sales = New York sales + Maine sales + Florida sales

4. calculate commission = total sales * 5%

5. display total sales and commission in the uiTotalSalesLabel and uiCommissionLabel controls

6. send the focus to the New York sales text box

Figure 3-39

e. Save the solution, then start the application. Test the application by calculating the total sales and commission for the following sales amounts:

New York sales:	15000
Maine sales:	25000
Florida sales:	10500

f. Click the Exit button to end the application, then close the Output window.

g. Code the form's Load event procedure so that it uses the InputBox function to ask the user for the commission rate before the form appears.

h. Save the solution, then start the application. When you are prompted to enter the commission rate, type .1 (the decimal equivalent of 10%) and then click the OK button. Test the application by calculating the total sales and commission for the following sales amounts:

New York sales:	26000
Maine sales:	34000
Florida sales:	17000

i. Click the Exit button to end the application.

j. Close the Output window, then close the solution.

4. In this exercise, you code an application for IMY Industries. The application should calculate the new hourly pay for each of three job codes, given the current hourly pay for each job code and the raise percentage (entered as a decimal number). The application should display the message "Raise percentage: XX" in a label control on the form. The XX in the message should be replaced by the actual raise percentage, formatted using the Percent format style.

a. If necessary, start Visual Studio .NET. Open the IMY Solution (IMY Solution.sln) file, which is contained in the VBNET\Chap03\IMY Solution folder.

b. Code the Exit button so that it ends the application when it is clicked.

c. Before the form appears, use the InputBox function to prompt the personnel clerk to enter the raise percentage. You will use the raise percentage to calculate the new hourly pay for each job code.

d. Use the pseudocode shown in Figure 3-40 to code the New Hourly Pay button's Click event procedure. Create a named constant for the "Raise percentage:" message. Format the new hourly pay using the Standard format style. Format the raise rate (in the message) using the Percent format style.

New Hourly Pay button

1. declare variables and constant

2. assign values to variables

3. calculate new hourly pay = current hourly pay * raise rate + current hourly pay

4. display new hourly pay in appropriate label controls

5. display message and raise rate in uiMessageLabel control

6. send the focus to the Job Code 1 text box

Figure 3-40

    e. Save the solution, then start the application. When you are prompted to enter the raise percentage, type .05 (the decimal equivalent of 5%) and then click the OK button. Use the following information to calculate the new hourly pay for each job code:

        Current hourly pay for job code 1:   5

        Current hourly pay for job code 2:   6.5

        Current hourly pay for job code 3:   8.75

    f. Click the Exit button to end the application.

    g. Close the Output window, then close the solution.

5. In this exercise, you modify the application that you coded in Exercise 4. The application now will allow the user to enter a separate raise percentage for each job code.

    a. If necessary, start Visual Studio .NET. Open the IMY Solution (IMY Solution.sln) file, which is contained in the VBNET\Chap03\IMY Solution folder.

    b. Modify the application's code so that it asks the personnel clerk to enter the raise for each job code separately. (*Hint*: Use three InputBox functions in the form's Load event procedure.)

    c. Display the following information on separate lines in the uiMessageLabel control (be sure to replace XX with the appropriate raise percentage):

        Job Code 1: XX%

        Job Code 2: XX%

        Job Code 3: XX%

    d. Save the solution, then start the application. When you are prompted to enter the raise percentages for the job codes, use .03 for job code 1, .05 for job code 2, and .045 for job code 3.

    e. Use the following information to calculate the new hourly pay for each job code:

        Current hourly pay for job code 1:   5

        Current hourly pay for job code 2:   6.5

        Current hourly pay for job code 3:   8.75

    f. Click the Exit button to end the application.

    g. Close the Output window, then close the solution.

Use the information shown in Figure 3-41 to complete Exercises 6 through 8.

Variable/Constant name	Contents
cityName	Madison
stateName	WI
zipCode	53711
MESSAGE	The capital of

Figure 3-41

6. Using the information shown in Figure 3-41, write an assignment statement that displays the string "Madison, WI" in the uiAddressLabel control.

7. Using the information shown in Figure 3-41, write an assignment statement that displays the string "The capital of WI is Madison." in the uiAddressLabel control.

8. Using the information shown in Figure 3-41, write an assignment statement that displays the string "My ZIP code is 53711." in the uiAddressLabel control. (The **zipCode** variable is a String variable.)

discovery ▶ 9. In this exercise, you learn about the CancelButton property of a Windows form.
   a. If necessary, start Visual Studio .NET. Open the Cancel Solution (Cancel Solution.sln) file, which is contained in the VBNET\Chap03\Cancel Solution folder.
   b. Open the Code Editor window and view the existing code.
   c. Start the application. Type your first name in the text box, then press Enter to select the Clear button, which is the form's default button. The Clear button removes your name from the text box.
   d. Click the Undo button. Your name reappears in the text box.
   e. Click the Exit button to end the application, then close the Output window.
   f. Return to the designer window. Set the form's CancelButton property to uiUndoButton. This tells the computer to process the code in the Undo button's Click event procedure when the user presses the Esc key.
   g. Save the solution, then start the application.
   h. Type your first name in the text box, then press Enter to select the Clear button.
   i. Press Esc to select the Undo button. Your name reappears in the text box.
   j. Click the Exit button to end the application.
   k. Close the Output window, then close the solution.

discovery ▶ 10. In this exercise, you learn about the Object Browser, which is a window that provides information about the various objects available to your application. The information includes properties, methods, events, and intrinsic constants.
   a. If necessary, start Visual Studio .NET. Open the Order Solution (Order Solution.sln) file, which is contained in the VBNET\Chap03\Order Solution folder.
   b. Open the Object Browser window by clicking View on the menu bar, and then clicking Object Browser. Click the Find Symbol button in the Object Browser window. (If you cannot locate the Find Symbol button, refer to Figure 3-42.) When the Find Symbol dialog box opens, type *math* in the Find what box, as shown in Figure 3-42.

Find Symbol button

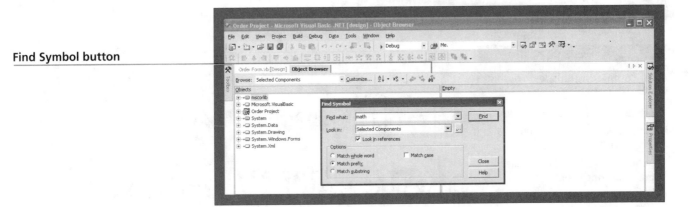

Figure 3-42

c. Click the Find button in the dialog box. The Find Symbol Results window opens.

d. Right-click Math (System) in the Find Symbol Results window, then click Browse Definition. Close the Find Symbol Results window.

e. Scroll to the bottom of the Members of 'Math' list box. What is the value assigned to the E named constant? What is the value assigned to the PI named constant?

f. Click the Find Symbol button. Use the Find Symbol dialog box to find the word *color*. Right-click Color (System.Drawing) in the Find Symbol Results window, then click Browse Definition. Close the Find Symbol Results window.

g. Scroll the Members of 'Color' list box to view the various color settings.

h. Close the Object Browser window, then close the solution.

LESSON C

After completing this lesson, you will be able to:

■ Include a static variable in code

■ Code the TextChanged event procedure

■ Create a procedure that handles more than one event

Modifying the Skate-Away Sales Application's Code

Modifying the Code in the Load and uiCalcButton Click Procedures

Mr. Cousard, the sales manager at Skate-Away Sales, asks you to make an additional change to the order form that you completed in Lesson B. Currently, the order form allows the user to enter the salesperson's name only once, when the application first starts. Mr. Cousard would like to have the order form ask for the salesperson's name each time an order is calculated. This way, while a salesperson is at lunch or on a break, another salesperson can use the same computer to take an order, without having to start the application again.

As you learned in Lesson B, before making modifications to an application's existing code, you should review the application's documentation and revise the necessary documents. First, view the revised TOE chart, which is shown in Figure 3-43. Changes made to the TOE chart from Lesson B are shaded in the figure. (Lesson B's TOE chart is shown in Figure 3-16.) Notice that the Calculate Order button's Click event procedure, rather than the OrderForm's Load event procedure, now is responsible for getting the salesperson's name.

Task	Object	Event
1. Get the salesperson's name	uiCalcButton	Click
2. Calculate the total skateboards ordered and the total price		
3. Display the total skateboards ordered and the total price in the uiTotalBoardsLabel and uiTotalPriceLabel		
4. Calculate the sales tax		
5. Display the message, sales tax, and salesperson's name in the uiMessageLabel		
Clear the screen for the next order	uiClearButton	Click
End the application	uiExitButton	Click
Display the total skateboards ordered (from uiCalcButton)	uiTotalBoardsLabel	None
Display the total price (from uiCalcButton)	uiTotalPriceLabel	None
Get and display the order information	uiNameTextBox, uiAddressTextBox, uiCityTextBox, uiStateTextBox, uiZipTextBox, uiPriceTextBox, uiRateTextBox, uiBlueTextBox, uiYellowTextBox	None
~~Get the salesperson's name~~	~~OrderForm~~	~~Load~~
Display the message, sales tax, and salesperson's name (from uiCalcButton)	uiMessageLabel	None

Figure 3-43: Revised TOE chart

Next, view the revised pseudocode for the Calculate Order button's Click event procedure, which is shown in Figure 3-44. Changes made to the pseudocode from Lesson B are shaded in the figure. (Lesson B's pseudocode is shown in Figure 3-18.)

Calculate Order button

1. declare variables and named constants

2. assign values to variables

3. get the salesperson's name

4. calculate total skateboards = blue skateboards + yellow skateboards

5. calculate subtotal = total skateboards * skateboard price

6. calculate sales tax = subtotal * sales tax rate

7. calculate total price = subtotal + sales tax

8. display total skateboards and total price in uiTotalBoardsLabel and uiTotalPriceLabel controls

9. display "The sales tax was" message, sales tax, and salesperson's name in the uiMessageLabel control

10. send the focus to the Clear Screen button

Figure 3-44: Revised pseudocode for the Calculate Order button

First, open the Skate-Away Sales application and move the code contained in the OrderForm's Load event procedure to the uiCalcButton's Click event procedure.

To open the application and move the code:

1. Start Microsoft Visual Studio .NET, if necessary, and close the Start Page window.

2. Open the **Order Solution** (Order Solution.sln) file contained in the VBNET\Chap03\Order Solution folder.

3. Open the Code Editor window.

4. Locate the OrderForm Load event procedure. Highlight the two Const statements in the procedure. Click **Edit** on the menu bar, and then click **Cut**.

It is customary to place any procedure-level constant declaration statements at the beginning of the procedure, above the Dim statements.

5. Locate the uiCalcButton Click event procedure. Position the insertion point in the blank line above the first Dim statement in the procedure, then press **Enter** to insert a new blank line. With the insertion point in the new blank line, click **Edit** on the menu bar, and then click **Paste** to paste the two Const statements into the procedure.

6. Return to the OrderForm Load event procedure. Highlight the second comment and the assignment statement. Click **Edit** on the menu bar, and then click **Cut**.

7. Return to the uiCalcButton Click event procedure. Position the insertion point in the blank line below the `salesTaxRate = Single.Parse(Me.uiRateTextBox.Text)` statement, then press **Enter** to insert a new blank line. With the insertion point in the new blank line, click **Edit** on the menu bar, and then click **Paste** to paste the comment and assignment statement into the procedure. Press **Enter** to insert a new blank line below the assignment statement.

8. Remove the word *module-level* from the comment. Figure 3-45 shows the current status of the uiCalcButton Click event procedure. (The procedure's `End Sub` statement does not appear in the figure.)

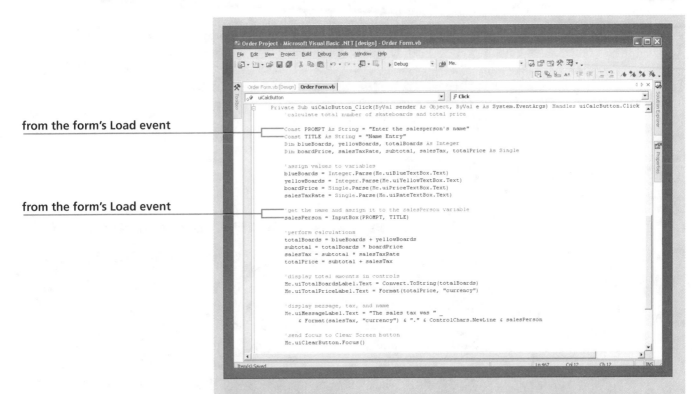

from the form's Load event

from the form's Load event

Figure 3-45: Current status of the uiCalcButton Click event procedure

9 Return to the OrderForm Load event procedure. Highlight the remaining lines in the procedure, beginning with the `Private Sub` line and ending with the `End Sub` line. Press **Delete** to delete the lines from the Code Editor window.

Now that you have moved the InputBox function from the OrderForm's Load event procedure to the uiCalcButton Click event procedure, only one procedure— the uiCalcButton Click event procedure—needs to use the `salesPerson` variable. Therefore, you can move the statement that declares the `salesPerson` variable from the form's Declarations section to the uiCalcButton Click event procedure. Additionally, you will need to change the keyword `Private` to the keyword `Dim`. Recall that you use the `Private` keyword to create module-level variables, and the `Dim` keyword to create procedure-level variables.

To move the `salesPerson` variable declaration statement, then modify the statement, and then save the solution and start the application:

1 Locate the form's Declarations section. Highlight the `'declare module-level variable` comment, then press **Delete** to delete the comment.

2 Highlight the `Private salesPerson As String` statement in the Declarations section. Click **Edit** on the menu bar, and then click **Cut**.

3 Locate the uiCalcButton Click event procedure. Position the insertion point in the blank line below the second Dim statement in the procedure. Click **Edit** on the menu bar, and then click **Paste** to paste the `Private` statement in the procedure, then press **Enter** to insert a blank line below the statement. Notice that a jagged line appears below the keyword `Private`. The jagged line indicates that there is something wrong with the statement. To determine the problem, you need simply to rest your mouse pointer somewhere on the word (or words) immediately above the jagged line.

4   Rest your mouse pointer on the word **Private**. A message appears in a box, as shown in Figure 3-46.

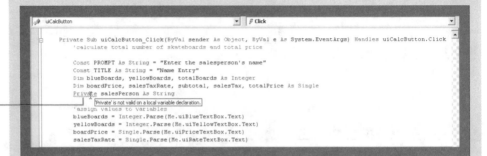

the jagged line indicates a syntax error in the code

Figure 3-46: Message that appears when you rest your mouse pointer on the word **Private**

The message indicates that the word **Private** is not valid on a local variable declaration.

5   Change **Private** in the variable declaration statement to **Dim**.

Now save the solution and start it to verify that the application works correctly.

6   Save the solution, then start the application. The order form appears.

7   Type **10** as the number of blue skateboards ordered, **10** as the number of yellow skateboards ordered, **100** as the skateboard price, and **.1** as the sales tax rate. Press **Enter** to calculate the order. The Name Entry dialog box created by the InputBox function appears.

8   Type your name in the Name Entry dialog box, then press **Enter**. "The sales tax was $200.00." and your name appear in the uiMessageLabel control.

9   Click the **Calculate Order** button. Notice that the Name Entry dialog box requires the user to enter the salesperson's name again. It would be more efficient for the user if the salesperson's name appeared as the default response the second and subsequent times the Calculate Order button is clicked.

10 Click the **Cancel** button in the dialog box. Notice that no name appears in the uiMessageLabel; this is because the InputBox function returns a zero-length (empty) string when you click the Cancel button in the dialog box.

11 Click the **Exit** button on the order form. When you return to the Code Editor window, close the Output window.

tip

Recall that when you click the Cancel button in the InputBox function's dialog box, the function returns a zero-length (empty) string.

Recall that the InputBox function allows you to specify a default response, which appears in the input area of the dialog box when the dialog box is opened. Observe the effect of using the contents of the `salesPerson` variable as the default response.

To modify the InputBox function:

1   Change the `salesPerson = InputBox(PROMPT, TITLE)` statement in the uiCalcButton Click event procedure to **salesPerson = InputBox(PROMPT, TITLE, salesPerson)**.

2   Save the solution, then start the application.

3   Enter the following order:

    blue skateboards ordered   5

    yellow skateboards ordered   5

    skateboard price   20

    sales tax rate   .05

4   Click the **Calculate Order** button to calculate the order. Type your name in the Name Entry dialog box, then press **Enter**. "The sales tax was $10.00." and your name appear in the uiMessageLabel control.

5   Click the **Calculate Order** button again. Notice that your name still does not appear in the input area of the dialog box. This is because the `salesPerson` variable is both created in and removed from the computer's internal memory each time you click the Calculate Order button. (Recall that the `Dim` statement creates the variable in memory, and the variable is removed from memory when the `End Sub` statement is processed.)

To display the salesperson's name in the dialog box when the Calculate Order button is clicked the second and subsequent times, you need to use a static variable.

6   Click the **Cancel** button in the dialog box, then click the **Exit** button on the order form to end the application. When you return to the Code Editor window, close the Output window.

Static Variables

A **static variable** is a procedure-level variable that retains its value even when the procedure in which it is declared ends. Similar to a module-level variable, a static variable is not removed from memory until the application ends. You declare a static variable using the `Static` keyword, like this: **Static** *variablename* [**As** *datatype*] [= *initialvalue*].

To declare the `salesPerson` variable as a static variable, then test the application:

1   Change the `Dim salesPerson As String` statement in the uiCalcButton Click event procedure to **Static salesPerson As String**. See Figure 3-47. (The Code Editor's font size was changed so that you could view more of the code in the figure. The `End Sub` line is not visible in the figure.)

static variable declaration ————————

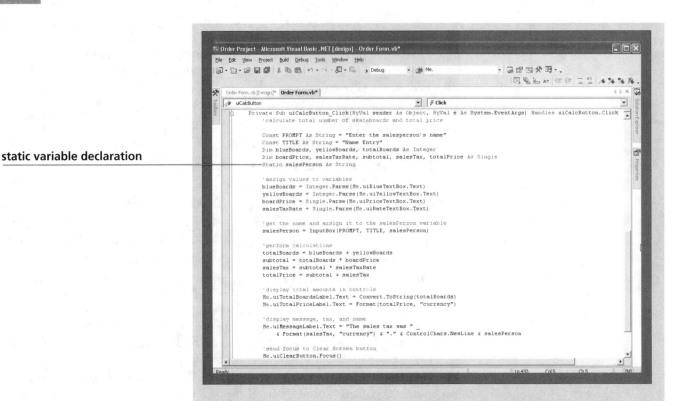

Figure 3-47: Static variable declared in the uiCalcButton Click event procedure

2 Save the solution, then start the application.

3 Enter the following order:

blue skateboards ordered	5
yellow skateboards ordered	5
skateboard price	20
sales tax rate	.05

4 Press **Enter** to calculate the order. Type your name in the Name Entry dialog box, and then press **Enter**. The application calculates and displays the total skateboards ordered (10), total price ($210.00), and sales tax ($10.00). "The sales tax was $10.00." and your name appear in the uiMessageLabel control.

5 Enter **20** as the number of blue skateboards ordered. Notice that, at this point, the total skateboards ordered, the total price, and the sales tax amount shown on the order form are incorrect, because they do not reflect the change in the order of blue skateboards. To display the correct amounts, you will need to recalculate the order by selecting the Calculate Order button.

6 Press **Enter** to recalculate the order. Notice that your name appears highlighted in the input area of the Name Entry dialog box. Press **Enter** to select the OK button in the Name Entry dialog box. The application calculates and displays the total skateboards ordered (25), total price ($525.00), and sales tax ($25.00). "The sales tax was $25.00." and your name appear in the uiMessageLabel control.

7 Click the **Exit** button to end the application. When you return to the Code Editor window, close the Output window.

Having the previously calculated figures remain on the screen when a change is made to the interface could be misleading. A better approach is to clear the total skateboards ordered, total price, and sales tax message when a change is made to one of the following input items: the number of blue skateboards ordered, the number of yellow skateboards ordered, the skateboard price, or the sales tax rate.

Coding the TextChanged Event Procedure

A control's **TextChanged event** occurs when the contents of a control's Text property change. This can happen as a result of either the user entering data into the control, or the application's code assigning data to the control's Text property. In the next set of steps, you code the uiBlueTextBox TextChanged event procedure so that it clears the contents of the uiTotalBoardsLabel, uiTotalPriceLabel, and uiMessageLabel controls when the user changes the number of blue skateboards ordered.

To code the uiBlueTextBox TextChanged event procedure, then test the procedure:

1 Click the **Class Name** list arrow in the Code Editor window, then click **uiBlueTextBox** in the list. Click the **Method Name** list arrow. Scroll the list until you see TextChanged, and then click **TextChanged**. The uiBlueTextBox's TextChanged event procedure appears in the Code Editor window.

2 Enter the comment and three assignment statements shown in Figure 3-48.

enter this comment and these lines of code

```
Private Sub uiBlueTextBox_TextChanged(ByVal sender As Object, ByVal e As System.EventArgs) Handles
    'clears the total boards, total price, and message

    Me.uiTotalBoardsLabel.Text = ""
    Me.uiTotalPriceLabel.Text = ""
    Me.uiMessageLabel.Text = ""

End Sub
```

Figure 3-48: Comment and assignment statements entered in the uiBlueTextBox's TextChanged event procedure

Now test the procedure to verify that it is working correctly.

3 Save the solution, then start the application.

4 Enter **5** as the number of blue skateboards ordered, **15** as the number of yellow skateboards ordered, **100** as the skateboard price, and **.05** as the sales tax rate. Press **Enter** to calculate the order.

5 Type your name in the Name Entry dialog box, then press **Enter** to select the OK button. The application calculates the total skateboards ordered (20), total price ($2,100.00), and sales tax ($100.00).

6 Change the number of blue skateboards ordered to 3. Notice that when you make a change to the number of blue skateboards ordered, the application clears the total skateboards ordered, total price, and message information from the form.

7 Click the **Exit** button to end the application. When you return to the Code Editor window, close the Output window.

Recall that you also want to clear the total skateboards ordered, total price, and message information when a change is made to the number of yellow skateboards ordered, skateboard price, or sales tax rate. You could code the TextChanged event procedure for the uiYellowTextBox, uiPriceTextBox, and uiRateTextBox controls separately, as you did with the uiBlueTextBox control.

However, an easier way is simply to create one procedure for the computer to process when the TextChanged event of any of these controls occurs.

Associating a Procedure With Different Objects or Events

As you learned in Chapter 1, the keyword `Handles` appears in a procedure header and indicates the object and event associated with the procedure. For example, the `Handles uiBlueTextBox.TextChanged` that appears at the end of the procedure header shown in Figure 3-49 indicates, not surprisingly, that the uiBlueTextBox_TextChanged procedure is associated with the TextChanged event of the uiBlueTextBox control. In other words, the uiBlueTextBox_TextChanged procedure will be processed when the TextChanged event of the uiBlueTextBox control occurs.

procedure name

Handles **keyword**

names of object and event

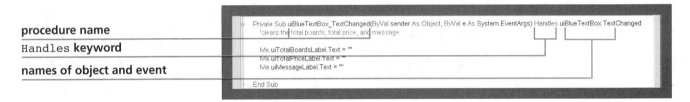

```
Private Sub uiBlueTextBox_TextChanged(ByVal sender As Object, ByVal e As System.EventArgs) Handles uiBlueTextBox.TextChanged
    'clears the total boards, total price, and message

    Me.uiTotalBoardsLabel.Text = ""
    Me.uiTotalPriceLabel.Text = ""
    Me.uiMessageLabel.Text = ""

End Sub
```

Figure 3-49: `Handles` keyword shown in the procedure

Although the procedure name (uiBlueTextBox_TextChanged) shown in Figure 3-49 contains the object name (uiBlueTextBox) and event name (TextChanged), both of which appear after the `Handles` keyword, that is not a requirement. You can change the name of the procedure to anything you like. You also can associate a procedure with more than one object and event. To do so, you simply list each object and event, separated by commas, in the `Handles` section of the procedure header. In the Skate-Away Sales application, you will change the name of the uiBlueTextBox_TextChanged procedure to ClearControls. You then will associate the ClearControls procedure with the uiBlueTextBox.TextChanged, uiYellowTextBox.TextChanged, uiPriceTextBox.TextChanged, and uiRateTextBox.TextChanged events.

To change the uiBlueTextBox_TextChanged procedure's name to ClearControls, and then associate the procedure with different objects and events:

1   Change `uiBlueTextBox_TextChanged`, which appears after `Private Sub` in the procedure header, to **ClearControls**.

2   In the ClearControls procedure header, position the insertion point immediately before the letter H in the word `Handles`. Type _ (the underscore, which is the line continuation character). Be sure there is a space between the ending parentheses and the underscore.

3   Press **Enter** to move the `Handles` portion of the procedure header to the next line in the procedure. Press **Tab** two times to indent the line.

4   Position the insertion point immediately after `Handles uiBlueTextBox.TextChanged`.

The ClearControls procedure is already associated with the uiBlueTextBox.TextChanged event. You just need to associate it with the uiYellowTextBox.TextChanged, uiPriceTextBox.TextChanged, and uiRateTextBox.TextChanged events.

5 Type , (a comma). Scroll the list of object names until you see uiYellowTextBox. Click **uiYellowTextBox** in the list, and then press **Tab** to enter the object name in the procedure.

6 Type . (a period), then scroll the list of event names until you see TextChanged. Click **TextChanged**, and then press **Tab**. Type , _ (a comma, a space, and an underscore) and press **Enter**.

7 Press the **Spacebar** to display the listing of object names, then enter the additional code shown in Figure 3-50.

enter this code

```
Private Sub ClearControls(ByVal sender As Object, ByVal e As System.EventArgs) _
     Handles uiBlueTextBox.TextChanged, uiYellowTextBox.TextChanged, _
        uiPriceTextBox.TextChanged, uiRateTextBox.TextChanged
     'clears the total boards, total price, and message

     Me.uiTotalBoardsLabel.Text = ""
     Me.uiTotalPriceLabel.Text = ""
     Me.uiMessageLabel.Text = ""

End Sub
```

Figure 3-50: Completed ClearControls procedure

Now test the ClearControls procedure to verify that it is working correctly.

To test the ClearControls procedure:

1 Save the solution, then start the application.

2 Enter 5 as the number of blue skateboards ordered, **10** as the number of yellow skateboards ordered, **100** as the skateboard price, and **.05** as the sales tax rate. Press **Enter** to calculate the order.

3 Type your name in the Name Entry dialog box, then press **Enter** to select the OK button. The application calculates the total skateboards ordered (15), total price ($1,575.00), and sales tax ($75.00).

4 Change the skateboard price to 50. When you do so, the application clears the total skateboards ordered, total price, and message information from the form.

5 Click the **Calculate Order** button, then click the **OK** button in the Name Entry dialog box.

6 On your own, verify that the ClearControls procedure clears the appropriate information when a change is made to the number of blue skateboards ordered, the number of yellow skateboards ordered, or the sales tax rate. As you are testing, be sure to enter a valid number in the text boxes for the blue and yellow skateboards ordered, as well as for the skateboard price and the sales tax rate. Currently, the program will not work correctly if one of the text boxes is empty, or if one contains a character that is not a number. This is because the Parse methods used in the uiCalcButton's Click event procedure cannot convert the empty string or a letter to a numeric value. You learn how to fix this problem in Chapter 4. For now, just be sure to enter valid data while you are testing the application.

7 When you have finished testing the application, click the **Exit** button. When you return to the Code Editor window, close the Output window.

8 Click **File** on the menu bar, and then click **Close Solution** to close the solution.

You now have completed Chapter 3. You can either take a break or complete the end-of-lesson questions and exercises.

SUMMARY

To create a static variable:

■ Use a declaration statement that follows the syntax **Static** *variablename* [**As** *datatype*] [= *initialvalue*].

To process code when the contents of a control have changed:

■ Enter the code in the control's TextChanged event.

To create a procedure for more than one object or event:

■ List each object and event (using the syntax *object*.*event*) after the `Handles` keyword in the procedure.

QUESTIONS

1. A _____ variable is a procedure-level variable that retains its value after the procedure in which it is declared ends.
   a. consistent
   b. constant
   c. static
   d. stationary
   e. term

2. Which of the following statements declares a procedure-level variable that retains its value after the procedure in which it is declared ends?
   a. `Const counter As Integer`
   b. `Dim counter As Constant`
   c. `Dim counter As Integer`
   d. `Static counter As Integer`
   e. `Term counter As Integer`

3. The _____ event occurs when the contents of a text box have changed.
   a. Change
   b. Changed
   c. Text
   d. TextChange
   e. TextChanged

4. Assume you have a procedure named GetNumber. Which of the following instructions indicates that the procedure should be processed when the user clicks either the uiNum1TextBox or the uiNum2TextBox?
   a. `Private Sub GetNumber(ByVal sender As Object, ByVal e As System.EventArgs) Handles uiNum1TextBox.Click, uiNum2TextBox.Click`
   b. `Private Sub GetNumber(ByVal sender As Object, ByVal e As System.EventArgs) Handles uiNum1TextBox, uiNum2TextBox`

c. `Private Sub GetNumber(ByVal sender As Object, ByVal e As System.EventArgs) Handles uiNum1TextBox.Click and uiNum2TextBox.Click`

d. `Private Sub GetNumber(ByVal sender As Object, ByVal e As System.EventArgs) Handles Click for uiNum1TextBox, uiNum2TextBox`

e. None of the above.

E X E R C I S E S

1. In this exercise, you code an application that allows the user to enter a person's first name and last name, and then uses string concatenation to display the last name, a comma, a space, and the first name in a label control.

    a. If necessary, start Visual Studio .NET. Open the Name Solution (Name Solution.sln) file, which is contained in the VBNET\Chap03\Name Solution folder.

    b. Code the form's Load event procedure so that it uses two InputBox functions to prompt the user to enter his or her first name and last name. Assign the results of both functions to variables.

    c. Code the Display button's Click event procedure so that it displays the user's last name, a comma, a space, and the user's first name in the uiNameLabel control.

    d. Save the solution, then start the application. Test the application by entering your first and last names, and then clicking the Display button.

    e. Click the Exit button to end the application.

    f. Close the Output window, then close the solution.

2. In this exercise, you create an application that allows the user to enter a number of pennies. The application then calculates the number of dollars, quarters, dimes, nickels, and pennies that the user would receive if he or she cashed in the pennies at a bank.

    a. If necessary, start Visual Studio .NET. Create a blank solution named Pennies Solution. Save the solution in the VBNET\Chap03 folder.

    b. Add a Visual Basic .NET Windows Application project to the solution. Name the project Pennies Project.

    c. Assign the filename Pennies Form.vb to the form file object.

    d. Assign the name MoneyForm to the Windows Form object.

    e. The design of the interface is up to you. Use the GUI design guidelines listed in Appendix B to verify that the interface you create adheres to the GUI standards outlined in this book. Code the application appropriately. (*Hint*: Review the arithmetic operators listed in Figure 2-34 in Chapter 2.)

    f. Save the solution, then start the application. Test the application twice, using the following data: 2311 pennies and 7333 pennies.

    g. Stop the application.

    h. Close the Output window, then close the solution.

3. In this exercise, you create an application that can help students in grades 1 through 6 learn how to make change. The application should allow the student to enter the amount of money the customer owes and the amount of money the customer paid. It then should calculate the amount of change, as well as how many dollars, quarters, dimes, nickels, and pennies to return to the customer. For now, you do not have to worry about the situation where the price is greater than what the customer pays. You can assume that the customer paid either the exact amount or more than the exact amount.

    a. If necessary, start Visual Studio .NET. Create a blank solution named Change Solution. Save the solution in the VBNET\Chap03 folder.

    b. Add a Visual Basic .NET Windows Application project to the solution. Name the project Change Project.

c. Assign the filename Change Form.vb to the form file object.

d. Assign the name ChangeForm to the Windows Form object.

e. The design of the interface is up to you. Use the GUI design guidelines listed in Appendix B to verify that the interface you create adheres to the GUI standards outlined in this book. Code the application appropriately. (*Hint*: Review the arithmetic operators listed in Figure 2-34 in Chapter 2.)

f. Save the solution, then start the application. Test the application three times, using the following data:

75.33 as the amount owed and 80.00 as the amount paid

39.67 as the amount owed and 50.00 as the amount paid

45.55 as the amount owed and 45.55 as the amount paid

g. Stop the application.

h. Close the Output window, then close the solution.

discovery ▶ 4. In this exercise, you experiment with a **Static** variable.

a. If necessary, start Visual Studio .NET. Open the Static Solution (Static Solution.sln) file, which is contained in the VBNET\Chap03\Static Solution folder. The application is supposed to count the number of times the Count button is pressed, but it is not working correctly.

b. Start the application. Click the Count button. The message indicates that you have pressed the Count button once, which is correct.

c. Click the Count button several more times. Notice that the message still displays the number 1.

d. Click the Exit button to end the application. Close the Output window.

e. Open the Code Editor window. The uiCountButton's Click event procedure first uses a **Dim** statement to declare a procedure-level variable named **counter**. It then adds 1 to the **counter** variable, and then displays the variable's value in the uiCounterLabel control on the form.

f. Modify the uiCountButton's Click event procedure so that it uses a static variable.

g. Save the solution, then start the application.

h. Click the Count button several times. Each time you click the Count button, the message changes to indicate the number of times the button was clicked.

i. Click the Exit button to end the application.

j. Close the Output window, then close the solution.

debugging 5. In this exercise, you debug an existing application. The purpose of this exercise is to demonstrate the problems that can occur when using the InputBox function.

a. If necessary, start Visual Studio .NET. Open the Debug Solution (Debug Solution.sln) file, which is contained in the VBNET\Chap03\Debug Solution folder.

b. Start the application. Click the Compute Sum button, then click the OK button in the First Number dialog box without entering a number. Read the error message that appears in a message box.

c. Click the Break button. Notice that the first assignment statement is causing the problem. Click Debug on the menu bar, and then click Stop Debugging.

d. Start the application again. Click the Compute Sum button. Type 3 in the input area of the First Number dialog box, then click the OK button. When the Second Number dialog box appears, click the Cancel button. Read the error message that appears in a message box.

e. Click the Break button. Notice that the second assignment statement is causing the problem. Click Debug on the menu bar, and then click Stop Debugging.

f. Use the Val function to correct the code so that the application does not result in an error message when the user clicks the OK button without entering any data, or when he or she clicks the Cancel button.

g. Start the application. Click the Compute Sum button, then click the OK button in the First Number dialog box without entering any data. Click the Cancel button in the second dialog box. The application should not result in an error message.

h. Stop the application. Close the output window, then close the solution.

The Selection Structure

Creating a Monthly Payment Calculator Application

case ▶ After weeks of car shopping, Herman Juarez still has not decided what car to purchase. Recently, Herman has noticed that many auto dealers, in an effort to boost sales, are offering buyers a choice of either a large cash rebate or an extremely low financing rate, much lower than the rate Herman would pay by financing the car through his local credit union. Herman is not sure whether to take the lower financing rate from the dealer, or take the rebate and then finance the car through the credit union. He has asked you to create an application that he can use to calculate and display the monthly payment on a car loan.

Previewing the Completed Application

Before creating the Monthly Payment Calculator application, you first preview the completed application.

To preview the completed application:

1   Use the Run command on the Windows Start menu to run the **Payment** (Payment.exe) file, which is contained in the VBNET\Chap04 folder on your computer's hard disk. The Monthly Payment Calculator application's user interface appears on the screen.

Calculate the monthly payment on a $9,000 loan at 5% interest for 3 years.

2   Type **9000** in the Principal text box, and then press **Tab**.

3   Type **5** in the Rate text box, and then press **Enter** to select the Calculate Monthly Payment button, which is the default button on the form. A message box containing the message "The principal, rate, and term must be numbers." appears on the screen, as shown in Figure 4-1. You learn how to create a message box in Lesson B.

message box

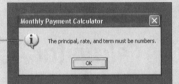

Figure 4-1: Monthly Payment Calculator application's user interface

4   Press **Enter** to select the OK button in the message box.

5   Press **Tab** to move the insertion point into the Term text box. Type **3** in the Term text box, then press **Enter**. The application calculates and displays a monthly payment amount of $268.62, as shown in Figure 4-2.

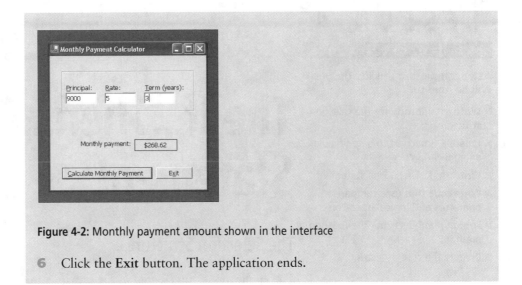

Figure 4-2: Monthly payment amount shown in the interface

6   Click the **Exit** button. The application ends.

Before you can begin coding the Monthly Payment Calculator application, you need to learn about the selection structure; you learn that structure in Lesson A. In Lesson B, you complete the Monthly Payment Calculator application's interface as you learn how to use a GroupBox control. You begin coding the application in Lesson B, and complete the application in Lesson C.

After completing this lesson, you will be able to:

- Write pseudocode for the selection structure
- Create a flowchart to help you plan an application's code
- Write an If...Then...Else statement
- Write code that uses comparison operators and logical operators
- Format numbers using the ToString method
- Change the case of a string

tip

As you may remember from Chapter 1, the selection structure is one of three programming structures. The other two programming structures are sequence, which was covered in the previous chapters, and repetition, which is covered in Chapter 6.

The If...Then...Else Statement

The Selection Structure

The applications you created in the previous three chapters used the sequence programming structure only, where a procedure's instructions are processed, one after another, in the order in which each appears in the procedure. In many applications, however, the next instruction processed depends on the result of a decision or comparison that the program must make. For example, a payroll program typically compares the number of hours the employee worked with the number 40 to determine whether the employee should receive overtime pay in addition to regular pay. Based on the result of that comparison, the program then selects either an instruction that computes regular pay only or an instruction that computes regular pay plus overtime pay.

You use the **selection structure**, also called the **decision structure**, when you want a program to make a decision or comparison and then select one of two paths, depending on the result of that decision or comparison. Although the idea of using the selection structure in a program is new, the concept of the selection structure is already familiar to you, because you use it each day to make hundreds of decisions. For example, every morning you have to decide if you are hungry and, if you are, what you are going to eat. Figure 4-3 shows other examples of selection structures you might use today.

	Example 1	Example 2
condition	if *it is raining*	if *you have a test tomorrow*
condition	wear a raincoat	study tonight
	bring an umbrella	otherwise
		watch a movie

Figure 4-3: Selection structures you might use today

In the examples shown in Figure 4-3, the portion in *italics*, called the **condition**, specifies the decision you are making and is phrased so that it results in either a true or false answer only. For example, either it is raining (true) or it is not raining (false); either you have a test tomorrow (true) or you do not have a test tomorrow (false).

If the condition is true, you perform a specific set of tasks. If the condition is false, on the other hand, you might or might not need to perform a different set of tasks. For instance, look at the first example shown in Figure 4-3. If it is raining (a true condition), then you will wear a raincoat and bring an umbrella. Notice that you do not have anything in particular to do if it is not raining (a false condition). Compare this with the second example shown in Figure 4-3. If you have a test tomorrow (a true condition), then you will study tonight. However, if you do not have a test tomorrow (a false condition), then you will watch a movie.

Like you, the computer also can evaluate a condition and then select the appropriate tasks to perform based on that evaluation. When using the selection structure in a program, the programmer must be sure to phrase the condition so that it results in either a true or a false answer only. The programmer also must specify the tasks to be performed when the condition is true and, if necessary, the tasks to be performed when the condition is false.

Visual Basic .NET provides four forms of the selection structure: If, If/Else, If/ElseIf/Else, and Case. You learn about If and If/Else selection structures in this chapter. If/ElseIf/Else and Case selection structures are covered in Chapter 5. (Chapter 5 also covers nested selection structures. A nested selection structure is a selection structure that is contained entirely within another selection structure.)

Writing Pseudocode for If and If/Else Selection Structures

An **If selection structure** contains only one set of instructions, which are processed when the condition is true. An **If/Else selection structure**, on the other hand, contains two sets of instructions: one set is processed when the condition is true and the other set is processed when the condition is false. Figure 4-4 shows examples of both the If and the If/Else structures written in pseudocode.

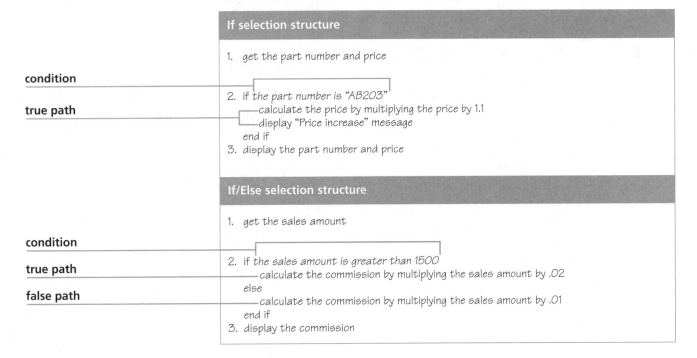

Figure 4-4: Examples of the If and If/Else structures written in pseudocode

Although pseudocode is not standardized—every programmer has his or her own version—you will find some similarities among the various versions. For example, many programmers begin the selection structure with the word "if" and end the structure with the two words "end if"; they also use the word "else" to designate the instructions to be performed when the condition is false.

In the examples shown in Figure 4-4, the italicized portion of the instruction indicates the condition to be evaluated. Notice that each condition results in either a true or a false answer only. In Example 1, either the part number is "AB203" or it isn't. In Example 2, either the sales amount is greater than the number 1500 or it isn't.

When the condition is true, the set of instructions following the condition is selected for processing. The instructions following the condition are referred to as the **true path**—the path you follow when the condition is true. The true path ends when you come to the "else" or, if there is no "else", when you come to the end of the selection structure (the "end if"). After the true path instructions are processed, the instruction following the "end if" is processed. In the examples shown in Figure 4-4, the display instructions are processed after the instructions in the true path.

The instructions processed when the condition is false depend on whether the selection structure contains an "else". When there is no "else", as in the first example shown in Figure 4-4, the selection structure ends when its condition is false, and processing continues with the instruction following the "end if". In the first example, for instance, the "display the part number and price" instruction is processed when the part number is not "AB203." In cases where the selection structure contains an "else", as in the second example shown in Figure 4-4, the instructions between the "else" and the "end if"—referred to as the **false path**—are processed before the instruction after the "end if" is processed. In the second example, the calculate the commission by multiplying the sales amount by .01 instruction is processed first, followed by the "display the commission" instruction.

Recall from Chapter 2 that, in addition to using pseudocode to plan algorithms, programmers also use flowcharts. In the next section, you learn how to show the If and If/Else selection structures in a flowchart.

Flowcharting the If and If/Else Selection Structures

Unlike pseudocode, which consists of short phrases, a flowchart uses standardized symbols to show the steps the computer must take to accomplish a task. Figure 4-5 shows Figure 4-4's examples in flowchart form.

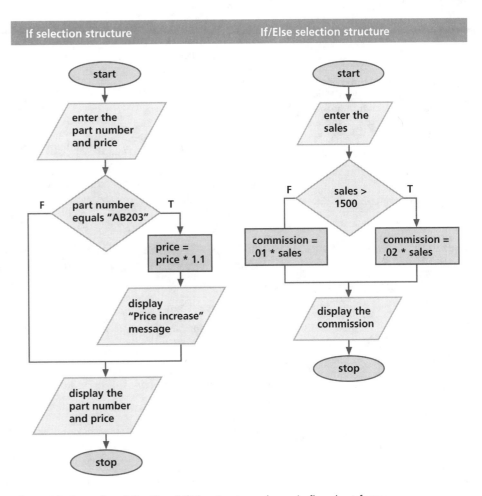

Figure 4-5: Examples of the If and If/Else structures drawn in flowchart form

tip

You also can mark the flow-lines leading out of the dia-mond with a "Y" and an "N" (for yes and no).

The flowcharts shown in Figure 4-5 contain four different symbols: an oval, a rectangle, a parallelogram, and a diamond. The symbols are connected with lines, called **flowlines**. The oval symbol is called the **start/stop symbol**. The start oval indicates the beginning of the flowchart, and the stop oval indicates the end of the flowchart. The rectangles that appear between the start and the stop ovals are called **process symbols**. You use the process symbol to represent tasks such as making calculations.

The parallelogram in a flowchart is called the **input/output symbol** and is used to represent input tasks, such as getting information from the user, and output tasks, such as displaying information. The first parallelogram in each example shown in Figure 4-5 represents an input task, and the last parallelogram represents an output task.

The diamond in a flowchart is called the **selection/repetition symbol**, because it is used to represent both selection and repetition. In Figure 4-5's flowcharts, the diamonds represent the selection structure. (You learn how to use the diamond to represent the repetition structure in Chapter 6.) Notice that inside each diamond is a comparison that evaluates to either true or false only. Each diamond also has one flowline entering the symbol and two flowlines leaving the symbol. The two flowlines leading out of the diamond should be marked so that anyone reading the flowchart can distinguish the true path from the false path. You mark the flowline leading to the true path with a "T" (for true), and you mark the flowline leading to the false path with an "F" (for false).

The start and stop ovals in a flowchart are associated with the procedure header and procedure footer, respectively.

To translate the flowchart into Visual Basic .NET code, you simply start at the top of the flowchart and write the code for each symbol as you follow the flowlines down to the bottom of the flowchart. Keep in mind that some symbols in a flowchart may require more than one line of code.

Next, you learn how to code the If and If/Else selection structures in Visual Basic .NET.

Coding the If and If/Else Selection Structures

You use the **If...Then...Else statement** to code the If and If/Else selection structures in Visual Basic .NET. Figure 4-6 shows the syntax of the If...Then...Else statement and includes two examples of using the statement to code the If and If/Else selection structures.

If...Then...Else statement used to code the If and If/Else selection structures
Syntax
If *condition* **Then**
statement block containing one or more statements to be processed when the condition is true
[Else
statement block containing one or more statements to be processed when the condition is false]
End If

Examples

```
If partNumber = "AB203" Then
     price = price * 1.1;
     me.uiMessageLabel.Text = "Price increase"
End If
```

If the partNumber variable contains the string "AB203", the first instruction in the true path multiplies the contents of the price variable by 1.1 and assigns the result to the price variable. The second instruction in the true path displays the message "Price increase" in the uiMessageLabel control.

```
If sales > 1500 Then
     commission = .02 * sales
Else
     commission = .01 * sales
End If
```

If the sales variable contains a number that is greater than 1500, the instruction in the true path multiplies the contents of the sales variable by .02; otherwise, the instruction in the false path multiplies the contents of the sales variable by .01.

Figure 4-6: Syntax and examples of the If...Then...Else statement used to code the If and If/Else structures

The items in square brackets in the syntax are optional. For example, you do not always need to include the Else portion of the syntax, referred to as the **Else clause**, in an If...Then...Else statement. Words in **bold**, however, are essential components of the statement. The words If, Then, and End If, for instance, must be included in the If...Then...Else statement. The word Else must be included only if the statement uses the Else clause.

Items in *italics* indicate where the programmer must supply information pertaining to the current application. For instance, the programmer must supply the *condition* to be evaluated. The *condition* must be a Boolean expression, which is an expression that results in a Boolean value (True or False). In addition to supplying the *condition*, the programmer also must supply the statements to be processed when the *condition* evaluates to true and, optionally, when the *condition* evaluates to false. The set of statements contained in the true path, as well as the set of statements contained in the false path, are referred to as a **statement block**.

The If...Then...Else statement's *condition* can contain variables, literal constants, named constants, properties, functions, methods, arithmetic operators, comparison operators, and logical operators. You already know about variables, literal constants, named constants, properties, functions, methods, and arithmetic operators. You learn about comparison operators and logical operators in the following sections.

In Visual Basic .NET, a statement block is a set of statements terminated by an Else, End If, Loop, or Next statement.

Comparison Operators

Visual Basic .NET provides nine **comparison operators**, also referred to as **relational operators**. Figure 4-7 lists the six most commonly used comparison operators. (You learn about the remaining three comparison operators—Is, TypeOf...Is, and Like—in Chapter 5.)

Operator	Operation
=	equal to
>	greater than
>=	greater than or equal to
<	less than
<=	less than or equal to
<>	not equal to

Figure 4-7: Most commonly used comparison operators

Unlike arithmetic operators, comparison operators do not have an order of precedence in Visual Basic .NET. If an expression contains more than one comparison operator, Visual Basic .NET evaluates the comparison operators from left to right in the expression. Keep in mind, however, that comparison operators are evaluated after any arithmetic operators in the expression. In other words, in the expression 5 - 2 > 1 + 2, the two arithmetic operators (-, +) are evaluated before the comparison operator (>). The result of the expression is the Boolean value False, as shown in Figure 4-8.

Evaluation steps	Result
Original expression	5 − 2 > 1 + 2
5 − 2 is evaluated first	3 > 1 + 2
1 + 2 is evaluated second	3 > 3
3 > 3 is evaluated last	False

Figure 4-8: Evaluation steps for an expression containing arithmetic and comparison operators

Figure 4-9 shows examples of using comparison operators in the If...Then...Else statement's *condition*.

If...Then...Else statement's *condition*	Meaning
`If price < 45.75 Then`	Compares the contents of the `price` variable to the number 45.75. The *condition* evaluates to True if the `price` variable contains a number that is less than 45.75; otherwise, it evaluates to False.
`If age >= 21 Then`	Compares the contents of the `age` variable to the number 21. The *condition* evaluates to True if the `age` variable contains a number that is greater than or equal to 21; otherwise, it evaluates to False.
`If num1 = num2 Then`	Compares the contents of the `num1` variable to the contents of the `num2` variable. The *condition* evaluates to True if the contents of both variables are equal; otherwise, it evaluates to False.
`If state <> "MA" Then`	Compares the contents of the `state` variable to the string "MA". The *condition* evaluates to True if the `state` variable does not contain the string "MA"; otherwise, it evaluates to False.

Figure 4-9: Examples of comparison operators in the If...Then...Else statement's *condition*

Notice that the expression contained in each *condition* shown in Figure 4-9 evaluates to one of two Boolean values—either True or False. All expressions containing a comparison operator will result in an answer of either True or False only.

Next, you view two examples of procedures that contain comparison operators in an If...Then...Else statement. The first procedure uses the If selection structure, and the second procedure uses the If/Else selection structure.

Using Comparison Operators—Swapping Numeric Values

Assume you want to create a procedure that displays both the lowest and highest of two numbers entered by the user. Figure 4-10 shows the pseudocode and flowchart for a procedure that will accomplish this task, and Figure 4-11 shows the corresponding Visual Basic .NET code. Figure 4.12 shows a sample run of the application that contains the procedure.

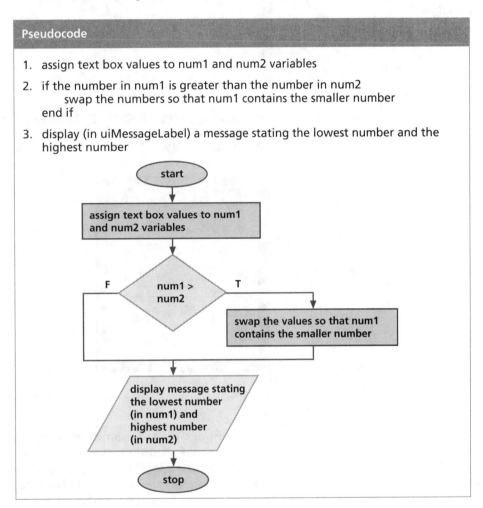

Pseudocode

1. assign text box values to num1 and num2 variables
2. if the number in num1 is greater than the number in num2
       swap the numbers so that num1 contains the smaller number
   end if
3. display (in uiMessageLabel) a message stating the lowest number and the highest number

Figure 4-10: Pseudocode and flowchart showing the If selection structure

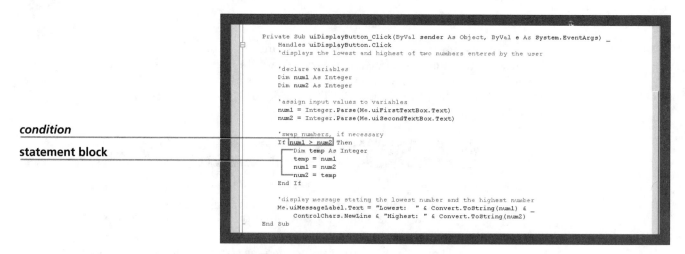

condition

statement block

```
Private Sub uiDisplayButton_Click(ByVal sender As Object, ByVal e As System.EventArgs) _
    Handles uiDisplayButton.Click
    'displays the lowest and highest of two numbers entered by the user

    'declare variables
    Dim num1 As Integer
    Dim num2 As Integer

    'assign input values to variables
    num1 = Integer.Parse(Me.uiFirstTextBox.Text)
    num2 = Integer.Parse(Me.uiSecondTextBox.Text)

    'swap numbers, if necessary
    If num1 > num2 Then
        Dim temp As Integer
        temp = num1
        num1 = num2
        num2 = temp
    End If

    'display message stating the lowest number and the highest number
    Me.uiMessageLabel.Text = "Lowest:   " & Convert.ToString(num1) & _
        ControlChars.NewLine & "Highest:  " & Convert.ToString(num2)
End Sub
```

Figure 4-11: Visual Basic .NET code showing the If selection structure

Figure 4-12: Sample run of the application that contains the procedure

Notice that the code shown in Figure 4-11 first declares two procedure-level Integer variables named num1 and num2; it then assigns the contents of two text boxes to the variables. The num1 > num2 *condition* in the If...Then...Else statement tells the computer to compare the contents of the num1 variable with the contents of the num2 variable. If the *condition* evaluates to True, it means that the value in the num1 variable is greater than the value in the num2 variable. In that case, the four instructions contained in the If...Then...Else statement's true path swap the values contained in those variables. Swapping the values places the smaller number in the num1 variable, and the larger number in the num2 variable. If the num1 > num2 *condition* evaluates to False, on the other hand, the true path instructions are skipped over. The instructions do not need to be processed because the num1 variable already contains a number that is smaller than (or possibly equal to) the one stored in num2. The last statement in the procedure displays a message that indicates the lowest number (which is contained in num1) and the highest number (which is contained in num2).

Study closely the instructions used to swap the values stored in the num1 and num2 variables. The first instruction, `Dim temp As Integer`, declares a variable named `temp`. Like the variables declared at the beginning of a procedure, variables declared within a statement block remain in memory until the procedure ends. However, unlike variables declared at the beginning of a procedure, variables declared within a statement block have block scope rather than procedure scope. Recall that when a variable has procedure scope, it can be used anywhere within the procedure. A variable that has **block scope**, on the other hand, can be used only within the statement block in which it is declared. In this case, for example, the num1 and num2 variables can be used anywhere within the uiDisplayButton's Click event procedure, but the `temp` variable can be used only within the If...Then...Else statement's true path. You may be wondering why the `temp` variable was not declared at the beginning of the procedure, along with the num1 and num2 variables. Although that would have been correct, the `temp` variable is not needed unless a swap is necessary, so there is no reason to create the variable until it is needed.

The second instruction in the If...Then...Else statement's true path, `temp = num1`, assigns the value in the num1 variable to the `temp` variable. The `temp` variable is necessary to store the contents of the num1 variable temporarily so that the swap can be made. If you did not store the num1 variable's value in the `temp` variable, the num1 variable's value would be lost when the computer processes the next statement, `num1 = num2`, which replaces the contents of the num1 variable with the contents of the num2 variable. Finally, the `num2 = temp` instruction assigns the value in the `temp` variable to the num2 variable. Figure 4-13 illustrates the concept of swapping, assuming the user entered the numbers eight and four in the uiFirstTextBox and uiSecondTextBox controls, respectively.

	temp	num1	num2
values stored in the variables immediately before the `temp = num1` instruction is processed	0	8	4
result of the `temp = num1` instruction	8	8	4
result of the `num1 = num2` instruction	8	4	4
result of the `num2 = temp` instruction, which completes the swapping process	8	4	8

values were swapped

Figure 4-13: Illustration of the swapping process

Using Comparison Operators—Displaying the Sum or Difference

Now assume you want to give the user the option of displaying either the sum of two numbers that he or she enters, or the difference between the two numbers. Figure 4-14 shows the pseudocode and flowchart for a procedure that will accomplish this task, and Figure 4-15 shows the corresponding Visual Basic .NET code. Figure 4-16 shows a sample run of the application that contains the procedure.

Pseudocode

1. assign text box values to operation, num1, and num2 variables

2. if the operation variable contains "1"
   calculate the sum by adding together the numbers contained in the num1 and num2 variables

   display (in uiAnswerLabel) the message "Sum:" and the sum
   else
   calculate the difference by subtracting the number contained in num2 from the number contained in num1

   display (in uiAnswerLabel) the message "Difference:" and the difference
   end if

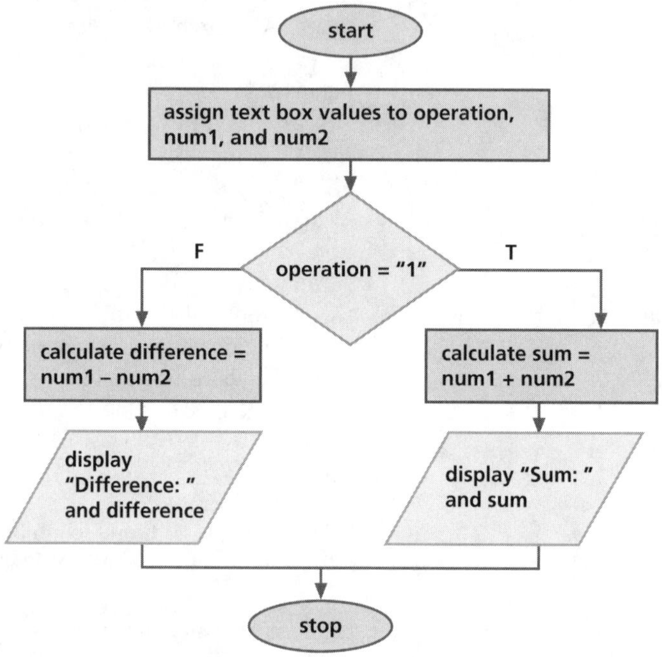

```
                    ┌─────────┐
                    │  start  │
                    └─────────┘
                         │
        ┌────────────────────────────────────┐
        │ assign text box values to operation,│
        │ num1, and num2                      │
        └────────────────────────────────────┘
                         │
        F          ◇ operation = "1" ◇          T
   ┌──────────────┐                      ┌──────────────┐
   │ calculate    │                      │ calculate    │
   │ difference = │                      │ sum =        │
   │ num1 – num2  │                      │ num1 + num2  │
   └──────────────┘                      └──────────────┘
          │                                     │
   ╱ display       ╲                     ╱ display "Sum: " ╲
   ╱ "Difference: " ╲                    ╱ and sum          ╲
   ╱ and difference  ╲                   ╱                   ╲
          │                                     │
          └──────────────┬──────────────────────┘
                    ┌─────────┐
                    │  stop   │
                    └─────────┘
```

Figure 4-14: Pseudocode and flowchart showing the If/Else selection structure

```
Private Sub uiCalcButton_Click(ByVal sender As Object, ByVal e As System.EventArgs) _
    Handles uiCalcButton.Click
    'calculates the sum of or difference between two numbers

    'declare variables
    Dim operation As String
    Dim num1 As Integer
    Dim num2 As Integer
    Dim answer As Integer

    'assign input values to variables
    operation = Me.uiOperationTextBox.Text
    num1 = Integer.Parse(Me.uiNum1TextBox.Text)
    num2 = Integer.Parse(Me.uiNum2TextBox.Text)

    'calculate and display sum or difference
    If operation = "1" Then
        answer = num1 + num2
        Me.uiAnswerLabel.Text = "Sum: " & Convert.ToString(answer)
    Else
        answer = num1 - num2
        Me.uiAnswerLabel.Text = "Difference: " & Convert.ToString(answer)
    End If
End Sub
```

condition

Figure 4-15: Visual Basic .NET code showing the If/Else selection structure

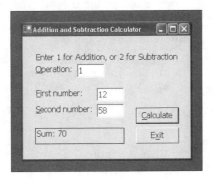

Figure 4-16: Sample run of the application that contains the procedure

The code shown in Figure 4-15 first declares four procedure-level variables: a String variable named `operation` and three Integer variables named `num1`, `num2`, and `answer`. The procedure then assigns the user's input to the `operation`, `num1`, and `num2` variables. The `operation = "1"` *condition* in the If...Then...Else statement tells the computer to compare the contents of the `operation` variable with the string "1". If the *condition* is true, then the selection structure calculates and displays the sum of the two numbers entered by the user. If the *condition* is false, however, the selection structure calculates and displays the difference between the two numbers.

Recall that you also can use logical operators in the If...Then...Else statement's *condition*.

Logical Operators

Logical operators, sometimes referred to as **Boolean operators,** allow you to combine two or more *conditions* into one compound *condition.* Visual Basic .NET has six logical operators, which are listed along with their order of precedence in Figure 4-17.

Operator	Operation	Precedence number
Not	reverses the value of the *condition*; True becomes False, and False becomes True	1
And	all conditions must be true for the compound condition to be true	2
AndAlso	same as the And operator, except performs short-circuit evaluation	2
Or	only one of the conditions must be true for the compound condition to be true	3
OrElse	same as the Or operator, except performs short-circuit evaluation	3
Xor	one and only one condition can be true for the compound condition to be true	4

Figure 4-17: Logical operators

The tables shown in Figure 4-18, called **truth tables,** summarize how Visual Basic .NET evaluates the logical operators in an expression. Like expressions containing comparison operators, expressions containing logical operators always evaluate to a Boolean value.

Truth table for the Not operator

value of *condition*	value of Not *condition*	
True	False	
False	True	

Truth table for the And operator

value of *condition1*	value of *condition2*	value of *condition1* And *condition2*
True	True	True
True	False	False
False	True	False
False	False	False

Truth table for the AndAlso operator

value of *condition1*	value of *condition2*	value of *condition1* AndAlso *condition2*
True	True	True
True	False	False
False	(not evaluated)	False

Figure 4-18: Truth tables for the logical operators

Truth table for the Or operator		
value of *condition1*	value of *condition2*	value of *condition1* Or *condition2*
True	True	True
True	False	True
False	True	True
False	False	False

Truth table for the OrElse operator		
value of *condition1*	value of *condition2*	value of *condition1* OrElse *condition2*
True	(not evaluated)	True
False	True	True
False	False	False

Truth table for the Xor operator		
value of *condition1*	value of *condition2*	value of *condition1* Xor *condition2*
True	True	False
True	False	True
False	True	True
False	False	False

Figure 4-18: Truth tables for the logical operators (continued)

As Figure 4-18 indicates, the Not operator reverses the truth-value of the *condition*. If the value of the *condition* is True, then the value of Not *condition* is False. Likewise, if the value of the *condition* is False, then the value of Not *condition* is True.

Now look at the truth tables for the And and AndAlso logical operators. When you use the And or AndAlso operators to combine two conditions, the resulting compound condition is True only when both conditions are True. If either condition is False or if both conditions are False, then the compound condition is False. The difference between the And and AndAlso operators is that the And operator always evaluates both conditions, while the AndAlso operator performs a **short-circuit evaluation**, which means that it does not always evaluate *condition2*. Because both conditions combined with the AndAlso operator need to be True for the compound condition to be True, the AndAlso operator does not evaluate *condition2* if *condition1* is False. Although the And and AndAlso operators produce the same results, the AndAlso operator is more efficient.

Now look at the truth tables for the Or and OrElse logical operators. When you combine conditions using the Or or OrElse operators, the compound condition is False only when both conditions are False. If either condition is True or if both conditions are True, then the compound condition is True. The difference between the Or and OrElse operators is that the Or operator always evaluates both conditions, while the OrElse operator performs a short-circuit evaluation. Because only one of the conditions combined with the OrElse operator needs to be True for the compound condition to be True, the OrElse operator does not evaluate *condition2* if *condition1* is True. Although the Or and OrElse operators produce the same results, the OrElse operator is more efficient.

Finally, look at the truth table for the Xor operator. When you combine conditions using the Xor operator, the compound condition is True only when one and only one condition is True. If both conditions are True or both conditions are False, then the compound condition is False. In the next section, you use the truth tables to determine which logical operator is appropriate for the If...Then...Else statement's compound condition.

Using the Truth Tables

Assume that you want to pay a bonus to every A-rated salesperson whose monthly sales total more than $10,000. To receive a bonus, the salesperson must be rated A and he or she must sell more than $10,000 in product. Assuming the two variables `rate` and `sales` contain the salesperson's rating and sales amount, you can phrase *condition1* as `rate = "A"` and *condition2* as `sales > 10000`. Now the question is, which logical operator should you use to combine both conditions into one compound condition? You can use the truth tables shown in Figure 4-18 to answer this question.

For a salesperson to receive a bonus, remember that both *condition1* (`rate = "A"`) and *condition2* (`sales > 10000`) must be True at the same time. If either condition is False, or if both conditions are False, then the compound condition should be False, and the salesperson should not receive a bonus. According to the truth tables, the And, AndAlso, Or, and OrElse operators evaluate the compound condition as True when both conditions are True. However, only the And and AndAlso operators evaluate the compound condition as False when either one or both of the conditions are False. The Or and OrElse operators, you will notice, evaluate the compound condition as False only when *both* conditions are False. Therefore, the correct compound condition to use here is either `rate = "A" And sales > 10000` or `rate = "A" AndAlso sales > 10000`. Recall, however, that the AndAlso operator is more efficient than the And operator.

Now assume that you want to send a letter to all A-rated salespeople and all B-rated salespeople. Assuming the rating is stored in the `rate` variable, you can phrase *condition1* as `rate = "A"` and *condition2* as `rate = "B"`. Now which operator do you use?

At first it might appear that either the And or the AndAlso operator is the correct one to use, because the example says to send the letter to "all A-rated salespeople and all B-rated salespeople." In everyday conversations, you will find that people sometimes use the word *and* when what they really mean is *or*. Although both words do not mean the same thing, using *and* instead of *or* generally does not cause a problem because we are able to infer what another person means. Computers, however, cannot infer anything; they simply process the directions you give them, word for word. In this case, you actually want to send a letter to all salespeople with either an A or a B rating (a salesperson cannot have both an A rating and a B rating), so you will need to use either the Or or the OrElse operator. As the truth tables indicate, the Or and OrElse operators are the only operators that evaluate the compound condition as True if one or more of the conditions is True. Therefore, the correct compound condition to use here is either `rate = "A" Or rate = "B"` or `rate = "A" OrElse rate = "B"`. Recall, however, that the OrElse operator is more efficient than the Or operator.

Finally, assume that, when placing an order, a customer is allowed to use only one of two coupons. Assuming the program uses the variables `coupon1` and `coupon2` to keep track of the coupons, you can phrase *condition1* as `coupon1 = "USED"` and *condition2* as `coupon2 = "USED"`. Now which operator should you use to combine both conditions? According to the truth tables, the Xor operator is the only operator that evaluates the compound condition as True when one and only one condition is True. Therefore, the correct compound condition to use here is `coupon1 = "USED" Xor coupon2 = "USED"`.

Figure 4-19 shows the order of precedence for the arithmetic, comparison, and logical operators you have learned so far.

Operator	Operation	Precedence number
^	exponentiation	1
–	negation	2
*, /	multiplication and division	3
\	integer division	4
Mod	modulus arithmetic	5
+, –	addition and subtraction	6
&	concatenation	7
=, >, >=, <, <=, <>	equal to, greater than, greater than or equal to, less than, less than or equal to, not equal to	8
Not	reverses truth value of condition	9
And, AndAlso	all conditions must be true for the compound condition to be true	10
Or, OrElse	only one condition needs to be true for the compound condition to be true	11
Xor	one and only one condition can be true for the compound condition to be true	12

Figure 4-19: Order of precedence for arithmetic, comparison, and logical operators

Notice that logical operators are evaluated after any arithmetic operators or comparison operators in an expression. In other words, in the expression $12 > 0$ AndAlso $12 < 10 * 2$, the arithmetic operator (*) is evaluated first, followed by the two comparison operators (> and <), followed by the logical operator (AndAlso). The expression evaluates to True, as shown in Figure 4-20.

Evaluation steps	Result
Original expression	12 > 0 AndAlso 12 < 10 * 2
10 * 2 is evaluated first	12 > 0 AndAlso 12 < 20
12 > 0 is evaluated second	True AndAlso 12 < 20
12 < 20 is evaluated third	True AndAlso True
True AndAlso True is evaluated last	True

Figure 4-20: Evaluation steps for an expression containing arithmetic, comparison, and logical operators

Next, you view the Visual Basic .NET code for a procedure that contains a logical operator in an If...Then...Else statement.

Using Logical Operators: Calculating Gross Pay

Assume you want to create a procedure that calculates and displays an employee's gross pay. To keep this example simple, assume that no one at the company works more than 40 hours per week, and everyone earns the same hourly rate, $10.65. Before making the gross pay calculation, the program should verify that the number of hours entered by the user is greater than or equal to zero, but less than or equal to 40. Programmers refer to the process of verifying that the input data is within the expected range as **data validation**. In this case, if the number of hours is valid, the program should calculate and display the gross pay; otherwise, it should display an error message alerting the user that the input data is incorrect. Figure 4-21 shows two ways of writing the Visual Basic .NET code for this procedure. Notice that the If...Then...Else statement in the first example uses the AndAlso logical operator, whereas the If...Then...Else statement in the second example uses the OrElse logical operator.

Example 1: using the AndAlso operator

```
'declare variables
Dim hoursWorked As Double
Dim grossPay As Double


'assign input to variable
hoursWorked = Double.Parse(Me.uiHoursTextBox.Text)


If hoursWorked >= 0.0 AndAlso hoursWorked <= 40.0 Then
    'calculate and display gross pay
    grossPay = hoursWorked * 10.65
    Me.uiGrossLabel.Text = Convert.ToString(grossPay)
Else
    'display error message
    Me.uiGrossLabel.Text = "Input Error"
End If
```

Figure 4-21: AndAlso and OrElse logical operators in the If...Then...Else statement

Example 2: using the OrElse operator

```
'declare variables
Dim hoursWorked As Double
Dim grossPay As Double

'assign input to variable
hoursWorked = Double.Parse(Me.uiHoursTextBox.Text)

If hoursWorked < 0.0 OrElse hoursWorked > 40.0 Then
    'display error message
        Me.uiGrossLabel.Text = "Input Error"
Else
    'calculate and display gross pay
    grossPay = hoursWorked * 10.65
    Me.uiGrossLabel.Text = Convert.ToString(grossPay)
End If
```

Figure 4-21: AndAlso and OrElse logical operators in the If...Then...Else statement (continued)

The compound condition in Example 1, hoursWorked >= 0.0 AndAlso hoursWorked <= 40.0, tells the computer to determine whether the value stored in the hoursWorked variable is greater than or equal to the number 0.0 and, at the same time, less than or equal to the number 40.0. If the compound condition evaluates to True, then the selection structure calculates and displays the gross pay; otherwise, it displays the "Input Error" message.

The compound condition in Example 2, hoursWorked < 0.0 OrElse hoursWorked > 40.0, tells the computer to determine whether the value stored in the hoursWorked variable is less than the number 0.0 or greater than the number 40.0. If the compound condition evaluates to True, then the selection structure displays the "Input Error" message; otherwise, it calculates and displays the gross pay.

Both If...Then...Else statements shown in Figure 4-21 produce the same results, and simply represent two different ways of performing the same task. Figure 4-22 shows a sample run of the application that contains either of the procedures shown in Figure 4-21.

the gross pay contains three decimal places

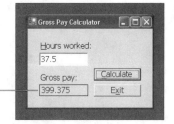

Figure 4-22: Sample run of the application that contains either procedure shown in Figure 4-21

Notice that the result of the gross pay calculation contains three decimal places. In Chapter 2, you learned how to use the Format function to display a dollar sign and two decimal places in a number. Although you can still use the Format function in Visual Basic .NET, most .NET programmers now use the ToString method.

Using the ToString Method to Format Numbers

As you learned in Chapter 1, a method is a predefined Visual Basic .NET procedure that you can call (or invoke) when needed. You already are familiar with one method, the Close method, which you use to end an application. In Visual Basic .NET, you can use the ToString method to format a number. Figure 4-23 shows the syntax of the ToString method and includes several examples of using the method to format numbers.

Using the ToString method to format a number

<u>Syntax</u>

variablename.**ToString**(*formatString*)

<u>Examples</u>

```
Me.uiCommissionLabel.Text = commission.ToString("C")
```

assuming that the `commission` variable contains the number 1250, the statement assigns the string "$1,250.00" to the Text property of the uiCommissionLabel control

```
Me.uiTotalLabel.Text = total.ToString("N2")
```

assuming that the `total` variable contains the number 123.675, the statement assigns the string "123.68" to the Text property of the uiTotalLabel control

```
Me.uiRateLabel.Text = rate.ToString("P")
```

assuming that the `rate` variable contains the number .06, the statement assigns the string "6 %" to the Text property of the uiRateLabel control

---

Figure 4-23: Syntax and examples of the ToString method

In the syntax shown in Figure 4-23, *variablename* is the name of a numeric variable, and *formatString* is a string that specifies the format you want to use. The *formatString* argument, which must be enclosed in double quotation marks, takes the form *Axx*, where *A* is an alphabetic character called the **format specifier**, and *xx* is a sequence of digits called the **precision specifier**. The format specifier must be one of the built-in format characters; the most commonly used format characters are listed in Figure 4-24. The precision specifier controls the number of significant digits or zeros to the right of the decimal point in the formatted number.

Format specifier	Name	Description
C or c	Currency	displays a number with a dollar sign; the precision specifier indicates the desired number of decimal places; if appropriate, displays a number with a thousand separator; negative numbers are enclosed in parentheses
D or d	Decimal	formats only integers; the precision specifier indicates the minimum number of digits desired; if required, the number is padded with zeros to its left to produce the number of digits specified by the precision specifier; if appropriate, displays a number with a thousand separator; negative numbers are preceded by a minus sign
F or f	Fixed-point	the precision specifier indicates the desired number of decimal places; negative numbers are preceded by a minus sign
N or n	Number	the precision specifier indicates the desired number of decimal places; if appropriate, displays a number with a thousand separator; negative numbers are preceded by a minus sign
P or p	Percent	the precision specifier indicates the desired number of decimal places; multiplies the number by 100 and displays the number with a percent sign; negative numbers are preceded by a minus sign

Figure 4-24: Most commonly used format specifiers

Notice that you can use either an uppercase letter or a lowercase letter as the format specifier. Figure 4-25 shows examples of how various *formatString*s format numeric values.

formatString	Value	Result
C	3764	$3,764.00
C0	3764	$3,764
C2	3764	$3,764.00
C2	456.783	$456.78
C2	456.785	$456.79
C2	-75.31	($75.31)
D	3764	3764
D	-53	-53
D3	8	008
D3	15	015
F	3764	3764.00

Figure 4-25: Examples of how various *formatString*s format numeric values

To learn how to create custom *formatStrings*, click Help on the menu bar, and then click Index. Click either Visual Basic or Visual Studio in the Filtered by list box, then type *custom numeric format strings* in the Look for text box, and then press Enter.

formatString	Value	Result
F0	3764	3764
F2	3764	3764.00
F2	456.783	456.78
F2	456.785	456.79
F2	-75.31	-75.31
N	3764	3,764.00
N0	3764	3,764
N2	3764	3,764.00
N2	456.783	456.78
N2	456.785	456.79
N2	-75.31	-75.31
P	.364	36.40 %
P	-.05	-5.00 %
P1	.3645	36.5 %
P2	1.1	110.00%

Figure 4-25: Examples of how various *formatStrings* format numeric values (continued)

Figure 4-26 shows how you can use the ToString method to format the gross pay displayed by the application shown earlier in Figure 4-22, and Figure 4-27 shows a sample run of the application containing the ToString method.

ToString method

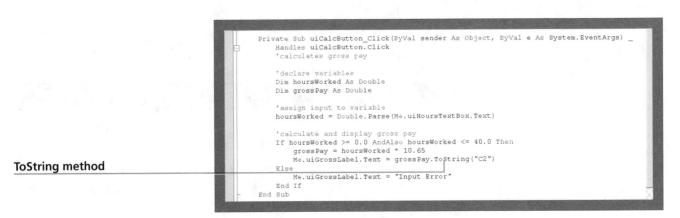

```
Private Sub uiCalcButton_Click(ByVal sender As Object, ByVal e As System.EventArgs) _
    Handles uiCalcButton.Click
    'calculates gross pay

    'declare variables
    Dim hoursWorked As Double
    Dim grossPay As Double

    'assign input to variable
    hoursWorked = Double.Parse(Me.uiHoursTextBox.Text)

    'calculate and display gross pay
    If hoursWorked >= 0.0 AndAlso hoursWorked <= 40.0 Then
        grossPay = hoursWorked * 10.65
        Me.uiGrossLabel.Text = grossPay.ToString("C2")
    Else
        Me.uiGrossLabel.Text = "Input Error"
    End If
End Sub
```

Figure 4-26: ToString method used in the Gross Pay Calculator application

the gross pay contains a dollar sign and two decimal places

Figure 4-27: Sample run of the Gross Pay Calculator application

In all of the procedures shown so far in this lesson, the If...Then...Else statement's *condition* compared numeric values. You also can use the If...Then...Else statement's *condition* to perform string comparisons involving letters.

Comparing Strings

Assume you want a procedure to display the word "Pass" if the user enters the letter P, and the word "Fail" if the user enters anything else. Figure 4-28 shows four ways of writing the Visual Basic .NET code for this procedure.

Example 1: using the OrElse operator

```
Dim letter As String
letter = Me.uiLetterTextBox.Text
If letter = "P" OrElse letter = "p" Then
    Me.uiResultLabel.Text = "Pass"
Else
    Me.uiResultLabel.Text = "Fail"
End if
```

Example 2: using the AndAlso operator

```
Dim letter As String
letter = Me.uiLetterTextBox.Text
If letter <> "P" AndAlso letter <> "p" Then
    Me.uiResultLabel.Text = "Fail"
Else
    Me.uiResultLabel.Text = "Pass"
End if
```

Example 3: correct, but less efficient, solution

```
Dim letter As String
letter = Me.uiLetterTextBox.Text
If letter = "P" OrElse letter = "p" Then
    Me.uiResultLabel.Text = "Pass"
End If
If letter <> "P" AndAlso letter <> "p" Then
    Me.uiResultLabel.Text = "Fail"
End if
```

Figure 4-28: Visual Basic .NET code showing string comparisons in the If...Then...Else statement's *condition*

Example 4: using the `ToUpper` method

```
Dim letter As String
letter = Me.uiLetterTextBox.Text
If letter.ToUpper() = "P" Then
    Me.uiResultLabel.Text = "Pass"
Else
    Me.uiResultLabel.Text = "Fail"
End if
```

Figure 4-28: Visual Basic .NET code showing string comparisons in the If...Then...Else statement's *condition* (continued)

tip

The uppercase letter P is stored in the computer's internal memory using the eight bits 01010000 (ASCII code 80), whereas the lowercase letter p is stored using the eight bits 01110000 (ASCII code 112). ASCII stands for American Standard Code for Information Interchange and is the coding scheme used by microcomputers to represent the numbers, letters, and symbols on the keyboard.

The first statement in each example shown in Figure 4-28 creates and initializes a String variable named `letter`. The second statement assigns the contents of the uiLetterTextBox to the `letter` variable. The `letter = "P" OrElse letter = "p"` compound condition in the first example tells the computer to determine whether the value stored in the `letter` variable is either the uppercase letter P or the lowercase letter p. If the compound condition is true, which means that the variable contains one of those two letters, then the selection structure displays the word "Pass" on the screen; otherwise, it displays the word "Fail". You may be wondering why you need to tell the computer to compare the contents of the `letter` variable to both the uppercase and lowercase version of the letter P. As is true in many programming languages, string comparisons in Visual Basic .NET are case sensitive. That means that the uppercase version of a letter is not the same as its lowercase counterpart. So, although a human being recognizes P and p as being the same letter, a computer does not; to a computer, a P is different from a p. The reason for this differentiation is that each character on the computer keyboard is stored differently in the computer's internal memory.

The `letter <> "P" AndAlso letter <> "p"` compound condition in the second example shown in Figure 4-28 tells the computer to determine whether the value stored in the `letter` variable is *not* equal to either the uppercase letter P or the lowercase letter p. If the compound condition is true, which means that the variable does not contain either of those two letters, then the selection structure displays the word "Fail" on the screen; otherwise, it displays the word "Pass".

Rather than using one If...Then...Else statement with an Else clause, as in Examples 1 and 2, Example 3 in Figure 4-28 uses two If...Then...Else statements with no Else clause in either one. Although the If...Then...Else statements in Example 3 produce the same results as the If...Then...Else statement in Examples 1 and 2, they do so less efficiently. To illustrate this point, assume that the user enters the letter P in the uiLetterTextBox. The compound condition in the first If...Then...Else statement shown in Example 3 determines whether the value stored in the `letter` variable is equal to either P or p. In this case, the compound condition evaluates to true, because the `letter` variable contains the letter P. As a result, the first If...Then...Else statement's true path displays the word "Pass" in the uiResultLabel control, and then the first If...Then...Else statement ends. Although the appropriate word ("Pass") already appears in the uiResultLabel control, the procedure instructs the computer to evaluate the second If...Then...Else statement's compound condition to determine whether to display the "Fail" message. The second evaluation is unnecessary and makes Example 3's code less efficient than the code shown in Examples 1 and 2.

The If...Then...Else statement shown in Example 4 in Figure 4-28 also contains a string comparison in its *condition*, but notice that the *condition* does not use a logical operator; rather, it uses the ToUpper method. You learn about the ToUpper method next.

Converting a String to Uppercase or Lowercase

As you learned earlier, string comparisons in Visual Basic .NET are case-sensitive, which means that the string "Yes" is not the same as the string "YES" or the string "yes". A problem occurs when you need to include a string, entered by the user, in a comparison, because you cannot control the case in which the user enters the string. Before using a string in a comparison, you should convert it to either uppercase or lowercase, and then use the converted string in the comparison.

Visual Basic .NET provides the ToUpper and ToLower methods that you can use to convert a string to uppercase and lowercase, respectively. Figure 4-29 shows the syntax of both methods and includes several examples of using the methods.

Using the ToUpper and ToLower methods

Syntax

string.**ToUpper()**

string.**ToLower()**

Examples

```
If letter.ToUpper() = "P" Then
```

compares the uppercase version of the string stored in the `letter` variable to the uppercase letter "P"

```
If state.ToLower() = "ca" Then
```

compares the lowercase version of the string stored in the `state` variable to the lowercase letters "ca"

```
If item1.ToUpper() <> item2.ToUpper() Then
```

compares the uppercase version of the string stored in the item1 variable to the uppercase version of the string stored in the item2 variable

```
If "reno" = Me.uiCityTextBox.Text.ToLower() Then
```

compares the lowercase letters "reno" to the lowercase version of the string stored in the uiCityTextBox control

```
name = name.ToUpper()
```

changes the contents of the `name` variable to uppercase

```
Me.uiNameTextBox.Text = Me.uiNameTextBox.Text.ToLower()
```

changes the contents of the uiNameTextBox control's Text property to lowercase

---

Figure 4-29: Syntax and examples of the ToUpper and ToLower methods

In each syntax shown in Figure 4-29, *string* typically is the name of a String variable that contains the string you want to convert; however, as the fourth example shows, *string* also can be the property of an object. Both methods temporarily convert the string to the appropriate case. For example, `letter.ToUpper()` temporarily converts the contents of the `letter` variable to uppercase, and `state.ToLower()` temporarily converts the contents of the `state` variable to lowercase.

You also can use the ToUpper and ToLower methods to permanently convert the contents of a String variable or property to uppercase or lowercase, respectively. To do so, you simply include the appropriate method in an assignment statement. For example, to permanently change the contents of the name variable to uppercase, you use the assignment statement `name = name.ToUpper()`. You use the assignment statement `Me.uiNameTextBox.Text = Me.uiNameTextBox.Text.ToLower()` to convert the contents of the uiNameTextBox control's Text property to lowercase.

When using the ToUpper method, be sure that everything you are comparing is uppercase. In other words, the clause `If letter.ToUpper() = "p" Then` will not work correctly: the *condition* will always evaluate to False, because the uppercase version of a letter will never be equal to its lowercase counterpart. Likewise, when using the ToLower method, be sure that everything you are comparing is lowercase.

In the next section, you view the Visual Basic .NET code for a procedure that uses the ToUpper and ToLower methods.

> The ToUpper and ToLower methods affect only characters that represent letters of the alphabet, as these are the only characters that have uppercase and lowercase forms.

Using the ToUpper and ToLower Methods: Displaying a Message

Assume you want to create a procedure that displays the message "We have a store in this state." if the user enters any of the following three state IDs: Il, In, Ky. If the user enters an ID other than these, you want to display the message "We do not have a store in this state." Figure 4-30 shows three ways of writing the Visual Basic .NET code for this procedure.

Example 1: using the ToUpper method

```
Dim state As String
state = Me.uiStateTextBox.Text
If state.ToUpper() = "IL" OrElse state.ToUpper() = "IN" _
        OrElse state.ToUpper() = "KY"
    Me.uiMessageLabel.Text = "We have a store in this state."
Else
    Me.uiMessageLabel.Text = "We do not have a store in this state."
End If
```

Example 2: using the ToUpper method

```
Dim state As String
state = Me.uiStateTextBox.Text.ToUpper()
If state = "IL" OrElse state = "IN" OrElse state = "KY"
    Me.uiMessagerLabel.Text = "We have a store in this state."
Else
    Me.uiMessagerLabel.Text = "We do not have a store in this state."
End If
```

Figure 4-30: Examples of using the ToUpper and ToLower methods in a procedure

Example 3: using the ToLower method

```
Dim state As String
state = Me.uiStateTextBox.Text.ToLower()
If state <> "il" AndAlso state <> "in" AndAlso state <> "ky"
    Me.uiMessagerLabel.Text = "We do not have a store in this state."
Else
    Me.uiMessagerLabel.Text = "We have a store in this state."
End If
```

Figure 4-30: Examples of using the ToUpper and ToLower methods in a procedure (continued)

When the computer processes the `state.ToUpper() = "IL" OrElse state.ToUpper() = "IN" OrElse state.ToUpper() = "KY"` compound condition shown in Example 1 in Figure 4-30, it first temporarily converts the contents of the `state` variable to uppercase, and then compares the result to the string "IL". If the comparison evaluates to False, the computer again temporarily converts the contents of the `state` variable to uppercase, this time comparing the result to the string "IN". If the comparison evaluates to False, it again converts the contents of the `state` variable to uppercase, and compares the result to the string "KY". Notice that, depending on the result of each *condition*, the computer might need to convert the contents of the `state` variable to uppercase three times. A more efficient way of writing Example 1's code is shown in Example 2 in Figure 4-30.

The `state = Me.uiStateTextBox.Text.ToUpper()` statement in Example 2 tells the computer to assign to the `state` variable the uppercase equivalent of the uiStateTextBox control's Text property. The `state = "IL" OrElse state = "IN" OrElse state = "KY"` compound condition first compares the contents of the `state` variable (which now contains uppercase letters) to the string "IL". If the condition evaluates to False, the computer compares the contents of the `state` variable to the string "IN". If this condition evaluates to False, the computer compares the contents of the `state` variable to the string "KY". Notice that, in this case, the computer converts the contents of the `state` variable to uppercase only once, rather than three times.

The `state = Me.uiStateTextBox.Text.ToLower()` statement in Example 3 tells the computer to assign to the `state` variable the lowercase equivalent of the uiStateTextBox control's Text property. The compound condition in Example 3 is processed similarly to the compound condition in Example 2. However, the comparisons are made using lowercase letters rather than uppercase letters, and the conditions test for inequality rather than equality. The three examples shown in Figure 4-30 produce the same results, and simply represent different ways of performing the same task.

tip

Although the code shown in Example 2 in Figure 4-30 is more efficient than the code shown in Example 1, there may be times when you will not want to change the case of the string stored in a variable. For example, you may need to display the variable's contents using the exact case entered by the user.

S U M M A R Y

To evaluate an expression containing arithmetic, comparison, and logical operators:

■ Evaluate the arithmetic operators first, then evaluate the comparison operators, and then evaluate the logical operators. Figure 4-19 shows the order of precedence for the arithmetic, comparison, and logical operators.

To create a flowchart:

■ Use the start/stop oval to mark the beginning and end of the flowchart.
■ Use the input/output parallelogram to represent input tasks, such as getting information from the user, and output tasks, such as displaying information.
■ Use the process rectangle to represent tasks such as making calculations.
■ Use the selection/repetition diamond to represent the selection and repetition programming structures.
■ Connect the flowchart symbols with flowlines.

To code a selection structure:

■ Use the If...Then...Else statement. The statement's syntax is shown in Figure 4-6.

To compare two values:

■ Use the comparison operators listed in Figure 4-7.

To swap the values contained in two variables:

■ Assign the value stored in the first variable to a temporary variable, then assign the value stored in the second variable to the first variable, and then assign the value stored in the temporary variable to the second variable.

To create a compound condition:

■ Use the logical operators listed in Figure 4-17, and the truth tables listed in Figure 4-18.

To format a number:

■ Use the ToString method. The method's syntax is *variablename*.**ToString**(*formatString*).

To convert a string to uppercase:

■ Use the ToUpper method. The method's syntax is *string*.**ToUpper**().

To convert a string to lowercase:

■ Use the ToLower method. The method's syntax is *string*.**ToLower**().

QUESTIONS

1. Which of the following is a valid condition for an If...Then...Else statement? (`sales` and `cost` are Integer variables, and `state` is a String variable.)
   a. `Integer.Parse(Me.uiAgeTextBox.Text > 65)`
   b. `Integer.Parse(Me.uiPriceLabel.Text) > 0 AndAlso < 10`
   c. `sales > 500 AndAlso < 800`
   d. `cost > 100 AndAlso cost <= 1000`
   e. `state.ToUpper() = "Alaska" OrElse state.ToUpper() = "Hawaii"`

2. You can use the _____ method to convert a string to uppercase.
   a. ToCaseupper
   b. ToCaseUpper
   c. ToUCase
   d. ToUpper
   e. ToUpperCase

3. Assume you want to compare the string contained in the Text property of the uiNameTextBox control with the name Bob. Which of the following conditions should you use in the If...Then...Else statement? (Be sure the condition will handle Bob, BOB, bob, and so on.)
   a. `Me.uiNameTextBox.Text = "BOB"`
   b. `Me.uiNameTextBox.Text = ToUpper("BOB")`
   c. `Me.uiNameTextBox.Text = ToUpper("Bob")`
   d. `ToUpper(Me.uiNameTextBox.Text) = "BOB"`
   e. `Me.uiNameTextBox.Text.ToUpper() = "BOB"`

4. The six logical operators are listed below. Indicate their order of precedence by placing a number (1, 2, and so on) on the line to the left of the operator. (If two or more operators have the same precedence, assign the same number to each.)

   _____ Xor

   _____ And

   _____ Not

   _____ Or

   _____ AndAlso

   _____ OrElse

5. An expression can contain arithmetic, comparison, and logical operators. Indicate the order of precedence for the three types of operators by placing a number (1, 2, or 3) on the line to the left of the operator type.

   _____ Arithmetic

   _____ Logical

   _____ Comparison

6. The expression 3 > 6 AndAlso 7 > 4 evaluates to _____.
   a. True
   b. False

7. The expression 4 > 6 OrElse 10 < 2 * 6 evaluates to _____.
   a. True
   b. False

8. The expression 7 >= 3 + 4 Or 6 < 4 And 2 < 5 evaluates to _____.
   a. True
   b. False

Use the following information to answer Questions 9–16:

   X=5, Y=3, Z=2, A=True, B=False

9. The expression X – Y = Z evaluates to _____.
   a. True
   b. False

10. The expression X * Z > X * Y AndAlso A evaluates to _____.
   a. True
   b. False

11. The expression: X * Z < X * Y Or A evaluates to _____.
   a. True
   b. False

12. The expression A AndAlso B evaluates to _____.
   a. True
   b. False

13. The expression A OrElse B evaluates to _____.
   a. True
   b. False

14. The expression X * Y > Y ^ Z evaluates to _____.
   a. True
   b. False

15. The expression X * Y > Y ^ Z And A Or B evaluates to _____.
   a. True
   b. False

16. The expression A Xor B evaluates to _____.
   a. True
   b. False

Use the following selection structure to answer Questions 17 and 18:

```
If number <= 100 Then
    number = number * 2
Else
    number = number * 3
End If
```

17. Assume the `number` variable contains the number 90. What value will be in the `number` variable after the above selection structure is processed?
   a. 0
   b. 90
   c. 180
   d. 270
   e. None of the above.

18. Assume the `number` variable contains the number 1000. What value will be in the `number` variable after the above selection structure is processed?
    a. 0
    b. 1000
    c. 2000
    d. 3000
    e. None of the above.

19. Which of the following flowchart symbols is used to represent the If...Then...Else selection structure?
    a. diamond
    b. hexagon
    c. oval
    d. parallelogram
    e. rectangle

20. The _____ symbol is used in a flowchart to represent a calculation task.
    a. input/output
    b. process
    c. selection/repetition
    d. start
    e. stop

21. The _____ symbol is used in a flowchart to represent an input task.
    a. input/output
    b. process
    c. selection/repetition
    d. start
    e. stop

22. The process symbol in a flowchart is the _____.
    a. diamond
    b. oval
    c. parallelogram
    d. rectangle
    e. square

23. The input/output symbol in a flowchart is the _____.
    a. diamond
    b. oval
    c. parallelogram
    d. rectangle
    e. square

24. The selection/repetition symbol in a flowchart is the _____.
    a. diamond
    b. oval
    c. parallelogram
    d. rectangle
    e. square

25. Assume that a Decimal variable named `sales` contains the number 12345.89. Which of the following displays the number as 12,345.89?

    a. `Me.uiSalesLabel.Text = sales.ToString("C2")`
    b. `Me.uiSalesLabel.Text = sales.ToString("N2")`
    c. `Me.uiSalesLabel.Text = sales.ToString("D2")`
    d. `Me.uiSalesLabel.Text = sales.ToString("F2")`
    e. `Me.uiSalesLabel.Text = sales.ToString()`

EXERCISES

1. Draw the flowchart that corresponds to the following pseudocode.

   ```
   if hours > 40
           display "Overtime pay"
   else
           display "Regular pay"
   end if
   ```

2. Write an If...Then...Else statement that displays the string "Pontiac" in the uiCarMakeLabel control if the uiCarTextBox control contains the string "Grand Am" (in any case).

3. Write an If...Then...Else statement that displays the string "Entry error" in the uiMessageLabel control if the `units` variable contains a number that is less than 0; otherwise, display the string "Valid Number". The `units` variable is an Integer variable.

4. Write an If...Then...Else statement that displays the string "Reorder" in the uiMessageLabel control if the `price` variable contains a number that is less than 10; otherwise, display the string "OK". The `price` variable is a Decimal variable.

5. Write an If...Then...Else statement that assigns the number 10 to the `bonus` variable if the `sales` variable contains a number that is less than or equal to $250; otherwise, assign the number 15. The `bonus` and `sales` variables are Integer variables.

6. Write an If...Then...Else statement that displays the number 25 in the uiShippingLabel control if the `state` variable contains the string "Hawaii" (in any case); otherwise, display the number 50.

7. Assume you want to calculate a 3% sales tax if the `state` variable contains the string "Colorado" (in any case); otherwise, you want to calculate a 4% sales tax. You can calculate the sales tax by multiplying the tax rate by the contents of the `sales` variable. Display the sales tax in the uiSalesTaxLabel control. The `sales` variable is a Double variable. Draw the flowchart, then write the Visual Basic .NET code.

8. Assume you want to calculate an employee's gross pay. Employees working more than 40 hours should receive overtime pay (time and one-half) for the hours over 40. Use the variables `hours`, `rate`, and `gross`. Display the contents of the `gross` variable in the uiGrossLabel control. The variables are Decimal variables. Write the pseudocode, then write the Visual Basic .NET code.

9. Write the If...Then...Else statement that displays the string "Dog" in the uiAnimalLabel control if the `animal` variable contains the letter "D" (in any case); otherwise, display the string "Cat". Draw the flowchart, then write the Visual Basic .NET code.

10. Assume you want to calculate a 10% discount on desks sold to customers in Colorado. Use the variables `item`, `state`, `sales`, and `discount`. The `item` and `state` variables are String variables; the `sales` and `discount` variables are Single variables. Use the ToString method to format the discount to show two decimal places and a comma (if necessary). Display the discount in the uiDiscountLabel control. Write the pseudocode, then write the Visual Basic .NET code.

11. Assume you want to calculate a 2% price increase on all red shirts, but a 1% price increase on all other items. In addition to calculating the price increase, also calculate the new price. You can use the variables `color`, `item`, `origPrice`, `increase`, and `newPrice`. The `color` and `item` variables are String variables; the remaining variables are Decimal variables. Use the ToString method to format the original price, price increase, and new price to show two decimal places and a comma (if necessary). Display the original price, price increase, and new price in the uiOriginalLabel, uiIncreaseLabel, and uiNewLabel controls, respectively. Write the Visual Basic .NET code.

12. Write the Visual Basic .NET code that swaps the values stored in two Single variables named `marySales` and `jeffSales`, but only if the value stored in the `marySales` variable is less than the value stored in the `jeffSales` variable.

The Monthly Payment Calculator Application

Completing the User Interface

Recall that Herman Juarez has asked you to create an application that he can use to calculate the monthly payment on a car loan. To make this calculation, the application must know the loan amount (principal), the annual percentage rate (APR) of interest, and the life of the loan (term) in years. The sketch of the application's user interface is shown in Figure 4-31.

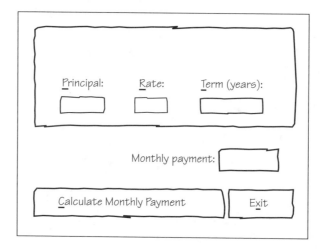

Figure 4-31: Sketch of the Monthly Payment Calculator user interface

The user interface contains a group box, three text boxes, five labels, and two buttons. To save you time, your computer's hard disk contains a partially completed Monthly Payment Calculator application. When you open the application, you will notice that most of the user interface has already been created and the properties of the existing objects have been set. You complete the user interface in this lesson.

To open the partially completed application:

1 Start Microsoft Visual Studio .NET, if necessary.

2 If necessary, close the Start Page window.

3 Open the **Payment Solution** (Payment Solution.sln) file, which is contained in the VBNET\Chap04\Payment Solution folder.

4 Auto-hide the Toolbox, Solution Explorer, and Properties windows, if necessary. The partially completed user interface is shown in Figure 4-32.

uildTermLabel
uildRateLabel
uildPrincipalLabel
uiPrincipalTextBox

uiRateTextBox

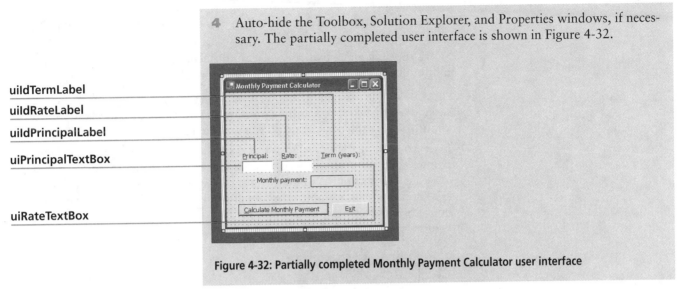

Figure 4-32: Partially completed Monthly Payment Calculator user interface

Only two controls are missing from the interface: a group box and a text box. You add the group box control first, and then you add the text box.

Adding a Group Box Control to the Form

You use the **GroupBox tool** in the Toolbox window to add a group box control to the interface. A **group box control** serves as a container for other controls. You can use a group box control to visually separate related controls from other controls on the form. In the Monthly Payment Calculator interface, for example, the group box control will visually separate the controls relating to the principal, rate, and term information from the rest of the controls.

Visual Basic .NET treats the group box and the controls contained in the group box as one unit. When you move the group box, the controls inside the group box also move, and when you delete the group box, the controls inside the group box also are deleted.

You can include an identifying label on a group box by setting the group box control's Text property. Labeling a group box is optional, but if you do, you should use sentence capitalization for the identifying label.

GUI Design Tips

Labeling a Group Box Control

• Use sentence capitalization for the optional identifying label, which is entered in the control's Text property.

To add a group box to the interface, and then drag several of the existing controls into the group box:

1 Click the **GroupBox** tool in the toolbox, and then drag a group box control onto the form.

2 Set the following properties for the group box control:

Name: **uiInfoGroupBox**

Location: 24, 24

Size: 272, 88

The group box control will not need an identifying label in this interface, so you can delete the contents of its Text property.

3 Delete the contents of the group box control's Text property.

Now drag the controls related to the principal, rate, and term into the group box control.

4   Select the following five controls: uiIdPrincipalLabel, uiPrincipalTextBox, uiIdRateLabel, uiRateTextBox, and uiIdTermLabel.

> HELP?   As you learned in Chapter 1, you can select more than one control by clicking the first control and then pressing and holding down the Ctrl (Control) key as you click the other controls you want to select.

5   Place your mouse pointer on one of the selected controls. The mouse pointer turns into ⊕. Press and hold down the left mouse button as you drag the selected controls into the group box, then release the mouse button. (The controls will not appear in the group box until you release the mouse button.) If necessary, drag the controls to position them as shown in Figure 4-33.

Figure 4-33: Controls dragged into the group box

6   Click the **form** to deselect the controls.

Also missing from the interface is a text box in which the user can enter the term information.

> **tip**
>
> As you learned in Chapter 1, the last control selected is used as the reference control when aligning and sizing controls.

To add the missing text box:

1   Click the **TextBox** tool in the toolbox, and then drag a text box control into the group box, immediately below the uiIdTermLabel.

2   Change the text box's Name property from TextBox1 to **uiTermTextBox**.

3   Delete the contents of the uiTermTextBox control's Text property.

4   With the uiTermTextBox control selected, press and hold down the Ctrl key as you click the **uiRateTextBox** control on the form. Both controls now should be selected.

5   Click **Format** on the menu bar, point to **Align**, and then click **Tops** to align the top border of the uiTermTextBox control with the top border of the uiRateTextBox control.

6   Click **Format** on the menu bar, point to **Make Same Size**, and then click **Both** to make the uiTermTextBox control the same size as the uiRateTextBox control.

7 Ctrl+click the **uiRateTextBox** control to deselect the control. The uiTermTextBox control should still be selected.

8 With the uiTermTextBox control selected, Ctrl+click the **uiIdTermLabel** control. Both controls should now be selected.

9 Click **Format** on the menu bar, point to **Align**, and then click **Lefts** to align the left border of the uiTermTextBox control with the left border of the uiIdTermLabel control.

10 Click the **form** to deselect the controls. Figure 4-34 shows the completed user interface.

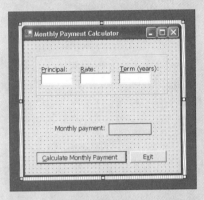

Figure 4-34: Completed user interface

Now that you have completed the user interface, you can lock the controls in place, and then set each control's TabIndex property appropriately.

Locking the Controls and Setting the TabIndex Property

As you learned in Chapter 2, when you have completed a user interface, you should lock the controls in place, and then set each control's TabIndex property.

To lock the controls, and then set each control's TabIndex property:

1 Right-click the **form**, and then click **Lock Controls** on the context menu.

2 Click **View** on the menu bar, and then click **Tab Order**. The current TabIndex value for each control appears in blue boxes on the form.

Notice that the TabIndex values of the controls contained within the group box begin with the number 9, which is the TabIndex value of the group box itself; this indicates that the controls belong to the group box rather than to the form. As mentioned earlier, if you move or delete the group box, the controls that belong to the group box also will be moved or deleted. The numbers that appear after the period in the controls' TabIndex values indicate the order in which each control was added to the group box.

3 Click the **uiInfoGroupBox** control. The number 0 replaces the number 9 in the TabIndex box, and the color of the box changes from blue to white to indicate that you have set the TabIndex value.

4 Click the **uiIdPrincipalLabel** control. The number 0.0 appears in the control's TabIndex box.

5 Click the **uiPrincipalTextBox** control. The number 0.1 appears in the control's TabIndex box.

6 Use the information in Figure 4-35 to set the TabIndex values for the remaining controls on the form.

Figure 4-35: Correct TabIndex values

7 Press **Esc** to remove the TabIndex boxes from the form.

8 Click **File** on the menu bar, and then click **Save All** to save the solution.

Recall that you also can click View on the menu bar and then click Tab Order to remove the TabIndex boxes.

Now you can begin coding the application. The TOE chart for the Monthly Payment Calculator application is shown in Figure 4-36.

Task	Object	Event
1. Calculate the monthly payment amount 2. Display the monthly payment amount in the uiPaymentLabel control	uiCalcPayButton	Click
End the application	uiExitButton	Click
Display the monthly payment amount (from uiCalcPayButton)	uiPaymentLabel	None
Get and display the principal, rate, and term amounts	uiPrincipalTextBox, uiRateTextBox, uiTermTextBox	None
Clear the contents of the uiPaymentLabel control	uiPrincipalTextBox, uiRateTextBox, uiTermTextBox	TextChanged
Prevent the user from typing a minus sign, dollar sign, percent sign, comma, or space in a text box	uiPrincipalTextBox, uiRateTextBox, uiTermTextBox	KeyPress

Figure 4-36: TOE chart for the Monthly Payment Calculator application

According to the TOE chart, the Click event procedures for the two buttons, and the TextChanged and KeyPress events for the three text boxes need to be coded. When you open the Code Editor window, you will notice that the uiExitButton's Click event procedure has been coded for you. In this lesson, you first code the uiCalcPayButton's Click event procedure, and then you code the TextChanged event for the text boxes. You code the KeyPress event in Lesson C.

Coding the uiCalcPayButton Click Event Procedure

According to the TOE chart shown in Figure 4-36, the uiCalcPayButton's Click event procedure is responsible for calculating the monthly payment amount, and then displaying the result in the uiPaymentLabel control. The pseudocode for the uiCalcPayButton's Click event procedure is shown in Figure 4-37.

---

uiCalcPayButton
1.   declare variables

2.   assign principal, rate, and term to variables

3.   if rate >= 1
         rate = rate /100
     end if

4.   if term >= 1
         calculate the monthly payment
         display the monthly payment in the uiPaymentLabel control
     else
         display the message "The term must be greater than or equal to 1." in a message box
     end if

Figure 4-37: Pseudocode for the uiCalcPayButton Click event procedure

To begin coding the uiCalcPayButton's Click event procedure:

1   Right-click the **form**, and then click **View Code** to open the Code Editor window. Notice that the uiExitButton's Click event procedure already contains the `Me.Close()` statement.

2   Replace the *<enter your name here>* and *<enter date here>* text with your name and the current date.

3   Open the code template for the uiCalcPayButton's Click event procedure.

4   Type '**calculates and displays a monthly payment** and press **Enter** twice.

The first step in the pseudocode shown in Figure 4-37 is to declare the necessary variables. The uiCalcPayButton's Click event procedure will use four Double variables named `principal`, `interestRate`, `loanTerm`, and `monthlyPayment`.

5   Type the following four Dim statements, and then press **Enter** twice.

   Dim principal As Double

   Dim interestRate As Double

   Dim loanTerm As Double

   Dim monthlyPayment As Double

Step 2 in the pseudocode is to assign the principal, rate, and term information to the appropriate variables.

6   Enter the comment and three assignment statements shown in Figure 4-38, then position the insertion point as shown in the figure.

tip

It is a good programming practice to use a blank line to separate related blocks of code in the Code Editor window; this makes your code more readable and easier to understand.

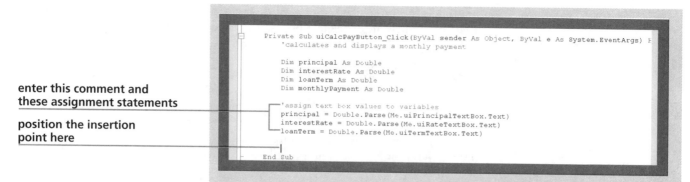

```
    Private Sub uiCalcPayButton_Click(ByVal sender As Object, ByVal e As System.EventArgs) H
        'calculates and displays a monthly payment

        Dim principal As Double
        Dim interestRate As Double
        Dim loanTerm As Double
        Dim monthlyPayment As Double

        'assign text box values to variables
        principal = Double.Parse(Me.uiPrincipalTextBox.Text)
        interestRate = Double.Parse(Me.uiRateTextBox.Text)
        loanTerm = Double.Parse(Me.uiTermTextBox.Text)

        |
    End Sub
```

enter this comment and these assignment statements

position the insertion point here

Figure 4-38: Comment and three assignment statements entered in the procedure

Now use a selection structure to handle Step 3 in the pseudocode—determining whether the application needs to convert the interest rate entered by the user to its decimal equivalent. This is necessary because the user might enter the rate as a whole number, or he or she might enter it as a decimal number. For example, an interest rate of 5% might be entered as either 5 or .05.

7   Type **'convert the rate to decimal form, if necessary** and press **Enter**.

8   Type **if interestrate >= 1.0 then** and press **Enter**. Notice that when you press Enter, the Code Editor automatically enters the End If statement in the window. Type **interestrate = interestrate / 100.0** between the If and End If statements.

9   Position the insertion point after the End If statement, and then press **Enter** twice to insert two blank lines after the statement.

Step 4 in the pseudocode is to determine whether the term amount entered by the user is greater than or equal to one year.

10   Type **'verify that the term is valid** and press **Enter**.

11   Type **if loanterm >= 1.0 then** and press **Enter**. Figure 4-39 shows the current status of the procedure.

```
    Private Sub uiCalcPayButton_Click(ByVal sender As Object, ByVal e As System.EventArgs) H
        'calculates and displays a monthly payment

        Dim principal As Double
        Dim interestRate As Double
        Dim loanTerm As Double
        Dim monthlyPayment As Double

        'assign text box values to variables
        principal = Double.Parse(Me.uiPrincipalTextBox.Text)
        interestRate = Double.Parse(Me.uiRateTextBox.Text)
        loanTerm = Double.Parse(Me.uiTermTextBox.Text)

        'convert the rate to decimal form, if necessary
        If interestRate >= 1.0 Then
            interestRate = interestRate / 100.0
        End If

        'verify that the term is valid
        If loanTerm >= 1.0 Then
            |
        End If
    End Sub
```

Figure 4-39: Current status of the uiCalcPayButton Click event procedure

According to the pseudocode, if the term is valid, the procedure should calculate the monthly payment, and then display the monthly payment in the uiPaymentLabel control. You can use the Financial.Pmt method to calculate the monthly payment.

Using the Financial.Pmt Method

You can use the Visual Basic .NET **Financial.Pmt method** to calculate a periodic payment on either a loan or an investment. Figure 4-40 shows the syntax of the Financial.Pmt method and lists the meaning of each argument included in the method. The figure also includes three examples of using the method.

Using the Financial.Pmt method

Syntax

Financial.Pmt(*Rate, NPer, PV*[, *FV, Due*]**)**

Argument	Meaning
Rate	interest rate per period
NPer	total number of payment periods (the term)
PV	present value of the loan or investment; the present value of a loan is the loan amount, whereas the present value of an investment is zero
FV	future value of the loan or investment; the future value of a loan is zero, whereas the future value of an investment is the amount you want to accumulate; if omitted, the number 0 is assumed
Due	due date of payments; can be either the constant `DueDate.EndOfPeriod` or the constant `DueDate.BegOfPeriod`; if omitted, `DueDate.EndOfPeriod` is assumed

Example 1 – Calculates the annual payment for a loan of $9,000 for 3 years at 5% interest. The payments are due at the end of each period (year).

Rate: .05

NPer: 3

PV: 9000

FV: 0

Due: `DueDate.EndOfPeriod`

Method: `Financial.Pmt(.05, 3, 9000, 0, DueDate.EndOfPeriod)`

or

`Financial.Pmt(.05, 3, 9000)`

Annual payment (rounded to the nearest cent): -3,304.88

Figure 4-40: Syntax, arguments, and examples of the Financial.Pmt method

<u>Example 2</u> – Calculates the monthly payment for a loan of $12,000 for 5 years at 6% interest. The payments are due at the beginning of each period (month).

Rate: .06/12

NPer: 5 * 12

PV: 12000

FV: 0

Due: `DueDate.BegOfPeriod`

Method: `Financial.Pmt(.06/12, 5 * 12, 12000, 0, DueDate.BegOfPeriod)`

Monthly payment (rounded to the nearest cent): -230.84

<u>Example 3</u> – Calculates the amount you need to save each month to accumulate $40,000 at the end of 20 years. The interest rate is 6%, and deposits are due at the beginning of each period (month).

Rate: .06/12

NPer: 20 * 12

PV: 0

FV: 40000

Due: `DueDate.BegOfPeriod`

Method: `Financial.Pmt(.06/12, 20 * 12, 0, 40000, DueDate.BegOfPeriod)`

Monthly payment (rounded to the nearest cent): -86.14

Figure 4-40: Syntax, arguments, and examples of the Financial.Pmt method (continued)

Notice that the Financial.Pmt method contains five arguments. Three of the arguments (*Rate*, *NPer*, and *PV*) are required, and two (*FV* and *Due*) are optional. If the *FV* (future value) argument is omitted, the method uses the default value, 0. If the *Due* argument is omitted, the method uses the constant `DueDate.EndOfPeriod` as the default value. The `DueDate.EndOfPeriod` constant indicates that payments are due at the end of each period.

Study closely the three examples shown in Figure 4-40. Example 1 uses the Financial.Pmt method to calculate the annual payment for a loan of $9,000 for 3 years at 5% interest, where payments are due at the end of each period; in this case, a period is a year. As the example indicates, the annual payment returned by the method and rounded to the nearest cent is -3,304.88. In other words, if you borrow $9,000 for 3 years at 5% interest, you would need to make three annual payments of $3,304.88 to pay off the loan. Notice that the Financial.Pmt method returns a negative number.

When calculating an annual payment, the *Rate* argument should specify the annual interest rate, and the *NPer* argument should specify the life of the loan or investment in years. In Example 1, the *Rate* argument is .05, which is the annual interest rate, and the *NPer* argument is the number 3, which is the number of years you have to pay off the loan. As the example indicates, you can use the method `Financial.Pmt(.05, 3, 9000, 0, DueDate.EndOfPeriod)` to calculate the annual payment. You also can use the method `Pmt(.05, 3, 9000)`, because the default values for the optional *FV* and *Due* arguments are 0 and `DueDate.EndOfPeriod`, respectively.

tip

The *Rate* and *NPer* arguments in the Financial.Pmt method must be expressed using the same units. For example, if *Rate* is a monthly interest rate, then *NPer* must specify the number of monthly payments. If *Rate* is an annual interest rate, then *NPer* must specify the number of annual payments.

The Financial.Pmt method shown in Example 2 in Figure 4-40 calculates the monthly payment for a loan of $12,000 for 5 years at 6% interest, where payments are due at the beginning of each period; in this case, a period is a month. Notice that the *Rate* and *NPer* arguments are expressed in monthly terms rather than in annual terms. The monthly payment for this loan, rounded to the nearest cent, is -230.84.

In addition to using the Financial.Pmt method to calculate the payments required to pay off a loan, you also can use the method to calculate the amount you would need to save each period to accumulate a specific sum. The method `Financial.Pmt(.06/12, 20 * 12, 0, 40000, DueDate.BegOfPeriod)` shown in Example 3 in Figure 4-40, for instance, indicates that you need to save 86.14 (rounded to the nearest cent) each month to accumulate $40,000 at the end of 20 years, assuming a 6% interest rate and the appropriate amount deposited at the beginning of each period.

In the current application, you will use the Financial.Pmt method to calculate a monthly payment on a car loan. When entering the method, you must convert the annual interest rate, which is stored in the `interestRate` variable, to a monthly rate; you do so by dividing the annual rate by 12. You also must multiply by 12 the term of the loan, which is expressed in years and stored in the `loanTerm` variable, to convert the number of years to the number of months. Additionally, because you want the monthly payment amount to appear as a positive number, you will precede the Financial.Pmt method with the negation operator (−).

tip

You learned about the negation operator in Chapter 2. The negation operator reverses the sign of the number: a negative number becomes a positive number and vice versa.

To continue coding the uiCalcPayButton Click event procedure:

1   In the blank line below the `If loanTerm >= 1.0 Then` instruction, type **'calculate and display the monthly payment** and press **Enter**.

2   Type **monthlypayment = -financial.pmt(interestrate/12, loanterm * 12, principal, 0, duedate.begofperiod)** and press **Enter**.

Now format the monthly payment amount to show a dollar sign and two decimal places, and then display the formatted amount in the uiPaymentLabel control.

3   Type **me.uipaymentlabel.text = monthlypayment.tostring("C2")** and press **Enter**. See Figure 4-41. (The size of the font used in the Code Editor window was changed so that you could view more of the code in the figure.)

true path

```
Private Sub uiCalcPayButton_Click(ByVal sender As Object, ByVal e As System.EventArgs) Handles uiCalcPayButton.C
    'calculates and displays a monthly payment

    Dim principal As Double
    Dim interestRate As Double
    Dim loanTerm As Double
    Dim monthlyPayment As Double

    'assign text box values to variables
    principal = Double.Parse(Me.uiPrincipalTextBox.Text)
    interestRate = Double.Parse(Me.uiRateTextBox.Text)
    loanTerm = Double.Parse(Me.uiTermTextBox.Text)

    'convert the rate to decimal form, if necessary
    If interestRate >= 1.0 Then
        interestRate = interestRate / 100.0
    End If

    'verify that the term is valid
    If loanTerm >= 1.0 Then
        'calculate and display the monthly payment
        monthlyPayment = -Financial.Pmt(interestRate / 12, loanTerm * 12, principal, 0, DueDate.BegOfPeriod)
        Me.uiPaymentLabel.Text = monthlyPayment.ToString("C2")

    End If
End Sub
```

Figure 4-41: Selection structure's true path coded in the procedure

4   Save the solution.

tip

In previous versions of Visual Basic, programmers used the MsgBox function to display a message box. Although the MsgBox function still is available in Visual Basic .NET, the MessageBox. Show method is the recommended way to display a message box.

According to the pseudocode shown in Figure 4-37, if the term entered by the user is not greater than or equal to 1, the uiCalcPayButton's Click event procedure should display an appropriate message in a message box. You can display the message using the MessageBox.Show method.

The MessageBox.Show Method

You can use the **MessageBox.Show method** to display a message box that contains text, one or more buttons, and an icon. Figure 4-42 shows the syntax of the MessageBox.Show method. It also lists the meaning of each argument used by the method, and includes two examples of using the method to create a message box.

Using the MessageBox.Show method	
Syntax	
MessageBox.Show(*text, caption, buttons, icon*[*, defaultButton*]**)**	
Argument	**Meaning**
text	text to display in the message box
caption	text to display in the title bar of the message box

buttons	buttons to display in the message box; can be one of the following constants:
	`MessageBoxButtons.AbortRetryIgnore`
	`MessageBoxButtons.OK`
	`MessageBoxButtons.OKCancel`
	`MessageBoxButtons.RetryCancel`
	`MessageBoxButtons.YesNo`
	`MessageBoxButtons.YesNoCancel`

icon	icon to display in the message box; typically, one of the following constants: `MessageBoxIcon.Exclamation` ⚠ `MessageBoxIcon.Information` ⓘ `MessageBoxIcon.Stop` ⊗

defaultButton	button automatically selected when the user presses Enter; can be one of the following constants:
	`MessageBoxDefaultButton.Button1` (default setting)
	`MessageBoxDefaultButton.Button2`
	`MessageBoxDefaultButton.Button3`

Example 1 – Displays an informational message box that contains the message "Record deleted.".
`MessageBox.Show("Record deleted.", "Payroll", _`
`    MessageBoxButtons.OK, MessageBoxIcon.Information)`	

Example 2 – Displays a warning message box that contains the message "Delete this record?".
`MessageBox.Show("Delete this record?", "Payroll", _`
`    MessageBoxButtons.YesNo, MessageBoxIcon.Exclamation, _`
`    MessageBoxDefaultButton.Button2)`	

Figure 4-42: Syntax, arguments, and examples of the MessageBox.Show method

As Figure 4-42 indicates, the *text* argument specifies the text to display in the message box. The *text* argument can be a String literal constant, String named constant, or String variable. The message in the *text* argument should be concise but clear, and should be entered using sentence capitalization. You should avoid using the words "error," "warning," or "mistake" in the message, as these words imply that the user has done something wrong.

The *caption* argument specifies the text to display in the title bar of the message box, and typically is the application's name. Like the *text* argument, the *caption* argument can be a String literal constant, String named constant, or String variable. Unlike the *text* argument, however, the *caption* argument is entered using book title capitalization.

The *buttons* argument indicates the buttons to display in the message box and can be one of six different constants. For example, a *buttons* argument of `MessageBoxButtons.AbortRetryIgnore` displays the Abort, Retry, and Ignore buttons in the message box. A *buttons* argument of `MessageBoxButtons.OK`, on the other hand, displays only the OK button in the message box.

The *icon* argument specifies the icon to display in the message box and typically is one of the following constants: `MessageBoxIcon.Exclamation`, `MessageBoxIcon.Information`, or `MessageBoxIcon.Stop`. A message box's icon indicates the type of message being sent to the user. The `MessageBoxIcon.Exclamation` constant, for example, displays the Warning Message icon, which alerts the user to a condition or situation that requires him or her to make a decision before the application can proceed. The message to the user can be phrased as a question, such as "Save changes to the document?"

The `MessageBoxIcon.Information` constant displays the Information Message icon, which indicates that the message in the message box is for information only and does not require the user to make a decision. An example of an informational message is "The changes were saved." A message box with an Information Message icon should contain only an OK button. In other words, you always use `MessageBoxButtons.OK` for the *buttons* argument when using `MessageBoxIcon.Information` for the *icon* argument. The user acknowledges the informational message by clicking the OK button.

The `MessageBoxIcon.Stop` constant displays the Stop Message icon, which alerts the user to a serious problem that requires intervention or correction before the application can continue. You would use the Stop Message icon in a message box that alerts the user that the disk in the disk drive is write-protected.

The *defaultButton* argument in the MessageBox.Show method identifies the default button, which is the button that is selected automatically when the user presses the Enter key on the computer keyboard. To designate the first button in the message box as the default button, you either set the *defaultButton* argument to `MessageBoxDefaultButton.Button1`, or you simply omit the argument. To have the second or third button be the default button, you set the *defaultButton* argument to `MessageBoxDefaultButton.Button2` or `MessageBoxDefaultButton.Button3`, respectively. The default button should be the button that represents the user's most likely action, as long as that action is not destructive.

Study closely the two examples shown in Figure 4-42. In the first example, the `MessageBox.Show("Record deleted.", "Payroll", MessageBoxButtons.OK, MessageBoxIcon.Information)` instruction displays the informational message box shown in Figure 4-43. Similarly, the `MessageBox.Show("Delete this record?", "Payroll", MessageBoxButtons.YesNo, MessageBoxIcon.Exclamation, MessageBoxDefaultButton.Button2)` instruction in the second example displays the warning message box shown in Figure 4-44.

Figure 4-43: Message box displayed by the first example shown in Figure 4-42

default button

Figure 4-44: Message box displayed by the second example shown in Figure 4-42

MessageBox.Show Method Standards

- Use sentence capitalization for the *text* argument, but book title capitalization for the *caption* argument. The name of the application typically appears in the *caption* argument.
- Avoid using the words "error," "warning," or "mistake" in the message, as these words imply that the user has done something wrong.
- Display the Warning Message icon ⚠ in a message box that alerts the user that he or she must make a decision before the application can continue. You can phrase the message as a question.
- Display the Information Message icon ⓘ in a message box that displays an informational message along with an OK button only.
- Display the Stop Message icon ⊗ when you want to alert the user of a serious problem that must be corrected before the application can continue.
- The default button in the dialog box should be the one that represents the user's most likely action, as long as that action is not destructive.

After displaying the message box, the MessageBox.Show method waits for the user to choose one of the buttons displayed in the message box. It then closes the message box and returns an integer that indicates which button the user chose.

Sometimes you are not interested in the value returned by the MessageBox.Show method. This is the case when the message box is for informational purposes only, like the message box shown in Figure 4-43. Recall that the only button in an informational message box is the OK button. Many times, however, the button selected by the user determines the next task performed by an application. For example, selecting the Yes button in the message box shown in Figure 4-44 tells the application to delete the record; selecting the No button tells the application not to delete the record.

Figure 4-45 lists the integer values returned by the MessageBox.Show method; each integer is associated with a button that can appear in a message box. The figure also lists the constant values assigned to each integer, and the meaning of the integers and constants. Additionally, the figure contains three examples of using the value returned by the MessageBox.Show method.

Values returned by the MessageBox.Show method		
Number	Constant	Meaning
1	DialogResult.OK	user chose the OK button
2	DialogResult.Cancel	user chose the Cancel button
3	DialogResult.Abort	user chose the Abort button
4	DialogResult.Retry	user chose the Retry button
5	DialogResult.Ignore	user chose the Ignore button
6	DialogResult.Yes	user chose the Yes button
7	DialogResult.No	user chose the No button

Example 1

```
Dim button As Integer
button = MessageBox.Show("Delete this record?", _
          "Payroll", MessageBoxButtons.YesNo, _
          MessageBoxIcon.Exclamation, _
          MessageBoxDefaultButton.Button2)
If button = DialogResult.Yes Then
       instructions to delete the record
End If
```

Example 2

```
If MessageBox.Show("Delete this record?", _
     "Payroll", MessageBoxButtons.YesNo, _
     MessageBoxIcon.Exclamation, _
     MessageBoxDefaultButton.Button2) = DialogResult.Yes Then
        instructions to delete the record
End If
```

Example 3
```
Dim button As Integer
button = MessageBox.Show("Play another game?", _
             "Math Monster", MessageBoxButtons.YesNo, _
             MessageBoxIcon.Exclamation)
If button = DialogResult.Yes Then
       instructions to start another game
Else   'DialogResult.No
       instructions to close the game application
End If
```

Figure 4-45: Values returned by the MessageBox.Show method

As Figure 4-45 indicates, the MessageBox.Show method returns the integer 6 when the user selects the Yes button in the message box. The integer 6 is represented by the constant DialogResult.Yes. When referring to the MessageBox.Show method's return value in code, you should use the constants listed in Figure 4-45 rather than the integers, because the constants make the code easier to understand.

Look closely at the three examples shown in Figure 4-45. In the first example, the value returned by the MessageBox.Show method is assigned to an Integer variable named button. If the user selects the Yes button in the message box, the number 6 is stored in the button variable; otherwise, the number 7 is stored in the variable to indicate that the user selected the No button. The selection structure in the example compares the contents of the button variable to the constant DialogResult.Yes. If the button variable contains the number 6, which is the value of the DialogResult.Yes constant, then the instructions to delete the record are processed; otherwise, the deletion instructions are skipped.

You do not have to store the value returned by the MessageBox.Show method in a variable, although doing so can make your code more readable. For instance, in the second example shown in Figure 4-45, the method's return value is not stored in a variable. Instead, the method appears in the selection structure's *condition*, where its return value is compared to the `DialogResult.Yes` constant.

The selection structure shown in the third example in Figure 4-45 performs one set of tasks when the user selects the Yes button, and another set of tasks when the user selects the No button. It is a good programming practice to document the Else portion of the selection structure as shown in the figure, because it makes it clear that the Else portion is processed only when the user selects the No button.

Recall that the uiCalcPayButton's Click event procedure should display the message "The term must be greater than or equal to 1." if the term entered by the user is not greater than or equal to 1. The message box is for informational purposes only. Therefore, it should contain the Information Message icon and the OK button, and you do not need to be concerned with its return value.

To complete the uiCalcPayButton Click event procedure:

1   Enter the additional code shown in Figure 4-46, which shows the completed uiCalcPayButton's Click event procedure.

```
Private Sub uiCalcPayButton_Click(ByVal sender As Object, ByVal e As System.EventArgs) Handles uiCalcPayButton.C
    'calculates and displays a monthly payment

    Dim principal As Double
    Dim interestRate As Double
    Dim loanTerm As Double
    Dim monthlyPayment As Double

    'assign text box values to variables
    principal = Double.Parse(Me.uiPrincipalTextBox.Text)
    interestRate = Double.Parse(Me.uiRateTextBox.Text)
    loanTerm = Double.Parse(Me.uiTermTextBox.Text)

    'convert the rate to decimal form, if necessary
    If interestRate >= 1.0 Then
        interestRate = interestRate / 100.0
    End If

    'verify that the term is valid
    If loanTerm >= 1.0 Then
        'calculate and display the monthly payment
        monthlyPayment = -Financial.Pmt(interestRate / 12, loanTerm * 12, principal, 0, DueDate.BegOfPeriod)
        Me.uiPaymentLabel.Text = monthlyPayment.ToString("C2")
    Else
        MessageBox.Show("The term must be greater than or equal to 1.",
            "Monthly Payment Calculator", MessageBoxButtons.OK, MessageBoxIcon.Information)
    End If
End Sub
```

line continuation character

enter these three lines of code

Figure 4-46: Completed uiCalcPayButton Click event procedure

2   Save the solution, then start the application. The Monthly Payment Calculator user interface appears on the screen.

Calculate the monthly payment for a loan of $12,000 for 5 years at 6% interest, where payments are due at the beginning of each month. (Recall that the *Due* argument in the Financial.Pmt method is `DueDate.BegOfPeriod`.)

3   Type **12000** in the Principal text box and press **Tab**. Type **6** in the Rate text box and press **Tab**. Type **5** in the Term text box and press **Enter** to select the Calculate Monthly Payment button, which is the default button on the form. The uiCalcPayButton's Click event procedure calculates and displays the monthly payment, as shown in Figure 4-47.

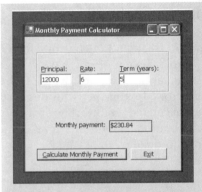

Figure 4-47: Monthly payment displayed in the interface

Next, verify that the application works correctly when the user enters an incorrect term.

4   Change the term from 5 to 0, and then press **Enter**. The application displays the message box shown in Figure 4-48.

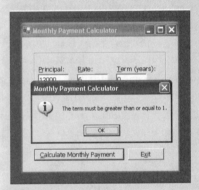

Figure 4-48: Message box created by the MessageBox.Show method

5   Press **Enter** to select the OK button in the message box. The message box closes.

6   Click the **Exit** button to end the application.

Now verify that the application works correctly when the user enters the interest rate as a decimal number.

7   Start the application. Enter **12000** in the Principal text box, **.06** in the Rate text box, and **5** in the Term text box. Press **Enter**. The uiCalcPayButton's Click event procedure calculates and displays a monthly payment of $230.84, which is the same monthly payment shown in Figure 4-47.

8   Click the **Exit** button to end the application. When you return to the Code Editor window, close the Output window.

According to the TOE chart shown earlier in Figure 4-36, you also need to code the TextChanged event for the three text boxes.

Coding the TextChanged Event

As you learned in Chapter 3, a control's TextChanged event occurs when the contents of a control's Text property have changed. This can happen as a result of either the user entering data into the control, or the application's code assigning data to the control's Text property. In this case, when the user makes a change to the information entered in the three text box controls, the Monthly Payment Calculator application should delete the monthly payment displayed in the uiPaymentLabel control.

To code the TextChanged event for the three text boxes:

1. Open the code template for the uiPrincipalTextBox control's TextChanged event.

2. Type **'clears monthly payment** and press **Enter** twice.

3. Type **me.uipaymentlabel.text = ""** and press **Enter**. This instruction tells the computer to remove the contents of the uiPaymentLabel control.

Next, assign the procedure a more meaningful name, and then tell the computer to process the procedure when the TextChanged event occurs for any of the three text boxes.

4. Change `uiPrincipalTextBox_TextChanged`, which appears after the words `Private Sub`, to **ClearLabel**.

5. Type **_** (an underscore, which is the line continuation character) immediately before the letter H in the word Handles, and then press **Enter**.

6. Press **Tab** twice to indent the Handles line, and then make the additional changes noted in Figure 4-49.

enter this additional code ───────────────

```
Private Sub ClearLabel(ByVal sender As Object, ByVal e As System.EventArgs) _
    Handles uiPrincipalTextBox.TextChanged, uiRateTextBox.TextChanged, uiTermTextBox.TextChanged
    'clears monthly payment

    Me.uiPaymentLabel.Text = ""

End Sub
```

Figure 4-49: Completed ClearLabel procedure

Now test the ClearLabel procedure to verify that it is working correctly.

To test the ClearLabel procedure:

1. Save the solution, then start the application.

2. Enter **30000** in the Principal text box, **8** in the Rate text box, and **5** in the Term text box. Press **Enter**. $604.26 appears in the Monthly payment label.

3. Change the term from 5 to 3. Notice that the $604.26 no longer appears in the Monthly payment label. This is because when you make a change to the Term text box, the text box's TextChanged event processes the `Me.uiPaymentLabel.Text = ""` instruction contained in the ClearLabel procedure.

4 Press **Enter**. $933.87 appears in the Monthly payment label.

5 On your own, verify that the monthly payment amount is removed from the interface when the user changes the principal and rate amounts. However, be sure to enter a number in each text box; otherwise, the application will not run correctly. You learn how to fix this problem in Lesson C.

6 Click the **Exit** button to end the application. When you return to the Code Editor window, close the Output window, and then close the Code Editor window.

7 Click **File** on the menu bar, and then click **Close Solution** to close the solution.

You now have completed Lesson B. You complete the Monthly Payment Calculator application in Lesson C. For now, you can either take a break or complete the end-of-lesson questions and exercises before moving on to the next lesson.

SUMMARY

To use a group box control to group controls together:

■ Use the GroupBox tool to add a group box control to the form. Drag controls from either the form or the Toolbox window into the group box control.

■ To include an optional identifying label on a group box control, set the group box control's Text property.

■ The TabIndex value of a control contained within a group box control is composed of two numbers separated by a period. The number to the left of the period is the TabIndex value of the group box itself. The number to the right of the period indicates the order in which the control was added to the group box.

To calculate a periodic payment on either a loan or an investment:

■ Use the Financial.Pmt method. The method's syntax is **Financial.Pmt(***Rate*, *NPer*, *PV*[, *FV*, *Due*]**)**. Refer to Figure 4-40 for a description of each argument and examples of using the method to calculate a periodic payment.

To display a message box that contains text, one or more buttons, and an icon:

■ Use the MessageBox.Show method. The method's syntax is **MessageBox.Show(***text*, *caption*, *buttons*, *icon*[, *defaultButton*]**)**. Refer to Figure 4-42 for a description of each argument and examples of using the method to display a message box.

■ Figure 4-45 lists the values returned by the MessageBox.Show method.

QUESTIONS

1. Which of the following statements is false?
    a. When you delete a group box control, the controls contained within the group box remain on the form.
    b. Use sentence capitalization for the group box control's identifying label.
    c. When you move a group box control, the controls contained within the group box also move.
    d. You can include an identifying label on a group box by setting the group box control's Text property.
    e. You can drag a control from the Toolbox window into a group box control.

2. Assume that the TabIndex value of a group box control is 5. If the uiNameTextBox control was the first control added to the group box, then its TabIndex value will be
    _____.
    a. 0.5
    b. 1
    c. 1.5
    d. 5.0
    e. 5.1

3. Which of the following calculates the monthly payment on a loan of $5,000 for 2 years at 4% interest? Payments are due at the end of the month and should be expressed as a positive number.
    a. `-Financial.Pmt(.04/12, 2 * 12, 5000)`
    b. `-Financial.Pmt(.04/12, 24, 5000)`
    c. `-Financial.Pmt(.04/12, 2 * 12, 5000, 0)`
    d. `-Financial.Pmt(.04/12, 24, 5000, 0,`
        `DueDate.EndOfPeriod)`
    e. All of the above.

4. Which of the following calculates the quarterly payment on a loan of $6,000 for 3 years at 9% interest? Payments are due at the beginning of the quarter and should be expressed as a negative number.
    a. `Financial.Pmt(.09/4, 3 * 12, 6000, 0,`
        `DueDate.BegOfPeriod)`
    b. `Financial.Pmt(.09/4, 3 * 4, 6000, 0,`
        `DueDate.BegOfPeriod)`
    c. `Financial.Pmt(.09/12, 3 * 12, 6000, 0,`
        `DueDate.BegOfPeriod)`
    d. `Financial.Pmt(.09/12, 12, 6000, 0,`
        `DueDate.BegOfPeriod)`
    e. None of the above.

5. Which of the following calculates the amount you need to save each month to accumulate $50,000 at the end of 10 years? The interest rate is 3% and deposits, which should be expressed as a positive number, are due at the beginning of the month.

    a. `Financial.Pmt(.03/12, 10 * 12, 0, 50000,`
       `DueDate.BegOfPeriod)`

    b. `-Financial.Pmt(.03/12, 10 * 12, 0, 50000,`
       `DueDate.BegOfPeriod)`

    c. `-Financial.Pmt(.03/12, 10 * 12, 50000, 0)`

    d. `Financial.Pmt(.03/12, 10 * 12, 50000, 0,`
       `DueDate.BegOfPeriod)`

    e. `-Financial.Pmt(.03/12, 120, 50000, 0, DueDate.BegOfPeriod)`

6. A message box's _____ argument indicates the type of message being sent.

    a. *buttons*

    b. *caption*

    c. *icon*

    d. *text*

    e. Both b and c.

7. You use the _____ constant to include the Warning Message icon in a message box.

    a. `MessageBox.Exclamation`

    b. `MessageBox.IconExclamation`

    c. `MessageBoxIcon.Exclamation`

    d. `MessageBox.IconWarning`

    e. `MessageBox.WarningIcon`

8. If a message is for informational purposes only and does not require the user to make a decision, the message box should display which of the following?

    a. an OK button and the Information Message icon

    b. an OK button and the Warning Message icon

    c. a Yes button and the Information Message icon

    d. any button and the Information Message icon

    e. an OK button and any icon

9. You can use the _____ method to display a message in a message box.

    a. `MessageBox.Display`

    b. `MessageBox.Open`

    c. `Message.Open`

    d. `Message.Show`

    e. None of the above.

10. If the user clicks the OK button in a message box, the message box returns the number 1, which is equivalent to which constant?

    a. `DialogResult.OK`

    b. `DialogResult.OKButton`

    c. `Message.OK`

    d. `MessageBox.OK`

    e. `MessageResult.OK`

EXERCISES

1. In this exercise, you code an application that uses the Financial.Pmt method to calculate the amount of money you need to save each week to accumulate a specific sum.

    a. If necessary, start Visual Studio .NET. Open the Weekly Savings Solution (Weekly Savings Solution.sln) file, which is contained in the VBNET\Chap04\Weekly Savings Solution folder. If necessary, open the designer window.

    b. Add a group box control to the interface. Name the group box control uiInfoGroupBox. Drag the uiIdGoalLabel, uiIdRateLabel, uiIdTermLabel, uiGoalTextBox, uiRateTextBox, and uiTermTextBox controls into the group box. Position the controls appropriately. Delete the contents of the group box's Text property.

    c. Lock the controls, and then set the TabIndex property appropriately.

    d. The user will enter the amount he or she wants to accumulate in the uiGoalTextBox. He or she will enter the annual interest rate and term (in years) in the uiRateTextBox and uiTermTextBox controls, respectively. Code the Calculate button so that it calculates the amount of money the user will need to save each week. Assume that each year has exactly 52 weeks, and that deposits are made at the end of the week. The weekly payment should show two decimal places and be displayed in the uiSavingsLabel control.

    e. Save the solution, then start the application. Test the application by calculating the amount the user needs to save to accumulate $10,000 at the end of two years, assuming a 4.5% interest rate.

    f. Click the Exit button to end the application.

    g. Close the Output window, then close the solution.

2. In this exercise, you code an application for Mingo Sales. The application calculates a 10% discount if the customer is a wholesaler.

    a. If necessary, start Visual Studio .NET. Open the Discount Solution (Discount Solution.sln) file, which is contained in the VBNET\Chap04\Discount Solution folder. If necessary, open the designer window.

    The user will enter the product number, quantity ordered, and price in the uiProductTextBox, uiQuantityTextBox, and uiPriceTextBox controls, respectively.

    b. Code the Calculate button so that it displays the message "Are you a wholesaler?" in a message box. If the user is a wholesaler, calculate a 10% discount on the total due, and then display the discount with two decimal places in the uiDiscountLabel control; otherwise, display 0.00 in the uiDiscountLabel control. Display the total due with a dollar sign and two decimal places in the uiTotalLabel control.

    c. Have the application remove the contents of the uiDiscountLabel and uiTotalLabel controls when a change is made to the contents of a text box on the form.

    d. Save the solution, then start the application. Test the application by calculating the total due for a wholesaler ordering four units of product number BCX12 at $10 per unit. Then test the application by calculating the total due for a non-wholesaler ordering two units of product number ABC34 at $5 per unit.

    e. Click the Exit button to end the application.

    f. Close the Output window, then close the solution.

discovery ▶ 3. In this exercise, you research the constants you can use to display an icon in a message box.

    a. If necessary, start Visual Studio .NET. Click Help on the menu bar, and then click Index. Click the Filtered by list arrow, and then click Visual Basic and Related in the list (this may take several seconds to load).

    b. Type MessageBoxIcon in the Look for text box, then click MessageBoxIcon enumeration in the list of topics. An enumeration is simply a set of related constants. In this case, the MessageBoxIcon enumeration contains the constants you can use in the MessageBox.Show method's *icon* argument.

    c. Read the MessageBoxIcon Enumeration Help screen. In addition to the MessageBoxIcon.Exclamation constant, what other constant displays the Warning Message icon in a message box? Which constants display the Information Message icon? Which constants display the Stop Message icon? Which constant displays a symbol consisting of a question mark in a circle?

    d. Close the Help window.

LESSON C

objectives

After completing this lesson, you will be able to:

- Specify the keys that a text box will accept
- Align the text in a label control
- Handle exceptions using a Try/Catch block

Completing the Monthly Payment Calculator Application

Coding the KeyPress Event

Recall that you still need to code the KeyPress event for the three text box controls in the Monthly Payment Calculator application. Before learning more about this event, open the Monthly Payment Calculator application that you worked on in Lesson B, and then view the template for the uiPrincipalTextBox control's KeyPress event procedure.

To open the Monthly Payment Calculator application, then view the template for the KeyPress event procedure:

1. Start Microsoft Visual Studio .NET, if necessary.

2. If necessary, close the Start Page window.

3. Open the **Payment Solution** (Payment Solution.sln) file, which is contained in the VBNET\Chap04\Payment Solution folder.

4. Auto-hide the Toolbox, Solution Explorer, and Properties windows, if necessary. See Figure 4-50.

Figure 4-50: Monthly Payment Calculator application

5 Open the Code Editor window, and then open the code template for the uiPrincipalTextBox control's KeyPress event procedure. See Figure 4-51. The items contained within parentheses in the procedure are called **parameters** and represent information passed to the procedure when the event occurs. (The font size in the Code Editor window was changed so that you could view more of the code in the figure.)

sender **parameter**

e **parameter**

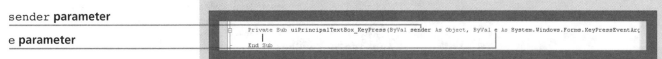

```
Private Sub uiPrincipalTextBox_KeyPress(ByVal sender As Object, ByVal e As System.Windows.Forms.KeyPressEventArg

End Sub
```

Figure 4-51: Code template for the uiPrincipalTextBox control's KeyPress event procedure

A control's KeyDown event also occurs when the user presses a key while the control has the focus. The KeyDown event occurs before the KeyPress event. When the user releases the key, the control's KeyUp event occurs.

A control's **KeyPress event** occurs when the user presses a key while the control has the focus. When the KeyPress event occurs, a character corresponding to the key that was pressed is sent to the KeyPress event's e parameter, which appears in the procedure header in every event procedure. For example, when you press the period (.) on your keyboard, a period is sent to the e parameter. Similarly, when you press the Shift key along with a letter key on your keyboard, the uppercase version of the letter is sent to the e parameter.

One popular use for the KeyPress event is to prevent users from entering inappropriate characters in a text box. For example, a text box for entering a person's age should contain numbers only; it should not contain letters or special characters, such as the dollar sign or percent sign. To prevent a text box from accepting inappropriate characters, you first use the e parameter's **KeyChar property** to determine the key that the user pressed. You then use the e parameter's **Handled property** to cancel the key if it is an inappropriate one. Figure 4-52 shows examples of using the KeyChar and Handled properties in the KeyPress event procedure.

KeyChar stands for "key character".

Using the KeyChar and Handled properties in the KeyPress event procedure

Example 1 - prevents the text box from accepting the dollar sign

```
Private Sub uiSalesTextBox_KeyPress(ByVal sender As Object, _
        ByVal e As System.Windows.Forms.KeyPressEventArgs) _
        Handles uiSalesTextBox.KeyPress
    If e.KeyChar = "$" Then
        e.Handled = True
    End If
End Sub
```

Example 2 – allows the text box to accept only numbers

```
Private Sub uiAgeTextBox_KeyPress(ByVal sender As Object, _
        ByVal e As System.Windows.Forms.KeyPressEventArgs) _
        Handles uiAgeTextBox.KeyPress
    If e.KeyChar < "0" OrElse e.KeyChar > "9" Then
        e.Handled = True
    End If
End Sub
```

Example 3 – allows the text box to accept only numbers and the Backspace key

```
Private Sub uiAgeTextBox_KeyPress(ByVal sender As Object, _
        ByVal e As System.Windows.Forms.KeyPressEventArgs) _
        Handles uiAgeTextBox.KeyPress
    If (e.KeyChar < "0" OrElse e.KeyChar > "9") _
        AndAlso e.KeyChar <> ControlChars.Back Then
        e.Handled = True
    End If
End Sub
```

Figure 4-52: Examples of using the KeyChar and Handled properties

The selection structure shown in Example 1 in Figure 4-52 prevents the uiSalesTextBox control from accepting the dollar sign. The `e.KeyChar = "$"` *condition* in the selection structure compares the contents of the e parameter's KeyChar property with a dollar sign ($). If the *condition* evaluates to True, which means that a dollar sign is stored in the KeyChar property, the `e.Handled = True` instruction cancels the key before it is entered in the uiSalesTextBox control.

You can use the selection structure shown in Example 2 to prevent a text box from accepting a character that is not a number. However, keep in mind that Example 2's selection structure also prevents the text box from accepting the Backspace key. In other words, when entering text in the uiAgeTextBox control, you will not be able to use the Backspace key to delete a character entered in the text box. You can, however, use the left and right arrow keys to position the insertion point immediately before the character you want to delete, and then use the Delete key to delete the character.

Like Example 2's selection structure, the selection structure shown in Example 3 in Figure 4-52 also prevents the uiAgeTextBox control from accepting a character that is not a number. However, unlike Example 2's selection structure, Example 3's selection structure allows the user to employ the Backspace key, which is represented by the constant **ControlChars.Back**. Basically, Example 3's selection structure tells the KeyPress event to cancel a key if it is not a number and, at the same time, it is not the Backspace key.

In the Monthly Payment Calculator application, you want the three text boxes to accept the numbers 0 through 9, the Backspace key, and the period; keys other than these should be canceled.

To allow the three text boxes to accept numbers, the Backspace key, and the period:

1   Change `uiPrincipalTextBox_KeyPress`, which appears in the procedure header, to **CancelKeys**.

2   Position the insertion point immediately before the letter H in the word Handles in the procedure header.

3   Type _ (the underscore, which is the line continuation character), and then press **Enter** to move the `Handles  uiPrincipalTextBox.KeyPress` text to the next line in the procedure.

4   Press **Tab** twice. Change `Handles uiPrincipalTextBox.KeyPress` to **Handles uiPrincipalTextBox.KeyPress, uiRateTextBox.KeyPress, uiTermTextBox.KeyPress**.

5   Enter the additional code shown in Figure 4-53. (The font size in the Code Editor window was changed so that you could view more of the code in the figure.)

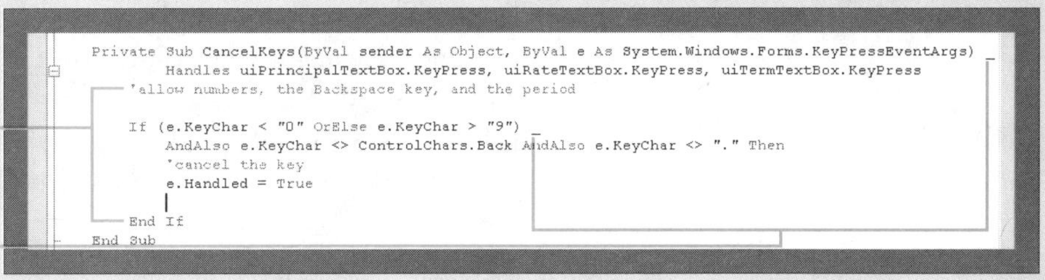

enter these comments and these lines of code

line continuation character

```
Private Sub CancelKeys(ByVal sender As Object, ByVal e As System.Windows.Forms.KeyPressEventArgs) _
        Handles uiPrincipalTextBox.KeyPress, uiRateTextBox.KeyPress, uiTermTextBox.KeyPress
    'allow numbers, the Backspace key, and the period

    If (e.KeyChar < "0" OrElse e.KeyChar > "9") _
        AndAlso e.KeyChar <> ControlChars.Back AndAlso e.KeyChar <> "." Then
        'cancel the key
        e.Handled = True

    End If
End Sub
```

Figure 4-53: Completed CancelKeys procedure

Now save the solution, then start the application and test the CancelKeys procedure.

To save the solution, then start the application and test the CancelKeys procedure:

1   Save the solution, then start the application.

2   Try entering a letter in the Principal text box, and then try entering a special character, such as a dollar sign.

3   Type **30000** in the Principal text box, then press **Backspace** to delete the last zero. The text box now contains 3000.

4   On your own, try entering a letter in the Rate text box, then try entering a special character.

5   Type **.045** in the Rate text box, then press **Backspace** to delete the number 5. The text box now contains .04.

6   On your own, try entering a letter in the Term text box, then try entering a special character.

7   Type **20** in the Term text box, then press **Backspace** to delete the zero. The text box now contains 2.

8   Press **Enter** to calculate the monthly payment amount. The number $129.84 appears in the uiPaymentLabel control.

Notice that the monthly payment amount aligns on the top and left sides of the label control. You can improve the appearance of the interface by centering the amount in the control. You learn how to align the text contained in a label control in the next section.

9   Click the **Exit** button to end the application. When you return to the Code Editor window, close the Output window.

Aligning the Text in a Label Control

The **TextAlign property** controls the placement of the text in a label control and can be set to TopLeft (the default), TopCenter, TopRight, MiddleLeft, MiddleCenter, MiddleRight, BottomLeft, BottomCenter, or BottomRight. In this case, you will change the uiPaymentLabel control's TextAlign property to MiddleCenter.

To change the TextAlign property to MiddleCenter, then test the application:

1   Click the **Payment Form.vb [Design]** tab to return to the designer window.

2   Click the **uiPaymentLabel** control on the form, then click **TextAlign** in the Properties window.

3   Click the list arrow in the Settings box. Buttons corresponding to the valid settings for the TextAlign property appear, as shown in Figure 4-54.

MiddleCenter setting —————————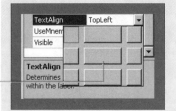

Figure 4-54: TextAlign property settings

4   Click the center button. MiddleCenter appears in the TextAlign property.

5   Save the solution, then start the application.

6   Type **9000** in the Principal text box, **5** in the Rate text box, and **3** in the Term text box. Press **Enter** to select the Calculate Monthly Payment button. The monthly payment amount, $268.62, appears centered in the uiPaymentLabel control, as shown in Figure 4-55.

Figure 4-55: Monthly payment amount centered in the label control

Now observe what happens if one of the text boxes is empty when you select the Calculate Monthly Payment button.

7 Delete the term from the Term text box, then click the **Calculate Monthly Payment** button. An error message appears in a dialog box, and the instruction causing the error appears highlighted in the Code Editor window. See Figure 4-56.

the Code Editor highlights the instruction that is causing the error

error

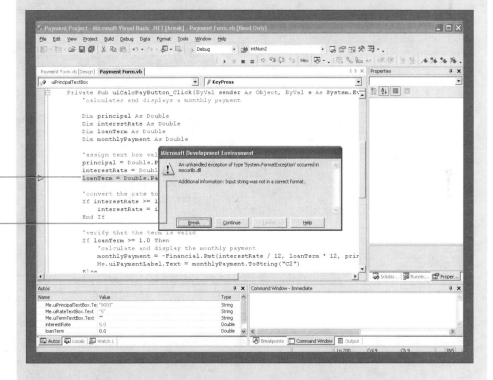

Figure 4-56: Screen showing the error message and the highlighted instruction

The error message first informs you that an unhandled exception occurred. It then gives you some additional information about the error; in this case, it displays the message *Input string was not in a correct format.*

The Convert methods you learned about in Chapter 3 also cannot convert an empty string to a number.

8   Click the **Break** button in the dialog box to close the dialog box. Highlighted in the Code Editor window is the `loanTerm = Double.Parse(Me.uiTermTextBox.Text)` statement, which is causing the error. The error occurs because the Parse method cannot convert an empty string to a number. (When a text box is empty, its Text property contains the empty string.) You learn how to handle this error in the next section.

9   Click **Debug** on the menu bar, and then click **Stop Debugging**.

10 Close the Output window.

When an error occurs in a procedure's code, programmers say that the procedure "threw an exception."

Using a Try/Catch Block

In Visual Basic .NET, an error that occurs while a program is running is called an **exception** and typically results in the program displaying an error message and then ending abruptly. You can use the **Try statement** to catch (or trap) an exception when it occurs in a program, and then use a **Catch statement** to have the computer take the appropriate action to resolve the problem. A block of code that uses both the Try and Catch statements is referred to as a **Try/Catch block**. Figure 4.57 shows the syntax of a Try/Catch block. It also lists common *exceptionTypes* and includes two examples of using a Try/Catch block to catch exceptions.

Using a Try/Catch Block

Syntax

Try
        one or more statements that might generate an exception
Catch [*variablename As exceptionType*]
            one or more statements that will execute when an exceptionType exception occurs
[**Catch** [*variablename As exceptionType*]
            one or more statements that will execute when an exceptionType exception occurs]
End Try

Common *exceptionTypes*	Caused By
ArithmeticException	an error in a calculation
IO.DirectoryNotFoundException	an invalid folder path
IO.FileNotFoundException	a file that cannot be located
Exception	any error
FormatException	an argument that does not meet the specifications of the invoked method

Figure 4-57: Syntax and examples of a Try/Catch block

Example 1

```
Try
     'calculate the square
      squareNum = Integer.Parse(Me.uiNumTextBox.Text) ^ 2
      Me.uiSquareLabel.Text = squareNum.ToString("N2")
Catch exFormat As FormatException
     'processed when the contents of the text box
     'cannot be converted to a number
     MessageBox.Show("Please enter a number.", _
          "Number", MessageBoxButtons.OK, _
          MessageBoxIcon.Information)
End Try
```

Example 2

```
Try
     'calculate and display the average
      average = Convert.ToDecimal(totalScores / numStudents)
      Me.uiAverageLabel.Text = average.ToString("N2")
Catch exArithmetic As ArithmeticException
     'processed when the average cannot be calculated
      Me.uiAverageLabel.Text = "0.00"
Catch ex As Exception
     'handles any other errors
     MessageBox.Show(ex.Message, "Average", _
          MessageBoxButtons.OK, MessageBoxIcon.Information)
End Try
```

Figure 4-57: Syntax and examples of a Try/Catch block (continued)

The Try statement begins with the keyword `Try` and ends with the keywords `End Try`. Within the Try statement you place the code that might generate an exception; you also list one or more Catch statements. Each Catch statement begins with the keyword `Catch`, followed by the name of a variable, the keyword `As`, and an exception type. A Catch statement ends when the computer reaches another Catch statement or the End Try clause.

A Try/Catch block can contain multiple Catch statements, with each Catch statement handling a different type of exception (error). When an exception occurs in the code included in the Try statement, only one of the Catch statements is processed; the appropriate Catch statement depends on the exception that occurred.

Study closely the examples shown in Figure 4-57. In Example 1, the Try section of the Try/Catch block contains two statements. The first statement, `squareNum = Integer.Parse(Me.uiNumTextBox.Text) ^ 2`, will generate a FormatException if the contents of the uiNumTextBox cannot be converted to a value of the Integer data type. If a FormatException does not occur, the computer squares the number stored in the text box and stores the result in the `squareNum` variable. It then processes the `Me.uiSquareLabel.Text = squareNum.ToString("N2")` statement, which displays the contents of the `squareNum` variable in the uiSquareLabel control. The computer then processes the End Try clause, which marks the end of the Try/Catch block. Notice that the computer skips over the Catch section of the Try/Catch block when a FormatException does not occur.

If, on the other hand, a FormatException does occur when processing the code shown in Example 1, the computer will process the MessageBox.Show method contained in the `Catch exFormat As FormatException` section of the Try/Catch block. That statement displays a message that prompts the user to enter a number. After displaying the message, the computer processes the End Try clause, which marks the end of the Try/Catch block.

In Example 2, the Try section of the Try/Catch block also contains two statements. The first statement, `average = Convert.ToDecimal(totalScores / numStudents)`, will generate an ArithmeticException if the `numStudents` variable contains the number zero, because division by zero is not mathematically possible. If an ArithmeticException does not occur, the computer calculates the average and stores the result in the `average` variable. It then processes the `Me.uiAverageLabel.Text = average.ToString("N2")` statement, which displays the average in the uiAverageLabel control. The computer then processes the End Try clause, which marks the end of the Try/Catch block. Notice that the computer skips over the Catch section of the Try/Catch block when an ArithmeticException does not occur.

If, on the other hand, an ArithmeticException does occur when processing the code shown in Example 2, the computer will process the `Me.uiAverageLabel.Text = "0.00"` statement contained in the `Catch exArithmetic As ArithmeticException` section of the Try/Catch block. That statement displays 0.00 in the uiAverageLabel control. After displaying the average, the computer processes the End Try clause, which marks the end of the Try/Catch block.

Example 2's code also contains a second Catch statement: `Catch ex As Exception`. This Catch statement will catch any errors that are not handled by any previous, more specific Catch statements listed in the Try/Catch block. It is a good programming practice to include a general Catch statement as the last Catch statement in a Try/Catch block. The purpose of the general Catch statement is to handle any unexpected exceptions (errors) that may arise. You can access a description of the exception that occurred using the syntax *variablename*.**Message**, where *variablename* is the name of the variable used in the Catch statement. For example, if the variable's name is **ex**, as it is in Example 2, you can display a description of the error by using **ex.Message** as the *text* argument in the MessageBox.Show method.

You will include a Try/Catch block in the Monthly Payment Calculator application.

To include a Try/Catch block in the Monthly Payment Calculator application, then test the application:

1   Click the **Payment Form.vb** tab to return to the Code Editor window.

2   Locate the uiCalcPayButton's Click event procedure, then enter the Try/Catch block shown in Figure 4-58. The instructions you should enter are shaded in the figure.

```vb
Private Sub uiCalcPayButton_Click(ByVal sender As Object, ByVal e As System.EventArgs) Handles
uiCalcPayButton.Click
    'calculates and displays a monthly payment

    Dim principal As Double
    Dim interestRate As Double
    Dim loanTerm As Double
    Dim monthlyPayment As Double

    Try
        'assign text box values to variables
        principal = Double.Parse(Me.uiPrincipalTextBox.Text)
        interestRate = Double.Parse(Me.uiRateTextBox.Text)
        loanTerm = Double.Parse(Me.uiTermTextBox.Text)

        'convert the rate to decimal form, if necessary
        If interestRate >= 1.0 Then
            interestRate = interestRate / 100.0
        End If

        'verify that the term is valid
        If loanTerm >= 1.0 Then
            'calculate and display the monthly payment
            monthlyPayment = -Financial.Pmt(interestRate / 12, loanTerm * 12, principal, 0,
            DueDate.BegOfPeriod)
            Me.uiPaymentLabel.Text = monthlyPayment.ToString("C2")
        Else
            MessageBox.Show("The term must be greater than or equal to 1.", _
                "Monthly Payment Calculator", MessageBoxButtons.OK, MessageBoxIcon.Information)
        End If

    Catch exFormat As FormatException
        'processed when the contents of a text box
        'cannot be converted to a number
        MessageBox.Show("The principal, rate, and term must be numbers.", _
            "Monthly Payment Calculator", MessageBoxButtons.OK, _
            MessageBoxIcon.Information)
    Catch ex As Exception
        MessageBox.Show(ex.Message, "Monthly Payment Calculator", _
            MessageBoxButtons.OK, MessageBoxIcon.Information)
    End Try

End Sub
```

Figure 4-58: Try/Catch block entered in the uiCalcPayButton's Click event procedure

3   Save the solution, then start the application.

4   Click the **Calculate Monthly Payment** button without entering any values in the text boxes. The Try/Catch block displays the message box shown in Figure 4-59.

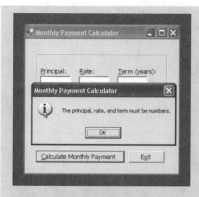

Figure 4-59: Message box displayed by the Try/Catch block

5 Click the **OK** button to close the message box.

6 On your own, verify that the message box shown in Figure 4-59 appears when only one of the text boxes is empty.

7 On your own, verify that the application displays a monthly payment of $268.62 for a $9,000 loan, at 5% interest, for 3 years.

8 Click the **Exit** button to end the application, then close the Output window.

You have finished coding the Monthly Payment Calculator application, so you can close the Code Editor window.

9 Close the Code Editor window, then use the File menu to close the solution.

You now have completed Chapter 4. You can either take a break or complete the end-of-lesson questions and exercises.

SUMMARY

To allow a text box to accept only certain keys:

▪ Code the text box's KeyPress event.

▪ The key the user pressed is stored in the KeyChar property of the KeyPress event procedure's e parameter. The `e.Handled = True` instruction cancels the key pressed by the user.

To align the text in a control:

▪ Set the control's TextAlign property.

To catch an exception, and then have the computer take the appropriate action:

▪ Use a Try/Catch block. Figure 4-57 shows the syntax and examples of a Try/Catch block.

QUESTIONS

1. A control's _____ event occurs when a user presses a key while the control has the focus.
   a. Key
   b. KeyPress
   c. Press
   d. PressKey
   e. None of the above.

2. When entered in the appropriate event, which of the following statements cancels the key pressed by the user?
   a. `Cancel = True`
   b. `e.Cancel = True`
   c. `e.Handled = True`
   d. `Handled = True`
   e. `Key = Null`

3. Which of the following can be used in an If...Then...Else statement to determine whether the user pressed the Backspace key?
   a. `If ControlChars.Back = True Then`
   b. `If e.KeyChar = Backspace Then`
   c. `If e.KeyChar = ControlChars.Backspace Then`
   d. `If KeyChar.ControlChars = Back Then`
   e. None of the above.

4. Which of the following can be used in an If...Then...Else statement to determine whether the user pressed the $ (dollar sign) key?
   a. `If ControlChars.DollarSign = True Then`
   b. `If e.KeyChar = "$" Then`
   c. `If e.KeyChar = Chars.DollarSign Then`
   d. `If KeyChar.ControlChars = "$" Then`
   e. None of the above.

5. You can center the contents of a label control by setting the control's _____ property to MiddleCenter.
   a. Align
   b. AlignLabel
   c. AlignText
   d. LabelAlign
   e. TextAlign

6. Which of the following can be used as a general Catch statement?
   a. `Catch exGeneral As General`
   b. `Catch ex As Exception`
   c. `Catch ex As GenException`
   d. `Catch exGeneral As GenException`
   e. `Catch exGeneral As GeneralException`

7. Which of the following assigns (to the message variable) a description of the exception that occurred?
   a. message = ex.Message
   b. message = ex.Description
   c. message = ex.Exception
   d. message = ex.GenException
   e. message = ex.GeneralException

8. What type of exception occurs when the computer cannot process a statement that contains a calculation?
   a. ArithmeticException
   b. CalculateException
   c. CalculationException
   d. MathException
   e. MathematicalException

9. What type of exception occurs when the Decimal.Parse method cannot convert a string to a number?
   a. ConversionException
   b. ConvertException
   c. FormatException
   d. NumericException
   e. StringConversionException

EXERCISES

1. In this exercise, you code an application that swaps two values entered by the user.
   a. If necessary, start Visual Studio .NET. Open the Swap Solution (Swap Solution.sln) file, which is contained in the VBNET\Chap04\Swap Solution folder. If necessary, open the designer window.
   b. Complete the code for the uiDisplayButton Click event procedure. The procedure should swap the two values entered by the user, but only if the first value is greater than the second value. Include a Try/Catch block in the procedure.
   c. Save the solution, then start the application. Test the application by clicking the Display button, and then entering the two values 10 and 7. Click the Display button again, then enter the two values 5 and 9.
   d. Click the Exit button to end the application.
   e. Close the Output window, then close the solution.

2. In this exercise, you code an application that either adds or subtracts two numbers.
   a. If necessary, start Visual Studio .NET. Open the Math Solution (Math Solution.sln) file, which is contained in the VBNET\Chap04\Math Solution folder. If necessary, open the designer window.
   b. Complete the code for the uiOperationButton's Click event procedure. The procedure should either add or subtract the two numbers entered by the user. Include a Try/Catch block in the procedure.
   c. Save the solution, then start the application. Test the application by clicking the Add or Subtract button. Use the application to add the two numbers 23 and 13. Click the Add or Subtract button again. Use the application to subtract the two numbers 23 and 13.
   d. Click the Exit button to end the application.
   e. Close the Output window, then close the solution.

3. In this exercise, you create an application for Micro Seminars. The application displays the total amount a company owes for a seminar. The seminar charge is $80 per person.

    a. If necessary, start Visual Studio .NET. Create a blank solution named Seminar Solution. Save the solution in the VBNET\Chap04 folder.

    b. Add a Visual Basic .NET Windows Application project to the solution. Name the project Seminar Project.

    c. Assign the filename Seminar Form.vb to the form file object.

    d. Assign the name SeminarForm to the Windows Form object.

    e. When designing the interface, provide a text box into which the user can enter the number of seminar registrants, and a label for displaying the total owed. Use the GUI design guidelines listed in Appendix B to verify that the interface you create adheres to the GUI standards outlined in this book.

    f. Code the application appropriately. The number of registrants should be less than 50 but greater than 0. Display an appropriate message if the number of registrants is invalid. Include a Try/Catch block in the procedure.

    g. Allow the user to press only numeric keys and the Backspace key when entering the number of registrants.

    h. When a change is made to the number of registrants entered in the text box, clear the contents of the label control that displays the total owed.

    i. Center the total owed in the label control, and display it with a dollar sign and two decimal places.

    j. Save the solution, then start the application. Test the application with both valid and invalid data.

    k. End the application.

    l. Close the Output window, then close the solution.

4. In this exercise, you code an application that allows the user to enter a state abbreviation.

    a. If necessary, start Visual Studio .NET. Open the State Solution (State Solution.sln) file, which is contained in the VBNET\Chap04\State Solution folder. If necessary, open the designer window.

    b. Set the text box's MaxLengh property to 2. Code the application so that it allows the user to enter only letters in the uiStateTextBox. Also allow the user to use the Backspace key.

    c. Save the solution, then start the application. Test the application with both valid data (uppercase and lowercase letters and the Backspace key) and invalid data (numbers and special characters).

    d. Click the Exit button to end the application.

    e. Close the Output window, then close the solution.

5. In this exercise, you code an application that calculates a customer's water bill.

    a. If necessary, start Visual Studio .NET. Open the Water Solution (Water Solution.sln) file, which is contained in the VBNET\Chap04\Water Solution folder. If necessary, open the designer window.

    b. Code the application so that it calculates and displays the gallons of water used and the water charge. Display the water charge with a dollar sign and two decimal places. The charge for water is $1.75 per 1000 gallons, or .00175 per gallon. Before making the calculations, verify that the meter readings entered by the user are valid. To be valid, the current meter reading must be greater than or equal to the previous meter reading. Display an appropriate message if the meter readings are not valid. Include a Try/Catch block in the procedure.

    c. Allow the user to enter only numbers in the uiCurrentTextBox and uiPreviousTextBox controls. Also allow the user to press the Backspace key when entering data in those two text boxes.

    d. Clear the contents of the uiGalUsedLabel and uiChargeLabel controls when a change is made to the contents of a text box on the form.

    e. Save the solution, then start the application. Test the application with both valid and invalid data.

    f. Click the Exit button to end the application.

    g. Close the Output window, then close the solution.

discovery ▶ **6.** In this exercise, you code an application that calculates a bonus.

    a. If necessary, start Visual Studio .NET. Open the Bonus Solution (Bonus Solution.sln) file, which is contained in the VBNET\Chap04\Bonus Solution folder. If necessary, open the designer window.

    b. The user will enter the sales amount in the uiSalesTextBox. The sales amount will always be an integer. Code the uiCalcButton's Click event procedure so that it calculates the salesperson's bonus. Include a Try/Catch block in the procedure. Display the bonus with a dollar sign and two decimal places in the uiBonusLabel control. The following rates should be used when calculating the bonus:

Sales amount ($)	Bonus
0-5000	1% of the sales amount
5001-10000	3% of the sales amount
Over 10000	7% of the sales amount

    (*Hint*: You can nest an If…Then…Else statement, which means you can place one If…Then…Else statement inside another If…Then…Else statement.)

    c. Allow the user to enter only numbers in the uiSalesTextBox control. Also allow the user to press the Backspace key when entering data in that text box.

    d. Clear the contents of the uiBonusLabel control when a change is made to the contents of the uiSalesTextBox control.

    e. Save the solution, then start the application. Test the application with both valid and invalid data.

    f. Click the Exit button to end the application.

    g. Close the Output window, then close the solution.

discovery ▶ **7.** In this exercise, you learn how to specify the maximum number of characters that can be entered in a text box.

    a. If necessary, start Visual Studio .NET. Open the Zip Solution (Zip Solution.sln) file, which is contained in the VBNET\Chap04\Zip Solution folder. If necessary, open the designer window.

    b. Click the uiZipTextBox. Scan the Properties list, looking for a property that allows you to specify the maximum number of characters that can be entered in the text box. When you locate the property, set its value to 10.

    c. Save the solution, then start the application. Test the application by trying to enter more than 10 characters in the text box.

    d. Click the Exit button to end the application.

    e. Close the Output window, then close the solution.

debugging 8. In this exercise, you debug an existing application. The purpose of this exercise is to demonstrate operator order of precedence.

a. If necessary, start Visual Studio .NET. Open the Debug Solution (Debug Solution.sln) file, which is contained in the VBNET\Chap04\Debug Solution folder. If necessary, open the designer window.

b. Open the Code Editor window and review the existing code. The uiCalcButton Click event procedure should calculate a 10% bonus when the code entered by the user is either 1 or 2 and, at the same time, the sales amount is greater than $10,000. Otherwise, the bonus rate is 5%. Also, the CancelKeys procedure should allow the user to enter only numbers, and also use the Backspace key, when entering data in the two text boxes on the form.

c. Start the application. Type the number 1 in the Code text box, then press Backspace. Notice that the Backspace key is not working correctly.

d. Click the Exit button to end the application.

e. Make the appropriate change to the CancelKeys procedure.

f. Save the solution, then start the application. Type the number 12 in the Code text box, then press Backspace to delete the 2. The Code text box now contains the number 1. Type 200 in the Sales amount text box, then click the Calculate Bonus button. A message box appears and indicates that the bonus amount is $20.00 (10% of $200), which is incorrect; it should be $10.00 (5% of $200).

g. Click the OK button to close the message box. Click the Exit button to end the application.

h. Make the appropriate change to the uiCalcButton's Click event procedure.

i. Save the solution, then start the application. Type the number 1 in the Code text box. Type 200 in the Sales amount text box, then click the Calculate Bonus button. The message box correctly indicates that the bonus amount is $10.00.

j. Click the Exit button to end the application.

k. Close the Output window, then close the solution.

More on the Selection Structure

Creating a Math Practice Application

case ▶ On Monday you meet with Susan Chen, the principal of a local primary school. Ms. Chen needs an application that the first and second grade students can use to practice both adding and subtracting numbers. The application should display the addition or subtraction problem on the screen, then allow the student to enter the answer, and then verify that the answer is correct. If the student's answer is not correct, the application should give him or her as many chances as necessary to answer the problem correctly.

The problems displayed for the first grade students should use numbers from 1 through 10 only. The problems for the second grade students should use numbers from 10 through 99. Because the first and second grade students have not learned about negative numbers yet, the subtraction problems should never ask them to subtract a larger number from a smaller one.

Ms. Chen also wants the application to keep track of how many correct and incorrect responses the student makes; this information will help her assess the student's math ability. Finally, she wants to be able to control the display of this information to keep students from being distracted or pressured by the number of right and wrong answers.

Previewing the Completed Application

Before you begin creating the Math Practice application, you first preview the completed application.

To preview the completed application:

1   Use the Run command on the Windows Start menu to run the **Math** (Math.exe) file, which is contained in the VBNET\Chap05 folder on your computer's hard disk. The Math Practice application's user interface appears on the screen. See Figure 5-1.

your numbers may differ

enter the answer here

check box

radio buttons

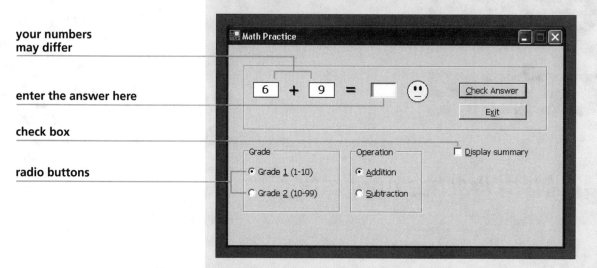

Figure 5-1: Math Practice application's user interface

Do not worry if the numbers on your screen do not match the ones shown in the figure. This application uses the Random object and the Random.Next method to display random numbers in the two label controls. You learn how to use the Random object and the Random.Next method in Lesson B.

The Math Practice application contains two new controls—radio buttons and a check box. You learn about these controls in Lesson B.

2   Type the correct answer to the addition problem appearing in the interface, then press **Enter** to select the Check Answer button, which is the default button on the form.

When you answer the math problem correctly, a happy face icon appears in the picture box control located to the left of the Check Answer button, and a new problem appears in the interface.

3   Click the **Display summary** check box to select it. A check mark appears inside the check box, and a group box control appears below the check box. The label controls contained in the group box display the number of correct and incorrect responses, as shown in Figure 5-2. In this case, you have made one correct response and zero incorrect responses.

new math problem
appears

happy face icon appears
when the answer is correct

number of correct and
incorrect responses

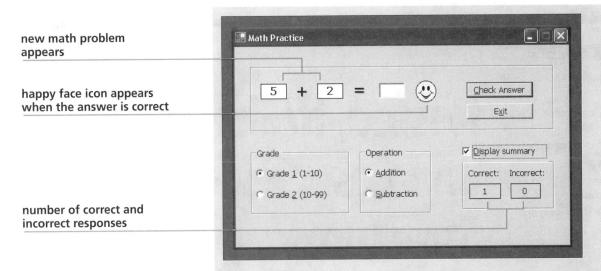

Figure 5-2: Interface showing that a correct response was made to the previous problem

4 Click the **Subtraction** radio button. A black dot appears in the center of the Subtraction radio button to indicate that the radio button is selected. The math problem changes to one involving subtraction.

5 Click inside the text box in which you enter the answer. Type an incorrect answer to the subtraction problem appearing on the screen, and then press **Enter**. The application replaces the happy face icon in the picture box control with an icon whose facial expression is neutral. It also displays the "Try again!" message in a message box.

6 Press **Enter** to close the message box. The application highlights the incorrect answer in the text box and gives you another chance to enter a correct response. The interface shows that you have made one correct response and one incorrect response.

7 Type the correct answer to the subtraction problem, then press **Enter**. The happy face icon reappears in the picture box control, and the number of correct responses now says 2. Additionally, a new math problem appears in the interface.

8 Click the **Display summary** check box to deselect it. The application removes the check mark from the check box and hides the group box control that contains the summary information.

9 Click the **Exit** button. The application ends.

Before you can begin coding the Math Practice application, you need to learn how to write nested and extended selection structures, as well as how to use the Is, TypeOf...Is, and Like comparison operators. You learn those structures and operators in Lesson A. In Lesson B you complete the Math Practice application's interface as you learn how to include radio button and check box controls in an interface. You begin coding the application in Lesson B, and complete the application in Lesson C.

After completing this lesson, you will be able to:

- Include a nested selection structure in pseudocode and in a flowchart
- Code a nested selection structure
- Desk-check an algorithm
- Recognize common logic errors in selection structures
- Code an If/ElseIf/Else selection structure
- Include a Case selection structure in pseudocode and in a flowchart
- Code a Case selection structure
- Write code that uses the Is, TypeOf...Is, and Like comparison operators

Nested, If/ElseIf/Else, and Case Selection Structures

Nested Selection Structures

As you learned in Chapter 4, you use the selection structure when you want a procedure to make a decision and then select one of two paths—either the true path or the false path—based on the result of that decision. Both paths in a selection structure can include instructions that declare and initialize variables, perform calculations, and so on; both also can include other selection structures. When either a selection structure's true path or its false path contains another selection structure, the inner selection structure is referred to as a **nested selection structure**, because it is contained (nested) within the outer selection structure.

You use a nested selection structure when more than one decision must be made before the appropriate action can be taken. For example, assume you want to create a procedure that determines whether a person can vote, and then, based on the result of that determination, displays one of three messages. The messages and the criteria for displaying each message are shown here:

Message	Criteria
"You are too young to vote."	person is younger than 18 years old
"You can vote."	person is at least 18 years old and is registered to vote
"You need to register before you can vote."	person is at least 18 years old but is not registered to vote

As the chart indicates, the person's age and voter registration status determine the appropriate message to display. If the person is younger than 18 years old, the procedure should display the message "You are too young to vote." However, if the person is at least 18 years old, the program should display one of two different messages. The correct message to display is determined by the person's voter registration status. If the person is registered, then the appropriate message is "You can vote."; otherwise, it is "You need to register before you can vote." Notice that determining the person's voter registration status is important only *after* his or her age is determined. You can think of the decision regarding the age as being the

primary decision, and the decision regarding the registration status as being the **secondary decision**, because whether the registration decision needs to be made depends on the result of the age decision. The primary decision is always made by the outer selection structure, while the secondary decision is always made by the inner (nested) selection structure.

Figure 5-3 shows the pseudocode and Visual Basic .NET code for a procedure that determines voter eligibility, and Figure 5-4 shows the corresponding flowchart. In both figures, the outer selection structure determines the age (the primary decision), and the nested selection structure determines the voter registration status (the secondary decision). Notice that the nested selection structure appears in the outer selection structure's true path in both figures.

Pseudocode

1. declare variables

2. get the age

3. if the age is greater than or equal to 18
        get the registration status
        if the registration status is Y
                display "You can vote."
        else
                display "You need to register before you can vote."
        end if
   else
        display "You are too young to vote."
   end if

Visual Basic .NET code

```
Dim ageInput As String
Dim status As String
ageInput = InputBox("Enter your age", "Age")
If Integer.Parse(ageInput) >= 18 Then
        status = InputBox("Are you registered to vote (Y or N)?", _
                "Registration", "Y")

    If status.ToUpper() = "Y" Then
            Me.uiMessageLabel.Text = "You can vote."
    Else
            Me.uiMessageLabel.Text = "You need to register before you can vote."
    End If

Else
        Me.uiMessageLabel.Text = "You are too young to vote."
End If
```

Figure 5-3: Pseudocode and Visual Basic .NET code showing the nested selection structure in the true path

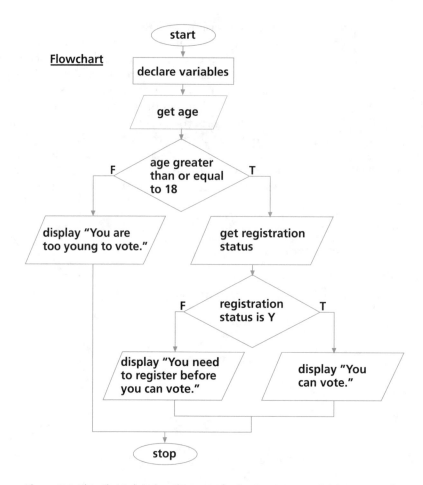

Flowchart

Figure 5-4: Flowchart showing the nested selection structure in the true path

As both figures indicate, the procedure begins by declaring the variables and then getting the age from the user. The condition in the outer selection structure then checks whether the age is greater than or equal to 18. If the condition is false, it means that the person is not old enough to vote. In that case, only one message—the "You are too young to vote." message—is appropriate. After the message is displayed, both the outer selection structure and the procedure end.

If the outer selection structure's condition is true, on the other hand, it means that the person *is* old enough to vote. Before displaying the appropriate message, the instructions in the outer selection structure's true path first get the registration status from the user. A nested selection structure then is used to determine whether the person is registered. If he or she is registered, the instruction in the nested selection structure's true path displays the "You can vote." message. Otherwise, the instruction in the nested selection structure's false path displays the "You need to register before you can vote." message. After the appropriate message is displayed, both selection structures and the procedure end. Notice that the nested selection structure in this procedure is processed only when the outer selection structure's condition is true.

Figure 5-5 shows the pseudocode and Visual Basic .NET code for a different version of the voter eligibility procedure, and Figure 5-6 shows the corresponding flowchart. As in the previous version, the outer selection structure in this version determines the age (the primary decision), and the nested selection structure determines the voter registration status (the secondary decision). In this version of the procedure, however, the nested selection structure appears in the false path of the outer selection structure.

Pseudocode

1. declare variables

2. get the age

3. if the age is less than 18
        display "You are too young to vote."
   else
        get the registration status
        if the registration status is Y
            display "You can vote."
        else
            display "You need to register before you can vote."
        end if
   end if

Visual Basic .NET code

```
Dim ageInput As String
Dim status As String
ageInput = InputBox("Enter your age", "Age")
If Integer.Parse(ageInput) < 18 Then
      Me.uiMessageLabel.Text = "You are too young to vote."
Else
      status = InputBox("Are you registered to vote (Y or N)?", _
            "Registration", "Y")

      If status.ToUpper() = "Y" Then
          Me.uiMessageLabel.Text = "You can vote."
      Else
          Me.uiMessageLabel.Text = "You need to register before you can vote."
      End If
End If
```

Figure 5-5: Pseudocode and Visual Basic .NET code showing the nested selection structure in the false path

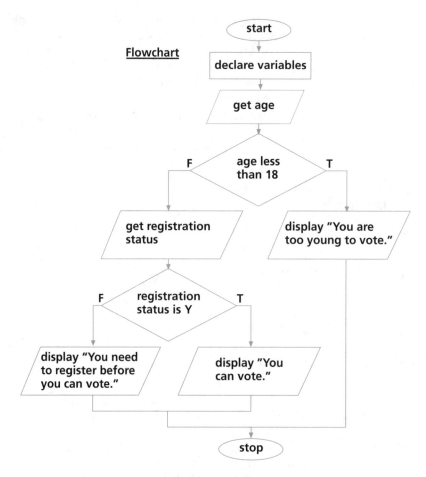

Flowchart

Figure 5-6: Flowchart showing the nested selection structure in the false path

Like the version shown earlier, this version of the voter eligibility procedure first declares the necessary variables and then gets the age from the user. However, rather than checking whether the age is greater than or equal to 18, the outer selection structure in this version checks whether the age is less than 18. If the condition is true, the instruction in the outer selection structure's true path displays the "You are too young to vote." message. If the condition is false, the instructions in the outer selection structure's false path first get the registration status from the user, and then use a nested selection structure to determine whether the person is registered. If the person is registered, the instruction in the nested selection structure's true path displays the "You can vote." message. Otherwise, the instruction in the nested selection structure's false path displays the "You need to register before you can vote." message. Unlike in the previous version, the nested selection structure in this version of the procedure is processed only when the outer selection structure's condition is false.

Notice that both versions of the voter eligibility procedure produce the same results. Neither version is better than the other; each simply represents a different way of solving the same problem.

In the next section, you learn some of the common logic errors made when writing selection structures. Being aware of these errors will help to prevent you from making them.

Logic Errors in Selection Structures

Typically, logic errors commonly made when writing selection structures are a result of one of the following mistakes:

1. Using a logical operator rather than a nested selection structure
2. Reversing the primary and secondary decisions
3. Using an unnecessary nested selection structure

The XYZ Company's vacation procedure can be used to demonstrate each of these logic errors. Assume that the company employs both full-time and part-time employees. Only full-time employees receive a paid vacation, as shown here:

Vacation weeks	Criteria
0	Part-time employees
2	Full-time employees working at the company for 5 years or fewer
3	Full-time employees working at the company for over 5 years

Your task is to create a procedure that allows the user to enter the employee's status—either F for full-time or P for part-time—and the number of years the employee has worked for the company. If the employee is full-time, the procedure should display the number of vacation weeks the employee has earned, and then the procedure should end. If the employee is not full-time, the procedure should simply end without displaying anything.

As the vacation chart indicates, the employee's status—either full-time or part-time—is a factor in determining whether the employee receives any paid vacation. If the employee is entitled to a paid vacation, then the number of years he or she has worked for the company determines the appropriate number of vacation weeks. In this case, the decision regarding the employee's status is the primary decision, and the decision regarding the years employed is the secondary decision, because whether the years employed decision needs to be made depends on the result of the status decision.

The pseudocode shown in Figure 5-7 represents a correct algorithm for the vacation procedure. An **algorithm** is simply the set of step-by-step instructions that accomplish a task.

tip

You also could have written the nested selection structure's condition in Figure 5-7 as follows: *if the years are less than or equal to 5*. The nested structure's true path then would contain the instruction *display "2-week vacation"*, and its false path would contain the instruction *display "3-week vacation"*.

Correct algorithm for the vacation procedure

```
1. declare variables

2. get the status and years

3. if the status is F
        if the years are greater than 5
                display "3-week vacation"
        else
                display "2-week vacation"
        end if
   end if
```

Figure 5-7: A correct algorithm for the vacation procedure

To observe why the algorithm shown in Figure 5-7 is correct, you will desk-check it. **Desk-checking**, also called **hand-tracing**, means that you use sample data to walk through each of the steps in the algorithm manually, just as if you were the computer. Programmers desk-check an algorithm to verify that it will work as intended. If any errors are found in the algorithm, the errors are corrected before the programmer begins coding the algorithm. You will use the following test data to desk-check the algorithm shown in Figure 5-7:

Data for first desk-check		Data for second desk-check		Data for third desk-check	
Status:	F	Status:	F	Status:	P
Years:	4	Years:	15	Years:	11

The algorithm should display the message "2-week vacation" for the first set of test data, the message "3-week vacation" for the second set, and nothing for the third set.

Using the first set of test data, the user enters F as the status and 4 as the years. The outer selection structure's condition determines whether the status is F; it is, so the nested selection structure's condition checks whether the years are greater than 5. The years are not greater than 5, so the nested selection structure's false path displays the message "2-week vacation," which is correct. After doing so, both selection structures and the procedure end.

Using the second set of test data, the user enters F as the status and 15 as the years. The outer selection structure's condition determines whether the status is F; it is, so the nested selection structure's condition checks whether the years are greater than 5. The years are greater than 5, so the nested selection structure's true path displays the message "3-week vacation," which is correct. After doing so, both selection structures and the procedure end.

Using the third set of test data, the user enters P as the status and 11 as the years. The outer selection structure's condition determines whether the status is F. The status is not F, so the outer selection structure and the procedure end. Notice that the nested selection structure is not processed when the outer selection structure's condition is false. Figure 5-8 shows the results of desk-checking the correct algorithm shown in Figure 5-7.

Desk-check	Result
First: using F as the status and 4 as the years	"2-week vacation" displayed
Second: using F as the status and 15 as the years	"3-week vacation" displayed
Third: using P as the status and 11 as the years	Nothing is displayed

Figure 5-8: Results of desk-checking the correct algorithm shown in Figure 5-7

In the next section, you view and desk-check another algorithm for the vacation procedure. You will find that the algorithm does not produce the desired results because it contains a logical operator instead of a nested selection structure.

Using a Logical Operator Rather Than a Nested Selection Structure

One common error made when writing selection structures is to use a logical operator in the outer selection structure's condition when a nested selection structure is needed. Figure 5-9 shows an example of this error in the vacation algorithm. The correct algorithm is included in the figure for comparison.

logical operator used rather than a nested selection structure

Correct algorithm	Incorrect algorithm
1. declare variables	1. declare variables
2. get the status and years	2. enter the status and years

3. if the status is F
    if the years are greater than 5
        display "3-week vacation"
    else
        display "2-week vacation"
    end if
end if
	3. if the status is F AndAlso the years are greater than 5
	        display "3-week vacation"
	    else
	        display "2-week vacation"
	    end if

Figure 5-9: Correct algorithm and an incorrect algorithm containing the first logic error

Notice that the incorrect algorithm uses one selection structure rather than two selection structures, and the selection structure's condition contains the AndAlso logical operator. Consider why the selection structure in the incorrect algorithm cannot be used in place of the selection structures in the correct algorithm. In the correct algorithm, the outer and nested selection structures indicate that a hierarchy exists between the status and years employed decisions: the status decision is always made first, followed by the years employed decision (if necessary). In the incorrect algorithm, on the other hand, the logical operator in the selection structure's condition indicates that no hierarchy exists between the status and years employed decisions; each has equal weight and neither is dependent on the other, which is incorrect. To better understand why this algorithm is incorrect, you will desk-check it using the same test data used to desk-check the correct algorithm.

After the user enters the first set of test data—F as the status and 4 as the years—the selection structure's condition in the incorrect algorithm determines whether the status is F and, at the same time, the years are greater than 5. Only one of these conditions is true, so the compound condition evaluates to false and the selection structure's false path displays the message "2-week vacation" before both the selection structure and the procedure end. Even though the algorithm's selection structure is phrased incorrectly, notice that the incorrect algorithm produces the same result as the correct algorithm using the first set of test data.

After the user enters the second set of test data—F as the status and 15 as the years—the selection structure's condition in the incorrect algorithm determines whether the status is F and, at the same time, the years are greater than 5. Both conditions are true, so the compound condition is true and the selection structure's true path displays the message "3-week vacation" before both the selection structure and the procedure end. Here again, using the second set of test data, the incorrect algorithm produces the same result as the correct algorithm.

After the user enters the third set of test data—P as the status and 11 as the years—the selection structure's condition in the incorrect algorithm determines whether the status is F and, at the same time, the years are greater than 5. Only one of these conditions is true, so the compound condition is false and the selection structure's false path displays the message "2-week vacation" before both the selection structure and the procedure end. Notice that the incorrect algorithm produces erroneous results for the third set of test data; according to Figure 5-8, the algorithm should not have displayed anything using this data. It is important to desk-check an algorithm several times using different test data. In this case, if you had used only the first two sets of data to desk-check the incorrect algorithm, you would not have discovered the error.

tip

As you learned in Chapter 4, when you use the AndAlso logical operator to combine two conditions in a selection structure, both conditions must be true for the compound condition to be true. If at least one of the conditions is false, then the compound condition is false and the instructions in the selection structure's false path (assuming there is a false path) are processed.

Figure 5-10 shows the results of desk-checking the incorrect algorithm shown in Figure 5-9. As indicated in the figure, the results of the first and second desk-checks are correct, but the result of the third desk-check is not correct.

Desk-check	Result
First: using F as the status and 4 as the years	"2-week vacation" displayed
Second: using F as the status and 15 as the years	"3-week vacation" displayed
Third: using P as the status and 11 as the years	"2-week vacation" displayed

correct results — First / Second (first row bracket)

incorrect result — Third

Figure 5-10: Results of desk-checking the incorrect algorithm shown in Figure 5-9

Next, you view and desk-check another algorithm for the vacation procedure. You will find that this algorithm also does not produce the desired results, because the primary and secondary decisions are reversed in the selection structures.

Reversing the Primary and Secondary Decisions

Another common error made when writing a selection structure that contains a nested selection structure is to reverse the primary and secondary decisions—in other words, put the secondary decision in the outer selection structure, and put the primary decision in the nested selection structure. Figure 5-11 shows an example of this error in the vacation algorithm. The correct algorithm is included in the figure for comparison.

Correct algorithm	Incorrect algorithm
1. declare variables	1. declare variables
2. get the status and years	2. get the status and years

3. if the status is F
        if the years are greater than 5
            display "3-week vacation"
        else
            display "2-week vacation"
        end if
    end if
	3. if the years are greater than 5
	        if the status is F
	            display "3-week vacation"
	        else
	            display "2-week vacation"
	        end if
	    end if

primary and secondary decisions reversed

Figure 5-11: Correct algorithm and an incorrect algorithm containing the second logic error

Unlike the selection structures in the correct algorithm, which determine the employment status before determining the number of years employed, the selection structures in the incorrect algorithm determine the number of years employed before determining the employment status. Consider how this difference changes the algorithm. In the correct algorithm, the selection structures indicate that only employees whose status is full-time receive a paid vacation, which is correct. The selection structures in the incorrect algorithm, on the other hand, indicate that all employees who have been with the company for more than five years receive a paid vacation, which is not correct. Desk-check the incorrect algorithm to see the results.

After the user enters the first set of test data—F as the status and 4 as the years—the condition in the outer selection structure determines whether the years are greater than 5. The years are not greater than 5, so both the outer selection structure and the procedure end. Notice that the incorrect algorithm does not display the expected message, "2-week vacation."

After the user enters the second set of test data—F as the status and 15 as the years—the condition in the outer selection structure determines whether the years are greater than 5; they are, so the condition in the nested selection structure checks whether the status is F. The status is F, so the nested selection structure's true path displays the message "3-week vacation," which is correct.

After the user enters the third set of test data—P as the status and 11 as the years—the condition in the outer selection structure determines whether the years are greater than 5; they are, so the condition in the nested selection structure checks whether the status is F. The status is not F, so the nested selection structure's false path displays the message "2-week vacation," which is not correct.

Figure 5-12 shows the results of desk-checking the incorrect algorithm shown in Figure 5-11. As indicated in the figure, only the results of the second desk-check are correct.

only this result is corrrect

Desk-check	Result
First: using F as the status and 4 as the years	Nothing is displayed
Second: using F as the status and 15 as the years	"3-week vacation" displayed
Third: using P as the status and 11 as the years	"2-week vacation" displayed

Figure 5-12: Results of desk-checking the incorrect algorithm shown in Figure 5-11

Next, you view and desk-check another algorithm for the vacation procedure. This algorithm contains the third logic error—using an unnecessary nested selection structure. Like the correct algorithm, this algorithm produces the desired results; however, it does so in a less efficient manner than the correct algorithm.

Using an Unnecessary Nested Selection Structure

Another common error made when writing selection structures is to include an unnecessary nested selection structure. In most cases, a selection structure containing this error still will produce the correct results. The only problem is that it does so less efficiently than selection structures that are properly structured. Figure 5-13 shows an example of this error in the vacation algorithm. The correct algorithm is included in the figure for comparison.

unnecessary nested selection structure

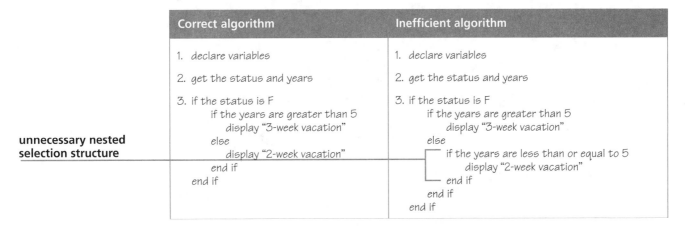

Correct algorithm	Inefficient algorithm
1. declare variables	1. declare variables
2. get the status and years	2. get the status and years

3. if the status is F
      if the years are greater than 5
          display "3-week vacation"
      else
          display "2-week vacation"
      end if
end if
	3. if the status is F
	      if the years are greater than 5
	          display "3-week vacation"
	      else
	          if the years are less than or equal to 5
	              display "2-week vacation"
	          end if
	      end if
	end if

Figure 5-13: Correct algorithm and an inefficient algorithm containing the third logic error

Unlike the correct algorithm, which contains two selection structures, the inefficient algorithm contains three selection structures. Notice that the condition in the third selection structure determines whether the years are less than or equal to 5, and is processed only when the condition in the second selection structure is false; in other words, it is processed only when the years are not greater than 5. However, if the years are not greater than 5, then they would have to be either less than or equal to 5, so the third selection structure is unnecessary. To better understand the error in the inefficient algorithm, you will desk-check it.

After the user enters the first set of test data—F as the status and 4 as the years—the first selection structure's condition determines whether the status is F; it is, so the second selection structure's condition determines whether the years are greater than 5. The years are not greater than 5, so the third selection structure's condition checks whether the years are less than or equal to 5—an unnecessary decision. In this case, 4 is less than 5, so the third selection structure's true path displays the message "2-week vacation," which is correct. After doing so, the three selection structures and the procedure end.

After the user enters the second set of test data—F as the status and 15 as the years—the first selection structure's condition determines whether the status is F; it is, so the second selection structure's condition determines whether the years are greater than 5. The years are greater than 5, so the second selection structure's true path displays the message "3-week vacation," which is correct. After doing so, the first and second selection structures and the procedure end.

After the user enters the third set of test data—P as the status and 11 as the years—the condition in the first selection structure determines whether the status is F; it isn't, so the first selection structure and the procedure end.

Figure 5-14 shows the results of desk-checking the inefficient algorithm shown in Figure 5-13. As indicated in the figure, although the results of the three desk-checks are correct, the result of the first desk-check is obtained in a less efficient manner.

correct result is obtained in a less efficient manner

Desk-check	Result
First: using F as the status and 4 as the years	"2-week vacation" displayed
Second: using F as the status and 15 as the years	"3-week vacation" displayed
Third: using P as the status and 11 as the years	Nothing is displayed

Figure 5-14: Results of desk-checking the inefficient algorithm shown in Figure 5-13

As you learned in Chapter 4, Visual Basic .NET provides four forms of the selection structure: If, If/Else, If/ElseIf/Else, and Case. You learned about the If and If/Else forms of the selection structure in Chapter 4. In this chapter, you learn about the If/ElseIf/Else and Case forms, which are commonly referred to as **extended selection structures** or **multiple-path selection structures**.

The If/ElseIf/Else Form of the Selection Structure

At times, you may need to create a selection structure that can choose from several alternatives. For example, assume you are asked to create a procedure that displays a message based on a letter grade that the user enters. Figure 5-15 shows the valid letter grades and their corresponding messages.

Letter grade	Message
A	Excellent
B	Above Average
C	Average
D	Below Average
F	Below Average

Figure 5-15: Letter grades and messages

As Figure 5-15 indicates, if the letter grade is an A, then the procedure should display the message "Excellent." If the letter grade is a B, then the procedure should display the message "Above Average," and so on. Figure 5-16 shows two versions of the Visual Basic .NET code for the grade procedure. The first version uses nested If/Else structures to display the appropriate message, while the second version uses the If/ElseIf/Else structure. As you do with the If/Else structure, you use the If...Then...Else statement to code the If/ElseIf/Else structure.

Version 1 – nested If/Else structures

```
Dim grade As String
grade = _
   InputBox("Grade?", "Grade")
grade = grade.ToUpper()

If grade = "A" Then
  Me.uiMsgLabel.Text = "Excellent"
Else
   If grade = "B" Then
      Me.uiMsgLabel.Text = "Above Average"
   Else
      If grade = "C" Then
        Me.uiMsgLabel.Text = "Average"
      Else
        If grade = "D" OrElse _
              grade = "F" Then
          Me.uiMsgLabel.Text = "Below Average"
        Else
            Me.uiMsgLabel.Text = "Error"
        End If
      End If
   End If
End If
```

Version 2 – If/ElseIf/Else structure

```
Dim grade As String
grade = _
   InputBox("Grade?", "Grade")
grade = grade.ToUpper()

If grade = "A" Then
    Me.uiMsgLabel.Text = "Excellent"
ElseIf grade = "B" Then
    Me.uiMsgLabel.Text = "Above Average"
ElseIf grade = "C" Then
    Me.uiMsgLabel.Text = "Average"
ElseIf grade = "D" OrElse _
     grade = "F" Then
    Me.uiMsgLabel.Text = "Below Average"
Else
    Me.uiMsgLabel.Text = "Error"
End If
```

you need four End If **statements to mark the end of the entire If/Else selection structure**

you need only one End If **statement to mark the end of the entire If/ElseIf/Else selection structure**

Figure 5-16: Two versions of the Visual Basic .NET code for the grade procedure

Although you can write the grade procedure using either nested If/Else structures (as shown in Version 1) or the If/ElseIf/Else structure (as shown in Version 2), the **If/ElseIf/Else structure** provides a much more convenient way of writing a multiple-path selection structure.

Next, you learn about the Case form of the selection structure.

The Case Form of the Selection Structure

It is often simpler and clearer to use the Case form of the selection structure, rather than the If/ElseIf/Else form, in situations where the selection structure has many paths from which to choose. Figure 5-17 shows the flowchart and pseudocode for the grade procedure, using the Case selection structure.

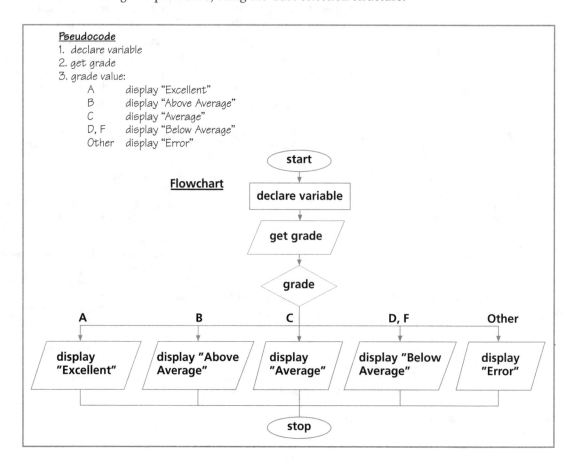

Figure 5-17: Flowchart and pseudocode showing the Case form of the selection structure

Notice that the flowchart symbol for the Case form of the selection structure is the same as the flowchart symbol for the If, If/Else, and If/ElseIf/Else forms—a diamond. Unlike the diamonds used in the other selection structures, however, the Case diamond does not contain a condition requiring a true or false answer. Instead, the Case diamond contains an expression whose value determines which path is chosen. In this case, the expression is grade.

Like the If, If/Else, and If/ElseIf/Else diamond, the Case diamond has one flowline leading into the symbol. Unlike the other diamonds, however, the Case diamond has many flowlines leading out of the symbol. Each flowline represents a possible path for the selection structure. The flowlines must be marked appropriately, indicating which value(s) are necessary for each path to be chosen.

In Visual Basic .NET, you use the **Select Case statement** to code the Case selection structure. Figure 5-18 shows the syntax of the Select Case statement. It also shows how you could use the Select Case statement to code the grade problem.

Syntax	Grade procedure

Select Case *selectorExpression*
    Case *expressionList1*
      [*instructions for the first Case*]
    [**Case** *expressionList2*
      [*instructions for the second Case*]]
    [**Case** *expressionListn*
      [*instructions for the nth case*]]
    [**Case Else**
      [*instructions for when the*
       selectorExpression does not match
       any of the expressionLists]]
End Select
	```Dim grade As String```
	```grade = InputBox("Grade?", "Grade")```
	```grade = grade.ToUpper()```
	
	```Select Case grade```
	``` Case "A"```
	``` Me.uiMsgLabel.Text = "Excellent"```
	``` Case "B"```
	``` Me.uiMsgLabel.Text = "Above Average"```
	``` Case "C"```
	``` Me.uiMsgLabel.Text = "Average"```
	``` Case "D", "F"```
	``` Me.uiMsgLabel.Text = "Below Average"```
	``` Case Else```
	``` Me.uiMsgLabel.Text = "Error"```
	```End Select```

Figure 5-18: Syntax and an example of the Select Case statement

tip

It is customary to indent each Case clause, as well as the instructions within each Case clause, as shown in Figure 5-18.

The Select Case statement begins with the Select Case clause and ends with the two words `End Select`. Between the Select Case clause and the `End Select` are the individual Case clauses. Each Case clause represents a different path that the selection structure can follow. You can have as many Case clauses as necessary in a Select Case statement. If the Select Case statement includes a `Case Else` clause, the `Case Else` clause must be the last clause in the statement.

Notice that the Select Case clause must include a *selectorExpression*. The *selectorExpression* can contain any combination of variables, constants, functions, methods, operators, and properties. In the grade procedure shown in Figure 5-18, the *selectorExpression* is a String variable named `grade`.

Each of the individual Case clauses, except the `Case Else` clause, must contain an *expressionList*, which can include one or more expressions. To include more than one expression in an *expressionList*, you simply separate each expression with a comma, as in the *expressionList* `Case "D", "F"`. The data type of the expressions must be compatible with the data type of the *selectorExpression*. In other words, if the *selectorExpression* is numeric, the expressions in the Case clauses should be numeric. Likewise, if the *selectorExpression* is a string, the expressions should be strings. In the grade procedure shown in Figure 5-18, the *selectorExpression* (`grade`) is a string, and so are the expressions—"A", "B", "C", "D", and "F"—as the quotation marks indicate.

When processing the Select Case statement, the computer first compares the value of the *selectorExpression* with the values listed in *expressionList1*. If a match is found, the computer processes the instructions for the first Case, stopping when it reaches either another Case clause (including the `Case Else` clause) or the `End Select` (which marks the end of the selection structure). It then skips to the instruction following the `End Select`. If a match is not found in *expressionList1*, the computer skips to the second Case clause, where it compares the *selectorExpression* with the values listed in *expressionList2*. If a match is found, the computer processes the instructions for the second Case clause and then skips to the instruction following the `End Select`. If a match is not found, the computer skips to the third Case clause, and so on. If the *selectorExpression* does not match any of the values listed in any of the *expressionLists*, the computer then processes the instructions listed in the `Case Else` clause or, if there is no `Case Else` clause, it processes the instruction following the `End Select`. Keep in mind that if the *selectorExpression* matches a value in more than one Case clause, only the instructions in the first match are processed.

To better understand the Select Case statement, you will desk-check the grade procedure shown in Figure 5-18.

Desk-Checking the Grade Procedure

Assume the user enters the letter C in response to the "Grade?" prompt. The grade procedure stores the letter C in the `grade` variable, which then is used as the *selectorExpression* in the procedure's Select Case statement. The computer compares the value of the *selectorExpression* ("C") with the expression listed in *expressionList1* ("A"). "C" does not match "A", so the computer compares the value of the *selectorExpression* ("C") with the expression listed in *expressionList2* ("B"). "C" does not match "B", so the computer compares the value of the *selectorExpression* ("C") with the expression listed in *expressionList3* ("C"). Here there is a match, so the computer processes the `Me.uiMsgLabel.Text = "Average"` instruction, which displays the string "Average" in the uiMsgLabel control. The computer then skips the remaining instructions in the Select Case statement and processes the instruction following the `End Select`. (In the grade procedure, the `End Sub`, which is not shown in Figure 5-18, would be processed.)

Now assume the user enters the letter F in response to the "Grade?" prompt. The grade procedure stores the letter F in the `grade` variable, which then is used as the *selectorExpression* in the procedure's Select Case statement. The computer compares the value of the *selectorExpression* ("F") with the expression listed in *expressionList1* ("A"). "F" does not match "A", so the computer compares the value of the *selectorExpression* ("F") with the expression listed in *expressionList2* ("B"). "F" does not match "B", so the computer compares the value of the *selectorExpression* ("F") with the expression listed in *expressionList3* ("C"). "F" does not match "C", so the computer compares the value of the *selectorExpression* ("F") with the expressions listed in *expressionList4* ("D", "F"). Here the computer finds a match, so it processes the `Me.uiMsgLabel.Text = "Below Average"` instruction, which displays the string "Below Average" in the uiMsgLabel control. The computer then processes the instruction following the `End Select`.

Finally, assume the user enters the letter X as the grade. In this situation, the computer processes the `Me.uiMsgLabel.Text = "Error"` instruction contained in the `Case Else` clause, because the *selectorExpression* ("X") does not match any of the expressions listed in the other Case clauses. The computer then processes the instruction following the `End Select`. Figure 5-19 shows the results of desk-checking the grade procedure shown in Figure 5-18.

tip

The *selectorExpression* needs to match only one of the expressions listed in an *expressionList*.

Desk-check	Result
First: using A	"Excellent" displayed
Second: using F	"Below Average" displayed
Third: using X	"Error" displayed

Figure 5-19: Results of desk-checking the grade procedure shown in Figure 5-18

You also can specify a range of values in an *expressionList*—such as the values 1 through 4, and values greater than 10. You can do so using the keywords To and Is.

Using To and Is in an *ExpressionList*

You can use either the keyword To or the keyword Is to specify a range of values in a Case clause's *expressionList*. You use the To keyword when you know both the upper and lower bounds of the range, and you use the Is keyword when you know only one end of the range—either the upper or lower end. For example, assume that the price of an item sold by ABC Corporation depends on the number of items ordered, as shown in the following table:

Number of items ordered	Price per item
1 – 5	$ 25
6 – 10	$ 23
More than 10	$ 20

Figure 5-20 shows the Select Case statement that assigns the appropriate price per item to the `itemPrice` variable.

tip

Because `numOrdered` is an Integer variable, you also can write the third Case clause in Figure 5-20 as `Case Is >= 11`, which specifies all numbers that are greater than or equal to the number 11.

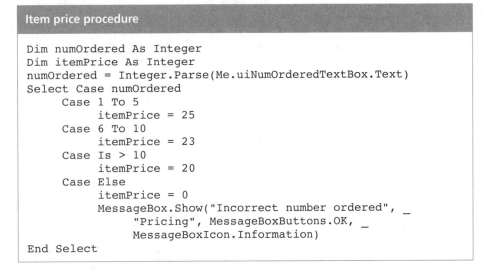

```
Item price procedure

Dim numOrdered As Integer
Dim itemPrice As Integer
numOrdered = Integer.Parse(Me.uiNumOrderedTextBox.Text)
Select Case numOrdered
    Case 1 To 5
        itemPrice = 25
    Case 6 To 10
        itemPrice = 23
    Case Is > 10
        itemPrice = 20
    Case Else
        itemPrice = 0
        MessageBox.Show("Incorrect number ordered", _
            "Pricing", MessageBoxButtons.OK, _
            MessageBoxIcon.Information)
End Select
```

Figure 5-20: Example of using the To and Is keywords in a Select Case statement

tip

When you use the To keyword, the value preceding the To always must be less than the value following the To; in other words, 10 To 6 is not a correct expression. Visual Basic .NET will not display an error message if the value preceding the To is greater than the value following the To. Instead, the Select Case statement simply will not give the correct results. This is another reason it always is important to test your code thoroughly.

According to the ABC Corporation table, the price for one to five items is $25 each. Therefore, you could have written the first Case clause in Figure 5-20 as `Case 1, 2, 3, 4, 5`. However, a more convenient way of writing that range of numbers is to use the keyword To in the Case clause, but you must follow this syntax to do so: **Case** *smallest value in the range* **To** *largest value in the range*. The expression `1 To 5` in the first Case clause, for example, specifies the range of numbers from one to five, inclusive. The expression `6 To 10` in the second Case clause specifies the range of numbers from six to 10, inclusive. Notice that both Case clauses state both the lower (1 and 6) and upper (5 and 10) ends of each range.

The third Case clause in Figure 5-20, `Case Is > 10`, contains the Is keyword rather than the To keyword. Recall that you use the Is keyword when you know only one end of the range of values—either the upper or lower end. In this case, for example, you know only the lower end of the range, 10. You always use

If you neglect to type the keyword Is in an expression, the Code Editor types it in for you. In other words, if you enter Case > 10, the Code Editor changes the clause to Case Is > 10.

the Is keyword in combination with one of the following comparison (relational) operators: =, <, <=, >, >=, <>. The `Case Is > 10` clause, for example, specifies all numbers that are greater than the number 10.

Notice that the `Case Else` clause shown in Figure 5-20 first assigns the number 0 to the `itemPrice` variable and then uses the MessageBox.Show method to display the message "Incorrect number ordered." The `Case Else` clause is processed when the `numOrdered` variable contains a value that is not included in any of the Case clauses—namely, a zero or a negative number.

In Chapter 4's Lesson A, you learned how to use six of the nine comparison operators available in Visual Basic .NET. You learn how to use the remaining three comparison operators in this lesson. You often will find these operators used in selection structures.

The Is, TypeOf...Is, and Like Comparison Operators

In addition to the =, <>, <, <=, >, >= comparison operators, which you learned about in Chapter 4, Visual Basic .NET also provides the Is, TypeOf...Is, and Like comparison operators. Figure 5-21 briefly describes these three comparison operators.

Operator	Operation
Is	determine whether two object references refer to the same object
TypeOf...Is	determine whether an object is a specified type
Like	use pattern matching to determine whether one string is equal to another string

Figure 5-21: Is, TypeOf...Is, and Like comparison operators

First, you learn about the Is comparison operator.

The Is Comparison Operator

You use the **Is operator** to determine whether two object references refer to the same object. An **object reference** is a memory address within the computer's internal memory; it indicates where in memory the object is stored. If both object references refer to the same object, the Is operator evaluates to True; otherwise, it evaluates to False.

Figure 5-22 shows the syntax of the Is operator. It also shows the CalcCommission procedure, which uses the Is operator in a selection structure to determine the button selected by the user.

Is operator

Syntax

objectReference1 **Is** *objectReference2*

The Is operator evaluates to True if *objectReference1* is the same as *objectReference2*; otherwise it evaluates to False.

Example

```
Private Sub CalcCommission(ByVal sender As Object, _
        ByVal e As System.EventArgs) _
        Handles uiCalc2Button.Click, uiCalc4Button.Click, _
        uiCalc7Button.Click

    Dim sales, commission As Double
    sales = Double.Parse(Me.uiSalesTextBox.Text)

    If sender Is uiCalc2Button Then
        commission = sales * .02
    ElseIf sender Is uiCalc4Button Then
        commission = sales * .04
    Else
        commission = sales * .07
    End If
    Me.uiCommLabel.Text = commission.ToString("C2")
End Sub
```

Handles section

compares memory addresses

Figure 5-22: Syntax and an example of the Is operator

The CalcCommission procedure shown in Figure 5-22 calculates and displays a commission amount. As the Handles section in the procedure header indicates, the procedure is processed when the user selects the uiCalc2Button, uiCalc4Button, or uiCalc7Button on the form. When one of these buttons is selected, its memory address is sent to the CalcCommission procedure's `sender` parameter. In this case, for example, the memory address of the uiCalc2Button is sent to the `sender` parameter when the user selects the uiCalc2Button. Likewise, when the user selects the uiCalc4Button, the uiCalc4Button's memory address is sent to the `sender` parameter. The uiCalc7Button's memory address is sent to the `sender` parameter when the user selects the uiCalc7Button.

Before the commission amount can be calculated, the procedure first must determine which button the user selected, because each button is associated with a different commission rate. The `sender Is uiCalc2Button` condition in the first If…Then…Else statement compares the memory address stored in the `sender` parameter with the memory address of the uiCalc2Button. If the condition evaluates to True, it means that both memory addresses are the same. If both memory addresses are the same, then the user selected the uiCalc2Button and the commission amount should be calculated by multiplying the sales amount by 2 percent.

If the `sender` parameter does not contain the address of the uiCalc2Button, the `sender Is uiCalc4Button` condition in the ElseIf clause compares the memory address stored in the `sender` parameter with the memory address of the uiCalc4Button. If both memory addresses are the same, then the user selected the uiCalc4Button and the commission amount is 4 percent of the sales amount. If both memory addresses are not the same, then the user must have selected the uiCalc7Button; in this case, the commission amount is 7 percent of the sales amount.

tip

The Is operator is not the same as the Is keyword used in the Select Case statement. Recall that the Is keyword is used in combination with one of the following comparison operators: =, <, <=, >, >=, <>.

Next, you learn about the TypeOf...Is comparison operator.

The TypeOf...Is Comparison Operator

You use the **TypeOf...Is operator** to determine whether an object is a specified type. For example, you can use the operator to determine whether an object is a TextBox or a Button. If the object's type matches the specified type, the TypeOf...Is operator evaluates to True; otherwise, it evaluates to False.

Figure 5-23 shows the syntax of the TypeOf...Is operator. It also shows the DisplayMessage procedure, which uses the TypeOf...Is operator in a selection structure to determine the type of control that invoked the procedure.

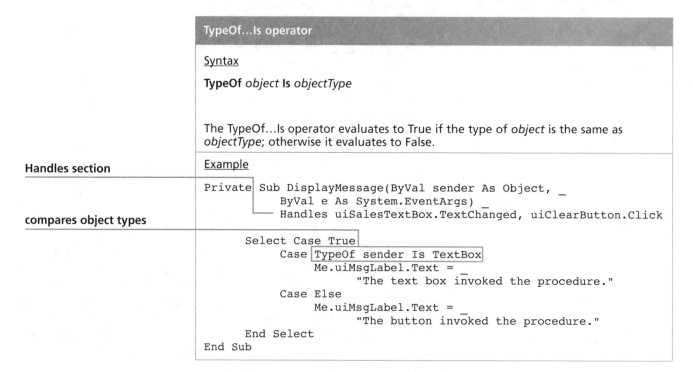

TypeOf...Is operator

Syntax

TypeOf *object* **Is** *objectType*

The TypeOf...Is operator evaluates to True if the type of *object* is the same as *objectType*; otherwise it evaluates to False.

Handles section

compares object types

Example

```
Private Sub DisplayMessage(ByVal sender As Object, _
        ByVal e As System.EventArgs) _
        Handles uiSalesTextBox.TextChanged, uiClearButton.Click

    Select Case True
        Case TypeOf sender Is TextBox
            Me.uiMsgLabel.Text = _
                "The text box invoked the procedure."
        Case Else
            Me.uiMsgLabel.Text = _
                "The button invoked the procedure."
    End Select
End Sub
```

Figure 5-23: Syntax and an example of the TypeOf...Is operator

The DisplayMessage procedure shown in Figure 5-23 displays a message in a label control. As the Handles section in the procedure header indicates, the procedure is processed when the uiSalesTextBox control's TextChanged event occurs, and also when the uiClearButton control's Click event occurs. When either of these events occurs, the memory address of the control associated with the event is sent to the DisplayMessage procedure's `sender` parameter. In this case, for example, the memory address of the uiSalesTextBox is sent to the `sender` parameter when the text box's TextChanged event occurs. Likewise, the memory address of the uiClearButton is sent to the `sender` parameter when the button's Click event occurs.

The Select Case statement in the procedure displays the appropriate message based on the type of control whose address is stored in the `sender` parameter. Notice that the Select Case statement uses the Boolean value True as the *selectorExpression*. It also uses the TypeOf...Is operator in the first Case clause to compare the `sender` parameter's type to the type, TextBox. If the `TypeOf sender Is TextBox` expression evaluates to True, it means that the `sender` parameter's type is TextBox. In this case, because the value of the expression (True) matches the value of the *selectorExpression* (True), the procedure displays the message "The text box invoked the procedure." in the uiMsgLabel control. If, on the other hand, the `TypeOf sender Is TextBox` expression evaluates to False, it means that the `sender` parameter's type is not TextBox. Here, because the value of the expression (False) does not match the value of the *selectorExpression* (True), the procedure displays the message "The button invoked the procedure." in the uiMsgLabel control.

Finally, you learn about the Like comparison operator.

The Like Comparison Operator

The **Like operator** allows you to use pattern matching to determine whether one string is equal to another string. To use the Like operator, you must follow the syntax *string* **Like** *pattern*. Both *string* and *pattern* must be String expressions; however, *pattern* can contain one or more of the pattern-matching characters described in Figure 5-24.

Pattern-matching characters	Matches in *string*
?	any single character
*	zero or more characters
#	any single digit (0-9)
[*charlist*]	any single character in the *charlist* (for example, [a-z] matches any lowercase letter)
[!*charlist*]	any single character not in the *charlist* (for example, [!a-z] matches any character that is not a lowercase letter)

Figure 5-24: Pattern-matching characters

Figure 5-25 shows the syntax of the Like operator and contains several examples of using the Like operator and its pattern-matching characters to compare strings.

Like operator	
Syntax *string* **Like** *pattern* The Like operator evaluates to True if *string* matches *pattern*; otherwise it evaluates to False.	
Examples	**Results**
<u>Example 1</u> `name.ToUpper() Like "B?LL"`	evaluates to True if the string stored in the name variable begins with the letter B, followed by one character and then the two letters LL; otherwise, it evaluates to False
<u>Example 2</u> `state Like "K*"`	evaluates to True if the string stored in the state variable begins with the letter K, followed by zero or more characters; otherwise, it evaluates to False

Figure 5-25: Syntax and examples of the Like operator

Examples	Results
Example 3 `id Like "###*"`	evaluates to True if the string stored in the `id` variable begins with three digits, followed by zero or more characters; otherwise, it evaluates to False
Example 4 `name.ToUpper() Like "T[OI]M"`	evaluates to True if the string stored in the `name` variable begins with the letter T, followed by either the letter O or the letter I, followed by the letter M; otherwise, it evaluates to False
Example 5 `letter Like "[a-z]"`	evaluates to True if the string stored in the `letter` variable is a lowercase letter; otherwise, it evaluates to False
Example 6 `letter Like "[!a-zA-Z]"`	evaluates to True if the string stored in the `letter` variable is not a letter; otherwise, it evaluates to False

Figure 5-25: Syntax and examples of the Like operator (continued)

Study closely each example shown in Figure 5-25. The `name.ToUpper() Like "B?LL"` expression in Example 1 contains the question mark (?) pattern-matching character, which is used to match one character in the *string*. Examples of *strings* that would make this expression evaluate to True include "Bill", "Ball", "bell", and "bull". Examples of *strings* for which the expression would evaluate to False include "BPL", "BLL", and "billy".

Example 2's expression, `state Like "K*"`, uses the asterisk (*) pattern-matching character to match zero or more characters. Examples of *strings* that would make this expression evaluate to True include "KANSAS", "Ky", and "Kentucky". Examples of *strings* for which the expression would evaluate to False include "kansas" and "ky".

Example 3's expression, `id Like "###*"`, contains two different pattern-matching characters: the number sign (#), which matches a digit, and the asterisk (*), which matches zero or more characters. Examples of *strings* that would make this expression evaluate to True include "178" and "983Ab". Examples of *strings* for which the expression would evaluate to False include "X34" and "34Z".

The `name.ToUpper() Like "T[OI]M"` expression in Example 4 in Figure 5-25 contains a *charlist* (character list)—in this case, the two letters O and I—enclosed in square brackets ([]). The expression evaluates to True if the string stored in the `name` variable is either "Tom" or "Tim" (entered in any case). If the `name` variable does not contain "Tom" or "Tim"—for example, if it contains "Tam" or "Tommy"—the expression evaluates to False.

Example 5's expression, `letter Like "[a-z]"`, also contains a *charlist* enclosed in square brackets; however, the *charlist* represents a range of values—in this case, the lowercase letters "a" through "z". Notice that you use a hyphen (-) to specify a range of values. In this case, if the string stored in the `letter` variable is a lowercase letter, then the expression evaluates to True; otherwise, it evaluates to False.

tip

When using the hyphen to specify a range of values, the value on the left side of the hyphen must have a lower ASCII value than the value on the right side of the hyphen. For example, you must use [a-z], and not [z-a], to specify the lowercase letters of the alphabet.

The `letter Like "[!a-zA-Z]"` expression shown in the last example in Figure 5-25 also contains a *charlist* that specifies a range of values; however, the *charlist* is preceded by an exclamation point (!), which stands for "not". The expression evaluates to True if the string stored in the `letter` variable is *not* a letter; otherwise, it evaluates to False.

You now have completed Lesson A. You can either take a break or complete the end-of-lesson questions and exercises before moving on to the next lesson.

S U M M A R Y

To create a selection structure that evaluates both a primary and a secondary decision:

■ Place (or nest) the selection structure for the secondary decision within either the true path or false path of the selection structure for the primary decision.

To verify that an algorithm works correctly:

■ Desk-check the algorithm. Desk-checking, also called hand-tracing, means that you use sample data to walk through each of the steps in the algorithm manually, just as if you were the computer.

To code a multiple-path (or extended) selection structure:

■ Use either the If...Then...Else statement or the Select Case statement.

To specify a range of values in a Case clause contained in a Select Case statement:

■ Use the keyword To when you know both the upper and lower bounds of the range. The syntax for using the To keyword is **Case** *smallest value in the range* **To** *largest value in the range*.
■ Use the keyword Is when you know only one end of the range—either the upper or lower end. The Is keyword is used in combination with one of the following comparison operators: =, <, <=, >, >=, <>.

To determine whether two object references refer to the same object:

■ Use the Is comparison operator. The syntax for using the Is operator is *objectReference1* **Is** *objectReference2*. The Is operator returns the Boolean value True if both *objectReferences* contain the same address; otherwise, the operator returns the Boolean value False.

To determine whether an object is a specified type:

■ Use the TypeOf...Is comparison operator. The syntax for using the TypeOf...Is operator is **TypeOf** *object* **Is** *objectType*.

To use pattern matching to determine whether one string is equal to another string:

■ Use the Like comparison operator. The syntax for using the Like operator is *string* **Like** *pattern*, where *pattern* can contain one or more pattern-matching characters. Refer to Figure 5-24 for the pattern-matching characters.

QUESTIONS

Use the following code to answer Questions 1 through 3.

```
If number <= 100 Then
      number = number * 2
ElseIf number > 500 Then
      number = number * 3
End If
```

1. Assume the number variable contains the number 90. What value will be in the number variable after the preceding code is processed?
   a. 0
   b. 90
   c. 180
   d. 270

2. Assume the number variable contains the number 1000. What value will be in the number variable after the preceding code is processed?
   a. 0
   b. 1000
   c. 2000
   d. 3000
   e. None of the above.

3. Assume the number variable contains the number 200. What value will be in the number variable after the preceding code is processed?
   a. 0
   b. 200
   c. 400
   d. 600
   e. None of the above.

Use the following code to answer Questions 4 through 7.

```
If id = 1 Then
      Me.uiNameLabel.Text = "Janet"
ElseIf id = 2 OrElse id = 3 Then
      Me.uiNameLabel.Text = "Paul"
ElseIf id = 4 Then
      Me.uiNameLabel.Text = "Jerry"
Else
      Me.uiNameLabel.Text = "Sue"
End If
```

4. What, if anything, will the preceding code display if the id variable contains the number 2?
   a. Janet
   b. Jerry
   c. Paul
   d. Sue
   e. nothing

5. What, if anything, will the preceding code display if the `id` variable contains the number 4?
    a. Janet
    b. Jerry
    c. Paul
    d. Sue
    e. nothing

6. What, if anything, will the preceding code display if the `id` variable contains the number 3?
    a. Janet
    b. Jerry
    c. Paul
    d. Sue
    e. nothing

7. What, if anything, will the preceding code display if the `id` variable contains the number 8?
    a. Janet
    b. Jerry
    c. Paul
    d. Sue
    e. nothing

8. A nested selection structure can appear in _____ of another selection structure.
    a. only the true path
    b. only the false path
    c. either the true path or the false path

9. Which of the following flowchart symbols represents the Case selection structure?
    a. diamond
    b. hexagon
    c. oval
    d. parallelogram
    e. rectangle

10. If the *selectorExpression* used in the Select Case statement is an Integer variable named `code`, which of the following Case clauses is valid?
    a. `Case 3`
    b. `Case Is > 7`
    c. `Case 3, 5`
    d. `Case 1 To 4`
    e. All of the above.

Use the following Case statement to answer Questions 11 through 13.

```
Select Case id
    Case 1
            Me.uiNameLabel.Text = "Janet"
        Case 2 To 4
            Me.uiNameLabel.Text = "Paul"
        Case 5, 7
            Me.uiNameLabel.Text = "Jerry"
        Case Else
            Me.uiNameLabel.Text = "Sue"
    End Select
```

11. What will the preceding Case statement display if the `id` variable contains the number 2?
    a. Jerry
    b. Paul
    c. Sue
    d. nothing

12. What will the preceding Case statement display if the `id` variable contains the number 3?
    a. Jerry
    b. Paul
    c. Sue
    d. nothing

13. What will the preceding Case statement display if the `id` variable contains the number 6?
    a. Jerry
    b. Paul
    c. Sue
    d. nothing

14. Which of the following can be used to determine whether the `sender` parameter contains the address of the uiNameTextBox?
    a. `If sender Is uiNameTextBox Then`
    b. `If sender = uiNameTextBox Then`
    c. `If sender Like uiNameTextBox Then`
    d. `If sender Is = uiNameTextBox Then`
    e. `If TypeOf sender Is uiNameTextBox Then`

15. Which of the following can be used to determine whether the `sender` parameter contains the address of a label control?
    a. `If sender Is Label Then`
    b. `If sender = Label Then`
    c. `If sender Like Label Then`
    d. `If sender Is = Label Then`
    e. `If TypeOf sender Is Label Then`

16. Which of the following can be used to determine whether a String variable named `partNum` contains two characters followed by a digit?
    a. `If partNum = "##?" Then`
    b. `If partNum Is = "**?" Then`
    c. `If partNum = "##?" Then`
    d. `If partNum Like "[0-9]" Then`
    e. None of the above.

17. Which of the following can be used to determine whether a String variable named `item` contains either the word "shirt" or the word "skirt"?
    a. `If item.ToUpper() = "SHIRT" OrElse item.ToUpper() = "SKIRT" Then`
    b. `If item.ToUpper() = "S[HK]IRT" Then`
    c. `If item.ToUpper() Like "S[HK]IRT" Then`
    d. `If item.ToUpper() Like "S[H-K]IRT" Then`
    e. a and c

18. Which of the following can be used to determine whether the percent sign (%) is the last character entered in the uiRateTextBox?
    a. `If "%" Like Me.uiRateTextBox.Text Then`
    b. `If "%" Like [Me.uiRateTextBox.Text] Then`
    c. `If Me.uiRateTextBox.Text Like "?%" Then`
    d. `If Me.uiRateTextBox.Text Like "*%" Then`
    e. `If Me.uiRateTextBox.Text Like [*%] Then`

19. Which of the following pattern-matching characters represents any single digit (0–9)?
    a. #
    b. *
    c. ?
    d. &
    e. @

20. Which of the following pattern-matching characters represents zero or more characters?
    a. #
    b. *
    c. ?
    d. &
    e. @

21. Assume that you need to create a procedure that displays the appropriate fee to charge a golfer. The fee is based on the following fee schedule:

Fee	Criteria
0	Club members
15	Non-members golfing on Monday through Thursday
25	Non-members golfing on Friday through Sunday

    In this procedure, which is the primary decision and which is the secondary decision? Why?

22. List the three errors commonly made when writing selection structures. Which error makes the selection structure inefficient, but not incorrect?

23. Explain what the term "desk-checking" means.

24. What is an object reference?

25. What is an algorithm?

EXERCISES

1. Write the Visual Basic .NET code for the algorithm shown in Figure 5-7 in this lesson. The employee's status and years employed are entered in the uiStatusTextBox and uiYearsTextBox controls, respectively. Store the text box values in String and Integer variables named `status` and `years`. Display the appropriate message in the uiMsgLabel control.

2. Modify the code from Exercise 1 so that it displays the message "No vacation" if the employee's status is part-time.

3. Write the Visual Basic .NET code that displays the message "Highest honors" if a student's test score is 90 or above. If the test score is 70 through 89, display the message "Good job". For all other test scores, display the message "Retake the test". Use the If/ElseIf/Else selection structure. The test score is stored in an Integer variable named `score`. Display the appropriate message in the uiMsgLabel control.

4. Write the Visual Basic .NET code that compares the contents of an Integer variable named `quantity` with the number 10. If the `quantity` variable contains a number that is equal to 10, display the string "Equal" in the uiMsgLabel control. If the `quantity` variable contains a number that is greater than 10, display the string "Over 10". If the `quantity` variable contains a number that is less than 10, display the string "Not over 10". Use the If/ElseIf/Else selection structure.

5. Write the Visual Basic .NET code that corresponds to the flowchart shown in Figure 5-26. Store the salesperson's code, which is entered in the uiCodeTextBox control, in an Integer variable named `code`. Store the sales amount, which is entered in the uiSalesTextBox control, in a Single variable named `sales`. Display the result of the calculation, or the error message, in the uiMsgLabel control.

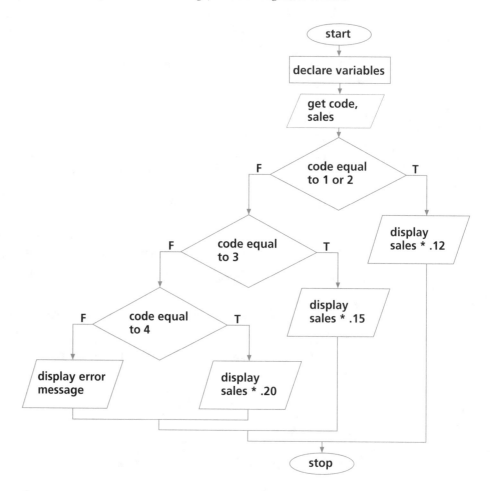

Figure 5-26

6. Write the Visual Basic .NET code that corresponds to the flowchart shown in Figure 5-27. Store the salesperson's code, which is entered in the uiCodeTextBox control, in an Integer variable named `code`. Store the sales amount, which is entered in the uiSalesTextBox control, in a Single variable named `sales`. Display the result of the calculation, or the error message, in the uiMsgLabel control.

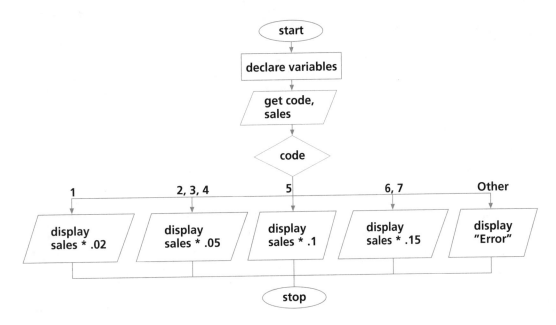

Figure 5-27

7. Assume that a procedure needs to display a shipping charge based on the state name stored in the `state` variable. (You can assume that the state name is stored using uppercase letters.) Write a Select Case statement that assigns the shipping charge to a Single variable named `shipCharge`. Use the following table to determine the appropriate shipping charge.

State entered in the `state` variable	Shipping charge
HAWAII	$25.00
OREGON	$30.00
CALIFORNIA	$32.50

Display an appropriate message in the uiMsgLabel control if the `state` variable contains a value that does not appear in the table. Also assign the number 0 to the `shipCharge` variable.

8. Rewrite the code from Exercise 7 using an If...Then...Else statement.

9. The price of a concert ticket depends on the seat location stored in the `seatLocation` variable. (You can assume that the seat location is stored using uppercase letters.) Write a Select Case statement that displays the price in the uiPriceLabel control. Use the following table to determine the appropriate price.

Seat location	Concert ticket price
BOX	$75.00
PAVILION	$30.00
LAWN	$21.00

Display an appropriate message in the uiPriceLabel control if the `seatLocation` variable contains a value that does not appear in the table.

10. Rewrite the code from Exercise 9 using an If...Then...Else statement.

11. Assume that a procedure needs to display a shipping charge based on the five-digit ZIP code stored in a String variable named `zipCode`. Write an If...Then...Else statement that assigns the shipping charge to a Double variable named `shipCharge`. Use the following table to determine the appropriate shipping charge. (*Hint*: Notice that the first two ZIP codes begin with "605", and the last three ZIP codes begin with "606".)

ZIP code entered in the `zipCode` variable	Shipping charge
60522	$25.00
60534	$25.00
60611	$30.00
60612	$30.00
60634	$30.00

All other ZIP codes are charged $35.00 for shipping.

12. Rewrite the code from Exercise 11 using a Select Case statement.

13. Assume that the DisplayCapital procedure is invoked when the Click event occurs for one of the following buttons: uiAlabamaButton, uiAlaskaButton, uiArizonaButton, and uiArkansasButton. Write an If...Then...Else statement that displays the name of the appropriate state's capital in the uiCapitalLabel control. Use the following table.

State	Capital
Alabama	Montgomery
Alaska	Juneau
Arizona	Phoenix
Arkansas	Little Rock

14. Rewrite the code from Exercise 13 using a Select Case statement.

15. In this exercise, you complete two procedures that display a message based on a code entered by the user.

    a. If necessary, start Visual Studio .NET. Open the Animal Solution (Animal Solution.sln) file, which is contained in the VBNET\Chap05\Animal Solution folder. If necessary, open the designer window.

    b. Open the Code Editor window. Complete the If...Then...Else button's Click event procedure by writing an If...Then...Else statement that displays the string "Dog" if the `animal` variable contains the number 1. Display the string "Cat" if the `animal` variable contains the number 2. Display the string "Bird" if the `animal` variable contains anything other than the number 1 or the number 2. Display the appropriate string in the uiMsgLabel control.

    c. Save the solution, then start the application. Test the application three times, using the numbers 1, 2, and 5.

    d. Click the Exit button to end the application.

    e. Complete the Select Case button's Click event procedure by writing a Select Case statement that displays the string "Dog" if the `animal` variable contains either the letter "D" or the letter "d". Display the string "Cat" if the `animal` variable contains either the letter "C" or the letter "c". Display the string "Bird" if the `animal` variable contains anything other than the letters "D", "d", "C", or "c". Display the appropriate string in the uiMsgLabel control.

    f. Save the solution, then start the application. Test the application three times, using the letters D, c, and x.

    g. Click the Exit button to end the application.

    h. Close the Output window, then close the solution.

16. In this exercise, you complete two procedures that display the name of the month corresponding to a number entered by the user.

    a. If necessary, start Visual Studio .NET. Open the Month Solution (Month Solution.sln) file, which is contained in the VBNET\Chap05\Month Solution folder. If necessary, open the designer window.

    b. Open the Code Editor window. Complete the If...Then...Else button's Click event procedure by writing an If...Then...Else statement that displays the name of the month corresponding to the number entered by the user. For example, if the user enters the number 1, the procedure should display the string "January". If the user enters an invalid number (one that is not in the range 1 through 12), display an appropriate message. Display the appropriate string in the uiMsgLabel control.

    c. Save the solution, then start the application. Test the application three times, using the numbers 3, 7, and 20.

    d. Click the Exit button to end the application.

    e. Now assume that the user will enter the first three characters of the month's name (rather than the month number) in the text box. Complete the Select Case button's Click event procedure by writing a Select Case statement that displays the name of the month corresponding to the characters entered by the user. For example, if the user enters the three characters "Jan" (in any case), the procedure should display the string "January". If the user enters "Jun", the procedure should display "June". If the three characters entered by the user do not match any of the expressions in the Case clauses, display an appropriate message. Display the appropriate string in the uiMsgLabel control.

    f. Save the solution, then start the application. Test the application three times, using the following data: jun, dec, xyz.

    g. Click the Exit button to end the application.

    h. Close the Output window, then close the solution.

17. In this exercise, you complete a procedure that calculates and displays a bonus amount.

    a. If necessary, start Visual Studio .NET. Open the Bonus Solution (Bonus Solution.sln) file, which is contained in the VBNET\Chap05\Bonus Solution folder. If necessary, open the designer window.

    b. Open the Code Editor window. Complete the Calculate button's Click event procedure by writing an If...Then...Else statement that assigns the number 25 to the bonus variable when the user enters a sales amount that is greater than or equal to $100, but less than or equal to $250. When the user enters a sales amount that is greater then $250, assign the number 50 to the bonus variable. When the user enters a sales amount that is less than 100, assign the number 0 as the bonus.

    c. Save the solution, then start the application. Test the application three times, using sales amounts of 100, 300, and 40.

    d. Click the Exit button to end the application.

    e. Close the Output window, then close the solution.

18. In this exercise, you complete a procedure that calculates and displays the total amount owed by a company.

    a. If necessary, start Visual Studio .NET. Open the Seminar Solution (Seminar Solution.sln) file, which is contained in the VBNET\Chap05\Seminar Solution folder. If necessary, open the designer window.

b. Open the Code Editor window. Assume you offer programming seminars to companies. Your price per person depends on the number of people the company registers, as shown in the following table. (For example, if the company registers seven people, then the total amount owed is $560, which is calculated by multiplying the number 7 by the number 80.) Use the Select Case statement to complete the Calculate button's Click event procedure.

Number of registrants	Criteria
1 - 4	$100 per person
5 - 10	$ 80 per person
11 or more	$ 60 per person
Less than 1	$ 0 per person

c. Save the solution, then start the application. Test the application four times, using the following data: 7, 4, 11, and -3.

d. Click the Exit button to end the application.

e. Close the Output window, then close the solution.

LESSON B
objectives

After completing this lesson, you will be able to:

- Include a group of radio buttons in an interface
- Designate a default radio button
- Include a check box in an interface
- Create a user-defined Sub procedure
- Generate random numbers using the Random object and the Random.Next method
- Call a user-defined Sub procedure
- Invoke a radio button control's Click event procedure from code
- Process code when a form is first loaded into the computer's memory

The Math Practice Application

Completing the User Interface

Recall that Susan Chen, the principal of a local primary school, wants an application that the first and second grade students can use to practice both adding and subtracting numbers. The application should display the addition or subtraction problem on the screen, then allow the student to enter the answer, and then verify that the answer is correct. If the student's answer is not correct, the application should give him or her as many chances as necessary to answer the problem correctly.

The problems displayed for the first grade students should use numbers from 1 through 10 only, and the problems for the second grade students should use numbers from 10 through 99. Because the students have not learned about negative numbers yet, the subtraction problems should never ask them to subtract a larger number from a smaller one.

Ms. Chen also wants the application to keep track of how many correct and incorrect responses the student makes. Recall that Ms. Chen wants the ability to control the display of this information. Figure 5-28 shows the sketch of the Math Practice application's user interface.

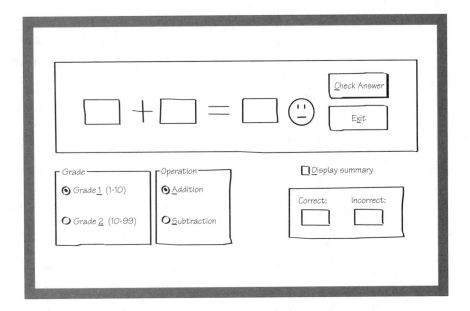

Figure 5-28: Sketch of the Math Practice application's user interface

The user interface contains one text box, four radio buttons, one check box, three picture box controls, four group box controls, and various label controls. To save you time, your computer's hard disk contains a partially completed Math Practice application. When you open the application, you will notice that most of the user interface has already been created and the properties of the existing objects have been set. You complete the user interface in this lesson.

To open the partially completed application:

1 Start Microsoft Visual Studio .NET, if necessary.

2 If necessary, close the Start Page window.

3 Open the **Math Solution** (Math Solution.sln) file, which is contained in the VBNET\Chap05\Math Solution folder.

4 Auto-hide the Toolbox, Solution Explorer, and Properties windows, if necessary. Figure 5-29 shows the partially completed user interface for the Math Practice application.

uiProblemGroupBox

uiOperationGroupBox

uiGradeGroupBox

uiSummaryGroupBox

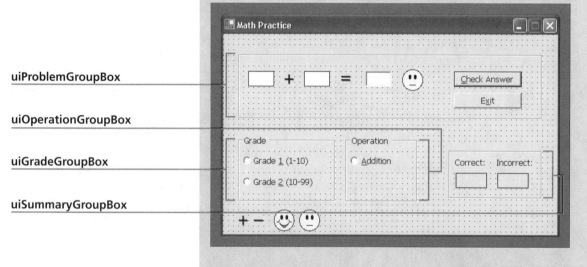

Figure 5-29: Partially completed user interface for the Math Practice application

As Figure 5-29 indicates, the names of the four group boxes are uiProblemGroupBox, uiGradeGroupBox, uiOperationGroupBox, and uiSummaryGroupBox. The uiProblemGroupBox control contains eight controls; the names of the controls (from left to right) are uiNum1Label, uiOperatorPictureBox, uiNum2Label, uiEqualPictureBox, uiAnswerTextBox, uiAnswerPictureBox, uiCheckAnswerButton, and uiExitButton. As you learned in Chapter 1, Visual Studio .NET comes with a variety of graphics files, which typically are located in the Program Files\Microsoft Visual Studio .NET 2003\ Common7\Graphics folder on either the local hard drive or the network drive. The graphics that appear in the uiOperatorPictureBox, uiEqualPictureBox, and uiAnswerPictureBox controls, for example, are stored in the MISC18.ICO, MISC22.ICO, and FACE01.ICO files within the Graphics\icons\Misc folder.

tip

Recall that you display a graphic in a picture box control by setting the control's Image property.

The uiGradeGroupBox control contains two radio buttons named uiGrade1RadioButton and uiGrade2RadioButton, and the uiOperationGroupBox control contains one radio button named uiAdditionRadioButton. The uiSummaryGroupBox control contains four label controls named uiIdCorrectLabel, uiCorrectLabel, uiIdIncorrectLabel, and uiIncorrectLabel.

In addition to the controls already mentioned, the form also contains four picture box controls positioned at the bottom of the form and named uiPlusPictureBox, uiMinusPictureBox, uiHappyPictureBox, and uiNeutralPictureBox. The graphics that appear in these controls are stored in the MISC18.ICO, MISC19.ICO, FACE03.ICO, and FACE01.ICO files within the Graphics\icons\Misc folder. For now, do not worry about these four picture box controls; you learn their purpose later in this lesson.

Only two controls are missing from the interface: the Subtraction radio button and the Display summary check box. You add the radio button first, and then you add the check box.

Adding a Radio Button to the Form

You also can use a ListBox control, CheckedListBox control, or ComboBox control to limit the user to only one choice in a group of two or more related and mutually exclusive choices.

You use the **RadioButton tool** in the toolbox to add a radio button control to the interface. A **radio button control** is the appropriate control to use when you want to limit the user to only one choice in a group of two or more related and mutually exclusive choices. In the Math Practice application, for example, you want the user to select one grade level (either Grade 1 or Grade 2) and one mathematical operation (either Addition or Subtraction), so the radio button control is the appropriate control to use in this situation.

Each radio button in an interface should be labeled so that the user knows its purpose. You enter the label using sentence capitalization in the radio button's Text property. Each radio button also should have a unique access key, which allows the user to select the button using the keyboard. In the next set of steps, you add the missing Subtraction radio button to the interface.

The uiSubtractionRadio Button control is an instance of the RadioButton class.

To add a radio button to the interface:

1 Click the **RadioButton** tool in the toolbox, and then drag a radio button control into the uiOperationGroupBox control, immediately below the uiAdditionRadioButton. The RadioButton1 control appears in the interface.

2 Set the following properties for the RadioButton1 control:

Name: **uiSubtractionRadioButton**

Location: 8, 59

Size: 96, 24

Text: **&Subtraction**

3 Click the form's **title bar**. Figure 5-30 shows the Subtraction radio button in the interface.

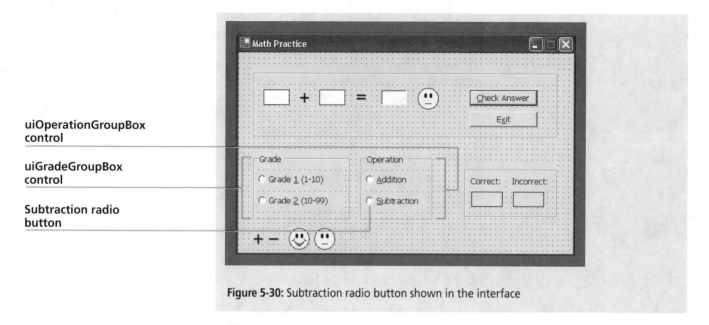

Figure 5-30: Subtraction radio button shown in the interface

uiOperationGroupBox control

uiGradeGroupBox control

Subtraction radio button

tip

If you have more than seven choices from which the user can choose, you should consider using a ListBox, CheckedListBox, or ComboBox control rather than radio buttons.

The Math Practice application contains two groups of radio buttons: one group allows the user to select the grade level, and the other allows him or her to select the mathematical operation. The minimum number of radio buttons in a group is two, because the only way to deselect a radio button is to select another radio button. The recommended maximum number of radio buttons in a group is seven. Notice that each group of radio buttons in the Math Practice application contains the minimum number of required radio buttons, two.

To include two groups of radio buttons in an interface, at least one of the groups must be placed within either a group box control or a panel control. Otherwise, the radio buttons are considered to be in the same group and only one can be selected at any one time. In this case, the radio buttons pertaining to the grade choice are contained in the uiGradeGroupBox control, and the radio buttons pertaining to the mathematical operation are contained in the uiOperationGroupBox control. Placing each group of radio buttons in a separate group box control allows the user to select one button from each group.

It is customary in Windows applications to have one of the radio buttons in each group of radio buttons already selected when the user interface first appears. The selected button is called the **default radio button** and is either the radio button that represents the user's most likely choice or the first radio button in the group. You designate a radio button as the default radio button by setting the button's **Checked property** to the Boolean value True. In the Math Practice application, you will make the first radio button in each group the default radio button.

To designate the first radio button in each group as the default radio button:

1 Click the **Grade 1** radio button to select it, and then set its Checked property to **True**. A black dot appears inside the circle in the Grade 1 radio button.

2 Now set the **Addition** radio button's Checked property to **True**. A black dot appears inside the circle in the Addition radio button.

GUI Design Tips

Radio Button Standards

- Use radio buttons when you want to limit the user to one of two or more related and mutually exclusive choices.
- The minimum number of radio buttons in a group is two, and the recommended maximum is seven.
- The label in the radio button's Text property should be entered using sentence capitalization.
- Assign a unique access key to each radio button in an interface.
- Use a group box control (or a panel control) to create separate groups of radio buttons. Only one button in each group can be selected at any one time.
- Designate a default radio button in each group of radio buttons.

Next, add the missing check box control to the interface.

Adding a Check Box Control to the Form

You use the **CheckBox tool** in the toolbox to add a check box control to the interface. Check boxes work like radio buttons in that they are either selected or deselected only; but that is where the similarity ends. You use radio button controls when you want to limit the user to only one choice from a group of related and mutually exclusive choices. You use **check box controls,** on the other hand, to allow the user to select any number of choices from a group of one or more independent and nonexclusive choices. Unlike radio buttons, where only one button in a group can be selected at any one time, any number of check boxes on a form can be selected at the same time.

As with radio buttons, each check box in an interface should be labeled so that the user knows its purpose. You enter the label using sentence capitalization in the check box's Text property. Each check box also should have a unique access key.

GUI Design Tips

Check Box Standards

- Use check boxes when you want to allow the user to select any number of choices from a group of one or more independent and nonexclusive choices.
- The label in the check box's Text property should be entered using sentence capitalization.
- Assign a unique access key to each check box in an interface.

The uiSummaryCheckBox control is an instance of the CheckBox class.

To add a check box to the interface:

1   Click the **CheckBox** tool in the toolbox, and then drag a check box control onto the form. Position the check box control immediately above the uiSummaryGroupBox control. (You can look ahead to Figure 5-31 for the exact location.) The CheckBox1 control appears in the interface.

2   Set the following properties for the CheckBox1 control:

Name:	uiSummaryCheckBox
Location:	352, 144
Size:	136, 32
Text:	&Display summary

3   Click the form's **title bar.** Figure 5-31 shows the Display summary check box in the interface.

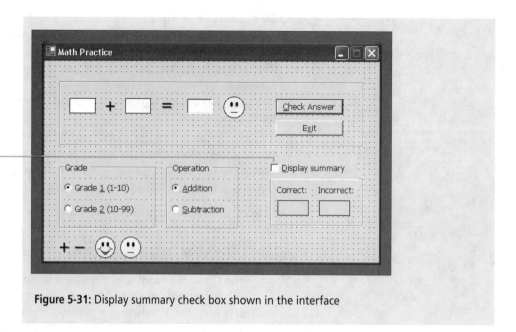

Display summary check box

Figure 5-31: Display summary check box shown in the interface

Now that you have completed the user interface, you can lock the controls in place, and then set each control's TabIndex property appropriately.

Locking the Controls and Setting the TabIndex Property

Recall that when you have completed a user interface, you should lock the controls in place and then set each control's TabIndex property appropriately.

To lock the controls, and then set each control's TabIndex property:

1 Right-click the **form**, and then click **Lock Controls** on the context menu.
2 **Click** View on the menu bar, and then click **Tab Order**. Use Figure 5-32 to set the TabIndex values for the controls on the form.

tip

As you learned in Chapter 2, picture box controls do not have a TabIndex property.

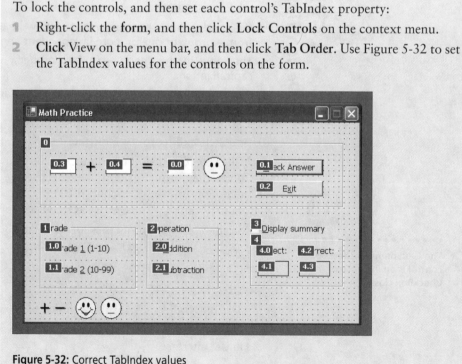

Figure 5-32: Correct TabIndex values

3   Press **Esc** to remove the TabIndex boxes from the form.

Now start the application to observe how you select and deselect radio buttons and check boxes.

To observe how you select and deselect radio buttons and check boxes:

1   Save the solution, and then start the application. Notice that the Grade 1 and Addition radio buttons already are selected, as the black dot inside each button's circle indicates. Also notice that the four picture box controls located at the bottom of the form, as well as the uiSummaryGroupBox control and its contents, do not appear in the interface when the application is started. This is because the Visible property of those controls is set to False in the Properties window. You learn more about the Visible property of a control in Lesson C.

You can select a different radio button control by clicking it. You can click either the circle or the text that appears inside the radio button.

2   Click the **Subtraction** radio button. Visual Basic .NET selects the Subtraction radio button as it deselects the Addition radio button. This is because both radio buttons belong to the same group and only one radio button in a group can be selected at any one time.

3   Click the **Grade 2** radio button. Visual Basic .NET selects the Grade 2 radio button as it deselects the Grade 1 radio button. Here again, the Grade 1 and Grade 2 radio buttons belong to the same group; so selecting one deselects the other.

After selecting a radio button in a group, you then can use the ↑ and ↓ keys on your keyboard to select another radio button in the group.

4   Press ↑ to select the Grade 1 radio button, and then press ↓ to select the Grade 2 radio button.

5   Press **Tab**. Notice that the focus moves to the Subtraction radio button rather than to the Addition radio button. In Windows applications, only the selected radio button in a group of radio buttons receives the focus.

You can select a check box control by clicking either the square or the text that appears inside the control.

6   Click the **Display summary** check box to select it. A check mark appears inside the check box to indicate that the check box is selected.

7   Click the **Display summary** check box to deselect it. Visual Basic .NET removes the check mark from the check box.

When a check box has the focus, you can use the spacebar on your keyboard to select and deselect it.

8   Press the **spacebar** to select the Display summary check box. A check mark appears inside the check box. Press the **spacebar** again to deselect the check box, which removes the check mark.

9   Click the **Exit** button to end the application. When you return to the designer window, close the Output window.

Now you can begin coding the application.

Coding the Math Practice Application

The TOE chart for the Math Practice application is shown in Figure 5-33.

Task	Object	Event
1. Display the plus sign in the uiOperatorPictureBox control 2. Generate and display two random numbers in the uiNum1Label and uiNum2Label controls	uiAdditionRadioButton	Click
Display either the happy face or the neutral face icon (from uiCheckAnswerButton)	uiAnswerPictureBox	None
Get and display the user's answer	uiAnswerTextBox	None
1. Calculate the correct answer to the math problem 2. Compare the correct answer to the user's answer 3. Display appropriate icon in the uiAnswerPictureBox 4. If the user's answer is correct, then generate and display two random numbers in the uiNum1Label and uiNum2Label controls 5. If the user's answer is incorrect, then display the "Try again!" message 6. Add 1 to the number of either correct or incorrect responses 7. Display the number of correct and incorrect responses in the uiCorrectLabel and uiIncorrectLabel controls, respectively	uiCheckAnswerButton	Click
Display the number of correct responses (from uiCheckAnswerButton)	uiCorrectLabel	None
Display the equal sign	uiEqualPictureBox	None
End the application	uiExitButton	Click
Display an addition problem when the form first appears on the screen	MathForm	Load
Generate and display two random numbers in the uiNum1Label and uiNum2Label controls	uiGrade1RadioButton, uiGrade2RadioButton	Click
Display the number of incorrect responses (from uiCheckAnswerButton)	uiIncorrectLabel	None
Display two random numbers (from uiGrade1RadioButton, uiGrade2RadioButton, uiAdditionRadioButton, uiSubtractionRadioButton, uiCheckAnswerButton)	uiNum1Label, uiNum2Label	None
Display either the plus sign or the minus sign (from uiAdditionRadioButton and uiSubtractionRadioButton)	uiOperatorPictureBox	None
1. Display the minus sign in the uiOperatorPictureBox control 2. Generate and display two random numbers in the uiNum1Label and uiNum2Label controls	uiSubtractionRadioButton	Click
Display or hide the uiSummaryGroupBox control	uiSummaryCheckBox	Click

Figure 5-33: TOE chart for the Math Practice application

According to the TOE chart, the Click event procedures for seven of the controls, as well as the Load event for the MathForm, need to be coded. In this lesson, you code all but the Click event procedures for the uiExitButton control (which already has been coded for you) and the uiCheckAnswerButton and uiSummaryCheckBox controls (which you code in Lesson C).

Notice that the task of generating and displaying two random numbers in the uiNum1Label and uiNum2Label controls appears in the Task column for five of the controls. For example, the task is listed as Step 2 for the uiAdditionRadioButton and uiSubtractionRadioButton controls. It is listed as the only task for the uiGrade1RadioButton and uiGrade2RadioButton controls, and it also appears as Step 4 for the uiCheckAnswerButton control. Rather than entering the appropriate code in the Click event procedures for each of the five controls, you will enter the code in a user-defined Sub procedure. You then will have the five Click event procedures call (or invoke) the Sub procedure. First, learn how to create a user-defined Sub procedure.

Creating a User-Defined Sub Procedure

Pascal is a programming language that was created by Niklaus Wirth in the late 1960s. It was named in honor of the seventeenth-century French mathematician Blaise Pascal, and is used to develop scientific applications.

A **user-defined Sub procedure** is a collection of code that can be invoked from one or more places in an application. When the code, or a portion of the code, for two or more objects is almost identical, it is more efficient to enter the code once, in a user-defined Sub procedure, instead of duplicating the code in various event procedures throughout the application.

The rules for naming a user-defined Sub procedure are the same as those for naming variables. (The naming rules are listed in Figure 3-4 in Chapter 3.) However, Sub procedure names should be entered using Pascal case, which means that you capitalize the first letter in the name and the first letter of each subsequent word in the name. You should select a descriptive name for the Sub procedure—one that indicates the task the procedure performs. It is a common practice to begin the name with a verb. For example, a good name for a Sub procedure that generates and displays two random numbers is GenerateAndDisplayNumbers.

To create a user-defined Sub procedure named GenerateAndDisplayNumbers:

1. Open the Code Editor window. Notice that the Exit button's Click event procedure already contains the appropriate code.

2. Replace the *<enter your name here>* and *<enter date here>* text with your name and the current date.

3. Click the blank line above the End Class statement, and then press Enter to insert another blank line.

As you learned in Chapter 1, every procedure begins with a procedure header and ends with a procedure footer. In this case, you will use `Private Sub GenerateAndDisplayNumbers()` as the procedure header, and `End Sub` as the procedure footer. Recall that the keyword Private indicates that the procedure can be used only within the class in which it is defined—in this case, only within the MathForm class. The keyword Sub indicates that the procedure is a Sub procedure.

In the GenerateAndDisplayNumbers procedure, an empty set of parentheses follows the procedure's name. The empty set of parentheses indicates that no items of information will be passed (sent) to the procedure when it is called. You learn how to pass information to a Sub procedure in Chapter 7.

4   In the new blank line, type **private sub GenerateAndDisplayNumbers**() and press **Enter**. When you press Enter, the Code Editor automatically enters the procedure footer for you, as shown in Figure 5-34.

procedure header

procedure footer

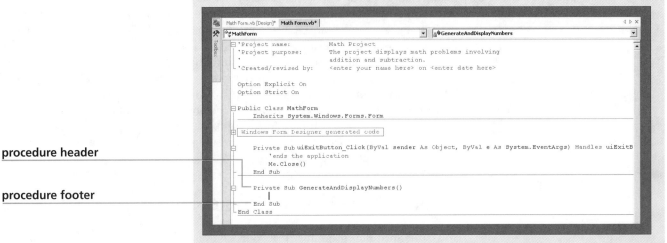

Figure 5-34: GenerateAndDisplayNumbers procedure header and footer

Figure 5-35 shows the pseudocode for the GenerateAndDisplayNumbers procedure.

GenerateAndDisplayNumbers
1. declare variables
2. if the Grade 1 radio button is selected
       generate two random numbers from 1 through 10
   else
       generate two random numbers from 10 through 99
   end if
3. if the Subtraction radio button is selected and the first random number is less
   than the second random number
       swap the two random numbers
   end if
4. display the random numbers in the uiNum1Label and uiNum2Label controls

Figure 5-35: Pseudocode for the GenerateAndDisplayNumbers procedure

The first step in the pseudocode is to declare the variables. The GenerateAndDisplayNumbers procedure will use two Integer variables to store the two random numbers generated by the procedure.

To begin coding the GenerateAndDisplayNumbers procedure:

1   Type **'generates and displays two random numbers** and press **Enter** twice.

2   Type **dim randomNum1 as integer** and press **Enter**. Then type **dim randomNum2 as integer** and press **Enter** twice.

Step 2 in the pseudocode is to determine whether the Grade 1 radio button is selected in the interface. You can determine whether a radio button is selected by comparing its Checked property to the Boolean value True. If the Checked property contains the Boolean value True, then the radio button is selected; if it contains the Boolean value False, then the radio button is not selected.

3 Type **'generate random numbers** and press **Enter**, then type **if me.uigrade1radiobutton.checked = true then** and press **Enter**.

If the Grade 1 radio button is selected, then the GenerateAndDisplayNumbers procedure should generate two random numbers from 1 through 10.

Generating Random Numbers

Visual Studio .NET provides a **pseudo-random number generator**, which is a device that produces a sequence of numbers that meet certain statistical requirements for randomness. To use the pseudo-random number generator in a procedure, you first create a Random object, typically using the syntax **Dim** *objectname* **As New Random**. The **Random object** represents the pseudo-random number generator in the procedure.

After creating a Random object, you can generate random integers using the **Random.Next method**. The syntax of the Random.Next method is *randomObject*.**Next**(*minValue*, *maxValue*), where *randomObject* is the name of a Random object. The *minValue* and *maxValue* arguments in the syntax must be integers, and *minValue* must be less than *maxValue*. The Random.Next method returns an integer that is greater than or equal to *minValue*, but less than *maxValue*. Figure 5-36 shows examples of using a Random object and the Random.Next method to generate random integers.

> **tip**
> Pseudo-random numbers are chosen with equal probability from a finite set of numbers. The chosen numbers are not completely random because a definite mathematical algorithm is used to select them, but they are sufficiently random for practical purposes.

Examples	Result

Example 1
`Dim randomGenerator As New Random`
`number = randomGenerator.Next(0, 51)`
	creates a Random object named randomGenerator, then assigns (to the number variable) a random integer that is greater than or equal to 0, but less than 51

Example 2
`Dim randomGenerator As New Random`
`number = randomGenerator.Next(50, 100)`
	creates a Random object named randomGenerator, then assigns (to the number variable) a random integer that is greater than or equal to 50, but less than 100

Example 3
`Dim randomGenerator As New Random`
`number = randomGenerator.Next(-10, 0)`
	creates a Random object named randomGenerator, then assigns (to the number variable) a random integer that is greater than or equal to –10, but less than 0

Figure 5-36: Examples of generating random integers

> **tip**
> In Discovery Exercise 4 at the end of this lesson, you learn how to use the R a n d o m . N e x t D o u b l e method to generate a random floating-point number.

The `Dim randomGenerator As New Random` statement in each example creates a Random object named randomGenerator. The randomGenerator object represents the pseudo-random number generator in the procedure. The `number = randomGenerator.Next(0, 51)` statement in Example 1 assigns (to the number variable) a random integer that is greater than or equal to 0, but less than 51. In Example 2, the `number = randomGenerator.Next(50, 100)` statement assigns a random integer that is greater than or equal to 50, but less than 100. In

In Discovery Exercise 5 at the end of this lesson, you learn how to generate random numbers using the Randomize statement and the Rnd function.

Example 3, the number = randomGenerator.Next(-10, 0) statement assigns a random integer that is greater than or equal to -10, but less than 0.

According to the pseudocode shown in Figure 5-35, if the Grade 1 radio button is selected in the Math Practice interface, then the GenerateAndDisplayNumbers procedure should generate two random numbers from 1 through 10. To generate numbers within that range, you use the number 1 as the *minValue* and the number 11 as the *maxValue*. If the Grade 1 radio button is not selected, then the Grade 2 button must be selected. In that case, the GenerateAndDisplayNumbers procedure should generate two random numbers from 10 through 99. To generate numbers within that range, you use the numbers 10 and 100 as the *minValue* and *maxValue*, respectively.

To continue coding the GenerateAndDisplayNumbers procedure:

1 Enter the additional code shown in Figure 5-37, then position the insertion point as shown in the figure.

enter this Dim
statement

enter these five
lines of code

position the insertion
point here

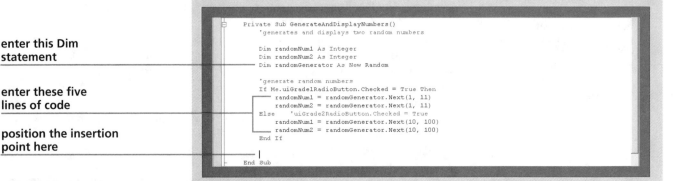

```
Private Sub GenerateAndDisplayNumbers()
    'generates and displays two random numbers

    Dim randomNum1 As Integer
    Dim randomNum2 As Integer
    Dim randomGenerator As New Random

    'generate random numbers
    If Me.uiGrade1RadioButton.Checked = True Then
        randomNum1 = randomGenerator.Next(1, 11)
        randomNum2 = randomGenerator.Next(1, 11)
    Else    'uiGrade2RadioButton.Checked = True
        randomNum1 = randomGenerator.Next(10, 100)
        randomNum2 = randomGenerator.Next(10, 100)
    End If

    |
End Sub
```

Figure 5-37: Random number generation code entered in the GenerateAndDisplayNumbers procedure

Step 3 in the pseudocode is to determine whether the Subtraction radio button is selected and, at the same time, to determine whether the first random number is less than the second random number. If both conditions are true, then the procedure should swap (interchange) the two random numbers, because no subtraction problem should result in a negative number.

2 Enter the additional code shown in Figure 5-38, then position the insertion point as shown in the figure.

```
Private Sub GenerateAndDisplayNumbers()
    'generates and displays two random numbers

    Dim randomNum1 As Integer
    Dim randomNum2 As Integer
    Dim randomGenerator As New Random

    'generate random numbers
    If Me.uiGrade1RadioButton.Checked = True Then
        randomNum1 = randomGenerator.Next(1, 11)
        randomNum2 = randomGenerator.Next(1, 11)
    Else    'uiGrade2RadioButton.Checked = True
        randomNum1 = randomGenerator.Next(10, 100)
        randomNum2 = randomGenerator.Next(10, 100)
    End If

    'swap numbers if the subtraction problem would result in a negative number
    If Me.uiSubtractionRadioButton.Checked = True AndAlso randomNum1 < randomNum2 Then
        Dim temp As Integer
        temp = randomNum1
        randomNum1 = randomNum2
        randomNum2 = temp
    End If

End Sub
```

enter this comment and six lines of code ⟶

position the insertion point here ⟶

Figure 5-38: Additional code entered in the GenerateAndDisplayNumbers procedure

The last step in the pseudocode shown in Figure 5-35 is to display the random numbers in the uiNum1Label and uiNum2Label controls.

3 Enter the additional code shown in Figure 5-39, which shows the completed GenerateAndDisplayNumbers procedure.

```
Private Sub GenerateAndDisplayNumbers()
    'generates and displays two random numbers

    Dim randomNum1 As Integer
    Dim randomNum2 As Integer
    Dim randomGenerator As New Random

    'generate random numbers
    If Me.uiGrade1RadioButton.Checked = True Then
        randomNum1 = randomGenerator.Next(1, 11)
        randomNum2 = randomGenerator.Next(1, 11)
    Else    'uiGrade2RadioButton.Checked = True
        randomNum1 = randomGenerator.Next(10, 100)
        randomNum2 = randomGenerator.Next(10, 100)
    End If

    'swap numbers if the subtraction problem would result in a negative number
    If Me.uiSubtractionRadioButton.Checked = True AndAlso randomNum1 < randomNum2 Then
        Dim temp As Integer
        temp = randomNum1
        randomNum1 = randomNum2
        randomNum2 = temp
    End If

    'display numbers in the label controls
    Me.uiNum1Label.Text = Convert.ToString(randomNum1)
    Me.uiNum2Label.Text = Convert.ToString(randomNum2)

End Sub
```

enter this comment and two lines of code ⟶

Figure 5-39: Completed GenerateAndDisplayNumbers procedure

4 Save the solution.

Next, code the Click event procedures for the Grade 1 and Grade 2 radio buttons.

Coding the uiGrade1RadioButton and uiGrade2RadioButton Click Event Procedures

According to the TOE chart shown in Figure 5-33, the uiGrade1RadioButton and uiGrade2RadioButton controls should generate and display two random numbers when clicked. Recall that the code to generate and display the random numbers is entered in the GenerateAndDisplayNumbers procedure. The uiGrade1RadioButton and uiGrade2RadioButton controls can use the code entered in the GenerateAndDisplayNumbers procedure simply by calling, or invoking, the procedure.

You can use the Visual Basic .NET **Call statement**, whose syntax is **Call** *procedurename([argumentlist])*, to call (invoke) a user-defined Sub procedure. The square brackets in the syntax indicate that the *argumentlist* is optional. If you have no information to pass to the procedure that you are calling, as is the case in the GenerateAndDisplayNumbers procedure, you simply include an empty set of parentheses after the *procedurename*.

Figure 5-40 shows two examples of including the `Call GenerateAndDisplayNumbers()` statement in the Click event procedures for the uiGrade1RadioButton and uiGrade2RadioButton controls.

Example 1

```
Private Sub uiGrade1RadioButton_Click(ByVal sender As Object, _
        ByVal e As System.EventArgs) Handles uiGrade1RadioButton.Click
    Call GenerateAndDisplayNumbers()
End Sub

Private Sub uiGrade2RadioButton_Click(ByVal sender As Object, _
        ByVal e As System.EventArgs) Handles uiGrade2RadioButton.Click
    Call GenerateAndDisplayNumbers()
End Sub
```

Example 2

```
Private Sub ProcessGradeRadioButtons(ByVal sender As Object, _
        ByVal e As System.EventArgs) _
        Handles uiGrade1RadioButton.Click, uiGrade2RadioButton.Click
    Call GenerateAndDisplayNumbers()
End Sub
```

Figure 5-40: Two examples of including the Call statement in the Click event procedures for the grade radio buttons

In the first example shown in Figure 5-40, the Call statement is entered in both Click event procedures. In the second example, the Call statement is entered in a procedure named ProcessGradeRadioButtons, which, according to its Handles section, is processed when the Click event occurs for either the uiGrade1RadioButton or uiGrade2RadioButton control. In this case, neither example is better than the other; both simply represent different ways of performing the same task.

To call the GenerateAndDisplayNumbers procedure when the Grade 1 and
Grade 2 radio buttons are clicked:

1 Open the code template for the uiGrade1RadioButton's Click event
procedure.

2 Change uiGrade1RadioButton_Click, which appears after `Private Sub` in
the procedure header, to **ProcessGradeRadioButtons**.

3 Click immediately before the word Handles in the procedure header. Type _
(the underscore, which is the line continuation character) and press **Enter**.

4 Press **Tab** twice to indent the line.

5 Enter the additional code shown in Figure 5-41, which shows the completed
ProcessGradeRadioButtons procedure.

enter this line of code

enter this code

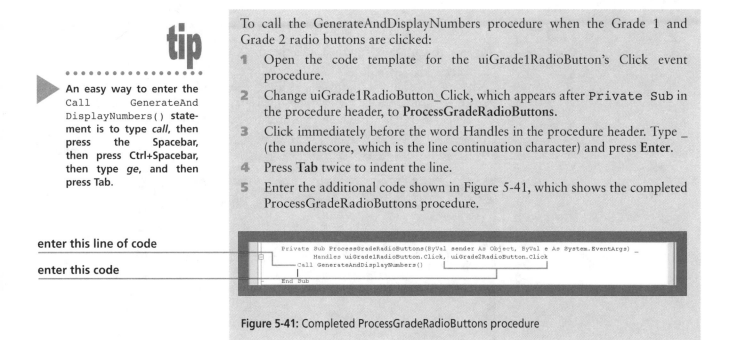

```
Private Sub ProcessGradeRadioButtons(ByVal sender As Object, ByVal e As System.EventArgs) _
       Handles uiGrade1RadioButton.Click, uiGrade2RadioButton.Click
    Call GenerateAndDisplayNumbers()

End Sub
```

Figure 5-41: Completed ProcessGradeRadioButtons procedure

When the user clicks either the Grade 1 radio button or the Grade 2 radio button, the computer processes the `Call GenerateAndDisplayNumbers()` statement contained in the ProcessGradeRadioButtons procedure. When the Call
statement is processed, the computer leaves the ProcessGradeRadioButtons procedure, temporarily, to process the instructions contained in the
GenerateAndDisplayNumbers procedure. When the GenerateAndDisplayNumbers
procedure ends, which is when the computer processes the procedure's `End Sub`
statement, the computer returns to the ProcessGradeRadioButtons procedure, to
the line below the Call statement. In the ProcessGradeRadioButtons procedure, the
line below the Call statement is the `End Sub` statement, which ends the procedure.
Figure 5-42 illustrates the concept of calling a procedure.

leave
ProcessGradeRadio-
Buttons procedure,
temporarily

return to
ProcessGradeRadio-
Buttons procedure

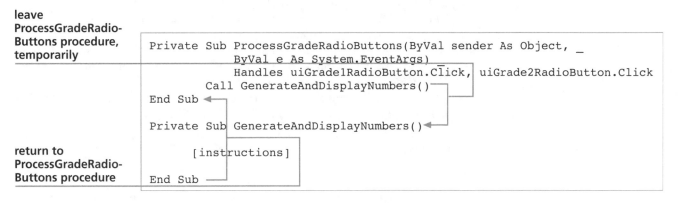

```
Private Sub ProcessGradeRadioButtons(ByVal sender As Object, _
       ByVal e As System.EventArgs) _
       Handles uiGrade1RadioButton.Click, uiGrade2RadioButton.Click
    Call GenerateAndDisplayNumbers()
End Sub

Private Sub GenerateAndDisplayNumbers()

    [instructions]

End Sub
```

Figure 5-42: Illustration of calling a procedure

Now test the grade radio buttons to verify that they are working correctly.

To test the grade radio buttons:

1 Save the solution, and then start the application.

2 Click the **Grade 2** radio button. The computer leaves the ProcessGradeRadioButtons procedure, temporarily, to process the instructions in the GenerateAndDisplayNumbers procedure. The GenerateAndDisplayNumbers procedure generates and displays two random integers from 10 through 99, as shown in Figure 5-43. (Do not be concerned if the numbers on your screen are different from the ones shown in the figure.)

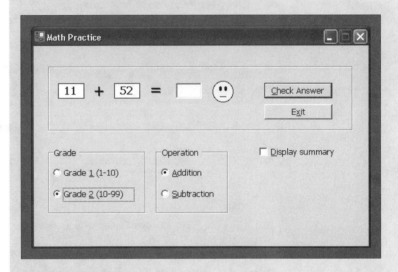

Figure 5-43: Two random numbers displayed in the interface

When the GenerateAndDisplayNumbers procedure ends, the computer returns to the ProcessGradeRadioButtons procedure, to the line immediately below the Call statement. That line is the `End   Sub` statement, which ends the ProcessGradeRadioButtons procedure.

3 Click the **Grade 1** radio button. The computer leaves the ProcessGradeRadioButtons procedure, temporarily, to process the instructions in the GenerateAndDisplayNumbers procedure. The GenerateAndDisplayNumbers procedure generates and displays two random integers from 1 through 10. When the GenerateAndDisplayNumbers procedure ends, the computer returns to the ProcessGradeRadioButtons procedure, to the line immediately below the Call statement. That line is the `End Sub` statement, which ends the ProcessGradeRadioButtons procedure.

4 Click the **Exit** button. When you return to the Code Editor window, close the Output window.

Next, code the Click event procedures for the Addition and Subtraction radio buttons.

tip

· · · · · · · · · · · · · · · · ·

▶ To remove a graphic from a picture box control while a procedure is running, set the picture box control's Image property to the keyword Nothing.

Coding the uiAdditionRadioButton and uiSubtractionRadioButton Click Event Procedures

According to the TOE chart shown in Figure 5-33, when the user clicks either the uiAdditionRadioButton control or the uiSubtractionRadioButton control, the control's Click event procedure should display the appropriate mathematical operator (either a plus sign or a minus sign) in the uiOperatorPictureBox control, and then generate and display two random numbers in the uiNum1Label and uiNum2Label controls. Figure 5-44 shows two examples of coding the Click event procedures for these radio buttons.

Example 1

```
Private Sub uiAdditionRadioButton_Click(ByVal sender As Object, _
     ByVal e As System.EventArgs) Handles uiAdditionRadioButton.Click
    Me.uiOperatorPictureBox.Image = Me.uiPlusPictureBox.Image
    Call GenerateAndDisplayNumbers()
End Sub

Private Sub uiSubtractionRadioButton_Click(ByVal sender As Object, _
     ByVal e As System.EventArgs) Handles uiSubtractionRadioButton.Click
    Me.uiOperatorPictureBox.Image = Me.uiMinusPictureBox.Image
    Call GenerateAndDisplayNumbers()
End Sub
```

Example 2

```
Private Sub ProcessOperationRadioButtons(ByVal sender As Object, _
     ByVal e As System.EventArgs) _
    Handles uiAdditionRadioButton.Click, uiSubtractionRadioButton.Click
    If sender Is Me.uiAdditionRadioButton Then
         Me.uiOperatorPictureBox.Image = Me.uiPlusPictureBox.Image
    Else 'uiSubtractionRadioButton is sender
         Me.uiOperatorPictureBox.Image = Me.uiMinusPictureBox.Image
    End If
    Call GenerateAndDisplayNumbers()
End Sub
```

Figure 5-44: Examples of coding the Click event procedures for the operation radio buttons

In Example 1 in Figure 5-44, both Click event procedures first display the appropriate operator in the uiOperatorPictureBox control. The Click event procedure for the uiAdditionRadioButton control displays the plus sign by assigning the Image property of the uiPlusPictureBox control, which is located at the bottom of the form, to the Image property of the uiOperatorPictureBox control. Likewise, the Click event procedure for the uiSubtractionRadioButton control displays the minus sign by assigning the Image property of the uiMinusPictureBox control, which also is located at the bottom of the form, to the Image property of the uiOperatorPictureBox control. After assigning the appropriate operator, the Click event procedures shown in Example 1 call the GenerateAndDisplayNumbers procedure to generate and display two random numbers in the uiNum1Label and uiNum2Label controls.

In the second example shown in Figure 5-44, the code to display the operator and random numbers is entered in the ProcessOperationRadioButtons procedure, rather than in the individual Click event procedures. According to the Handles section, the ProcessOperationRadioButtons procedure is processed when either the uiAdditionRadioButton Click event or the uiSubtractionRadioButton Click event occurs. Notice that the procedure uses a selection structure to determine whether the `sender` parameter contains the address of the uiAdditionRadioButton control. If it does, then the procedure displays the plus sign in the uiOperatorPictureBox control; otherwise, it displays the minus sign in the control. Here again, neither example is better than the other; both simply represent two different ways of performing the same task.

To code the uiAdditionRadioButton and uiSubtractionRadioButton Click event procedures, then test the application:

1   Open the code template for the uiAdditionRadioButton's Click event procedure.

2   Change uiAdditionRadioButton_Click, which appears after `Private Sub` in the procedure header, to **ProcessOperationRadioButtons**.

3   Click immediately before the word Handles in the procedure header. Type _ (the underscore, which is the line continuation character) and press **Enter**.

4   Press **Tab** twice to indent the line.

5   Enter the additional code shown in Figure 5-45, which shows the completed ProcessOperationRadioButtons procedure.

enter these comments and lines of code

enter this code

```
Private Sub ProcessOperationRadioButtons(ByVal sender As Object, ByVal e As System.EventArgs) _
        Handles uiAdditionRadioButton.Click, uiSubtractionRadioButton.Click
    'display appropriate operator
    If sender Is Me.uiAdditionRadioButton Then
        Me.uiOperatorPictureBox.Image = Me.uiPlusPictureBox.Image
    Else    'uiSubtractionRadioButton is sender
        Me.uiOperatorPictureBox.Image = Me.uiMinusPictureBox.Image
    End If
    Call GenerateAndDisplayNumbers()
End Sub
```

Figure 5-45: Completed ProcessOperationRadioButtons procedure

Now test the application's code.

6   Save the solution, then start the application. Notice that, even though the Grade 1 and Addition radio buttons are selected in the interface, an addition problem does not automatically appear in the interface. You fix that in the next section.

7   Click the **Subtraction** radio button. A minus sign appears in the uiOperatorPictureBox control, and two new random integers from 1 through 10 appear in the interface.

8   Click the **Addition** radio button. A plus sign appears in the uiOperatorPictureBox control, and two new random integers from 1 through 10 appear in the interface.

9   Click the **Grade 2** radio button. Two new random integers from 10 through 99 appear in the interface.

10 Click the **Exit** button. When you return to the Code Editor window, close the Output window.

To click a Button control from code, you use the syntax *button*.PerformClick().

In the Math Practice application, you want an addition problem to be displayed automatically when the form first appears on the screen. You can accomplish this task in two ways: either you can use the Call statement to call the GenerateAndDisplayNumbers procedure, or you can use the PerformClick method to invoke the uiAdditionRadioButton control's Click event procedure. Whichever way you choose, the appropriate code must be entered in the form's Load event procedure, which is the last procedure you code in this lesson.

Coding the Form's Load Event Procedure

Instructions entered in the form's **Load event procedure** are processed when the application is started and the form is loaded into memory. The form is not displayed on the screen until all of the instructions in its Load event procedure are processed. To automatically display an addition problem when the Math Practice interface first appears, you can enter either the statement `Call GenerateAndDisplayNumbers()` or the statement `Me.uiAdditionRadioButton.PerformClick()` in the MathForm's Load event procedure. The latter statement uses the **RadioButton.PerformClick method**, whose syntax is *radiobutton*.**PerformClick()**, to invoke the Addition radio button's Click event, which causes the code in the Click event procedure to be processed by the computer.

To automatically display an addition problem when the Math Practice interface first appears:

1 Click the **Class Name** list arrow in the Code Editor window, and then click (**MathForm Events**) in the list. Click the **Method Name** list arrow, and then click **Load** in the list. The template for the MathForm's Load event procedure appears in the Code Editor window.

2 Enter the Call statement shown in Figure 5-46, which shows the completed Load event procedure.

enter this statement ⟶

```
Private Sub MathForm_Load(ByVal sender As Object, ByVal e As System.EventArgs) Handles MyBase.Load
    Call GenerateAndDisplayNumbers()

End Sub
```

Figure 5-46: Completed Load event procedure

3 Save the solution, then start the application. When the Math Practice interface appears on the screen, it displays an addition problem, as shown in Figure 5-47.

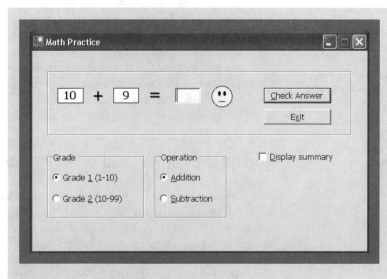

Figure 5-47: Addition problem displayed when the form first appears

4　Click the **Exit** button to end the application. When you return to the Code Editor window, close the Output window, and then close the Code Editor window.

5　Click **File** on the menu bar, and then click **Close Solution** to close the solution.

You now have completed Lesson B. You can either take a break or complete the end-of-lesson questions and exercises before moving on to the next lesson. You complete the Math Practice application in Lesson C.

SUMMARY

To limit the user to only one choice in a group of two or more related and mutually exclusive choices:

■　Use the RadioButton tool to add a radio button control to the interface.

■　To include two groups of radio buttons in an interface, at least one of the groups must be placed within either a group box control or a panel control.

To allow the user to select any number of choices from a group of one or more independent and nonexclusive choices:

■　Use the CheckBox tool to add a check box control to the interface.

To create a collection of code that can be invoked from one or more places in a program:

■　Create a user-defined Sub procedure. The Sub procedure's name should begin with a verb and indicate the task performed by the procedure.

To generate random numbers that are integers:

■　Create a Random object to represent the Visual Studio .NET pseudo-random number generator. Typically, the syntax for creating a Random object is **Dim** *objectname* **As New Random**.

Use the Random.Next method to generate a random integer. The syntax of the Random.Next method is *randomObject*.**Next**(*minValue, maxValue*), where *randomObject* is the name of the Random object, and *minValue* and *maxValue* are integers. The Random.Next method returns an integer that is greater than or equal to *minValue*, but less than *maxValue*.

To call (invoke) a user-defined Sub procedure:

Use the Call statement. The syntax of the Call statement is **Call** *procedurename* ([*argumentlist*]), where *procedurename* is the name of the procedure you want to call, and *argumentlist* (which is optional) contains the information you want to send to the Sub procedure.

To process code when the form is loaded into memory:

Enter the code in the form's Load event procedure.

To invoke a radio button control's Click event procedure from code:

Use the RadioButton.PerformClick method. The syntax of the RadioButton.PerformClick method is *radiobutton*.**PerformClick**(), where *radiobutton* is the name of the radio button whose Click event you want invoked.

Q U E S T I O N S

1. The minimum number of radio buttons in a group is _____.
   a. one
   b. two
   c. three
   d. four
   e. seven

2. The minimum number of check boxes in an interface is _____.
   a. one
   b. two
   c. three
   d. four
   e. seven

3. The text appearing in check box and radio button controls should be entered using _____.
   a. book title capitalization
   b. sentence capitalization
   c. either book title capitalization or sentence capitalization

4. It is customary in Windows applications to designate a default check box.
   a. True
   b. False

5. To create three groups of radio buttons in an interface, what is the minimum number of groups that must be placed in a separate group box or panel control?
   a. zero
   b. one
   c. two
   d. three

6. To create three groups of check boxes in an interface, what is the minimum number of groups that must be placed in a separate group box or panel control?
   a. zero
   b. one
   c. two
   d. three

7. Assume that a form contains two group box controls, each containing three radio buttons. How many radio buttons can be selected on the form?
   a. one
   b. two
   c. three
   d. five
   e. six

8. Assume that a form contains two group box controls, each containing three check boxes. How many check boxes can be selected on the form?
   a. one
   b. two
   c. three
   d. five
   e. six

9. If a radio button is selected, its _____ property contains the Boolean value True.
   a. Checked
   b. Dot
   c. On
   d. Selected
   e. Value

10. You can use the radio button control to limit the user to only one choice in a group of two or more related and mutually exclusive choices.
    a. True
    b. False

11. You can use the check box control to allow the user to select any number of independent and nonexclusive choices.
    a. True
    b. False

12. Which of the following statements declares an object that can represent the Visual Studio .NET pseudo-random number generator in a procedure?
    a. `Dim generator As New RandomNumber`
    b. `Dim numberGenerator As New Generator`
    c. `Dim numberRandom As New Random`
    d. `Dim numberRandom As Random`
    e. `Dim number As New RandomObject`

13. Which of the following statements generates a random number from 1 to 25, inclusive? (The Random object's name is randomGenerator.)
    a. `number = randomGenerator(1, 25)`
    b. `number = randomGenerator.Get(1, 25)`
    c. `number = randomGenerator.Next(1, 25)`
    d. `number = randomGenerator.Next(1, 26)`
    e. `number = randomGenerator.NextNumber(1, 26)`

14. You can use the _____ statement to invoke a user-defined Sub procedure.
     a. Call
     b. DoProcedure
     c. Get
     d. Invoke
     e. ProcedureCall

15. The _____ event occurs when a form is being read into the computer's internal memory.
     a. BringIn
     b. Change
     c. Load
     d. MemoryInit
     e. Read

16. Which of the following statements invokes the uiAlaskaRadioButton control's Click event procedure?
     a. `Me.uiAlaskaRadioButton.Click()`
     b. `Me.uiAlaskaRadioButton.ClickIt`
     c. `Me.Click.uiAlaskaRadioButton()`
     d. `Me.PerformClick.uiAlaskaRadioButton`
     e. None of the above.

EXERCISES

1. In this exercise, you use the RadioButton.PerformClick method to invoke a radio button's Click event procedure.
     a. If necessary, start Visual Studio .NET. Open the Practice Solution (Practice Solution.sln) file, which is contained in the VBNET\Chap05\Practice Solution folder. If necessary, open the designer window.
     b. Modify the form's Load event procedure so that it uses the RadioButton.PerformClick method to invoke the Addition radio button's Click event procedure.
     c. Save the solution, then start the application. An addition problem automatically appears in the interface.
     d. Click the Exit button to end the application.
     e. Close the Output window, then close the solution.

2. In this exercise, you code an application for Woodland School. The application allows a student to select the name of a state and the name of a capital city. After making his or her selections, the student can click the Verify Answer button to verify that the selected city is the capital of the selected state.
     a. If necessary, start Visual Studio .NET. Open the Capitals Solution (Capitals Solution.sln) file, which is contained in the VBNET\Chap05\Capitals Solution folder. If necessary, open the designer window.
     b. Designate the first radio button in each group as the default radio button for the group.
     c. Enter the code to invoke the Click event for the two default radio buttons when the form is read into the computer's internal memory.
     d. Declare two module-level String variables named `capital` and `choice`.
     e. Code the State radio buttons' Click event procedures so that each assigns the appropriate capital to the `capital` variable, and each removes the contents of the uiMsgLabel control.

f. Code the Capital radio buttons' Click event procedures so that each assigns the selected capital to the choice variable, and each removes the contents of the uiMsgLabel control.

g. Code the Verify Answer button's Click event procedure so that it displays the word "Correct" in the uiMsgLabel control if the student selected the appropriate capital; otherwise, display the word "Incorrect".

h. Save the solution, then start the application. Test the application by selecting Illinois from the State group and Salem from the Capital group. Click the Verify Answer button. The word "Incorrect" appears in the uiMsgLabel control. Now select Wisconsin from the State group and Madison from the Capital group. Click the Verify Answer button. The word "Correct" appears in the uiMsgLabel control.

i. Click the Exit button to end the application.

j. Close the Output window, then close the solution.

3. In this exercise, you code an application for Professor Juarez. The application displays a letter grade based on the average of three test scores entered by the professor.

a. If necessary, start Visual Studio .NET. Open the Grade Solution (Grade Solution.sln) file, which is contained in the VBNET\Chap05\Grade Solution folder. If necessary, open the designer window.

b. Code the Display Grade button's Click event procedure so that it displays the appropriate letter grade based on the average of three test scores. Each test is worth 100 points. Use the following information to complete the procedure:

Test average	Grade
90–100	A
80–89	B
70–79	C
60–69	D
below 60	F

c. When the user makes a change to the contents of a text box, the application should remove the contents of the uiGradeLabel control. Code the appropriate event procedures.

d. Save the solution, then start the application. Test the application three times. For the first test, use scores of 90, 95, and 100. For the second test, use scores of 83, 72, and 65. For the third test, use scores of 40, 30, and 20.

e. Click the Exit button to end the application.

f. Close the Output window, then close the solution.

discovery ▶ 4. In this exercise, you generate and display random floating-point numbers.

a. If necessary, start Visual Studio .NET. Open the Random Float Solution (Random Float Solution.sln) file, which is contained in the VBNET\Chap05\Random Float Solution folder. If necessary, open the designer window.

b. You can use the Random.NextDouble method to return a floating-point random number that is greater than or equal to 0.0, but less than 1.0. The syntax of the Random.NextDouble method is *randomObject*.**NextDouble**. Code the Display Random Number button's Click event procedure so that it displays a random floating-point number in the uiNumberLabel control.

c. Save the solution, then start the application. Click the Display Random Number button several times. Each time you click the button, a random number that is greater than or equal to 0.0, but less than 1.0, appears in the uiNumberLabel control.

d. Click the Exit button to end the application.

e. You can use the following formula to generate random floating-point numbers within a specified range: (*maxValue* − *minValue* + 1) * *randomObject*.**NextDouble** + *minValue*. For example, assuming the Random object's name is randomGenerator, the formula (10 − 1 + 1) * randomGenerator.NextDouble + 1 generates floating-point numbers that are greater than or equal to 1.0, but less than 11.0. Modify the

Display Random Number button's Click event procedure so that it displays a random floating-point number that is greater than or equal to 25.0, but less than 51.0. Display two decimal places in the floating-point number.

f. Save the solution, then start the application. Click the Display Random Number button several times. Each time you click the button, a random number that is greater than or equal to 25.0, but less than 51.0, appears in the uiNumberLabel control.

g. Click the Exit button to end the application.

h. Close the Output window, then close the solution.

discovery ▶ **5.** In this exercise, you use the Randomize statement and Rnd function, which are used in previous versions of Visual Basic to generate and display random numbers. You also can use the Randomize statement and Rnd function in Visual Basic .NET.

a. If necessary, start Visual Studio .NET. Open the Randomize Solution (Randomize Solution.sln) file, which is contained in the VBNET\Chap05\Randomize Solution folder. If necessary, open the designer window.

In addition to using a Random object and the Random.Next method to generate random numbers, you also can use the Randomize statement and the Rnd function. The Randomize statement initializes (gives a beginning value to) the random number generator, and the Rnd function generates the random number. The syntax of the Randomize statement is **Randomize**, and the syntax of the Rnd function is **Rnd()**. The Rnd function produces floating-point numbers within the 0.0 to 1.0 range, including 0.0 but not including 1.0. For example, the statement `Me.uiNumberLabel.Text = Convert.ToString(Rnd())` displays a random floating-point number that is greater than or equal to 0.0, but less than 1.0. You can use the following formula to generate random floating-point numbers in a range other than 0.0 to 1.0: (*maxValue* − *minValue* + 1) * **Rnd()** + *minValue*. To generate random integers within a specified range, you simply include the Convert.ToInt32 method in the formula, like this: **Convert.ToInt32**((*maxValue* − *minValue* + 1) * **Rnd()** + *minValue*). The Convert.ToInt32 method returns the integer portion of a number. For example, the formula `Convert.ToInt32((10 - 1 + 1) * Rnd() + 1)` returns random integers from 1 through 10.

b. Complete the Display Random Number button's Click event procedure by entering the Randomize statement immediately below the Dim statement. Then use the Rnd function to assign, to the `number` variable, a random integer from 10 through 100.

c. Save the solution, then start the application. Click the Display Random Number button several times. Each time you click the button, a random number that is greater than or equal to 10, but less than or equal to 100, appears in the uiNumberLabel control.

d. Click the Exit button to end the application.

e. Close the Output window, then close the solution.

After completing this lesson, you will be able to:

- Select the existing text in a text box control
- Code a check box control's Click event procedure
- Display and hide a control

Completing the Math Practice Application

Coding the uiCheckAnswerButton Click Event Procedure

Recall that to complete the Math Practice application, you still need to code the Click event procedures for the uiCheckAnswerButton and the uiDisplaySummaryCheckBox controls. Before you can code these procedures, you need to open the Math Practice application from Lesson B.

To open the Math Practice application from Lesson B:

1 Start Microsoft Visual Studio .NET, if necessary.

2 If necessary, close the Start Page window.

3 Open the **Math Solution** (Math Solution.sln) file contained in the VBNET\Chap05\Math Solution folder. Figure 5-48 shows the user interface for the Math Practice application.

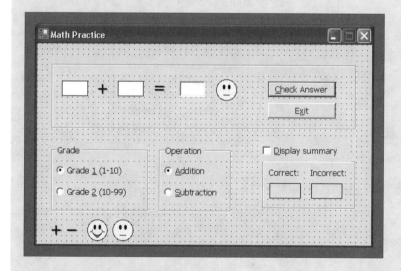

Figure 5-48: User interface for the Math Practice application

Figure 5-49 shows the pseudocode for the uiCheckAnswerButton control's Click event procedure.

```
uiCheckAnswerButton
1.  declare variables
include the following in the Try section of a Try/Catch block:
2.  assign random numbers and user's answer to variables
3.  if the Addition radio button is selected
        add the two random numbers together, and assign the result to a variable
    else
        subtract the second random number from the first random number, and assign the
        result to a variable
    end if
4.  if the user's answer is correct
        display the happy face icon in the uiAnswerPictureBox control
        add 1 to the number of correct responses
        clear the contents of the uiAnswerTextBox control
        call the GenerateAndDisplayNumbers procedure to generate and display two
        random numbers
    else
        display the neutral face icon in the uiAnswerPictureBox control
        add 1 to the number of incorrect responses
        display the "Try again!" message in a message box
        select the existing text in the uiAnswerTextBox control
    end if
5.  send the focus to the uiAnswerTextBox control
6.  display the number of correct and incorrect responses in the uiCorrectLabel and
    uiIncorrectLabel controls

include the following in the Catch section of a Try/Catch block
1.  use a Catch statement to handle the FormatException
        if a FormatException error occurs, display the message "The answer must be numeric." in a message box
2.  use a general Catch statement to handle any other errors
        if an error occurs, display a description of the error in a message box
```

Figure 5-49: Pseudocode for the uiCheckAnswerButton control's Click event procedure

The first step in the pseudocode is to declare the variables. The uiCheckAnswerButton control's Click event procedure will use the six Integer variables listed in Figure 5-50.

Name	Purpose
randomNum1	store the random number contained in the uiNum1Label control
randomNum2	store the random number contained in the uiNum2Label control
userAnswer	store the user's answer, which is contained in the uiAnswerTextBox
correctAnswer	store the correct answer
numberCorrect	store the number of correct responses made by the user; declare as a static variable
numberIncorrect	store the number of incorrect responses made by the user; declare as a static variable

Figure 5-50: Variables used by the uiCheckAnswerButton control's Click event procedure

Notice that the `numberCorrect` and `numberIncorrect` variables must be declared as static variables. As you learned in Chapter 3, a static variable is a local variable that retains its value even when the procedure in which it is declared ends. In this case, the `numberCorrect` and `numberIncorrect` variables need to be static variables because they must keep a running tally of the number of correct and incorrect responses.

To begin coding the uiCheckAnswerButton Click event procedure:

1 Open the Code Editor window, then open the code template for the uiCheckAnswerButton's Click event procedure.

2 Type **'calculates the correct answer, and then compares the correct answer to the user's answer** and press Enter.

3 Type **'keeps track of the number of correct and incorrect answers** and press Enter twice.

4 Type **dim randomNum1 as integer** and press Enter, then type **dim randomNum2 as integer** and press Enter.

5 Type **dim userAnswer as integer** and press Enter, then type **dim correctAnswer as integer** and press Enter.

6 Type **static numberCorrect as integer** and press Enter, then type **static numberIncorrect as integer** and press Enter twice.

Next, include a Try/Catch block in the procedure.

7 Enter the Try/Catch block shown in Figure 5-51, and then position the insertion point as shown in the figure.

position the insertion point here

enter these lines of code

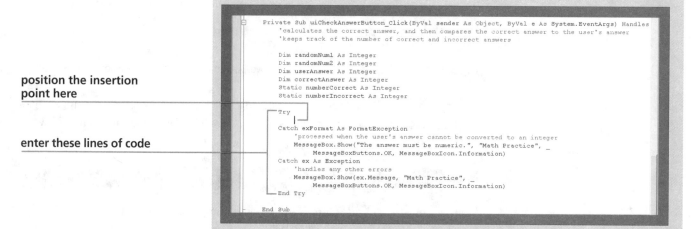

```
Private Sub uiCheckAnswerButton_Click(ByVal sender As Object, ByVal e As System.EventArgs) Handles
    'calculates the correct answer, and then compares the correct answer to the user's answer
    'keeps track of the number of correct and incorrect answers

    Dim randomNum1 As Integer
    Dim randomNum2 As Integer
    Dim userAnswer As Integer
    Dim correctAnswer As Integer
    Static numberCorrect As Integer
    Static numberIncorrect As Integer

    Try

    Catch exFormat As FormatException
        'processed when the user's answer cannot be converted to an integer
        MessageBox.Show("The answer must be numeric.", "Math Practice", _
            MessageBoxButtons.OK, MessageBoxIcon.Information)
    Catch ex As Exception
        'handles any other errors
        MessageBox.Show(ex.Message, "Math Practice", _
            MessageBoxButtons.OK, MessageBoxIcon.Information)
    End Try

End Sub
```

Figure 5-51: Try/Catch block entered in the procedure

Now assign the two random numbers and the user's answer to the appropriate variables.

8 Enter the comment and three assignment statements shown in Figure 5-52.

```
Private Sub uiCheckAnswerButton_Click(ByVal sender As Object, ByVal e As System.EventArgs) Handles
    'calculates the correct answer, and then compares the correct answer to the user's answer
    'keeps track of the number of correct and incorrect answers

    Dim randomNum1 As Integer
    Dim randomNum2 As Integer
    Dim userAnswer As Integer
    Dim correctAnswer As Integer
    Static numberCorrect As Integer
    Static numberIncorrect As Integer

    Try
        'assign random numbers and user's answer to variables
        randomNum1 = Integer.Parse(Me.uiNum1Label.Text)
        randomNum2 = Integer.Parse(Me.uiNum2Label.Text)
        userAnswer = Integer.Parse(Me.uiAnswerTextBox.Text)

    Catch exFormat As FormatException
        'processed when the user's answer cannot be converted to an integer
        MessageBox.Show("The answer must be numeric.", "Math Practice", _
            MessageBoxButtons.OK, MessageBoxIcon.Information)
    Catch ex As Exception
        'handles any other errors
        MessageBox.Show(ex.Message, "Math Practice", _
            MessageBoxButtons.OK, MessageBoxIcon.Information)
    End Try

End Sub
```

enter this comment and assignment statements

Figure 5-52: Comment and assignment statements entered in the procedure

Step 3 in the pseudocode is to determine whether the Addition radio button is selected in the interface. If it is, then the procedure should add the two random numbers together; otherwise, it should subtract the second random number from the first random number. In either case, the result of the calculation should be assigned to a variable.

9 Enter the comment and selection structure shown in Figure 5-53, then position the insertion point as shown in the figure. (You also could use an If...Then...Else statement rather than a Select Case statement to determine whether the Addition radio button is selected.)

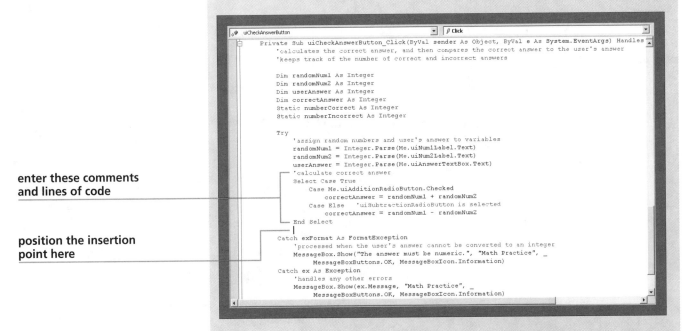

```
uiCheckAnswerButton                              Click

Private Sub uiCheckAnswerButton_Click(ByVal sender As Object, ByVal e As System.EventArgs) Handles
    'calculates the correct answer, and then compares the correct answer to the user's answer
    'keeps track of the number of correct and incorrect answers

    Dim randomNum1 As Integer
    Dim randomNum2 As Integer
    Dim userAnswer As Integer
    Dim correctAnswer As Integer
    Static numberCorrect As Integer
    Static numberIncorrect As Integer

    Try
        'assign random numbers and user's answer to variables
        randomNum1 = Integer.Parse(Me.uiNum1Label.Text)
        randomNum2 = Integer.Parse(Me.uiNum2Label.Text)
        userAnswer = Integer.Parse(Me.uiAnswerTextBox.Text)
        'calculate correct answer
        Select Case True
            Case Me.uiAdditionRadioButton.Checked
                correctAnswer = randomNum1 + randomNum2
            Case Else    'uiSubtractionRadioButton is selected
                correctAnswer = randomNum1 - randomNum2
        End Select

    Catch exFormat As FormatException
        'processed when the user's answer cannot be converted to an integer
        MessageBox.Show("The answer must be numeric.", "Math Practice", _
            MessageBoxButtons.OK, MessageBoxIcon.Information)
    Catch ex As Exception
        'handles any other errors
        MessageBox.Show(ex.Message, "Math Practice", _
            MessageBoxButtons.OK, MessageBoxIcon.Information)
```

enter these comments and lines of code

position the insertion point here

Figure 5-53: Comments and selection structure entered in the procedure

10 Save the solution.

Step 4 in the pseudocode shown in Figure 5-49 is to determine whether the user's answer is correct. You can do so by comparing the contents of the userAnswer variable to the contents of the correctAnswer variable.

To continue coding the uiCheckAnswerButton Click event procedure:

1   The insertion point should be positioned below the **End Select** statement. Type **'determine whether the user's answer is correct** and press **Enter**, then type **if useranswer = correctanswer then** and press **Enter**. (You also could use a Select Case statement to compare the contents of both variables.)

If the user's answer is correct, the procedure should perform the following four tasks: display the happy face icon in the uiAnswerPictureBox control, add the number 1 to the number of correct responses, clear the contents of the uiAnswerTextBox control, and call the GenerateAndDisplayNumbers procedure to generate and display two random numbers.

2   Enter the additional code shown in Figure 5-54.

enter these four lines of code

Figure 5-54: Additional code entered in the procedure

If the user's answer is not correct, the procedure should perform the following four tasks: display the neutral face icon in the uiAnswerPictureBox control, add the number 1 to the number of incorrect responses, display the "Try again!" message in a message box, and select the existing text in the uiAnswerTextBox control. You can use the **SelectAll method** to select all of the text contained in a text box. The syntax of the SelectAll method is *textbox*.**SelectAll**(), where *textbox* is the name of the text box whose text you want to select.

3   Complete the If...Then...Else statement by entering the additional code shown in Figure 5-55, then position the insertion point as shown in the figure.

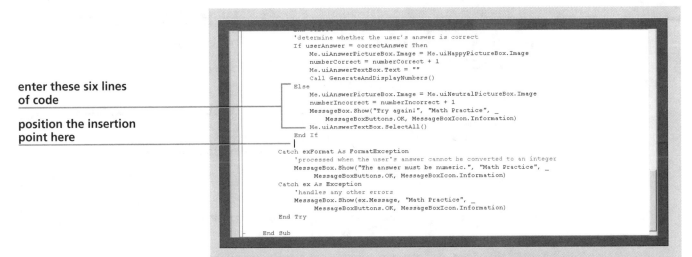

enter these six lines
of code

position the insertion
point here

```
                        'determine whether the user's answer is correct
                        If userAnswer = correctAnswer Then
                                Me.uiAnswerPictureBox.Image = Me.uiHappyPictureBox.Image
                                numberCorrect = numberCorrect + 1
                                Me.uiAnswerTextBox.Text = ""
                                Call GenerateAndDisplayNumbers()
                        Else
                                Me.uiAnswerPictureBox.Image = Me.uiNeutralPictureBox.Image
                                numberIncorrect = numberIncorrect + 1
                                MessageBox.Show("Try again!", "Math Practice", _
                                    MessageBoxButtons.OK, MessageBoxIcon.Information)
                                Me.uiAnswerTextBox.SelectAll()
                        End If

                Catch exFormat As FormatException
                        'processed when the user's answer cannot be converted to an integer
                        MessageBox.Show("The answer must be numeric.", "Math Practice", _
                            MessageBoxButtons.OK, MessageBoxIcon.Information)
                Catch ex As Exception
                        'handles any other errors
                        MessageBox.Show(ex.Message, "Math Practice", _
                            MessageBoxButtons.OK, MessageBoxIcon.Information)
                End Try

        End Sub
```

Figure 5-55: Completed If...Then...Else statement shown in the procedure

The last two steps in the pseudocode shown in Figure 5-49 are to send the focus to the uiAnswerTextBox control and then display the number of correct and incorrect responses in the uiCorrectLabel and uiIncorrectLabel controls.

4   Type **me.uianswertextbox.focus()** and press **Enter**.

5   Type **me.uicorrectlabel.text = convert.tostring(numbercorrect)** and press **Enter**.

6   Type **me.uiincorrectlabel.text = convert.tostring(numberincorrect)** and press **Enter**. Figure 5-56 shows the completed uiCheckAnswerButton Click event procedure.

```
    Private Sub uiCheckAnswerButton_Click(ByVal sender As Object, ByVal e As
System.EventArgs) Handles uiCheckAnswerButton.Click
        'calculates the correct answer, and then compares the correct answer to
the user's answer
        'keeps track of the number of correct and incorrect answers

        Dim randomNum1 As Integer
        Dim randomNum2 As Integer
        Dim userAnswer As Integer
        Dim correctAnswer As Integer
        Static numberCorrect As Integer
        Static numberIncorrect As Integer

        Try
            'assign random numbers and user's answer to variables
            randomNum1 = Integer.Parse(Me.uiNum1Label.Text)
            randomNum2 = Integer.Parse(Me.uiNum2Label.Text)
            userAnswer = Integer.Parse(Me.uiAnswerTextBox.Text)
            'calculate correct answer
            Select Case True
                Case Me.uiAdditionRadioButton.Checked
                    correctAnswer = randomNum1 + randomNum2
                Case Else    'uiSubtractionRadioButton is selected
                    correctAnswer = randomNum1 - randomNum2
            End Select
            'determine whether the user's answer is correct
```

Figure 5-56: Completed uiCheckAnswerButton Click event procedure

```
            If userAnswer = correctAnswer Then
                Me.uiAnswerPictureBox.Image = Me.uiHappyPictureBox.Image
                numberCorrect = numberCorrect + 1
                Me.uiAnswerTextBox.Text = ""
                Call GenerateAndDisplayNumbers()
            Else
                Me.uiAnswerPictureBox.Image = Me.uiNeutralPictureBox.Image
                numberIncorrect = numberIncorrect + 1
                MessageBox.Show("Try again!", "Math Practice", _
                    MessageBoxButtons.OK, MessageBoxIcon.Information)
                Me.uiAnswerTextBox.SelectAll()
            End If
            Me.uiAnswerTextBox.Focus()
            Me.uiCorrectLabel.Text = Convert.ToString(numberCorrect)
            Me.uiIncorrectLabel.Text = Convert.ToString(numberIncorrect)

        Catch exFormat As FormatException
            'processed when the user's answer cannot be converted to an integer
            MessageBox.Show("The answer must be numeric.", "Math Practice", _
                MessageBoxButtons.OK, MessageBoxIcon.Information)
        Catch ex As Exception
            'handles any other errors
            MessageBox.Show(ex.Message, "Math Practice", _
                MessageBoxButtons.OK, MessageBoxIcon.Information)
        End Try

    End Sub
```

Figure 5-56: Completed uiCheckAnswerButton Click event procedure (continued)

7   Save the solution.

Before testing the code in the Check Answer button's Click event procedure, you will code the uiSummaryCheckBox control's Click event procedure.

Coding the uiSummaryCheckBox Click Event Procedure

tip

As you learned in Chapter 4, Visual Basic .NET treats the group box and the controls contained in the group box as one unit. Hiding the group box also hides the controls contained within the group box.

Recall that the four picture box controls located at the bottom of the form do not appear in the interface when the Math Practice application is started. This is because the Visible property of those controls is set to False in the Properties window. The Visible property of the uiSummaryGroupBox control is also set to False, which explains why you do not see the control and its contents when the form appears on the screen.

According to the TOE chart shown earlier in Figure 5-33, the uiSummaryCheckBox control's Click event procedure is responsible for both displaying and hiding the uiSummaryGroupBox control. The procedure should display the group box control when the user selects the check box, and it should hide the group box control when the user deselects the check box. You can use a check box control's Checked property to determine whether the check box was selected or deselected by the user. If the Checked property contains the Boolean value True, then the check box was selected. If it contains the Boolean value False, then the check box was deselected.

Unlike the Click event procedure for a radio button, the Click event procedure for a check box will always contain a selection structure that determines whether the check box was selected or deselected by the user. The selection structure is not necessary in a radio button's Click event procedure, because clicking a radio button always selects the button; the user cannot deselect a radio button by clicking it.

To code the uiSummaryCheckBox control's Click event procedure:

1   Open the code template for the uiSummaryCheckBox's Click event procedure.

2   Type **if me.uisummarycheckbox.checked = true then** and press **Enter**. (You also could use the Select Case statement rather than the If...Then...Else statement to compare the Checked property to the Boolean value True.)

If the user selected the uiSummaryCheckBox control, then the procedure should display the uiSummaryGroupBox control. You can do so by setting the uiSummaryGroupBox control's Visible property to the Boolean value True.

3   Type **me.uisummarygroupbox.visible = true** and press **Enter**.

If the user deselected the uiSummaryCheckBox control, then the procedure should hide the uiSummaryGroupBox control. You can do so by setting the uiSummaryGroupBox control's Visible property to the Boolean value False.

4   Enter the additional code shown in Figure 5-57, which shows the completed uiSummaryCheckBox Click event procedure.

enter these two lines of code

```
Private Sub uiSummaryCheckBox_Click(ByVal sender As Object, ByVal e As System.EventArgs) Handles u:
    If Me.uiSummaryCheckBox.Checked = True Then
        Me.uiSummaryGroupBox.Visible = True
    Else
        Me.uiSummaryGroupBox.Visible = False
    End If
End Sub
```

Figure 5-57: Completed uiSummaryCheckBox Click event procedure

Now verify that the Click event procedures for the uiCheckAnswerButton and uiSummaryCheckBox controls are working correctly.

To test the application's code:

1   Save the solution, then start the application.

2   Type the correct answer to the addition problem appearing in the interface, then press **Enter** to select the Check Answer button, which is the default button on the form. The happy face icon and a new addition problem appear in the interface.

3   Click the **Display summary** check box to select it. A check mark appears in the check box, and the uiSummaryGroupBox control and its contents appear in the interface. Notice that the label controls within the group box indicate that you have made one correct response and zero incorrect responses.

4   Click inside the text box in which you enter the answer. Type an incorrect answer to the current addition problem, then press **Enter**. A neutral face icon appears in the interface, and a message box appears on the screen, as shown in Figure 5-58.

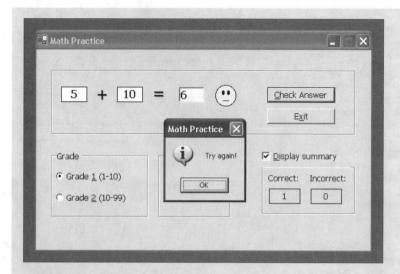

Figure 5-58: Result of entering an incorrect response to the addition problem

5   Click the **OK** button to close the message box. Notice that the number of incorrect responses changes from 0 to 1. Also notice that the incorrect answer is selected in the uiAnswerTextBox control. You can remove the incorrect answer simply by typing another answer in the text box.

6   Type the correct answer to the current addition problem, then press **Enter**. The number of correct responses changes from 1 to 2, and the happy face icon appears in the interface.

7   Click the **Display summary** check box to deselect it. The check mark is removed from the check box, and the uiSummaryGroupBox and its contents disappear from the interface.

8   Click the **Exit** button to end the application. When you return to the Code Editor window, close the Output window, and then close the Code Editor window.

9   Click **File** on the menu bar, and then click **Close Solution**.

You now have completed Chapter 5. You can either take a break or complete the end-of-lesson questions and exercises.

SUMMARY

To select the existing text in a text box:

■ Use the SelectAll method. The method's syntax is *textbox*.**SelectAll**(), where *textbox* is the name of the text box whose text you want to select.

To display or hide a control:

■ Set the control's Visible property to the Boolean value True to display the control. Set the control's Visible property to the Boolean value False to hide the control.

To code a check box control's Click event procedure:

■ Use a selection structure to determine whether the check box was either selected or deselected by the user.

QUESTIONS

1. Which of the following statements selects all of the text contained in the uiNameTextBox control?
   a. `Me.uiNameTextBox.Select()`
   b. `Me.uiNameTextBox.SelectAll()`
   c. `Me.Select.uiNameTextBox()`
   d. `Me.SelectAll.uiNameTextBox()`
   e. None of the above.

2. Which of the following statements hides the uiDivisionPictureBox control?
   a. `Me.uiDivisionPictureBox.Hide`
   b. `Me.uiDivisionPictureBox.Hide = True`
   c. `Hide.uiDivisionPictureBox`
   d. `Hide.uiDivisionPictureBox = True`
   e. None of the above.

3. If a check box is deselected, its _____ property contains the Boolean value False.
   a. Checked
   b. Deselected
   c. On
   d. Value
   e. None of the above.

4. When coded, a check box's Click event procedure will always contain a selection structure that determines whether the check box is selected or deselected.
   a. True
   b. False

5. Like a check box, a radio button can be deselected by clicking it.
   a. True
   b. False

EXERCISES

1. In this exercise, you modify the selection structures contained in the Math Practice application.

   a. Use Windows to make a copy of the Math Solution folder, which is contained in the VBNET\Chap05 folder. Rename the folder Math Solution2.

   b. If necessary, start Visual Studio .NET. Open the Math Solution (Math Solution.sln) file, which is contained in the VBNET\Chap05\Math Solution2 folder. Open the designer window.

   c. Change the If...Then...Else statement in the uiSummaryCheckBox control's Click event procedure to a Select Case statement.

   d. Change the first selection structure in the uiCheckAnswerButton control's Click event procedure to an If...Then...Else statement.

   e. Change the second selection structure in the uiCheckAnswerButton control's Click event procedure to a Select Case statement.

   f. Change the If...Then...Else statement in the uiProcessOperationRadioButtons procedure to a Select Case statement.

   g. Save the solution, then start the application. Test the application to verify that it is working correctly.

   h. Click the Exit button to end the application.

   i. Close the Output window, then close the solution.

2. In this exercise, you code an application for Willow Health Club. The application calculates a member's monthly dues.

   a. If necessary, start Visual Studio .NET. Open the Health Solution (Health Solution.sln) file, which is contained in the VBNET\Chap05\Health Solution folder. If necessary, open the designer window.

   b. Declare a module-level variable named additionalCharges.

   c. Code each check box's Click event procedure so that it adds the appropriate additional charge to the additionalCharges variable when the check box is selected, and subtracts the appropriate additional amount from the additionalCharges variable when the check box is deselected. The additional charges are $30 per month for tennis, $25 per month for golf, and $20 per month for racquetball. Each check box's Click event procedure should display the contents of the additionalCharges variable in the uiAdditionalLabel control, and also remove the contents of the uiTotalLabel control.

   d. Code the Calculate button's Click event procedure so that it calculates the monthly dues. The dues are calculated by adding the basic fee to the total additional charge. Display the total due with a dollar sign and two decimal places.

   e. When the user makes a change to the contents of the uiBasicTextBox, the application should remove the contents of the uiTotalLabel control. Code the appropriate event procedure.

   f. Save the solution, then start the application. Test the application by entering 80 in the text box, and then selecting the Golf check box. The number 25 appears in the uiAdditionalLabel control. Click the Calculate button. $105.00 appears in the uiTotalLabel control.

   g. Now select the Tennis and Racquetball check boxes and deselect the Golf check box. The number 50 appears in the uiAdditionalLabel control. Click the Calculate button. $130.00 appears in the uiTotalLabel control.

   h. Click the Exit button to end the application.

   i. Close the Output window, then close the solution.

3. In this exercise, you create an application for Washington High School. The application displays a class rank, which is based on the code entered by the user. Use the following information to code the application:

Code	Rank
1	Freshman
2	Sophomore
3	Junior
4	Senior

  a. If necessary, start Visual Studio .NET. Create a blank solution named Washington Solution. Save the solution in the VBNET\Chap05 folder.

  b. Add a Visual Basic .NET Windows Application project to the solution. Name the project Washington Project.

  c. Assign the filename Washington Form.vb to the form file object.

  d. Assign the name WashingtonForm to the Windows Form object.

  e. When designing the interface, provide a text box for the user to enter the code, and a label control for displaying the rank. Use the GUI design guidelines listed in Appendix B to verify that the interface you create adheres to the GUI standards outlined in this book.

  f. Code the application appropriately. Allow the user to press only the numeric keys 1, 2, 3, and 4 and the Backspace key when entering the code. Also, set the text box's MaxLength property to the number 1; this allows the user to enter only one character in the text box.

  g. When a change is made to the code entered in the text box, clear the contents of the label control that displays the rank.

  h. Center the rank in the label control.

  i. Save the solution, then start the application. Test the application using codes of 1, 2, 3, and 4. Also test the code using an empty text box (which should not display a rank in the label control). Additionally, try to enter characters other than 1, 2, 3, or 4 in the text box.

  j. End the application.

  k. Close the Output window, then close the solution.

4. In this exercise, you create an application for Barren Community Center. The application displays a seminar fee, which is based on the membership status and age entered by the user. Use the following information to code the application:

Seminar fee	Criteria
10	Club member younger than 65 years old
5	Club member at least 65 years old
20	Non-member

  a. If necessary, start Visual Studio .NET. Create a blank solution named Barren Solution. Save the solution in the VBNET\Chap05 folder.

  b. Add a Visual Basic .NET Windows Application project to the solution. Name the project Barren Project.

  c. Assign the filename Barren Form.vb to the form file object.

  d. Assign the name BarrenForm to the Windows Form object.

  e. Design an appropriate interface. Use the GUI design guidelines listed in Appendix B to verify that the interface you create adheres to the GUI standards outlined in this book. Use radio button controls for the status and age choices. Display the seminar fee in a label control. When the user clicks a radio button, clear the contents of the label control that displays the fee.

  f. Code the application.

  g. Save the solution, then start the application. Test the application appropriately.

  h. End the application.

  i. Close the Output window, then close the solution.

5. In this exercise, you create an application for Golf Pro, a U.S. company that sells golf equipment both domestically and abroad. Each of Golf Pro's salespeople receives a commission based on the total of his or her domestic and international sales. The application you create should allow the user to enter the amount of domestic sales and the amount of international sales. It then should calculate and display the commission. Use the following information to code the application:

Sales	Commission
1 – 100,000	2% * sales
100,001 – 400,000	2,000 + 5% * sales over 100,000
400,001 and over	17,000 + 10% * sales over 400,000

a. If necessary, start Visual Studio .NET. Create a blank solution named Golf Pro Solution. Save the solution in the VBNET\Chap05 folder.

b. Add a Visual Basic .NET Windows Application project to the solution. Name the project Golf Pro Project.

c. Assign the filename Golf Pro Form.vb to the form file object.

d. Assign the name GolfProForm to the Windows Form object.

e. Design an appropriate interface. Use the GUI design guidelines listed in Appendix B to verify that the interface you create adheres to the GUI standards outlined in this book.

f. Code the application. Keep in mind that the sales amounts may contain decimal places.

g. Save the solution, then start the application. Test the application using both valid and invalid data.

h. End the application.

i. Close the Output window, then close the solution.

6. In this exercise, you create an application for Marshall Sales Corporation. Each of the company's salespeople receives a commission based on the amount of his or her sales. The application you create should allow the user to enter the sales amount. It then should calculate and display the commission. Use the following information to code the application:

Sales	Commission
1 – 100,000	2% * sales
100,001 – 200,000	4% * sales
200,001 – 300,000	6% * sales
300,001 – 400,000	8% * sales
400,001 and over	10% * sales

a. If necessary, start Visual Studio .NET. Create a blank solution named Marshall Solution. Save the solution in the VBNET\Chap05 folder.

b. Add a Visual Basic .NET Windows Application project to the solution. Name the project Marshall Project.

c. Assign the filename Marshall Form.vb to the form file object.

d. Assign the name MarshallForm to the Windows Form object.

e. Design an appropriate interface. Use the GUI design guidelines listed in Appendix B to verify that the interface you create adheres to the GUI standards outlined in this book.

f. Code the application. Keep in mind that the sales amount may contain decimal places.

g. Save the solution, then start the application. Test the application using both valid and invalid data.

h. End the application.

i. Close the Output window, then close the solution.

7. In this exercise, you create an application for Jasper Springs Health Club. The application allows the user to enter a specific food's total calories and grams of fat. It then calculates and displays the food's fat calories (the number of calories attributed to fat) and its fat percentage (the ratio of the food's fat calories to its total calories). You can calculate the number of fat calories in a food by multiplying the number of fat grams contained in the food by the number nine, because each gram of fat contains nine calories. To calculate the fat percentage, you divide the food's fat calories by its total calories, and then multiply the result by 100.

   a. If necessary, start Visual Studio .NET. Create a blank solution named Jasper Solution. Save the solution in the VBNET\Chap05 folder.

   b. Add a Visual Basic .NET Windows Application project to the solution. Name the project Jasper Project.

   c. Assign the filename Jasper Form.vb to the form file object.

   d. Assign the name JasperForm to the Windows Form object.

   e. Design an appropriate interface. Use the GUI design guidelines listed in Appendix B to verify that the interface you create adheres to the GUI standards outlined in this book.

   f. Code the application. Display the message "Low-fat food" if the fat percentage is less than or equal to 30%; otherwise, display the message "High-fat food".

   g. Save the solution, then start the application. Test the application using both valid and invalid data.

   h. End the application.

   i. Close the Output window, then close the solution.

8. In this exercise, you create an application that displays the number of daily calories needed to maintain your current weight. Use the following information to code the application:

Moderately active female: total calories per day = weight multiplied by 12 calories per pound

Relatively inactive female: total calories per day = weight multiplied by 10 calories per pound

Moderately active male: total calories per day = weight multiplied by 15 calories per pound

Relatively inactive male: total calories per day = weight multiplied by 13 calories per pound

   a. If necessary, start Visual Studio .NET. Create a blank solution named Calories Solution. Save the solution in the VBNET\Chap05 folder.

   b. Add a Visual Basic .NET Windows Application project to the solution. Name the project Calories Project.

   c. Assign the filename Calories Form.vb to the form file object.

   d. Assign the name CaloriesForm to the Windows Form object.

   e. Design an appropriate interface. Use the GUI design guidelines listed in Appendix B to verify that the interface you create adheres to the GUI standards outlined in this book.

   f. Code the application.

   g. Save the solution, then start the application. Test the application using both valid and invalid data.

   h. End the application.

   i. Close the Output window, then close the solution.

9. In this exercise, you create an application for Johnson Products. The application calculates and displays the price of an order, based on the number of units ordered and the customer's status (either wholesaler or retailer). The price per unit is as follows:

Wholesaler		Retailer	
Number of units	Price per unit ($)	Number of units	Price per unit ($)
1 – 4	10	1 – 3	15
5 and over	9	4 – 8	14
		9 and over	12

  a. If necessary, start Visual Studio .NET. Create a blank solution named Johnson Solution. Save the solution in the VBNET\Chap05 folder.

  b. Add a Visual Basic .NET Windows Application project to the solution. Name the project Johnson Project.

  c. Assign the filename Johnson Form.vb to the form file object.

  d. Assign the name JohnsonForm to the Windows Form object.

  e. Design an appropriate interface. Use the GUI design guidelines listed in Appendix B to verify that the interface you create adheres to the GUI standards outlined in this book.

  f. Code the application. Use a Select Case statement to determine the customer's status. Use an If...Then...Else statement to determine the price per unit.

  g. Save the solution, then start the application. Test the application using both valid and invalid data.

  h. End the application.

  i. Close the Output window, then close the solution.

10. Jacques Cousard has been playing the lottery for four years and has yet to win any money. He wants an application that will select the six lottery numbers for him. Each lottery number can range from 1 to 54 only. (An example of six lottery numbers would be: 4, 8, 35, 15, 20, 3.)

  a. If necessary, start Visual Studio .NET. Create a blank solution named Lottery Solution. Save the solution in the VBNET\Chap05 folder.

  b. Add a Visual Basic .NET Windows Application project to the solution. Name the project Lottery Project.

  c. Assign the filename Lottery Form.vb to the form file object.

  d. Assign the name LotteryForm to the Windows Form object.

  e. Design an appropriate interface. Use the GUI design guidelines listed in Appendix B to verify that the interface you create adheres to the GUI standards outlined in this book.

  f. Code the application. (For now, do not worry if the lottery numbers are not unique. You learn how to display unique numbers in Chapter 11.)

  g. Save the solution, then start the application. Test the application.

  h. End the application.

  i. Close the Output window, then close the solution.

11. Ferris Seminars offers computer seminars to various companies. The owner of Ferris Seminars wants an application that the registration clerks can use to calculate the registration fee for each customer. Many of Ferris Seminars' customers are companies that register more than one person for a seminar. The registration clerk will need to enter the number registered for the seminar, then select either the Seminar 1 radio button or the

Seminar 2 radio button. If a company is entitled to a 10 percent discount, the clerk will need to click the 10% discount check box. After the selections are made, the clerk will click the Calculate Total Due button to calculate the total registration fee. Seminar 1 is $100 per person, and Seminar 2 is $120 per person.

a. If necessary, start Visual Studio .NET. Open the Ferris Solution (Ferris Solution.sln) file, which is contained in the VBNET\Chap05\Ferris Solution folder. If necessary, open the designer window.

b. Code the application appropriately.

c. Save the solution, then start the application. Test the application.

d. End the application.

e. Close the Output window, then close the solution.

12. Western Veterinarians wants an application that its receptionist can use to display the doctor's fee for performing a specific medical procedure. Use the following information to code the application:

Procedure	Fee
Fecal Check	$5
Heartworm Test	15
Office Visit	15
Other Shots	5
Rabies Vaccination	15
Teeth Cleaning	50

a. If necessary, start Visual Studio .NET. Open the Western Solution (Western Solution.sln) file, which is contained in the VBNET\Chap05\Western Solution folder. If necessary, open the designer window.

b. Code the application appropriately.

c. Save the solution, then start the application. Test the application.

d. End the application.

e. Close the Output window, then close the solution.

13. Wholesome Veterinarians wants an application that its receptionist can use to display the total amount a customer owes. Use the following information to code the application:

Procedure	Fee
Fecal Check	$5
Heartworm Test	15
Office Visit	15
Other Shots	5
Rabies Vaccination	15
Teeth Cleaning	50

a. If necessary, start Visual Studio .NET. Open the Wholesome Solution (Wholesome Solution.sln) file, which is contained in the VBNET\Chap05\Wholesome Solution folder. If necessary, open the designer window.

b. Code the application appropriately.

c. Save the solution, then start the application. Test the application.

d. End the application.

e. Close the Output window, then close the solution.

discovery ▶ 14. In this exercise, you learn about a text box control's Enter event.

    a. If necessary, start Visual Studio .NET. Open the Name Solution (Name Solution.sln) file, which is contained in the VBNET\Chap05\Name Solution folder. If necessary, open the designer window.

    b. Start the application. Type your first name in the First text box, then press Tab. Type your last name in the Last text box, then press Tab. Click the Concatenate Name button. Your full name appears in the uiFullNameLabel control.

    c. Press Tab twice to move the focus to the First text box. Notice that the insertion point appears after your first name in the text box. It is customary in Windows applications to have a text box's existing text selected (highlighted) when the text box receives the focus. You can select a text box's existing text by entering the SelectAll method in the text box's Enter event. (You also can enter the SelectAll method in the text box's GotFocus event. The Enter event occurs before the GotFocus event.)

    d. Click the Exit button to end the application.

    e. Open the Code Editor window. Enter the SelectAll method in the Enter event procedure for the uiFirstTextBox and uiLastTextBox controls.

    f. Save the solution, then start the application. Enter your first name in the First text box, then press Tab. Enter your last name in the Last text box. Click the Concatenate Name button. Your full name appears in the uiFullNameLabel control.

    g. Press Tab twice to move the focus to the First text box. Notice that your first name is selected in the text box. Press Tab to move the focus to the Last text box. Notice that your last name is selected in the text box.

    h. Click the Exit button to end the application.

    i. Close the Output window, then close the solution.

debugging 15. In this exercise, you debug an existing application. The purpose of this exercise is to demonstrate the importance of testing an application thoroughly.

    a. If necessary, start Visual Studio .NET. Open the Debug Solution (Debug Solution.sln) file, which is contained in the VBNET\Chap05\Debug Solution folder. If necessary, open the designer window. The application displays a shipping charge, which is based on the total price entered by the user. If the total price is greater than or equal to $100 but less than $501, the shipping charge is $10. If the total price is greater than or equal to $501 but less than $1001, the shipping charge is $7. If the total price is greater than or equal to $1001, the shipping charge is $5. No shipping charge is due if the total price is less than $100.

    b. Start the application. Test the application using the following total prices: 100, 501, 1500, 500.75, 30, 1000.33. You will notice that the application does not display the correct shipping charge for some of these total prices.

    c. Click the Exit button to end the application.

    d. Correct the application's code, then save the solution and start the application. Test the application using the total prices listed in Step b.

    e. Click the Exit button to end the application.

    f. Close the Output window, then close the solution.

The Repetition Structure

Creating the Shoppers Haven Application

case ▶ The manager of Shoppers Haven wants an application that the store clerks can use to calculate the discounted price of an item, using discount rates from 10% through 30% in increments of 5%. The clerks will enter the item's original price. The application should display the discount rates and the discounted prices in the interface.

Previewing the Completed Application

Before creating the Shoppers Haven application, you first preview the completed application.

To preview the completed application:

1   Use the Run command on the Windows Start menu to run the **Shoppers** (Shoppers.exe) file, which is contained in the VBNET\Chap06 folder on your computer's hard disk. The user interface for the Shoppers Haven application appears on the screen.

2   Type **56.99** in the Original price text box, then click the **Calculate** button. The discount rates and discounted prices appear in the interface, as shown in Figure 6-1. Notice that the text in the text box is selected (highlighted). You learn how to select the existing text in a text box in Lesson C.

the text is selected in the text box

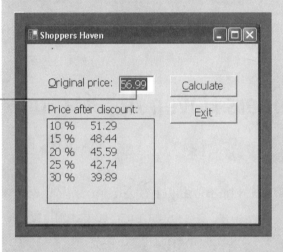

Figure 6-1: Rates and prices shown in the Shoppers Haven application

3   Click the **Exit** button. A message box containing the message "Do you want to exit?" appears. Click the **No** button. Notice that the application remains open. You learn how to prevent a form from being closed in Lesson C.

4   Click the **Exit** button, then click the **Yes** button in the message box. The application closes.

The Shoppers Haven application uses the repetition structure, which you learn about in Lessons A and B. You code the Shoppers Haven application in Lesson C.

LESSON A
objectives

After completing this lesson, you will be able to:

- Code the repetition structure using the For...Next and Do...Loop statements
- Write pseudocode for the repetition structure
- Create a flowchart for the repetition structure
- Initialize and update counters and accumulators

The Repetition Structure (Looping)

The Repetition Structure

As you learned in Chapter 1, the three programming structures are sequence, selection, and repetition. Every program contains the sequence structure, in which the program instructions are processed, one after another, in the order in which each appears in the program. Most programs also contain the selection structure, which you learned about in Chapters 4 and 5. Recall that programmers use the selection structure when they need the computer to make a decision and then take the appropriate action based on the result of that decision.

In addition to including the sequence and selection structures, many programs also include the repetition structure. Programmers use the **repetition structure**, referred to more simply as a **loop**, when they need the computer to repeatedly process one or more program instructions until some condition is met, at which time the loop ends. For example, you may want to process a set of instructions—such as the instructions to calculate net pay—for each employee in a company. Or, you may want to process a set of instructions until the user enters a negative sales amount, which indicates that he or she has no more sales amounts to enter.

A repetition structure can be either a pretest loop or a posttest loop. In both types of loops, the condition is evaluated with each repetition, or iteration, of the loop. In a **pretest loop,** the evaluation occurs before the instructions within the loop are processed, while in a **posttest loop,** the evaluation occurs after the instructions within the loop are processed. Depending on the result of the evaluation, the instructions in a pretest loop may never be processed. The instructions in a posttest loop, however, always will be processed at least once. Of the two types of loops, the pretest loop is the most commonly used.

You code a repetition structure (loop) in Visual Basic .NET using one of the following statements: For...Next, Do...Loop, and For Each...Next. You learn about the For...Next and Do...Loop statements in this lesson, and about the For Each...Next statement in Chapter 10.

> **tip**
>
> As with the sequence and selection structures, you already are familiar with the repetition structure. For example, shampoo bottles typically include a direction that tells you to repeat the "apply shampoo to hair," "lather," and "rinse" steps until your hair is clean.

> **tip**
>
> Pretest and posttest loops also are called top-driven and bottom-driven loops, respectively.

The For...Next Statement

You can use the **For...Next statement** to code a loop whose instructions you want processed a precise number of times. The loop created by the For...Next statement is a pretest loop, because the loop's condition is evaluated before the instructions in the loop are processed. Figure 6-2 shows the syntax of the For...Next statement and includes two examples of using the statement.

Syntax

For *counter* = *startvalue* **To** *endvalue* [**Step** *stepvalue*]

      [*statements*]

Next *counter*

Examples

```
Dim num As Integer
Dim numSquared As Integer
For num = 1 To 3
    numSquared = num * num
    MessageBox.Show(Convert.ToString(num) & " squared is " _
        & Convert.ToString(numSquared), "Number Squared", _
        MessageBoxButtons.OK, MessageBoxIcon.Information)
Next num
```
displays the squares of the numbers 1, 2, and 3 in message boxes

```
Dim num As Integer
Dim numSquared As Integer
For num = 3 To 1 Step -1
    numSquared = num * num
    MessageBox.Show(Convert.ToString(num) & " squared is " _
        & Convert.ToString(numSquared), "Number Squared", _
        MessageBoxButtons.OK, MessageBoxIcon.Information)
Next num
```
displays the squares of the numbers 3, 2, and 1 in message boxes

Figure 6-2: Syntax and examples of the For...Next statement

The For...Next statement begins with the For clause and ends with the Next clause. Between the two clauses, you enter the instructions you want the loop to repeat.

In the syntax for the For...Next statement, *counter* is the name of the numeric variable that the computer will use to keep track of the number of times it processes the loop instructions. The *startvalue*, *endvalue*, and *stepvalue* items control how many times the loop instructions are processed. The *startvalue* tells the computer where to begin, the *endvalue* tells the computer when to stop, and the *stepvalue* tells the computer how much to add to (or subtract from if the *stepvalue* is a negative number) the *counter* variable each time the loop is processed. If you omit the *stepvalue*, a *stepvalue* of positive 1 is used. In the first example shown in Figure 6-2, the *startvalue* is 1, the *endvalue* is 3, and the *stepvalue* (which is omitted) is 1. Those values tell the computer to start counting at 1 and, counting by 1s, stop at 3—in other words, count 1, 2, and then 3. The computer will process the loop instructions shown in the first example three times.

The For clause's *startvalue*, *endvalue*, and *stepvalue* must be numeric and can be either positive or negative, integer or non-integer. If *stepvalue* is positive, then *startvalue* must be less than or equal to *endvalue* for the loop instructions to be processed. In other words, the instruction `For count = 1 To 3` is correct, but the instruction `For count = 3 To 1` is not correct, because you cannot count from 3 (the *startvalue*) to 1 (the *endvalue*) by adding increments of 1 (the *stepvalue*). If, on the other hand, *stepvalue* is negative, then *startvalue* must be greater than or equal to *endvalue* for the loop instructions to be processed. For example, the instruction `For count = 3 To 1 Step -1` is correct, but the instruction `For count = 1 To 3 Step -1` is not correct, because you cannot count from 1 to 3 by subtracting increments of 1.

When processing the For...Next statement, the computer performs the following three tasks:

1. The computer initializes the numeric *counter* variable to the *startvalue*. This is done only once, at the beginning of the loop.
2. If the *stepvalue* is positive, the computer checks whether the value in the *counter* is greater than the *endvalue*. (Or, if the *stepvalue* is negative, the loop checks whether the value in the *counter* is less than the *endvalue*.) If it is, the computer stops processing the loop; processing continues with the statement following the Next clause. If it is not, the computer processes the instructions within the loop, and then the next task, task 3, is performed. (Notice that the computer evaluates the loop condition before processing the statements within the loop.)
3. The computer adds the *stepvalue* to the *counter*. It then repeats tasks 2 and 3 until the *counter* is greater than (or less than, if the *stepvalue* is negative) the *endvalue*.

Figure 6-3 describes how the computer processes the code shown in the first example in Figure 6-2. Notice that when the For...Next statement in that example ends, the value stored in the num variable is 4.

Processing steps for the first example in Figure 6-2

1. The computer creates and initializes the num and numSquared variables in memory.

2. The computer initializes the *counter*, num, to 1 (*startvalue*).

3. The computer checks whether the value in num is greater than 3 (*endvalue*). It's not.

4. The assignment statement multiplies the value in num by itself and assigns the result to numSquared.

5. The MessageBox.Show method displays the message "1 squared is 1".

6. The computer processes the Next clause, which adds 1 (*stepvalue*) to num, giving 2.

7. The computer checks whether the value in num is greater than 3 (*endvalue*). It's not.

8. The assignment statement multiplies the value in num by itself and assigns the result to numSquared.

9. The MessageBox.Show method displays the message "2 squared is 4".

10. The computer processes the Next clause, which adds 1 (*stepvalue*) to num, giving 3.

11. The computer checks whether the value in num is greater than 3 (*endvalue*). It's not.

12. The assignment statement multiplies the value in num by itself and assigns the result to numSquared.

13. The MessageBox.Show method displays the message "3 squared is 9".

14. The computer processes the Next clause, which adds 1 (*stepvalue*) to num, giving 4.

15. The computer checks whether the value in num is greater than 3 (*endvalue*). It is, so the computer stops processing the For...Next statement. Processing continues with the statement following the Next clause.

Figure 6-3: Processing steps for the code shown in the first example in Figure 6-2

Figure 6-4 shows the pseudocode and flowchart corresponding to the first example in Figure 6-2.

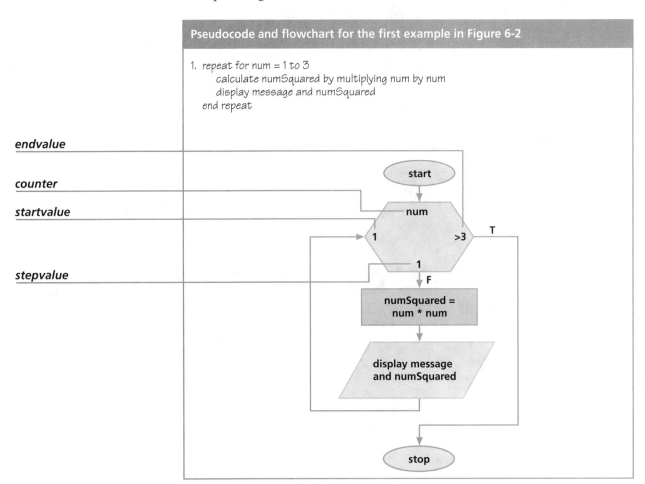

Pseudocode and flowchart for the first example in Figure 6-2

1. repeat for num = 1 to 3
       calculate numSquared by multiplying num by num
       display message and numSquared
   end repeat

endvalue

counter

startvalue

stepvalue

Figure 6-4: Pseudocode and flowchart for the first example shown in Figure 6-2

If the *stepvalue* is a negative number, a less-than sign (<) should precede the *endvalue* in the hexagon, as a loop with a negative *stepvalue* stops when the value in the *counter* variable is less than the *endvalue*.

The For...Next loop is represented in a flowchart by a hexagon, which is a six-sided figure. Four values are recorded inside the hexagon: the name of the *counter* variable, the *startvalue*, the *stepvalue*, and the *endvalue*. Notice that the *endvalue* in the hexagon shown in Figure 6-4 is preceded by a greater-than sign (>). The greater-than sign reminds you that the loop stops when the value in the *counter* variable is greater than the *endvalue*.

Next, you view the Monthly Payment Calculator application, which uses the For...Next statement.

The Monthly Payment Calculator Application

Figure 6-5 shows the code for a procedure that calculates and displays a monthly car payment, using annual interest rates of 5%, 6%, 7%, 8%, 9%, and 10% and a term of five years, and Figure 6-6 shows a sample run of the Monthly Payment Calculator application that contains the procedure.

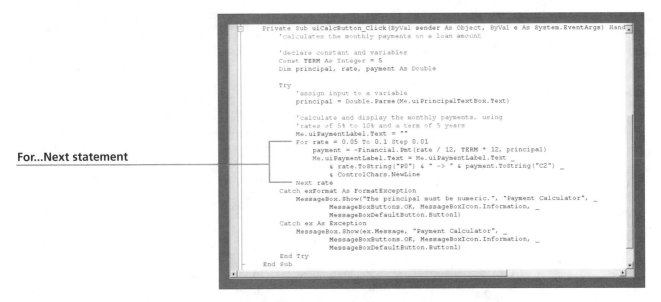

For...Next statement

```
Private Sub uiCalcButton_Click(ByVal sender As Object, ByVal e As System.EventArgs) Hand
    'calculates the monthly payments on a loan amount

    'declare constant and variables
    Const TERM As Integer = 5
    Dim principal, rate, payment As Double

    Try
        'assign input to a variable
        principal = Double.Parse(Me.uiPrincipalTextBox.Text)

        'calculate and display the monthly payments, using
        'rates of 5% to 10% and a term of 5 years
        Me.uiPaymentLabel.Text = ""
        For rate = 0.05 To 0.1 Step 0.01
            payment = -Financial.Pmt(rate / 12, TERM * 12, principal)
            Me.uiPaymentLabel.Text = Me.uiPaymentLabel.Text _
                & rate.ToString("P0") & " -> " & payment.ToString("C2") _
                & ControlChars.NewLine
        Next rate
    Catch exFormat As FormatException
        MessageBox.Show("The principal must be numeric.", "Payment Calculator", _
            MessageBoxButtons.OK, MessageBoxIcon.Information, _
            MessageBoxDefaultButton.Button1)
    Catch ex As Exception
        MessageBox.Show(ex.Message, "Payment Calculator", _
            MessageBoxButtons.OK, MessageBoxIcon.Information, _
            MessageBoxDefaultButton.Button1)
    End Try
End Sub
```

Figure 6-5: Code for the uiCalcButton's Click event procedure

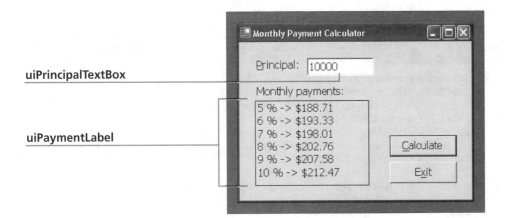

uiPrincipalTextBox

uiPaymentLabel

Figure 6-6: Sample run of the application that contains the procedure

The For...Next statement shown in Figure 6-5 repeats its instructions six times, using annual interest rates of .05, .06, .07, .08, .09, and .1. The first instruction in the For...Next statement uses the Financial.Pmt method, which you learned about in Chapter 4, to calculate the monthly payment. Notice that the negation operator precedes the method; this changes the negative number returned by the method to a positive number. Also notice that the For...Next statement's *counter* variable (`rate`), which keeps track of the annual interest rates, is divided by 12 and used as the *Rate* argument in the method. It is necessary to divide the annual interest rate by 12 to get a monthly rate, because you want to display monthly payments rather than an annual payment. The TERM constant, on the other hand, is multiplied by 12 to get the number of monthly payments; this result is used as the *Nper* argument in the method. Lastly, the `principal` variable, which stores the principal entered by the user, is used as the *PV* argument in the method.

The second instruction in the For...Next statement is an assignment statement that concatenates the current contents of the uiPaymentLabel control to the following items: the annual interest rate converted to a string and formatted to a percentage with zero decimal places, the string " -> " (a space, a hyphen, a greater than sign, and a space), the monthly payment amount converted to a string and formatted with a dollar sign and two decimal places, and the `ControlChars.NewLine` constant. As you learned in Chapter 3, the `ControlChars.NewLine` constant advances the insertion point to the next line in a control. Figure 6-6 shows the output displayed by the uiCalcButton's Click event procedure when the user clicks the Calculate button after entering 10000 in the uiPrincipalTextBox.

Recall that you also can use the Do...Loop statement to code a repetition structure in Visual Basic .NET.

The Do...Loop Statement

You can use the `Exit Do` statement to exit the Do...Loop statement prematurely—in other words, exit it before the loop has finished processing. You may need to do so if the loop encounters an error when processing its instructions.

Unlike the For...Next statement, the **Do...Loop statement** can be used to code both a pretest loop and a posttest loop. Figure 6-7 shows two slightly different versions of the Do...Loop statement's syntax. You use the first version to code a pretest loop, and the second version to code a posttest loop. Figure 6-7 also includes an example of using each syntax to display the numbers 1, 2, and 3 in a message box.

You can nest Do...Loop statements, which means that you can place one Do...Loop statement within another Do...Loop statement.

As both examples shown in Figure 6-7 indicate, you do not type the braces ({}) or the pipe symbol (|) when entering the Do...Loop statement.

Do...Loop Statement

Do...Loop syntax (pretest loop)
Do {While | Until} *condition*
    [instructions to be processed either while the condition is true or until
    the condition becomes true]
Loop

Do...Loop syntax (posttest loop)
Do
    [instructions to be processed either while the condition is true or until
    the condition becomes true]
Loop {While | Until} *condition*

Pretest loop example

```
Dim num As Integer = 1
Do While num <= 3
    MessageBox.Show(Convert.ToString(num), "Numbers", _
        MessageBoxButtons.OK, MessageBoxIcon.Information)
    num = num + 1
Loop
```

Posttest loop example

```
Dim num As Integer = 1
Do
    MessageBox.Show(Convert.ToString(num), "Numbers", _
        MessageBoxButtons.OK, MessageBoxIcon.Information)
    num = num + 1
Loop Until num > 3
```

Figure 6-7: Syntax and examples of the Do...Loop statement

Notice that the Do...Loop statement begins with the Do clause and ends with the Loop clause. Between both clauses, you enter the instructions you want the computer to repeat.

The {**While** | **Until**} portion of each syntax shown in Figure 6-7 indicates that you can select only one of the keywords appearing within the braces. In this case, you can choose either the keyword While or the keyword Until. You follow the keyword with a *condition*, which can contain variables, constants, properties, methods, and operators. Like the *condition* used in the If...Then...Else statement, the *condition* used in the Do...Loop statement also must evaluate to a Boolean value—either True or False. The *condition* determines whether the computer processes the loop instructions. The keyword While indicates that the loop instructions should be processed while the *condition* is true. The keyword Until, on the other hand, indicates that the loop instructions should be processed until the *condition* becomes true. Notice that the keyword (either While or Until) and the *condition* appear in the Do clause in a pretest loop, but in the Loop clause in a posttest loop.

Figure 6-8 describes how the computer processes the code shown in the examples in Figure 6-7.

Processing steps for the pretest loop example in Figure 6-7

1. The computer creates the num variable and initializes it to 1.
2. The computer processes the Do clause, which checks whether the value in num is less than or equal to 3. It is.
3. The MessageBox.Show method displays 1 (the contents of the num variable).
4. The num = num + 1 statement adds 1 to num, giving 2.
5. The computer processes the Loop clause, which returns processing to the Do clause (the beginning of the loop).
6. The computer processes the Do clause, which checks whether the value in num is less than or equal to 3. It is.
7. The MessageBox.Show method displays 2 (the contents of the num variable).
8. The num = num + 1 statement adds 1 to num, giving 3.
9. The computer processes the Loop clause, which returns processing to the Do clause (the beginning of the loop).
10. The computer processes the Do clause, which checks whether the value in num is less than or equal to 3. It is.
11. The MessageBox.Show method displays 3 (the contents of the num variable).
12. The num = num + 1 statement adds 1 to num, giving 4.
13. The computer processes the Loop clause, which returns processing to the Do clause (the beginning of the loop).
14. The computer processes the Do clause, which checks whether the value in num is less than or equal to 3. It isn't, so the computer stops processing the Do...Loop statement. Processing continues with the statement following the Loop clause.

Figure 6-8: Processing steps for the code shown in the examples in Figure 6-7

Processing steps for the posttest loop example in Figure 6-7

1. The computer creates the `num` variable and initializes it to 1.
2. The computer processes the Do clause, which marks the beginning of the loop.
3. The MessageBox.Show method displays 1 (the contents of the `num` variable).
4. The `num = num + 1` statement adds 1 to `num`, giving 2.
5. The computer processes the Loop clause, which checks whether the value in `num` is greater than 3. It isn't, so processing returns to the Do clause (the beginning of the loop).
6. The MessageBox.Show method displays 2 (the contents of the `num` variable).
7. The `num = num + 1` statement adds 1 to `num`, giving 3.
8. The computer processes the Loop clause, which checks whether the value in `num` is greater than 3. It isn't, so processing returns to the Do clause (the beginning of the loop).
9. The MessageBox.Show method displays 3 (the contents of the `num` variable).
10. The `num = num + 1` statement adds 1 to `num`, giving 4.
11. The computer processes the Loop clause, which checks whether the value in `num` is greater than 3. It is, so the computer stops processing the Do...Loop statement. Processing continues with the statement following the Loop clause.

Figure 6-8: Processing steps for the code shown in the examples in Figure 6-7 (continued)

Figure 6-9 shows the flowcharts associated with the examples in Figure 6-7; the pseudocode for each example is shown in Figure 6-10.

Flowchart for the pretest loop example

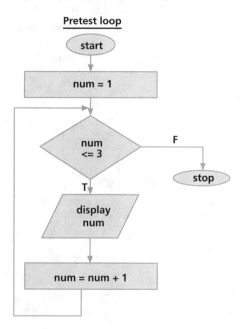

Figure 6-9: Flowcharts for the examples shown in Figure 6-7

Flowchart for the posttest loop example

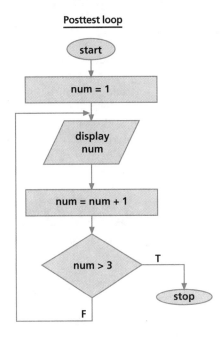

Figure 6-9: Flowcharts for the examples shown in Figure 6-7 (continued)

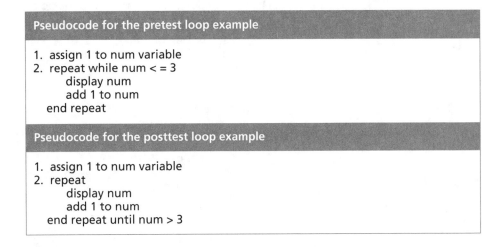

Pseudocode for the pretest loop example

1. assign 1 to num variable
2. repeat while num < = 3
     display num
     add 1 to num
   end repeat

Pseudocode for the posttest loop example

1. assign 1 to num variable
2. repeat
     display num
     add 1 to num
   end repeat until num > 3

Figure 6-10: Pseudocode for the examples shown in Figure 6-7

Notice that a diamond represents the loop condition in both flowcharts shown in Figure 6-9. As with the selection structure diamond, which you learned about in Chapter 4, the repetition structure diamond contains a comparison that evaluates to either True or False only. The result of the comparison determines whether the computer processes the instructions within the loop.

Like the selection diamond, the repetition diamond has one flowline entering the diamond and two flowlines leaving the diamond. The two flowlines leaving the diamond should be marked with a "T" (for True) and an "F" (for False).

In the flowchart of the pretest loop shown in Figure 6-9, the flowline entering the repetition diamond, as well as the symbols and flowlines within the True path, form a circle or loop. In the posttest loop's flowchart shown in Figure 6-9, the loop is formed by all of the symbols and flowlines in the False path. It is this loop, or circle, that distinguishes the repetition structure from the selection structure in a flowchart.

Although it appears that the pretest and posttest loops produce the same results—in this case, for instance, both examples shown in Figure 6-7 display the numbers 1 through 3—that will not always be the case. In other words, the two loops are not always interchangeable. The difference between both loops is demonstrated in the examples shown in Figure 6-11.

Examples and processing steps

Pretest loop example

```
Dim num As Integer = 10
Do While num <= 3
    MessageBox.Show(Convert.ToString(num), "Numbers", _
        MessageBoxButtons.OK, MessageBoxIcon.Information)
    num = num + 1
Loop
```

Processing steps for the pretest loop

1. The computer creates the num variable and initializes it to 10.

2. The computer processes the Do clause, which checks whether the value in num is less than or equal to 3. It isn't, so the computer stops processing the Do...Loop statement. Processing continues with the statement following the Loop clause.

Posttest loop example

```
Dim num As Integer = 10
Do
    MessageBox.Show(Convert.ToString(num), "Numbers", _
        MessageBoxButtons.OK, MessageBoxIcon.Information)
    num = num + 1
Loop Until num > 3
```

Processing steps for the posttest loop

1. The computer creates the num variable and initializes it to 10.

2. The computer processes the Do clause, which marks the beginning of the loop.

3. The MessageBox.Show method displays 10 (the contents of the num variable).

4. The num = num + 1 statement adds 1 to num, giving 11.

5. The computer processes the Loop clause, which checks whether the value in num is greater than 3. It is, so the computer stops processing the Do...Loop statement. Processing continues with the statement following the Loop clause.

Figure 6-11: Examples showing that the pretest and posttest loops do not always produce the same results

Comparing the processing steps shown in both examples in Figure 6-11, you will notice that the instructions in the pretest loop are not processed. This is because the num <= 3 condition, which is evaluated *before* the instructions are processed, evaluates to False. The instructions in the posttest loop, on the other hand, are processed one time, because the num > 3 condition is evaluated *after* (rather than *before*) the loop instructions are processed.

Many times an application will need to display a subtotal, a total, or an average. You calculate this information using a repetition structure that includes a counter, or an accumulator, or both.

Using Counters and Accumulators

Counters and accumulators are used within a repetition structure to calculate subtotals, totals, and averages. A **counter** is a numeric variable used for counting something—such as the number of employees paid in a week. An **accumulator** is a numeric variable used for accumulating (adding together) something—such as the total dollar amount of a week's payroll.

Two tasks are associated with counters and accumulators: initializing and updating. **Initializing** means to assign a beginning value to the counter or accumulator. Typically, counters and accumulators are initialized to zero; however, they can be initialized to any number, depending on the value required by the application. The initialization task is done before the loop is processed, because it needs to be done only once.

Updating, also called **incrementing**, means adding a number to the value stored in the counter or accumulator. The number can be either positive or negative, integer or non-integer. A counter is always incremented by a constant value—typically the number 1—whereas an accumulator is incremented by a value that varies. The assignment statement that updates a counter or an accumulator is placed within the loop in a procedure, because the update task must be performed each time the loop instructions are processed. The Sales Express application, which you view next, includes a counter and an accumulator, as well as a repetition structure.

The Sales Express Application

Assume that Sales Express wants an application that the sales manager can use to display the average amount the company sold during the prior year. The sales manager will enter the amount of each salesperson's sales. The application will use a counter to keep track of the number of sales amounts entered by the sales manager, and an accumulator to total those sales amounts. After all of the sales amounts are entered, the application will calculate the average sales amount by dividing the value stored in the accumulator by the value stored in the counter; it then will display the average sales amount on the screen. Figure 6-12 shows the pseudocode for a possible solution to the Sales Express problem.

tip

Counters are used to answer the question, "How many?"—for example, "How many salespeople live in Virginia?" Accumulators are used to answer the question, "How much?"—for example, "How much did the salespeople sell this quarter?"

priming read

Pseudocode for the Sales Express application

include the following in the Try section of a Try/Catch block:
1. get a sales amount from the user

2. repeat while the user entered a sales amount
    　　　add 1 to the counter variable
    　　　add the sales amount to the accumulator variable
    　　　get a sales amount from the user
    end repeat

3. if the counter variable contains a value that is greater than zero
    　　　calculate the average sales by dividing the accumulator variable by the
    　　　counter variable
    　　　display the average sales in the uiAvgLabel control
    else
    　　　display the number 0 in the uiAvgLabel control
    　　　display an appropriate message in a message box
    end if

include the following in the Catch section of a Try/Catch block
1. use a Catch statement to handle the FormatException
    　　　if a FormatException error occurs, display the message "The sales
    　　　amount must be numeric." in a message box

2. use a general Catch statement to handle any other errors
    　　　if an error occurs, display a description of the error in a message box

Figure 6-12: Pseudocode for the Sales Express application

Step 1 in the pseudocode is to get a sales amount from the user. Step 2 is a pretest loop whose instructions are processed as long as the user enters a sales amount. The loop instructions increment the counter variable by one, then increment the accumulator variable by the sales amount, and then request another sales amount from the user. The computer then checks whether a sales amount was entered to determine whether the loop instructions should be processed again. When the user has finished entering sales amounts, the loop ends and processing continues with Step 3 in the pseudocode.

Step 3 in the pseudocode is a selection structure that checks whether the counter variable contains a value that is greater than zero. Before using a variable as the divisor in an expression, you always should verify that the variable does not contain the number zero because, as in math, division by zero is not mathematically possible. Dividing by zero in a program will cause the program to end abruptly with an error.

As Step 3 indicates, if the counter variable contains a value that is greater than zero, the average sales amount is calculated and then displayed in the uiAvgLabel control. Otherwise, the number zero is displayed in the uiAvgLabel control and an appropriate message is displayed in a message box.

Notice that "get a sales amount from the user" appears twice in the pseudocode shown in Figure 6-12: immediately above the loop and also within the loop. The "get a sales amount from the user" entry that appears above the loop is referred to as the **priming read**, because it is used to prime (prepare or set up) the loop. In this case, the priming read gets only the first salesperson's sales amount from the user. Because the loop in Figure 6-12 is a pretest loop, this first value determines whether the loop instructions are processed at all. The "get a sales amount from the user" entry that appears within the loop gets the sales amounts for the remaining salespeople (if any) from the user.

Figure 6-13 shows the Visual Basic .NET code for the Sales Express application.

Code corresponding to the pseudocode shown in Figure 6-12

```
Dim sales As String
Dim salesCount As Integer   'counter
Dim salesTotal As Double    'accumulator
Dim salesAverage As Double

Try
    'get the first sales amount
    sales = InputBox("Enter a sales amount. Click Cancel when finished.", _
        "Sales Entry")

    'verify that the user entered a sales amount
    Do While sales <> ""
        'update counter
        salesCount = salesCount + 1
        'update accumulator
        salesTotal = salesTotal + Double.Parse(sales)
        'get another sales amount
        sales = InputBox("Enter a sales amount. Click Cancel when finished.", _
            "Sales Entry")
    Loop

    'verify that the counter contains a value greater than 0
    If salesCount > 0 Then
        'calculate and display the average sales amount
        salesAverage = salesTotal / Convert.ToDouble(salesCount)
        Me.uiAvgLabel.Text = salesAverage.ToString("C2")
    Else
        Me.uiAvgLabel.Text = "0"
        MessageBox.Show("You didn't enter any sales amounts.", _
            "Sales Entry", MessageBoxButtons.OK, MessageBoxIcon.Information)
    End If

Catch exFormat As FormatException
    MessageBox.Show("The sales amount must be numeric.", "Sales Entry", _
        MessageBoxButtons.OK, MessageBoxIcon.Information)
Catch ex As Exception
    MessageBox.Show(ex.Message, "Sales Entry", _
        MessageBoxButtons.OK, MessageBoxIcon.Information)
End Try
```

priming read

Figure 6-13: Code for the Sales Express application

tip

....

If you forget to enter the sales = InputBox("Enter a sales amount. Click Cancel when finished.", "Sales Entry") instruction within the loop, you will create an endless or infinite loop. To stop an endless loop, click Debug on the menu bar, and then click Stop Debugging.

The code begins by declaring four variables: sales, salesCount, salesTotal, and salesAverage. The sales variable will store the sales amounts entered by the user. The salesCount variable is the counter variable that will keep track of the number of sales amounts entered. The salesTotal variable is the accumulator variable that the computer will use to total the sales amounts. The remaining variable, salesAverage, will store the average sales amount after it has been calculated.

Recall that counters and accumulators must be initialized, or given a beginning value; typically, the beginning value is the number zero. Because the Dim statement automatically assigns a zero to Integer and Double variables when the variables are created, you do not need to enter any additional code to initialize the salesCount counter or the salesTotal accumulator. If you want to initialize a counter or an accumulator to a value other than zero, however, you can do so either in the Dim statement that declares the variable or in an assignment statement. For example, to initialize the salesCount counter variable to the number one, you could use either the declaration statement Dim salesCount As Integer = 1 or the assignment statement salesCount = 1 in your code. (To use the assignment statement, the variable must already be declared.)

The InputBox function in the code displays a dialog box that prompts the user to either enter a sales amount or click the Cancel button, which indicates that the user has no more sales amounts to enter. As you learned in Chapter 3, the value returned by the InputBox function depends on whether the user clicks the dialog box's OK button, Cancel button, or Close button. In this case, if the user enters a sales amount and then clicks the OK button in the dialog box, the InputBox function returns (as a string) the sales amount contained in the input area of the dialog box. However, if the user fails to enter a sales amount before clicking the OK button, or if he or she clicks either the dialog box's Cancel button or its Close button, the function returns a zero-length string (""). The assignment statement that contains the InputBox function assigns the function's return value to the `sales` variable, which has a String data type.

Next, the computer evaluates the loop *condition* in the Do...Loop statement to determine whether the loop instructions should be processed. In this case, the `sales <> ""` *condition* compares the contents of the `sales` variable to a zero-length string. If the `sales` variable does not contain a zero-length string, the loop *condition* evaluates to True and the computer processes the loop instructions. If, on the other hand, the `sales` variable contains a zero-length string, the loop *condition* evaluates to False and the computer skips over the loop instructions.

Now take a closer look at the instructions within the loop. The first instruction in the loop, `salesCount = salesCount + 1`, updates the counter variable by adding a constant value of one to it. Notice that the counter variable, `salesCount`, appears on both sides of the assignment operator. The statement tells the computer to add one to the contents of the `salesCount` variable, then place the result back in the `salesCount` variable. The `salesCount` variable's value will be incremented by one each time the loop is processed. The second instruction in the loop, `salesTotal = salesTotal + Double.Parse(sales)`, updates the accumulator variable by adding a sales amount to it. Notice that the accumulator variable, `salesTotal`, also appears on both sides of the assignment operator. The statement tells the computer to add the contents of the `sales` variable (converted to Double) to the contents of the `salesTotal` variable, then place the result back in the `salesTotal` variable. The `salesTotal` variable's value will be incremented by a sales amount, which will vary, each time the loop is processed.

The last instruction in the loop, `sales = InputBox ("Enter a sales amount. Click Cancel when finished.", "Sales Entry")`, displays a dialog box that prompts the user for another sales amount. Notice that the instruction appears twice in the code—before the Do...Loop statement and within the Do...Loop statement. Recall that the instruction located above the loop is referred to as the priming read, and its task is to get only the first sales amount from the user. The instruction located within the loop gets each of the remaining sales amounts (if any) from the user.

After the user enters another sales amount, the computer returns to the Do clause, where the loop *condition* is tested again. If the *condition* evaluates to True, the loop instructions are processed again. If the *condition* evaluates to False, the loop stops and the instruction after the Loop clause is processed. That instruction is a selection structure that determines whether the counter variable, `salesCount`, contains a value that is greater than zero. Recall that before using a variable as the divisor in an expression, you first should verify that the variable does not contain the number zero, because division by zero is mathematically impossible and will cause the program to end with an error. In this case, if the counter variable is greater than zero, the instructions in the selection structure's true path calculate the average sales amount and assign the result to the `salesAverage` variable, and then display the contents of the variable in the uiAvgLabel control. However, if the counter variable is not greater than zero, the instructions in the selection structure's false path display the number zero in the uiAvgLabel control and display an appropriate message in a message box.

You now have completed Lesson A. You can either take a break or complete the end-of-lesson questions and exercises before moving on to the next lesson.

SUMMARY

To have the computer repeat a set of instructions until some condition is met:

■ Use a repetition structure (loop). You can code a repetition structure in Visual Basic .NET using one of the following statements: For...Next, Do...Loop, and For Each...Next.

To use the For...Next statement to code a loop:

■ Refer to Figure 6-2 for the syntax of the For...Next statement. The For...Next statement can be used to code pretest loops only. In the syntax, *counter* is the name of the numeric variable that will be used to keep track of the number of times the loop instructions are processed. The *startvalue*, *endvalue*, and *stepvalue* items control how many times the loop instructions are processed. The *startvalue*, *endvalue*, and *stepvalue* items must be numeric and can be positive or negative, integer or non-integer. If you omit the *stepvalue*, a *stepvalue* of positive 1 is used.

■ The For...Next statement performs the following three tasks:

1. The loop initializes the *counter* (the numeric variable) to the *startvalue*. This is done only once, at the beginning of the loop.

2. If the *stepvalue* is positive, the loop checks whether the value in the *counter* is greater than the *endvalue*. (Or, if the *stepvalue* is negative, the loop checks whether the value in the *counter* is less than the *endvalue*.) If it is, the loop stops, and processing continues with the statement following the Next clause. If it is not, the instructions within the loop are processed and the next task, task 3, is performed.

3. The loop adds the *stepvalue* to the *counter*. It then repeats tasks 2 and 3 until the *counter* is greater than (or less than, if the *stepvalue* is negative) the *endvalue*.

To flowchart a For...Next loop:

■ Use a hexagon that shows the name of the *counter*, the *startvalue*, the *stepvalue*, and the *endvalue*.

To use the Do...Loop statement to code a loop:

■ Refer to Figure 6-7 for the two versions of the Do...Loop statement's syntax. The Do...Loop statement can be used to code pretest and posttest loops. In a pretest loop, the loop condition appears in the Do clause; it appears in the Loop clause in a posttest loop.

■ The loop condition must evaluate to a Boolean value.

To flowchart the Do...Loop statement:

■ Use the selection/repetition diamond. The two flowlines leading out of the diamond should be marked with a "T" (for True) and an "F" (for False).

To use a counter:

- Initialize the counter, if necessary.
- Update the counter using an assignment statement within a repetition structure. You update a counter by incrementing (or decrementing) its value by a constant amount.

To use an accumulator:

- Initialize the accumulator, if necessary.
- Update the accumulator using an assignment statement within a repetition structure. You update an accumulator by incrementing (or decrementing) its value by an amount that varies.

QUESTIONS

1. Which of the following flowchart symbols represents the For...Next loop?
   a. diamond
   b. hexagon
   c. oval
   d. parallelogram
   e. rectangle

2. Which of the following flowchart symbols represents the *condition* in the Do...Loop statement?
   a. diamond
   b. hexagon
   c. oval
   d. parallelogram
   e. rectangle

3. Assuming count is a numeric variable, how many times will the instructions within the For...Next statement be processed?

   ```
   For count = 1 To 6
        [instructions]
   Next count
   ```

   a. 0
   b. 1
   c. 5
   d. 6
   e. 7

4. What is the value stored in the count variable when the loop in Question 3 stops?
   a. 1
   b. 5
   c. 6
   d. 7
   e. 8

5. Assuming `count` is a numeric variable, how many times will the instructions within the For...Next loop be processed?

    ```
    For count = 4 To 11 Step 2
            [instructions]
    Next count
    ```

    a. 0
    b. 3
    c. 4
    d. 5
    e. 12

6. What is the value stored in the `count` variable when the loop in Question 5 stops?
    a. 4
    b. 6
    c. 10
    d. 11
    e. 12

7. When the *stepvalue* in a For...Next statement is positive, the instructions within the loop are processed only when the *counter* is _____ the *endvalue*.
    a. equal to
    b. greater than
    c. greater than or equal to
    d. less than
    e. less than or equal to

8. Which of the following is a valid For clause, assuming `temp` is an Integer variable?
    a. `For temp = 1.5 To 5 Step .5`
    b. `For temp = 5 To 1 Step .25`
    c. `For temp = 1 To 3 Step -1`
    d. `For temp = 3 To 1`
    e. `For temp = 1 To 10`

9. The For...Next statement performs three tasks, as shown below. Put these tasks in their proper order by placing the numbers 1 through 3 on the line to the left of the task.

    _____ Adds the *stepvalue* to the *counter*.

    _____ Initializes the *counter* to the *startvalue*.

    _____ Checks whether the value in the *counter* is greater (less) than the *endvalue*.

10. Assume that you do not know the precise number of times the loop instructions should be processed. You can use the _____ statement to code this loop.
    a. Do...Loop
    b. For...Next
    c. a or b

11. Assume that you know the precise number of times the loop instructions should be processed. You can use the _____ statement to code this loop.
    a. Do...Loop
    b. For...Next
    c. a or b

12. The _____ loop processes the loop instructions at least once, whereas the _____ loop instructions might not be processed at all.
    a. posttest, pretest
    b. pretest, posttest

13. Counters and accumulators must be initialized and _____.
    a. added
    b. counted
    c. displayed
    d. printed
    e. updated

14. Which of the following statements will correctly update a counter variable named number?
    a. `number = 0`
    b. `number = 1`
    c. `number = number + number`
    d. `number = number + sales`
    e. `number = number + 1`

15. Which of the following statements will correctly update an accumulator variable named total?
    a. `total = 0`
    b. `total = 1`
    c. `total = total + total`
    d. `total = total + sales`
    e. `total = total + 1`

16. Which of the following clauses stops the loop when the value in the age variable is less than the number 0?
    a. `Do While age >= 0`
    b. `Do Until age < 0`
    c. `Loop While age >= 0`
    d. `Loop Until age < 0`
    e. All of the above.

17. How many times will the instructions in the following code be processed?
```
Dim count As Integer
Do While count > 3
      [instructions]
      count = count + 1
Loop
```
    a. 0
    b. 1
    c. 2
    d. 3
    e. 4

18. How many times will the instructions in the following code be processed?

```
Dim count As Integer
Do
    [instructions]
    count = count + 1
Loop While count > 3
```

a. 0

b. 1

c. 2

d. 3

e. 4

Refer to Figure 6-14 to answer Questions 19 through 22.

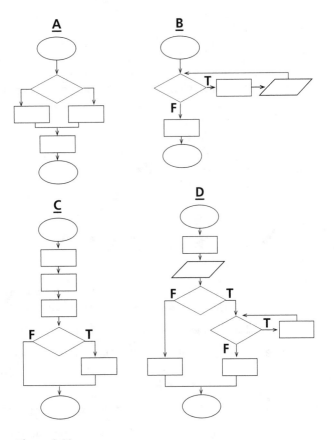

Figure 6-14

19. Which of the following programming structures are used in flowchart A in Figure 6-14? (Select all that apply.)

a. sequence

b. selection

c. repetition

20. Which of the following programming structures are used in flowchart B in Figure 6-14? (Select all that apply.)
   a. sequence
   b. selection
   c. repetition

21. Which of the following programming structures are used in flowchart C in Figure 6-14? (Select all that apply.)
   a. sequence
   b. selection
   c. repetition

22. Which of the following programming structures are used in flowchart D in Figure 6-14? (Select all that apply.)
   a. sequence
   b. selection
   c. repetition

23. Assume that a program allows the user to enter one or more numbers. The first input instruction will get the first number only and is referred to as the _____ read.
   a. entering
   b. initializer
   c. priming
   d. starter
   e. starting

E X E R C I S E S

1. Write a Visual Basic .NET Do clause that processes the loop instructions as long as the value in the `quantity` variable is greater than the number 0. Use the While keyword.

2. Rewrite the Do clause from Exercise 1 using the Until keyword.

3. Write a Visual Basic .NET Do clause that stops the loop when the value in the `inStock` variable is less than or equal to the value in the `reorder` variable. Use the Until keyword.

4. Rewrite the Do clause from Exercise 3 using the While keyword.

5. Write a Visual Basic .NET Loop clause that processes the loop instructions as long as the value in the `letter` variable is either Y or y. Use the While keyword.

6. Rewrite the Loop clause from Exercise 5 using the Until keyword.

7. Write a Visual Basic .NET Do clause that processes the loop instructions as long as the value in the `name` variable is not "Done" (in any case). Use the While keyword.

8. Rewrite the Do clause from Exercise 7 using the Until keyword.

9. Write a Visual Basic .NET assignment statement that updates the `quantity` counter variable by 2.

10. Write a Visual Basic .NET assignment statement that updates the `total` counter variable by -3.

11. Write a Visual Basic .NET assignment statement that updates the `totalPurchases` accumulator variable by the value stored in the `purchases` variable.

12. Write a Visual Basic .NET assignment statement that subtracts 100 from the `sales` accumulator variable.

13. Assume that a procedure declares an Integer variable named `evenNum` and initializes it to 2. Write the Visual Basic .NET code for a pretest loop that uses the `evenNum` variable to display the even integers between 1 and 9 in the uiNumbersLabel control. Use the For...Next statement. Display each number on a separate line in the control.

14. Rewrite the pretest loop from Exercise 13 using the Do...Loop statement.

15. Change the pretest loop from Exercise 14 to a posttest loop.

16. Write the Visual Basic .NET code that corresponds to the flowchart shown in Figure 6-15. (Display the calculated results on separate lines in the uiCountLabel control.)

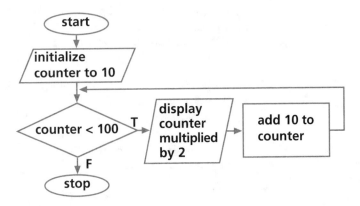

Figure 6-15

17. Write a For...Next statement that displays the numbers from 0 through 117, in increments of 9, in the uiNumbersLabel control. Display each number on a separate line in the control.

18. Write a For...Next statement that calculates and displays the squares of the even numbers from 2 through 12. Display the results in the uiNumbersLabel control. Display each number on a separate line in the control.

19. Complete the following code, which should display the word "Hello" 10 times:

```
Dim count As Integer = 1
Do _____
    MessageBox.Show("Hello")
    count = count + 1
Loop
```

20. Complete the following code, which should display the word "Hello" 10 times:

```
Dim count As Integer = 1
Do
    MessageBox.Show("Hello")
    count = count + 1
Loop _____
```

21. What will the following code display?

```
Dim x As Integer
Do While x < 5
    MessageBox.Show(Convert.ToString(x))
    x = x + 1
Loop
```

22. What will the following code display?

```
Dim x As Integer
Do
    MessageBox.Show(Convert.ToString(x))
    x = x + 1
Loop Until x > 5
```

23. An instruction is missing from the following code. What is the missing instruction and where does it belong in the code?

```
Dim num As Integer = 1
Do While num < 5
    MessageBox.Show(Convert.ToString(num))
Loop
```

24. An instruction is missing from the following code. What is the missing instruction and where does it belong in the code?

```
Dim num As Integer = 10
Do
    MessageBox.Show(Convert.ToString(num))
Loop Until num = 0
```

25. The following code should display a 10% commission for each sales amount that is entered. The code is not working properly because an instruction is missing. What is the missing instruction and where does it belong in the code?

```
Dim salesInput As String, sales As Double
salesInput = InputBox("Enter a sales amount", "Sales")
sales = Double.Parse(salesInput)
Do While sales > 0
    MessageBox.Show("Commission: " & sales * .1)
    sales = Double.Parse(salesInput)
Loop
```

26. The following code should display a 10% commission for each sales amount that is entered. The code is not working properly. What is wrong with the code and how will you fix it?

```
Dim salesInput As String, sales As Double
salesInput = InputBox("Enter a sales amount", "Sales")
sales = Double.Parse(salesInput)
Do
    salesInput = InputBox("Enter a sales amount", "Sales")
    sales = Double.Parse(salesInput)
    MessageBox.Show("Commission: " & sales * .1)
Loop Until sales <= 0
```

27. What will the following code display?

```
Dim totEmp As Integer
Do While totEmp <= 5
    MessageBox.Show(Convert.ToString(totEmp))
    totEmp = totEmp + 2
Loop
```

28. What will the following code display?

```
Dim totEmp As Integer = 1
Do
    MessageBox.Show(Convert.ToString(totEmp))
    totEmp = totEmp + 2
Loop Until totEmp >= 3
```

29. In this exercise, you modify the repetition structure contained in the Monthly Payment Calculator application.

    a. Use Windows to make a copy of the Payment Solution folder, which is contained in the VBNET\Chap06 folder. Rename the folder Payment Solution Ex29.

    b. If necessary, start Visual Studio .NET. Open the Payment Solution (Payment Solution.sln) file, which is contained in the VBNET\Chap06\Payment Solution Ex29 folder. Open the designer window.

    c. Change the For...Next statement to a Do...Loop statement.

    d. Save the solution, then start the application. Test the application to verify that it is working correctly.

    e. Click the Exit button to end the application.

    f. Close the Output window, then close the solution.

30. In this exercise, you modify the repetition structure contained in the Sales Express application.

    a. Use Windows to make a copy of the Sales Express Solution folder, which is contained in the VBNET\Chap06 folder. Rename the folder Sales Express Solution Ex30.

    b. If necessary, start Visual Studio .NET. Open the Sales Express Solution (Sales Express Solution.sln) file, which is contained in the VBNET\Chap06\Sales Express Solution Ex30 folder. Open the designer window.

    c. Change the Do...Loop statement to a For...Next statement. Assume the user will enter five sales amounts.

    d. Save the solution, then start the application. Test the application to verify that it is working correctly.

    e. Click the Exit button to end the application.

    f. Close the Output window, then close the solution.

Nested Repetition Structures

Nesting Repetition Structures

Although both loops in Figure 6-16 are pretest loops, you also could write the logic using two posttest loops or a combination of a pretest and a posttest loop.

In Chapter 5, you learned how to nest selection structures. You also can nest repetition structures. In a nested repetition structure, one loop, referred to as the **inner loop**, is placed entirely within another loop, called the **outer loop**. Although the idea of nested loops may sound confusing, you already are familiar with the concept. A clock, for instance, uses nested loops to keep track of the time. For simplicity, consider a clock's second and minute hands only. You can think of the second hand as being the inner loop and the minute hand as being the outer loop. As you know, the second hand on a clock moves one position, clockwise, for every second that has elapsed. Only after the second hand completes its processing—in this case, only after it moves 60 positions—does the minute hand move one position, clockwise. The second hand then begins its journey around the clock again. Figure 6-16 illustrates the logic used by a clock's second and minute hands.

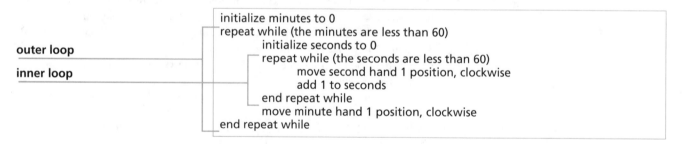

outer loop

inner loop

```
initialize minutes to 0
repeat while (the minutes are less than 60)
        initialize seconds to 0
        repeat while (the seconds are less than 60)
                move second hand 1 position, clockwise
                add 1 to seconds
        end repeat while
        move minute hand 1 position, clockwise
end repeat while
```

Figure 6-16: Nested loops used by a clock

As indicated in Figure 6-16, the outer loop corresponds to a clock's minute hand, and the inner loop corresponds to a clock's second hand. Notice that the entire inner loop is contained within the outer loop, which must be true for the loops to be nested and to work correctly.

Next, you view another version of the Monthly Payment Calculator application that you viewed in Lesson A. This version uses two For...Next statements, one nested within the other.

Monthly Payment Calculator Application—Nested For...Next Statements

Figure 6-17 shows the code for the uiCalcButton's Click event procedure, which uses a nested repetition structure to calculate and display monthly car payments, and Figure 6-18 shows a sample run of the Monthly Payment Calculator application that contains the procedure.

```
Private Sub uiCalcButton_Click(ByVal sender As Object, ByVal e As System.EventArgs)
Handles uiCalcButton.Click
    'calculates the monthly payments on a loan amount

    'declare variables
    Dim term As Integer
    Dim principal, rate, payment As Double

    Try
        'assign input to a variable
        principal = Double.Parse(Me.uiPrincipalTextBox.Text)

        'display the years in the heading
        Me.uiPaymentLabel.Text = "            3 yrs       4 yrs       5 yrs" _
            & ControlChars.NewLine

        'calculate and display the monthly payments, using
        'rates of 5% to 10% and terms of 3 to 5 years
        For rate = 0.05 To 0.1 Step 0.01
            'display the current rate
            Me.uiPaymentLabel.Text = Me.uiPaymentLabel.Text & rate.ToString("P0") _
                & "    "
            For term = 3 To 5
                payment = -Financial.Pmt(rate / 12, term * 12, principal)
                Me.uiPaymentLabel.Text = Me.uiPaymentLabel.Text _
                    & payment.ToString("N2") & "      "
            Next term
            Me.uiPaymentLabel.Text = Me.uiPaymentLabel.Text & ControlChars.NewLine
        Next rate

    Catch exFormat As FormatException
        MessageBox.Show("The principal must be numeric.", "Payment Calculator", _
            MessageBoxButtons.OK, MessageBoxIcon.Information, _
            MessageBoxDefaultButton.Button1)
    Catch ex As Exception
        MessageBox.Show(ex.Message, "Payment Calculator", _
            MessageBoxButtons.OK, MessageBoxIcon.Information, _
            MessageBoxDefaultButton.Button1)
    End Try
End Sub
```

outer loop *(label pointing to the For rate loop)*

inner loop *(label pointing to the For term loop)*

Figure 6-17: Nested repetition structure shown in the Calculate button's Click event procedure

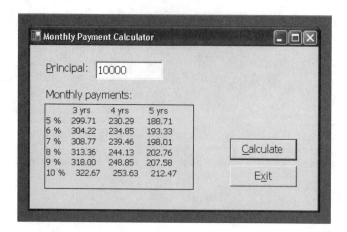

Figure 6-18: Sample run of the application that contains the procedure

Notice that the code shown in Figure 6-17 uses two For...Next statements to calculate and display the monthly car payments. The outer For...Next statement controls the interest rates, which range from 5% to 10%. The inner For...Next statement controls the terms, which range from three to five years.

When processing the `For rate = 0.05 To 0.1 Step 0.01` clause, the computer assigns the number 0.05 to the `rate` variable. It then checks whether the `rate` variable contains a value that is greater than 0.1; at this point, it doesn't. Therefore, the computer processes the instructions contained in the outer loop.

The first instruction in the outer loop displays the current rate in the uiPaymentLabel control. When processing the next instruction, `For term = 3 To 5`, the computer initializes the `term` variable to 3. It then checks whether the `term` variable contains a value that is greater than 5; at this point, it doesn't. Therefore, the computer processes the instructions contained in the inner loop.

The first instruction in the inner loop calculates the monthly car payment, using 0.05 as the rate and 3 as the term. The second instruction displays the monthly car payment in the uiPaymentLabel control. The `Next term` clause increments the `term` variable by 1, giving 4. The computer then processes the `For term = 3 To 5` clause. This time, however, the computer simply checks whether the value in the `term` variable is greater than 5; it's not. Therefore, the computer again processes the instructions contained in the inner loop. Those instructions calculate the monthly car payment (using 0.05 as the rate and 4 as the term) and display the result in the uiPaymentLabel control.

The `Next term` clause is processed next and increments the `term` variable by 1, giving 5. Then the computer processes the `For term = 3 To 5` clause, which checks whether the value in the `term` variable is greater than 5; it's not. As a result, the computer processes the instructions contained in the inner loop. Those instructions calculate the monthly car payment (using 0.05 as the rate and 5 as the term) and display the result in the uiPaymentLabel control.

The `Next term` clause is processed next and increments the `term` variable by 1, giving 6. Then the computer processes the `For term = 3 To 5` clause, which checks whether the value in the `term` variable is greater than 5; it is. As a result, the inner For...Next statement ends, and the computer processes the instruction located immediately after the `Next term` clause; that instruction moves the cursor to the next line in the uiPaymentLabel control.

The computer then processes the `Next rate` instruction, which increments the `rate` variable by 0.01, giving 0.06. It then processes the `For rate = 0.05 To 0.1 Step 0.01` instruction, which checks whether the `rate` variable contains a value that is greater than 0.1; it doesn't. Therefore the computer again processes the instructions contained in the outer loop. Recall that those instructions display the rate in the uiPaymentLabel control, and then use a For...Next statement to calculate and display the monthly car payments—this time using a rate of 0.06 and terms of three to five years. The outer For...Next statement ends when the value in the `rate` variable is 0.11.

In the next section, you view the Grade Calculator application, which uses a For...Next statement nested within a Do...Loop statement.

The Grade Calculator Application

Assume that Professor Arkins needs an application that allows him to assign a grade to any number of students. Each student's grade is based on three test scores, with each test worth 100 points. The application should total the test scores and then assign the appropriate grade, using the following chart:

Total points earned	Grade
270–300	A
240–269	B
210–239	C
180–209	D
below 180	F

Figure 6-19 shows the code for the uiAssignGradeButton's Click event procedure, which allows Professor Arkins to enter each student's test scores, and then assign the appropriate grade. Figure 6-20 shows a sample run of the Grade Calculator application that contains the procedure.

```
Private Sub uiAssignGradeButton_Click(ByVal sender As Object, ByVal e As
System.EventArgs) Handles uiAssignGradeButton.Click
    'calculates the total points earned, displays the total points earned
    'and the grade

    'declare variables
    Dim testNumber As Integer    'counter-keeps track of the number of tests
    Dim totalPoints As Integer   'accumulator-keeps track of the total points
    Dim button As Integer        'used by the MessageBox.Show method
    Dim testScore As String      'stores the user's input
    Dim grade As String          'stores the grade

    Try
        Do
            'initialize total points accumulator
            totalPoints = 0

            'clear label control
            Me.uiPointsGradeLabel.Text = ""

            'get and accumulate test scores
            For testNumber = 1 To 3
                testScore = InputBox("Enter the points earned on test " _
                    & testNumber & ":", "Grade Calculator", "0")
                If testScore = "" Then
                    Exit For
                Else
                    'update the accumulator
                    totalPoints = totalPoints + Integer.Parse(testScore)
                    'display the test score in the uiPointsGradeLabel
                    Me.uiPointsGradeLabel.Text = Me.uiPointsGradeLabel.Text _
                        & testScore & ControlChars.NewLine
                End If
            Next testNumber

            'assign grade
            Select Case totalPoints
                Case Is >= 270
                    grade = "A"
                Case Is >= 240
                    grade = "B"
                Case Is >= 210
                    grade = "C"
                Case Is >= 180
                    grade = "D"
                Case Else
                    grade = "F"
            End Select

            'display total points earned and grade
            Me.uiPointsGradeLabel.Text = Me.uiPointsGradeLabel.Text _
                & Convert.ToString(totalPoints) & " -> " & grade

            'determine whether the user wants to calculate the grade for
            another student
```

outer loop

inner loop

Figure 6-19: Nested repetition structure shown in the Assign Grade button's Click event procedure

```
        button = MessageBox.Show("Calculate another student's grade?", _
            "Grade Calculator", MessageBoxButtons.YesNo, _
            MessageBoxIcon.Exclamation, MessageBoxDefaultButton.Button1)
    Loop While button = DialogResult.Yes

Catch exFormat As FormatException
    MessageBox.Show("The test score must be numeric.", _
        "Grade Calculator", MessageBoxButtons.OK, _
        MessageBoxIcon.Information)
Catch ex As Exception
    MessageBox.Show(ex.Message, "Grade Calculator", _
        MessageBoxButtons.OK, MessageBoxIcon.Information)
    End Try
End Sub
```

Figure 6-19: Nested repetition structure shown in the Assign Grade button's Click event procedure (continued)

controlled by the inner loop

controls the outer loop

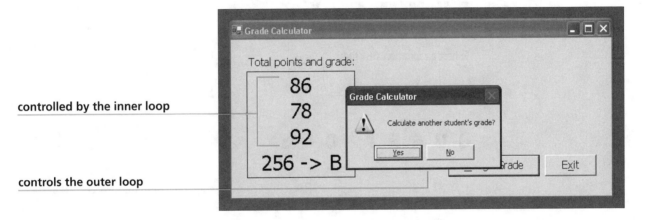

Figure 6-20: Sample run of the application that contains the procedure

tip

As you learned in Chapter 3, when the user clicks either the Cancel button in the dialog box or the Close button on the dialog box's title bar, the InputBox function returns a zero-length (or empty) string.

The procedure shown in Figure 6-19 contains two loops, one nested within the other. A For...Next statement controls the inner loop, and a Do...Loop statement controls the outer loop. The inner loop is a pretest loop, while the outer loop is a posttest loop.

First, the outer loop initializes the total points accumulator to the number zero. It then clears the label control that displays the test score, total points, and grade. Next, it uses a For...Next loop that repeats its instructions three times. The first instruction in the loop uses the InputBox function to get a test score from the user, assigning the test score to the testScore variable. If the testScore variable contains the empty string, it means that the user clicked either the Cancel button in the dialog box or the Close button on the dialog box's title bar. In that case, the Exit For statement in the selection structure's true path exits the For...Next loop and processing continues with the instruction following the Next testNumber statement. However, if the testScore variable does not contain the empty string, the instructions in the selection structure's false path add the test score to the accumulator variable and then display the test score in the uiPointsGradeLabel control.

When the computer finishes processing the For...Next statement, the instructions in the Select Case statement (which is part of the outer loop) assign the appropriate grade to the grade variable. The next instruction in the outer loop displays both the total points earned and the grade in the uiPointsGradeLabel control. Next, the MessageBox.Show method displays the message box shown in Figure 6-20. As you learned in Chapter 4, when the user clicks a button in the message box, the MessageBox.Show method returns an integer that indicates which button the user chose. For example, when the user clicks the Yes button in the message box, the message box closes and the MessageBox.Show method returns the integer 6. Recall that each integer is associated with a constant; the integer 6, for example, is associated with the constant `DialogResult.Yes`.

After the user responds to the prompt in the message box, the computer processes the `Loop While button = DialogResult.Yes` clause. This clause tells the computer to repeat the outer loop, which processes another student's information, as long as the user clicked the Yes button in the dialog box.

You now have completed Lesson B. You can either take a break or complete the end-of-lesson questions and exercises before moving on to the next lesson.

SUMMARY

To nest a repetition structure:

■ Place the entire inner loop within the outer loop.

QUESTIONS

1. What appears in the uiAsterisksLabel control when the computer processes the following code?

```
For x = 1 To 2
    For y = 1 To 3
        Me.uiAsterisksLabel.Text = _
            Me.uiAsterisksLabel.Text & "*"
    Next y
    Me.uiAsterisksLabel.Text = _
        Me.uiAsterisksLabel.Text & _
        ControlChars.NewLine
Next x
```

a. ```
   ***
   ***
   ```

b. ```
   ***
   ***
   ***
   ```

c. ```
   **
   **
   **
   ```

d. ```
   ***
   ***
   ***
   ***
   ```

e. ```
   **
   **
   ```
   ```

2. What number appears in the uiSumLabel control when the computer processes the following code?

```
Dim sum As Integer
Dim x, y As Integer
Do While y < 3
        For x = 1 To 4
                sum = sum + x
        Next x
        y = y + 1
Loop
Me.uiSumLabel.Text = Convert.ToString(sum)
```

a. 5

b. 8

c. 15

d. 30

EXERCISES

1. In this exercise, you modify one of the repetition structures contained in the Monthly Payment Calculator application.
   a. Use Windows to make a copy of the Payment Solution Nested folder, which is contained in the VBNET\Chap06 folder. Rename the folder Payment Solution Nested Ex1.
   b. If necessary, start Visual Studio .NET. Open the Payment Solution (Payment Solution.sln) file, which is contained in the VBNET\Chap06\Payment Solution Nested Ex1 folder. Open the designer window.
   c. Change the For...Next statement that controls the term to a Do...Loop statement.
   d. Save the solution, then start the application. Test the application to verify that it is working correctly.
   e. Click the Exit button to end the application.
   f. Close the Output window, then close the solution.

2. In this exercise, you modify both repetition structures contained in the Monthly Payment Calculator application.
   a. Use Windows to make a copy of the Payment Solution Nested folder, which is contained in the VBNET\Chap06 folder. Rename the folder Payment Solution Nested Ex2.
   b. If necessary, start Visual Studio .NET. Open the Payment Solution (Payment Solution.sln) file, which is contained in the VBNET\Chap06\Payment Solution Nested Ex2 folder. Open the designer window.
   c. Change both For...Next statements to Do...Loop statements.
   d. Save the solution, then start the application. Test the application to verify that it is working correctly.
   e. Click the Exit button to end the application.
   f. Close the Output window, then close the solution.

3. In this exercise, you modify both repetition structures contained in the Grade Calculator application.

   a. Use Windows to make a copy of the Grade Calculator Solution folder, which is contained in the VBNET\Chap06 folder. Rename the folder Grade Calculator Solution Ex3.

   b. If necessary, start Visual Studio .NET. Open the Grade Calculator Solution (Grade Calculator Solution.sln) file, which is contained in the VBNET\Chap06\Grade Calculator Solution Ex3 folder. Open the designer window.

   c. Change the For...Next statement to a Do...Loop statement.

   d. Save the solution, then start the application. Test the application to verify that it is working correctly.

   e. Click the Exit button to end the application.

   f. Close the Output window, then close the solution.

Coding the Shoppers Haven Application

Shoppers Haven

Recall that the manager of Shoppers Haven wants an application that the store clerks can use to calculate the discounted price of an item, using discount rates from 10% through 30% in increments of 5%. The clerks will enter the item's original price. The application should display the discount rates and the discounted prices in the interface.

To open the partially completed application:

1 Start Microsoft Visual Studio .NET, if necessary.

2 If necessary, close the Start Page window.

3 Open the **Shoppers Haven Solution** (Shoppers Haven Solution.sln) file, which is contained in the VBNET\Chap06\Shoppers Haven Solution folder.

4 Auto-hide the Toolbox, Solution Explorer, and Properties windows, if necessary. Figure 6-21 shows the user interface for the Shoppers Haven application.

uiOriginalTextBox

uiDiscPricesLabel

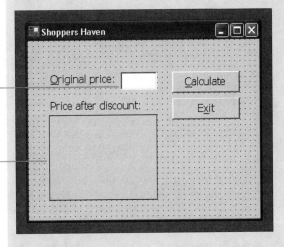

Figure 6-21: User interface for the Shoppers Haven application

The TOE chart for the Shoppers Haven application is shown in Figure 6-22.

Task	Object	Event
1. Calculate the discounted prices using rates of 10% through 30%, in increments of 5% 2. Display the discount rates and discounted prices in the uiDiscPricesLabel control	uiCalcButton	Click
End the application	uiExitButton	Click
Display the discount rates and discounted prices (from uiCalcButton)	uiDiscPricesLabel	None
Get and display the item's original price Select the existing text Clear the uiDiscPricesLabel control	uiOriginalTextBox	None Enter TextChanged
Verify that the user wants to exit the application, then take the appropriate action based on the user's response	ShoppersForm	Closing

Figure 6-22: TOE chart for the Shoppers Haven application

According to the TOE chart, five event procedures need to be coded. However, you will code only four of them, because the Click event procedure for the uiExitButton control has already been coded for you.

Figure 6-23 shows the pseudocode for the uiCalcButton's Click event procedure.

---

uiCalcButton

include the following in the Try section of a Try/Catch block:
1. clear the contents of the uiDiscPricesLabel control

2. if the uiOriginalTextBox contains data
      assign the contents of the text box to a variable
      repeat for discount rates of 10% through 30% in increments of 5%
          calculate the discounted price by multiplying the original price by the current discount rate, and then subtracting the result from the original price

          display the discount rate and discounted price in uiDiscPricesLabel
      end repeat
   else
      display a message requesting the user to enter the original price
   end if

3. send the focus to the uiOriginalTextBox control

include the following in the Catch section of a Try/Catch block:
1. use a general Catch statement to handle any errors
      if an error occurs, display a description of the error in a message box

Figure 6-23: Pseudocode for the Calculate button's Click event procedure

To begin coding the Calculate button's Click event procedure:

1 Open the Code Editor window. Notice that the Exit button's Click event procedure already contains the appropriate code.

2 Replace the *<enter your name here>* and *<enter date here>* text with your name and the current date.

3 Open the code template for the uiCalcButton's Click event procedure.

4 Type **'calculates the discounted prices using discount rates of 10% through** and press **Enter**.

5 Type **'30%, in increments of 5%** and press **Enter** twice.

First, declare the necessary variables. The Calculate button's Click event procedure will use three variables.

6 Type **'declare variables** and press **Enter**, then type **dim originalPrice as double** and press **Enter**. The procedure will use the `originalPrice` variable to store the original price entered by the user.

7 Type **dim discountPrice as double** and press **Enter**, then type **dim discountRate as double** and press **Enter** twice. The procedure will use the `discountPrice` variable to store each discounted price. The `discountRate` variable will be used in a For...Next statement to keep track of the discount rates.

Next, enter a Try/Catch block.

8 Type **try** and press **Enter**.

The first step in the pseudocode is to clear the contents of the uiDiscPricesLabel control, which will display the discount rates and discounted prices.

9 Type **'clear the contents of the uiDiscPricesLabel control** and press **Enter**, then type **me.uidiscpriceslabel.text = ""** and press **Enter** twice.

If the uiOriginalTextBox contains data, the data should be assigned to a variable—in this case, to the `originalPrice` variable.

10 Type **'if the text box contains data, then assign input to** and press **Enter**, then type **'variable and display the discounted prices** and press **Enter**.

11 Type **if me.uioriginaltextbox.text <> ""** **then** and press **Enter**, then type **originalprice = double.parse(me.uioriginaltextbox.text)** and press **Enter**.

Next, the selection structure's true path should use a repetition structure that calculates the discounted price using discount rates of 10% through 30% in increments of 5%. The repetition structure also should display the discount rate and discounted price in the uiDiscPricesLabel.

12 Type the repetition structure shown in Figure 6-24, and then position the insertion point as shown in the figure.

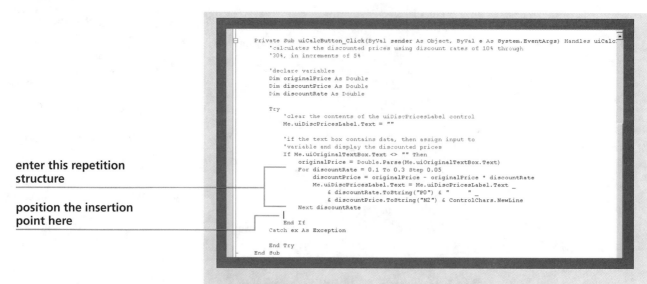

enter this repetition structure

position the insertion point here

```
Private Sub uiCalcButton_Click(ByVal sender As Object, ByVal e As System.EventArgs) Handles uiCalc
    'calculates the discounted prices using discount rates of 10% through
    '30%, in increments of 5%

    'declare variables
    Dim originalPrice As Double
    Dim discountPrice As Double
    Dim discountRate As Double

    Try
        'clear the contents of the uiDiscPricesLabel control
        Me.uiDiscPricesLabel.Text = ""

        'if the text box contains data, then assign input to
        'variable and display the discounted prices
        If Me.uiOriginalTextBox.Text <> "" Then
            originalPrice = Double.Parse(Me.uiOriginalTextBox.Text)
            For discountRate = 0.1 To 0.3 Step 0.05
                discountPrice = originalPrice - originalPrice * discountRate
                Me.uiDiscPricesLabel.Text = Me.uiDiscPricesLabel.Text _
                    & discountRate.ToString("P0") & "       " _
                    & discountPrice.ToString("N2") & ControlChars.NewLine
            Next discountRate
        |
        End If
    Catch ex As Exception

    End Try
End Sub
```

Figure 6-24: Repetition structure shown in the procedure

If the uiOriginalTextBox does not contain data, the selection structure's false path should display a message requesting the user to enter the original price.

13 Type the additional lines of code shown in Figure 6-25, then position the insertion point as shown in the figure.

enter the selection structure's false path

position the insertion point here

```
        'if the text box contains data, then assign input to
        'variable and display the discounted prices
        If Me.uiOriginalTextBox.Text <> "" Then
            originalPrice = Double.Parse(Me.uiOriginalTextBox.Text)
            For discountRate = 0.1 To 0.3 Step 0.05
                discountPrice = originalPrice - originalPrice * discountRate
                Me.uiDiscPricesLabel.Text = Me.uiDiscPricesLabel.Text _
                    & discountRate.ToString("P0") & "       " _
                    & discountPrice.ToString("N2") & ControlChars.NewLine
            Next discountRate
        Else
            MessageBox.Show("Please enter the original price.", _
                "Shoppers Haven", MessageBoxButtons.OK, _
                MessageBoxIcon.Information)
        End If
    Catch ex As Exception

    End Try

    |
End Sub
```

Figure 6-25: Selection structure's false path shown in the procedure

Step 3 in the pseudocode is to send the focus to the uiOriginalTextBox control.

14 Type **'set the focus** and press **Enter**, then type **me.uioriginaltextbox.focus()** and press **Enter**.

Finally, you complete the Catch section of the Try/Catch block.

15 Type the MessageBox.Show method indicated in Figure 6-26.

```
Private Sub uiCalcButton_Click(ByVal sender As Object, ByVal e As
System.EventArgs) Handles uiCalcButton.Click
    'calculates the discounted prices using discount rates of 10% through
    '30%, in increments of 5%

    'declare variables
    Dim originalPrice As Double
    Dim discountPrice As Double
    Dim discountRate As Double

    Try
        'clear the contents of the uiDiscPricesLabel control
        Me.uiDiscPricesLabel.Text = ""

        'if the text box contains data, then assign input to
        'variable and display the discounted prices
        If Me.uiOriginalTextBox.Text <> "" Then
            originalPrice = Double.Parse(Me.uiOriginalTextBox.Text)
            For discountRate = 0.1 To 0.3 Step 0.05
                discountPrice = originalPrice - originalPrice * discountRate
                Me.uiDiscPricesLabel.Text = Me.uiDiscPricesLabel.Text _
                    & discountRate.ToString("P0") & "        " _
                    & discountPrice.ToString("N2") & ControlChars.NewLine
            Next discountRate
        Else
            MessageBox.Show("Please enter the original price.", _
                "Shoppers Haven", MessageBoxButtons.OK, _
                MessageBoxIcon.Information)
        End If
    Catch ex As Exception
        MessageBox.Show(ex.Message, "Shoppers Haven", MessageBoxButtons.OK, _
            MessageBoxIcon.Information)
    End Try

    'set the focus
    Me.uiOriginalTextBox.Focus()

End Sub
```

**enter this
MessageBox.
Show method**

Figure 6-26: Completed uiCalcButton's Click event procedure

16 Save the solution, and then start the application. The blinking insertion point indicates that the uiOriginalTextBox has the focus.

First, calculate the discounted prices for an item costing $100. The discounted prices should be 90.00, 85.00, 80.00, 75.00, and 70.00. These prices represent the original price ($100) multiplied by the discount rates (10%, 15%, 20%, 25%, and 30%).

17 Type **100** and then click the **Calculate** button. The uiCalcButton's Click event procedure calculates the discounted prices and displays the prices in the uiDiscPricesLabel control. The procedure also sends the focus to the uiOriginalTextBox, as shown in Figure 6-27.

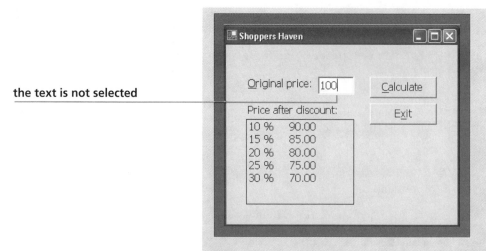

the text is not selected

Figure 6-27: Discounted prices shown in the Shoppers Haven application

Notice that the existing text is not highlighted (selected) in the text box. It is customary in Windows applications to highlight the existing text when a text box receives the focus. You learn how to select the existing text in the next section.

18   Click the **Exit** button to end the application, and then close the Output window.

Next, you learn how to select the existing text in a text box.

Selecting the Existing Text in a Text Box

When you select the existing text in a text box, the user can remove the text simply by pressing a key—for example, the letter "n" on the keyboard. The key that is pressed—in this case, the letter "n"—replaces the selected text in the text box.

You use the **SelectAll method** to select all of the text contained in a text box. The method's syntax is *textbox*.**SelectAll**(), where *textbox* is the name of the text box whose text you want to select. Typically, you enter the SelectAll method in a text box control's **Enter event**, which occurs when the user tabs to the control, and when the Focus method is used in code to send the focus to the control. According to the TOE chart for the Shoppers Haven application (shown earlier in Figure 6-22), the uiOriginalTextBox control's Enter event is responsible for highlighting the existing text in the control.

Highlighting Existing Text

- It is customary in Windows applications to highlight (select) the existing text in a text box when the text box receives the focus.

To code the uiOriginalTextBox's Enter event procedure, then test the application:

1 Open the code template for the uiOriginalTextBox control's Enter event procedure.

2 Type the comment and instruction shown in Figure 6-28.

enter this comment and line of code

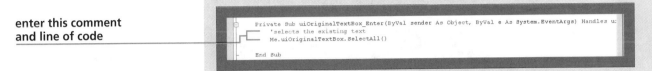

```
Private Sub uiOriginalTextBox_Enter(ByVal sender As Object, ByVal e As System.EventArgs) Handles u:
    'selects the existing text
    Me.uiOriginalTextBox.SelectAll()

End Sub
```

Figure 6-28: Completed Enter event procedure for the uiOriginalTextBox

3 Save the solution, and then start the application.

4 Type **20** in the uiOriginalTextBox, and then click the **Calculate** button. The uiCalcButton's Click event procedure calculates the discounted prices and displays the prices in the uiDiscPricesLabel control. When the procedure sends the focus to the uiOriginalTextBox, the instruction in the text box's Enter event procedure selects the existing text, as shown in Figure 6-29.

the text is selected

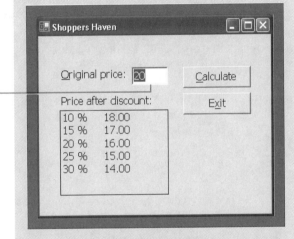

Figure 6-29: Text selected in the Shoppers Haven application

Notice that the existing text is now selected (highlighted) in the text box.

5 Type the number **5**. Notice that the number 5 replaces the existing text in the text box. Also notice that, at this point, the discounted prices in the uiDiscPricesLabel control are incorrect. As you learned in Chapter 3, having the previously calculated figures remain on the screen when a change is made to the interface could be misleading. A better approach is to clear the contents of the uiDiscPricesLabel control when a change is made to the original price. You will enter the appropriate code in the next section.

6 Click the **Exit** button to end the application, and then close the Output window.

Next, you code the uiOriginalTextBox control's TextChanged event procedure.

Coding the TextChanged Event Procedure

As you learned in Chapter 3, a control's TextChanged event occurs when the contents of a control's Text property change. You will use the uiOriginalTextBox's TextChanged event to clear the contents of the uiDiscPricesLabel when the user changes the original price.

To code the uiOriginalTextBox's TextChanged event:

1   Open the code template for the uiOriginalTextBox's TextChanged event procedure.

2   Type the comment and instruction shown in Figure 6-30.

enter this comment and line of code

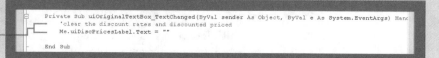

```
Private Sub uiOriginalTextBox_TextChanged(ByVal sender As Object, ByVal e As System.EventArgs) Hand
     'clear the discount rates and discounted priced
     Me.uiDiscPricesLabel.Text = ""

End Sub
```

Figure 6-30: Completed TextChanged event procedure for the uiOriginalTextBox

3   Save the solution, and then start the application.

4   Type 20 in the uiOriginalTextBox, and then click the **Calculate** button. The uiCalcButton's Click event procedure calculates the discounted prices and displays the prices in the uiDiscPricesLabel control. It then sends the focus to the uiOriginalTextBox control.

5   Type the number 5. The number 5 replaces the existing text in the text box, and the text box's TextChanged event procedure clears the contents of the uiDiscPricesLabel control.

6   Click the **Exit** button to end the application, and then close the Output window.

The last procedure you need to code is the form's Closing event procedure.

Coding the ShoppersForm's Closing Event Procedure

A form's **Closing event** occurs when a form is about to be closed. You can close a form using either the Close button on its title bar, or the `Me.Close()` statement in code. In the Shoppers Haven application, the Closing event procedure is responsible for verifying that the user wants to exit the application, and then taking the appropriate action based on the user's response. (Refer to the TOE chart shown earlier in Figure 6-22.) Figure 6-31 shows the pseudocode for this procedure.

ShoppersForm

1. declare the button variable

2. ask the user whether he or she wants to exit the application, then assign the response to the button variable

3. if the user does not want to exit the application
      set the Cancel property of the procedure's e parameter to True
   end if

Figure 6-31: Pseudocode for the ShoppersForm's Closing event procedure

To code the ShoppersForm's Closing event procedure:

1 Click the **Class Name** list arrow, then click (**ShoppersForm Events**) in the list. Click the **Method Name** list arrow, then click **Closing** in the list. The code template for the ShoppersForm's Closing event procedure appears in the Code Editor window.

2 Type '**verify that the user wants to exit the application** and press **Enter** twice.

First, declare the `button` variable.

3 Type **dim button as integer** and press **Enter**.

Now use the MessageBox.Show method to ask the user if he or she wants to exit the application. Include Yes and No buttons and the Warning Message icon in the message box. Designate the Yes button as the default button, and assign the user's response to the `button` variable.

4 Type **button = messagebox.show("Do you want to exit?", "Shoppers Haven", _** (be sure to type the line continuation character) and press **Enter**.

5 Press **Tab**, then type **messageboxbuttons.yesno, messageboxicon.exclamation, _** and press **Enter**.

6 Type **messageboxdefaultbutton.button1)** and press **Enter** twice.

If the user selects the No button in the message box, then the Closing procedure should prevent the form from being closed; you do so by setting the Cancel property of the procedure's **e** parameter to True.

7 Type the comment and selection structure indicated in Figure 6-32, which shows the completed Closing event procedure.

enter this comment
and selection structure

```
Private Sub ShoppersForm_Closing(ByVal sender As Object, ByVal e As System.ComponentModel.CancelEve
    'verify that the user wants to exit the application

    Dim button As Integer
    button = MessageBox.Show("Do you want to exit?", "Shoppers Haven", _
        MessageBoxButtons.YesNo, MessageBoxIcon.Exclamation, _
        MessageBoxDefaultButton.Button1)

    'if the user selects the No button, don't close the form
    If button = DialogResult.No Then
        e.Cancel = True
    End If
End Sub
```

Figure 6-32: Completed Closing event procedure for the ShoppersForm

8 Save the solution, then start the application.

9   Click the **Close** button on the form's title bar. A message box containing the message "Do you want to exit?" appears on the screen, as shown in Figure 6-33.

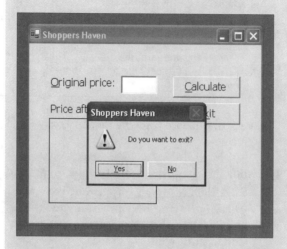

Figure 6-33: Message box displayed by the form's Closing event

10   Click the **No** button. The form remains on the screen.

11   Click the **Exit** button. Here again, the form's Closing event procedure displays a message box containing the "Do you want to exit?" message. This time, click the **Yes** button. The application ends.

12   When you return to the Code Editor window, close the Output window, then close the Code Editor window.

13   Click **File** on the menu bar, and then click **Close Solution**.

You now have completed Chapter 6. You can either take a break or complete the end-of-lesson questions and exercises.

SUMMARY

To process code when the user tabs to a control, or when the Focus method is used in code to send the focus to the control:

■ Enter the code in the control's Enter event procedure.

To process code when a form is about to be closed:

■ Enter the code in the form's Closing event procedure. The Closing event occurs when the user clicks the Close button on a form's title bar. It also occurs when the `Me.Close()` statement is used in code.

To prevent a form from being closed:

■ Set the Cancel property of the Closing event procedure's `e` parameter to True.

QUESTIONS

1. The _____ event is triggered when you click a form's Close button.
   a. Close
   b. Closing
   c. FormClose
   d. FormClosing
   e. Unloading

2. The _____ event is triggered when you use the statement `Me.Close()` to close a form.
   a. Close
   b. Closing
   c. FormClose
   d. FormClosing
   e. Unloading

3. The _____ event occurs when the user tabs to a text box.
   a. Enter
   b. Focus
   c. Tab
   d. Tabbing
   e. None of the above.

4. Which of the following statements prevents a form from being closed?
   a. `e.Cancel = False`
   b. `e.Cancel = True`
   c. `e.Close = False`
   d. `sender.Cancel = True`
   e. `sender.Cancel = False`

5. Which of the following statements selects the contents of the uiNameTextBox control?
   a. `Me.uiNameTextBox.Enter()`
   b. `Me.uiNameTextBox.SelectAll()`
   c. `Me.uiNameTextBox.SelectText()`
   d. `SelectAll(Me.uiNameTextBox)`
   e. None of the above.

EXERCISES

1. In this exercise, you modify the repetition structure contained in the Shoppers Haven application.
   a. Use Windows to make a copy of the Shoppers Haven Solution folder, which is contained in the VBNET\Chap06 folder. Rename the folder Shoppers Haven Solution Ex1.
   b. If necessary, start Visual Studio .NET. Open the Shoppers Haven Solution (Shoppers Haven Solution.sln) file, which is contained in the VBNET\Chap06\Shoppers Haven Solution Ex1 folder. Open the designer window.
   c. Change the For...Next statement in the uiCalcButton's Click event procedure to a Do...Loop statement.
   d. Save the solution, then start the application. Test the application to verify that it is working correctly.
   e. Click the Exit button to end the application.
   f. Close the Output window, then close the solution.

2. Powder Skating Rink holds a weekly ice-skating competition. Competing skaters must perform a two-minute program in front of a panel of judges. The number of judges varies from week to week. At the end of a skater's program, each judge assigns a score of zero through 10 to the skater. The manager of the ice rink wants an application that can be used to calculate and display a skater's average score. The application also should display the skater's total score and the number of scores entered.

   a. If necessary, start Visual Studio .NET. Create a blank solution named Powder Skating Solution. Save the solution in the VBNET\Chap06 folder.

   b. Add a Visual Basic .NET Windows Application project to the solution. Name the project Powder Skating Project.

   c. Assign the filename Powder Skating Form.vb to the form file object.

   d. Assign the name PowderForm to the Windows Form object.

   e. Design an appropriate interface. Use the GUI design guidelines listed in Appendix B to verify that the interface you create adheres to the GUI standards outlined in this book.

   f. Code the application. Code the form's Closing event so that it verifies that the user wants to exit the application.

   g. Save the solution, then start the application. Test the application using your own sample data.

   h. End the application.

   i. Close the Output window, then close the solution.

3. In this exercise, you code an application that allows the user 10 chances to guess a random number generated by the computer. Each time the user makes an incorrect guess, the application will display a message that tells the user either to guess a higher number or to guess a lower number. When the user guesses the random number, the application should display a "Congratulations!" message. However, if the user is not able to guess the random number after 10 tries, the application should display the random number in a message.

   a. If necessary, start Visual Studio .NET. Create a blank solution named Guessing Game Solution. Save the solution in the VBNET\Chap06 folder.

   b. Add a Visual Basic .NET Windows Application project to the solution. Name the project Guessing Game Project.

   c. Assign the filename Guessing Game Form.vb to the form file object.

   d. Assign the name GameForm to the Windows Form object.

   e. Design an appropriate interface. Use the GUI design guidelines listed in Appendix B to verify that the interface you create adheres to the GUI standards outlined in this book.

   f. Code the application. Code the form's Closing event so that it verifies that the user wants to exit the application.

   g. Save the solution, then start the application. Test the application appropriately.

   h. End the application.

   i. Close the Output window, then close the solution.

discovery ▶ 4. Sonheim Manufacturing Company wants an application that the accountant can use to calculate an asset's annual depreciation. The accountant will enter the asset's cost, useful life (in years), and salvage value (which is the value of the asset at the end of its useful life). The application should use the double-declining balance method to calculate the annual depreciation amounts, and then display the amounts in the interface.

In this exercise, you learn how to use a text box control's Multiline, ScrollBars, and ReadOnly properties. The Multiline property allows you to display more than one line of text in a text box. The ScrollBars property allows you to display scroll bars on a text box, and the ReadOnly property allows you to prevent the user from changing the data stored in a text box.

Additionally, you learn how to use the Financial.DDB function to calculate an asset's depreciation using the double-declining balance method. The syntax of the Financial.DDB function is **Financial.DDB**(*cost*, *salvage*, *life*, *period*). In the syntax, the *cost*, *salvage*, and *life* arguments are the asset's cost, salvage value, and useful life, respectively. The *period* argument is the period for which you want the depreciation amount calculated. The function returns the depreciation amount as a Double number. Figure 6-34 shows examples of using the Financial.DDB function to calculate depreciation amounts on an asset with a cost of $1000, a salvage value of $100, and a useful life of four years.

Examples of using the Financial.DDB function to calculate depreciation

```
depreciation = Financial.DDB(1000, 100, 4, 1)
```

calculates the depreciation amount for the first year of the asset's useful life, and then assigns the result (500) to the depreciation variable

```
depreciation = Financial.DDB(1000, 100, 4, 3)
```

calculates the depreciation amount for the third year of the asset's useful life, and then assigns the result (125) to the depreciation variable

---

Figure 6-34

a. If necessary, start Visual Studio .NET. Open the Sonheim Manufacturing Solution (Sonheim Manufacturing Solution.sln) file, which is contained in the VBNET\Chap06\Sonheim Manufacturing Solution folder. If necessary, open the designer window.

b. Set the uiDepreciationTextBox control's Multiline and ReadOnly properties to True, then set its ScrollBars property to Vertical. Set its Size property to 192, 216.

c. Code the application.

d. Save the solution, then start the application. Use the application to display the depreciation schedule for an asset with a cost of $1000, a salvage value of $100, and a useful life of four years. The application should display the depreciation schedule shown in Figure 6-35.

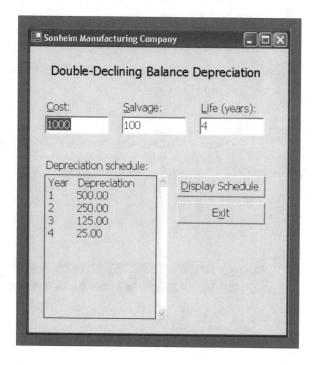

Figure 6-35

    e. Click the Exit button to end the application.

    f. Close the Output window, then close the solution.

5. In this exercise, you debug an existing application.

    a. If necessary, start Visual Studio .NET. Open the Debug Solution (Debug Solution.sln) file, which is contained in the VBNET\Chap06\Debug Solution folder. If necessary, open the designer window.

    b. Open the Code Editor window and study the existing code.

    c. Test the application.

    d. Click the Exit button to end the application. Correct any errors in the program.

    e. Close the Output window, then close the solution.

Sub and Function Procedures

Creating a Payroll Application

case Currently, Jefferson Williams, the payroll manager at Nelson Industries, manually calculates each employee's weekly gross pay, federal withholding tax (FWT), Social Security and Medicare (FICA) tax, and net pay—a very time-consuming process and one that is prone to mathematical errors. Mr. Williams has asked you to create an application that he can use to perform the payroll calculations both efficiently and accurately.

Previewing the Completed Application

Before creating the Payroll application, you first preview the completed application.

To preview the completed application:

1 Use the Run command on the Windows Start menu to run the **Payroll** (Payroll.exe) file, which is contained in the VBNET\Chap07 folder on your computer's hard disk. A copyright screen similar to the one that you created in Chapter 1 appears on the screen. In a few seconds, the copyright screen closes and the user interface for the payroll application appears on the screen. (Recall that the copyright screen from Chapter 1 contains a timer control that removes the form from the screen after eight seconds have elapsed.)

2 Type your name in the Name text box.

3 Scroll down the Hours list box until you see the number 41, then click **41** in the list.

4 Scroll down the Rate list box until you see the number 10.50, then click **10.50** in the list.

5 Click the **Single** radio button, and then click **1** in the Allowances list box.

6 Click the **Calculate** button. The application calculates and displays the amount of your gross pay, federal withholding tax (FWT), Social Security and Medicare (FICA) tax, and net pay. See Figure 7-1.

your name will appear here

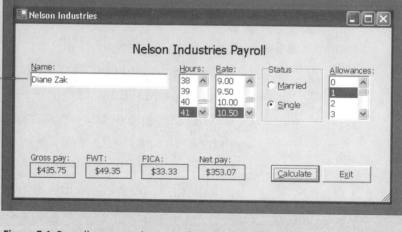

Figure 7-1: Payroll amounts shown in the Payroll application

7 Click the **Exit** button. The application closes.

The payroll application uses list boxes and a user-defined Function procedure. You learn about user-defined procedures in Lesson A, and about list boxes in Lesson B. You begin coding the payroll application in Lesson B and complete it in Lesson C.

LESSON A
objectives

After completing this lesson, you will be able to:

- Explain the difference between a Sub procedure and a Function procedure
- Create a procedure that receives information passed to it
- Explain the difference between passing data by value and by reference
- Create a Function procedure

Creating Sub and Function Procedures

Procedures

A **procedure** is a block of program code that performs a specific task. Procedures in Visual Basic .NET can be either Sub procedures or Function procedures. The difference between both types of procedures is that a **Function procedure** returns a value after performing its assigned task, whereas a **Sub procedure** does not return a value. Although you have been using Sub procedures since Chapter 1, this lesson provides a more in-depth look into their creation and use. After exploring the topic of Sub procedures, you then learn how to create and use Function procedures.

Sub Procedures

There are two types of Sub procedures in Visual Basic .NET: event procedures and user-defined Sub procedures. Most of the procedures that you coded in previous chapters were event procedures. An event procedure is a Sub procedure that is associated with a specific object and event, such as a button's Click event or a text box's KeyPress event. Recall that the computer automatically processes an event procedure when the event occurs.

You learned how to create a user-defined Sub procedure in Chapter 5. Unlike an event procedure, a user-defined Sub procedure is independent of any object and event, and is processed only when called, or invoked, from code. Recall that you invoke a user-defined Sub procedure using the Call statement.

A Sub procedure can contain one or more parameters in its procedure header. Each parameter stores data that is passed to the procedure when it is invoked. For example, all event procedures contain two parameters: sender and e. The sender parameter contains the internal memory address of the object that raised the event, and the e parameter contains any additional information provided by the object. For instance, when a button's Click event occurs, the address of the button is passed to the Click event procedure and stored in the procedure's sender parameter. No additional information is passed when a Click event occurs, so no information is stored in a Click event procedure's e parameter.

Now consider what happens when the user types the letter B in a text box named uiNameTextBox. As you learned in Chapter 4, typing a letter in a text box causes the text box's KeyPress event to occur. When the uiNameTextBox control's KeyPress event occurs, the address of the text box is passed to the KeyPress event procedure and stored in the procedure's sender parameter. Two additional items of information also are passed to the KeyPress event procedure. These items, KeyChar="B" and Handled=False, are stored in the procedure's e parameter.

tip

To determine the items of information passed to an event procedure's e parameter, first display the event procedure's code template in the Code Editor window. Then type the letter e followed by a period in the procedure; this displays a list that includes the properties of the e parameter. Each property in the list is designated by [icon] and represents an item passed to the procedure's e parameter. You can use the MessageBox.Show method to display the value of a property.

(Recall that the KeyChar property contains the character corresponding to the key that was pressed, and the Handled property determines whether the text box accepts the key contained in the KeyChar property.)

Like the procedure header for an event procedure, the procedure header for a user-defined Sub procedure also can include one or more parameters.

Including Parameters in a User-Defined Sub Procedure

Figure 7-2 shows the syntax you use to create a user-defined Sub procedure.

Sub procedure syntax
{**Private** | **Public**} **Sub** *procedurename*([*parameterlist*])
[*statements*]
End Sub

procedure header —
procedure footer —

Figure 7-2: Syntax for creating a user-defined Sub procedure

> **tip**
>
> A Sub procedure also can begin with a keyword other than the ones shown in Figure 7-2. The other keywords are beyond the scope of this book.

> **tip**
>
> As you learned in Chapter 5, Sub procedure names should be entered using Pascal case. Also, it is a common practice to begin a procedure's name with a verb.

> **tip**
>
> Visual Basic .NET allows you to specify that an argument in the Call statement is optional. If the argument is not provided, a default value is used for the corresponding parameter in the *parameterlist*. You learn more about optional arguments in Discovery Exercise 11 at the end of this lesson.

As do all procedures, user-defined Sub procedures have both a procedure header and procedure footer. The procedure header usually begins with either the keyword `Private` or the keyword `Public`. You use the keyword `Private` to indicate that only the procedures in the current form can access the procedure. You use the keyword `Public` when you want to allow unlimited access to the procedure.

Following the keyword `Private` or `Public` in the procedure header is the keyword `Sub`. The `Sub` keyword identifies the procedure as a Sub procedure, which is a procedure that does not return a value after performing its assigned task. After the keyword `Sub` is the *procedurename* and a set of parentheses that contains an optional *parameterlist*. The *parameterlist* lists the data type and name of memory locations used by the procedure to store the information passed to it. The *parameterlist* also specifies how each item of information is passed—either *by value* or *by reference*. You learn more about the *parameterlist*, as well as passing information *by value* and *by reference*, later in this lesson.

Unlike the procedure header, which varies with each procedure, the procedure footer for a Sub procedure is always `End Sub`. Between the procedure header and the procedure footer, you enter the instructions you want the computer to process when the procedure is invoked.

As you learned in Chapter 5, you can use the Call statement to call (or invoke) a Sub procedure. Recall that the syntax of the Call statement is **Call** *procedurename* ([*argumentlist*]), where *procedurename* is the name of the procedure you are calling, and *argumentlist* (which is optional) is a comma-separated list of arguments you want passed to the procedure. The number of arguments listed in the Call statement's *argumentlist* should agree with the number of parameters listed in the *parameterlist* in the procedure header. If the *argumentlist* includes one argument, then the procedure header should have one parameter in its *parameterlist*. Similarly, a procedure that is passed three arguments when called requires three parameters in its *parameterlist*. (Refer to the last tip on this page for an exception to this general rule.)

In addition to having the same number of parameters as arguments, the data type and position of each parameter in the *parameterlist* must agree with the data type and position of its corresponding argument in the *argumentlist*. For instance, if the argument is an integer, then the parameter in which the integer will be stored should have a data type of Integer, Short, or Long, depending on the size of the integer. Likewise, if two arguments are passed to a procedure—the first one being a String variable and the second one being a Single variable—the first parameter should have a data type of String and the second parameter should have a data type of Single.

You can pass a literal constant, named constant, keyword, or variable to a user-defined Sub procedure; in most cases, you will pass a variable.

Passing Variables

Each variable you declare in an application has both a value and a unique address that represents the location of the variable in the computer's internal memory. Visual Basic .NET allows you to pass either the variable's value (referred to as **passing by value**) or its address (referred to as **passing by reference**) to the receiving procedure. The method you choose—*by value* or *by reference*—depends on whether you want the receiving procedure to have access to the variable in memory—in other words, whether you want to allow the receiving procedure to change the contents of the variable.

Although the idea of passing information *by value* and *by reference* may sound confusing at first, it is a concept with which you already are familiar. To illustrate, assume that you have a savings account at a local bank. During a conversation with a friend, you mention the amount of money you have in the account. Telling someone the amount of money in your account is similar to passing a variable *by value*. Knowing the balance in your account does not give your friend access to your bank account; it merely gives your friend some information that he or she can use—perhaps to compare to the amount of money he or she has saved.

The savings account example also provides an illustration of passing information *by reference*. To deposit money to or withdraw money from your account, you must provide the bank teller with your account number. The account number represents the location of your account at the bank and allows the teller to change the account balance. Giving the teller your bank account number is similar to passing a variable *by reference*. The account number allows the teller to change the contents of your bank account, similar to the way the variable's address allows the receiving procedure to change the contents of the variable passed to the procedure.

First, you learn how to pass a variable *by value*.

Passing Variables by Value

To pass a variable *by value* in Visual Basic .NET, you include the keyword `ByVal` before the variable's corresponding parameter in the *parameterlist*; `ByVal` stands for "by value." When you pass a variable *by value*, the computer passes only the contents of the variable to the receiving procedure. When only the contents are passed, the receiving procedure is not given access to the variable in memory, so it cannot change the value stored inside the variable. You pass a variable *by value* when the receiving procedure needs to *know* the variable's contents, but the receiving procedure does not need to *change* the contents. Unless specified otherwise, variables are passed *by value* in Visual Basic .NET.

Figure 7-3 shows two examples of passing variables *by value*. The *argumentlist* in each Call statement, and the *parameterlist* in each procedure header, are shaded in the figure.

tip

The internal memory of a computer is like a large post office, where each memory cell, like each post office box, has a unique address.

tip

In previous versions of Visual Basic, the default method for passing variables is *by reference*.

Examples – passing *by value*

Example 1
```
Private Sub GetInfoButton_Click(ByVal sender As Object, _
        ByVal e As System.EventArgs) Handles uiGetInfoButton.Click
    Dim name, age As String
    name = InputBox("Pet's name:", "Name")
    age = InputBox("Pet's age (years):", "Age")
    Call DisplayMsg(name, age)
End Sub

Private Sub DisplayMsg(ByVal pet As String, ByVal years As String)
    Me.uiMessageLabel.Text = "Your pet " & pet & " is " _
        & years & " years old."
End Sub
```

Example 2
```
Private Sub uiCalcButton_Click(ByVal sender As Object, _
        ByVal e As System.EventArgs) Handles uiCalcButton.Click
    Dim region1, region2 As Integer, bonusRate As Double
    region1 = Integer.Parse(Me.uiRegion1TextBox.Text)
    region2 = Integer.Parse(Me.uiRegion2TextBox.Text)
    bonusRate = Double.Parse(Me.uiBonusRateTextBox.Text)
    Call CalcAndDisplayBonus(region1, region2, bonusRate)
End Sub

Private Sub CalcAndDisplayBonus(ByVal sale1 As Integer, _
                                ByVal sale2 As Integer, _
                                ByVal rate As Double)
    Dim total As Integer, bonus As Double
    total = sale1 + sale2
    bonus = total * rate
    Me.uiBonusLabel.Text = bonus.ToString("C2")
End Sub
```

Figure 7-3: Examples of passing variables *by value*

Notice that the number, data type, and sequence of the arguments in the Call statement in both examples match the number, data type, and sequence of the corresponding parameters in the procedure header. Also notice that the names of the parameters do not need to be identical to the names of the arguments to which they correspond. In fact, for clarity, it usually is better to use different names for the arguments and parameters.

Study closely the code shown in Example 1 in Figure 7-3. The uiGetInfoButton control's Click event procedure first declares two String variables named name and age. The next two statements in the procedure use the InputBox function to prompt the user to enter the name and age (in years) of his or her pet. Assume that the user enters "Spot" as the name and "4" as the age. The computer stores the string "Spot" in the name variable and the string "4" in the age variable.

Next, the Call DisplayMsg(name, age) statement calls the DisplayMsg procedure, passing it the name and age variables *by value*, which means that only the contents of the variables—in this case, "Spot" and "4"—are passed to the procedure. You know that the variables are passed *by value* because the keyword ByVal appears before each variable's corresponding parameter in the DisplayMsg procedure header. At this point, the computer temporarily leaves the uiGetInfoButton's Click event procedure to process the code contained in the DisplayMsg procedure.

The first instruction processed in the DisplayMsg procedure is the procedure header. When processing the procedure header, the computer creates the pet and years variables (which are listed in the *parameterlist*) in its internal memory, and stores the information passed to the procedure in those variables. In this case, the computer stores the string "Spot" in the pet variable and the string "4" in the years variable. The pet and years variables are local to the DisplayMsg procedure, which means they can be used only by the procedure.

After processing the DisplayMsg procedure header, the computer processes the assignment statement contained in the procedure. The assignment statement uses the values stored in the procedure's parameters—pet and years—to display the appropriate message in the uiMessageLabel control. In this case, the statement displays the message "Your pet Spot is 4 years old."

Next, the computer processes the DisplayMsg procedure footer, which ends the DisplayMsg procedure. At this point, the pet and years variables are removed from the computer's internal memory. (Recall that a local variable is removed from the computer's memory when the procedure in which it is declared ends.) The computer then returns to the uiGetInfoButton's Click event procedure, to the statement immediately following the Call DisplayMsg(name, age) statement. This statement, End Sub, ends the uiGetInfoButton's Click event procedure. The computer then removes the procedure's local variables (name and age) from its internal memory.

Now study closely the code shown in Example 2 in Figure 7-3. The uiCalcButton's Click event procedure first declares two Integer variables named region1 and region2, and a Double variable named bonusRate. The next three statements in the procedure assign the contents of three text boxes to the variables. Assume that the user entered the number 1000 in the uiRegion1TextBox, the number 3000 in the uiRegion2TextBox, and the number .1 in the uiBonusRateTextBox. The computer stores the number 1000 in the region1 variable, the number 3000 in the region2 variable, and the number .1 in the bonusRate variable.

Next, the Call CalcAndDisplayBonus(region1, region2, bonusRate) statement calls the CalcAndDisplayBonus procedure, passing it three variables *by value*, which means that only the contents of the variables—in this case, 1000, 3000, and .1—are passed to the procedure. Here again, you know that the variables are passed *by value* because the keyword ByVal appears before each variable's corresponding parameter in the CalcAndDisplayBonus procedure header. At this point, the computer temporarily leaves the uiCalcButton's Click event procedure to process the code contained in the CalcAndDisplayBonus procedure.

The first instruction processed in the CalcAndDisplayBonus procedure is the procedure header. When processing the procedure header, the computer creates the three local variables listed in the *parameterlist*, and stores the information passed to the procedure in those variables. In this case, the computer stores the number 1000 in the sale1 variable, the number 3000 in the sale2 variable, and the number .1 in the rate variable.

After processing the CalcAndDisplayBonus procedure header, the computer processes the statements contained in the procedure. The first statement declares two additional local variables named total and bonus. The next statement adds the value stored in the sale1 variable (1000) to the value stored in the sale2 variable (3000), and assigns the sum (4000) to the total variable. The third statement in the procedure multiplies the value stored in the total variable (4000) by the value stored in the rate (.1) variable, and assigns the result (400) to the bonus variable. The fourth statement in the procedure displays the bonus in the uiBonusLabel control; in this case, the statement displays $400.00.

Next, the computer processes the CalcAndDisplayBonus procedure footer, which ends the CalcAndDisplayBonus procedure. At this point, the procedure's local variables—sale1, sale2, rate, total, and bonus—are removed from the computer's internal memory. The computer then returns to the uiCalcButton's Click event procedure, to the statement immediately following the Call statement. This statement, End

Sub, ends the uiCalcButton's Click event procedure. The computer then removes the region1, region2, and bonusRate variables from its internal memory.

Next, you learn how to pass variables *by reference*.

Passing Variables by Reference

In addition to passing a variable's value to a procedure, you also can pass a variable's address—in other words, its location in the computer's internal memory. Passing a variable's address is referred to as passing *by reference*, and it gives the receiving procedure access to the variable being passed. You pass a variable *by reference* when you want the receiving procedure to change the contents of the variable.

To pass a variable *by reference* in Visual Basic .NET, you include the keyword ByRef before the name of the variable's corresponding parameter in the procedure header; ByRef stands for "by reference." The ByRef keyword tells the computer to pass the variable's address rather than its contents.

Figure 7-4 shows two examples of passing variables *by reference*. The *argumentlist* in each Call statement, and the *parameterlist* in each procedure header, are shaded in the figure.

Examples – passing *by reference*

Example 1
```
Private Sub uiDisplayButton_Click(ByVal sender As Object, _
        ByVal e As System.EventArgs) Handles uiDisplayButton.Click
    Dim name, age As String

    Call GetInfo(name, age)
    Me.uiMessageLabel.Text = "Your pet " & name & " is " _
        & age & " years old."
End Sub

Private Sub GetInfo(ByRef pet As String, ByRef years As String)
    pet = InputBox("Pet's name:", "Name")
    years = InputBox("Pet's age (years):", "Age")
End Sub
```

Example 2
```
Private Sub uiBonusButton_Click(ByVal sender As Object, _
        ByVal e As System.EventArgs) Handles uiBonusButton.Click
    Dim region1, region2 As Integer, bonus As Double
    region1 = Integer.Parse(Me.uiRegion1TextBox.Text)
    region2 = Integer.Parse(Me.uiRegion2TextBox.Text)
    Call CalcBonus(region1, region2, .05, bonus)
    Me.uiBonusLabel.Text = bonus.ToString("C2")
End Sub

Private Sub CalcBonus(ByVal sale1 As Integer, _
                ByVal sale2 As Integer, _
                ByVal rate As Double, _
                ByRef dollars As Double)
    Dim total As Integer
    total = sale1 + sale2
    dollars = total * rate
End Sub
```

Figure 7-4: Examples of passing variables *by reference*

You cannot determine by looking at the Call statement whether a variable is being passed *by value* or *by reference*. You must look at the procedure header to make the determination.

The `name` and `age` variables are local to the uiDisplayButton's Click event procedure. The `pet` and `years` variables, on the other hand, are local to the GetInfo procedure.

Notice that, in both examples, the number, data type, and sequence of the arguments in the Call statement match the number, data type, and sequence of the corresponding parameters in the procedure header. Also notice that the names of the parameters do not need to be identical to the names of the arguments to which they correspond.

Study closely the code shown in Example 1 in Figure 7-4. The uiDisplayButton's Click event procedure first declares two String variables named `name` and `age`. The next statement in the procedure calls the GetInfo procedure, passing it the `name` and `age` variables *by reference*, which means that each variable's address in memory, rather than its contents, is passed to the procedure. You know that the variables are passed *by reference* because the keyword `ByRef` appears before each variable's corresponding parameter in the GetInfo procedure header. At this point, the computer temporarily leaves the uiDisplayButton's Click event procedure to process the code contained in the GetInfo procedure.

The first instruction processed in the GetInfo procedure is the procedure header. The `ByRef` keyword that appears before each parameter's name in the procedure header indicates that the procedure will be receiving the addresses of two variables. When you pass a variable's address to a procedure, the computer uses the address to locate the variable in memory. It then assigns the name appearing in the procedure header to the memory location. In this case, for example, the computer first locates the `name` and `age` variables in memory; after doing so, it assigns the names `pet` and `years`, respectively, to these locations. At this point, each of the two memory locations has two names: one assigned by the uiDisplayButton's Click event procedure, and the other assigned by the GetInfo procedure.

After processing the GetInfo procedure header, the computer processes the two assignment statements contained in the procedure. Those statements prompt the user to enter the name and age of his or her pet, and then store the user's responses in the `pet` and `years` variables. Assume that the user entered "Simba" as the name and "9" as the age. The computer stores the string "Simba" in the `pet` variable and the string "9" in the `years` variable. Figure 7-5 shows the contents of memory after the two assignment statements in the GetInfo procedure are processed. Notice that changing the contents of the `pet` and `years` variables also changes the contents of the `name` and `age` variables, respectively. This is because the names refer to the same locations in memory.

memory location names	name (uiDisplayButton Click event procedure) pet (GetInfo procedure)	age (uiDisplayButton Click event procedure) years (GetInfo procedure)
memory location contents	Simba	9

Figure 7-5: Contents of memory after the two assignment statements in the GetInfo procedure are processed

As Figure 7-5 indicates, the two memory locations belong to both the uiDisplayButton's Click event procedure and the GetInfo procedure. Although both procedures can access the two memory locations, each procedure uses a different name to do so. The uiDisplayButton's Click event procedure, for example, uses the names `name` and `age` to refer to these memory locations. The GetInfo procedure, on the other hand, uses the names `pet` and `years`.

The `End Sub` statement in the GetInfo procedure is processed next and ends the procedure. At this point, the computer removes the `pet` and `years` names assigned to the memory locations. Now, each memory location shown in Figure 7-5 has only one name.

The computer then returns to the uiDisplayButton's Click event procedure, to the statement located immediately below the Call statement. This statement displays the message "Your pet Simba is 9 years old." in the uiMessageLabel control. Next, the computer processes the End Sub statement in the uiDisplayButton's Click event procedure, which ends the procedure. The computer then removes the name and age variables from its internal memory.

Now study the code shown in Example 2 in Figure 7-4. The uiBonusButton's Click event procedure first declares two Integer variables named region1 and region2, and a Double variable named bonus. The next two statements assign the contents of two text boxes to the region1 and region2 variables. Assume that the user entered the numbers 500 and 200 in the text boxes. The computer stores the number 500 in the region1 variable and the number 200 in the region2 variable.

Next, the Call CalcBonus(region1, region2, .05, bonus) statement calls the CalcBonus procedure. The CalcBonus procedure header indicates that the first three arguments in the Call statement will be passed *by value*, whereas the last argument will be passed *by reference*. The items passed *by value* should be stored in the sale1, sale2, and rate variables. The item passed *by reference* should be stored in a variable named dollars.

When the computer processes the CalcBonus procedure header, it first creates the sale1, sale2, and rate variables in memory. It then stores the numbers 500, 200, and .05, respectively, in the variables. Next, the computer locates the bonus variable (which is declared in the uiBonusButton's Click event procedure) in memory, and assigns the name dollars to the memory location.

After processing the CalcBonus procedure header, the computer processes the statements contained in the procedure. The first statement declares a local variable named total. The next statement adds the value stored in the sale1 variable (500) to the value stored in the sale2 variable (200), and then assigns the sum (700) to the total variable. The third statement in the procedure multiplies the value stored in the total variable (700) by the value stored in the rate variable (.05), and then assigns the result (35) to the dollars variable. The End Sub statement in the CalcBonus procedure then ends the procedure. At this point, the computer removes the sale1, sale2, rate, and total variables from its internal memory. It also removes the dollars name assigned to the bonus memory location.

When the CalcBonus procedure ends, the computer returns to the uiBonusButton's Click event procedure, to the statement located immediately below the Call statement. This statement displays the number $35.00 in the uiBonusLabel control. Finally, the computer processes the End Sub statement in the uiBonusButton's Click event procedure, which ends the procedure. The computer then removes the region1, region2, and bonus variables from its internal memory.

As you learned earlier, in addition to creating Sub procedures, you also can create Function procedures in Visual Basic .NET.

tip

Notice that you can pass a literal constant—in this case, the number .05—to a procedure. Literal constants are usually passed *by value* to a procedure.

Function Procedures

Like a Sub procedure, a **Function procedure**, typically referred to simply as a **function**, is a block of code that performs a specific task. However, unlike a Sub procedure, a function returns a value after completing its task. Some functions, such as the Val and InputBox functions, are intrinsic to Visual Basic .NET. Recall that the Val function returns the numeric equivalent of a string, and the InputBox function returns the user's response to a prompt that appears in a dialog box.

Functions typically are called from statements that display the function's return value, use the return value in a calculation, or assign the return value to a variable.

You also can create your own functions, referred to as **user-defined functions**, in Visual Basic .NET. After creating a user-defined function, you then can invoke it from one or more places in the application. You invoke a user-defined function in exactly the same way as you invoke a built-in function—simply by including the function's name in a statement. You also can pass (send) information to a user-defined function, and the information can be passed either *by value* or *by reference*.

Figure 7-6 shows the syntax you use to create a user-defined function. It also includes an example of using the syntax to create a user-defined function.

procedure header

procedure footer

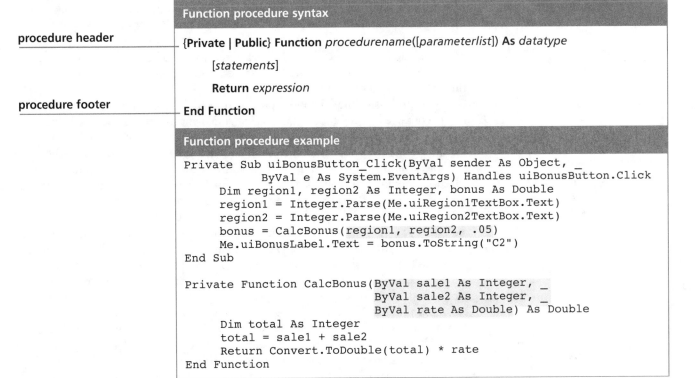

Function procedure syntax

{**Private** | **Public**} **Function** *procedurename*([*parameterlist*]) **As** *datatype*

   [*statements*]

   Return *expression*

End Function

Function procedure example

```
Private Sub uiBonusButton_Click(ByVal sender As Object, _
        ByVal e As System.EventArgs) Handles uiBonusButton.Click
    Dim region1, region2 As Integer, bonus As Double
    region1 = Integer.Parse(Me.uiRegion1TextBox.Text)
    region2 = Integer.Parse(Me.uiRegion2TextBox.Text)
    bonus = CalcBonus(region1, region2, .05)
    Me.uiBonusLabel.Text = bonus.ToString("C2")
End Sub

Private Function CalcBonus(ByVal sale1 As Integer, _
                           ByVal sale2 As Integer, _
                           ByVal rate As Double) As Double
    Dim total As Integer
    total = sale1 + sale2
    Return Convert.ToDouble(total) * rate
End Function
```

Figure 7-6: User-defined function syntax and example

Like Sub procedures, Function procedures have both a procedure header and procedure footer. The procedure header for a Function procedure is almost identical to the procedure header for a Sub procedure, except it includes the keyword `Function` rather than the keyword `Sub`. The keyword `Function` identifies the procedure as a Function procedure—one that returns a value after completing its task.

Also different from a Sub procedure header, a Function procedure header includes the **As** *datatype* clause. You use this clause to specify the data type of the value returned by the function. For example, if the function returns a string, you include `As String` at the end of the procedure header. Similarly, if the function returns a decimal number, you include `As Single`, `As Decimal`, or `As Double` at the end of the procedure header. The *datatype* you use depends on the size of the number, and whether you want the number stored with a fixed decimal point or a floating decimal point.

The procedure footer in a Function procedure is always `End Function`. Between the procedure header and the procedure footer, you enter the instructions you want the computer to process when the function is invoked. In most cases, the last statement in a Function procedure is **Return** *expression*, where *expression* represents the one and only value that will be returned to the statement that called the function. The data type of the *expression* in the Return statement must agree with the data type specified in the **As** *datatype* clause in the procedure header. The **Return statement** alerts the computer that the function has completed its task and ends the function after returning the value of its *expression*.

Study closely the example shown in Figure 7-6. The uiBonusButton's Click event procedure first declares two Integer variables named `region1` and `region2`, and a Double variable named `bonus`. The next two statements assign the contents of two text boxes to the `region1` and `region2` variables. Assume that the user entered the numbers 500 and 200 in the text boxes. The computer stores the number 500 in the `region1` variable and the number 200 in the `region2` variable.

Next, the `bonus = CalcBonus(region1, region2, .05)` statement calls the CalcBonus procedure, passing it the values 500, 200, and .05. The computer stores the values in the `sale1`, `sale2`, and `rate` variables, which appear in the CalcBonus procedure header.

After processing the CalcBonus procedure header, the computer processes the statements contained in the function. The first statement declares a local variable named `total`. The next statement adds the value stored in the `sale1` variable (500) to the value stored in the `sale2` variable (200), and then assigns the sum (700) to the `total` variable. The `Return Convert.ToDouble(total) * rate` statement in the function multiplies the value stored in the `total` variable (700) by the value stored in the `rate` variable (.05), and then returns the result (35) to the statement that called the function; in this case, it returns the result to the `bonus = CalcBonus(region1, region2, .05)` statement in the uiBonusButton's Click event procedure. After processing the Return statement, the CalcBonus function ends and the computer removes the `sale1`, `sale2`, `rate`, and `total` variables from its internal memory.

The `bonus = CalcBonus(region1, region2, .05)` statement assigns the CalcBonus function's return value (35) to the `bonus` variable. The `Me.uiBonusLabel.Text = bonus.ToString("C2")` statement then displays $35.00 in the uiBonusLabel control. Finally, the computer processes the `End Sub` statement in the uiBonusButton's Click event procedure, which ends the procedure. The computer then removes the `region1`, `region2`, and `bonus` variables from its internal memory.

The code shown in the example in Figure 7-6 is similar to the code shown in Example 2 in Figure 7-4. Both examples differ only in the way each assigns the appropriate bonus amount to the `bonus` variable. In Figure 7-6, the uiBonusButton's Click event procedure calls a function to calculate the bonus amount, and then assigns the amount to the `bonus` variable. In Example 2 in Figure 7-4, on the other hand, the uiBonusButton's Click event procedure passes the `bonus` variable *by reference* to the CalcBonus Sub procedure. The CalcBonus Sub procedure assigns the appropriate amount to the `bonus` variable. Both examples simply represent two different ways of performing the same task.

You now have completed Lesson A. You can either take a break or complete the end-of-lesson questions and exercises before moving on to the next lesson.

SUMMARY

To create a user-defined Sub procedure:

■ Refer to the syntax shown in Figure 7-2.

To create a user-defined Function procedure:

■ Refer to the syntax shown in Figure 7-6.

To pass information to a Sub or Function procedure:

- Include the information in the Call statement's *argumentlist*. In the procedure header's *parameterlist*, include the names of memory locations that will store the information.
- The number, data type, and sequence of the arguments listed in the Call statement's *argumentlist* should agree with the number, data type, and sequence of the parameters listed in the *parameterlist* in the procedure header.

To pass a variable by value to a procedure:

- Include the keyword `ByVal` before the parameter name in the procedure header's *parameterlist*. Because only the value stored in the variable is passed, the receiving procedure cannot access the variable.

To pass a variable by reference:

- Include the keyword `ByRef` before the parameter name in the procedure header's *parameterlist*. Because the address of the variable is passed, the receiving procedure can change the contents of the variable.

QUESTIONS

1. Which of the following is false?
   a. A Function procedure can return one or more values to the statement that called it.
   b. An event procedure is a Sub procedure that is associated with a specific object and event.
   c. A procedure can accept one or more items of data passed to it.
   d. The *parameterlist* in a procedure header is optional.
   e. At times, a memory location inside the computer's internal memory may have more than one name.

2. When the uiCodeRadioButton's Click event occurs, the address of the uiCodeRadioButton is stored in the event procedure's _____ parameter.
   a. `address`
   b. `button`
   c. `e`
   d. `object`
   e. `sender`

3. The items listed in the Call statement are called _____.
   a. arguments
   b. constraints
   c. events
   d. passers
   e. None of the above.

4. Each memory location listed in the *parameterlist* in the procedure header is referred to as _____.
   a. an address
   b. a constraint
   c. an event
   d. a parameter
   e. None of the above.

5. To determine whether a variable is being passed *by value* or *by reference* to a procedure, you will need to examine _____.
a. the Call statement
b. the procedure header
c. the procedure footer
d. the statements entered in the procedure
e. Either a or b.

6. Which of the following statements can be used to call the CalcArea procedure, passing it two variables *by value*?
a. `Call CalcArea(length, width)`
b. `Call CalcArea(ByVal length, width)`
c. `Call CalcArea(length, width ByVal)`
d. `Call ByVal CalcArea(length, width)`
e. `Call CalcArea(ByVal length, ByVal width)`

7. Which of the following procedure headers receives the value stored in a String variable?
a. `Private Sub DisplayName(name As String)`
b. `Private Sub DisplayName(ByValue name As String)`
c. `Private Sub DisplayName(ByRef name As String)`
d. `Private Sub DisplayName(name ByVal As String)`
e. None of the above.

8. Which of the following is a valid procedure header for a procedure that receives an integer first and a number with a decimal place second?
a. `Private Sub CalcFee(base As Integer, rate As Single)`
b. `Private Sub CalcFee(ByRef base As Integer, ByRef rate As Single)`
c. `Private Sub CalcFee(ByVal base As Integer, ByVal rate As Single)`
d. `Private Sub CalcFee(base As Integer ByVal, rate As Single ByVal)`
e. None of the above.

9. A function procedure can return _____.
a. one value only
b. one or more values

10. The procedure header specifies the procedure's _____.
a. accessibility
b. name
c. parameters
d. type (either Sub or Function)
e. All of the above.

11. Which of the following is false?
a. In most cases, the number of arguments should agree with the number of parameters.
b. The data type of each argument should match the data type of its corresponding parameter.
c. The name of each argument should be identical to the name of its corresponding parameter.
d. When you pass information to a procedure *by value*, the procedure stores the value of each item it receives in a separate memory location.
e. The sequence of the arguments listed in the Call statement should agree with the sequence of the parameters listed in the procedure header.

12. Which of the following instructs a function to return the contents of the `stateTax` variable to the statement that called the function?

    a. `Restore stateTax`

    b. `Restore ByVal stateTax`

    c. `Return stateTax`

    d. `Return ByVal stateTax`

    e. `Return ByRef stateTax`

13. Which of the following is a valid procedure header for a procedure that receives the value stored in an Integer variable first and the address of a Single variable second?

    a. `Private Sub CalcFee(ByVal base As Integer, ByAdd rate`
       `As Single)`

    b. `Private Sub CalcFee(Val(base As Integer), Add(rate As`
       `Single))`

    c. `Private Sub CalcFee(ByVal base As Integer, ByRef rate`
       `As Single)`

    d. `Private Sub CalcFee(Value of base As Integer, Address of`
       `rate As Single)`

    e. None of the above.

14. Which of the following is a valid procedure header for a procedure that receives the number .09?

    a. `Private Function CalcTax(ByVal rate As Double) As Double`

    b. `Private Function CalcTax(ByAdd rate As Double) As Double`

    c. `Private Sub CalcTax(ByVal rate As Double)`

    d. `Private Sub CalcTax(ByAdd rate As Double)`

    e. `Both a and c.`

15. If the statement `Call CalcNet(net)` passes the address of the `net` variable to the CalcNet procedure, the variable is said to be passed _____.

    a. *by address*

    b. *by content*

    c. *by reference*

    d. *by value*

    e. *by variable*

16. Which of the following is false?

    a. When you pass a variable *by reference*, the receiving procedure can change its contents.

    b. When you pass a variable *by value*, the receiving function creates a local variable that it uses to store the passed value.

    c. Unless specified otherwise, all variables in Visual Basic .NET are passed *by value*.

    d. To pass a variable *by reference* in Visual Basic .NET, you include the keyword `ByRef` before the variable's name in the Call statement.

    e. None of the above.

17. Assume that a Sub procedure named CalcEndingInventory is passed the values stored in four Integer variables named beginAmt, sales, purchases, and endAmt. The procedure's task is to calculate the ending inventory, based on the beginning inventory, sales, and purchase amounts passed to the procedure. The procedure should store the result in the endAmt memory location. Which of the following procedure headers is correct?
    a. `Private Sub CalcEndingInventory(ByVal b As Integer, ByVal s As Integer, ByVal p As Integer, ByRef e As Integer)`
    b. `Private Sub CalcEndingInventory(ByVal b As Integer, ByVal s As Integer, ByVal p As Integer, ByVal e As Integer)`
    c. `Private Sub CalcEndingInventory(ByRef b As Integer, ByRef s As Integer, ByRef p As Integer, ByVal e As Integer)`
    d. `Private Sub CalcEndingInventory(ByRef b As Integer, ByRef s As Integer, ByRef p As Integer, ByRef e As Integer)`
    e. None of the above.

18. Which of the following statements should you use to call the CalcEndingInventory procedure described in Question 17?
    a. `Call CalcEndingInventory(beginAmt, sales, purchases, endAmt)`
    b. `Call CalcEndingInventory(ByVal beginAmt, ByVal sales, ByVal purchases, ByRef endAmt)`
    c. `Call CalcEndingInventory(ByRef beginAmt, ByRef sales, ByRef purchases, ByRef endAmt)`
    d. `Call CalcEndingInventory(ByVal beginAmt, ByVal sales, ByVal purchases, ByVal endAmt)`
    e. `Call CalcEndingInventory(ByRef beginAmt, ByRef sales, ByRef purchases, ByVal endAmt)`

19. The memory locations listed in the *parameterlist* in a procedure header are local to the procedure and are removed from the computer's internal memory when the procedure ends.
    a. True
    b. False

20. What is the difference between a Sub procedure and a Function procedure?

EXERCISES

1. Write the Visual Basic .NET code for a Sub procedure that receives an integer passed to it. The procedure, named HalveNumber, should divide the integer by 2, and then display the result in the uiAnswerLabel control.

2. Write the Visual Basic .NET code for a Sub procedure that prompts the user to enter the name of a city, and then stores the user's response in the String variable whose address is passed to the procedure. Name the procedure GetCity.

3. Write the Visual Basic .NET code for a Sub procedure that receives four Integer variables: the first two *by value* and the last two *by reference*. The procedure should calculate the sum and the difference of the two variables passed *by value*, and then store the results in the variables passed *by reference*. (When calculating the difference, subtract the contents of the second variable from the contents of the first variable.) Name the procedure CalcSumAndDiff.

4. Write the Visual Basic .NET code for a Sub procedure that receives three Single variables: the first two *by value* and the last one *by reference*. The procedure should divide the first variable by the second variable, and then store the result in the third variable. Name the procedure CalcQuotient.

5. Write the Visual Basic .NET code for a Function procedure that receives the value stored in an Integer variable named number. The procedure, named DivideNumber, should divide the integer by 2, and then return the result (which may contain a decimal place). Use the num variable in the *parameterlist*.

6. Write an appropriate statement to call the DivideNumber function created in Exercise 5. Assign the value returned by the function to the answer variable.

7. Write the Visual Basic .NET code for a Function procedure that prompts the user to enter the name of a state, and then returns the user's response to the calling procedure. Name the procedure GetState.

8. Write the Visual Basic .NET code for a Function procedure that receives four integers. The procedure should calculate the average of the four integers, and then return the result (which may contain a decimal place). Name the procedure CalcAverage.

9. Write the Visual Basic .NET code for a Function procedure that receives two numbers that both have a decimal place. The procedure should divide the first number by the second number, and then return the result. Name the procedure CalcQuotient.

discovery ▶ **10.** In this exercise, you experiment with passing variables *by value* and *by reference*.

    a. If necessary, start Visual Studio .NET. Open the Passing Solution (Passing Solution.sln) file, which is contained in the VBNET\Chap07\Passing Solution folder. If necessary, open the designer window.

    b. Open the Code Editor window. Study the application's existing code. Notice that the name variable is passed *by value* to the GetName procedure.

    c. Start the application. Click the Display Name button. When prompted to enter a name, type your name and press Enter. Explain why the uiDisplayButton control's Click event procedure does not display your name in the uiNameLabel control. Click the Exit button to end the application.

    d. Modify the application's code so that it passes the name variable *by reference* to the GetName procedure.

    e. Save the solution, then start the application. Click the Display Name button. When prompted to enter a name, type your name and press Enter. This time, your name appears in the uiNameLabel control. Explain why the uiDisplayButton control's Click event procedure now works correctly.

    f. Click the Exit button to end the application.

    g. Close the Output window, then close the solution.

discovery ▶ **11.** In this exercise, you learn how to specify that one or more arguments are optional in a Call statement.

    a. If necessary, start Visual Studio .NET. Open the Optional Solution (Optional Solution.sln) file, which is contained in the VBNET\Chap07\Optional Solution folder. If necessary, open the designer window.

    b. Open the Code Editor window. Study the application's existing code. Notice that the uiCalcButton's Click event procedure contains two Call statements. The first Call statement passes three variables (sales, bonus, and rate) to the GetBonus procedure. The second Call statement, however, passes only two variables (sales and bonus) to the procedure. (Do not be concerned about the jagged line that appears below the second Call statement.) Notice that the rate variable is omitted from the second Call statement. You indicate that the rate variable is optional in the Call statement by including the keyword Optional before the variable's corresponding parameter in the procedure header. You also assign a default value that the procedure will use for the missing parameter when the procedure is called. In this case, you will assign the number .1 as the default value for the rate variable. (Optional parameters must be listed at the end of the procedure header.)

c. Change the `ByVal bonusRate As Double` in the procedure header to
`Optional ByVal bonusRate As Double = .1`.

d. Save the solution, then start the application. Type the letter A in the Code
text box, then type 1000 in the Sales text box. Click the Calculate button.
When the Rate Entry dialog box appears, type .05 and press Enter. The `Call`
`GetBonus(sales, bonus, rate)` statement calls the GetBonus procedure,
passing it the number 1000, the address of the bonus variable, and the number .05.
The GetBonus procedure stores the number 1000 in the `totalSales` variable. It
also assigns the name `bonusAmount` to the bonus variable, and stores the number
.05 in the `bonusRate` variable. The procedure then multiplies the contents of the
`totalSales` variable (1000) by the contents of the `bonusRate` variable (.05),
and assigns the result (50) to the `bonusAmount` variable. The
`Me.uiBonusLabel.Text = bonus.ToString("C2")` statement then displays
$50.00 in the uiBonusLabel control.

e. Now type the letter B in the Code text box, then type 2000 in the Sales text box.
Click the Calculate button. The `Call GetBonus(sales, bonus)` statement
calls the GetBonus procedure, passing it the number 2000 and the address of the
bonus variable. The GetBonus procedure stores the number 2000 in the
`totalSales` variable, and assigns the name `bonusAmount` to the bonus variable. Because the Call statement did not supply a value for the `bonusRate` variable, the default value (.1) is assigned to the variable. The procedure then multiplies
the contents of the `totalSales` variable (2000) by the contents of the
`bonusRate` variable (.1), and assigns the result (200) to the `bonusAmount` variable. The `Me.uiBonusLabel.Text = bonus.ToString("C2")` statement
then displays $200.00 in the uiBonusLabel control.

f. Click the Exit button to end the application.

g. Close the Output window, then close the solution.

LESSON B
objectives

After completing this lesson, you will be able to:

- Add a list box to a form
- Add items to a list box
- Sort the contents of a list box
- Select a list box item from code
- Determine the selected item in a list box
- Round a number
- Code a list box's SelectedValueChanged event

Using a List Box Control

Completing the Payroll Application's User Interface

Recall that your task in this chapter is to create a payroll application for Jefferson Williams, the payroll manager at Nelson Industries. The application should allow Mr. Williams to enter an employee's name, hours worked, rate of pay, marital status (either "Married" or "Single"), and number of withholding allowances. The application should calculate the employee's weekly gross pay, federal withholding tax (FWT), Social Security and Medicare (FICA) tax, and net pay.

On your computer's hard disk is a partially completed payroll application. You complete the application's user interface in this lesson.

To open the payroll application:

1 Start Microsoft Visual Studio .NET, if necessary.

2 If necessary, close the Start Page window.

3 Open the **Payroll Solution** (Payroll Solution.sln) file, which is contained in the VBNET\Chap07\Payroll Solution folder.

4 Auto-hide the Toolbox, Solution Explorer, and Properties windows, if necessary. Figure 7-7 shows the partially completed user interface for the payroll application.

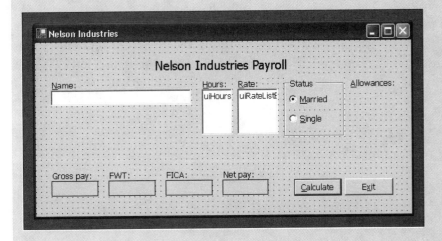

Figure 7-7: Partially completed user interface for the payroll application

The interface contains one text box for the employee's name, and two list boxes for the employee's hours worked and pay rate. It also contains two radio buttons that allow the user to specify the employee's marital status. Missing from the interface is the list box that allows the payroll manager to select the number of withholding allowances.

Adding a List Box to a Form

You learn how to use the MultiSimple and Multi-Extended settings in Discovery Exercise 7 at the end of this lesson.

You can use a **list box control** to display a list of choices from which the user can select zero choices, one choice, or more than one choice. The number of choices the user is allowed to select is controlled by the list box control's **SelectionMode property**. The default value for this property is One, which allows the user to select only one choice at a time in the list box. However, you also can set the property to None, MultiSimple, or MultiExtended. The None setting allows the user to scroll the list box, but not make any selections in it. The MultiSimple and MultiExtended settings allow the user to select more than one choice.

If you have only two options to offer the user, you should use radio buttons instead of a list box.

You can make a list box any size you want. If you have more items than fit into the list box, the control automatically displays scroll bars that you can use to view the complete list of items. The Windows standard for list boxes is to display a minimum of three selections and a maximum of eight selections at a time. In the next set of steps, you add the missing list box control to the Payroll application's user interface.

To add a list box control to the form, then lock the controls and set the TabIndex property:

1   Click the **ListBox tool** in the toolbox, and then drag a list box control to the form. Position the list box control immediately below the Allowances: label.

As you do with a text box, you use a label control to identify a list box. In this case, the Allowances label identifies the contents of the list box located below the label.

2   Set the ListBox1 control's Name property to **uiAllowListBox**. Set its Location property to **488, 72**, and set its Size property to **64, 68**. (Do not be concerned that the list box's name, uiAllowListBox, appears inside the list box. The name will not appear when you start the application.)

Now that the interface is complete, you can lock the controls on the form, and then set the TabIndex property for each control.

3   Right-click the **form**, then click **Lock Controls**.

4   Click **View** on the menu bar, and then click **Tab Order**. Use Figure 7-8 to set each control's TabIndex property to the appropriate value.

The uiAllowListBox, uiHours-ListBox, and uiRateListBox controls on the form are instances of the ListBox class.

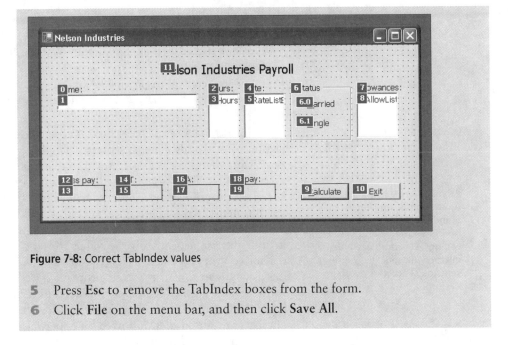

Figure 7-8: Correct TabIndex values

5 Press **Esc** to remove the TabIndex boxes from the form.

6 Click **File** on the menu bar, and then click **Save All**.

Next, you learn how to specify the items to display in a list box.

Adding Items to a List Box

The items in a list box belong to the **Items collection**. A **collection** is simply a group of one or more individual objects treated as one unit. The first item in the Items collection appears as the first item in the list box, the second item appears as the second item in the list box, and so on. Each item in a collection is identified by a unique number called an **index**. The first item in the Items collection—and, therefore, the first item in the list box—has an index of zero; the second item has an index of one, and so on.

You use the Items collection's **Add method** to specify the items you want displayed in a list box control. The syntax of the Add method is *object*.**Items.Add**(*item*), where *object* is the name of the control to which you want the item added, and *item* is the text you want displayed in the control. Figure 7-9 shows examples of using the Add method to display items in a list box.

You also can use the Items collection's Insert method to add an item at a desired position in the list box. The syntax of the Insert method is *object*.Items. Insert(*position*, *item*). For example, the statement Me.uiNameListBox.Items .Insert(0, "Carol") inserts "Carol" as the first name in the uiNameListBox.

Examples	Results
`Me.uiAnimalListBox.Items.Add("Dog")`	displays the string "Dog" in the uiAnimalListBox
`Me.uiAgeListBox.Items.Add(35)`	displays the number 35 in the uiAgeListBox

`For rate = 0 To 5 Step .5`
`    Me.uiRateListBox.Items.Add(rate)`
`Next rate`
	displays the numbers from 0 through 5, in increments of .5, in the uiRateListBox

Figure 7-9: Examples of using the Items collection's Add method

List Box Standards

- A list box should contain a minimum of three selections.
- A list box should display a minimum of three selections and a maximum of eight selections at a time.
- Use a label control to provide keyboard access to the list box. Set the label control's TabIndex property to a value that is one less than the list box's TabIndex value.

As you learned in Chapter 4, ASCII stands for American Standard Code for Information Interchange and is the coding scheme used by microcomputers to represent the characters on your keyboard.

The `Me.uiAnimalListBox.Items.Add("Dog")` statement shown in Figure 7-9 adds the string "Dog" to the uiAnimalListBox. The `Me.uiAgeListBox.Items.Add(35)` statement adds the number 35 to the uiAgeListBox. The `Me.uiRateListBox.Items.Add(rate)` statement in the For...Next loop displays numbers from zero through five, in increments of .5, in the uiRateListBox.

When you use the Add method to add an item to a list box, the position of the item in the list depends on the value stored in the list box's **Sorted property**. If the Sorted property contains its default value, False, the item is added to the end of the list. However, if the Sorted property is set to True, the item is sorted along with the existing items, and then placed in its proper position in the list. Visual Basic .NET sorts the list box items in ascending ASCII order, which means that numbers are sorted first, followed by uppercase letters, and then lowercase letters.

Whether you display the list box items in sorted order, or display them in the order in which they are added to the list box, depends on the application. If several list items are selected much more frequently than other items, you typically leave the list box's Sorted property set to False, and then add the frequently used items first, so that the items appear at the beginning of the list. However, if the list box items are selected fairly equally, you typically set the list box's Sorted property to True, because it is easier to locate items when they appear in a sorted order.

Order of List Box Items

- List box items are either arranged by use, with the most used entries appearing first in the list, or sorted in ascending order.

If a list box's Sorted property is set to True, the items 1, 2, 3, and 10 will appear in the following order in the list box: 1, 10, 2, and 3. This is because items in a list box are treated as strings rather than as numbers, and strings are sorted based on the ASCII value of the leftmost character in the string.

You will use the Items collection's Add method to add the appropriate items to the three list boxes in the payroll application's user interface. Because you want each list box to display its values when the interface first appears on the screen, you will enter the appropriate Add methods in the form's Load event procedure. Recall that the Load event occurs when an application is started and the form is loaded into the computer's internal memory. The computer automatically executes the instructions contained in the Load event procedure when the Load event occurs.

To add items to the list boxes in the payroll application's user interface:

1 Open the Code Editor window. Replace the *<enter your name here>* and *<enter date here>* text with your name and the current date.

Notice that two event procedures have already been coded for you. The uiExitButton's Click event procedure contains the `Me.Close()` statement, which ends the application. The uiNameTextBox's Enter event procedure contains the `Me.uiNameTextBox.SelectAll()` statement, which selects the existing text in the text box when the user tabs to the control, and when the Focus method is used in code to send the focus to the control.

2 Click the **Class Name** list arrow, and then click (**PayrollForm Events**) in the list. Click the **Method Name** list arrow, and then click **Load** the list. The code template for the Payroll form's Load event procedure appears in the Code Editor window.

3 Type '**fill the list boxes with data, then select a default item in each list** and press **Enter** twice.

4 Type the following three variable declaration statements. Press **Enter** twice after typing the last statement.

> **dim hours as integer**
> **dim allow as integer**
> **dim rate as double**

The payroll manager at Nelson Industries wants the uiHoursListBox to display numbers from one through 50, because that is the minimum and maximum number of hours an employee can work. The easiest way to display those values is to use a For...Next loop.

5 Type the comment and For...Next loop shown in Figure 7-10, then position the insertion point as shown in the figure.

enter this comment and these lines of code

position the insertion point here

```
Private Sub PayrollForm_Load(ByVal sender As Object, ByVal e As System.EventArgs) Handle
    'fill the list boxes with data, then select a default item in each list

    Dim hours As Integer
    Dim allow As Integer
    Dim rate As Double

    'display hours
    For hours = 1 To 50
        Me.uiHoursListBox.Items.Add(hours)
    Next hours

End Sub
```

Figure 7-10: Code for displaying values in the uiHoursListBox

The payroll manager wants the uiRateListBox to display pay rates from 6.00 through 12.00, in increments of .50. You will format the rates so that each contains two decimal places.

6 Type the comment and For...Next loop shown in Figure 7-11, then position the insertion point as shown in the figure.

enter this comment and these lines of code

position the insertion point here

```
Private Sub PayrollForm_Load(ByVal sender As Object, ByVal e As System.EventArgs) Handle
    'fill the list boxes with data, then select a default item in each list

    Dim hours As Integer
    Dim allow As Integer
    Dim rate As Double

    'display hours
    For hours = 1 To 50
        Me.uiHoursListBox.Items.Add(hours)
    Next hours
    'display pay rates
    For rate = 6 To 12 Step 0.5
        Me.uiRateListBox.Items.Add(rate.ToString("N2"))
    Next rate

End Sub
```

Figure 7-11: Code for displaying values in the uiRateListBox

Next, you will display numbers from 0 through 10 in the uiAllowListBox.

7 Type the comment and For...Next loop shown in Figure 7-12, then position the insertion point as shown in the figure.

```
Private Sub PayrollForm_Load(ByVal sender As Object, ByVal e As System.EventArgs) Handle
    'fill the list boxes with data, then select a default item in each list

    Dim hours As Integer
    Dim allow As Integer
    Dim rate As Double

    'display hours
    For hours = 1 To 50
        Me.uiHoursListBox.Items.Add(hours)
    Next hours
    'display pay rates
    For rate = 6 To 12 Step 0.5
        Me.uiRateListBox.Items.Add(rate.ToString("N2"))
    Next rate
    'display withholding allowances
    For allow = 0 To 10
        Me.uiAllowListBox.Items.Add(allow)
    Next allow
    |
End Sub
```

enter this comment and
these lines of code

position the insertion
point here

Figure 7-12: Code for displaying values in the uiAllowListBox

Now test the code in the Load event procedure.

8 Save the solution, and then start the application. The interface appears on the screen, as shown in Figure 7-13.

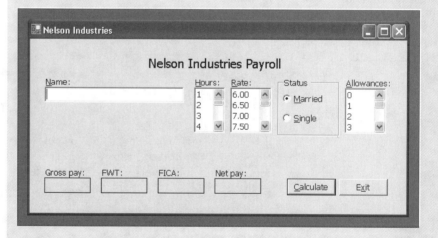

Figure 7-13: List boxes shown in the interface

9 Scroll down each of the list boxes to verify that each contains the appropriate values.

10 Scroll to the top of the Rate list box, then click **6.00** in the list. Notice that when you select an item in a list box, the item appears highlighted in the list. Additionally, the item's value (in this case, the number 6.00) is stored in the uiRateListBox control's SelectedItem property, and the item's index (in this case, the number 0) is stored in the uiRateListBox control's SelectedIndex property. You learn more about the SelectedItem and SelectedIndex properties in the next section.

11 Click the **Exit** button. When you return to the Code Editor window, close the Output window.

If a list box allows the user to select only one item at a time, it is customary in Windows applications to have one of the items in the list box selected when the interface appears. You can accomplish this task using either a list box's SelectedItem property or its SelectedIndex property. (If a list box allows the user to select more than one item at a time, it is customary to have no items selected in the list when the interface appears.)

The SelectedItem and SelectedIndex Properties

A list box's **SelectedItem property** and its **SelectedIndex property** can be used both to determine the item selected in the list box and to select a list box item from code. Figure 7-14 shows examples of using these properties.

SelectedItem property examples	Results
Example 1 `numAllow = Convert.ToInt32(Me.uiAllowListBox.SelectedItem)`	assigns the contents of the uiAllowListBox control's SelectedItem property to the numAllow variable
Example 2 `If Convert.ToInt32(Me.uiHoursListBox.SelectedItem) > 40 Then`	compares the contents of the uiHoursListBox control's SelectedItem property with the number 40 to determine whether the selected item's value is greater than 40
Example 3 `Me.uiRateListBox.SelectedItem = 7.00`	selects the number 7.00 in the uiRateListBox control
SelectedIndex property examples	Results
Example 4 `item = Me.uiAllowListBox.SelectedIndex`	assigns the contents of the uiAllowListBox control's SelectedIndex property to the item variable
Example 5 `If Me.uiHoursListBox.SelectedIndex = 0 Then`	compares the contents of the uiHoursListBox control's SelectedIndex property with the number 0 to determine whether the first item is selected in the control
Example 6 `Me.uiRateListBox.SelectedIndex = 2`	selects the third item (7.00) in the uiRateListBox control

Figure 7-14: Examples of the SelectedItem and SelectedIndex properties

The statement shown in Example 1 in Figure 7-14 assigns the contents of the uiAllowListBox control's SelectedItem property to the numAllow variable. If the number 5 is selected in the control, the statement assigns the number 5 to the variable.

GUI

Design Tips

Default List Box Item

- If a list box allows the user to make only one selection at a time, then a default item should be selected in the list box when the interface first appears. The default item should be either the most used selection or the first selection in the list. However, if a list box allows more than one selection at a time, you do not select a default item.

In Example 2, the If clause compares the contents of the uiHoursListBox control's SelectedItem property with the number 40 to determine whether the employee worked more than 40 hours. You can use the `Me.uiRateListBox.SelectedItem = 7.00` statement shown in Example 3 to select the third item (in this case, the number 7.00) in the uiRateListBox.

The statement shown in Example 4 in Figure 7-14 assigns the contents of the uiAllowListBox control's SelectedIndex property to the `item` variable. If the second item is selected in the control, the statement assigns the number 1 to the variable. In Example 5, the If clause compares the contents of the uiHoursListBox control's SelectedIndex property with the number 0 to determine whether the first item is selected in the control. You can use the `Me.uiRateListBox.SelectedIndex = 2` statement shown in Example 6 to select the third item (in this case, the number 7.00) in the uiRateListBox.

As mentioned earlier, if a list box allows the user to select only one item at a time, it is customary in Windows applications to have an item in the list box selected when the interface appears. The selected item, called the **default list box item**, should be either the most used selection or, if all of the selections are used fairly equally, the first selection in the list. In the payroll application, you will select the number 40 in the Hours list box, because most of the employees at Nelson Industries work 40 hours. In the Rate and Allowances list boxes, you will select the first item in the list, because the selections in these list boxes are used fairly equally.

To select a default item in each list box, then test the Load event procedure:

1 The insertion point should be positioned below the `Next allow` clause in the PayrollForm's Load event procedure. Type **'select a default item in each list box** and press **Enter**.

First, use the SelectedItem property to select the number 40 in the Hours list box.

2 Type **me.uihourslistbox.selecteditem = 40** and press **Enter**.

Next, use the SelectedIndex property to select the first item in the Rate and Allowances list boxes.

3 Type the two additional instructions shown in Figure 7-15, which shows the completed Load event procedure.

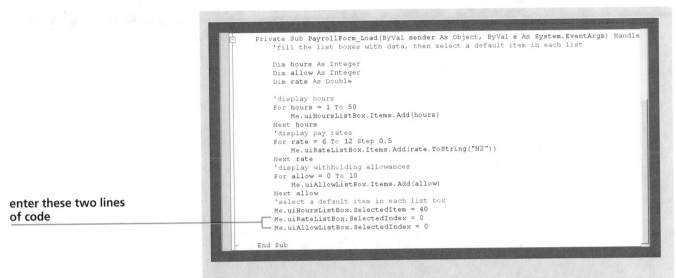

```
Private Sub PayrollForm_Load(ByVal sender As Object, ByVal e As System.EventArgs) Handle
    'fill the list boxes with data, then select a default item in each list

    Dim hours As Integer
    Dim allow As Integer
    Dim rate As Double

    'display hours
    For hours = 1 To 50
        Me.uiHoursListBox.Items.Add(hours)
    Next hours
    'display pay rates
    For rate = 6 To 12 Step 0.5
        Me.uiRateListBox.Items.Add(rate.ToString("N2"))
    Next rate
    'display withholding allowances
    For allow = 0 To 10
        Me.uiAllowListBox.Items.Add(allow)
    Next allow
    'select a default item in each list box
    Me.uiHoursListBox.SelectedItem = 40
    Me.uiRateListBox.SelectedIndex = 0
    Me.uiAllowListBox.SelectedIndex = 0

End Sub
```

enter these two lines of code

Figure 7-15: Completed Load event procedure

Now test the Load event procedure to verify that it is working correctly.

4   Save the solution, then start the application. A default item is selected in each list box, as shown in Figure 7-16.

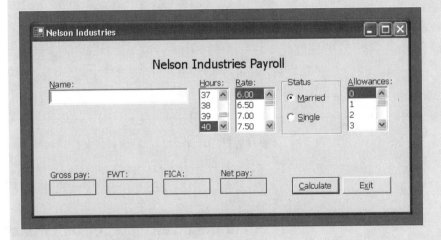

Figure 7-16: Default list box items selected in the interface

5   Click the **Exit** button to end the application. When you return to the Code Editor window, close the Output window.

In addition to the uiExitButton's Click event procedure, the uiNameTextBox's Enter event procedure, and the PayrollForm's Load event procedure, several other procedures in the payroll application also need to be coded. These procedures are shaded in the TOE chart shown in Figure 7-17.

Task	Object	Event
1. Calculate gross pay 2. Calculate federal withholding tax (FWT) 3. Calculate Social Security and Medicare (FICA) tax 4. Calculate net pay 5. Display gross pay, FWT, FICA, and net pay in uiGrossLabel, uiFwtLabel, uiFicaLabel, and uiNetLabel controls	uiCalculateButton	Click
End the application	uiExitButton	Click
Display the gross pay, FWT, FICA, and net pay (from uiCalculateButton)	uiGrossLabel, uiFwtLabel, uiFicaLabel, uiNetLabel	None
Clear the contents of the uiGrossLabel, uiFwtLabel, uiFicaLabel, and uiNetLabel controls	uiNameTextBox	TextChanged
	uiHoursListBox, uiRateListBox, uiAllowListBox	SelectedValueChanged
	uiMarriedRadioButton, uiSingleRadioButton	Click
Highlight (select) the existing text	uiNameTextBox	Enter
Get and display the name, hours worked, pay rate, marital status, and number of withholding allowances	uiNameTextBox, uiHoursListBox, uiRateListBox, uiMarriedRadioButton, uiSingleRadioButton, uiAllowListBox	None
1. Fill uiHoursListBox, uiRateListBox, and uiAllowListBox controls with data 2. Select a default item in each list box	PayrollForm	Load

Figure 7-17: TOE chart for the payroll application

First, you will code the uiCalculateButton Click event procedure.

Coding the uiCalculateButton Click Event Procedure

Figure 7-18 shows the pseudocode for the uiCalculateButton control's Click event procedure.

```
uiCalculateButton
1.  declare variables
2.  assign the item selected in the uiHoursListBox to a variable
3.  assign the item selected in the uiRateListBox to a variable
4.  if the hours worked are less than or equal to 40
        calculate gross pay = hours worked * pay rate
    else
        calculate gross pay = 40 * pay rate + (hours worked - 40) * pay rate * 1.5
    end if
5.  call a function to calculate the FWT
6.  calculate the FICA tax = gross pay * 7.65%
7.  round the gross pay, FWT, and FICA tax to two decimal places
8.  calculate the net pay = gross pay - FWT - FICA
9.  display the gross pay, FWT, FICA, and net pay in the uiGrossLabel, uiFwtLabel, uiFicaLabel,
    and uiNetLabel controls
```

Figure 7-18: Pseudocode for the uiCalculateButton control's Click event procedure

To begin coding the uiCalculateButton control's Click event procedure:

1 Open the code template for the uiCalculateButton's Click event procedure. Type **'calculates and displays gross pay, taxes, and net pay** and press **Enter** twice.

Step 1 in the pseudocode is to declare the variables. The procedure will use one Integer variable to store the number of hours worked, and five Double variables to store the pay rate, gross pay, FWT, FICA tax, and net pay amounts.

2 Type the following variable declaration statements. Press **Enter** twice after typing the last statement.

> **dim hours as integer**
> **dim rate as double**
> **dim gross as double**
> **dim fedWithTax as double**
> **dim fica as double**
> **dim net as double**

Step 2 in the pseudocode is to assign to a variable the item that is selected in the uiHoursListBox, and Step 3 is to assign to a variable the item that is selected in the uiRateListBox. Recall that the item selected in a list box is stored in the list box's SelectedItem property.

3 Type **'assign selected items to variables** and press **Enter**.

4 Type **hours = convert.toint32(me.uihourslistbox.selecteditem)** and press **Enter**, then type **rate = convert.todouble(me.uiratelistbox.selecteditem)** and press **Enter** twice.

Step 4 in the pseudocode is a selection structure that first compares the number of hours worked to the number 40, and then calculates the gross pay based on the result.

5 Type **'calculate gross pay** and press **Enter**, then type **if hours <= 40 then** and press **Enter**.

If the number of hours worked is less than or equal to 40, then the procedure should calculate the gross pay by multiplying the number of hours worked by the pay rate.

6 Type **gross = hours * rate** and press **Enter**.

If, on the other hand, the number of hours worked is greater than 40, then the employee is entitled to his or her regular pay rate for the hours worked up to and including 40, and then time and one-half for the hours worked over 40.

7 Type **else** and press **Enter**.

8 Type the additional line of code shown in Figure 7-19, then position the insertion point as shown in the figure.

enter this line of code

position the insertion point here

```
Private Sub uiCalculateButton_Click(ByVal sender As Object, ByVal e As System.EventArgs)
    'calculates and displays gross pay, taxes, and net pay

    Dim hours As Integer
    Dim rate As Double
    Dim gross As Double
    Dim fedWithTax As Double
    Dim fica As Double
    Dim net As Double

    'assign selected items to variables
    hours = Convert.ToInt32(Me.uiHoursListBox.SelectedItem)
    rate = Convert.ToDouble(Me.uiRateListBox.SelectedItem)

    'calculate gross pay
    If hours <= 40 Then
        gross = hours * rate
    Else
        gross = 40 * rate + (hours - 40) * rate * 1.5
    End If

End Sub
```

Figure 7-19: Current status of the uiCalculateButton Click event procedure

9 Save the solution.

Step 5 in the pseudocode shown in Figure 7-18 is to call a function to calculate the FWT (federal withholding tax). Before entering the appropriate instruction, you will create the function, which you will name GetFwtTax.

Coding the GetFwtTax Function

The amount of federal withholding tax (FWT) to deduct from an employee's weekly gross pay is based on the employee's filing status—either single (including head of household) or married—and his or her weekly taxable wages. You calculate the weekly taxable wages by first multiplying the number of withholding allowances by $55.77 (the value of one withholding allowance), and then subtracting the result from the weekly gross pay. For example, if your weekly gross pay is $400 and you have two withholding allowances, your weekly taxable wages are $288.46 (400 minus 111.54, which is the product of 2 times 55.77). You use the weekly taxable wages, along with the filing status and the weekly Federal Withholding Tax tables, to determine the amount of tax to withhold. Figure 7-20 shows the weekly FWT tables.

FWT Tables – Weekly Payroll Period

Single person (including head of household)

If the taxable wages are:		The amount of income tax to withhold is		
Over	**But not over**	**Base amount**	**Percentage**	**Of excess over**
	$ 51	0		
$ 51	$ 552	0	15%	$ 51
$ 552	$1,196	$ 75.15 plus	28%	$ 552
$1,196	$2,662	$ 255.47 plus	31%	$1,196
$2,662	$5,750	$ 709.93 plus	36%	$2,662
$5,750		$1,821.61 plus	39.6%	$5,750

Married person

If the taxable wages are:		The amount of income tax to withhold is		
Over	**But not over**	**Base amount**	**Percentage**	**Of excess over**
	$ 124	0		
$ 124	$ 960	0	15%	$ 124
$ 960	$2,023	$ 125.40 plus	28%	$ 960
$2,023	$3,292	$ 423.04 plus	31%	$2,023
$3,292	$5,809	$ 816.43 plus	36%	$3,292
$5,809		$1,722.55 plus	39.6%	$5,809

Figure 7-20: Weekly FWT tables

Notice that both tables shown in Figure 7-20 contain five columns of information. The first two columns list various ranges, also called brackets, of taxable wage amounts. The first column—the Over column—lists the amount that a taxable wage in that range must be over, and the second column—the But not over column—lists the maximum amount included in the range. The remaining three columns (Base amount, Percentage, and Of excess over) tell you how to calculate the tax for each range. For example, assume that you are married and your weekly taxable wages are $288.46. Before you can calculate the amount of your tax, you need to locate your taxable wages in the first two columns of the Married table. In this case, your taxable wages fall within the $124 through $960 range. After locating the range that contains your taxable wages, you then use the remaining three columns in the table to calculate your tax. According to the table, taxable wages in the $124 through $960 bracket have a tax of 15% of the amount over $124; therefore, your tax is $24.67, as shown in Figure 7-21.

Taxable wages	$ 288.46	
Of excess over	−124.00	
	164.46	
Percentage	* .15	
	24.67	
Base amount	+ 0.00	
Tax	$ 24.67	

Figure 7-21: FWT calculation for a married taxpayer with taxable wages of $288.46

As Figure 7-21 indicates, you calculate the tax first by subtracting 124 (the amount shown in the Of excess over column) from your taxable wages of 288.46, giving 164.46. You then multiply 164.46 by 15% (the amount shown in the Percentage column), giving 24.67. You add the amount shown in the Base amount column—in this case, 0—to that result, giving $24.67 as your tax.

Now assume that your taxable wages are $600 per week and you are single. Figure 7-22 shows how the correct tax amount of $88.59 is calculated.

Taxable wages	$ 600.00	
Of excess over	−552.00	
	48.00	
Percentage	* .28	
	13.44	
Base amount	+ 75.15	
Tax	$ 88.59	

Figure 7-22: FWT calculation for a single taxpayer with taxable wages of $600

To calculate the federal withholding tax, the GetFwtTax function needs to know the employee's gross pay amount, as well as his or her marital status and number of withholding allowances. The function will get the gross pay amount from the uiCalculateButton's Click event procedure, which will pass the value stored in its gross variable when it calls the function. The function can use the Checked properties of the Married and Single radio buttons to determine the marital status, and the uiAllowListBox control's SelectedItem property to determine the number of withholding allowances. After the GetFwtTax function calculates the appropriate federal withholding tax, it will return the tax amount to the uiCalculateButton's Click event procedure. Figure 7-23 shows the pseudocode for the GetFwtTax function.

GetFwtTax function
1. declare variables
2. assign the item selected in the uiAllowListBox to a variable
3. calculate the taxable wages = gross pay – number of withholding allowances * 55.77
4. if the uiSingleRadioButton is selected
    taxable wages value:
        <= 51
            tax = 0
        <= 552
            calculate tax = 0.15 * (taxable wages - 51)
        <= 1196
            calculate tax = 75.15 + 0.28 * (taxable wages - 552)
        <= 2662
            calculate tax = 255.47 + 0.31 * (taxable wages - 1196)
        <= 5750
            calculate tax = 709.93 + .36 * (taxable wages - 2662)
        other
            calculate tax = 1821.61 + 0.396 * (taxable wages - 5750)
    else
    taxable wages value:
        <= 124
            tax = 0
        <= 960
            calculate tax = 0.15 * (taxable wages - 124)
        <= 2023
            calculate tax = 125.4 + 0.28 * (taxable wages - 960)
        <= 3292
            calculate tax = 423.04 + 0.31 * (taxable wages - 2023)
        <= 5809
            calculate tax = 816.43 + .36 * (taxable wages - 3292)
        other
            calculate tax = 1722.55 + 0.396 * (taxable wages - 5809)
    end if
5. return tax

Figure 7-23: Pseudocode for the GetFwtTax function

To code the GetFwtTax function:

1   Insert two blank lines above the `End Class` statement, which appears as the last line in the Code Editor window.

Recall that the uiCalculateButton's Click event procedure will pass to the GetFwtTax function the value stored in the `gross` variable. In this case, you are passing the variable's value rather than its address because you do not want the GetFwtTax function to change the contents of the variable. You will store the value passed to the function in a Double variable named `weekPay`.

2   In the blank line immediately above the `End Class` statement, type **private function GetFwtTax(byval weekPay as double) as double** and press **Enter**. Notice that the Code Editor automatically enters the procedure footer (`End Function`) for you.

3   Type '**calculates and returns the federal withholding tax** and press **Enter** twice.

Step 1 in the pseudocode shown in Figure 7-23 is to declare the variables. In addition to the `weekPay` variable, which is declared in the procedure header, the GetFwtTax function will use an Integer variable named `allowances` to store the number of withholding allowances. The procedure also will use a Double variable named `taxWages` to store the taxable wages amount, and a Double variable named `tax` to store the federal withholding tax amount.

4 Type the following variable declaration statements. Press **Enter** twice after typing the last statement.

> **dim allowances as integer**
> **dim taxWages as double**
> **dim tax as double**

Step 2 in the pseudocode is to assign the item that is selected in the uiAllowListBox to a variable. The selected item represents the number of the employee's withholding allowances.

5 Type **'assign number of withholding allowances to a variable** and press **Enter**, then type **allowances = convert.toint32(me.uiallowlistbox. selecteditem)** and press **Enter** twice.

Now calculate the taxable wages by multiplying the number of withholding allowances by $55.77, and then subtracting the result from the gross pay amount.

6 Type **'calculate taxable wages** and press **Enter**, then type **taxwages = weekpay - allowances * 55.77** and press **Enter** twice.

Next, determine whether the uiSingleRadioButton is selected.

7 Type **'determine marital status, then calculate FWT** and press **Enter**, then type **if me.uisingleradiobutton.checked = true then** and press **Enter**. Notice that the Code Editor enters the End If clause for you.

If the Single radio button is selected, the procedure should calculate the federal withholding tax using the information from the Single tax table.

8 Type the Select Case statement shown in Figure 7-24, then position the insertion point as shown in the figure.

enter the Select Case statement

position the insertion point here

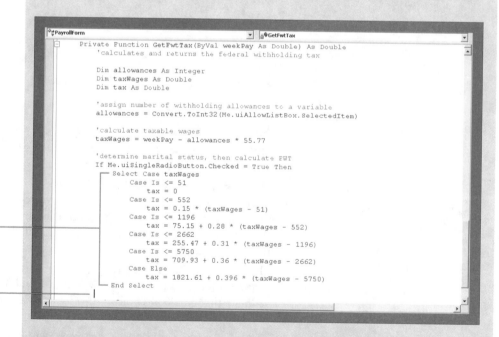

```
PayrollForm                                          GetFwtTax
     Private Function GetFwtTax(ByVal weekPay As Double) As Double
         'calculates and returns the federal withholding tax

         Dim allowances As Integer
         Dim taxWages As Double
         Dim tax As Double

         'assign number of withholding allowances to a variable
         allowances = Convert.ToInt32(Me.uiAllowListBox.SelectedItem)

         'calculate taxable wages
         taxWages = weekPay - allowances * 55.77

         'determine marital status, then calculate FWT
         If Me.uiSingleRadioButton.Checked = True Then
             Select Case taxWages
                 Case Is <= 51
                     tax = 0
                 Case Is <= 552
                     tax = 0.15 * (taxWages - 51)
                 Case Is <= 1196
                     tax = 75.15 + 0.28 * (taxWages - 552)
                 Case Is <= 2662
                     tax = 255.47 + 0.31 * (taxWages - 1196)
                 Case Is <= 5750
                     tax = 709.93 + 0.36 * (taxWages - 2662)
                 Case Else
                     tax = 1821.61 + 0.396 * (taxWages - 5750)
             End Select
```

Figure 7-24: FWT calculations for taxpayers whose marital status is Single

If the Single radio button is not selected, it means that the Married radio button is selected. In that case, the procedure should calculate the federal withholding tax using the information from the Married tax table.

9 Type **else** and press **Tab**, then type **'uiMarriedRadioButton is selected** and press **Enter**.

10 Type the Select Case statement shown in Figure 7-25, then position the insertion point as shown in the figure.

enter the Select Case statement

position the insertion point here

```
Else      'uiMarriedRadioButton is selected
   Select Case taxWages
      Case Is <= 124
         tax = 0
      Case Is <= 960
         tax = 0.15 * (taxWages - 124)
      Case Is <= 2023
         tax = 125.4 + 0.28 * (taxWages - 960)
      Case Is <= 3292
         tax = 423.04 + 0.31 * (taxWages - 2023)
      Case Is <= 5809
         tax = 816.43 + 0.36 * (taxWages - 3292)
      Case Else
         tax = 1722.55 + 0.396 * (taxWages - 5809)
   End Select
End If

   |
      End Function
End Class
```

Figure 7-25: FWT calculations for taxpayers whose marital status is Married

The last step in the pseudocode shown in Figure 7-23 is to return the federal withholding tax amount, which is stored in the **tax** variable, to the statement that invoked the function.

11 Type **'return FWT** and press **Enter**, then type **return tax**. Figure 7-26 shows the completed GetFwtTax function.

```
Private Function GetFwtTax(ByVal weekPay As Double) As Double
    'calculates and returns the federal withholding tax

    Dim allowances As Integer
    Dim taxWages As Double
    Dim tax As Double

    'assign number of withholding allowances to a variable
    allowances = Convert.ToInt32(Me.uiAllowListBox.SelectedItem)

    'calculate taxable wages
    taxWages = weekPay - allowances * 55.77

    'determine marital status, then calculate FWT
    If Me.uiSingleRadioButton.Checked = True Then
        Select Case taxWages
            Case Is <= 51
                tax = 0
            Case Is <= 552
                tax = 0.15 * (taxWages - 51)
            Case Is <= 1196
                tax = 75.15 + 0.28 * (taxWages - 552)
            Case Is <= 2662
                tax = 255.47 + 0.31 * (taxWages - 1196)
            Case Is <= 5750
                tax = 709.93 + 0.36 * (taxWages - 2662)
            Case Else
                tax = 1821.61 + 0.396 * (taxWages - 5750)
        End Select
    Else     'uiMarriedRadioButton is selected
        Select Case taxWages
            Case Is <= 124
                tax = 0
            Case Is <= 960
                tax = 0.15 * (taxWages - 124)
            Case Is <= 2023
                tax = 125.4 + 0.28 * (taxWages - 960)
            Case Is <= 3292
                tax = 423.04 + 0.31 * (taxWages - 2023)
            Case Is <= 5809
                tax = 816.43 + 0.36 * (taxWages - 3292)
            Case Else
                tax = 1722.55 + 0.396 * (taxWages - 5809)
        End Select
    End If

    'return FWT
    Return tax
End Function
```

Figure 7-26: Completed GetFwtTax function

Recall that you still need to complete the uiCalculateButton's Click event procedure.

Completing the uiCalculateButton's Click Event Procedure

Now that you have created the GetFwtTax function, you can call the function from the uiCalculateButton's Click event procedure. Calling the GetFwtTax function is Step 5 in the event procedure's pseudocode (shown earlier in Figure 7-18).

To complete the uiCalculateButton's Click event procedure, then test the procedure:

1   Position the insertion point in the blank line above the End Sub statement in the uiCalculateButton's Click event procedure. If necessary, press **Tab** twice to align the insertion point with the letter E in the End If statement.

2   Type **'calculate FWT** and press **Enter**.

Recall that the uiCalculateButton's Click event procedure needs to pass the value stored in its gross variable to the GetFwtTax function. The procedure should store the value returned by the function in the fedWithTax variable.

3   Type **fedwithtax = getfwttax(gross)** and press **Enter** twice.

Step 6 in the pseudocode for the uiCalculateButton's Click event procedure is to calculate the FICA tax by multiplying the gross pay amount by 7.65%.

4   Type **'calculate FICA tax** and press **Enter**, then type **fica = gross * .0765** and press **Enter** twice.

Step 7 in the pseudocode is to round the gross pay, FWT, and FICA tax amounts to two decimal places. You can use Visual Basic .NET's **Math.Round function** to return a number rounded to a specific number of decimal places. The syntax of the Math.Round function is **Math.Round(**value[, digits]**)**, where value is a numeric expression, and digits, which is optional, is an integer indicating how many places to the right of the decimal are included in the rounding. For example, Math.Round(3.235, 2) returns the number 3.24, but Math.Round(3.234, 2) returns the number 3.23. Notice that the Math.Round function rounds a number up only if the number to its right is 5 or greater; otherwise the Math.Round function truncates the excess digits. If the digits argument is omitted, the Math.Round function returns an integer.

5   Type **'round gross pay, FWT, and FICA tax** and press **Enter**.

6   Type the following three assignment statements. Press **Enter** twice after typing the last statement.

```
gross = math.round(gross, 2)
fedwithtax = math.round(fedwithtax, 2)
fica = math.round(fica, 2)
```

Step 8 in the pseudocode is to calculate the net pay by subtracting the FWT and FICA amounts from the gross pay amount.

7   Type **'calculate net pay** and press **Enter**, then type **net = gross - fedwithtax - fica** and press **Enter** twice.

The last step in the pseudocode for the uiCalculateButton's Click event procedure is to display the gross pay, FWT, FICA, and net pay in the appropriate label controls in the interface.

8   Type the additional comment and lines of code shaded in Figure 7-27, which shows the completed uiCalculateButton Click event procedure.

```
Private Sub uiCalculateButton_Click(ByVal sender As Object, ByVal e As
  System.EventArgs) Handles uiCalculateButton.Click
        'calculates and displays gross pay, taxes, and net pay

      Dim hours As Integer
      Dim rate As Double
      Dim gross As Double
      Dim fedWithTax As Double
      Dim fica As Double
      Dim net As Double

      'assign selected items to variables
      hours = Convert.ToInt32(Me.uiHoursListBox.SelectedItem)
      rate = Convert.ToDouble(Me.uiRateListBox.SelectedItem)

      'calculate gross pay
      If hours <= 40 Then
          gross = hours * rate
      Else
          gross = 40 * rate + (hours - 40) * rate * 1.5
      End If

      'calculate FWT
      fedWithTax = GetFwtTax(gross)

      'calculate FICA tax
      fica = gross * 0.0765

      'round gross pay, FWT, and FICA tax
      gross = Math.Round(gross, 2)
      fedWithTax = Math.Round(fedWithTax, 2)
      fica = Math.Round(fica, 2)

      'calculate net pay
      net = gross - fedWithTax - fica

      'display calculated amounts
      Me.uiGrossLabel.Text = gross.ToString("C2")
      Me.uiFwtLabel.Text = fedWithTax.ToString("C2")
      Me.uiFicaLabel.Text = fica.ToString("C2")
      Me.uiNetLabel.Text = net.ToString("C2")

End Sub
```

enter this comment and these lines of code

Figure 7-27: Completed uiCalculateButton Click event procedure

Now test the uiCalculateButton's Click event procedure and the GetFwtTax function to verify that both are working correctly.

9 Save the solution, then start the application.

Calculate the weekly gross pay, taxes, and net pay for Karen Douglas. Last week, Karen worked 40 hours. She earns $10 per hour, and her marital status is Married. She claims two withholding allowances.

10 Type **Karen Douglas** in the Name text box. Click **10.00** in the Rate list box, then click **2** in the Allowances list box. Click the **Calculate** button. The application calculates and displays Karen's gross pay, FWT, FICA, and net pay amounts, as shown in Figure 7-28.

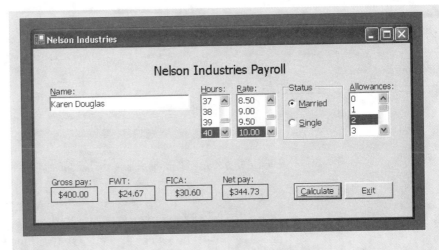

Figure 7-28: Payroll calculations displayed in the interface

11 Click the **Exit** button to end the application. When you return to the Code Editor window, close the Output window.

When the user changes the value entered in the uiNameTextBox, or when he or she selects a different item in the uiHoursListBox, uiRateListBox, or uiAllowListBox, the payroll application should clear the contents of the uiGrossLabel, uiFwtLabel, uiFicaLabel, and uiNetLabel controls in the interface. The contents of those label controls also should be cleared when the user selects a different radio button in the interface.

Clearing the Contents of the Label Controls

According to the payroll application's TOE chart (shown earlier in Figure 7-17), the contents of the uiGrossLabel, uiFwtLabel, uiFicaLabel, and uiNetLabel controls should be cleared when the uiNameTextBox's TextChanged event occurs, or when either the uiMarriedRadioButton's Click event or the uiSingleRadioButton's Click event occurs. The label controls also should be cleared when the SelectedValueChanged event occurs for one of the list boxes in the interface. A list box's **SelectedValueChanged event** occurs each time a different value is selected in the list box. (A list box's **SelectedIndexChanged event** also occurs each time a different item is selected in a list box.)

To clear the appropriate label controls in the interface, then test the application:

1 Open the code template for the uiNameTextBox's TextChanged event procedure.

2 Change the name of the procedure from `uiNameTextBox_TextChanged` to **ClearLabels**.

3 Change the Handles portion of the ClearLabels procedure header as shown in Figure 7-29, then enter the comment and four assignment statements shown in the figure.

change the Handles
portion

enter this comment and
assignment statements

```
Private Sub ClearLabels(ByVal sender As Object, ByVal e As System.EventArgs) _
    Handles uiNameTextBox.TextChanged, uiHoursListBox.SelectedValueChanged, _
    uiRateListBox.SelectedValueChanged, uiAllowListBox.SelectedValueChanged, _
    uiMarriedRadioButton.Click, uiSingleRadioButton.Click
    'clears the gross, taxes, and net

    Me.uiGrossLabel.Text = ""
    Me.uiFwtLabel.Text = ""
    Me.uiFicaLabel.Text = ""
    Me.uiNetLabel.Text = ""
End Sub
```

Figure 7-29: Completed ClearLabels procedure

Now test the ClearLabels procedure to verify that it is working correctly.

4   Save the solution, then start the application.

5   Type **Helen Stone** in the Name text box, then click the **Calculate** button.

6   Change the name in the Name text box to **Helen Stoner**. The **ClearLabels** procedure clears the gross pay, FWT, FICA, and net pay amounts from the label controls.

7   Click the **Calculate** button, then click the number 30 in the Hours list box. The ClearLabels procedure clears the gross pay, FWT, FICA, and net pay amounts from the label controls.

8   Click the **Calculate** button. On your own, verify that the gross pay, FWT, FICA, and net pay amounts are cleared from the label controls when you select a different pay rate, marital status, and number of withholding allowances.

9   Click the **Exit** button to end the application. When you return to the Code Editor window, close the Output window, then close the Code Editor window.

10   Click **File** on the menu bar, and then click **Close Solution** to close the solution.

You now have completed Lesson B. In Lesson C, you add to the payroll application a copyright screen that is similar to the one you created in Chapter 1. For now, you can either take a break or complete the end-of-lesson questions and exercises before moving on to the next lesson.

SUMMARY

To add a list box control to a form:

■   Use the ListBox tool in the toolbox.

To specify whether the user can select zero choices, one choice, or more than one choice in a list box:

■   Set the list box's SelectionMode property to None, One, MultiSimple, or MultiExtended.

To add items to a list box:

■   Use the Items collection's Add method. The syntax of the method is
object.**Items.Add**(*item*), where *object* is the name of the control to which you want the item added, and *item* is the text you want displayed in the control.

To automatically sort the items in a list box:

■ Set the list box's Sorted property to True.

To determine the item selected in a list box, or to select a list box item from code:

■ Set either the list box's SelectedItem property or its SelectedIndex property.

To round a number to a specific number of decimal places:

■ Use the Math.Round function. The function's syntax is **Math.Round**(*value*[, *digits*]), where *value* is a numeric expression, and *digits*, which is optional, is an integer indicating how many places to the right of the decimal are included in the rounding. If the *digits* argument is omitted, the Math.Round function returns an integer.

To process code when a different value is selected in a list box:

■ Enter the code in either the list box's SelectedValueChanged event procedure or its SelectedIndexChanged event procedure.

QUESTIONS

1. You use the _____ method to include items in a list box control.
   a. Add
   b. AddList
   c. Item
   d. ItemAdd
   e. ListAdd

2. You use the _____ property to specify whether the user can select zero or more choices from a list box.
   a. Choices
   b. Number
   c. Selection
   d. SelectionMode
   e. SelectionNumber

3. The items in a list box belong to the _____ collection.
   a. Items
   b. List
   c. ListBox
   d. Values
   e. None of the above.

4. The _____ property stores the index of the item that is selected in a list box.
   a. Index
   b. SelectedIndex
   c. SelectedItem
   d. Selection
   e. SelectionIndex

5. When you select an item in a list box, the item is stored in the list box's
   _____ property.
   a. Item
   b. SelectedItem
   c. Selection
   d. SelectionItem
   e. SelectionList

6. Which of the following adds the word DESK to a list box named uiOfficeListBox?
   a. `Me.uiOfficeListBox.Add("DESK")`
   b. `Me.uiOfficeListBox.AddItems("DESK")`
   c. `Me.uiOfficeListBox.Item.Add("DESK")`
   d. `Me.uiOfficeListBox.ItemAdd("DESK")`
   e. None of the above.

7. The second item in a list box has an index of _____.
   a. 1
   b. 2
   c. 3

8. Which of the following selects the number 3, which is the first item in a list box named uiTermListBox?
   a. `Me.uiTermListBox.SelectedIndex = 0`
   b. `Me.uiTermListBox.SelectedIndex = 3`
   c. `Me.uiTermListBox.SelectedItem = 0`
   d. `Me.uiTermListBox.SelectedItem = 3`
   e. Both a and d.

9. You use the _____ property to arrange list box items in ascending ASCII order.
   a. Alphabetical
   b. Arrange
   c. ASCII
   d. ListOrder
   e. Sorted

10. The _____ event occurs when the user selects a different value in a list box.
   a. ChangeItem
   b. ChangeValue
   c. SelectNewItem
   d. ValueChanged
   e. None of the above.

EXERCISES

1. In this exercise, you modify the payroll application you created in this lesson so that it uses a user-defined Sub procedure rather than a Function procedure.
   a. Use Windows to make a copy of the Payroll Solution folder, which is contained in the VBNET\Chap07 folder. Change the name of the folder to Nelson Solution.
   b. If necessary, start Visual Studio .NET. Open the Payroll Solution (Payroll Solution.sln) file, which is contained in the VBNET\Chap07\Nelson Solution folder. Open the designer window.

c. Modify the application's code so that it displays pay rates from 6.00 through 40.00, in increments of .50, in the Rate list box.

d. Change the GetFwtTax Function procedure to a user-defined Sub procedure, then modify the statement that calls the procedure.

e. Save the solution, then start the application. Test the application by entering Karen Douglas in the Name text box. Then click 10.00 in the Rate list box, and 2 in the Allowances list box. Click the Calculate button. The calculated amounts should be identical to those shown in Lesson B's Figure 7-28.

f. Click the Exit button to end the application.

g. Close the Output window, then close the solution.

2. In this exercise, you code an application that displays the telephone extension corresponding to the name selected in a list box. The names and extensions are shown here:

Smith, Joe	3388
Jones, Mary	3356
Adkari, Joel	2487
Lin, Sue	1111
Li, Vicky	2222

a. If necessary, start Visual Studio .NET. Open the Phone Solution (Phone Solution.sln) file, which is contained in the VBNET\Chap07\Phone Solution folder. If necessary, open the designer window.

b. Set the list box's Sorted property to True.

c. Code the form's Load event procedure so that it adds the five names shown above to the uiNamesListBox. Select the first name in the list.

d. Code the list box's SelectedValueChanged event procedure so that it assigns the item selected in the uiNameListBox to a variable. The procedure then should use the Select Case statement to display the telephone extension that corresponds to the name stored in the variable.

e. Save the solution, then start the application. Test the application by clicking each name in the list box.

f. Click the Exit button to end the application.

g. Close the Output window, then close the solution.

3. In this exercise, you modify the application that you coded in Exercise 2. The application will now assign the index of the selected item, rather than the selected item itself, to a variable.

a. Use Windows to make a copy of the Phone Solution folder, which is contained in the VBNET\Chap07 folder. Change the name of the folder to Phone2 Solution.

b. If necessary, start Visual Studio .NET. Open the Phone Solution (Phone Solution.sln) file, which is contained in the VBNET\Chap07\Phone2 Solution folder. Open the designer window.

c. Modify the list box's SelectedValueChanged event procedure so that it assigns the index of the item selected in the uiNameListBox to a variable. The procedure then should use the Select Case statement to display the telephone extension that corresponds to the index stored in the variable.

d. Save the solution, then start the application. Test the application by clicking each name in the list box.

e. Click the Exit button to end the application.

f. Close the Output window, then close the solution.

4. In this exercise, you code an application that allows the user to display an image that corresponds to the item selected in a list box.

   a. If necessary, start Visual Studio .NET. Open the Image Solution (Image Solution.sln) file, which is contained in the VBNET\Chap07\Image Solution folder. If necessary, open the designer window.

   b. Set the list box's Sorted property to True.

   c. In the form's Load event procedure, fill the uiElementListBox with the following items: Cloud, Rain, Snow, Sun, and Lightning, then select the first item in the list.

   d. Code the list box's SelectedValueChanged event procedure so that it displays, in the uiElementPictureBox control, the image that corresponds to the item selected in the list box.

   e. Save the solution, then start the application. Test the application by clicking each item in the list box.

   f. Click the Exit button to end the application.

   g. Close the Output window, then close the solution.

5. In this exercise, you modify the Grade Calculator application that you viewed in Chapter 6. The modified application will use a Function procedure to determine the grade.

   a. If necessary, start Visual Studio .NET. Open the Grade Calculator Solution (Grade Calculator Solution.sln) file, which is contained in the VBNET\Chap07\Grade Calculator Solution folder. Open the designer window.

   b. Modify the application's code so that it uses a Function procedure to determine the student's grade. Return the grade to the uiAssignGradeButton's Click event procedure, which should display the grade in the uiPointsGradeLabel control.

   c. Save the solution, then start the application. Test the application to verify that it is working correctly.

   d. Click the Exit button to end the application.

   e. Close the Output window, then close the solution.

6. In this exercise, you modify the application that you coded in Exercise 5. The application will now use a user-defined Sub procedure rather than a Function procedure.

   a. Use Windows to make a copy of the Grade Calculator Solution folder, which is contained in the VBNET\Chap07 folder. Change the name of the folder to Grade Calculator2 Solution.

   b. If necessary, start Visual Studio .NET. Open the Grade Solution (Grade Solution.sln) file, which is contained in the VBNET\Chap07\Grade Calculator2 Solution folder. Open the designer window.

   c. Modify the application's code so that it uses a Sub procedure, rather than a Function procedure, to determine the student's grade.

   d. Save the solution, then start the application. Test the application to verify that it is working correctly.

   e. Click the Exit button to end the application.

   f. Close the Output window, then close the solution.

discovery ▶ 7. In this exercise, you learn how to create a list box that allows the user to select more than one item at a time.

   a. If necessary, start Visual Studio .NET. Open the Multi Solution (Multi Solution.sln) file, which is contained in the VBNET\Chap07\Multi Solution folder. If necessary, open the designer window. The interface contains a list box named uiNamesListBox. The list box's Sorted property is set to True, and its SelectionMode property is set to One.

   b. Open the Code Editor window. Notice that the form's Load event procedure adds five names to the uiNamesListBox.

c. Code the uiSingleButton's Click event procedure so that it displays, in the uiResultLabel control, the item that is selected in the uiNamesListBox. For example, if the user clicks Debbie in the list box and then clicks the Single Selection button, the name Debbie should appear in the uiResultLabel control.

d. Save the solution, then start the application. Click Debbie in the list box, then click Ahmad, and then click Bill. Notice that, when the list box's SelectionMode property is set to One, you can select only one item at a time in the list.

e. Click the Single Selection button. The name "Bill" appears in the uiResultLabel control.

f. Click the Exit button to end the application, then close the Output window.

g. Change the list box's SelectionMode property to MultiSimple. Save the solution, then start the application. Click Debbie in the list box, then click Ahmad, then click Bill, and then click Ahmad. Notice that, when the list box's SelectionMode property is set to MultiSimple, you can select more than one item at a time in the list. Also notice that you click to both select and deselect an item. (You also can use Ctrl+click and Shift+click, as well as press the Spacebar, to select and deselect items when the list box's SelectionMode property is set to MultiSimple.)

h. Click the Exit button to end the application, then close the Output window.

i. Change the list box's SelectionMode property to MultiExtended. Save the solution, then start the application.

j. Click Debbie in the list box, then click Jim. Notice that, in this case, clicking Jim deselects Debbie. When a list box's SelectionMode property is set to MultiExtended, you use Ctrl+click to select multiple items in the list. You also use Ctrl+click to deselect items in the list. Click Debbie in the list, then Ctrl+click Ahmad, and then Ctrl+click Debbie.

k. Next, click Bill in the list, then Shift+click Jim; this selects all of the names from Bill through Jim.

l. Click the Exit button to end the application, then close the Output window.

As you know, when a list box's SelectionMode property is set to One, the item selected in the list box is stored in the SelectedItem property, and the item's index is stored in the SelectedIndex property. However, when a list box's SelectionMode property is set to either MultiSimple or MultiExtended, the items selected in the list box are stored (as strings) in the SelectedItems property, and the indices of each item are stored (as integers) in the SelectedIndices property.

m. Code the MultiButton Click event procedure so that it clears the contents of the uiResultLabel control. The procedure should then display the selected names (which are stored in the SelectedItems property) on separate lines in the uiResultLabel control.

n. Save the solution, then start the application.

o. Click Ahmad in the list box, then Shift+click Jim. Click the Multi-Selection button. The five names should appear on separate lines in the uiResultLabel control.

p. Click the Exit button to end the application.

q. Close the Output window, then close the solution.

After completing this lesson, you will be able to:

■ Add an existing form to a solution

■ Add a new module to a solution

■ Code the Sub Main procedure

■ Create an instance of a form

■ Display a form object using the ShowDialog method

Completing the Payroll Application

Adding an Existing Form to a Solution

In Chapter 1, you created a copyright screen for Interlocking Software Company. Recall that the copyright screen is to be the splash screen for each custom application created by the company. The copyright screen identifies the application's author and copyright year and includes the Interlocking Software Company logo. In the next set of steps, you add the copyright screen to the payroll application.

tip

You also can click Project on the menu bar, and then click Add Existing Item to open the Add Existing Item – Payroll Project dialog box.

tip

The Open button in the Add Existing Item – *projectname* dialog box also allows you to add to a solution a link to an existing file, rather than the file itself. You learn how to add a link in Discovery Exercise 2 at the end of this lesson.

To add the copyright screen to the payroll application:

1 Start Microsoft Visual Studio .NET, if necessary.

2 If necessary, close the Start Page window.

3 Open the **Payroll Solution** (Payroll Solution.sln) file, which is contained in the VBNET\Chap07\Payroll Solution folder.

4 Auto-hide the Toolbox, Solution Explorer, and Properties windows, if necessary.

5 Click **File** on the menu bar, and then click **Add Existing Item**. The Add Existing Item – Payroll Project dialog box opens.

6 Open the Copyright Project folder, which is contained in the VBNET\Chap07\Copyright Solution folder on your computer's hard disk, and then click **Copyright Form.vb**.

7 Click the **Open** button to add the Copyright Form.vb file to the Payroll application.

8 Right-click **Copyright Form.vb** in the Solution Explorer window, then click **View Designer**. See Figure 7-30.

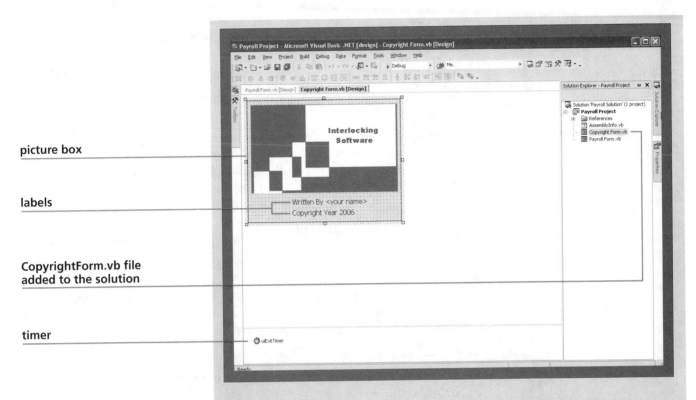

Figure 7-30: Copyright form

As Figure 7-30 indicates, the Copyright form contains a picture box, two labels, and a timer control.

9 Click the **uiAuthorLabel control** on the Copyright screen. Replace <your name> in the control's Text property with your name.

10 Save the solution.

As you may recall, the timer control's Interval property is set to 8000 milliseconds, which means that the code in the control's Tick event procedure is processed every eight seconds. View the Tick event procedure's code.

11 Open the Code Editor window. Figure 7-31 shows the uiExitTimer's Tick event procedure.

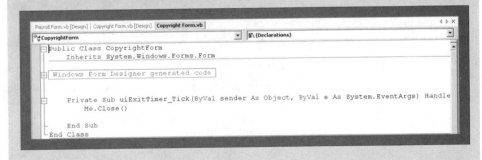

Figure 7-31: uiExitTimer's Tick event procedure

Notice that the Tick event procedure contains the statement `Me.Close()`, which closes the Copyright form.

12 Close the Code Editor window, then close the Copyright form's designer window.

The Copyright form should be the first interface that appears when the payroll application is started. When the uiExitTimer control closes the Copyright form, the computer should display the Payroll form. You can control the display of both forms by coding the Sub Main procedure.

Coding the Sub Main Procedure

Sub Main is a special procedure in Visual Basic .NET, because it can be declared as the "starting point" for an application. In other words, you can tell the computer to process the Sub Main procedure automatically when an application is started. You enter the Sub Main procedure in a **module**, which is a file that contains code that is not associated with any specific object in the interface.

> You also can click Project on the menu bar, and then click Add New Item to open the Add New Item – *projectname* dialog box.

To add a module and the Sub Main procedure to the payroll application:

1 Click **File** on the menu bar, and then click **Add New Item**. The Add New Item – Payroll Project dialog box opens.

2 Click **Module** in the Templates list box. In the Name text box, change the module name from Module1.vb to **Payroll Module**.

3 Click the **Open** button to add the Payroll Module to the application, then temporarily display the Solution Explorer window. As Figure 7-32 indicates, a module begins with the module header and ends with the module footer.

module header

module footer

module file added to the solution

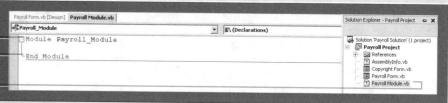

Figure 7-32: Payroll Module added to the application

Next, enter the Sub Main procedure's header and footer.

4 Position the insertion point in the blank line between the module's header and footer. If necessary, press **Tab** to indent the line, then type **Sub Main** and press **Enter**. Notice that the Code Editor enters the procedure footer (`End Sub`) for you.

Now specify that the Sub Main procedure should be processed automatically when the application is started.

5 Right-click **Payroll Project** in the Solution Explorer window, and then click **Properties**. The Payroll Project Property Pages dialog box opens.

6 Click the **Startup object** list arrow, and then click **Sub Main** in the list. Click the **OK** button to close the dialog box.

Before you can complete the Sub Main procedure, you need to learn how to create an instance of a form.

Creating an Instance of a Form

If you look closely at the code shown earlier in Figure 7-31, you will notice that the code begins with the instruction `Public Class CopyrightForm` and ends with the instruction `End Class`. As you learned in Chapter 1, a block of code that begins with the `Public Class` clause and ends with the `End Class` clause is called a class definition. Recall that a class definition, more simply referred to as a class, specifies (or defines) the attributes and behaviors of an object. The CopyrightForm class shown in Figure 7-31, for example, specifies the attributes and behaviors of a CopyrightForm object.

Figure 7-33 shows the code contained in the PayrollForm, with each procedure collapsed to make the figure more readable. Notice that the code contains the class definition for a PayrollForm object.

class definition

```
Public Class PayrollForm
    Inherits System.Windows.Forms.Form

Windows Form Designer generated code

    Private Sub uiExitButton_Click(ByVal sender As Object, ByVal e As System.EventArgs) Hand

    Private Sub uiNameTextBox_Enter(ByVal sender As Object, ByVal e As System.EventArgs) Han

    Private Sub PayrollForm_Load(ByVal sender As Object, ByVal e As System.EventArgs) Handle

    Private Sub uiCalculateButton_Click(ByVal sender As Object, ByVal e As System.EventArgs)

    Private Function GetFwtTax(ByVal weekPay As Double) As Double...

    Private Sub ClearLabels(ByVal sender As Object, ByVal e As System.EventArgs) _
        Handles uiNameTextBox.TextChanged, uiHoursListBox.SelectedValueChanged, _
        uiRateListBox.SelectedValueChanged, uiAllowListBox.SelectedValueChanged, _
        uiMarriedRadioButton.Click, uiSingleRadioButton.Click...
End Class
```

Figure 7-33: Code contained in the PayrollForm

When an application is started, Visual Basic .NET automatically processes the code contained in one object: the Startup object. For example, if the CopyrightForm is specified as the Startup object, Visual Basic .NET automatically processes the code contained in the CopyrightForm class definition. The code creates a CopyrightForm object and then displays the object on the screen. If you need to display a different form on the screen—for example, the PayrollForm—after the application is started, you first instruct the computer to create a PayrollForm object by processing the code entered in the PayrollForm class definition, and then instruct the computer to display the form object on the screen.

Similarly, if the PayrollForm is specified as the Startup object, Visual Basic .NET automatically processes the code contained in the PayrollForm class definition. In this case, the code creates a PayrollForm object and then displays the object on the screen. If you need to display a different form on the screen after the application is started, you first instruct the computer to create the form object by processing the code entered in the appropriate class definition, and then instruct the computer to display the form object on the screen.

When the Sub Main procedure is the Startup object, as it is in this case, neither the CopyrightForm class definition nor the PayrollForm class definition will be processed automatically. To allow the payroll application to display the forms associated with these classes, the Sub Main procedure will need first to instruct the computer to create the objects, and then instruct the computer to display the objects on the screen.

You use the syntax **Dim** *variablename* **As New** *classname* to instruct the computer to create an object from a class. In the syntax, *classname* is the name of the class, and *variablename* is the name of a variable that will store the object's address. Storing the address in a variable allows the computer to locate the object when it is referred to in code. The statement `Dim copyForm As New CopyrightForm`, for example, instructs the computer to use the CopyrightForm class to create a CopyrightForm object. When the object is created, its address in the computer's internal memory is stored in the `copyForm` variable. Similarly, the statement `Dim payForm As New PayrollForm` instructs the computer to use the PayrollForm class to create a PayrollForm object. When the object is created, its address in the computer's internal memory is stored in the `payForm` variable.

To create a CopyrightForm object and a PayrollForm object:

1   Enter the two Dim statements shown in Figure 7-34.

enter these two lines of code

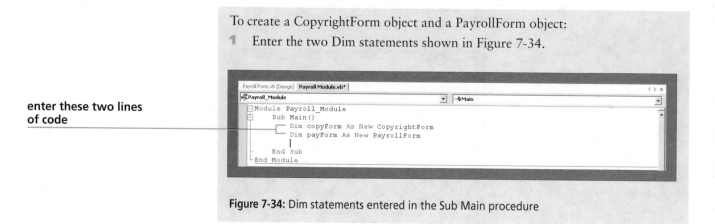

Figure 7-34: Dim statements entered in the Sub Main procedure

The Dim statements shown in Figure 7-34 create the CopyrightForm and PayrollForm objects and assign their addresses to variables. However, they do not display the form objects on the screen. You use a form object's ShowDialog method to display the form objects.

Using a Form Object's ShowDialog Method

The form object's **ShowDialog method** allows you to display a form object on the screen. The syntax of the ShowDialog method is *form*.**ShowDialog**(), where *form* is the name of the variable that contains the form object's address. For example, to display the CopyrightForm object, whose address is stored in the `copyForm` variable, you use the statement `copyForm.ShowDialog()`. Likewise, to display the PayrollForm object, whose address is stored in the `payForm` variable, you use the statement `payForm.ShowDialog()`.

To complete the Sub Main procedure:

1 Enter the two additional statements shown in Figure 7-35, which shows the completed Sub Main procedure.

enter these two lines of code

```
Module Payroll_Module
    Sub Main()
        Dim copyForm As New CopyrightForm
        Dim payForm As New PayrollForm
        copyForm.ShowDialog()
        payForm.ShowDialog()
    End Sub
End Module
```

Figure 7-35: Completed Sub Main procedure

2 Save the solution, then start the application. The Dim statements entered in the Sub Main procedure create a CopyrightForm object and a PayrollForm object. Then the `copyForm.ShowDialog()` statement displays the copyright form on the screen. After eight seconds have elapsed, the `Me.Close()` statement in the uiExitTimer's Tick event procedure closes the copyright form. The computer then returns to the Sub Main procedure to process the `payForm.ShowDialog()` statement, which displays the payroll form on the screen.

3 Click the **Exit** button to close the payroll form. The computer returns to the Sub Main procedure to process the `End Sub` instruction, which ends the procedure and the application.

4 When you return to the Code Editor window, close the Output window, then close the Code Editor window.

5 Click **File** on the menu bar, and then click **Close Solution**.

You now have completed Chapter 7. You can either take a break or complete the end-of-lesson questions and exercises.

S U M M A R Y

To add an existing item to an application:

▪ Click File on the menu bar, and then click Add Existing Item. You also can click Project on the menu bar, and then click Add Existing Item.

To add a new item to an application:

▪ Click File on the menu bar, and then click Add New Item. You also can click Project on the menu bar, and then click Add New Item.

To process code automatically when an application is started:

▪ Add a module to the application, then create a Sub Main procedure in the module. Right-click the project's name in the Solution Explorer window, then click Properties. Click the Startup object list arrow, then click Sub Main in the list.

To create an instance of an object from a class:

■ Use the syntax **Dim** *variablename* **As New** *classname*, where *classname* is the name of the class corresponding to the object you want to create, and *variablename* is the name of a variable that will store the object's address.

To display a form object on the screen:

■ Use the form object's ShowDialog method. Its syntax is *form*.**ShowDialog**(), where *form* is the name of the variable that contains the form object's address.

QUESTIONS

1. You can tell the computer to automatically process the code contained in the _____ procedure when an application is started.
   a. Auto
   b. AutoProcess
   c. Process
   d. Sub Main
   e. Sub Auto

2. The procedure from Question 1 is entered in a _____, which is a file that contains code that is not associated with any specific object in the interface.
   a. form
   b. global file
   c. module
   d. subroutine
   e. None of the above.

3. You can use the File menu to add both new and existing items to an application.
   a. True
   b. False

4. Which of the following statements creates an InventoryForm object and stores the object's address in a variable named invForm?
   a. `Dim invForm As New Class`
   b. `Dim invForm As New InventoryForm`
   c. `Dim inv As New Object`
   d. `Dim InventoryForm As New inv`
   e. None of the above.

5. Which of the following statements displays the InventoryForm object created in Question 4 on the screen?
   a. `InventoryForm.Display()`
   b. `InventoryForm.ShowDialog()`
   c. `invForm.Display()`
   d. `invForm.ShowDialog()`
   e. `invForm.ShowForm()`

E X E R C I S E S

1. In this exercise, you add the copyright screen to the Shoppers Haven application that you created in Chapter 6.
    a. Use Windows to make a copy of the Shoppers Haven Solution folder, which is contained in the VBNET\Chap06 folder. Change the name of the folder to Shoppers Haven2 Solution. Move the Shoppers Haven2 Solution folder to the VBNET\Chap07 folder.
    b. If necessary, start Visual Studio .NET. Open the Shoppers Haven Solution (Shoppers Haven Solution.sln) file, which is contained in the VBNET\Chap07\Shoppers Haven2 Solution folder. Open the designer window.
    c. Add the copyright form, which is contained in the VBNET\Chap07\Copyright Solution\Copyright Project folder, to the application.
    d. View the copyright form in the designer window. Change <your name> in the uiAuthorLabel control's Text property to your name.
    e. Add a module named Shoppers Haven2 Module to the application. Add a Sub Main procedure to the module. Code the Sub Main procedure so that it displays the copyright form first, and then displays the Shoppers Haven form.
    f. Change the Startup object to Sub Main.
    g. Save the solution, then start the application. The copyright form should appear first on the screen. After eight seconds, the copyright form should close and the Shoppers Haven form should appear.
    h. Click the Exit button to end the application, then click the Yes button.
    i. Close the Output window, then close the solution.

discovery ▶ 2. In this exercise, you learn how to include, in an application, a link to an existing file. When an application contains a link to a file, rather than the file itself, changes made to the linked file automatically appear in each application in which it is linked.
    a. If necessary, start Visual Studio .NET. Open the Hoover Solution (Hoover Solution.sln) file, which is contained in the VBNET\Chap07\Hoover Solution folder. If necessary, open the designer window.
    b. Click File on the menu bar, and then click Add Existing Item.
    c. Open the First Screen Project folder, which is contained in the VBNET\Chap07\First Screen Solution folder. Click First Screen Form.vb in the list of filenames.
    d. Click the Open button's list arrow, and then click Link File. This creates a link to the First Screen Form.vb file.
    e. Right-click First Screen Form.vb in the Solution Explorer window, then click View Designer. Notice that the text "Hoover Industries" appears in the label control on the form.
    f. Save the solution, then close the solution.
    g. Open the First Screen Solution (First Screen Solution.sln) file, which is contained in the VBNET\Chap07\First Screen Solution folder. If necessary, right-click First Screen Form.vb in the Solution Explorer window, then click View Designer.
    h. Change the contents of the label control from "Hoover Industries" to "Hoover Company".
    i. Save the solution, then close the solution.
    j. Open the Hoover Solution (Hoover Solution.sln) file, which is contained in the VBNET\Chap07\Hoover Solution folder. View the First Screen Form in the designer window. Notice that the First Screen Form in the Hoover application reflects the change you made to the form in Step h. This is because the Hoover application contains a link to the First Screen Form.vb file.
    k. Close the solution.

debugging   3. In this exercise, you debug an existing application. The purpose of this exercise is to demonstrate a common error made when using functions.

a. If necessary, start Visual Studio .NET. Open the Debug Solution (Debug Solution.sln) file, which is contained in the VBNET\Chap07\Debug Solution folder. If necessary, open the designer window.

b. Open the Code Editor window and study the existing code.

c. Start the application. Click 20 in the Length list box, then click 30 in the Width list box. Click the Calculate Area button, which should display the area of a rectangle having a length of 20 feet and a width of 30 feet. Notice that the application is not working properly.

d. Click the Exit button to end the application.

e. Correct the application's code, then save the solution and start the application. Click 20 in the Length list box, then click 30 in the Width list box. Click the Calculate Area button, which should display the area of a rectangle having a length of 20 feet and a width of 30 feet.

f. Click the Exit button to end the application.

g. Close the Output window, then close the solution.

Manipulating Strings

Creating a Hangman Game Application

case ▶ On days when the weather is bad and the students cannot go outside to play, Mr. Mitchell, who teaches second grade at Hinsbrook School, spends recess time playing a simplified version of the Hangman game with his class. Mr. Mitchell feels that the game is both fun (the students love playing the game) and educational (the game allows the students to observe how letters are used to form words). Mr. Mitchell has asked you to write an application that two students can use to play the game on the computer.

Mr. Mitchell's simplified version of the Hangman game requires two people to play. Currently, Mr. Mitchell thinks of a word that has five letters. He then draws five dashes on the chalkboard—one for each letter in the word. One student then is chosen to guess the word, letter by letter. If the student guesses a correct letter, Mr. Mitchell replaces the appropriate dash or dashes with the letter. For example, if the original word is *moose* and the student guesses the letter *o*, Mr. Mitchell changes the fives dashes on the chalkboard to -*oo*--. The game is over when the student guesses all of the letters in the word, or when he or she makes 10 incorrect guesses, whichever comes first.

Previewing the Completed Application

Before creating the Hangman Game application, you first preview the completed application.

To preview the completed application:

1   Use the Run command on the Windows Start menu to run the **Hangman** (Hangman.exe) file, which is contained in the VBNET\Chap08 folder on your computer's hard disk. The Hangman Game application's user interface appears on the screen. See Figure 8-1.

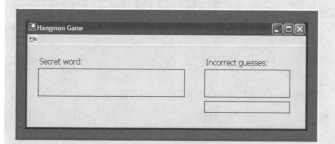

Figure 8-1: Hangman Game application

Notice that the interface contains a File menu. You learn how to include a menu in an interface in Lesson B.

2   Click **File** on the menu bar, and then click **New Game**. A dialog box opens and prompts you to enter a 5-letter word.

3   Type **puppy** and press **Enter**. Five dashes (hyphens)—one for each letter in the word "puppy"—appear in the application's interface. Additionally, a different dialog box opens and prompts you to enter a letter.

Your first guess will be the letter "Y".

4   Type y and press **Enter**. The application replaces the last dash in the interface with the letter "Y". This indicates that the letter "Y" is the last letter in the word.

Now guess the letter X.

5   Type **x** and press **Enter**. Because the letter X does not appear in the word "puppy", the application displays the number one as the number of incorrect guesses. Additionally, the letter X appears below the number of incorrect guesses in the interface; this reminds the user that the letter has already been guessed.

6   Type **p** and press **Enter**. The application replaces three of the five dashes in the interface with the letter P.

7   Type **u** and press **Enter**. The application replaces the remaining dash in the interface with the letter U. The application then displays the "Great guessing!" message in a message box.

8   Click the **OK** button to close the message box. See Figure 8-2.

Figure 8-2: Result of guessing the word

9   Click **File** on the menu bar, and then click **Exit** to end the application.

Before you can begin coding the Hangman Game application, you need to learn how to manipulate strings in Visual Basic .NET and how to create a menu. You learn about string manipulation in Lesson A and about the MainMenu tool in Lesson B. You complete the Hangman Game application in Lesson C.

LESSON A
objectives

After completing this lesson, you will be able to:

- Determine the number of characters contained in a string
- Remove characters from a string
- Determine whether a string begins or ends with one or more specific characters
- Access characters from the beginning, middle, and end of a string
- Replace one or more characters in a string
- Insert characters within a string
- Search a string for one or more characters

tip

You also can use the Len function to determine the number of characters contained in a string. You learn about the Len function in Discovery Exercise 17 at the end of this lesson.

String Manipulation

Manipulating Strings in Visual Basic .NET

Many times, an application will need to manipulate (process) string data. For example, an application may need to verify that an inventory part number begins with a specific letter. Or, it may need to determine whether the last three characters in an employee number are valid. In this chapter, you learn several ways of manipulating strings in Visual Basic .NET. You begin by learning how to determine the number of characters contained in a string.

Determining the Number of Characters Contained in a String

In many applications, it is necessary to determine the number of characters contained in a string. For example, an application that expects the user to enter a 10-digit phone number needs to verify that the user entered the required number of characters. You can use a string's **Length property** to determine the number of characters contained in the string. The syntax of the Length property is shown in Figure 8-3 along with several examples of using the property.

Syntax
To determine the number of characters contained in a string: *string*.**Length**
Examples and results

`Dim numChars As Integer`
`numChars = Me.uiZipTextBox.Text.Length`
assigns to the `numChars` variable the number of characters contained in the uiZipTextBox's Text property

`Dim numChars As Integer`
`Dim name As String = "Paul Blackfeather"`
`numChars = name.Length`
assigns the number 17 to the `numChars` variable

`Dim phone As String`
`phone = InputBox("10-digit phone number", "Phone")`
`Do While phone.Length <> 10`
`    phone = InputBox("10-digit phone number", "Phone")`
`Loop`
gets a phone number from the user until the number of characters contained in the phone number is equal to the number 10

Figure 8-3: Syntax and examples of the Length property

Examples and results

```
Dim part As String
part = InputBox("Part number", "Part Number")
If part.Length >= 4 Then
        instructions to process when the condition evaluates to True
Else
        instructions to process when the condition evaluates to False
End If
```

gets a part number from the user, and then determines whether the part number contains at least four characters

Figure 8-3: Syntax and examples of the Length property (continued)

In the first example in Figure 8-3, the numChars = Me.uiZipTextBox. Text.Length statement assigns to the numChars variable the number of characters contained in the uiZipTextBox's Text property. (Recall that the Text property of a control is treated as a string.) Assuming the user enters the ZIP code 60111 in the uiZipTextBox, the statement assigns the number five to the variable.

The Dim name As String = "Paul Blackfeather" statement in the second example assigns the string "Paul Blackfeather" to a String variable named name. The numChars = name.Length statement then uses the name variable's Length property to determine the number of characters contained in the variable, assigning the result to the numChars variable. In this case, the number 17 will be assigned, because the name variable contains 17 characters.

The pretest loop shown in the third example in Figure 8-3 processes the loop instruction, which prompts the user to enter a phone number, until the phone number entered contains 10 characters, at which time the loop ends. The code shown in the last example prompts the user to enter a part number, and stores the user's response in a String variable named part. The selection structure in the code then determines whether the part variable contains at least four characters.

Next, you learn how to remove characters from a string.

Removing Characters from a String

tip

You also can use the LTrim, RTrim, and Trim functions to remove any spaces from the beginning and/or end of a string. You learn about these functions in Discovery Exercise 18 at the end of this lesson.

At times, an application may need to remove one or more characters from an item of data entered by the user. For example, an application may need to remove a dollar sign from the beginning of a sales amount. Or, it may need to remove a percent sign from the end of a tax rate.

You can use the **TrimStart method** to remove one or more characters from the beginning of a string, and the **TrimEnd method** to remove one or more characters from the end of a string. To remove one or more characters from both the beginning and end of a string, you use the **Trim method**. Each method returns a string with the appropriate characters removed (trimmed).

Figure 8-4 shows the syntax of the TrimStart, TrimEnd, and Trim methods and includes several examples of using each method.

Syntax
To remove characters from the beginning of a string: *string*.**TrimStart(**[*trimChars*]**)**   To remove characters from the end of a string: *string*.**TrimEnd(**[*trimChars*]**)**   To remove characters from both the beginning and end of a string: *string*.**Trim(**[*trimChars*]**)**

Examples and results
| ```
Dim name As String
name = Me.uiNameTextBox.Text.TrimStart()
```<br> assigns the contents of the uiNameTextBox's Text property, excluding any leading spaces, to the `name` variable |
| ```
Me.uiNameTextBox.Text = Me.uiNameTextBox.Text.TrimStart()
```<br> removes any leading spaces from the uiNameTextBox's Text property |
| ```
Dim name As String
name = Me.uiNameTextBox.Text.TrimEnd()
```<br> assigns the contents of the uiNameTextBox's Text property, excluding any trailing spaces, to the `name` variable |
| ```
Dim inputRate As String, rate As Decimal
inputRate = InputBox("Rate:", "Rate")
rate = Decimal.Parse(inputRate.TrimEnd("%"c, " "c))
```<br> assigns the contents of the `inputRate` variable, excluding any trailing percent signs and spaces, to the `rate` variable |
| ```
Me.uiNameTextBox.Text = Me.uiNameTextBox.Text.Trim()
```<br> removes any leading and trailing spaces from the uiNameTextBox's Text property |
| ```
Dim num As String
num = InputBox("Number:", "Number")
num = num.Trim("$"c, " "c, "%"c)
```<br> removes any leading and trailing dollar signs, spaces, and percent signs from the `num` variable |

Figure 8-4: Syntax and examples of the TrimStart, TrimEnd, and Trim methods

In each syntax, *trimChars* is a comma-separated list of characters that you want removed (trimmed) from the *string*. Notice that the *trimChars* argument is optional in each syntax. If you omit the *trimChars* argument, Visual Basic .NET assumes that you want to remove one or more spaces from the beginning and/or end of the *string*. In other words, the default value for the *trimChars* argument is the space character (" ").

Study closely the examples shown in Figure 8-4. When processing the `name = Me.uiNameTextBox.Text.TrimStart()` statement, which is shown in the first example, the computer first makes a temporary copy of the string stored in the uiNameTextBox's Text property. It then removes any leading spaces from the temporary copy of the string, and assigns the resulting string to the `name` variable. Assuming the user enters the string " Karen" (two spaces followed by the name Karen) in the uiNameTextBox, the statement assigns the name "Karen" to the `name` variable; however, the uiNameTextBox's Text property still contains " Karen" (two spaces followed by the name Karen). After the statement is processed, the computer removes the temporary copy of the string from its internal memory.

Notice that the `name = Me.uiNameTextBox.Text.TrimStart()` statement does not remove the leading spaces from the uiNameTextBox's Text property. To remove the leading spaces from the Text property, you use the statement shown in the second example in Figure 8-4: `Me.uiNameTextBox.Text` = `Me.uiNameTextBox.Text.TrimStart()`.

When processing the statement shown in the third example in Figure 8-4, `name = Me.uiNameTextBox.Text.TrimEnd()`, the computer first makes a temporary copy of the string stored in the uiNameTextBox's Text property. It then removes any trailing spaces from the copied string, assigning the result to the `name` variable. After the statement is processed, the computer removes the copied string from its internal memory. Assuming the user enters the string "Ned Yander   " (the name Ned Yander followed by four spaces) in the uiNameTextBox, the statement assigns the name "Ned Yander" to the `name` variable. However, the statement does not change the contents of the uiNameTextBox's Text property.

When processing the `rate = Decimal.Parse(inputRate.TrimEnd("%"c, " "c))` statement shown in the fourth example in Figure 8-4, the computer first makes a copy of the string stored in the `inputRate` variable. It then removes any trailing percent signs and spaces from the copied string, and assigns the resulting string, treated as a Decimal number, to the `rate` variable. For example, if the `inputRate` variable contains the string "3 %" (the number 3, a space, and a percent sign), the statement assigns the number 3 to the `rate` variable, but it does not change the value stored in the `inputRate` variable. Likewise, if the `inputRate` variable contains the string "15% " (the number 15, a percent sign, and two spaces), the statement assigns the number 15 to the `rate` variable, but leaves the contents of the `inputRate` variable unchanged. The letter c that appears after each string in the *trimChars* argument is one of the literal type characters you learned about in Chapter 3. Recall that a literal type character forces a literal constant to assume a different data type. In this case, the c forces each string in the *trimChars* argument to assume the Char (character) data type.

You can use the `Me.uiNameTextBox.Text = Me.uiNameTextBox.Text.Trim()` statement, which is shown in the fifth example in Figure 8-4, to remove any leading and trailing spaces from the uiNameTextBox's Text property. Likewise, you can use the `num = num.Trim("$"c, " "c, "%"c)` statement, which is shown in the last example, to remove any leading and trailing dollar signs, spaces, and percent signs from the `num` variable.

Next, you learn how to use the Remove method to remove characters that are not located at the beginning or end of a string.

> **The literal type characters are listed in Figure 3-7 in Chapter 3.**

The Remove Method

You can use the **Remove method** to remove one or more characters located anywhere in a string. Figure 8-5 shows the syntax of the Remove method and includes several examples of using the method. Like the TrimStart, TrimEnd, and Trim methods, the Remove method returns a string with the appropriate characters removed.

Syntax
To remove characters from anywhere in a string: *string*.**Remove(***startIndex, count***)**

Examples and results

```Dim name As String = "John Cober"```
```Me.uiNameTextBox.Text = name.Remove(0, 5)```
 	
assigns the string "Cober" to the uiNameTextBox's Text property

```Dim name As String = "John"```
```Me.uiNameTextBox.Text = name.Remove(2, 1)```
 	
assigns the string "Jon" to the uiNameTextBox's Text property

```Dim name As String = "Janis"```
```name = name.Remove(3, 2)```
 	
assigns the string "Jan" to the name variable

Figure 8-5: Syntax and examples of the Remove method

Each character in a string is assigned a unique number, called an **index**, that indicates the character's position in the string. The first character in a string has an index of zero, the second character has an index of one, and so on. In the Remove method's syntax, *startIndex* is the index of the first character you want removed from the *string*, and *count* is the number of characters you want removed. For example, to remove only the first character from a string, you use the number zero as the *startIndex*, and the number one as the *count*. To remove the fourth through eighth characters, you use the number three as the *startIndex*, and the number five as the *count*.

Study closely the three examples shown in Figure 8-5. When processing the `Me.uiNameTextBox.Text = name.Remove(0, 5)` statement shown in the first example, the computer makes a copy of the string stored in the `name` variable. It then removes the first five characters from the copied string; in this case, the computer removes the letters J, o, h, and n, and the space character. The computer then assigns the resulting string ("Cober") to the uiNameTextBox's Text property before removing the copied string from its internal memory. The contents of the `name` variable are not changed as a result of processing the `Me.uiNameTextBox.Text = name.Remove(0, 5)` statement.

When processing the `Me.uiNameTextBox.Text = name.Remove(2, 1)`, statement, which is shown in the second example in Figure 8-5, the computer makes a copy of the string stored in the `name` variable. It then removes one character, beginning with the character whose index is 2, from the copied string. The character with an index of 2 is the third character in the string—in this case, the letter h. The computer then assigns the resulting string ("Jon") to the uiNameTextBox's Text property. Here again, the statement does not change the string stored in the `name` variable.

You can use the `name = name.Remove(3, 2)` statement shown in the last example in Figure 8-5 to remove two characters, beginning with the character whose index is 3, from the string stored in the `name` variable. In this case, the letters i and s are removed, changing the contents of the `name` variable from "Janis" to "Jan".

Next, you learn how to determine whether a string begins or ends with a specific sequence of characters.

Determining Whether a String Begins or Ends with a Specific Sequence of Characters

In many applications, it is necessary to determine whether a string begins or ends with a specific character or characters. For example, an application may need to determine whether a phone number entered by the user begins with area code "312". Or, an application may need to determine whether a tax rate entered by the user ends with a percent sign.

Visual Basic .NET provides the **StartsWith method** for determining whether a specific sequence of characters occurs at the beginning of a string, and provides the **EndsWith method** for determining whether a specific sequence of characters occurs at the end of a string. Figure 8-6 shows the syntax of the StartsWith and EndsWith methods along with examples of using each method.

Syntax

To determine whether a specific sequence of characters occurs at the beginning of a string:
string.**StartsWith**(*subString*)

To determine whether a specific sequence of characters occurs at the end of a string:
string.**EndsWith**(*subString*)

Examples and results

```
Dim pay As String
pay = InputBox("Pay rate", "Pay")
If pay.StartsWith("$") Then
    pay = pay.TrimStart("$"c)
End If
```

determines whether the string stored in the pay variable begins with the dollar sign; if it does, the dollar sign is removed from the string

```
Dim phone As String
phone = InputBox("10-digit phone number", "Phone")
Do While phone.StartsWith("312")
    MessageBox.Show(phone)
    phone = InputBox("10-digit phone number", "Phone")
Loop
```

determines whether the string stored in the phone variable begins with "312"; if it does, the contents of the phone variable are displayed in a message box and the user is prompted to enter another phone number

```
Dim cityState As String = Me.uiCityStateTextBox.Text.ToUpper()
If cityState.EndsWith("CA") Then
    Me.uiStateLabel.Text = "California customer"
End If
```

determines whether the string stored in the cityState variable ends with "CA"; if it does, the string "California customer" is displayed in the uiStateLabel control

---

Figure 8-6: Syntax and examples of the StartsWith and EndsWith methods

Examples and results

```
Dim name As String
name = InputBox("Your name:", "Name")
name = name.ToUpper()
If Not name.EndsWith("SMITH") Then
     Me.uiNameLabel.Text = name
End If
```

determines whether the string stored in the name variable ends with "SMITH"; if it does not, the variable's value is displayed in the uiNameLabel control

```
Dim name As String
name = InputBox("Your name:", "Name")
If Not name.ToUpper().EndsWith("SMITH") Then
     Me.uiNameLabel.Text = name
End If
```

determines whether the string stored in the name variable ends with "SMITH"; if it does not, the variable's value is displayed in the uiNameLabel control

Figure 8-6: Syntax and examples of the StartsWith and EndsWith methods (continued)

In the syntax for the StartsWith and EndsWith methods, *subString* is a string that represents the sequence of characters you want to search for either at the beginning or end of the *string*. The StartsWith method returns the Boolean value True if *subString* is located at the beginning of *string*; otherwise, it returns the Boolean value False. Likewise, the EndsWith method returns the Boolean value True if *subString* is located at the end of *string*; otherwise, it returns the Boolean value False.

In the first example shown in Figure 8-6, the If pay.StartsWith("$") Then clause determines whether the string stored in the pay variable begins with the dollar sign. If it does, the pay = pay.TrimStart("$"c) statement removes the dollar sign from the variable's contents. You also can write the If clause in this example as If pay.StartsWith("$") = True Then.

Notice that, in the first example, "$" is used as the *subString* argument in the StartsWith method, but "$"c is used as the *trimChars* argument in the TrimStart method. This is because the *subString* argument must be a string, while the *trimChars* argument must be a listing of one or more characters.

In the second example shown in Figure 8-6, the Do While phone.StartsWith("312") clause determines whether the string stored in the phone variable begins with "312". If it does, the contents of the variable are displayed in a message box and the user is prompted to enter another phone number. You also can write the Do clause in this example as Do While phone.StartsWith("312") = True.

In the third example shown in Figure 8-6, the code displays the string "California customer" in the uiStateLabel control if the string stored in the cityState variable ends with "CA". Here again, you also can write the If clause in this example as If cityState.EndsWith("CA") = True Then.

The name = name.ToUpper() statement shown in the fourth example in Figure 8-6 changes the contents of the name variable to uppercase. The If Not name.EndsWith("SMITH") Then clause then compares the contents of the name variable to the string "SMITH". If the name variable does not end with the string "SMITH", the Me.uiNameLabel.Text = name statement displays the contents of the name variable in the uiNameLabel control. You also can write the If clause in this example as If name.EndsWith("SMITH") = False Then.

The code shown in the last example in Figure 8-6 is similar to the code shown in the fourth example, except the ToUpper method is included in the If clause rather than in an assignment statement. When processing the `If Not name.ToUpper().EndsWith("SMITH") Then` clause shown in the last example, the computer first makes a copy of the string stored in the name variable; it then converts the copied string to uppercase. The computer then determines whether the copied string ends with the string "SMITH". Notice that the computer processes the methods from left to right; in other words, it processes the ToUpper method before processing the EndsWith method. If the copied string does not end with the string "SMITH", the `Me.uiNameLabel.Text = name` statement displays the contents of the name variable in the uiNameLabel control. Unlike the code in the fourth example, the code in this example does not permanently change the contents of the name variable to uppercase. The If clause in this example also can be written as `If name.ToUpper().EndsWith("SMITH") = False Then`.

Next you learn how to access characters contained in a string.

Accessing Characters Contained in a String

At times, an application may need to access one or more characters contained in a string. For example, an application may need to determine whether the letter K appears as the third character in a string; or, it may need to display only the string's first five characters. You can use the **Substring method** to access any number of characters in a string. Figure 8-7 shows the syntax of the Substring method and includes several examples of using the method.

Syntax
To access one or more characters contained in a string: *string*.**Substring**(*startIndex*[, *count*])

Examples and results
| ```
Dim name As String = "Peggy Ryan"
first = name.Substring(0, 5)
last = name.Substring(6)
``` |
| assigns "Peggy" to the first variable, and assigns "Ryan" to the last variable |
| ```
Dim sales As String
sales = Me.uiSalesTextBox.Text
If sales.StartsWith("$") Then
     sales = sales.Substring(1)
End If
``` |
| determines whether the string stored in the sales variable begins with the dollar sign; if it does, assigns the contents of the variable, excluding the dollar sign, to the sales variable |

Figure 8-7: Syntax and examples of the Substring method

Examples and results

```
Dim inputRate As String, rate As Double
inputRate = InputBox("Enter rate", "Tax Rate")
If inputRate.EndsWith("%") Then
    rate = Double.Parse(inputRate.Substring(0, _
        inputRate.Length - 1))
Else
    rate = Double.Parse(inputRate)
End If
```

determines whether the string stored in the inputRate variable ends with the percent sign; if it does, assigns the contents of the inputRate variable, excluding the percent sign and treated as a Double number, to the rate variable; otherwise, assigns the contents of the inputRate variable, treated as a Double number, to the rate variable

Figure 8-7: Syntax and examples of the Substring method (continued)

tip

You also can use the Left, Right, and Mid functions, which you learn about in Discovery Exercise 19 at the end of this lesson, to access characters contained in a string.

The Substring method contains two arguments: *startIndex* and *count*. *StartIndex* is the index of the first character you want to access in the *string*. As you learned earlier, the first character in a string has an index of zero, the second character has an index of one, and so on. The *count* argument, which is optional, specifies the number of characters you want to access. The Substring method returns a string that contains *count* number of characters, beginning with the character whose index is *startIndex*. If you omit the *count* argument, the Substring method returns all characters from the *startIndex* position through the end of the string.

Study closely the three examples shown in Figure 8-7. In the first example, the first = name.Substring(0, 5) statement assigns the first five characters contained in the name variable ("Peggy") to the first variable. The last = name.Substring(6) statement assigns all of the characters contained in the name variable, beginning with the character whose index is 6, to the last variable. In this case, the statement assigns "Ryan" to the last variable.

The code shown in the second example in Figure 8-7 uses the StartsWith method to determine whether the string stored in the sales variable begins with the dollar sign. If it does, the sales = sales.Substring(1) statement assigns all of the characters from the sales variable, beginning with the character whose index is 1, to the sales variable. The sales = sales.Substring(1) statement is equivalent to the statement sales = sales.Remove(0, 1), as well as to the statement sales = sales.TrimStart("$"c).

The code shown in the last example in Figure 8-7 uses the EndsWith method to determine whether the string stored in the inputRate variable ends with the percent sign. If it does, the statement rate = Double.Parse(inputRate.Substring(0, inputRate.Length - 1)) assigns all of the characters contained in the inputRate variable, excluding the last character (which is the percent sign), to the rate variable. The rate = Double.Parse(inputRate.Substring(0, inputRate.Length - 1)) statement is equivalent to the statement rate = Double.Parse(inputRate.Remove(inputRate.Length - 1, 1)), as well as to the statement rate = Double.Parse(inputRate.TrimEnd("%"c)).

Next, you learn how to replace a sequence of characters in a string with another sequence of characters.

Replacing Characters in a String

You can use the **Replace method** to replace a sequence of characters in a string with another sequence of characters. For example, you can use the Replace method to replace area code "800" with area code "877" in a phone number. Or, you can use it to replace the dashes in a Social Security number with the empty string. Figure 8-8 shows the syntax of the Replace method and includes several examples of using the method.

Syntax
To replace all occurrences of a sequence of characters in a string with another sequence of characters: *string*.**Replace(**oldValue, newValue**)**

Examples and results
``Dim phone As String = "1-800-111-0000"
Dim newPhone As String
newPhone = phone.Replace("800", "877")```
assigns the string "1-877-111-0000" to the `newPhone` variable
``Dim social As String = "000-11-9999"
social = social.Replace("-", "")```
assigns the string "000119999" to the `social` variable
``Dim word As String = "latter"
word = word.Replace("t", "d")```
assigns the string "ladder" to the `word` variable

Figure 8-8: Syntax and examples of the Replace method

tip

If the `phone` variable shown in the first example in Figure 8-8 contained "1-800-111-0800", the string "1-877-111-0877" would be assigned to the `newPhone` variable, because the Replace method replaces all occurrences of *oldValue* with *newValue*.

In the syntax, *oldValue* is the sequence of characters that you want to replace in the *string*, and *newValue* is the replacement characters. The Replace method returns a string with all occurrences of *oldValue* replaced with *newValue*.

When processing the `newPhone = phone.Replace("800", "877")` statement, which is shown in the first example in Figure 8-8, the computer first makes a copy of the string stored in the `phone` variable. It then replaces "800" with "877" in the copied string, and then assigns the result—in this case, "1-877-111-0000"—to the `newPhone` variable.

In the second example shown in Figure 8-8, the `social = social.Replace("-", "")` statement replaces each dash (hyphen) in the string stored in the `social` variable with a zero-length (empty) string. After the statement is processed, the `social` variable contains the string "000119999".

In the last example in Figure 8-8, the `word = word.Replace("t", "d")` statement replaces each letter "t" in the string stored in the `word` variable with the letter "d". The statement changes the contents of the `word` variable from "latter" to "ladder".

The Replace method replaces all occurrences of *oldValue* with *newValue*. At times, however, you may need to replace only a specific occurrence of *oldValue* with *newValue*; for this, you use the Mid statement rather than the Replace method.

The Mid Statement

You can use the **Mid statement** to replace a specified number of characters in a string with characters from another string. Figure 8-9 shows the syntax of the Mid statement and includes several examples of using the statement.

Syntax
To replace a specific number of characters in a string with characters from another string: **Mid**(*targetString, start* [, *count*]) = *replacementString*
Examples and results
`Dim name As String = "Rob Smith"` `Mid(name, 7, 1) = "y"`
changes the contents of the `name` variable to "Rob Smyth"
`Dim name As String = "Rob Smith"` `Mid(name, 7) = "y"`
changes the contents of the `name` variable to "Rob Smyth"
`Dim name As String = "Ann Johnson"` `Mid(name, 5) = "Paul"`
changes the contents of the `name` variable to "Ann Paulson"
`Dim name As String = "Earl Cho"` `Mid(name, 6) = "Liverpool"`
changes the contents of the `name` variable to "Earl Liv"

Figure 8-9: Syntax and examples of the Mid statement

In the Mid statement's syntax, *targetString* is the string in which you want characters replaced, and *replacementString* contains the replacement characters. *Start* is the character position of the first character you want replaced in the *targetString*. The first character in the *targetString* is in character position one, the second is in character position two, and so on. (Notice that the character position is not the same as the index, which begins with zero.) The *count* argument, which is optional in the Mid statement, specifies the number of characters to replace in the *targetString*. If *count* is omitted, the Mid statement replaces the lesser of either the number of characters in the *replacementString*, or the number of characters in the *targetString* from position *start* through the end of the *targetString*.

Study closely the examples shown in Figure 8-9. In the first example, the `Mid(name, 7, 1) = "y"` statement replaces the letter "i", which is located in character position seven in the `name` variable, with the letter "y". After the statement is processed, the `name` variable contains the string "Rob Smyth".

You also can omit the *count* argument and use the `Mid(name, 7) = "y"` statement, which is shown in the second example in Figure 8-9, to replace the letter "i" in the `name` variable with the letter "y". Recall that when the *count* argument is omitted from the Mid statement, the statement replaces the lesser of either the number of characters in the *replacementString* (in this case, one) or the number of characters in the *targetString* from position *start* through the end of the *targetString* (in this case, three).

The `Mid(name, 5) = "Paul"` statement in the third example in Figure 8-9 replaces four characters in the `name` variable, beginning with the character located in character position five in the variable (the letter J). Here again, because the *count* argument is omitted from the Mid statement, the statement replaces the lesser of either the number of characters in the *replacementString* (in this case, four) or the number of characters in the *targetString* from position *start* through the end of the *targetString* (in this case, seven). After the statement is processed, the `name` variable contains the string "Ann Paulson".

The `Mid(name, 6) = "Liverpool"` statement in the last example in Figure 8-9 replaces three characters in the `name` variable, beginning with the character located in character position six in the variable (the letter C). Here again, because the *count* argument is omitted from the Mid statement, the statement replaces the lesser of either the number of characters in the *replacementString* (in this case, nine) or the number of characters in the *targetString* from position *start* through the end of the *targetString* (in this case, three). After the statement is processed, the `name` variable contains the string "Earl Liv".

Next you learn how to insert characters at the beginning and end of a string.

Inserting Characters at the Beginning and End of a String

You can use the PadLeft and PadRight methods to pad a string with a character until the string is a specified length; both methods return the padded string. The **PadLeft method** pads the string on the left—in other words, it inserts the padded characters at the beginning of the string; doing so right-aligns the characters within the string. The **PadRight method**, on the other hand, pads the string on the right, which inserts the padded characters at the end of the string and left-aligns the characters within the string. Figure 8-10 shows the syntax of the PadLeft and PadRight methods and includes several examples of using the methods.

Syntax
To insert characters at the beginning of a string: *string*.**PadLeft**(*length*[, *character*])
To insert characters at the end of a string: *string*.**PadRight**(*length*[, *character*])

Examples and results
``` Dim num as Integer = 42 Dim numString As String numString = Convert.ToString(num) numString = numString.PadLeft(5) ``` assigns "   42" (three spaces and the string "42") to the `numString` variable
``` Dim num as Integer = 42 Dim numString As String numString = num.ToString().PadLeft(5) ``` assigns "   42" (three spaces and the string "42") to the `numString` variable
``` Dim netPay As Decimal = 767.89D Dim net As String net = netPay.ToString("C2").PadLeft(15, "*"c) ``` assigns "********$767.89" to the `net` variable
``` Dim name As String = "Sue", newName As String newName = name.PadRight(10) ``` assigns "Sue   " (the string "Sue" and seven spaces) to the `newName` variable
``` Dim name As String = "Sue" name = name.PadRight(10) ``` assigns "Sue   " (the string "Sue" and seven spaces) to the `name` variable

Figure 8-10: Syntax and examples of the PadLeft and PadRight methods

In each syntax, *length* is an integer that represents the desired length of the *string*—in other words, the total number of characters you want the *string* to contain. The *character* argument is the character that each method uses to pad the *string* until it reaches the desired *length*. Notice that the *character* argument is optional in each syntax; if omitted, the default *character* is the space character.

The code shown in the first two examples in Figure 8-10 produces the same results; both assign five characters—three space characters, the character 4, and the character 2—to the `numString` variable. However, the first example uses two assignment statements to accomplish the task, while the second example uses one assignment statement. The first assignment statement in the first example, `numString = Convert.ToString(num)`, assigns the contents of the num variable, converted to a String, to the `numString` variable. When processing the second assignment statement in the first example, `numString = numString.PadLeft(5)`, the computer first makes a copy of the string stored in the `numString` variable. It then pads the copied string with space characters until the string contains exactly five characters. In this case, the computer uses three space characters, which it inserts at the beginning of the string. The computer then assigns the resulting string—" 42"—to the `numString` variable.

When processing the `numString = num.ToString().PadLeft(5)` assignment statement in the second example, the computer first makes a copy of the value stored in the num variable. It then converts the copied value to a string, then inserts space characters at the beginning of the string until the string has exactly five characters, and then assigns the result to the `numString` variable. Here again, notice that when two methods appear in an expression, the computer processes the methods from left to right. In this case, the computer processes the ToString method before processing the PadLeft method.

When processing the `net = netPay.ToString("C2").PadLeft(15, "*"c)` statement shown in the third example in Figure 8-10, the computer first makes a copy of the number stored in the `netPay` variable. It then converts the number to a string and formats it with a dollar sign and two decimal places. The computer then pads the string with asterisks until the string contains exactly 15 characters. In this case, the computer inserts eight asterisks at the beginning of the string. The computer assigns the resulting string ("********$767.89") to the `net` variable.

When processing the `newName = name.PadRight(10)` statement shown in the fourth example in Figure 8-10, the computer first makes a copy of the string stored in the `name` variable. It then pads the copied string with space characters until the string contains exactly 10 characters. In this case, the computer uses seven space characters, which it inserts at the end of the string. The computer then assigns the resulting string—"Sue   "—to the `newName` variable. The `newName = name.PadRight(10)` statement does not change the contents of the `name` variable. To assign "Sue   " to the `name` variable, you would need to use the `name = name.PadRight(10)` statement shown in the last example in Figure 8-10.

The PadLeft and PadRight methods can be used to insert characters only at the beginning or end of a string; neither can be used to insert characters within a string. Visual Basic .NET provides the Insert method for inserting characters anywhere within a string.

Inserting Characters Within a String

You can use the **Insert method** to insert characters within a string. For example, you can use the Insert method to insert an employee's middle initial within his or her name. Or, you can use it to insert parentheses around the area code in a phone number. Figure 8-11 shows the syntax of the Insert method and includes two examples of using the method.

Syntax

To insert characters within a string: *string*.**Insert**(*startIndex*, *value*)

Examples and results

```
Dim name As String = "Rob Smith"
Dim newName As String
newName = name.Insert(4, "T. ")
```

assigns the string "Rob T. Smith" to the newName variable

```
Dim phone As String = "3120501111"
phone = phone.Insert(0, "(")
phone = phone.Insert(4, ")")
phone = phone.Insert(8, "-")
```

changes the contents of the phone variable to "(312)050-1111"

Figure 8-11: Syntax and examples of the Insert method

In the Insert method's syntax, *startIndex* specifies where in the *string* you want the *value* inserted. To insert the *value* at the beginning of the *string*, you use the number zero as the *startIndex*. To insert the *value* as the second character in the *string*, you use the number one as the *startIndex*, and so on. The Insert method returns a string with the appropriate characters inserted.

When processing the `newName = name.Insert(4, "T. ")` statement shown in the first example in Figure 8-11, the computer first makes a copy of the string stored in the `name` variable, and then inserts the *value* "T. " (the letter T, a period, and a space) in the copied string. The letter T is inserted in *startIndex* position 4, which makes it the fifth character in the string. The period and space are inserted in *startIndex* positions 5 and 6, making them the sixth and seventh characters in the string. After the statement is processed, the `newName` variable contains the string "Rob T. Smith"; however, the `name` variable still contains "Rob Smith".

In the second example shown in Figure 8-11, the `phone = phone.Insert(0, "(")` statement changes the contents of the `phone` variable from "3120501111" to "(3120501111". The `phone = phone.Insert(4, ")")` statement then changes the contents of the variable from "(3120501111" to "(312)0501111", and the `phone = phone.Insert(8, "-")` statement changes the contents of the variable from "(312)0501111" to "(312)050-1111".

Next, you learn how to search a string to determine whether it contains a specific sequence of characters.

> You also can use the Instr function to determine whether a string contains a specific sequence of characters. You learn about the Instr function in Discovery Exercise 20 at the end of this lesson.

Searching a String

You can use the **IndexOf method** to search a string to determine whether it contains a specific sequence of characters. For example, you can use the IndexOf method to determine whether the area code "312" appears in a phone number, or whether the street name "Elm Street" appears in an address. Figure 8-12 shows the syntax of the IndexOf method and includes several examples of using the method.

Syntax
To search a string to determine whether it contains a specific sequence of characters: *string*.**IndexOf**(*value*[, *startIndex*])

Examples and results
| ```
Dim msg As String = "Have a nice day"
Dim indexNum As Integer
indexNum = msg.IndexOf("nice", 0)
```<br>assigns the number 7 to the indexNum variable |
| ```
Dim msg As String = "Have a nice day"
Dim indexNum As Integer
indexNum = msg.IndexOf("nice")
```<br>assigns the number 7 to the indexNum variable |
| ```
Dim msg As String = "Have a nice day"
Dim indexNum As Integer
indexNum = msg.IndexOf("Nice")
```<br>assigns the number -1 to the indexNum variable |
| ```
Dim msg As String = "Have a nice day"
Dim indexNum As Integer
indexNum = msg.ToUpper().IndexOf("NICE")
```<br>assigns the number 7 to the indexNum variable |
| ```
Dim msg As String = "Have a nice day"
Dim indexNum As Integer
indexNum = msg.IndexOf("nice", 5)
```<br>assigns the number 7 to the indexNum variable |
| ```
Dim msg As String = "Have a nice day"
Dim indexNum As Integer
indexNum = msg.IndexOf("nice", 8)
```<br>assigns the number -1 to the indexNum variable |

Figure 8-12: Syntax and examples of the IndexOf method

In the syntax, *value* is the sequence of characters for which you are searching in the *string*, and *startIndex* is the index of the character at which the search should begin—in other words, *startIndex* specifies the starting position for the search. Recall that the first character in a string has an index of zero, the second character has an index of one, and so on. Notice that the *startIndex* argument is optional in the IndexOf method's syntax. If you omit the *startIndex* argument, the IndexOf method begins the search with the first character in the *string*.

The IndexOf method searches for *value* within *string*, beginning with the character whose index is *startIndex*. If the IndexOf method does not find the *value*, it returns the number -1; otherwise, it returns the index of the starting position of *value* within *string*.

You can use either the `indexNum = msg.IndexOf("nice", 0)` statement shown in the first example in Figure 8-12, or the `indexNum = msg.IndexOf("nice")` statement shown in the second example, to search for the word "nice" in the `msg` variable, beginning with the first character in the variable. In each case, the word "nice" begins with the eighth character in the variable. The eighth character has an index of seven, so both statements assign the number seven to the `indexNum` variable.

The IndexOf method performs a case-sensitive search, as the third example in Figure 8-12 indicates. In this example, the `indexNum = msg.IndexOf("Nice")` statement assigns the number -1 to the `indexNum` variable, because the word "Nice" is not contained in the `msg` variable.

You can use the `indexNum = msg.ToUpper().IndexOf("NICE")` statement shown in the fourth example in Figure 8-12 to perform a case-insensitive search for the word "nice". The ToUpper method in the statement is processed first and temporarily converts the string stored in the `msg` variable to uppercase. The IndexOf method then searches the uppercase string for the word "NICE". The statement assigns the number seven to the `indexNum` variable because, ignoring case, the word "nice" begins with the character whose index is seven.

The `indexNum = msg.IndexOf("nice", 5)` statement shown in the fifth example in Figure 8-12 searches for the word "nice" in the `msg` variable, beginning with the character whose index is five; that character is the second letter "a". The statement assigns the number seven to the `indexNum` variable, because the word "nice" begins with the character whose index is seven.

The `indexNum = msg.IndexOf("nice", 8)` statement shown in the last example in Figure 8-12 searches for the word "nice" in the `msg` variable, beginning with the character whose index is eight; that character is the letter "i". Notice that the word "nice" does not appear anywhere in the "ice day" portion of the string stored in the `msg` variable. Therefore, the statement assigns the number -1 to the `indexNum` variable.

Figure 8-13 summarizes the string manipulation techniques you learned in this lesson. It also includes the Like operator, which you learned about in Chapter 5. Recall that the Like operator allows you to use pattern-matching characters to determine whether one string is equal to another string.

Technique	Syntax	Purpose
EndsWith method	*string*.**EndsWith**(*subString*)	determine whether a string ends with a specific sequence of characters
IndexOf method	*string*.**IndexOf**(*value*[, *startIndex*])	search a string to determine whether it contains a specific sequence of characters
Insert method	*string*.**Insert**(*startIndex*, *value*)	insert characters within a string
Length property	*string*.**Length**	determine the number of characters in a string
Like operator	*string* **Like** *pattern*	use pattern-matching characters to determine whether one string is equal to another string
Mid statement	**Mid**(*targetString*, *start* [, *count*]) = *replacementString*	replace a specific number of characters in a string with characters from another string
PadLeft method	*string*.**PadLeft**(*length*[, *character*])	pad the beginning of a string with a character until the string is a specified length
PadRight method	*string*.**PadRight**(*length*[, *character*])	pad the end of a string with a character until the string is a specified length
Remove method	*string*.**Remove**(*startIndex*, *count*)	remove characters from anywhere in a string
Replace method	*string*.**Replace**(*oldValue*, *newValue*)	replace all occurrences of a sequence of characters in a string with another sequence of characters

Figure 8-13: String manipulation techniques

Technique	Syntax	Purpose
StartsWith method	*string*.**StartsWith(***subString***)**	determine whether a string begins with a specific sequence of characters
Substring method	*string*.**Substring(***startIndex***[, *count*])**	access one or more characters contained in a string
Trim method	*string*.**Trim([***trimChars***])**	remove characters from both the beginning and end of a string
TrimEnd method	*string*.**TrimEnd([***trimChars***])**	remove characters from the end of a string
TrimStart method	*string*.**TrimStart([***trimChars***])**	remove characters from the beginning of a string

Figure 8-13: String manipulation techniques (continued)

You now have completed Lesson A. You can either take a break or complete the end-of-lesson questions and exercises before moving on to the next lesson.

SUMMARY

To determine the number of characters contained in a string:

- Use the Length property in the following syntax: *string*.**Length**.

To remove one or more characters from the beginning and/or end of a string:

- Use the TrimStart method to remove one or more characters from the beginning of a string. The method's syntax is *string*.**TrimStart**([*trimChars*]), where *trimChars* is a comma-separated list of characters that you want removed from the *string*.
- Use the TrimEnd method to remove one or more characters from the end of a string. The method's syntax is *string*.**TrimEnd**([*trimChars*]), where *trimChars* is a comma-separated list of characters that you want removed from the *string*.
- Use the Trim method to remove one or more characters from both the beginning and end of a string. The method's syntax is *string*.**Trim**([*trimChars*]), where *trimChars* is a comma-separated list of characters that you want removed from the *string*.
- The TrimStart, TrimEnd, and Trim methods return a string with the appropriate characters removed (trimmed).

To remove one or more characters from anywhere in a string:

- Use the Remove method. The method's syntax is *string*.**Remove**(*startIndex*, *count*), where *startIndex* is the index of the first character you want removed from the *string*, and *count* is the number of characters you want removed. The first character in a string has an index of zero, the second character an index of one, and so on.
- The Remove method returns a string with the appropriate characters removed.

To determine whether a specific sequence of characters occurs at either the beginning or end of a string:

- Use the StartsWith method to determine whether a string begins with a specific sequence of characters. The method's syntax is *string*.**StartsWith**(*subString*), where *subString* is the sequence of characters that the method should search for at the beginning of the *string*. The StartsWith method returns the Boolean value True if *subString* is located at the beginning of *string*; otherwise, it returns the Boolean value False.

- Use the EndsWith method to determine whether a string ends with a specific sequence of characters. The method's syntax is *string*.**EndsWith**(*subString*), where *subString* is the sequence of characters that the method should search for at the end of the *string*. The EndsWith method returns the Boolean value True if *subString* is located at the end of *string*; otherwise, it returns the Boolean value False.

To access one or more characters contained in a string:

- Use the Substring method. The method's syntax is *string*.**Substring**(*startIndex*[, *count*]), where *startIndex* is the index of the first character you want to access in the *string*, and *count* (which is optional) specifies the number of characters to access.
- The Substring method returns a string that contains *count* number of characters, beginning with the character whose index is *startIndex*. If you omit the *count* argument, the Substring method returns all characters from the *startIndex* position through the end of the string.

To replace all occurrences of a sequence of characters in a string with another sequence of characters:

- Use the Replace method. The method's syntax is *string*.**Replace**(*oldValue*, *newValue*), where *oldValue* is the sequence of characters that you want replaced in the *string*, and *newValue* is the replacement characters.
- The Replace method returns a string with all occurrences of *oldValue* replaced with *newValue*.

To replace a specific number of characters in a string with characters from another string:

- Use the Mid statement. The statement's syntax is **Mid**(*targetString*, *start* [, *count*]) = *replacementString*, where *targetString* is the string in which you want characters replaced, and *replacementString* contains the replacement characters. *Start* is the character position of the first character you want replaced in the *targetString*. The first character in the *targetString* is in character position one, the second is in character position two, and so on. The *count* argument, which is optional, specifies the number of characters to replace in the *targetString*. If the *count* argument is omitted, the Mid statement replaces the lesser of either the number of characters in the *replacementString*, or the number of characters in the *targetString* from position *start* through the end of the *targetString*.
- The Mid statement replaces *count* number of characters in *targetString*, beginning with the character in character position *start*. The characters are replaced with *replacementString*.

To pad a string with a character until the string is a specified length:

- Use the PadLeft method to pad a string on the left, and the PadRight method to pad a string on the right.
- The syntax of the PadLeft method is *string*.**PadLeft**(*length*[, *character*]). The syntax of the PadRight method is *string*.**PadRight**(*length*[, *character*]). In each syntax, *length* is an integer that represents the desired length of the *string*, and *character* is the character that each method uses to pad the *string* until it reaches the desired *length*. If the *character* argument is omitted, the default *character* is the space character.
- The PadLeft method right-aligns the characters within a *string*, and the PadRight method left-aligns the characters.

To insert characters within a string:

- Use the Insert method. The method's syntax is *string*.**Insert**(*startIndex*, *value*), where *startIndex* specifies where in the *string* you want the *value* inserted. For example, to insert the *value* at the beginning of the *string*, you use the number zero as the *startIndex*.
- The Insert method returns a string with the appropriate characters inserted.

To search a string to determine whether it contains a specific sequence of characters:

- Use the IndexOf method. The method's syntax is *string*.**IndexOf**(*value*[, *startIndex*]), where *value* is the sequence of characters for which you are searching in the *string*, and *startIndex* (which is optional) specifies the index of the character at which the search should begin. If you omit the *startIndex* argument, the IndexOf method begins the search with the first character in the *string*.

- The IndexOf method returns the number -1 if *value* is not contained on or after the character in position *startIndex* in *string*; otherwise, it returns the index of the starting position of *value* within *string*.

QUESTIONS

1. You can use the _____ to determine the number of characters in a string.
   a. Length method
   b. Length property
   c. NumChars property
   d. Size method
   e. Size property

2. Assume that the `amount` variable contains the string "$56.55". Which of the following removes the dollar sign from the variable's contents?
   a. `amount = amount.Remove("$")`
   b. `amount = amount.Remove(0, 1)`
   c. `amount = amount.TrimStart(0, 1)`
   d. `amount = amount.TrimStart("$"c)`
   e. Both b and d.

3. Assume that the `state` variable contains the string "MI   " (the letters M and I followed by three spaces). Which of the following removes the three spaces from the variable's contents?
   a. `state = state.Remove(2, 3)`
   b. `state = state.Remove(3, 3)`
   c. `state = state.TrimEnd(2, 3)`
   d. `state = state.TrimEnd(3, 3)`
   e. Both a and c.

4. Which of the following removes any dollar signs and percent signs from the beginning and end of the string stored in the `amount` variable?
   a. `amount = amount.Trim("$"c, "%"c)`
   b. `amount = amount.Trim("$, %"c)`
   c. `amount = amount.TrimAll("$"c, "%"c)`
   d. `amount = amount.TrimAll("$, %"c)`
   e. None of the above.

5. The `name = Me.uiNameTextBox.Text.TrimEnd()` statement changes the contents of both the name variable and the uiNameTextBox control.
   a. True
   b. False

6. The index of the first character in a string is _____.
   a. 0 (zero)
   b. 1 (one)

7. Which of the following can be used to determine whether the string stored in the `part` variable begins with the letter A?

    a. `part.Begins("A")`

    b. `part.BeginsWith("A")`

    c. `part.Starts("A")`

    d. `part.StartsWith("A")`

    e. `part.StartsWith = "A"`

8. Which of the following can be used to determine whether the string stored in the `part` variable ends with either the letter B or the letter b?

    a. `part.Ends("B, b")`

    b. `part.Ends("B", "b")`

    c. `part.EndsWith("B", "b")`

    d. `part.ToUpper().EndsWith("B")`

    e. `part.ToUpper().EndsWith = "B"`

9. Which of the following assigns the first three characters in the `part` variable to the `code` variable?

    a. `code = part.Assign(0, 3)`

    b. `code = part.Sub(0, 3)`

    c. `code = part.Substring(0, 3)`

    d. `code = part.Substring(1, 3)`

    e. None of the above.

10. Assume that the `word` variable contains the string "Bells". Which of the following changes the contents of the `word` variable to "Bell"?

    a. `word = word.Remove(word.Length - 1, 1)`

    b. `word = word.Substring(0, word.Length - 1)`

    c. `word = word.TrimEnd("s"c)`

    d. `word = word.Replace("s", "")`

    e. All of the above.

11. Which of the following changes the contents of the `zip` variable from "60121" to "60323"?

    a. `Replace(zip, "1", "3")`

    b. `zip.Replace("1", "3")`

    c. `zip = zip.Replace("1", "3")`

    d. `zip = zip.Replace("3", "1")`

    e. None of the above.

12. Which of the following changes the contents of the `zip` variable from "60537" to "60536"?

    a. `Mid(zip, "7", "6")`

    b. `Mid(zip, 4, "6")`

    c. `zip = Mid(zip, 4, "6")`

    d. `zip.Mid("7", "6")`

    e. None of the above.

13. Which of the following changes the contents of the `word` variable from "men" to "mean"?

    a. `word = word.AddTo(2, "a")`

    b. `word = word.Insert(2, "a")`

    c. `word = word.Insert(3, "a")`

    d. `word = word.Replace(2, "a")`

    e. `word = word.Replace(3, "a")`

14. Assuming that the `msg` variable contains the string "Happy holidays", the `msg.IndexOf("day")` method returns _____.
    a. -1
    b. 0
    c. 10
    d. 11
    e. day

15. Assume that the `msg` variable contains the string "Good morning". The statement `Mid(msg, 6) = "night"` changes the contents of the `msg` variable to _____.

    a. Good mnight
    b. Good mnightg
    c. Good night
    d. Good nightng
    e. nightG

16. Which of the following If clauses can be used to determine whether the `amount` variable contains a comma?
    a. `If amount.Contains(",") Then`
    b. `If amount.Substring(",") Then`
    c. `If amount.IndexOf(",") = 0 Then`
    d. `If amount.IndexOf(",") > -1 Then`
    e. None of the above.

17. Which of the following can be used to assign the fifth character in the `word` variable to the `letter` variable?
    a. `letter = word.Substring(4)`
    b. `letter = word.Substring(5, 1)`
    c. `letter = word(5).Substring`
    d. `letter = Substring(word, 5)`
    e. None of the above.

18. Assume that the `state` variable contains the string "Florida". Which of the following assigns six spaces followed by the contents of the `state` variable to the `state` variable?
    a. `state = state.Pad(13)`
    b `state = state.PadLeft(6)`
    c. `state = state.PadLeft(13)`
    d. `state = state.PadRight(6)`
    e. None of the above.

19. Assume that the `msg` variable contains the string "Great job". Which of the following assigns the contents of the `msg` variable followed by four exclamation points (!) to the `newMsg` variable?
    a. `newMsg = msg.PadLeft(4, "!")`
    b. `newMsg = msg.PadLeft(13, "!")`
    c. `newMsg = msg.PadRight(4, "!")`
    d. `newMsg = msg.PadRight(13, "!")`
    e. None of the above.

EXERCISES

1. Write the Visual Basic .NET statement that displays in the uiSizeLabel control the number of characters contained in the `msg` variable.

2. Write the Visual Basic .NET statement that removes the leading spaces from the `city` variable.

3. Write the Visual Basic .NET statement that removes the leading and trailing spaces from the `num` variable.

4. Write the Visual Basic .NET statement that removes any trailing spaces, commas, and periods from the `amount` variable.

5. Write the Visual Basic .NET statement that uses the Remove method to remove the first two characters from the `name` variable.

6. Write the Visual Basic .NET code that uses the EndsWith method to determine whether the string stored in the `rate` variable ends with the percent sign. If it does, the code should use the TrimEnd method to remove the percent sign from the variable's contents.

7. Assume that the `part` variable contains the string "ABCD34G". Write the Visual Basic .NET statement that assigns the number 34 in the `part` variable to the `code` variable.

8. Assume that the `amount` variable contains the string "3,123,560". Write the Visual Basic .NET statement that assigns the contents of the variable, excluding the commas and treated as a Decimal number, to the `salesAmount` variable.

9. Write the Mid statement that changes the contents of the `word` variable from "mouse" to "mouth".

10. Write the Visual Basic .NET statement that uses the Insert method to change the contents of the `word` variable from "mend" to "amend".

11. Write the Visual Basic .NET statement that uses the IndexOf method to determine whether the `address` variable contains the street name "Elm Street" (entered in uppercase, lowercase, or a combination of uppercase and lowercase). Begin the search with the first character in the `address` variable, and assign the method's return value to the `indexNum` variable.

12. In this exercise, you complete an application that displays a shipping charge based on the ZIP code entered by the user.
    a. If necessary, start Visual Studio .NET. Open the Zip Solution (Zip Solution.sln) file, which is contained in the VBNET\Chap08\Zip Solution folder. If necessary, open the designer window.
    b. The Display Shipping Charge button's Click event procedure should display the appropriate shipping charge based on the ZIP code entered by the user. To be valid, the ZIP code must contain exactly five digits, and the first three digits must be either "605" or "606". All ZIP codes beginning with "605" have a $25 shipping charge. All ZIP codes beginning with "606" have a $30 shipping charge. All other ZIP codes are invalid and the procedure should display an appropriate message. Code the procedure appropriately.
    c. Save the solution, then start the application. Test the application using the following ZIP codes: 60677, 60511, and 60344.
    d. Click the Exit button to end the application, then close the solution.

13. In this exercise, you complete an application that displays the name of the month corresponding to three letters entered by the user.

    a. If necessary, start Visual Studio .NET. Open the Month Solution (Month Solution.sln) file, which is contained in the VBNET\Chap08\Month Solution folder. If necessary, open the designer window.

    b. The user will enter the first three characters of the month's name in the uiMonthTextBox control. The Display Month button's Click event procedure should display the name of the month corresponding to the characters entered by the user. For example, if the user enters the three characters "Jan" (in any case), the procedure should display the string "January" in the uiMonthLabel control. If the user enters "Jun", the procedure should display "June". If the three characters entered by the user do not match any of the 12 months, or if the user does not enter exactly three characters, the procedure should display an appropriate message.

    c. Save the solution, then start the application. Test the application using the following data: jun, dec, xyz, july.

    d. Click the Exit button to end the application, then close the solution.

14. In this exercise, you code an application that displays the color of an item.

    a. If necessary, start Visual Studio .NET. Open the Color Solution (Color Solution.sln) file, which is contained in the VBNET\Chap08\Color Solution folder. If necessary, open the designer window.

    b. The Display Color button's Click event procedure should display the color of the item whose item number is entered by the user. All item numbers contain exactly five characters. All items are available in four colors: blue, green, red, and white. The third character in the item number indicates the item's color, as follows:

Character	Color
B or b	Blue
G or g	Green
R or r	Red
W or w	White

For example, if the user enters 12b45, the procedure should display the word "Blue" in the uiColorLabel control. If the item number does not contain exactly five characters, or if the third character is not one of the characters listed above, the procedure should display an appropriate message in a message box.

    c. Save the solution, then start the application. Test the application using the following item numbers: 12x, 12b45, 99G44, abr55, 78w99, and 23abc.

    d. Click the Exit button to end the application, then close the solution.

15. In this exercise, you code an application that allows the user to enter a name (the first name followed by a space and the last name). The application then displays the name (the last name followed by a comma, a space, and the first name).

    a. Build an appropriate interface. Name the solution Reverse Name Solution. Name the project Reverse Name Project. Save the application in the VBNET\Chap08 folder.

    b. Code the application.

    c. Save the solution, and then start the application. Test the application using the following names: Carol Smith, Jose Martinez, and Sven Miller.

    d. Click the Exit button to end the application, then close the solution.

16. In this exercise, you code an application that allows the user to enter a phone number. The application then removes any hyphens and parentheses from the phone number before displaying the phone number.

    a. Build an appropriate interface. Name the solution Phone Solution. Name the project Phone Project. Save the application in the VBNET\Chap08 folder.

    b. Code the application.

    c. Save the solution, then start the application. Test the application using the following phone numbers: (555)-111-1111, 555-5555, and 123-456-1111.

    d. Click the Exit button to end the application, then close the solution.

discovery ▶ 17. In addition to using the Length property, you also can use the Len function to determine the number of characters contained in a string. The syntax of the Len function is **Len**(*string*). For example, you can rewrite Example 1 in Figure 8-3 as `numChars = Len(Me.uiZipTextBox.Text)`. Rewrite Examples 2 through 4 in Figure 8-3 using the Len function.

discovery ▶ 18. In addition to using the TrimStart, TrimEnd, and Trim methods, you also can use the LTrim, RTrim, and Trim functions, respectively, to remove any leading and/or trailing spaces from a string. The syntax of the LTrim function is **LTrim**(*string*). The syntax of the RTrim function is **RTrim**(*string*), and the syntax of the Trim function is **Trim**(*string*). Each function returns a string with the appropriate spaces removed. For example, you can remove the leading spaces from the `name` variable using the statement `name = LTrim(name)`.

    a. Write a statement that uses the LTrim function to remove the leading spaces from the uiNameTextBox's Text property. The statement should assign the resulting string to the `name` variable.

    b. Write a statement that uses the RTrim function to remove the trailing spaces from a String variable named `zip`. The statement should assign the resulting string to the `zip` variable.

    c. Write a statement that uses the Trim function to remove the leading and trailing spaces from a String variable named `inputNumber`. The statement should assign the resulting string, treated as a Decimal number, to the `number` variable.

discovery ▶ 19. In addition to using the Substring method, you also can use the Left, Right, and Mid functions to access one or more characters in a string. The syntax of the Left function is **Left**(*string*, *length*), and the syntax of the Right function is **Right**(*string*, *length*). The Left function returns the leftmost *length* number of characters in the *string*, and the Right function returns the rightmost *length* number of characters in the *string*. For example, assuming the `name` variable contains the string "Jose Tom Marsales", the statement `firstName = Left(name, 4)` assigns the string "Jose" to the `firstName` variable, and the statement `lastName = Right(name, 8)` assigns the string "Marsales" to the `lastName` variable.

The syntax of the Mid function is **Mid**(*string*, *start* [, *length*]). The Mid function returns *length* number of characters from a *string*, beginning with the *start* character. If *length* is omitted, the function returns all characters from the *start* position through the end of the *string*. The first character in a string is in character position one, the second is in character position two, and so on. For example, assuming the `name` variable contains the string "Jose Tom Marsales", the statement `middleName = Mid(name, 6, 3)` assigns the string "Tom" to the `middleName` variable.

a. Assuming that the `progName` variable contains the string "Visual Basic .NET", what will the following functions return?

1) `Left("January", 3)`
2) `Right("January", 2)`
3) `Left(progName, 6)`
4) `Right(progName, 10)`
5) `Mid("January", 2, 1)`
6) `Mid("January", 4, 2)`
7) `Mid(progName, 8, 1)`
8) `Mid(progName, 8)`

b. Write the Left function that returns the first three characters contained in the `part` variable.

c. Write the Right function that returns the last character contained in the `part` variable.

d. Write the Mid function that returns the second through fifth characters contained in the `part` variable.

discovery ▶ 20. In addition to using the IndexOf method, you also can use the Instr ("in string") function to determine whether a specific sequence of characters appears in a string. The syntax of the Instr function is **Instr**(*start, string1, string2*[, *compare*]), where *start* specifies the character position at which the search should begin. The first character in a string is in character position one, the second is in character position two, and so on. *String1* in the syntax is the string to be searched, and *string2* is the sequence of characters being sought. The *compare* argument, which is optional, indicates whether the function should perform a case-sensitive or case-insensitive search. If the *compare* argument is either omitted or set to the number zero, the function performs a case-sensitive search. If the *compare* argument is set to the number one, on the other hand, the function performs a case-insensitive search. If *string2* is not contained within *string1*, then the Instr function returns the number zero; otherwise, it returns the starting character position of *string2* within *string1*. For example, the `Instr(1, "Have a nice day", "nice", 0)` function returns the number eight, and the `Instr(1, "Have a nice day", "nice", 10)` function returns the number zero.

a. Assuming that the `msg` variable contains the string "Don't forget to VOTE for your favorite candidate", what will the following Instr functions return?

1) `Instr(1, msg, "vote", 0)`
2) `Instr(1, msg, "vote", 1)`
3) `Instr(10, msg, "vote", 1)`
4) `Instr(10, msg, "vote", 0)`

After completing this lesson, you will be able to:

■ Add a main menu control to a form

■ Add menu elements to a main menu control

■ Assign access keys and shortcut keys to menu elements

■ Code a menu item's Click event procedure

Using a Main Menu Control

Completing the Hangman Game Application's User Interface

Recall that your task in this chapter is to create a simplified version of the Hangman game for Mr. Mitchell, who teaches second grade at Hinsbrook School. On your computer's hard disk is a partially completed Hangman Game application. You complete the application's user interface in this lesson, and also begin coding the application.

To open the Hangman Game application:

1   Start Microsoft Visual Studio .NET, if necessary.

2   If necessary, close the Start Page window.

3   Open the **Hangman Solution** (Hangman Solution.sln) file, which is contained in the VBNET\Chap08\ Hangman Solution folder.

4   Auto-hide the Toolbox, Solution Explorer, and Properties windows, if necessary. Figure 8-14 shows the partially completed user interface for the Hangman Game application.

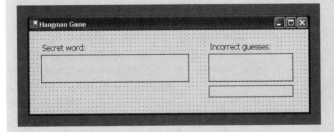

Figure 8-14: Partially completed interface for the Hangman Game application

You complete the interface by adding a main menu control to it.

Adding a Main Menu Control to a Form

You use a **main menu control** to include one or more menus in an application. Each menu contains a **menu title**, which appears on the menu bar at the top of a Windows form. When you click a menu title, its corresponding menu opens and displays a list of options, called **menu items**. The menu items can be commands (such as Open or Exit), separator bars, or submenu titles. As in all Windows applications, clicking a command on a menu executes the command, and clicking a submenu title opens an additional menu of options. Each of the options on a submenu is referred to as a **submenu item**. The purpose of a **separator bar** is to visually group together the related items on a menu or submenu. Figure 8-15 identifies the location of these menu elements.

separator bar

separator bar

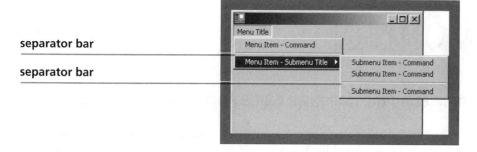

Figure 8-15: Location of menu elements

Each menu element is considered an object and has a set of properties associated with it. The most commonly used properties for a menu element are the Name and Text properties. The Name property is used by the programmer to refer to the menu element in code. The Text property, on the other hand, stores the menu element's caption, which is the text that the user sees when he or she is working with the menu. The caption indicates the purpose of the menu element. Examples of familiar captions for menu elements include Edit, Save As, Copy, and Exit.

Menu title captions should be one word only, with the first letter capitalized. Each menu title should have a unique access key. Menu item captions, on the other hand, can be from one to three words. Use book title capitalization for the menu item captions, and assign each menu item a unique access key. If a menu item requires additional information from the user, the Windows standard is to place an ellipsis (...) at the end of the caption. The ellipsis alerts the user that the menu item requires more information before it can perform its task.

When designing a menu, you must be sure to follow the standard conventions used in Windows applications. For example, the File menu is always the first menu on the menu bar, and typically contains commands for opening, saving, and printing files, as well as exiting the application. Cut, Copy, and Paste commands, on the other hand, are placed on an Edit menu, which typically is the second menu on the menu bar.

Before you can create a menu, you first must add a main menu control to the application.

tip

Although you can create many levels of submenus, it is best to use only one level in your application, because too many layers of submenus can be confusing to the user.

tip

You learned about access keys in Chapter 2. A menu title's access key allows the user to open the menu by pressing the Alt key in combination with the access key. A menu item's access key, however, allows the user to select the item simply by pressing the access key when the menu is open.

To add a main menu control to the Hangman Game application:

1   Click the **MainMenu tool** in the toolbox, and then drag a main menu control to the form. When you release the mouse button, the main menu control appears in the component tray, and the words "Type Here" appear on the form's title bar, as shown in Figure 8-16.

enter the first menu
title here

main menu control appears
in the component tray

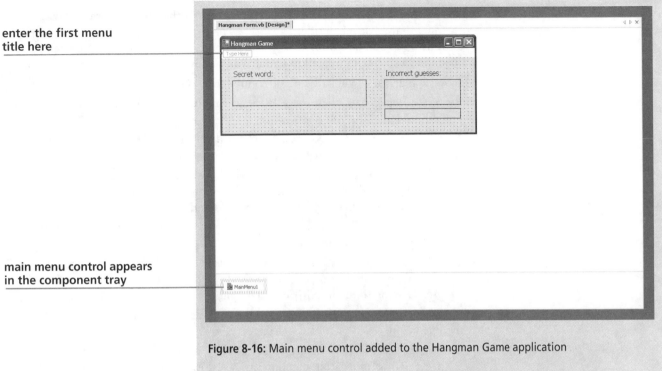

Figure 8-16: Main menu control added to the Hangman Game application

HELP? Do not be concerned if the words "Type Here" are highlighted on the menu bar.

2   Temporarily display the Properties window. Click (**Name**) in the Properties list, and then type **uiHangmanMainMenu** and press **Enter**.

You will include one menu—a File menu—on the Hangman Game application's menu bar. The File menu will contain three menu items: a New Game command, an Exit command, and a separator bar.

To create the File menu:

1   Click **Type Here** on the menu bar.

As is customary in Windows applications, you use the letter F as the File menu's access key.

2   Type **&File**. See Figure 8-17.

first menu title

first menu item on
the first menu

second menu title

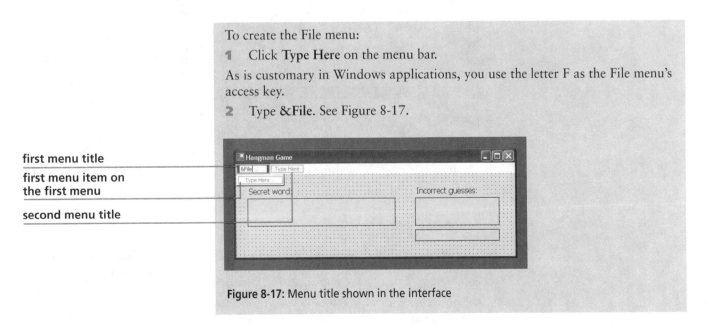

Figure 8-17: Menu title shown in the interface

Notice that the words "Type Here" appear below the File menu title and also to the right of the File menu title. The "Type Here" that appears below the menu title allows you to add a menu item to the File menu. The "Type Here" that appears to the right of the menu title allows you to add another menu title to the menu bar.

Now change the menu title's name to uiFileMenuTitle.

3 Press **Enter**, then click the **File** menu title. Change the menu title's name to **uiFileMenuTitle** and press **Enter**.

Next, you will include a New Game menu item on the File menu. The letter N is the standard access key for the New option on a File menu.

4 Click the **Type Here** that appears below the File menu title, then type **&New Game**. Press **Enter**, then click the **New Game** menu item. Change the New Game menu item's name to **uiFileNewMenuItem** and press **Enter**.

Now include an Exit menu item on the File menu. The letter X is the standard access key for the Exit option.

5 Click the **Type Here** that appears below the New Game menu item, and then type **E&xit**. Press **Enter**, then click the **Exit** menu item. Change the menu item's name to **uiFileExitMenuItem** and press **Enter**.

Next, you will insert a separator bar between the New Game and Exit options on the File menu.

6 Right-click the **Exit** menu item. A context menu opens and displays options for deleting an existing menu item, inserting a new menu item, and inserting a separator bar. In this case, you want to insert a separator bar.

7 Click **Insert Separator**. Notice that the separator bar is inserted above the menu item that you right-clicked; in this case, it is inserted above the Exit menu item.

8 Change the separator bar's name to **uiFileSeparator**, then click the **File** menu title on the menu. The File menu is shown in Figure 8-18.

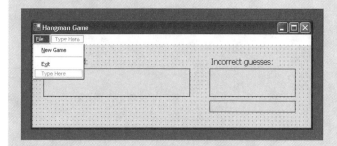

Figure 8-18: File menu

In addition to assigning access keys to menu items, you also can assign shortcut keys.

Assigning Shortcut Keys

Shortcut keys appear to the right of a menu item and allow you to select an item without opening the menu. For example, in Windows applications you can select the Save command when the File menu is closed by pressing Ctrl + S. You should assign shortcut keys only to commonly used menu items. In the Hangman Game application, you will assign a shortcut key to the New Game option on the File menu.

To assign a shortcut key to the New Game option:

1   Click the **New Game** menu item on the File menu. Temporarily display the Properties window, and then click **Shortcut** in the Properties list.

2   Click the **Shortcut** list arrow to display a list of shortcut keys. Scroll the list until you see CtrlN, then click **CtrlN** in the list. When you start the application and open the File menu, Ctrl+N will appear to the right of the New Game menu item. You verify that fact next.

3   Save the solution, then start the application. Click **File** on the Hangman Game application's menu bar. The shortcut key, Ctrl+N, appears to the right of the New Game menu item, as shown in Figure 8-19.

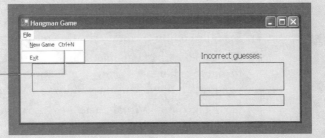

shortcut key

Figure 8-19: Shortcut key displayed on the File menu

4   Click the **Close** button on the Hangman Game application's title bar.

5   When you return to the designer window, close the Output window.

Designing Menus

- Menu title captions, which appear on the menu bar, should be one word, with the first letter capitalized. Each menu title should have a unique access key.

- Menu item captions, which appear on a menu, can be from one to three words. Use book title capitalization and assign a unique access key to each menu item. Assign shortcut keys to commonly used menu items.

- If a menu item requires additional information from the user, place an ellipsis (…) at the end of the item's caption, which is entered in the item's Text property.

- Follow the Windows standards for the placement of menu titles and items.

- Use a separator bar to separate groups of related menu items.

Now that the interface is complete, you can begin coding the application. In this lesson, you code only the Exit menu item's Click event procedure. You code the remaining procedures in Lesson C.

Coding the Click Event Procedure for the Exit Menu Item

When the user clicks the Exit item on the File menu, the item's Click event procedure should end the Hangman Game application.

To code the Exit menu item's Click event procedure, then test the procedure:

1   Open the Code Editor window. Replace the `<enter your name here>` and `<enter the date here>` text with your name and the current date.

2   Open the code template for the uiFileExitMenuItem's Click event procedure.

3   Enter the comment and statement shown in Figure 8-20.

enter this comment and statement

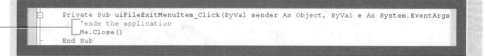

```
Private Sub uiFileExitMenuItem_Click(ByVal sender As Object, ByVal e As System.EventArgs
    'ends the application
    Me.Close()
End Sub
```

Figure 8-20: Completed uiFileExitMenuItem Click event procedure

4   Save the solution, and then start the application.

5   Click **File** on the Hangman Game application's menu bar, and then click **Exit** to end the Hangman Game application. When you return to the Code Editor window, close the Output window, then close the Code Editor window.

6   Click **File** on the Visual Basic .NET menu bar, and then click **Close Solution**.

You now have completed Lesson B. You finish coding the Hangman Game application in Lesson C. For now, you can either take a break or complete the end-of-lesson questions and exercises before moving on to the next lesson.

SUMMARY

To add a main menu control to a form:

■   Use the MainMenu tool in the toolbox.

To create a menu:

■   Replace the words "Type Here" with the menu element's caption.

■   Assign a meaningful name to each menu element.

■   Assign a unique access key to each menu element, excluding menu items that are separator bars.

To insert a separator bar in a menu:

■   Right-click a menu item, and then click Insert Separator. The separator bar will be inserted above the menu item.

To assign a shortcut key to a menu item:

■   Set the menu item's Shortcut property.

Q U E S T I O N S

1. A menu can contain a _____.
    a. command
    b. menu title
    c. separator bar
    d. submenu title
    e. All of the above.

2. The horizontal line in a menu is called _____.
    a. a dashed line
    b. a hyphen
    c. a menu bar
    d. a separator bar
    e. an item separator

3. The underlined letter in a menu element's caption is called a(n) _____.
    a. access key
    b. dash
    c. menu key
    d. open key
    e. shortcut key

4. A(n) _____ key allows you to access a menu item without opening the menu.
    a. access
    b. dash
    c. menu item
    d. open
    e. shortcut

5. Which of the following is false?
    a. Menu titles appear on the menu bar.
    b. Menu titles should be one word only.
    c. Each menu title should have a unique access key.
    d. You should assign a shortcut key to commonly used menu titles.
    e. Menu items should be entered using book title capitalization.

6. Explain the difference between a menu item's access key and its shortcut key.

E X E R C I S E S

1. In this exercise, you create a File menu and an Edit menu.
    a. If necessary, start Visual Studio .NET. Open the Menu Solution (Menu Solution.sln) file, which is contained in the VBNET\Chap08\Menu Solution folder. If necessary, open the designer window.
    b. Include a main menu control in the application. Change the control's name to uiPracticeMainMenu.
    c. Create the menu titles and menu items shown in Figure 8-21. Use appropriate names for the menu titles and menu items (including the separator bars).

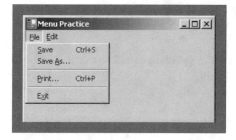

Figure 8-21

    d. Include the Undo, Paste, Copy, and Cut menu items on the Edit menu. Be sure to position the menu items in the correct order, and use a separator bar if appropriate. Also be sure to use the standard access keys and shortcut keys for the menu items. (*Hint*: You can use the Visual Basic .NET Edit menu to determine the standards for an Edit menu in a Windows application.)

    e. Code the Exit menu item so that it ends the application when the user clicks it.

    f. Save the solution, then start the application. Click File on the application's menu bar, and then click Exit to end the application.

    g. Close the Output window, then close the solution.

2. In this exercise, you include a menu in the Shoppers Haven application that you created in Chapter 6.

    a. Use Windows to make a copy of the Shoppers Haven Solution folder, which is contained in the VBNET\Chap06 folder. Change the name of the folder to Shoppers Haven Menu Solution. Move the Shoppers Haven Menu Solution folder to the VBNET\Chap08 folder.

    b. If necessary, start Visual Studio .NET. Open the Shoppers Haven Solution (Shoppers Haven Solution.sln) file, which is contained in the VBNET\Chap08\Shoppers Haven Menu Solution folder. Open the designer window.

    c. Add a File menu and a Calculate menu to the application. Include an Exit menu item on the File menu, and a Discounted Prices menu item on the Calculate menu. Allow the user to select the Discounted Prices menu item when the Calculate menu is not open.

    d. Move the comment and `Me.Close()` statement from the Exit button's Click event procedure to the Exit menu item's Click event procedure, then remove the Exit button's Click event procedure from the Code Editor window.

    e. Move the instructions contained in the Calculate button's Click event procedure (excluding the procedure header and footer) to the Discounted Prices menu item's Click event procedure, then remove the Calculate button's Click event procedure from the Code Editor window.

    f. Remove the Calculate and Exit buttons from the interface.

    g. Save the solution, then start the application. Test the Discounted Prices menu item to verify that it is working correctly.

    h. Click File on the application's menu bar, and then click Exit to end the application. Click the Yes button.

    i. Close the Output window, then close the solution.

3. In this exercise, you include a menu in the Monthly Payment Calculator application that you created in Chapter 4.

    a. Use Windows to make a copy of the Payment Solution folder, which is contained in the VBNET\Chap04 folder. Change the name of the folder to Payment Menu Solution. Move the Payment Menu Solution folder to the VBNET\Chap08 folder.

  b. If necessary, start Visual Studio .NET. Open the Payment Solution (Payment Solution.sln) file, which is contained in the VBNET\Chap08\Payment Menu Solution folder. Open the designer window.

  c. Add a File menu and a Calculate menu to the application. Include an Exit menu item on the File menu. Include two menu items on the Calculate menu: Annual Payment and Monthly Payment.

  d. When the user clicks the Exit menu item, the application should end. When the user clicks the Annual Payment menu item, the application should calculate and display the annual payment. When the user clicks the Monthly Payment menu item, the application should calculate and display the monthly payment. Modify the application's code appropriately.

  e. Remove the Calculate Monthly Payment and Exit buttons from the interface. Modify the interface appropriately.

discovery ▶ f. Save the solution, and then start the application. Test the Annual Payment and Monthly Payment menu items to verify that they are working correctly.

  g. Click File on the application's menu bar, and then click Exit to end the application.

  h. Close the Output window, and then close the solution.

4. In this exercise, you learn about a menu item's Checked property.

  a. If necessary, start Visual Studio .NET. Open the Check1 Solution (Check1 Solution.sln) file, which is contained in the VBNET\Chap08\Check1 Solution folder.

  b. If necessary, open the designer window. The interface contains two label controls (uiIdCarsLabel and uiIdRocketLabel) and two picture boxes (uiCarsPictureBox and uiRocketPictureBox). It also contains a File menu and a Display menu. The File menu contains an Exit menu item, which has already been coded for you. The Display menu contains two options: Cars and Rocket.

In Windows applications, a check mark next to a menu item indicates that the menu item is active. For example, in the Microsoft Word Window menu, a check mark indicates which of several open documents is currently displayed on the screen. In the Check1 application, you will use the check mark to indicate which label and picture box is currently displayed on the screen.

  c. Set the Visible property for the uiIdCarsLabel and uiCarsPictureBox controls to False.

  d. Click the Rocket menu item, and then set the menu item's Checked property to True. Notice that a check mark appears next to the Rocket menu item.

  e. Save the solution, and then start the application. Notice that only the uiIdRocketLabel and uiRocketPictureBox appear on the screen. Click the Display menu. Notice that a check mark appears next to the Rocket menu item.

  f. Click File on the application's menu bar, and then click Exit to end the application. Close the Output window.

  g. When the user clicks the Cars menu item, the item's Click event procedure should display the uiIdCarsLabel and uiCarsPictureBox controls, and hide the uiIdRocketLabel and uiRocketPictureBox controls. The procedure also should place a check mark next to the Cars menu item, and remove the check mark from the Rocket menu item. Code the Click event procedure for the uiDisplayCarsMenuItem.

  h. When the user clicks the Rocket menu item, the item's Click event procedure should display the uiIdRocketLabel and uiRocketPictureBox controls, and hide the uiIdCarsLabel and uiCarsPictureBox controls. The procedure also should place a check mark next to the Rocket menu item, and remove the check mark from the Cars menu item. Code the Click event procedure for the uiDisplayRocketMenuItem appropriately.

  i. Save the solution, and then start the application. Click Display, and then click Cars. Only the uiIdCarsLabel and uiCarsPictureBox controls appear on the screen. Click Display. A check mark appears next to the Cars menu item.

j. Click Rocket. Only the uiIdRocketLabel and uiRocketPictureBox controls appear on the screen. Click Display. A check mark appears next to the Rocket menu item.

k. Click File on the application's menu bar, and then click Exit to end the application.

l. Close the Output window, and then close the solution.

In the Check1 application, only one of the menu items can be selected at a time; recall that selecting one menu item on the Display menu deselected the other menu item on the menu. In the next application, however, the user can select some, none, or all of the menu items on a menu.

m. Open the Check2 Solution (Check2 Solution.sln) file, which is contained in the VBNET\Chap08\Check2 Solution folder. If necessary, open the designer window. The Check2 application's interface is identical to the Check1 application's interface.

n. Set the Visible property for the two label controls and two picture boxes to False.

o. Code the application so that it displays the uiIdRocketLabel and uiRocketPictureBox controls when the Rocket menu item is selected, and hides both controls when the Rocket menu item is deselected.

p. Code the application so that it displays the uiIdCarsLabel and uiCarsPictureBox controls when the Cars menu item is selected, and hides both controls when the Cars menu item is deselected.

q. Save the solution, and then start the application. No labels or picture boxes should appear in the interface. Open the Display menu. No check mark should appear next to either menu item on the Display menu.

r. Practice selecting and deselecting the Cars and Rocket menu items. When you select a menu item, its corresponding label and picture box should appear on the form, and a check mark should appear next to the menu item. When you deselect a menu item, its corresponding label and picture box should be hidden, and the check mark should be removed from the menu item.

s. Click File on the application's menu bar, and then click Exit to end the application.

t. Close the Output window, and then close the solution.

LESSON C

objectives

After completing this lesson, you will be able to:

- Include the Substring method in a procedure
- Include the Mid statement in a procedure
- Include the IndexOf method in a procedure

Completing the Hangman Game Application

The Hangman Game Application

Recall that Mr. Mitchell has asked you to write an application that two students can use to play a simplified version of the Hangman game on the computer. The application should allow one of the students to enter a five-letter word, and then allow the other student to guess the word, letter by letter. The game is over when the second student guesses all of the letters in the word, or when he or she makes 10 incorrect guesses, whichever comes first.

To open the Hangman Game application:

1. Start Microsoft Visual Studio .NET, if necessary.
2. If necessary, close the Start Page window.
3. Open the **Hangman Solution** (Hangman Solution.sln) file, which is contained in the VBNET\Chap08\ Hangman Solution folder.
4. Auto-hide the Toolbox, Solution Explorer, and Properties windows, if necessary. The user interface for the Hangman Game application is shown in Figure 8-22. Recall that the File menu contains the New Game command, the Exit command, and a separator bar.

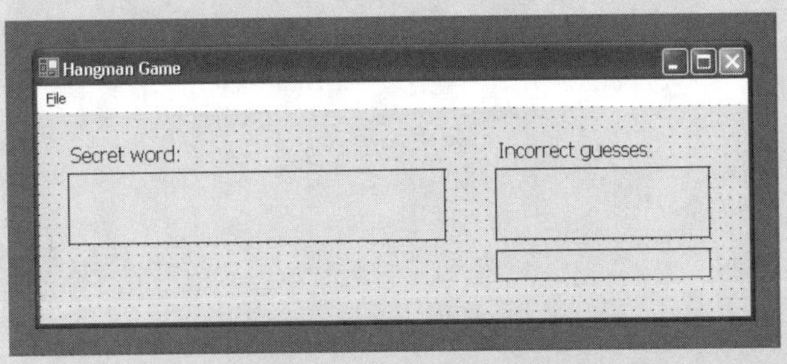

Figure 8-22: Hangman Game application's user interface

Figure 8-23 shows the TOE chart for the Hangman Game application.

Task	Object	Event
1. Get a five-letter word from player 1 2. Display five dashes in the uiWordLabel control 3. Clear the uiIncorrectGuessLabel and uiIncorrectLettersLabel controls 4. Get a letter from player 2 5. Search the word for the letter 6. If the letter is contained in the word, replace the appropriate dash(es) 7. If the letter is not contained in the word, add 1 to the number of incorrect guesses, and display the letter in the uiIncorrectLettersLabel control 8. If all of the dashes have been replaced, the game is over, so display the message "Great guessing!" in a message box 9. If the user makes 10 incorrect guesses, the game is over, so display the message "Sorry, the word is" and the word in a message box, and display the "Game Over" message in the uiWordLabel control.	uiFileNewMenuItem	Click
End the application	uiFileExitMenuItem	Click
Display the original word as hyphens and/or letters	uiWordLabel	None
Display the number of incorrect guesses	uiIncorrectGuessLabel	None
Display the incorrect letters	uiIncorrectLettersLabel	None

Figure 8-23: TOE chart for the Hangman Game application

Recall that you coded the uiFileExitMenuItem's Click event procedure in Lesson B. To complete the Hangman Game application, you need to code the Click event procedure for the uiFileNewMenuItem's Click event procedure.

Coding the Click Event Procedure for the uiFileNewMenuItem

Each time the user wants to begin a new Hangman game, he or she will need to click File on the application's menu bar and then click New Game. Figure 8-24 shows the pseudocode for the uiFileNewMenuItem's Click event procedure.

```
uiFileNewMenuItem
1. repeat
      get a five-letter word from player 1
   end repeat until the word contains five letters
2. convert word to uppercase
3. display five dashes in the uiWordLabel control
4. clear the uiIncorrectGuessLabel and uiIncorrectLettersLabel controls
5. repeat while the game is not over
      get a letter from player 2, then convert letter to uppercase
      repeat for each character in the word
          if the current character is equal to the letter entered by player 2
              replace the appropriate dash in the uiWordLabel control
              set the dashReplaced variable to True
          end if
      end repeat
      if a dash was replaced in the uiWordLabel control
          if the uiWordLabel control does not contain any dashes
              set the gameOver variable to True
              display the "Great guessing!" message in a message box
          else
              reset the dashReplaced variable to False
          end if
      else
          display the letter entered by the user in the uiIncorrectLettersLabel control
          add 1 to the incorrectGuesses counter variable
          display the incorrectGuesses variable's value in uiIncorrectGuessLabel
          if the user made 10 incorrect guesses
              set the gameOver variable to True
              display the "Game Over" message in the uiWordLabel control
              display the "Sorry, the word is" message and the word in a message box
          end if
      end if
   end repeat
```

Figure 8-24: Pseudocode for the uiFileNewMenuItem's Click event procedure

To code the uiFileNewMenuItem's Click event procedure:

1 Open the Code Editor window.

2 Open the code template for the uiFileNewMenuItem Click event procedure. Type '**simulates the Hangman game** and press **Enter** twice.

First you will declare the procedure's variables. The procedure will use two String variables named `word` and `letter`, two Boolean variables named `dashReplaced` and `gameOver`, and two Integer variables named `incorrectGuesses` and `indexNum`. The `word` variable will store the word to be guessed, and the `letter` variable will store the letter guesses. The `dashReplaced` variable will indicate whether a dash was replaced in the word, and the `gameOver` variable will indicate whether the game is over. The `incorrectGuesses` variable will keep track of the number of incorrect guesses, and the `indexNum` variable will control the loop that searches the word for the letter guessed by the user.

3 Type the Dim statements and comments shown in Figure 8-25, and then position the insertion point as shown in the figure.

enter these Dim statements
and comments

position the insertion point here

```
Private Sub uiFileNewMenuItem_Click(ByVal sender As Object, ByVal e As System.EventArgs)
    'simulates the Hangman game

    Dim word As String              'stores the word to be guessed
    Dim letter As String            'stores the letter guesses
    Dim dashReplaced As Boolean     'indicates whether a dash was replaced
    Dim gameOver As Boolean         'indicates whether the game is over
    Dim incorrectGuesses As Integer 'keeps track of the number of incorrect guesses
    Dim indexNum As Integer         'controls the loop that searches the word

    |
End Sub
```

Figure 8-25: Dim statements and comments entered in the procedure

According to the pseudocode shown in Figure 8-24, the Click event procedure should use a posttest loop to get a five-letter word from player 1. As you learned in Lesson A, the number of characters contained in a string is stored in the string's Length property.

4   Type the comment and loop shown in Figure 8-26, and then position the insertion point as shown in the figure.

```
Private Sub uiFileNewMenuItem_Click(ByVal sender As Object, ByVal e As System.EventArgs)
    'simulates the Hangman game

    Dim word As String              'stores the word to be guessed
    Dim letter As String            'stores the letter guesses
    Dim dashReplaced As Boolean     'indicates whether a dash was replaced
    Dim gameOver As Boolean         'indicates whether the game is over
    Dim incorrectGuesses As Integer 'keeps track of the number of incorrect guesses
    Dim indexNum As Integer         'controls the loop that searches the word

    'get a 5-letter word from the first player
    Do
        word = InputBox("Enter a 5-letter word", "Hangman Game")
    Loop Until word.Length = 5
    |
End Sub
```

enter this comment and loop

position the insertion point here

Figure 8-26: Comment and posttest loop entered in the procedure

Step 2 is to convert the word to uppercase.

5   Type **'convert word to uppercase** and press **Enter**, then type **word = word.toupper()** and press **Enter** twice.

Step 3 is to display five dashes in the uiWordLabel control.

6   Type **'display five dashes in uiWordLabel control** and press **Enter**, then type **me.uiwordlabel.text = "-----"** and press **Enter** twice.

Step 4 is to clear the uiIncorrectGuessLabel and uiIncorrectLettersLabel controls.

7   Type **'clear the label controls** and press **Enter**. Type **me.uiincorrectguesslabel. text = ""** and press **Enter**, then type **me.uiincorrectletterslabel.text = ""** and press **Enter** twice.

Step 5 is a pretest loop that repeats its instructions while the game is not over.

8   Type the comments and loop shown in Figure 8-27, and then position the insertion point as shown in the figure.

```
Private Sub uiFileNewMenuItem_Click(ByVal sender As Object, ByVal e As System.EventArgs)
    'simulates the Hangman game

    Dim word As String                 'stores the word to be guessed
    Dim letter As String               'stores the letter guesses
    Dim dashReplaced As Boolean        'indicates whether a dash was replaced
    Dim gameOver As Boolean            'indicates whether the game is over
    Dim incorrectGuesses As Integer    'keeps track of the number of incorrect guesses
    Dim indexNum As Integer            'controls the loop that searches the word

    'get a 5-letter word from the first player
    Do
        word = InputBox("Enter a 5-letter word", "Hangman Game")
    Loop Until word.Length = 5
    'convert word to uppercase
    word = word.ToUpper()

    'display five dashes in uiWordLabel control
    Me.uiWordLabel.Text = "-----"

    'clear the label controls
    Me.uiIncorrectGuessLabel.Text = ""
    Me.uiIncorrectLettersLabel.Text = ""

    'allow player 2 to guess a letter
    'the game is over when either the word is guessed or
    'player 2 makes 10 incorrect guesses
    Do While Not gameOver

    Loop
```

enter these comments and the pretest loop ——————

position the insertion point here ——————

Figure 8-27: Comments and pretest loop entered in the procedure

The first instructions in the loop should get a letter from player 2, and then convert the letter to uppercase.

9 Type '**get a letter from player 2** and press **Enter**, then type **letter = inputbox("Enter a letter:", "Letter", "", 500, 500)** and press **Enter**.

10 Type '**convert letter to uppercase** and press **Enter**, then type **letter = letter.toupper()** and press **Enter** twice.

Next is a nested loop that repeats its instructions for each character in the word.

11 Type '**search the word for the letter** and press **Enter**, then type **for indexnum = 0 to word.length – 1** and press **Enter**.

The nested loop contains a selection structure that compares the current letter in the word with the letter guessed by player 2. If the current letter is the same as the letter guessed by player 2, the selection structure's true path should replace the dash in the uiWordLabel control with the letter. It then should assign the Boolean value True to the `dashReplaced` variable to indicate that a replacement was made.

12 Type the selection structure shown in Figure 8-28, and also change the `Next` statement to **Next indexNum**. Then position the insertion point as shown in the figure.

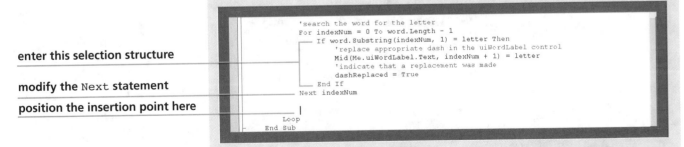

enter this selection structure ——————

modify the `Next` **statement** ——————

position the insertion point here ——————

```
    'search the word for the letter
    For indexNum = 0 To word.Length - 1
        If word.Substring(indexNum, 1) = letter Then
            'replace appropriate dash in the uiWordLabel control
            Mid(Me.uiWordLabel.Text, indexNum + 1) = letter
            'indicate that a replacement was made
            dashReplaced = True
        End If
    Next indexNum

    Loop
End Sub
```

Figure 8-28: Selection structure entered in the procedure

Next, the procedure should use a selection structure to determine whether any dashes were replaced in the word.

13 Type **'determine whether a replacement was made** and press **Enter**, then type **if dashreplaced then** and press **Enter**.

If at least one dash was replaced in the word, the selection structure's true path should use a nested selection structure to determine whether the word contains any more dashes. If the word does not contain any dashes, it means that the user guessed the word. In that case, the nested selection structure's true path should assign the Boolean value True to the `gameOver` variable to indicate that the game is over. It also should display the "Great guessing!" message in a message box. If, on the other hand, the word does contain at least one dash, the selection structure's false path should assign the Boolean value False to the `dashReplaced` variable.

14 Type the comments and nested selection structure shown in Figure 8-29, and then position the insertion point as shown in the figure.

```
                'search the word for the letter
                For indexNum = 0 To word.Length - 1
                    If word.Substring(indexNum, 1) = letter Then
                        'replace appropriate dash in the uiWordLabel control
                        Mid(Me.uiWordLabel.Text, indexNum + 1) = letter
                        'indicate that a replacement was made
                        dashReplaced = True
                    End If
                Next indexNum

                'determine whether a replacement was made
                If dashReplaced Then
                    'if the word does not contain any dashes, then
                    'the user guessed the word, so the game is over
                    If Me.uiWordLabel.Text.IndexOf("-") = -1 Then
                        gameOver = True
                        MessageBox.Show("Great guessing!", "Hangman Game", _
                            MessageBoxButtons.OK, MessageBoxIcon.Information)
                    Else    'reset the dashReplaced variable
                        dashReplaced = False
                    End If

                End If
            Loop
        End Sub
```

enter these comments and nested selection structure

position the insertion point here

Figure 8-29: Comments and nested selection structure entered in the procedure

If no dashes were replaced in the word, the selection structure's false path should display (in the uiIncorrectLettersLabel control) the letter entered by the user. It also should add the number one to the `incorrectGuesses` counter variable and display the variable's value in the uiIncorrectGuessLabel control.

15 Type **else** and press **Tab**, then type **'processed when no dash was replaced** and press **Enter**.

16 Type **'display incorrect letter** and press **Enter**.

17 Type **me.uiincorrectletterslabel.text = _** and press **Enter**, then press **Tab**. Type **me.uiincorrectletterslabel.text & " " & letter** and press **Enter**.

18 Type **'update the counter variable, then display the result** and press **Enter**, then type **incorrectguesses = incorrectguesses + 1** and press **Enter**.

19 Type **me.uiincorrectguesslabel.text = convert.tostring(incorrectguesses)** and press **Enter**.

Next, the selection structure's false path should use a nested selection structure to determine whether player 2 has made 10 incorrect guesses. If he or she has, it means that the game is over. In that case, the nested selection structure's true path should assign the Boolean value True to the gameOver variable. It also should display the message "Game Over" in the uiWordLabel control and display the message "Sorry, the word is" along with the word in a message box.

20 Type the comment and nested selection structure shown in Figure 8-30.

enter this comment and nested selection structure

```
          Else    'processed when no dash was replaced
              'display incorrect letter
              Me.uiIncorrectLettersLabel.Text = _
                  Me.uiIncorrectLettersLabel.Text & "   " & letter
              'update the counter variable, then display the result
              incorrectGuesses = incorrectGuesses + 1
              Me.uiIncorrectGuessLabel.Text = Convert.ToString(incorrectGuesses)
              'determine whether player 2 made 10 incorrect guesses
              If incorrectGuesses = 10 Then
                  'the game is over
                  gameOver = True
                  Me.uiWordLabel.Text = "Game Over"
                  MessageBox.Show("Sorry, the word is " & word, "Hangman Game", _
                      MessageBoxButtons.OK, MessageBoxIcon.Information)
              End If
          End If
      Loop
  End Sub
```

Figure 8-30: Comment and nested selection structure entered in the procedure

Figure 8-31 shows the completed uiFileNewMenuItem Click event procedure.

```
Private Sub uiFileNewMenuItem_Click(ByVal sender As Object, ByVal e As System.EventArgs)
Handles uiFileNewMenuItem.Click
      'simulates the Hangman game

      Dim word As String                  'stores the word to be guessed
      Dim letter As String                'stores the letter guesses
      Dim dashReplaced As Boolean         'indicates whether a dash was replaced
      Dim gameOver As Boolean             'indicates whether the game is over
      Dim incorrectGuesses As Integer    'keeps track of the number of incorrect guesses
      Dim indexNum As Integer             'controls the loop that searches the word

      'get a 5-letter word from the first player
      Do
          word = InputBox("Enter a 5-letter word", "Hangman Game")
      Loop Until word.Length = 5
      'convert word to uppercase
      word = word.ToUpper()

      'display five dashes in uiWordLabel control
      Me.uiWordLabel.Text = "-----"

      'clear the label controls
      Me.uiIncorrectGuessLabel.Text = ""
      Me.uiIncorrectLettersLabel.Text = ""

      'allow player 2 to guess a letter
      'the game is over when either the word is guessed or
      'player 2 makes 10 incorrect guesses
      Do While Not gameOver
          'get a letter from player 2
          letter = InputBox("Enter a letter:", "Letter", "", 500, 500)
          'convert letter to uppercase
          letter = letter.ToUpper()
```

Figure 8-31: Completed uiFileNewMenuItem Click event procedure

```
                  'search the word for the letter
                  For indexNum = 0 To word.Length - 1
                      If word.Substring(indexNum, 1) = letter Then
                          'replace appropriate dash in the uiWordLabel control
                          Mid(Me.uiWordLabel.Text, indexNum + 1) = letter
                          'indicate that a replacement was made
                          dashReplaced = True
                      End If
                  Next indexNum

                  'determine whether a replacement was made
                  If dashReplaced Then
                      'if the word does not contain any dashes, then
                      'the user guessed the word, so the game is over
                      If Me.uiWordLabel.Text.IndexOf("-") = -1 Then
                          gameOver = True
                          MessageBox.Show("Great guessing!", "Hangman Game", _
                              MessageBoxButtons.OK, MessageBoxIcon.Information)
                      Else    'reset the dashReplaced variable
                          dashReplaced = False
                      End If
                  Else    'processed when no dash was replaced
                      'display incorrect letter
                      Me.uiIncorrectLettersLabel.Text = _
                          Me.uiIncorrectLettersLabel.Text & "  " & letter
                      'update the counter variable, then display the result
                      incorrectGuesses = incorrectGuesses + 1
                      Me.uiIncorrectGuessLabel.Text = Convert.ToString(incorrectGuesses)
                      'determine whether player 2 made 10 incorrect guesses
                      If incorrectGuesses = 10 Then
                          'the game is over
                          gameOver = True
                          Me.uiWordLabel.Text = "Game Over"
                          MessageBox.Show("Sorry, the word is " & word, "Hangman Game", _
                              MessageBoxButtons.OK, MessageBoxIcon.Information)
                      End If
                  End If
              Loop
      End Sub
```

Figure 8-31: Completed uiFileNewMenuItem Click event procedure (continued)

Now test the uiFileNewMenuItem's Click event procedure to verify that it is working correctly.

To test the uiFileNewMenuItem's Click event procedure:

1 Save the solution, then start the application.

2 Click **File** on the Hangman Game application's menu bar, and then click **New Game**. The uiFileNewMenuItem's Click event procedure displays the Hangman Game dialog box, which prompts you to enter a five-letter word. See Figure 8-32.

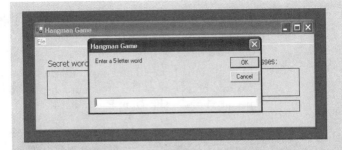

Figure 8-32: Hangman Game dialog box

First, enter a word that has less than five characters.

3 Type **dog** and press **Enter**. The procedure displays the Hangman Game dialog box again.

Now enter a word that has more than five characters.

4 Type **balloon** and press **Enter**. The procedure displays the Hangman Game dialog box again.

Next, enter a word that has exactly five letters.

5 Type **moose** and press **Enter**. The procedure displays five dashes in the uiWordLabel control. The procedure also displays the Letter dialog box shown in Figure 8-33.

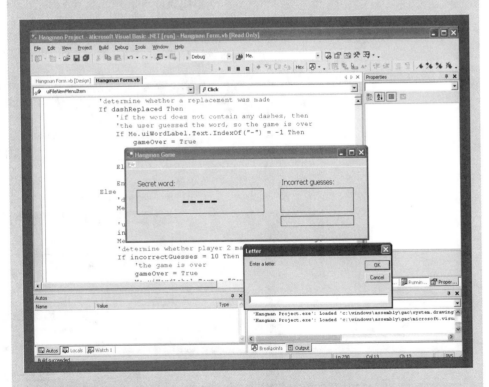

Figure 8-33: Result of entering a word that has exactly five characters

First, observe what happens when the user guesses the original word.

6 Type **e** in the Letter dialog box and press **Enter**. The procedure replaces the last dash in the uiWordLabel control with the letter E.

7   Type **o** in the Letter dialog box and press **Enter**. The procedure replaces the second dash in the uiWordLabel control with the letter O, and also replaces the third dash with the letter O.

8   Type **m** in the Letter dialog box and press **Enter**, then type **s** in the Letter dialog box and press **Enter**. The procedure displays the message "Great guessing!" in a message box, as shown in Figure 8-34.

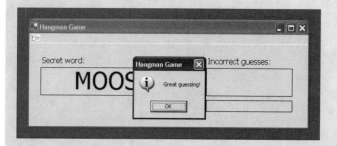

Figure 8-34: Result of guessing the word entered by player 1

9   Press **Enter** to close the message box.

10   Click **File** on the application's menu bar, and then click **New Game**. When you are prompted to enter a word, type **seven** and press **Enter**.

Now observe what happens when the user makes an incorrect guess.

11   Type **a** in the Letter dialog box and press **Enter**. The number one appears in the uiIncorrectGuessLabel control and the letter "A" appears in the uiIncorrectLettersLabel control. See Figure 8-35.

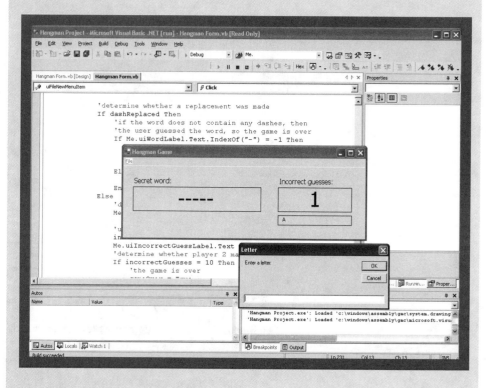

Figure 8-35: Result of making an incorrect guess

Next, you will make nine more incorrect guesses. This will allow you to observe what happens when the user does not guess the word.

12 Use the Letter dialog box to enter the following incorrect letters: **b, c, d, f, g, h, i, j, k.** Figure 8-36 shows the result of making 10 incorrect guesses. Notice that the procedure displays the message "Game Over" in the uiWordLabel control, and displays the message "Sorry, the word is SEVEN" in a message box.

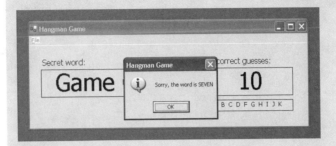

Figure 8-36: Result of making 10 incorrect guesses

13 Press **Enter** to close the message box.

14 Click **File** on the application's menu bar, and then click **Exit** to end the application.

15 When you return to the Code Editor window, close the Output window, then close the Code Editor window.

16 Click **File** on the menu bar, and then click **Close Solution**.

You now have completed Chapter 8. You can either take a break or complete the end-of-lesson questions and exercises.

SUMMARY

To access each character in a string:

■ Use the Substring method.

To replace a character in a string with another character:

■ Use the Mid statement.

To determine whether a specific character is contained in a string:

■ Use the IndexOf method.

QUESTIONS

1. Which of the following For clauses can be used to access each character contained in the name variable, character by character? The variable contains 10 characters.
   a. `For indexNum = 0 To 10`
   b. `For indexNum = 0 To name.Length`
   c. `For indexNum = 0 To name.Length - 1`
   d. `For indexNum = 1 To 10`
   e. `For indexNum = 1 To name.Length - 1`

2. Which of the following can be used to change the first letter in the name variable from "K" to "C"?
   a. `Mid(name, 0, "C")`
   b. `Mid(name, 0) = "C"`
   c. `Mid(name, 1, "C")`
   d. `Mid(name, 1) = "C"`
   e. `name = Mid(1, "C")`

3. If the word variable contains the string "Irene Turner", the `word.IndexOf("r")` method returns _____.
   a. -1
   b. 2
   c. 3
   d. r
   e. None of the above.

EXERCISES

1. In this exercise, you modify the Hangman Game application so that it allows the first student to enter a word that contains any number of characters.
   a. Use Windows to make a copy of the Hangman Solution folder, which is contained in the VBNET\Chap08 folder. Change the name of the folder to Hangman Ex1 Solution.
   b. If necessary, start Visual Studio .NET. Open the Hangman Solution (Hangman Solution.sln) file, which is contained in the VBNET\Chap08\Hangman Ex1 Solution folder. Open the designer window.
   c. Modify the application's code appropriately. The number of incorrect guesses the user is allowed to make should be four more than the total number of characters in the original word. For example, if the original word contains seven characters, allow the user to make 11 incorrect guesses.
   d. Save the solution, and then start the application. Click File on the application's menu bar, and then click New Game. Test the application using the word "telephone".
   e. Click File on the application's menu bar, and then click Exit to end the application.
   f. Close the Output window, and then close the solution.

2. In this exercise, you modify the Hangman Game application so that it stops the game when the user clicks the Cancel button in the Letter dialog box.

   a. Use Windows to make a copy of the Hangman Solution folder, which is contained in the VBNET\Chap08 folder. Change the name of the folder to Hangman Ex2 Solution.

   b. If necessary, start Visual Studio .NET. Open the Hangman Solution (Hangman Solution.sln) file, which is contained in the VBNET\Chap08\Hangman Ex2 Solution folder. Open the designer window.

   c. Modify the application's code appropriately.

   d. Save the solution, and then start the application. Click File on the application's menu bar, and then click New Game. Test the application to verify that it is working correctly.

   e. Click File on the application's menu bar, and then click Exit to end the application.

   f. Close the Output window, and then close the solution.

3. Credit card companies typically assign a special digit, called a check digit, to the end of each customer's credit card number. Many methods for creating the check digit have been developed. One simple method is to multiply every other number in the credit card number by two, then add the products to the remaining numbers to get the total. You then take the last digit in the total and append it to the end of the number, as illustrated in Figure 8-37.

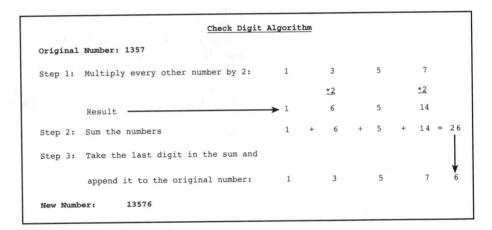

Figure 8-37

   a. If necessary, start Visual Studio .NET. Open the Georgetown Solution (Georgetown Solution.sln) file, which is contained in the VBNET\Chap08\Georgetown Solution folder. If necessary, open the designer window.

   b. Code the application so that it allows the user to enter a five-digit credit card number; assume that the fifth digit is the check digit. The application should use the method illustrated in Figure 8-37 to verify that the credit card number is valid. Display appropriate messages indicating whether the credit card number is valid or invalid.

   c. Save the solution, and then start and test the application.

   d. Stop the application.

   e. Close the Output window, and then close the solution.

4. In this exercise, you code an application that creates a new password.

   a. If necessary, start Visual Studio .NET. Open the Jacobson Solution (Jacobson Solution.sln) file, which is contained in the VBNET\Chap08\Jacobson Solution folder. If necessary, open the designer window.

   b. Code the application so that it allows the user to enter a password that contains five, six, or seven characters. The application then should create a new password as follows:

      1. Replace all vowels (A, E, I, O, and U) with the letter X.
      2. Replace all numbers with the letter Z.
      3. Reverse the characters in the password.

   c. Save the solution, and then start and test the application.

   d. Stop the application.

   e. Close the Output window, and then close the solution.

5. Each salesperson at BobCat Motors is assigned an ID number, which consists of four characters. The first character is either the letter F or the letter P. The letter F indicates that the salesperson is a full-time employee; the letter P indicates that he or she is a part-time employee. The middle two characters are the salesperson's initials, and the last character is either a 1 or a 2. A 1 indicates that the salesperson sells new cars, and a 2 indicates that the salesperson sells used cars.

   a. If necessary, start Visual Studio .NET. Open the BobCat Solution (BobCat Solution.sln) file, which is contained in the VBNET\Chap08\BobCat Solution folder. If necessary, open the designer window.

   b. Code the application so that it allows the sales manager to enter a salesperson's ID and the number of cars the salesperson sold during the month. The application should allow the sales manager to enter this information for as many salespeople as needed. The application should calculate and display the total number of cars sold by each of the following four categories of employees: full-time employees, part-time employees, employees selling new cars, and employees selling used cars.

   c. Save the solution, and then start and test the application.

   d. Stop the application.

   e. Close the Output window, and then close the solution.

6. In this exercise, you code an application that allows the user to guess a letter chosen randomly by the computer.

   a. If necessary, start Visual Studio .NET. Open the Random Solution (Random Solution.sln) file, which is contained in the VBNET\Chap08\Random Solution folder. If necessary, open the designer window.

   b. Study the application's existing code. Notice that the Play Game button's Click event procedure assigns the letters of the alphabet to the `alphabet` variable. It also prompts the user to enter a letter, and stores the user's response in the `letter` variable. Complete the procedure by entering instructions to do the following:

   ■ Generate a random integer that can be used to select one of the letters from the `alphabet` variable, and assign the selected letter to the `randomLetter` variable.

   ■ Verify that the user entered exactly one character.

   ■ If the user did not enter exactly one character, display an appropriate message in a message box.

   ■ If the user entered exactly one character, compare the lowercase version of the character to the letter stored in the `randomLetter` variable.

   ■ Allow the user to enter a character until he or she guesses the random letter stored in the `randomLetter` variable.

   ■ If the character entered by the user is the same as the letter stored in the `randomLetter` variable, display the message "You guessed the correct letter.".

■ If the letter stored in the `randomLetter` variable appears after the user's letter in the alphabet, display the message "The correct letter comes after the letter", followed by a space, the user's letter, and a period.

■ If the letter stored in the `randomLetter` variable appears before the user's letter in the alphabet, display the message "The correct letter comes before the letter", followed by a space, the user's letter, and a period.

  c. Save the solution, then start the application. Click the Play Game button, then enter one or more letters until the message "You guessed the correct letter." appears.

  d. Click the Exit button to end the application.

  e. Close the Output window, then close the solution.

discovery ▶ **7.** In this exercise, you code an application that displays a message indicating whether a portion of a string begins with another string.

  a. If necessary, start Visual Studio .NET. Open the String Solution (String Solution.sln) file, which is contained in the VBNET\Chap08\String Solution folder. If necessary, open the designer window.

  b. The application allows the user to enter a name (first name followed by a space and the last name) and the search text. If the last name begins with the search text (entered in any case), the Display Message button should display the message "The last name begins with" followed by a space and the search text. If the characters in the last name come before the search text in the ASCII coding scheme, display the message "The last name comes before" followed by a space and the search text. Finally, if the characters in the last name come after the search text in the ASCII coding scheme, display the message "The last name comes after" followed by a space and the search text.

  c. Save the solution, then start the application. To test the application, enter Helga Swanson as the name, then use the following strings for the search text: g, ab, he, s, SY, sw, swan, and wan.

  d. Click the Exit button to end the application.

  e. Close the Output window, then close the solution.

discovery ▶ **8.** In this exercise, you learn how to use a ColorDialog control.

  a. If necessary, start Visual Studio .NET. Create a blank solution named Dialog Solution. Save the solution in the VBNET\Chap08 folder.

  b. Add a Visual Basic .NET Windows Application project to the solution. Name the project Dialog Project.

  c. Assign the filename Dialog Form.vb to the form file object.

  d. Assign the name DialogForm to the Windows Form object. Change the form's StartPosition property to CenterScreen. Change its Text property to Color Dialog Example.

  e. Change the project's Startup object to DialogForm.

  f. Add a label control to the interface. Name the label control uiColorLabel. Set the label control's BorderStyle property to FixedSingle. Remove the contents of the label control's Text property.

  g. Add a MainMenu control to the interface. Name the control uiColorMainMenu. Include two menu titles in the interface: File and Format. The File menu should contain an Exit option. The Format menu should contain a Color… option. Use appropriate names and access keys for the menu titles and menu items.

  h. Add a ColorDialog control to the form. Name it uiColorDialog1.

  i. Code the File menu's Exit option so that it ends the application when it is clicked.

  j. Enter the following two lines of code in the Click event procedure for the Format menu's Color option:

```
Me.uiColorDialog1.ShowDialog()
Me.uiColorLabel.BackColor = Me.uiColorDialog1.Color
```

k. Close the Code Editor window.

l. Save the solution, then start the application. Click Format on the application's menu bar, and then click Color. The Color dialog box opens and displays a palette of colors. Click a color square, and then click the OK button. The background color of the uiColorLabel control changes accordingly.

m. Use the Exit option on the File menu to end the application.

n. Close the Output window, then close the solution.

debugging   9. In this exercise, you debug an existing application. The purpose of this exercise is to demonstrate a common error made when manipulating strings.

a. If necessary, start Visual Studio .NET. Open the Debug Solution (Debug Solution.sln) file, which is contained in the VBNET\Chap08\Debug Solution folder. If necessary, open the designer window.

b. Open the Code Editor window and study the existing code.

c. Start the application. Enter Tampa, Florida in the Address text box, then click the Display City button. The button displays the letter T in a message box, which is incorrect; it should display the word Tampa. Close the message box. Click the Exit button to end the application.

d. Correct the application's code, then save the solution and start the application.

e. Enter Tampa, Florida in the Address text box, then click the Display City button. The button displays the word Tampa in a message box. Close the message box.

f. Click the Exit button to end the application.

g. Close the Output window, then close the solution.

CHAPTER

9

Sequential Access Files and Printing

Creating the PAO Application

case ▶ During July and August of each year, the Political Awareness Organization (PAO) sends a questionnaire to the voters in their district. The questionnaire asks the voter to provide his or her political party (Democrat, Republican, Independent) and age. From the returned questionnaires, the organization's secretary tabulates the number of Democrats, Republicans, and Independents in the district—a time-consuming and tedious job. The organization's president has asked for your help in simplifying this process.

Previewing the Completed Application

Before creating the PAO application, you first preview the completed application.

To preview the completed application:

1 Use the Run command on the Windows Start menu to run the **PAO** (PAO.exe) file, which is contained in the VBNET\Chap09 folder on your computer's hard disk. The PAO application's user interface appears on the screen along with a dialog box that asks whether you want to create a new file. See Figure 9-1.

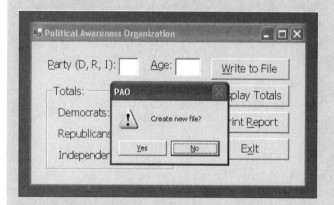

Figure 9-1: PAO application's user interface and dialog box

2 Click the **Yes** button. The application creates a sequential access file named pao.txt on your computer's hard disk.

3 Type **d** in the Party text box, then press **Tab**. Type **34** in the Age text box, then press **Tab**. Press **Enter** to select the Write to File button, which writes the party and age to the pao.txt file.

4 Use the application to write the following five records to the file:

    d   23
    r   50
    r   43
    i   21
    d   56

5 Click the **Display Totals** button. The button's Click event procedure opens the pao.txt file. It then calculates the total number of Democrats, Republicans, and Independents stored in the file and displays the results in label controls in the interface, as shown in Figure 9-2.

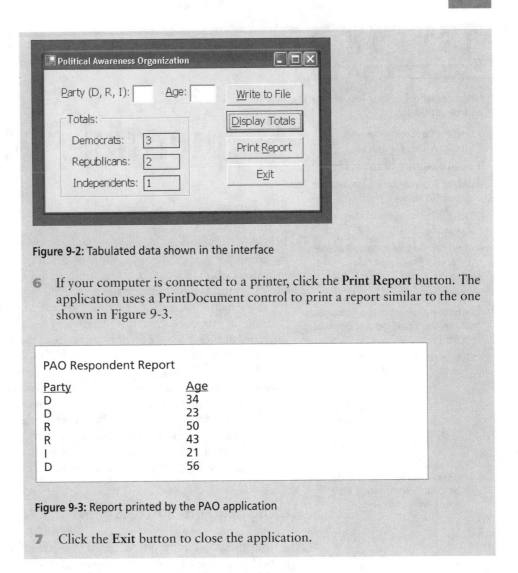

Figure 9-2: Tabulated data shown in the interface

6 If your computer is connected to a printer, click the **Print Report** button. The application uses a PrintDocument control to print a report similar to the one shown in Figure 9-3.

PAO Respondent Report

Party	Age
D	34
D	23
R	50
R	43
I	21
D	56

Figure 9-3: Report printed by the PAO application

7 Click the **Exit** button to close the application.

You learn about sequential access files in Lesson A. You begin coding the PAO application in Lesson B and complete it in Lesson C. Also in Lesson C, you learn how to use the PrintDocument control to print the contents of a sequential access file.

After completing this lesson, you will be able to:

- Declare StreamReader and StreamWriter variables
- Open a sequential access file
- Determine whether a sequential access file exists
- Write information to a sequential access file
- Align the text written to a sequential access file
- Read information from a sequential access file
- Determine whether the computer has finished reading a sequential access file
- Close a sequential access file

tip

▶ A chapter on Random Access Files is available on the Course Technology Web site at *www.course.com*.

Sequential Access Files

File Types

In addition to getting information from the keyboard and sending information to the computer screen, an application also can get information from and send information to a file on a disk. Getting information from a file is referred to as "reading the file," and sending information to a file is referred to as "writing to the file." Files to which information is written are called **output files**, because the files store the output produced by an application. Files that are read by the computer are called **input files**, because an application uses the information in these files as input.

You can create three different types of files in Visual Basic .NET: sequential, random, and binary. The file type refers to how the information in the file is accessed. The information in a sequential access file is always accessed sequentially—in other words, in consecutive order from the beginning of the file through the end of the file. The information stored in a random access file can be accessed either in consecutive order or in random order. The information in a binary access file can be accessed by its byte location in the file. You learn about sequential access files in this chapter. Random access and binary access files are used less often in programs, so these file types are not covered in this book.

Using Sequential Access Files

A **sequential access file** is often referred to as a **text file**, because it is composed of lines of text. The text might represent an employee list, as shown in Example 1 in Figure 9-4. Or, it might be a memo or a report, as shown in Examples 2 and 3 in the figure.

Examples
Example 1 – employee list
Bonnel, Jacob Carlisle, Donald Eberg, Jack Hou, Chang
Example 2 – memo
To all employees: Effective January 1, 2006, the cost of dependent coverage will increase from $35 to $38.50 per month. Jefferson Williams Insurance Manager

Figure 9-4: Examples of text stored in a sequential access file

Examples

Example 3 – report

```
ABC Industries Sales Report

State       Sales
California   15000
Montana      10000
Wyoming       7000
            -----
Total sales:  $32000
```

Figure 9-4: Examples of text stored in a sequential access file (continued)

Sequential access files are similar to cassette tapes in that each line in the file, like each song on a cassette tape, is both stored and retrieved in consecutive order (sequentially). In other words, before you can record (store) the fourth song on a cassette tape, you first must record songs one through three. Likewise, before you can write (store) the fourth line in a sequential access file, you first must write lines one through three. The same holds true for retrieving a song from a cassette tape and a line of text from a sequential access file. To listen to the fourth song on a cassette tape, you must play (or fast-forward through) the first three songs. Likewise, to read the fourth line in a sequential access file, you first must read the three lines that precede it.

Figure 9-5 shows the procedure you follow when using a sequential access file in an application.

Sequential access file procedure

1. declare either a StreamWriter or StreamReader variable

2. create a StreamWriter or StreamReader object by opening a file; assign the object's address to the variable declared in Step 1

3. use the StreamWriter object to write one or more lines of text to the file, or use the StreamReader object to read one or more lines of text from the file

4. use the StreamWriter or StreamReader object to close the file

Figure 9-5: Procedure for using a sequential access file

Step 1 in Figure 9-5 is to declare either a StreamWriter or StreamReader variable. The appropriate variable to declare depends on whether you want to write information to the file or read information from the file.

Declaring StreamWriter and StreamReader Variables

In Visual Basic .NET, you use a **StreamWriter object** to write a sequence of characters to a sequential access file. The sequence of characters is referred to as a **stream of characters** or, more simply, a **stream**. Similarly, you use a **StreamReader object** to read a stream (sequence of characters) from a sequential access file. Before you create the appropriate object, you first declare a variable to store the address of the object in the computer's internal memory. You use a StreamWriter variable to store the address of a StreamWriter object, and a StreamReader variable to store the address of a StreamReader object. Figure 9-6 shows the syntax you use to declare StreamWriter and StreamReader variables. The figure also includes examples of declaring the variables.

Syntax
{**Dim** | **Private**} *variablename* **As IO.***objecttype*
Examples and results
`Dim letterStreamWriter As IO.StreamWriter` declares a procedure-level StreamWriter variable named `letterStreamWriter`
`Private memoStreamWriter As IO.StreamWriter` declares a module-level StreamWriter variable named `memoStreamWriter`
`Dim reportStreamReader As IO.StreamReader` declares a procedure-level StreamReader variable named `reportStreamReader`
`Private textStreamReader As IO.StreamReader` declares a module-level StreamReader variable named `textStreamReader`

Figure 9-6: Syntax and examples of declaring StreamWriter and StreamReader variables

The {**Dim** | **Private**} portion of the syntax shown in Figure 9-6 indicates that you can select only one of the keywords appearing within the braces. In this case, you can select either Dim or Private. The appropriate keyword to use depends on whether the variable is a procedure-level or module-level variable. *Variablename* in the syntax is the name of the variable, and *objecttype* is either StreamWriter or StreamReader. The IO in the syntax stands for "Input/Output".

After you declare the appropriate variable, you then create a StreamWriter or StreamReader object and assign the object's address to the variable; this is Step 2 in the procedure shown in Figure 9-5. You create a StreamWriter or StreamReader object by opening a sequential access file.

Opening a Sequential Access File

When you open a sequential access file, the computer creates an object that represents the file in the program. You assign the object's address to a StreamWriter or StreamReader variable, and then use the variable to refer to the object, and therefore the file, in the program.

Figure 9-7 shows the syntax you use to open a sequential access file and assign the resulting object's address to a variable. The figure also describes the methods that are used to open a sequential access file. In addition, the figure includes several examples of using the syntax.

Syntax		
variablename = **IO.File.***method*(*filename*)		
method	Object created	Description
OpenText	StreamReader	opens an existing sequential access file for input, which allows the computer to read the information stored in the file; if the file does not exist, the computer displays an error message
CreateText	StreamWriter	opens a sequential access file for output, which creates a new, empty file to which data can be written; if the file already exists, its contents are erased before the new data is written
AppendText	StreamWriter	opens a sequential access file for append, which allows the computer to write new data to the end of the existing data in the file; if the file does not exist, the file is created before data is written to it

Examples and results
`reportStreamReader = IO.File.OpenText("a:\reports\pay.txt")`
opens for input the pay.txt file contained in the reports folder on the A drive; creates a StreamReader object and assigns its address to the `reportStreamReader` variable
`reportStreamReader = IO.File.OpenText("pay.txt")`
opens the pay.txt file for input; creates a StreamReader object and assigns its address to the `reportStreamReader` variable
`memoStreamWriter = IO.File.CreateText("memo.txt")`
opens the memo.txt file for output; creates a StreamWriter object and assigns its address to the `memoStreamWriter` variable
`textStreamWriter = IO.File.AppendText("sales.txt")`
opens the sales.txt file for append; creates a StreamWriter object and assigns its address to the `textStreamWriter` variable

Figure 9-7: Syntax and examples of opening a sequential access file

tip

You also can declare the appropriate variable and open a sequential access file in one statement. For example, you can use the statement `Dim reportStreamReader As IO.StreamReader = IO.File.OpenText ("pay.txt")` to declare the `reportStreamReader` variable and open the pay.txt file for input.

In the syntax, *variablename* is the name of either a StreamReader or StreamWriter variable, and *filename* is the name of the file you want to open. When you open a sequential access file, the computer creates either a StreamReader or StreamWriter object, depending on the *method* specified in the syntax. The **OpenText method**, for example, opens an existing sequential access file for input and allows the computer to read the information stored in the file. If the file does not exist when the OpenText method is processed, the computer displays an error message in a message box. The OpenText method creates a StreamReader object and can be used to open input files only.

You use the **CreateText method** to create a new, empty sequential access file to which data can be written. If the file already exists, the computer erases the contents of the file before writing any data to it. You use the **AppendText method** when you want to add data to the end of an existing sequential access file. If the file does not exist, the computer creates the file for you. Unlike the OpenText method, the CreateText and AppendText methods create StreamWriter objects and are used to open output files only.

When the computer processes the statement shown in the first example in Figure 9-7, it first searches the reports folder on the A drive for a file named pay.txt. If it cannot locate the pay.txt file, the computer displays an error message in a message box. Otherwise, it opens the file for input, creates a StreamReader object, and assigns the object's address to the `reportStreamReader` variable. Notice that the statement shown in the second example is identical to the statement shown in the first example, except the *filename* argument does not specify a folder path. If you do not include a folder path in the *filename* argument, the computer will search for the file in the current project's bin folder. For example, if the current project is stored in the VBNET\Chap09\Payroll Solution\Payroll Project folder, the computer will search for the pay.txt file in the VBNET\Chap09\Payroll Solution\Payroll Project\bin folder.

When processing the statement shown in the third example in Figure 9-7, the computer searches the current project's bin folder for a file named memo.txt. If the memo.txt file exists, its contents are erased and the file is opened for output. Otherwise, a new, empty file is created and opened for output. In addition to opening the memo.txt file, the statement shown in the third example also creates a StreamWriter object and assigns the object's address to the `memoStreamWriter` variable.

When the computer processes the statement shown in the last example in Figure 9-7, it searches the current project's bin folder for a file named sales.txt. If it locates the sales.txt file, the computer opens the file for append, which allows new information to be written to the end of the file. If the computer cannot locate the sales.txt file, it creates a new, empty file and opens the file for append. The statement also creates a StreamWriter object and assigns the object's address to the `textStreamWriter` variable.

The computer uses a file pointer to keep track of the next character either to read in or write to a file. When you open a file for input, the computer positions the file pointer at the beginning of the file, immediately before the first character. When you open a file for output, the computer also positions the file pointer at the beginning of the file, but recall that the file is empty. (As you learned earlier, opening a file for output tells the computer to create a new, empty file or erase the contents of an existing file.) However, when you open a file for append, the computer positions the file pointer immediately after the last character in the file. Figure 9-8 illustrates the position of the file pointer when files are opened for input, output, and append.

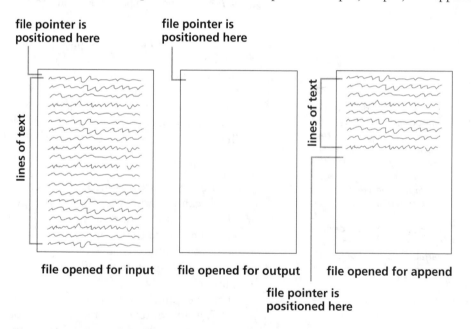

Figure 9-8: Position of the file pointer when files are opened for input, output, and append

Recall that the computer displays an error message if you use the OpenText method to open a file that does not exist. It is a good programming practice to verify that a file exists before you attempt to open the file for input.

Determining Whether a File Exists

You can use the **Exists method** to determine whether a file exists before you attempt to open it. Figure 9-9 shows the syntax of the Exists method and includes two examples of using the method. Both examples shown in the figure produce the same result and simply represent two different ways of accomplishing the same task.

Syntax
IO.File.Exists(*filename***)**
Examples and results

<pre>If IO.File.Exists("pay.txt") Then
        reportStreamReader = IO.File.OpenText("pay.txt")
        [instructions for processing the file]
Else
        MessageBox.Show("File does not exist", "Payroll", _
            MessageBoxButtons.OK, MessageBoxIcon.Information)
End If</pre>

opens and then processes the pay.txt file if the file exists; otherwise, displays the "File does not exist" message in a message box

<pre>If Not IO.File.Exists("pay.txt") Then
        MessageBox.Show("File does not exist", "Payroll", _
            MessageBoxButtons.OK, MessageBoxIcon.Information)
Else
        reportStreamReader = IO.File.OpenText("pay.txt")
        [instructions for processing the file]
End If</pre>

displays the "File does not exist" message in a message box if the pay.txt file does not exist; otherwise, opens and then processes the file

Figure 9-9: Syntax and examples of the Exists method

You also can write the If clause shown in the first example as If IO.File. Exists("pay.txt") = True Then, and the If clause shown in the second example as If IO.File. Exists("pay.txt") = False Then.

In the syntax shown in Figure 9-9, *filename* is the name of the file whose existence you want to verify. The *filename* argument can include an optional folder path. If the folder path is omitted, the computer searches for the file in the current project's bin folder. The Exists method returns the Boolean value True if *filename* exists; otherwise, it returns the Boolean value False.

Step 3 in the procedure shown earlier in Figure 9-5 is to use the StreamWriter object to write one or more lines of text to the file, or use the StreamReader object to read one or more lines of text from the file. First, you learn how to write information to a sequential access file.

Writing Information to a Sequential Access File

You can use either the Write method or the WriteLine method to write information to a sequential access file. Figure 9-10 shows the syntax of both methods and includes examples of using the methods to write information to sequential access files. The figure also indicates the placement of the file pointer after the method in each example is processed.

Syntax
variablename.**Write**(*data*) *variablename*.**WriteLine**(*data*)

Examples and results

file pointer

```
textStreamWriter.Write("Hello")
```
Hello

file pointer

```
textStreamWriter.WriteLine("Hello")
```
Hello

```
textStreamWriter.Write("The top salesperson is ")
textStreamWriter.WriteLine(name & ".")
textStreamWriter.WriteLine()
textStreamWriter.Write("ABC Sales")
```

(assuming the name *variable contains "Carolyn")*

file pointer

The top salesperson is Carolyn.

ABC Sales

```
textStreamWriter.Write("Total price: ")
textStreamWriter.WriteLine(price.ToString("C2"))
```

(assuming the price *variable contains 25)*

file pointer

Total price: $25.00

```
textStreamWriter.WriteLine(Space(10) & "A" & Space(5) & "B")
```
file pointer
          A   B

Figure 9-10: Syntax and examples of the Write and WriteLine methods

In each syntax shown in Figure 9-10, *variablename* is the name of a StreamWriter variable, and *data* is the information you want written to the file associated with the variable. The difference between the Write and WriteLine methods is the location of the file pointer after the *data* is written to the file. The **Write method** positions the file pointer at the end of the last character it writes to the file. The **WriteLine method**, on the other hand, positions the file pointer at the beginning of the next line in the file. It does so by appending a **line terminator character**, which is simply a carriage return followed by a line feed, to the end of the *data*.

The textStreamWriter.Write("Hello") statement shown in the first example in Figure 9-10 writes the string "Hello" to the file and then positions the file pointer immediately after the last letter in the string, as indicated in the example. The textStreamWriter.WriteLine("Hello") statement in the second example writes the string "Hello" and a line terminator character to the file. The line terminator character positions the file pointer at the beginning of the next line in the file, as indicated in the example.

The `textStreamWriter.Write("The top salesperson is ")` statement shown in the third example writes the string "The top salesperson is " to the file and then positions the file pointer after the last character in the string (in this case, after the space character). The `textStreamWriter.WriteLine(name & ".")` statement in the example first concatenates the contents of the `name` variable with a period. It then writes the concatenated string and a line terminator character to the file; the line terminator character moves the file pointer to the next line in the file. The next statement in the example, `textStreamWriter.WriteLine()`, writes only a line terminator character to the file; you can use this statement to insert a blank line in a file. The last statement in the example, `textStreamWriter.Write("ABC Sales")`, writes the string "ABC Sales" to the file, and then positions the file pointer after the last character in the string, as indicated in the example.

The two statements shown in the fourth example write the string "Total price: " and the contents of the `price` variable (formatted with a dollar sign and two decimal places) on the same line in the file. The file pointer is then positioned at the beginning of the next line in the file.

The last example in Figure 9-10 shows how you can use the **Space function** to write a specific number of spaces to a file. The syntax of the Space function is **Space**(*number*), where *number* represents the number of spaces you want to write. The `textStreamWriter.WriteLine(Space(10) & "A" & Space(5) & "B")` statement writes 10 spaces, the letter "A", five spaces, the letter "B", and the line terminator character to the file. After the statement is processed, the file pointer is positioned at the beginning of the next line in the file.

Next, you learn how to align columns of information in a sequential access file.

Aligning Columns of Information

In Chapter 8, you learned how to use the PadLeft and PadRight methods to pad a string with a character until the string is a specified length. Recall that the syntax of the PadLeft method is *string*.**PadLeft**(*length*[, *character*]), and the syntax of the PadRight method is *string*.**PadRight**(*length*[, *character*]). In each syntax, *length* is an integer that represents the desired length of the *string*, and *character* (which is optional) is the character that each method uses to pad the *string* until it reaches the desired *length*. If the *character* argument is omitted, the default *character* is the space character. Figure 9-11 shows examples of using the PadLeft and PadRight methods to align columns of information written to a sequential access file.

Examples and results

```
Dim sales As String, salesNum As Double
Dim reportStreamWriter As IO.StreamWriter
For region = 1 To 3
    sales = InputBox("Sales amount", "Sales")
    salesNum = Double.Parse(sales)
    sales = salesNum.ToString("N2")
    reportStreamWriter.WriteLine(sales.PadLeft(8))
Next region
```

(assuming the user enters the following sales amounts: 645.75, 1200, 40.80)
```
  645.75
1,200.00
   40.80
```

Figure 9-11: Examples of aligning columns of information in a sequential access file

Examples and results

```
Dim name As String, age As String
Dim reportStreamWriter As IO.StreamWriter
reportStreamWriter.WriteLine("Name" & Space(11) & "Age")
name = InputBox("Name:", "Name")
Do While name <> ""
    age = InputBox("Age:", "Age")
    reportStreamWriter.WriteLine(name.PadRight(15) & age)
    name = InputBox("Name:", "Name")
Loop
```

(assuming the user enters the following names and ages: Janice, 23, Sue, 67)

```
Name            Age
Janice          23
Sue             67
```

Figure 9-11: Examples of aligning columns of information in a sequential access file
(continued)

The code in the first example shows how you can align a column of numbers by the decimal point. First, you format each number in the column to ensure that each has the same number of digits to the right of the decimal point. You then use the PadLeft method to insert spaces at the beginning of the number; this right-aligns the number within the column. Because each number has the same number of digits to the right of the decimal point, aligning each number on the right will, in effect, align each by its decimal point.

The code in the second example in Figure 9-11 shows how you can align the second column of information when the first column contains strings whose lengths vary. To align the second column, you first use either the PadRight or PadLeft method to ensure that each string in the first column contains the same number of characters. You then concatenate the padded string to the information in the second column before writing the concatenated string to the file. The code shown in the second example, for instance, uses the PadRight method to ensure that each name in the first column contains exactly 15 characters. It then concatenates the 15 characters with the age stored in the age variable, and then writes the concatenated string to the file. Because each name has 15 characters, each age will automatically appear beginning in character position 16 in the file.

In the next section, you learn how to read information from a sequential access file.

Reading Information from a Sequential Access File

You use the **ReadLine method** to read a line of text from a sequential access file. A **line** is defined as a sequence of characters followed by the line terminator character. The string returned by the ReadLine method contains only the sequence of characters contained in the line; it does not include the line terminator character. Figure 9-12 shows the syntax of the ReadLine method and includes examples of using the method to read lines of text from a sequential access file. In the syntax, *variablename* is the name of a StreamReader variable.

Syntax
variablename.**ReadLine()**

Examples and results
| ```
line = textStreamReader.ReadLine()
``` |
| reads a line from a sequential access file, and then assigns the line (excluding the line terminator character) to the `line` variable |
| ```
Do Until textStreamReader.Peek() = -1
    line = textStreamReader.ReadLine()
    MessageBox.Show(line, "Line", _
        MessageBoxButtons.OK, MessageBoxIcon.Information)
Loop
``` |
| reads a sequential access file, line by line; assigns each line (excluding the line terminator character) to the `line` variable and displays each line in a message box |

Figure 9-12: Syntax and examples of the ReadLine method

In the first example shown in Figure 9-12, the `line = textStreamReader.ReadLine()` statement reads a line of text from a sequential access file and assigns the line, excluding the line terminator character, to the `line` variable.

In most cases, an application will need to read each line of text contained in a sequential access file, one line at a time. You can do so using a repetition structure along with the Peek method, as shown in the second example in Figure 9-12. The syntax of the Peek method is *variablename*.**Peek()**, where *variablename* is the name of a StreamReader variable. The **Peek method** "peeks" into the file to see whether the file contains another character to read. If the file contains another character, the Peek method returns the character; otherwise, it returns the number -1. The `Do Until textStreamReader.Peek() = -1` clause shown in the second example tells the computer to process the loop instructions until the Peek method returns the number -1, which indicates that there are no more characters to read. The loop instructions read a line of text and then display the line (excluding the line terminator character) in a message box.

The last step in the sequential access file procedure (shown earlier in Figure 9-5) is to use the StreamWriter or StreamReader object to close the file.

Closing a Sequential Access File

To prevent the loss of data, you should use the **Close method** to close a sequential access file as soon as you are finished using it. Figure 9-13 shows the syntax of the Close method and includes examples of using the method to close sequential access files. In the syntax, *variablename* is the name of either a StreamReader or StreamWriter variable.

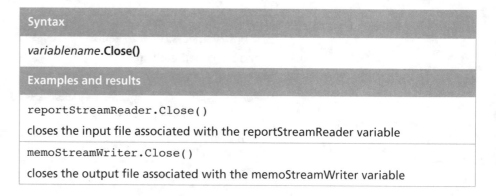

Syntax
variablename.**Close()**

Examples and results
`reportStreamReader.Close()` closes the input file associated with the reportStreamReader variable
`memoStreamWriter.Close()` closes the output file associated with the memoStreamWriter variable

Figure 9-13: Syntax and examples of the Close method

In the first example shown in Figure 9-13, the Close method closes the input file associated with the reportStreamReader variable. In the second example, the Close method closes the output file associated with the memoStreamWriter variable.

Next, you view an application that demonstrates most of what you have learned so far about files.

The Friends Application

Assume you want to create an application that allows the user to write the names of his or her friends to a sequential access file, and also read the names from the file. The user interface for this application is shown in Figure 9-14.

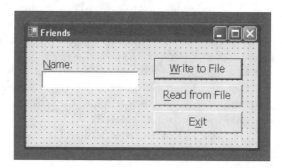

Figure 9-14: User interface for the Friends application

The user interface for the Friends application contains a text box for entering the names, and three buttons labeled Write to File, Read from File, and Exit. You use the Write to File button to write the name entered in the Name text box to a sequential access file named friends.txt. You use the Read from File button to read each name in the friends.txt file and display each name in a message box. You use the Exit button to end the application. Figure 9-15 shows the pseudocode for the Write to File and Read from File buttons, and Figure 9-16 shows the application's code.

Write to File button
1. open a sequential access file named friends.txt for append
2. write the name entered in the Name text box to the file
3. close the file
4. clear the Name text box
5. send the focus to the Name text box

Read from File button
1. if the friends.txt file exists
       open the file for input
       repeat until there are no more characters to read
             read a name from the file
             display the name in a message box
       end repeat
       close the file
   else
       display a message informing the user that the friends.txt file does not exist
   end if

Figure 9-15: Pseudocode for the Write to File and Read from File buttons

```
'Project name:          Friends Project
'Project purpose:       The project allows the user to write information
'                       to a sequential access file, and also read information
'                       from a sequential access file.
'Created/revised by:    <enter your name here> on <enter date here>

Option Explicit On
Option Strict On

[Windows Form Designer generated code]

    Private Sub uiExitButton_Click(ByVal sender As Object, _
            ByVal e As System.EventArgs) Handles uiExitButton.Click
        'ends the application
        Me.Close()
    End Sub


    Private Sub uiWriteButton_Click(ByVal sender As Object, _
            ByVal e As System.EventArgs) Handles uiWriteButton.Click
        'writes information to a sequential access file

        'declare a StreamWriter variable
        Dim friendsStreamWriter As IO.StreamWriter

        'create a StreamWriter object by opening the file for append
        friendsStreamWriter = IO.File.AppendText("friends.txt")

        'write the name entered in the Name text box
        'on a separate line in the file
        friendsStreamWriter.WriteLine(Me.uiNameTextBox.Text)
```

Figure 9-16: Code for the Friends application

```
          'close the file
          friendsStreamWriter.Close()

          'clear the Name text box, then send the focus to the text box
          Me.uiNameTextBox.Text = ""
          Me.uiNameTextBox.Focus()

     End Sub

     Private Sub uiReadButton_Click(ByVal sender As Object, _
             ByVal e As System.EventArgs) Handles uiReadButton.Click
          'reads information from a sequential access file

          'declare variables
          Dim name As String
          Dim friendsStreamReader As IO.StreamReader

          'determine whether the friends.txt file exists
          If IO.File.Exists("friends.txt") Then
              'create a StreamReader object by opening the file for input
              friendsStreamReader = IO.File.OpenText("friends.txt")

              'process the loop instructions until there are
              'no more characters to read
              Do Until friendsStreamReader.Peek() = -1
                  'read a name from the file--each name
                  'appears on a separate line in the file
                  name = friendsStreamReader.ReadLine()
                  'display the name in a message box
                  MessageBox.Show(name, "Friend", _
                      MessageBoxButtons.OK, MessageBoxIcon.Information)
              Loop

              'close the file
              friendsStreamReader.Close()
          Else
              'display an appropriate message
              MessageBox.Show("The friends.txt file does not exist.", _
                  "Friend", MessageBoxButtons.OK, _
                  MessageBoxIcon.Information)
          End If

     End Sub
End Class
```

Figure 9-16: Code for the Friends application (continued)

Notice that the uiWriteButton's Click event procedure declares a StreamWriter variable named `friendsStreamWriter`. It then uses the AppendText method to open the friends.txt file; this creates a StreamWriter object. The procedure assigns the StreamWriter object's address to the `friendsStreamWriter` variable. Next, the procedure uses the WriteLine method to write the contents of the Name text box on a separate line in the friends.txt file. The procedure then uses the Close method to close the friends.txt file. After closing the file, the procedure clears the contents of the Name text box and also sends the focus to the text box. If you start the Friends application and enter three names (Janice, Carl, and William), clicking the Write to File button after entering each name, the uiWriteButton's Click event procedure will write each name on a separate line in the friends.txt file. You can verify that the records were written correctly by viewing the contents of the file in a separate window in the IDE. Figure 9-17 shows the procedure you follow to view the contents of a sequential access file, and Figure 9-18 shows the contents of the friends.txt file.

Viewing the contents of a sequential access file

1. Click File on the menu bar.

2. Point to Open, then click File. The Open File dialog box opens.

3. Open the bin folder contained in the application's project folder.

4. Click the name of the sequential access file in the list of filenames.

5. Click the Open button to view the contents of the file in a separate window.

6. To close the window, click its Close button.

Figure 9-17: Procedure for viewing the contents of a sequential access file

Figure 9-18: Contents of the friends.txt file displayed in a window

tip

You can use the window shown in Figure 9-18 to add, delete, or edit the information contained in the friends.txt sequential access file. To save the modifications, you click File on the menu bar and then click Save friends.txt.

The uiReadButton's Click event procedure shown earlier in Figure 9-16 declares a StreamReader variable named `friendsStreamReader`. It then uses the Exists method to determine whether the friends.txt file exists. If the file does not exist, the procedure displays the message "The friends.txt file does not exist." in a message box. However, if the file does exist, the procedure uses the OpenText method to open the file; this creates a StreamReader object. The procedure assigns the StreamReader object's address to the `friendsStreamReader` variable. Next, the procedure uses a repetition structure, the Peek method, the ReadLine method, and the MessageBox.Show method to read each name in the file and display each name in a message box. After each name in the file has been displayed, the procedure uses the Close method to close the friends.txt file. Assuming the friends.txt file exists, Figure 9-19 shows the message box that will appear when the user clicks the Read from File button the first time.

Figure 9-19: Message box containing the first name read from the file

As you learned earlier, the computer displays an error message when the OpenText method tries to open an input file that does not exist. Recall that you can prevent this error from occurring by using the Exists method to verify that the file exists before you attempt to open it. Unfortunately, trying to open a nonexistent input file is not the only error that can occur when using sequential access files. For example, the AppendText and CreateText methods will result in an error if the file you are trying to open is read-only, or if the folder path specified in the *filename* argument does not exist. You can handle these errors using a Try/Catch block. Figure 9-20 shows a Try/Catch block entered in the Click event procedures for the uiWriteButton and uiReadButton controls in the Friends application.

```
'Project name:          Friends Project
'Project purpose:       The project allows the user to write information
'                       to a sequential access file, and also read information
'                       from a sequential access file.
'Created/revised by:    <enter your name here> on <enter date here>

Option Explicit On
Option Strict On

Public Class FriendsForm
    Inherits System.Windows.Forms.Form

[Windows Form Designer generated code]


    Private Sub uiExitButton_Click(ByVal sender As Object, _
            ByVal e As System.EventArgs) Handles uiExitButton.Click
        'ends the application
        Me.Close()
    End Sub


    Private Sub uiWriteButton_Click(ByVal sender As Object, _
            ByVal e As System.EventArgs) Handles uiWriteButton.Click
        'writes information to a sequential access file

        'declare a StreamWriter variable
        Dim friendsStreamWriter As IO.StreamWriter

        Try
            'create a StreamWriter object by opening the file for append
            friendsStreamWriter = IO.File.AppendText("friends.txt")
```

Figure 9-20: Try/Catch blocks included in the Friends application

```vb
                    'write the name entered in the Name text box
                    'on a separate line in the file
                    friendsStreamWriter.WriteLine(Me.uiNameTextBox.Text)

                    'close the file
                    friendsStreamWriter.Close()

                    'clear the Name text box, then send the focus to the text box
                    Me.uiNameTextBox.Text = ""
                    Me.uiNameTextBox.Focus()

            Catch ex As Exception
                'handles any errors
                MessageBox.Show(ex.Message, "Friends", _
                    MessageBoxButtons.OK, MessageBoxIcon.Information)
            End Try

        End Sub

        Private Sub uiReadButton_Click(ByVal sender As Object, _
                ByVal e As System.EventArgs) Handles uiReadButton.Click
            'reads information from a sequential access file

            'declare variables
            Dim name As String
            Dim friendsStreamReader As IO.StreamReader

            Try
                    'create a StreamReader object by opening the file for input
                    friendsStreamReader = IO.File.OpenText("friends.txt")

                    'process the loop instructions until there are
                    'no more characters to read
                    Do Until friendsStreamReader.Peek() = -1
                        'read a name from the file—each name
                        'appears on a separate line in the file
                        name = friendsStreamReader.ReadLine()
                        'display the name in a message box
                        MessageBox.Show(name, "Friend", _
                            MessageBoxButtons.OK, MessageBoxIcon.Information)
                    Loop

                    'close the file
                    friendsStreamReader.Close()

            Catch exFile As IO.FileNotFoundException
                'processed when the file cannot be found
                MessageBox.Show("Cannot locate the friends.txt file.", _
                    "Friends", MessageBoxButtons.OK, _
                    MessageBoxIcon.Information)
            Catch ex As Exception
                'handles any other errors
                MessageBox.Show(ex.Message, "Friends", _
                    MessageBoxButtons.OK, MessageBoxIcon.Information)

            End Try

        End Sub
End Class
```

Figure 9-20: Try/Catch blocks included in the Friends application (continued)

You now have completed Lesson A. You can either take a break or complete the end-of-lesson questions and exercises before moving on to the next lesson.

SUMMARY

To use a sequential access file in an application:

- Follow the procedure shown in Figure 9-5.

To declare a StreamWriter or StreamReader variable:

- Use the syntax {**Dim** | **Private**} *variablename* **As IO.***objecttype*, where *variablename* is the name of the variable, and *objecttype* is either StreamWriter or StreamReader.

To open a sequential access file for input:

- Use the syntax **IO.File.OpenText**(*filename*), where *filename* is the name of the file (including an optional folder path) that you want to open. If *filename* does not exist, the computer displays an error message in a message box.
- The OpenText method creates a StreamReader object and allows the computer to read the file.

To open a sequential access file for append:

- Use the syntax **IO.File.AppendText**(*filename*), where *filename* is the name of the file (including an optional folder path) that you want to open. If *filename* does not exist, the computer creates the file for you.
- The AppendText method creates a StreamWriter object and allows the computer to write information to the end of the file.

To open a sequential access file for output:

- Use the syntax **IO.File.CreateText**(*filename*), where *filename* is the name of the file (including an optional folder path) that you want to open. If *filename* exists, its contents are erased before any data is written to the file.
- The CreateText method creates a StreamWriter object and allows the computer to write information to a new, empty file.

To assign the object created by the OpenText, CreateText, and AppendText methods to a variable:

- Use the syntax *variablename* = **IO.File.***method*(*filename*), where *variablename* is the name of either a StreamReader or StreamWriter object, and *filename* is the name of the file you want to open, create, or append to.

To determine whether a file exists:

- Use the Exists method. The method's syntax is **IO.File.Exists**(*filename*), where *filename* is the name of the file (including an optional folder path) whose existence you want to verify. The Exists method returns the Boolean value True if *filename* exists; otherwise, it returns the Boolean value False.

To write information to a sequential access file:

- Use either the Write method or the WriteLine method.
- The syntax of the Write method is *variablename*.**Write**(*data*), where *variablename* is the name of a StreamWriter variable. The Write method writes the *data* to the file and then positions the file pointer at the end of the last character written.
- The syntax of the WriteLine method is *variablename*.**WriteLine**(*data*), where *variablename* is the name of a StreamWriter variable. The WriteLine method writes the *data* and a line terminator character to the file. The line terminator character positions the file pointer at the beginning of the next line in the file.

To write spaces to a sequential access file:

- Use the Space function. The function's syntax is **Space**(*number*), where *number* represents the number of spaces you want to write.

To pad a string with a character until the string is a specified length:

- Use the PadLeft method to pad a string on the left, and the PadRight method to pad a string on the right.
- The PadLeft method right-aligns the characters within a string, and the PadRight method left-aligns the characters.

To read a line of text from a sequential access file:

- Use the ReadLine method. The method's syntax is *variablename*.**ReadLine**(), where *variablename* is the name of a StreamReader variable.
- The ReadLine method returns a string that contains all of the characters in the line, excluding the line terminator character.

To determine whether a sequential access file contains another character to read:

- Use the Peek method. The method's syntax is *variablename*.**Peek**(), where *variablename* is the name of a StreamReader variable.
- If the file contains another character to read, the Peek method returns the character; otherwise, it returns the number -1.

To close a sequential access file:

- Use the Close method. The method's syntax is *variablename*.**Close**(), where *variablename* is the name of either a StreamReader or StreamWriter variable.

Q U E S T I O N S

1. Which of the following creates a variable that can be used when reading a sequential access file?
   a. Dim lineCharReader As IO.CharReader
   b. Dim lineCharacterReader As IO.CharacterReader
   c. Dim lineFileReader As IO.FileReader
   d. Dim lineSequenceReader As IO.SequenceReader
   e. Dim lineStreamReader As IO.StreamReader

2. Which of the following opens the names.txt file and allows the computer to write information to the end of the existing data in the file?
   a. `IO.File.AddText("names.txt")`
   b. `IO.File.AppendText("names.txt")`
   c. `IO.File.CreateText("names.txt")`
   d. `IO.File.InsertText("names.txt")`
   e. `IO.File.OpenText("names.txt")`

3. The OpenText method creates a _____.
   a. StreamReader object
   b. StreamReader variable
   c. StreamWriter object
   d. StreamWriter variable
   e. Both a and c.

4. If the file you want to open exists, the _____ method erases the file's contents.
   a. AddText
   b. AppendText
   c. CreateText
   d. InsertText
   e. OpenText

5. If the file you want to open does not exist, the _____ method displays an error message in a message box.
   a. AddText
   b. AppendText
   c. CreateText
   d. InsertText
   e. OpenText

6. Which of the following can be used to determine whether the "employ.txt" file exists?
   a. `If IO.File.Exists("employ.txt") Then`
   b. `If IO.File("employ.txt").Exists Then`
   c. `If IO.Exists("employ.txt") Then`
   d. `If IO.Exists.File("employ.txt") Then`
   e. None of the above.

7. Which of the following can be used to write the string "Your pay is $56" to a sequential access file? (Assume that the pay variable contains the number 56.)
   a. `objStreamWriter.Write("Your pay is $")`
      `objStreamWriter.WriteLine(pay)`
   b. `objStreamWriter.WriteLine("Your pay is $" & pay)`
   c. `objStreamWriter.Write("Your ")`
      `objStreamWriter.Write("pay is ")`
      `objStreamWriter.WriteLine("$" & pay)`
   d. `objStreamWriter.WriteLine("Your pay is $" & pay.ToString())`
   e. All of the above.

8. Which of the following can be used to write 15 space characters to a sequential access file?
   a. `textStreamWriter.WriteLine(Blank(15))`
   b. `textStreamWriter.WriteLine(Chars(15))`
   c. `textStreamWriter.WriteLine(Blank(15, " "))`
   d. `textStreamWriter.WriteLine(Space(15))`
   e. `textStreamWriter.WriteLine(Space(15, " "))`

9. Assume that the `state` variable contains the string "Florida". Which of the following assigns six spaces followed by the contents of the `state` variable to the `state` variable?
   a. `state = Space(6) & state`
   b. `state = state.PadLeft(13)`
   c. `state = state.PadLeft(6)`
   d. Both a and b.
   e. Both a and c.

10. You use the _____ method to left-align the characters in a string.
    a. AlignLeft
    b. CharLeft
    c. PadLeft
    d. StringLeft
    e. None of the above.

11. Assume that the `msg` variable contains the string "Great job". Which of the following assigns the contents of the `msg` variable followed by four exclamation points (!) to the `newMsg` variable?
    a. `newMsg = msg.PadLeft(4, "!")`
    b. `newMsg = msg.PadLeft(13, "!")`
    c. `newMsg = msg.PadRight(4, "!")`
    d. `newMsg = msg.PadRight(13, "!")`
    e. `newMsg = msg.PadRight("!!!!")`

12. Which of the following assigns the contents of the `age` variable, converted to a string, to the `ageInput` variable?
    a. `ageInput = age.ToString()`
    b. `ageInput = String(age)`
    c. `ageInput = ToString(age)`
    d. `ageInput = ToString().age`
    e. None of the above.

13. Which of the following reads a line of text from a sequential access file, and assigns the line (excluding the line terminator character) to the `textLine` variable?
    a. `textStreamReader.Read(textLine)`
    b. `textStreamReader.ReadLine(textLine)`
    c. `textLine = textStreamReader.ReadLine()`
    d. `textLine = textStreamReader.ReadLine(line)`
    e. `textLine = textStreamReader.Read(line)`

14. The Peek method returns _____ if the sequential access file does not contain any more characters to read.
    a. -1
    b. 0 (zero)
    c. 1 (one)
    d. the last character read
    e. the line terminator character

15. You can use the Close method to close files opened for _____.
    a. append
    b. input
    c. output
    d. All of the above.

E X E R C I S E S

1. Write the statement to declare a local StreamReader variable named `salesStreamReader`.

2. Write the statement to open a sequential access file named jansales.txt for input. Assign the resulting StreamReader object to the `salesStreamReader` variable.

3. Write the statement to open a sequential access file named firstQtr.txt for append. Assign the resulting StreamWriter object to the `salesStreamWriter` variable.

4. Write the statement to open a sequential access file named febsales.txt for output. Assign the resulting StreamWriter object to the `salesStreamWriter` variable.

5. Write the Visual Basic .NET code to determine whether the jansales.txt file exists. If it does, the code should display the string "File exists" in the uiMsgLabel control; otherwise, it should display the string "File does not exist" in the uiMsgLabel control.

6. Assume you want to write the string "Employee" and the string "Name" to the sequential access file associated with the `textStreamWriter` variable. Each string should appear on a separate line in the file. Write the Visual Basic .NET code to accomplish this task.

7. Assume you want to write the contents of the `capital` variable followed by 20 spaces, the contents of the `state` variable, and the line terminator character to the sequential access file associated with the `textStreamWriter` variable. Write the Visual Basic .NET code to accomplish this task.

8. Assume that a Double variable named `sales` contains the number 2356.75. Write the statement to assign the contents of the `sales` variable, formatted with a dollar sign and two decimal places, to the `salesString` variable. The statement also should right-align the contents of the `salesString` variable, which should contain a total of 15 characters.

9. Assume you want a String variable named `award` to contain 10 characters, which should be right-aligned in the variable. Write the statement to accomplish this task. Use the asterisk character to pad the variable.

10. Write the statement that will ensure that the `name` variable contains 30 characters, which should be left-aligned in the variable. Use the space character to pad the variable.

11. Write the statement to read a line of text from the sequential access file associated with the `textStreamReader` variable. Assign the line of text (excluding the line terminator character) to the `textInput` variable.

12. Assume you want to read a sequential access file, line by line, and then display each line in a message box. The file is associated with the `textStreamReader` variable. Write the Visual Basic .NET code to accomplish this task.

13. Write the statement to close the jansales.txt file, which is associated with the `textStreamWriter` variable.

discovery ▶ **14.** In this exercise, you modify the Friends application that you viewed in Figure 9-16. The modified application allows the user to either create a new file or append information to the end of an existing file.

a. If necessary, start Visual Studio .NET. Open the Friends Solution (Friends Solution.sln) file, which is contained in the VBNET\Chap09\Friends Solution folder. If necessary, open the designer window.

b. Open the Code Editor window. Change the filename in the uiReadButton's Click event procedure from "friends.txt" to "friends2.txt". (You will need to change the name in four places.)

c. Change the filename in the uiWriteButton's Click event procedure from "friends.txt" to "friends2.txt".

d. When the uiWriteButton's Click event procedure is processed the first time, the procedure should determine whether the friends2.txt exists before the file is opened. If the file exists, the procedure should use the MessageBox.Show method to ask the user if he or she wants to replace the existing file. Include Yes and No buttons in the message box. The procedure should take the appropriate action based on the user's response.

e. Save the solution, then start the application. Type Jan in the Name text box, and then press Enter.

f. Click the Exit button to end the application, then start the application again. Type Carol in the Name text box, and then press Enter. The application should ask if you want to replace the existing file. Click the No button.

g. Click the Exit button to end the application, then use the File menu to open the friends2.txt file in a window. The file should contain two names: Jan and Carol. Close the friends2.txt window.

h. Start the application again. Type Richard in the Name text box, and then press Enter. The application should ask if you want to replace the existing file. Click the Yes button.

i. Click the Exit button to end the application, then use the File menu to open the friends2.txt file in a window. The file should contain one name: Richard. Close the friends2.txt window.

j. Close the Output window, then close the solution.

Records In a Sequential Access File

Writing and Reading Records

In some applications, a sequential access file is used to store fields and records. A **field** is a single item of information about a person, place, or thing—for example, a name, a salary, a Social Security number, or a price. A **record** is one or more related fields that contain all of the necessary data about a specific person, place, or thing. The college you are attending keeps a student record on you. Your student record might contain the following fields: your Social Security number, name, address, phone number, credits earned, grades earned, grade point average, and so on. The place where you are employed also keeps a record on you. Your employee record might contain your Social Security number, name, address, phone number, starting date, salary or hourly wage, and so on.

When writing records to a sequential access file, you typically write each record on a separate line in the file. If the records contain more than one field, programmers separate each field with a special character, such as a comma or the number symbol (#); this is done to distinguish one field from the next when reading the record later. Figure 9-21 shows examples of writing records to a sequential access file.

Examples and results
`textStreamWriter.WriteLine(Me.uiCityTextBox.Text & "," & Me.uiStateTextBox.Text)`
assuming the uiCityTextBox and uiStateTextBox controls contain Miami and Florida, respectively, the statement writes the following record on a separate line in the file associated with the `textStreamWriter` variable: Miami,Florida
`textStreamWriter.WriteLine(last & "#" & first)`
assuming the `last` and `first` variables contain Smithson and Carol, respectively, the statement writes the following record on a separate line in the file associated with the `textStreamWriter` variable: Smithson#Carol

Figure 9-21: Examples of writing a record to a sequential access file

The statement shown in the first example in Figure 9-21 writes a record that consists of two fields—a city field and a state field—separated by a comma. The comma indicates where the city field ends in the record and where the state field begins. The WriteLine method in the statement ensures that the record appears on a separate line in the file.

The statement shown in the second example also writes a record that contains two fields: a last name field and a first name field. In this example, however, the fields are separated by the # character, which indicates where the last name ends and the first name begins.

Figure 9-22 shows examples of reading records from a sequential access file. More specifically, the examples in Figure 9-22 can be used to read the records from Figure 9-21.

You learned about the IndexOf and Substring methods in Chapter 8.

Examples and results

```
Do Until textStreamReader.Peek() = -1
        'read a record from the file
        record = textStreamReader.ReadLine()
        'display the city name
        indexNum = record.IndexOf(",")
        cityName = record.Substring(0, indexNum)
        MessageBox.Show(cityName, "City Name", _
                MessageBoxButtons.OK, MessageBoxIcon.Information)
Loop
```

assuming the file contains the record *Miami,Florida*, the code displays *Miami* in a message box

```
Do Until textStreamReader.Peek() = -1
        'read a record from the file
        record = textStreamReader.ReadLine()
        'display the first name
        indexNum = record.IndexOf("#")
        firstName = record.Substring(indexNum + 1)
        MessageBox.Show(firstName, "First Name", _
                MessageBoxButtons.OK, MessageBoxIcon.Information)
Loop
```

assuming the file contains the record *Smithson#Carol*, the code displays *Carol* in a message box

Figure 9-22: Examples of reading records from a sequential access file

The loop shown in the first example in Figure 9-22 processes its instructions until there are no more characters to read from the file. The first instruction in the loop uses the ReadLine method to read a line of text from the file, and it assigns the text to the `record` variable. In this case, the line of text represents a record that contains a city name field, followed by a comma and a state name field. The `indexNum = record.IndexOf(",")` statement in the loop searches for the comma in the `record` variable and assigns the comma's index to the `indexNum` variable. Assuming the `record` variable contains *Miami,Florida*, the statement assigns the number five to the `indexNum` variable. The `cityName = record.Substring(0, indexNum)` statement in the loop tells the computer to assign `indexNum` characters from the `record` variable, beginning with the first character. Assuming the `record` and `indexNum` variables contain *Miami,Florida* and *5*, respectively, the statement assigns *Miami* (the city name) to the `cityName` variable. Lastly, the MessageBox.Show method displays the city name in a message box.

The loop shown in the second example in Figure 9-22 also processes its instructions until there are no more characters to read from the file. Here again, the first instruction in the loop uses the ReadLine method to read a line of text from the file, and it assigns the text to the `record` variable. In this case, however, the line of text represents a record that contains a last name field, followed by the # character and a first name field. The `indexNum = record.IndexOf("#")` statement in the loop searches for the # character in the record and assigns the character's index to the `indexNum` variable. Assuming the `record` variable contains *Smithson#Carol*, the statement assigns the number eight to the `indexNum` variable. The `firstName = record.Substring(indexNum + 1)` statement in the loop tells the computer to assign all of the characters from the `record` variable, beginning with the character immediately after the # character. Assuming the `record` and `indexNum` variables contain *Smithson#Carol* and *8*, respectively, the statement assigns *Carol* (the first name) to the `firstName` variable. Lastly, the MessageBox.Show method displays the first name in a message box.

Now you can begin creating the application for the PAO (Political Awareness Organization).

Creating the PAO Application

Recall that your task in this chapter is to create an application for the PAO (Political Awareness Organization). The application should allow the organization's secretary to save (to a sequential access file) a voter's political party and age. It also should allow the secretary to tabulate the number of Democrats, Republicans, and Independents entered in the file, and also print the contents of the file.

To open the PAO application:

1   Start Microsoft Visual Studio .NET, if necessary.

2   If necessary, close the Start Page window.

3   Open the **Pao Solution** (Pao Solution.sln) file, which is contained in the VBNET\Chap09\ Pao Solution folder.

4   Auto-hide the Toolbox, Solution Explorer, and Properties windows, if necessary. Figure 9-23 shows the user interface for the PAO application.

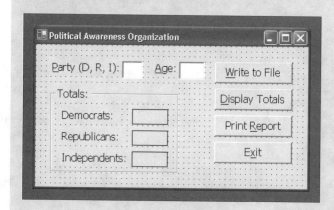

Figure 9-23: Interface for the PAO application

Figure 9-24 shows the TOE chart for the PAO application.

Task	Object	Event
1. Open a sequential access file named pao.txt for append 2. Write the political party and age to a sequential access file 3. Close the sequential access file 4. Clear the text boxes 5. Send the focus to the uiPartyTextBox control	uiWriteButton	Click
1. Open a sequential access file named pao.txt for input 2. Read each record in the sequential access file 3. If the current record begins with D, then add 1 to the Democrat counter 4. If the current record begins with R, then add 1 to the Republican counter 5. If the current record begins with I, then add 1 to the Independent counter 6. Close the sequential access file 7. Display the number of Democrats, Republicans, and Independents in uiTotalDemLabel, uiTotalRepLabel, and uiTotalIndLabel	uiDisplayButton	Click
End the application	uiExitButton	Click
Display the total number of Democrats (from uiDisplayButton)	uiTotalDemLabel	None
Display the total number of Republicans (from uiDisplayButton)	uiTotalRepLabel	None
Display the total number of Independents (from uiDisplayButton)	uiTotalIndLabel	None
Get the political party Allow text box to accept only D, R, I, and the Backspace key	uiPartyTextBox	None KeyPress
Get the age Allow text box to accept only numbers and the Backspace key	uiAgeTextBox	None KeyPress
1. Ask the user if he or she wants to create a new file 2. Create a new sequential access file (if necessary)	PaoForm	Load
Use the uiReportPrintDocument control to print the contents of the sequential access file	uiPrintButton	Click
1. Print the report header 2. Read and print each line in the sequential access file	uiReportPrintDocument	PrintPage

Figure 9-24: TOE chart for the PAO application

In this lesson, you code only the form's Load event procedure, as well as the Click event procedures for the uiWriteButton and uiDisplayButton controls. You code the uiPrintButton's Click event procedure and the uiReportPrintDocument's PrintPage event procedure in Lesson C. The uiExitButton's Click event procedure and the KeyPress event procedure for the uiPartyTextBox and uiAgeTextBox controls have already been coded for you.

Coding the PaoForm Load Event Procedure

The pseudocode for the PaoForm's Load event procedure is shown in Figure 9-25.

PaoForm
1. declare variables
2. ask the user if he or she wants to create a new file
3. if the user wants to create a new file
       include the following in the Try section of a Try/Catch block:
         create a sequential access file named pao.txt
         close the pao.txt file
       include the following in the Catch section of a Try/Catch block:
         use a general Catch statement to handle any errors
           if an error occurs, display a description of the error in a message box
   end if

Figure 9-25: Pseudocode for the PaoForm's Load event procedure

To code the PaoForm's Load event procedure, then test the procedure:

1. Open the Code Editor window. Notice that the Code Editor window contains the code for the uiExitButton's Click event procedure, the uiPartyTextBox's KeyPress event procedure, and the uiAgeTextBox's KeyPress event procedure. Replace the `<enter your name here>` and `<enter date here>` text with your name and the current date.

2. Open the code template for the PaoForm's Load event procedure. Type **'asks the user if he or she wants to create a new file** and press **Enter** twice.

The first step in the pseudocode is to declare the variables. The Load event procedure will use two variables: an Integer variable named `button` and a StreamWriter variable named `paoStreamWriter`.

3. Type the following two Dim statements, then press **Enter** twice.

   dim button as integer

   dim paoStreamWriter as io.streamwriter

Next, use the MessageBox.Show method to ask the user whether he or she wants to create a new file. Assign the user's response to the `button` variable.

4. Type **'determine whether the user wants to create a new file** and press **Enter**, then type **button = messagebox.show("Create new file?", "PAO", _** and press **Enter**. (Be sure to type the line continuation character.)

5. Press **Tab**, then type **messageboxbuttons.yesno, messageboxicon.exclamation, _** and press **Enter**. (Be sure to include a space before the line continuation character.) Type **messageboxdefaultbutton.button2)** and press **Enter**.

If the user wants to create a new file, then the Load event procedure should open a file named pao.txt for output. Recall that opening a file for output creates a new, empty file if the file does not exist. If the file does exist, opening the file for output erases the contents of the file before the file is opened. After opening the pao.txt file for output, which simply ensures that the file is empty, the procedure should immediately close the file. As you learned in Lesson A, you should close a sequential access file as soon as you are finished using it. In this case, after the Load event procedure creates (or erases the contents of) the pao.txt file, the procedure no longer needs the file.

6. Type the comment and Try/Catch block shown in Figure 9-26.

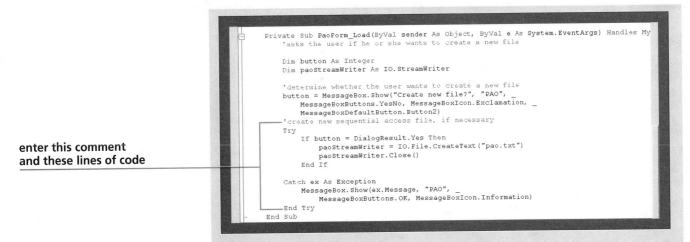

enter this comment and these lines of code

```
Private Sub PaoForm_Load(ByVal sender As Object, ByVal e As System.EventArgs) Handles My
    'asks the user if he or she wants to create a new file

    Dim button As Integer
    Dim paoStreamWriter As IO.StreamWriter

    'determine whether the user wants to create a new file
    button = MessageBox.Show("Create new file?", "PAO", _
        MessageBoxButtons.YesNo, MessageBoxIcon.Exclamation, _
        MessageBoxDefaultButton.Button2)
    'create new sequential access file, if necessary
    Try
        If button = DialogResult.Yes Then
            paoStreamWriter = IO.File.CreateText("pao.txt")
            paoStreamWriter.Close()
        End If

    Catch ex As Exception
        MessageBox.Show(ex.Message, "PAO", _
            MessageBoxButtons.OK, MessageBoxIcon.Information)
    End Try
End Sub
```

Figure 9-26: Completed PaoForm's Load event procedure

Now test the procedure to verify that it is working correctly.

7   Save the solution, then start the application. The dialog box shown in Figure 9-27 appears on the screen.

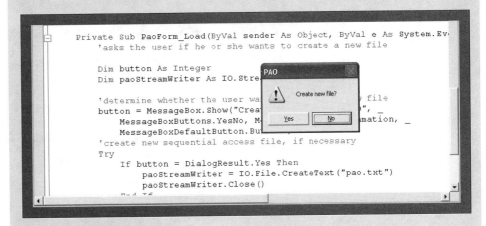

Figure 9-27: Dialog box created in the PaoForm's Load event procedure

8   Click the **No** button. The dialog box closes and the PAO application's user interface appears on the screen.

Notice that the PaoForm does not appear on the screen until after you close the dialog box created by the MessageBox.Show method in the Load event procedure. This is because Visual Basic .NET does not display a form until all of the instructions in the form's Load event procedure are processed. However, you can use a form's Show method to tell Visual Basic .NET to display the form immediately. You enter the Show method in the next set of steps.

9   Click the **Exit** button to end the application. When you return to the Code Editor window, close the Output window.

At times, as in the case of the PAO application, you may want a form to appear on the screen before all of the instructions in its Load event procedure have been processed. You can do so using the form's **Show method**, which tells Visual

Basic .NET to display the form on the screen immediately. The syntax of the form's Show method is simply **Me.Show()**.

To complete the PaoForm's Load event procedure, then test the procedure:

1   Type the additional comment and statement shown in Figure 9-28, which shows the completed PaoForm's Load event procedure.

enter this comment and line of code

```
Private Sub PaoForm_Load(ByVal sender As Object, ByVal e As System.EventArgs) Handles My
    'asks the user if he or she wants to create a new file

    Dim button As Integer
    Dim paoStreamWriter As IO.StreamWriter

    'display the form immediately
    Me.Show()

    'determine whether the user wants to create a new file
    button = MessageBox.Show("Create new file?", "PAO", _
        MessageBoxButtons.YesNo, MessageBoxIcon.Exclamation, _
        MessageBoxDefaultButton.Button2)
    'create new sequential access file, if necessary
    Try
        If button = DialogResult.Yes Then
            paoStreamWriter = IO.File.CreateText("pao.txt")
            paoStreamWriter.Close()
        End If

    Catch ex As Exception
        MessageBox.Show(ex.Message, "PAO", _
            MessageBoxButtons.OK, MessageBoxIcon.Information)
    End Try
End Sub
```

Figure 9-28: Completed PaoForm's Load event procedure

2   Save the solution, then start the application. This time, the PaoForm is displayed first, followed by the dialog box, as shown in Figure 9-29.

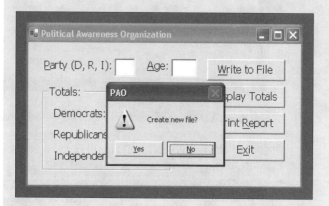

Figure 9-29: PaoForm and dialog box shown on the screen

3   Click the **Yes** button, which closes the dialog box and creates a sequential access file named pao.txt.

4   Click the **Exit** button to end the application. When you return to the Code Editor window, close the Output window.

Now verify that the Load event procedure created the pao.txt file.

5   Click **File** on the menu bar, point to **Open**, and then click **File**. Open the **bin** folder, which is contained in the VBNET\Chap09\PAO Solution\PAO Project folder. Notice that the bin folder contains a file named pao.txt. Click the **Cancel** button to close the Open File dialog box.

Next, you will code the uiWriteButton's Click event procedure.

Coding the uiWriteButton Click Event Procedure

Figure 9-30 shows the pseudocode for the uiWriteButton's Click event procedure.

---

uiWriteButton

1. declare variables

include the following in the Try section of a Try/Catch block:
2. open the pao.txt file for append
3. write the contents of the uiPartyTextBox control, 10 spaces, and the contents of the uiAgeTextBox control to the pao.txt file
4. close the pao.txt file
5. clear the contents of the uiPartyTextBox and uiAgeTextBox controls
6. send the focus to the uiPartyTextBox control

include the following in the Catch section of a Try/Catch block:
1. use a general Catch statement to handle any errors
        if an error occurs, display a description of the error in a message box

---

Figure 9-30: Pseudocode for the uiWriteButton's Click event procedure

To code the uiWriteButton's Click event procedure, then test the procedure:

1   Open the code template for the uiWriteButton's Click event procedure. Type **'writes information to a sequential access file** and press **Enter** twice.

The first step in the pseudocode is to declare the variables. The Click event procedure will use only one variable: a StreamWriter variable named `paoStreamWriter`.

2   Type **dim paoStreamWriter as io.streamwriter** and press **Enter** twice.

Next, open the pao.txt file for append, then write the contents of the uiPartyTextBox control, followed by 10 spaces and the contents of the uiAgeTextBox control to the file. After writing the information to the file, close the file.

3   Type the additional comments and lines of code shown in Figure 9-31.

enter these comments and lines of code

```
Private Sub uiWriteButton_Click(ByVal sender As Object, ByVal e As System.EventArgs) Han
    'writes information to a sequential access file

    Dim paoStreamWriter As IO.StreamWriter

    Try
        'create a StreamWriter object by opening the file for append
        paoStreamWriter = IO.File.AppendText("pao.txt")

        'write the party affiliation and age to the file
        paoStreamWriter.WriteLine(Me.uiPartyTextBox.Text & _
            Space(10) & Me.uiAgeTextBox.Text)

        'close the file
        paoStreamWriter.Close()

    Catch ex As Exception
        'handles any errors
        MessageBox.Show(ex.Message, "PAO", _
            MessageBoxButtons.OK, MessageBoxIcon.Information)
    End Try
End Sub
```

Figure 9-31: Additional comments and lines of code entered in the uiWriteButton's Click event procedure

Steps 5 and 6 in the pseudocode shown in Figure 9-30 are to clear the contents of the text boxes and then send the focus to the uiPartyTextBox control.

4   Type the additional comments and lines of code shown in Figure 9-32, which shows the completed uiWriteButton's Click event procedure.

enter these comments
and these lines of code

```
Private Sub uiWriteButton_Click(ByVal sender As Object, ByVal e As System.EventArgs) Han
    'writes information to a sequential access file

    Dim paoStreamWriter As IO.StreamWriter

    Try
        'create a StreamWriter object by opening the file for append
        paoStreamWriter = IO.File.AppendText("pao.txt")

        'write the party affiliation and age to the file
        paoStreamWriter.WriteLine(Me.uiPartyTextBox.Text & _
            Space(10) & Me.uiAgeTextBox.Text)

        'close the file
        paoStreamWriter.Close()

        'clear the text boxes
        Me.uiPartyTextBox.Text = ""
        Me.uiAgeTextBox.Text = ""

        'set the focus
        Me.uiPartyTextBox.Focus()

    Catch ex As Exception
        'handles any errors
        MessageBox.Show(ex.Message, "PAO", _
            MessageBoxButtons.OK, MessageBoxIcon.Information)
    End Try
End Sub
```

Figure 9-32: Completed uiWriteButton's Click event procedure

Now test the procedure to verify that it is working correctly.

5   Save the solution, then start the application. Click the **No** button in the PAO dialog box.

6   Type **r** in the Party text box, then press **Tab**. Type **34** in the Age text box, then press **Tab**. Press **Enter** to select the Write to File button.

7   Type **d** in the Party text box, then press **Tab**. Type **42** in the Age text box, then press **Tab**. Press **Enter** to select the Write to File button.

8   Click the **Exit** button to end the application. When you return to the Code Editor window, close the Output window.

Now verify that the uiWriteButton's Click event procedure wrote the appropriate information to the pao.txt file.

9   Click **File** on the menu bar, point to **Open**, and then click **File**. Open the **pao.txt** file, which is contained in the VBNET\Chap09\PAO Solution\PAO Project\bin folder. See Figure 9-33.

party

age

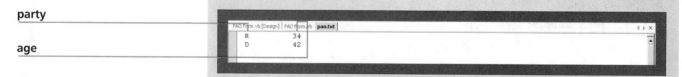

Figure 9-33: Contents of the pao.txt file

10   Close the pao.txt window.

The last procedure you will code in this lesson is the uiDisplayButton's Click event procedure.

Coding the uiDisplayButton Click Event Procedure

Figure 9-34 shows the pseudocode for the uiDisplayButton's Click event procedure.

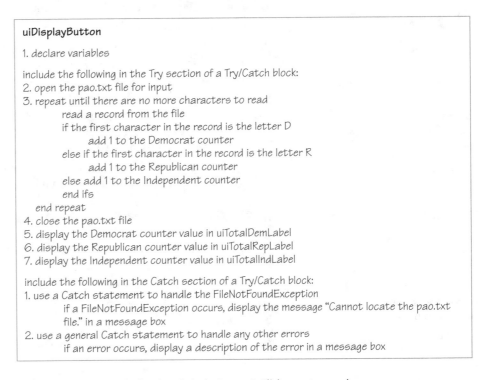

uiDisplayButton

1. declare variables

include the following in the Try section of a Try/Catch block:
2. open the pao.txt file for input
3. repeat until there are no more characters to read
      read a record from the file
      if the first character in the record is the letter D
         add 1 to the Democrat counter
      else if the first character in the record is the letter R
         add 1 to the Republican counter
      else add 1 to the Independent counter
      end ifs
  end repeat
4. close the pao.txt file
5. display the Democrat counter value in uiTotalDemLabel
6. display the Republican counter value in uiTotalRepLabel
7. display the Independent counter value in uiTotalIndLabel

include the following in the Catch section of a Try/Catch block:
1. use a Catch statement to handle the FileNotFoundException
      if a FileNotFoundException occurs, display the message "Cannot locate the pao.txt
      file." in a message box
2. use a general Catch statement to handle any other errors
      if an error occurs, display a description of the error in a message box

Figure 9-34: Pseudocode for the uiDisplayButton's Click event procedure

To code the uiDisplayButton's Click event procedure, then test the procedure:

1 Open the code template for the uiDisplayButton's Click event procedure. Type **'displays the total number of Democrats, Republicans, and Independents** and press **Enter** twice.

The first step in the pseudocode is to declare the variables. The Click event procedure will use five variables: one String variable, one StreamReader variable, and three Integer variables. The String variable, named `record`, will store a record as it is read from the pao.txt file. The StreamReader variable will be named `paoStreamReader` and will store the address of the StreamReader object that represents the pao.txt file. The three Integer variables will keep track of the number of Democrats, Republicans, and Independents stored in the pao.txt file. The Integer variables will be named `totalDem`, `totalRep`, and `totalInd`.

2   Type the following comments and Dim statements, then press **Enter** twice.

'declare a StreamReader variable
dim paoStreamReader as io.streamreader

dim record as string
dim totalDem as integer   'counter for total Democrats
dim totalRep as integer   'counter for total Republicans
dim totalInd as integer   'counter for total Independents

Next, open the pao.txt file for input.

3   Type **try** and press **Enter**. Type **'create a StreamReader object by opening the file for input** and press **Enter**, then type **paostreamreader = io.file.opentext("pao.txt")** and press **Enter** twice.

Step 3 in the pseudocode is a loop that repeats its instructions until there are no more characters to read from the file. The loop instructions read a record from the file and then update the appropriate counter. The counter to update depends on the party entry in the record.

4   Type the additional comments and lines of code shown in Figure 9-35, then position the insertion point as shown in the figure.

enter these comments
and lines of code

position the
insertion point here

Figure 9-35: Additional comments and lines of code entered in the uiDisplayButton's Click event procedure

Step 4 in the pseudocode is to close the pao.txt file.

5   Type **'close the file** and press **Enter**, then type **paostreamreader.close()** and press **Enter** twice.

Steps 5 through 7 are to display in the appropriate label controls the values stored in the three counter variables.

6   Type the additional comments and lines of code shaded in Figure 9-36.

```
Private Sub uiDisplayButton_Click(ByVal sender As Object, ByVal e As System.EventArgs)
Handles uiDisplayButton.Click
        'displays the total number of Democrats, Republicans, and Independents

        'declare a StreamReader variable
        Dim paoStreamReader As IO.StreamReader

        Dim record As String
        Dim totalDem As Integer          'counter for total Democrats
        Dim totalRep As Integer          'counter for total Republicans
        Dim totalInd As Integer          'counter for total Independents

        Try
            'create a StreamReader object by opening the file for input
            paoStreamReader = IO.File.OpenText("pao.txt")

            'process the loop instructions until there are
            'no more characters to read
            Do Until paoStreamReader.Peek() = -1
                'read a record from the file
                record = paoStreamReader.ReadLine()

                'update the appropriate counter
                If record.StartsWith("D") Then
                    totalDem = totalDem + 1
                ElseIf record.StartsWith("R") Then
                    totalRep = totalRep + 1
                Else
                    totalInd = totalInd + 1
                End If
            Loop

            'close the file
            paoStreamReader.Close()

            'display the totals
            Me.uiTotalDemLabel.Text = Convert.ToString(totalDem)
            Me.uiTotalRepLabel.Text = Convert.ToString(totalRep)
            Me.uiTotalIndLabel.Text = Convert.ToString(totalInd)

        Catch exFile As IO.FileNotFoundException
            'processed when the file cannot be found
            MessageBox.Show("Cannot locate the pao.txt file.", _
                "PAO", MessageBoxButtons.OK, _
                MessageBoxIcon.Information)
        Catch ex As Exception
            'handles any other errors
            MessageBox.Show(ex.Message, "PAO", _
                MessageBoxButtons.OK, MessageBoxIcon.Information)
        End Try
    End Sub
```

Figure 9-36: Completed uiDisplayButton's Click event procedure

Now test the procedure to verify that it is working correctly.

7   Save the solution, then start the application. Click the **No** button in the PAO dialog box.

8   Click the **Display Totals** button. The uiDisplayButton's Click event procedure calculates the number of Democrats, Republicans, and Independents stored in the pao.txt file. It then displays the results in the interface, as shown

in Figure 9-37. (Recall that you wrote two records to the pao.txt file when you tested the Write to File button.)

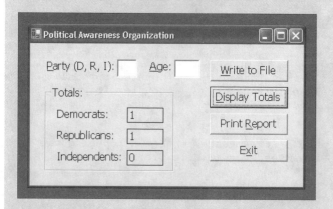

Figure 9-37: Counter values displayed in the interface

9 Click the **Exit** button to end the application. When you return to the Code Editor window, close the Output window, then close the Code Editor window.

10 Click **File** on the menu bar, and then click **Close Solution** to close the solution.

You now have completed Lesson B. In Lesson C, you add a PrintDocument control to the PAO application. You also finish coding the application. For now, you can either take a break or complete the end-of-lesson questions and exercises before moving on to the next lesson.

SUMMARY

To write a record to a sequential access file:

■ You typically write each record on a separate line in the file. If the records contain more than one field, programmers separate each field with a special character, such as a comma or the number symbol (#); this is done to distinguish one field from the next when reading the record later.

To read a record from a sequential access file:

■ Use the ReadLine method to read a line of text from the file; the line of text is the record. To separate the record into fields, search for the special character that separates one field from the next.

To display a form immediately:

■ Use the form's Show method as follows: **Me.Show()**.

QUESTIONS

1. Which of the following can be used to write a record that contains two fields: a book title field and an author field?
   a. `bookStreamWriter.WriteLine(title & "#" & author)`
   b. `bookStreamWriter.WriteLine(title & "," & author)`
   c. `bookStreamWriter.WriteLine(title & "$" & author)`
   d. `bookStreamWriter.WriteLine(title & Space(5) & author)`
   e. All of the above.

2. Assume that each record stored in a sequential access file contains two fields separated by the # character. Which of the following can be used to read a record from the file?
   a. `record = bookStreamReader.ReadLine()`
   b. `bookStreamReader.ReadLine(record)`
   c. `record = bookStreamReader.ReadLine("#")`
   d. `bookStreamReader.Read(record)`
   e. None of the above.

3. You can use the _____ method to display a form immediately.
   a. Display
   b. DisplayForm
   c. ShowForm
   d. Show
   e. None of the above.

EXERCISES

1. In this exercise, you complete an application that saves names and birth dates to a sequential access file.
   a. If necessary, start Visual Studio .NET. Open the Birthday Solution (Birthday Solution.sln) file, which is contained in the VBNET\Chap09\Birthday Solution folder. If necessary, open the designer window.
   b. The application allows the user to enter a person's name and birth date. Code the Add to File button's Click event procedure so that it writes the name and birth date to a sequential access file named birthday.txt. The name and birth date should appear on the same line in the file, but in two separate columns. The birth date should be right aligned in its column. The procedure also should send the focus to the uiNameTextBox control.
   c. Save the solution, then start the application. Test the application by entering the following names and birth dates: Kareem Abdula, 4/6/1980, Jefferson Williams, 12/8/1978, Jessica Jones, 9/30/1982.
   d. Click the Exit button to end the application.
   e. Open the birthday.txt file, which is contained in the VBNET\Chap09\Birthday Solution\Birthday Project\bin folder. The file should contain two columns of information. The first column should contain three names, and the second column should contain three birth dates. The birth dates should be right aligned in the column.
   f. Close the birthday.txt window. Close the Output window, then close the solution.

2. In this exercise, you complete an application that saves invoice numbers and amounts to a sequential access file.

   a. If necessary, start Visual Studio .NET. Open the Invoice Solution (Invoice Solution.sln) file, which is contained in the VBNET\Chap09\Invoice Solution folder. If necessary, open the designer window.

   b. The application allows the user to enter an invoice number and amount. Code the Save button's Click event procedure so that it writes the information entered by the user to a sequential access file named invoice.txt. The invoice number and amount should appear on the same line in the file, but in two separate columns. Align the information appropriately. (Recall from Lesson A that you typically align a column of numbers by their decimal point.) The procedure also should send the focus to the uiNumberTextBox control.

   c. Save the solution, then start the application. Test the application by entering the following invoice numbers and amounts:

Number	Amount
34NB	1389.56
124AC	6.35
12B	567

   d Click the Exit button to end the application.

   e. Open the invoice.txt file, which is contained in the VBNET\Chap09\Invoice Solution\Invoice Project\bin folder. The file should contain two columns of information.

   f. Close the invoice.txt window. Close the Output window, then close the solution.

3. In this exercise, you complete an application that saves names to a sequential access file.

   a. If necessary, start Visual Studio .NET. Open the Names Solution (Names Solution.sln) file, which is contained in the VBNET\Chap09\Names Solution folder. If necessary, open the designer window.

   b. The application allows the user to enter a first and last name. Code the Write to File button's Click event procedure so that it writes the last name followed by a comma and the first name to a sequential access file named names.txt. (For example, if the first name is Mary and the last name is Smith, the procedure should write Smith,Mary to the file.) The procedure also should send the focus to the uiFirstTextBox control.

   c. Save the solution, then start the application. Test the application by entering the following names: Mary Smith, Carol Carter, Jeff Reise, and Sam Tenny.

   d. Click the Exit button to end the application.

   e. Open the names.txt file, which is contained in the VBNET\Chap09\Names Solution\Names Project\bin folder. The file should contain four lines of information.

   f. Close the names.txt window. Close the Output window, then close the solution.

4. In this exercise, you modify the application that you coded in Exercise 3.

   a. Use Windows to make a copy of the Names Solution folder, which is contained in the VBNET\Chap09 folder. Change the name of the folder to Modified Names Solution.

   b. If necessary, start Visual Studio .NET. Open the Names Solution (Names Solution.sln) file, which is contained in the VBNET\Chap09\Modified Names Solution folder. Open the designer window.

   c. Modify the Write to File button's Click event procedure so that it ensures that the first and last names begin with an uppercase letter before the names are written to the file. The remaining letters in the names should be lowercase.

   d. Save the solution, then start the application. Test the application by entering the following names: mary smith, CAROL CARTER, JeFF rEISE, and Sam Tenny.

   e. Click the Exit button to end the application.

   f. Open the names.txt file, which is contained in the VBNET\Chap09\Modified Names Solution\Names Project\bin folder. The file should contain four lines of information. Each first and last name in the last four lines should begin with an uppercase letter; the remaining letters in the name should be lowercase.

   g. Close the names.txt window. Close the Output window, then close the solution.

After completing this lesson, you will be able to:

■ Add a PrintDocument control to a form

■ Print text using the Print and e.Graphics.DrawString methods

■ Code a PrintDocument control's PrintPage event procedure

Printing a Sequential Access File

Adding a PrintDocument Control to the Form

To complete the PAO application, which you began coding in Lesson B, you need to add a PrintDocument control to the form, and then code the Print Report button's Click event procedure and the PrintDocument control's PrintPage event procedure.

To open the PAO application, then add a PrintDocument control to the form:

1   Start Microsoft Visual Studio .NET, if necessary.

2   If necessary, close the Start Page window.

3   Open the **Pao Solution** (Pao Solution.sln) file, which is contained in the VBNET\Chap09\ Pao Solution folder.

4   Auto-hide the Toolbox, Solution Explorer, and Properties windows, if necessary.

Next, add a PrintDocument control to the form.

5   Click the **PrintDocument** tool in the toolbox, then drag a PrintDocument control to the form. The PrintDocument1 control appears in the component tray, as shown in Figure 9-38.

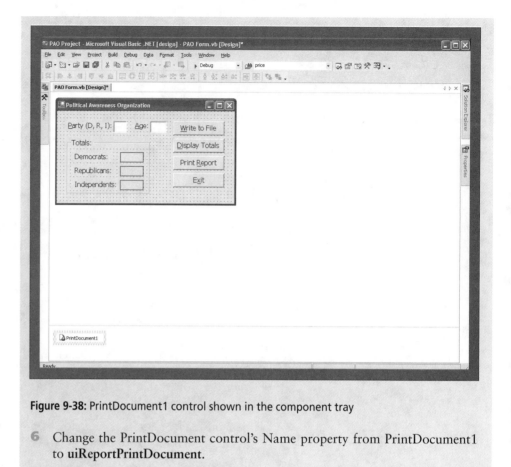

Figure 9-38: PrintDocument1 control shown in the component tray

6   Change the PrintDocument control's Name property from PrintDocument1 to **uiReportPrintDocument**.

Now code the Print Report button's Click event procedure.

Coding the Print Report Button Click Event Procedure

Figure 9-39 shows the pseudocode for the Print Report button's Click event procedure, which is responsible for using the uiReportPrintDocument control to print the contents of the pao.txt sequential access file.

```
uiPrintButton

if the pao.txt file exists
        print the contents of the file
else
        display an appropriate message
end if
```

Figure 9-39: Pseudocode for the Print Report button's Click event procedure

To code the Print Report button's Click event procedure:

1 Open the Code Editor window, then open the code template for the uiPrintButton's Click event procedure.

2 Type **'print the file, but only if it exists** and press **Enter** twice.

3 Type **if io.file.exists("pao.txt") then** and press **Enter**.

If the pao.txt file exists, the procedure should print the document. You print a document using the PrintDocument control's **Print method**. The method's syntax is *printdocument*.**Print()**, where *printdocument* is the name of a PrintDocument control.

4 Type **me.uireportprintdocument.print()** and press **Enter**.

If the pao.txt file does not exist, the procedure should display an appropriate message.

5 Type the additional lines of code indicated in Figure 9-40, which shows the completed uiPrintButton's Click event procedure.

enter these lines of code

```
Private Sub uiPrintButton_Click(ByVal sender As Object, ByVal e As System.EventArgs) Han
    'print the file, but only if it exists

    If IO.File.Exists("pao.txt") Then
        Me.uiReportPrintDocument.Print()
    Else
        MessageBox.Show("File does not exist.", "PAO", _
            MessageBoxButtons.OK, MessageBoxIcon.Information)
    End If
End Sub
```

Figure 9-40: Completed uiPrintButton Click event procedure

The Print method causes the PrintDocument control's PrintPage event to occur. You use the **PrintPage event** to indicate the information you want to print, as well as how you want the information to appear in the printout.

Coding the PrintPage Event Procedure

In this case, the PrintPage event procedure should print the contents of the pao.txt file in a report format. The report should contain a report header and two columns of information. The first column should list the party, and the second column the age. Figure 9-41 shows the pseudocode for the uiReportPrintDocument's PrintPage event procedure.

---

uiReportPrintDocument

1. declare variables
2. print the report header
3. open the pao.txt file for input
4. assign 10 to the horizontal variable, which controls the horizontal position of each print line
5. assign 80 to the vertical variable, which controls the vertical position of each print line
6. repeat until there are no more characters to read
   　　read a line of text from the file
   　　print the line of text
   　　add 15 to the vertical variable
   end repeat
7. close the pao.txt file

Figure 9-41: Pseudocode for the uiReportPrintDocument's PrintPage event procedure

To begin coding the uiReportPrintDocument's PrintPage event procedure:

1 Open the code template for the uiReportPrintDocument's PrintPage event procedure. Type **'prints the report** and press **Enter** twice.

First, declare the variables. The PrintPage event procedure will use five variables: a StreamReader variable for opening the pao.txt file, a String variable for reading a line of text from the file, two Integer variables for controlling the position of the text on the printed page, and a Font variable that indicates the name, size, and style of the font to use when printing the text.

2 Type the following five Dim statements, then press **Enter** twice.

```
dim reportStreamReader as io.streamreader
dim line as string
dim horizontal as integer
dim vertical as integer
dim reportFont as new font("courier new", 12, fontstyle.regular)
```

The next step in the pseudocode is to print the report header. You use the e.Graphics.DrawString method to print text on the printer.

The e.Graphics.DrawString Method

You use the **e.Graphics.DrawString method** to print text on the printer. The method's syntax is **e.Graphics.DrawString**(*string*, *font*, **Brushes.Black**, *horizontalPosition*, *verticalPosition*). In the syntax, *string* is the text to print, and *font* is a Font variable that indicates the name, size, and style of the print font. The *horizontalPosition* argument determines the location of the text from the left edge of the printed page, and the *verticalPosition* controls the location of the text from the top edge of the printed page.

Some print fonts are proportionally spaced, while others are fixed-spaced, often referred to as mono-spaced. **Fixed-spaced fonts** use the same amount of space to print each character, whereas proportionally spaced fonts use varying amounts of space to print characters. For example, with a fixed-spaced font, such as Courier New, the wide letter W and the narrow letter l occupy the same amount of print space. However, with a proportionally spaced font, such as Microsoft Sans Serif, the letter W occupies more print space than the letter l does. In most cases, you use a fixed-spaced font when printing a report on the printer, because a fixed-spaced font allows you to align the text that appears in a printout.

Figure 9-42 shows the report header that should appear at the top of the PAO report.

report title

column headings

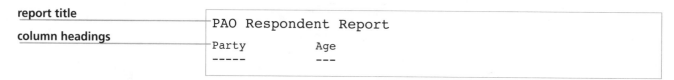

```
PAO Respondent Report

Party          Age
-----          ---
```

Figure 9-42: PAO report header

The first line in the report header contains the report title, which describes the contents of the report. An empty line follows the report title line. The third line in the report header contains the column headings, which identify the information listed in each column. The fourth line simply separates the column headings from the information listed in each column.

To continue coding the PrintPage event:

1   Type the lines of code indicated in Figure 9-43, then position the insertion point as shown in the figure.

enter this comment and these lines of code

position the insertion point here

```
Private Sub uiReportPrintDocument_PrintPage(ByVal sender As Object, ByVal e As System.Dr
    'prints the report

    Dim reportStreamReader As IO.StreamReader
    Dim line As String
    Dim horizontal As Integer
    Dim vertical As Integer
    Dim reportFont As New Font("courier new", 12, FontStyle.Regular)

    'print report header
    e.Graphics.DrawString("PAO Respondent Report", reportFont, Brushes.Black, 10, 10)
    e.Graphics.DrawString("Party        Age", reportFont, Brushes.Black, 10, 55)
    e.Graphics.DrawString("-----        ---", reportFont, Brushes.Black, 10, 65)

End Sub
```

Figure 9-43: Code to print the report header

The next step in the pseudocode shown in Figure 9-41 is to open the pao.txt file for input.

2   Type 'open the file and press **Enter**, then type **reportstreamreader = io.file.opentext("pao.txt")** and press **Enter**.

Next, assign the number 10 to the `horizontal` variable, which controls the horizontal position of the text on the printed page. Also assign 80 to the `vertical` variable, which controls the vertical position of the text on the printed page.

3   Type 'set the horizontal position of each print line and press **Enter**, then type **horizontal = 10** and press **Enter**.

4   Type 'set the vertical position of the next print line and press **Enter**, then type **vertical = 80** and press **Enter** twice.

Now enter a loop whose instructions should be repeated until there are no more characters to read in the file. The loop instructions should read a line of text from the file, then print the line of text on the printer, and then add the number 15 to the `vertical` variable. Updating the `vertical` variable in this manner advances the printer to the next print line. When the repetition structure has finished processing, the PrintPage procedure should close the pao.txt file.

5   Type the lines of code shaded in Figure 9-44, which shows the completed uiReportPrintDocument PrintPage event procedure.

```
Private Sub uiReportPrintDocument_PrintPage(ByVal sender As Object, ByVal e As
System.Drawing.Printing.PrintPageEventArgs) Handles uiReportPrintDocument.PrintPage
        'prints the report

        Dim reportStreamReader As IO.StreamReader
        Dim line As String
        Dim horizontal As Integer
        Dim vertical As Integer
        Dim reportFont As New Font("courier new", 12, FontStyle.Regular)

        'print report header
        e.Graphics.DrawString("PAO Respondent Report", reportFont, Brushes.Black, 10, 10)
        e.Graphics.DrawString("Party      Age", reportFont, Brushes.Black, 10, 55)
        e.Graphics.DrawString("-----      ---", reportFont, Brushes.Black, 10, 65)

        'open the file
        reportStreamReader = IO.File.OpenText("pao.txt")
        'set the horizontal position of each print line
        horizontal = 10
        'set the vertical position of the next print line
        vertical = 80

        'repeat the loop instructions until there are no more characters to read
        Do Until reportStreamReader.Peek = -1
            'read a line of text from the file, then print the line
            line = reportStreamReader.ReadLine()
            e.Graphics.DrawString(line, reportFont, Brushes.Black, _
                horizontal, vertical)
            'update the vertical position for the next print line
            vertical = vertical + 15
        Loop
        'close the file
        reportStreamReader.Close()
    End Sub
```

Figure 9-44: Completed uiReportPrintDocument PrintPage event procedure

Now verify that the uiPrintButton's Click event procedure and the uiReportPrintDocument's PrintPage event procedure work correctly.

6   Save the solution, then start the application. Click the **No** button in the PAO dialog box.

7   If your computer is connected to a printer, click the **Print Report** button. The printer prints a report similar to the one shown in Figure 9-45.

```
PAO Respondent Report

Party      Age
-----      ---
R          34
D          42
```

Figure 9-45: PAO Respondent Report

8   Click the **Exit** button to end the application. When you return to the Code Editor window, close the Output window, then close the Code Editor window.

9   Click **File** on the menu bar, and then click **Close Solution**.

You now have completed Chapter 9. You can either take a break or complete the end-of-lesson questions and exercises.

SUMMARY

To print text within a Visual Basic .NET application:

- Include a PrintDocument control in the application.
- Use the Print method to print the document. The Print method's syntax is *printdocument*.**Print**(), where *printdocument* is the name of a PrintDocument control. The Print method invokes the control's PrintPage event.
- Use the PrintPage event procedure to indicate the information you want to print, as well as how you want the information to appear in the printout.
- Use the syntax **e.Graphics.DrawString**(*string*, *font*, **Brushes.Black,** *horizontalPosition*, *verticalPosition*) to print the document. In the syntax, *string* is the text to print, and *font* is a Font variable that indicates the name, size, and style of the print font. The *horizontalPosition* argument determines the location of the text from the left edge of the printed page, and the *verticalPosition* argument controls the location of the text from the top edge of the printed page.

QUESTIONS

1. You use the _____ method to print a document within a Visual Basic .NET application.
   a. DocumentPrint
   b. DocumentPrintPage
   c. PagePrint
   d. Print
   e. PrintPage

2. You use the _____ method to describe the text you want to print.
   a. e.Graphics.DrawString
   b. e.Graphics.Document
   c. e.Graphics.DocumentPrintPage
   d. e.Graphics.PrintDocument
   e. e.Graphics.PrintPage

3. The method from Question 2 allows you to specify the horizontal and vertical position of the text in the printout.
   a. True
   b. False

4. A _____ font uses varying amounts of space to print characters.
   a. changeable-spaced
   b. fixed-spaced
   c. permanent-spaced
   d. proportionally spaced
   e. varying-spaced

5. In most cases, you should use a _____ font to print a report.
   a. changeable-spaced
   b. fixed-spaced
   c. permanent-spaced
   d. proportionally spaced
   e. varying-spaced

EXERCISES

1. In this exercise, you modify the application that you coded in Exercise 1 in Lesson B. The modified application will allow the user to print the contents of the sequential access file.
   a. If necessary, start Visual Studio .NET. Open the Birthday Solution (Birthday Solution.sln) file, which is contained in the VBNET\Chap09\Birthday Solution folder. If necessary, open the designer window.
   b. Add a PrintDocument control and a Print button to the form. (Be sure to reset the TabIndex properties.) Code the application so that it prints the contents of the birthday.txt file. Display an appropriate message if the birthday.txt file does not exist.
   c. Save the solution, then start the application. Click the Print button.
   d. Click the Exit button to end the application.
   e. Close the Output window, then close the solution.

2. In this exercise, you modify the application that you coded in Exercise 2 in Lesson B. The modified application will allow the user to print the contents of the sequential access file.
   a. If necessary, start Visual Studio .NET. Open the Invoice Solution (Invoice Solution.sln) file, which is contained in the VBNET\Chap09\Invoice Solution folder. If necessary, open the designer window.
   b. Add a PrintDocument control and a Print button to the form. (Be sure to reset the TabIndex properties.) Code the application so that it prints the contents of the invoice.txt file. Include an appropriate heading above each column in the printout. Display an appropriate message if the invoice.txt file does not exist.
   c. Save the solution, then start the application. Click the Print button.
   d. Click the Exit button to end the application.
   e. Close the Output window, then close the solution.

3. In this exercise, you modify the application that you coded in Exercise 3 in Lesson B. The modified application will allow the user to print the contents of the sequential access file.
   a. If necessary, start Visual Studio .NET. Open the Names Solution (Names Solution.sln) file, which is contained in the VBNET\Chap09\Names Solution folder. If necessary, open the designer window.
   b. Add a PrintDocument control and a Print button to the form. (Be sure to reset the TabIndex properties.)
   c. Open the names.txt file, which is contained in the VBNET\Chap09\Names Solution\Names Project\bin folder. Notice that each line in the file contains a last name followed by a comma and a first name. Close the names.txt window.
   d. Code the application so that it prints the contents of the names.txt file. Print the first name followed by a space and the last name. (For example, print Mary Smith.) Display an appropriate message if the names.txt file does not exist.

    e. Save the solution, then start the application. Click the Print button.

    f. Click the Exit button to end the application.

    g. Close the Output window, then close the solution.

4. In this exercise, you modify the PAO application that you coded in this chapter. The modified application will include the report header in the sequential access file.

    a. Use Windows to make a copy of the PAO Solution folder, which is contained in the VBNET\Chap09 folder. Change the name of the folder to PAO Solution Ex 4.

    b. If necessary, start Visual Studio .NET. Open the PAO Solution (PAO Solution.sln) file, which is contained in the VBNET\Chap09\PAO Solution Ex 4 folder. Open the designer window.

    c. Open the Code Editor window and locate the uiReportPrintDocument's PrintPage event procedure. Remove the three statements that print the report header. Also remove the 'print report header comment.

    d. Modify the form's Load event procedure so that it writes the report header to the pao.txt file, but only if the user wants to create a new file.

    e. Save the solution, then start the application. Click the Yes button to indicate that you want to create a new file. Use the application to enter the following information:

Party	Age
R	23
D	34
I	43

    f. Click the Print Report button, then click the Exit button to end the application.

    g. Close the Output window, then close the solution.

5. In this exercise, you code an application that prints a multiplication table.

    a. If necessary, start Visual Studio .NET. Open the Multiplication Solution (Multiplication Solution.sln) file, which is contained in the VBNET\Chap09\ Multiplication Solution folder. If necessary, open the designer window.

    b. Code the application so that it prints a multiplication table similar to the one shown in Figure 9-46. The first column of the table will always contain the numbers one through nine. The number in the third column, however, will be the number that the user enters in the Number text box. For example, if the user enters the number 12 in the Number text box, the number 12 should appear in the third column. If the user enters the number 3, the number 3 should appear in the third column.

```
Multiplication Table

1       X       6       =       6
2       X       6       =       12
3       X       6       =       18
4       X       6       =       24
5       X       6       =       30
6       X       6       =       36
7       X       6       =       42
8       X       6       =       48
9       X       6       =       54
```

Figure 9-46

    c. Save the solution, then start the application. Type 6 in the Number text box, then click the Print button.

    d. Click the Exit button to end the application.

    e. Close the Output window, then close the solution.

6. In this exercise, you code an application that assigns the contents of a sequential access file to a list box.

   a. If necessary, start Visual Studio .NET. Open the State Solution (State Solution.sln) file, which is contained in the VBNET\Chap09\State Solution folder. If necessary, open the designer window.

   b. Open the state.txt file, which is contained in the VBNET\Chap09\State Solution\State Project\bin folder. The file contains the names of five states. Close the state.txt window.

   c. Code the form's Load event procedure so that it reads the state.txt file and stores each state name in the uiStateListBox control.

   d. Save the solution, then start the application. The five state names appear in the list box.

   e. Click the Exit button to end the application.

   f. Close the Output window, then close the solution.

7. In this exercise, you modify the PAO application that you coded in this chapter. The modified application will verify the age entry and also display the total number of voters in each of four age groups.

   a. Use Windows to make a copy of the PAO Solution folder, which is contained in the VBNET\Chap09 folder. Change the name of the folder to PAO Solution Ex 7.

   b. If necessary, start Visual Studio .NET. Open the PAO Solution (PAO Solution.sln) file, which is contained in the VBNET\Chap09\PAO Solution Ex 7 folder. Open the designer window.

   c. Modify the application so that it also verifies that the age entered in the uiAgeTextBox is at least 18. If the age is not valid, don't write the record; rather, display an appropriate error message.

   d. Modify the application so that it also displays the total number of voters in each of the following four age groups: 18-35, 36-50, 51-65, and Over 65.

   e. Save the solution, then start and test the application.

   f. Click the Exit button to end the application, then close the solution.

discovery ▶ 8. In this exercise, you modify the PAO application that you coded in this chapter. The modified application will display a message informing the user that the file has been printed.

   a. Use Windows to make a copy of the PAO Solution folder, which is contained in the VBNET\Chap09 folder. Change the name of the folder to EndPrint PAO Solution.

   b. If necessary, start Visual Studio .NET. Open the PAO Solution (PAO Solution.sln) file, which is contained in the VBNET\Chap09\EndPrint PAO Solution folder. Open the designer window.

   c. The PrintDocument control's EndPrint event occurs when the last page in the document has printed. Code the EndPrint event procedure so that it assigns the filename ("pao.txt") to the PrintDocument control's DocumentName property. The procedure also should display the message "*filename* has finished printing", where *filename* is the name of the document. Display the message in a message box.

   d. Save the solution, then start the application. Click the No button to indicate that you do not want to create a new file. Click the Print Report button. The message "pao.txt has finished printing" appears in a message box. Click the OK button to close the message box.

   e. Click the Exit button to end the application.

   f. Close the Output window, then close the solution.

discovery ▶ 9. In this exercise, you update the contents of a sequential access file.

    a. If necessary, start Visual Studio .NET. Open the Pay Solution (Pay Solution.sln) file, which is contained in the VBNET\Chap09\Pay Solution folder. If necessary, open the designer window.

    b. Study the application's existing code. Also, open the payrates.txt file and view its contents, then close the payrates.txt window.

    c. Code the Increase button's Click event procedure so that it increases by 10% each pay rate. Save the increased prices in a sequential access file named updated.txt.

    d. Save the solution, then start the application. Click the Increase button to update the pay rates.

    e. Click the Exit button to end the application.

    f. Open the payrates.txt file. Also open the updated.txt file. The pay rates contained in the updated.txt file should be 10% more than the pay rates contained in the payrates.txt file.

    g. Close the updated.txt and payrates.txt windows, then close the solution.

debugging 10. In this exercise, you debug an existing application. The purpose of this exercise is to demonstrate a common error made when using files.

    a. If necessary, start Visual Studio .NET. Open the Debug Solution (Debug Solution.sln) file, which is contained in the VBNET\Chap09\Debug Solution folder. If necessary, open the designer window.

    b. Open the Code Editor window and study the existing code.

    c. Start the application. Type your name in the Name text box, then click the Write to File button.

    d. Click the Exit button to end the application.

    e. Open the debug.txt file, which is contained in the VBNET\Chap09\Debug Solution\ Debug Project\bin folder. Notice that the file is empty. Close the debug.txt window.

    f. Start the application. Type your name in the Name text box, then click the Write to File button. Type your name again in the Name text box, then click the Write to File button. An error message appears in a message box. Close the message box, then click the Exit button to end the application.

    g. Correct the application's code, then save the solution and start the application. Type your name in the Name text box, then click the Write to File button. Type your name again in the Name text box, then click the Write to File button.

    h. Click the Exit button to end the application.

    i. Open the debug.txt file. Your name appears twice in the file.

    j. Close the debug.txt window, then close the Output window.

    k. Close the solution.

Arrays

Creating a Tax Calculator Application

case ▶ John Blackfeather is the owner and manager of the Perrytown Gift Shop. Every Friday afternoon, Mr. Blackfeather calculates the weekly pay for his six employees. The most time-consuming part of this task, and the one prone to the most errors, is the calculation of the federal withholding tax (FWT). Mr. Blackfeather has asked you to create an application that he can use to quickly and accurately calculate the FWT.

Previewing the Tax Calculator Application

Before creating the Tax Calculator application, you first preview the completed application.

To preview the completed application:

1   Use the Run command on the Windows Start menu to run the **Perrytown** (Perrytown.exe) file, which is contained in the VBNET\Chap10 folder on your computer's hard disk. Use the Tax Calculator application to calculate the FWT for a married employee who has taxable wages of $288.46.

2   Type **288.46** in the Taxable wages text box, then click the **Calculate Tax** button. The application calculates the FWT of $13.45, as shown in Figure 10-1.

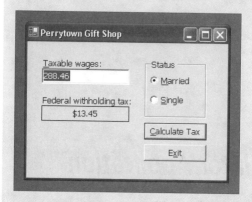

Figure 10-1: FWT for a married employee with taxable wages of $288.46

Next, calculate the FWT for a single employee who has taxable wages of $600.

3   Type **600** in the Taxable wages text box, then click the **Single** radio button. Click the **Calculate Tax** button. See Figure 10-2.

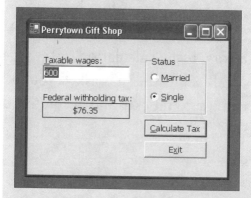

Figure 10-2: FWT for a single employee with taxable wages of $600

4   Click the **Exit** button to end the application.

Before you can begin coding the Tax Calculator application, you need to learn how to create and use an array. You learn about one-dimensional arrays in Lessons A and B, and two-dimensional arrays in Lesson C. You code the Tax Calculator application in Lesson C.

After completing this lesson, you will be able to:

- Declare and initialize a one-dimensional array

- Store data in a one-dimensional array

- Display the contents of a one-dimensional array

- Code a loop using the For Each...Next statement

- Access an element in a one-dimensional array

- Search a one-dimensional array

- Compute the average of a one-dimensional array's contents

- Find the highest entry in a one-dimensional array

- Update the contents of a one-dimensional array

- Sort a one-dimensional array

> The variables in an array are stored in consecutive memory locations in the computer's internal memory.

> It takes longer for the computer to access the information stored in a disk file, because the computer must wait for the disk drive to locate the needed information and then read the information into internal memory.

Using a One-Dimensional Array

Arrays

All of the variables you have used so far have been simple variables. A **simple variable**, also called a **scalar variable**, is one that is unrelated to any other variable in memory. In many applications, however, you may need to reserve a block of variables, referred to as an array.

An **array** is a group of variables that have the same name and data type and are related in some way. For example, each variable in the array might contain an inventory quantity, or each might contain a state name, or each might contain an employee record (name, Social Security number, pay rate, and so on). It may be helpful to picture an array as a group of small, adjacent boxes inside the computer's memory. You can write information to the boxes and you can read information from the boxes; you just cannot *see* the boxes.

Programmers use arrays to temporarily store related data in the internal memory of the computer. Examples of data stored in an array would be the federal withholding tax tables in a payroll program, and a price list in an order entry program. Storing data in an array increases the efficiency of a program, because data can be both written to and read from internal memory much faster than it can be written to and read from a file on a disk. Additionally, after the data is entered into an array, which typically is done at the beginning of the program, the program can use the data as many times as desired. A payroll program, for example, can use the federal withholding tax tables stored in an array to calculate the amount of each employee's federal withholding tax.

The most commonly used arrays are one-dimensional and two-dimensional. You learn about one-dimensional arrays in Lessons A and B, and two-dimensional arrays in Lesson C. Arrays having more than two dimensions, which are used in scientific and engineering applications, are beyond the scope of this book.

One-Dimensional Arrays

You can visualize a **one-dimensional** array as a column of variables. Each variable in a one-dimensional array is identified by a unique number, called a **subscript**, which the computer assigns to the variable when the array is created. The subscript indicates the variable's position in the array. The first variable in a one-dimensional array is assigned a subscript of 0 (zero), the second a subscript of 1 (one), and so on. You refer to each variable in an array by the array's name and the variable's subscript, which is specified in a set of parentheses immediately following the array name. For example, to refer to the first variable in a one-dimensional array named states, you use `states(0)`—read "states sub zero." Similarly, to refer to the third variable in the `states` array, you use `states(2)`. Figure 10-3 illustrates this naming convention.

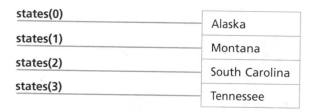

states(0) ——— Alaska

states(1) ——— Montana

states(2) ——— South Carolina

states(3) ——— Tennessee

Figure 10-3: Names of the variables in a one-dimensional array named `states`

Before you can use an array, you first must declare (create) it. Figure 10-4 shows two versions of the syntax you use to declare a one-dimensional array in Visual Basic .NET. The figure also includes examples of using each syntax.

You also can visualize a one-dimensional array as a row of variables, rather than as a column of variables.

A subscript is also called an index.

Syntax
Version 1 {**Dim** | **Private**} *arrayname*(*highestSubscript*) **As** *datatype* **Version 2** {**Dim** | **Private**} *arrayname*() **As** *datatype* = {*initialValues*}

Examples and results
`Dim cities(3) As String` declares a four-element procedure-level array named `cities`; each element is automatically initialized using the keyword `Nothing`
`Private numbers(5) As Integer` declares a six-element module-level array named `numbers`; each element is automatically initialized to the number zero
`Private states() As String = {"Hawaii", "Alaska", "Maine"}` declares and initializes a three-element module-level array named `states`
`Dim sales() As Decimal = {75.30D, 9.65D, 23.55D, 6.89D}` declares and initializes a four-element procedure-level array named `sales`

Figure 10-4: Syntax versions and examples of declaring a one-dimensional array

The {**Dim** | **Private**} portion of the syntax shown in Figure 10-4 indicates that you can select only one of the keywords appearing within the braces. In this case, you can select either `Dim` or `Private`. The appropriate keyword to use depends on whether you are creating a procedure-level or module-level array. *Arrayname* in the syntax is the name of the array, and *datatype* is the type of data the array variables, referred to as **elements**, will store. Recall that each of the elements (variables) in an array has the same data type.

In Version 1 of the syntax, *highestSubscript* is an integer that specifies the highest subscript in the array. When the array is created, it will contain one element more than the number specified in the *highestSubscript* argument; this is because the first element in an array has a subscript of zero. For instance, the `Dim cities(3) As String` statement, which is shown in the first example in Figure 10-4, creates a procedure-level one-dimensional array named `cities`. The `cities` array contains four elements with subscripts of 0, 1, 2, and 3; each element can store a string. Similarly, the statement shown in the second example, `Private numbers(5) As Integer`, creates a module-level Integer array named `numbers`. The `numbers` array contains six elements with subscripts of 0, 1, 2, 3, 4, and 5; in this case, each element can store an integer.

When you use the syntax shown in Version 1 to declare an array, the computer automatically initializes each element in the array when the array is created. If the array's data type is String, each element in the array is initialized using the keyword `Nothing`. As you learned in Chapter 3, variables initialized to `Nothing` do not actually contain the word "Nothing"; rather, they contain no data at all. Elements in a numeric array are initialized to the number zero, and elements in a Boolean array are initialized to the Boolean value False. Date array elements are initialized to 12:00 AM January 1, 0001.

You use the syntax shown in Version 2 in Figure 10-4 to declare an array and, at the same time, specify each element's initial value. You list the initial values in the *initialValues* section of the syntax, using commas to separate the values; you enclose the list of values in braces ({}). Notice that the syntax shown in Version 2 does not include the *highestSubscript* argument; rather, an empty set of parentheses follows the array name. The computer automatically calculates the highest subscript based on the number of values listed in the *initialValues* section. If the *initialValues* section contains five values, the highest subscript in the array is 4. Likewise, if the *initialValues* section contains 100 values, the highest subscript in the array is 99. Notice that the highest subscript is always one number less than the number of values listed in the *initialValues* section; this is because the first subscript in a one-dimensional array is the number zero.

The statement shown in the third example in Figure 10-4, `Private states() As String = {"Hawaii", "Alaska", "Maine"}`, declares a module-level one-dimensional String array named `states`. The `states` array contains three elements with subscripts of 0, 1, and 2. When the array is created, the computer assigns the string "Hawaii" to the `states(0)` element, "Alaska" to the `states(1)` element, and "Maine" to the `states(2)` element. Similarly, the statement shown in the last example, `Dim sales() As Decimal = {75.30D, 9.65D, 23.55D, 6.89D}`, declares a procedure-level one-dimensional Decimal array named `sales`. The `sales` array contains four elements with subscripts of 0, 1, 2, and 3. The computer assigns the number 75.30 to the `sales(0)` element, 9.65 to the `sales(1)` element, 23.55 to the `sales(2)` element, and 6.89 to the `sales(3)` element.

After declaring the array, you can use an assignment statement to store data in the array.

Storing Data in a One-Dimensional Array

In most cases, you use an assignment statement to enter data into an existing array. Figure 10-5 shows the syntax of such an assignment statement and includes several examples of using the syntax to enter data into the arrays declared in Figure 10-4. In the syntax, *arrayname*(*subscript*) is the name and subscript of the array variable to which you want the *value* (data) assigned.

Syntax
arrayname(*subscript*) = *value*

Examples and results
| ```
cities(0) = "Madrid"
cities(1) = "Paris"
cities(2) = "Rome"
```<br>assigns the strings "Madrid", "Paris", and "Rome" to the `cities` array |
| ```
Dim x As Integer
For x = 1 To 6
    numbers(x - 1) = x * x
Next x
```<br>assigns the squares of the numbers from one through six to the `numbers` array |
| ```
Dim x As Integer
Dim numStreamReader As IO.StreamReader
numStreamReader = IO.File.OpenText("numbers.txt")
Do Until x > 5 OrElse numStreamReader.Peek() = -1
    numbers(x) = _
        Integer.Parse(sortStreamReader.ReadLine())
        x = x + 1
Loop
numStreamReader.Close()
```<br>assigns the numbers stored in a sequential access file named numbers.txt to the `numbers` array |
| `states(1) = "Virginia"`
assigns the string "Virginia" to the second element in the `states` array |
| `sales(0) = Decimal.Parse(Me.uiSalesTextBox.Text)`
assigns the value entered in the uiSalesTextBox (converted to Decimal) to the first element in the `sales` array |

Figure 10-5: Syntax and examples of assignment statements used to enter data into a one-dimensional array

The three assignment statements shown in the first example in Figure 10-5 assign the strings "Madrid", "Paris", and "Rome" to the `cities` array, replacing the values stored in the array elements when the array was created. The code shown in the second example assigns the squares of the numbers from one through six to the `numbers` array, writing over the array's initial values. Notice that the number one must be subtracted from the value stored in the **x** variable when assigning the squares to the array. This is because the first array element has a subscript of zero rather than one.

The code shown in the third example in Figure 10-5 reads the numbers from the numbers.txt file, assigning each number to an element in the `numbers` array. In the fourth example, the statement `states(1) = "Virginia"` assigns the string "Virginia" to the second element in the `states` array, replacing the string "Alaska" that was stored in the element when the array was created. In the last example, the statement `sales(0) = Decimal.Parse(Me.uiSalesTextBox.Text)` replaces the value stored in the first element in the `sales` array (75.30) with the value entered in the uiSalesTextBox control (treated as a Decimal).
```

Now that you know how to declare and enter data into a one-dimensional array, you learn how to manipulate an array in a program.

Manipulating One-Dimensional Arrays

The variables (elements) in an array can be used just like any other variables. For example, you can assign values to them, use them in calculations, display their contents, and so on. In the next several sections, you view sample procedures that demonstrate how one-dimensional arrays are used in an application. More specifically, the procedures will show you how to perform the following tasks using a one-dimensional array:

1. Display the contents of an array
2. Access an array element using its subscript
3. Search the array
4. Calculate the average of the data stored in a numeric array
5. Find the highest value stored in an array
6. Update the array elements
7. Sort the array elements

Begin by viewing a procedure that displays the contents of a one-dimensional array.

In most applications, the values stored in an array come from a file on the computer's disk, and are assigned to the array after it is declared. However, so that you can follow the code and its results more easily, most of the procedures you view in this chapter use the Dim statement to assign the appropriate values to the array.

Displaying the Contents of a One-Dimensional Array

Figure 10-6 shows the uiDisplayButton's Click event procedure, which demonstrates how you can display the contents of an array in a label control.

Pseudocode

1. declare a String array named months
2. declare an Integer variable named x
3. repeat for each element in the months array
   display the contents of the current array element in the uiMonthsLabel control
   end repeat

Visual Basic .NET code

```
Dim months() As String = {"JAN", "FEB", "MAR", "APR", _
     "MAY", "JUN", "JUL", "AUG", "SEP", "OCT", "NOV", "DEC"}
Dim x As Integer

For x = 0 To 11
     Me.uiMonthsLabel.Text = Me.uiMonthsLabel.Text & months(x) _
          & ControlChars.NewLine
Next x
```

displays the contents of the months array in the uiMonthsLabel control

---

Figure 10-6: uiDisplayButton's Click event procedure

The procedure shown in Figure 10-6 declares a 12-element String array named months, using the names of the 12 months to initialize the array; it also declares an Integer variable named x. The procedure uses a loop, along with the x variable, to display the contents of each array element in the uiMonthsLabel control. The first time the loop is processed, the `x` variable contains the number zero, and the `Me.uiMonthsLabel.Text = Me.uiMonthsLabel.Text & months(x) & ControlChars.NewLine` statement displays the contents of the `months(0)` element—JAN—in the uiMonthsLabel control, and then advances the insertion point to the next line in the uiMonthsLabel control. The `Next x` statement then adds the number one to the value stored in the `x` variable, giving one. When the loop is processed the second time, the `Me.uiMonthsLabel.Text = Me.uiMonthsLabel.Text & months(x) & ControlChars.NewLine` statement adds the contents of the `months(1)` element—FEB—to the uiMonthsLabel control, and so on. The computer repeats the loop instructions for each element in the `months` array, beginning with the element whose subscript is zero and ending with the element whose subscript is 11. The computer stops processing the loop when the value contained in the `x` variable is 12, which is one number more than the highest subscript in the array. Figure 10-7 shows the results of processing the uiDisplayButton's Click event procedure.

Figure 10-7: Result of processing the uiDisplayButton's Click event procedure

The uiDisplayButton's Click event procedure shown in Figure 10-6 uses the For...Next statement to display each array element. You also could use the Do...Loop statement (which you learned about in Chapter 6) or the For Each...Next statement (which you learn about next).

The For Each...Next Statement

You can use the **For Each...Next statement** to code a loop whose instructions you want processed for each element in a group—for example, for each array variable in an array. Figure 10-8 shows the syntax of the For Each...Next statement. It also shows how you can rewrite the uiDisplayButton's Click event procedure from Figure 10-6 using the For Each...Next statement.

tip

....

▶ As you learned in Chapter 6, you can code a repetition structure (loop) in Visual Basic .NET using the For...Next, Do...Loop, or For Each...Next statement.

Syntax

```
For Each element In group
       [statements]
Next element
```

Example and result

```
Dim months() As String = {"JAN", "FEB", "MAR", "APR", _
       "MAY", "JUN", "JUL", "AUG", "SEP", "OCT", "NOV", "DEC"}
Dim element As String

For Each element In months
       Me.uiMonthsLabel.Text = Me.uiMonthsLabel.Text & element _
              & ControlChars.NewLine
Next element
```

displays the contents of the months array in the uiMonthsLabel control

Figure 10-8: Syntax and an example of the For Each...Next statement

You can use the Exit For statement to exit the For Each...Next statement prematurely—in other words, to exit it before it has finished processing. You may need to do so if the loop encounters an error when processing its instructions.

You can nest For Each... Next statements, which means that you can place one For Each...Next statement within another For Each...Next statement.

The For Each...Next statement begins with the For Each clause and ends with the Next clause. Between the two clauses you enter the instructions that you want the loop to repeat for each *element* in the *group*.

When using the For Each...Next statement to process an array, *element* is the name of a variable that the computer can use to keep track of each array variable, and *group* is the name of the array. The data type of the *element* must match the data type of the *group*. For example, if the *group* is an Integer array, then the *element*'s data type must be Integer. Likewise, if the *group* is a String array, then the *element*'s data type must be String. In the example shown in Figure 10-8, *group* is a String array named months, and *element* is a String variable named element.

In the example shown in Figure 10-8, the Me.uiMonthsLabel.Text = Me.uiMonthsLabel.Text & element & ControlChars.NewLine statement, which displays the current array element in the uiMonthsLabel control, will be processed for each element in the months array. The example will display the same result as shown earlier in Figure 10-7.

Next, you view a procedure that uses the array subscript to access the appropriate element in an array.

Using the Subscript to Access an Element in a One-Dimensional Array

Assume that XYZ Corporation pays its managers based on six different salary codes, 1 through 6. Each code corresponds to a different salary amount. Figure 10-9 shows the uiSalaryButton's Click event procedure, which displays the salary amount corresponding to the code entered by the user.

Pseudocode

1. declare an Integer array named salaries
2. declare an Integer variable named code
3. assign the code in the uiCodeTextBox control to the code variable
4. if the code stored in the code variable is not 1 through 6
　　　display the message "Invalid code" in the uiSalaryLabel control
　else
　　　display, in the uiSalaryLabel control, the salary stored in the array element located in position (code – 1)
　end if

Visual Basic .NET code

```
Dim salaries() As Integer = {25000, 35000, 55000, _
                             70000, 80200, 90500}
Dim code As Integer

code = Integer.Parse(Me.uiCodeTextBox.Text)
If code < 1 OrElse code > 6 Then
      Me.uiSalaryLabel.Text = "Invalid code"
Else
      Me.uiSalaryLabel.Text = _
            Convert.ToString(salaries(code - 1))
End If
```

Results (displayed in the uiSalaryLabel control)

55000　　　　(assuming the user enters the number 3)
Invalid code　(assuming the user enters the number 8)

Figure 10-9: uiSalaryButton's Click event procedure

tip
••••••••••••••••••••

Before accessing an array element, a procedure always should verify that the subscript is valid—in other words, that it is in range. If the procedure uses a subscript that is not in range, Visual Basic .NET displays an error message and the procedure ends abruptly.

The procedure shown in Figure 10-9 declares an Integer array named `salaries`, using six salary amounts to initialize the array. The salary amount for code 1 is stored in `salaries(0)`. Code 2's salary amount is stored in `salaries(1)`, and so on. Notice that the code is one number more than its corresponding array subscript.

After creating and initializing the array, the procedure declares an Integer variable named `code`. It then assigns the salary code entered in the uiCodeTextBox to the `code` variable. The selection structure in the procedure determines whether the code entered by the user is invalid. In this case, invalid codes are numbers that are less than one or greater than six. If the code is not valid, the procedure displays an appropriate message; otherwise, it displays the corresponding salary from the `salaries` array. Notice that, to access the correct element in the `salaries` array, the number one must be subtracted from the contents of the `code` variable. This is because the code entered by the user is one number more than its associated array subscript. As Figure 10-9 indicates, the procedure displays the number 55000 if the user enters a code of 3. If the user enters a code of 8, the program displays the message "Invalid code".

In the next section, you learn how to search a one-dimensional array.

Searching a One-Dimensional Array

Assume that the sales manager at Jacobsen Motors wants a procedure that allows him to determine the number of salespeople selling above a certain amount, which he will enter. To accomplish this task, the procedure will need to search the array, looking for values that are greater than the amount entered by the sales manager. The uiSearchButton's Click event procedure shown in Figure 10-10 shows you how to search an array.

Pseudocode

1. declare an Integer array named sales
2. declare Integer variables named amount, counter, and searchFor
3. assign the sales amount in the uiSearchTextBox control to the searchFor variable
4. repeat for each element in the sales array
      if the value in the current array element is greater than the value in the searchFor variable
         add 1 to the counter variable
     end if
    end repeat
5. display the contents of the counter variable in the uiCountLabel control

Visual Basic .NET code

```
Dim sales() As Integer = {45000, 35000, 25000, 60000, 23000}
Dim amount As Integer        'represents an array element
Dim counter As Integer       'counter variable
Dim searchFor As Integer     'number to search for

searchFor = Integer.Parse(Me.uiSearchTextBox.Text)
For Each amount in sales
        If amount > searchFor Then
             counter = counter + 1
        End If
Next amount
Me.uiCountLabel.Text = "Count: " & Convert.ToString(counter)
```

Results (displayed in the uiCountLabel control)

Count: 2   (assuming the user enters the number 40000)
Count: 0   (assuming the user enters the number 60000)

Figure 10-10: uiSearchButton's Click event procedure

The uiSearchButton's Click event procedure declares an Integer array named `sales`, using five sales amounts to initialize the array. The procedure also declares three Integer variables named `amount`, `counter`, and `searchFor`. After declaring the array and variables, the procedure assigns the sales amount entered in the uiSearchTextBox to the `searchFor` variable. The loop in the procedure then repeats its instructions for each element in the `sales` array. Notice that the loop uses the `amount` variable to represent each element in the array.

The selection structure in the loop compares the contents of the current array element with the contents of the `searchFor` variable. If the array element contains a number that is greater than the number stored in the `searchFor` variable, the selection structure's true path adds the number one to the value stored in the `counter` variable. In the uiSearchButton's Click event procedure, the `counter` variable is used as a counter to keep track of the number of salespeople selling over the amount entered by the sales manager.

When the loop ends, which is when there are no more array elements to search, the procedure displays the contents of the `counter` variable in the uiCountLabel control. As Figure 10-10 indicates, the procedure displays the number two if the sales manager enters 40000 as the sales amount, and it displays the number zero if he enters 60000 as the sales amount.

Next, you learn how to calculate the average of the data stored in a numeric array.

Calculating the Average Amount Stored in a One-Dimensional Numeric Array

Professor Jeremiah wants a procedure that calculates and displays the average test score earned by his students on the final exam. The uiCalcAvgButton's Click event procedure shown in Figure 10-11 can be used to accomplish this task.

Pseudocode

1. declare an Integer array named scores
2. declare Integer variables named x and total
3. declare a Decimal variable named average
4. repeat for each element in the scores array
      add the contents of the current array element to the total variable
  end repeat
5. calculate the average score by dividing the contents of the total variable by the number of array elements, and assign the result to the average variable
6. display the contents of the average variable in the uiAverageLabel control

Visual Basic .NET code

```
Dim scores() As Integer = {98, 100, 56, 74, 35}
Dim x As Integer          'keeps track of subscripts
Dim total As Integer      'accumulator variable
Dim average As Decimal    'average score

For x = 0 To 4
     total = total + scores(x)
Next x

average = Convert.ToDecimal(total / scores.Length)
Me.uiAverageLabel.Text = "Average: " & average.ToString("N1")
```

Results (displayed in the uiAverageLabel control)
Average: 72.6

Figure 10-11: uiCalcAvgButton's Click event procedure

You also can use the statement average = Convert.ToDecimal(total / x) to calculate the average test score in the uiCalcAvgButton's Click event procedure shown in Figure 10-11.

You also can write the For clause shown in Figure 10-11 as For x = 0 To scores.Length - 1.

The procedure shown in Figure 10-11 declares an Integer array named scores, using five test scores to initialize the array. It also declares two Integer variables named x and total, and a Decimal variable named average. The loop in the procedure repeats its instruction for each element in the scores array, beginning with the element whose subscript is zero and ending with the element whose subscript is four. The instruction in the loop adds the score contained in the current array element to the total variable, which is used as an accumulator to add up the test scores. When the loop ends, which is when the x variable contains the number five, the average = Convert.ToDecimal(total / scores.Length) statement uses the array's Length property to calculate the average test score. An array's **Length property**, whose syntax is *arrayname*.**Length**, stores an integer that represents the number of elements in the array. In this case, the Length property stores the number five, because the scores array contains five elements. The uiCalcAvgButton's Click event procedure then displays the average test score in the uiAverageLabel control. As Figure 10-11 indicates, the procedure displays the number 72.6.

In the next section, you learn how to determine the highest value stored in a one-dimensional array.

Determining the Highest Value Stored in a One-Dimensional Array

Sharon Johnson keeps track of the amount of money she earns each week. She would like a procedure that displays the highest amount earned in a week. Similar to the uiSearchButton's Click event procedure shown earlier in Figure 10-10, the uiHighestButton's Click event procedure will need to search the array. However, rather than looking in the array for values that are greater than a specific amount, the procedure will look for the highest amount in the array, as shown in Figure 10-12.

Pseudocode

1. declare a Decimal array named dollars
2. declare a Decimal variable named high, and initialize the variable to the contents of the first element in the dollars array
3. declare an Integer variable named x, and initialize the variable to 1 (the second subscript)
4. repeat while x is less than the number of elements in the array

    if the value in the current array element is greater than the value in the high variable

        assign the value in the current array element to the high variable

    end if

    add 1 to the x variable

    end repeat
5. display the contents of the high variable in the uiHighestLabel control

---

Visual Basic .NET code

```
Dim dollars() As Decimal = {25.60D, 30.25D, 50D, 20D, 25.45D}
Dim high As Decimal = dollars(0)      'stores the highest value
Dim x As Integer = 1                  'begins search with second element

Do While x < dollars.Length
     If dollars(x) > high Then
          high = dollars(x)
     End If
     x = x + 1
Loop
Me.uiHighestLabel.Text = "High: " & high.ToString("C2")
```

Results (displayed in the uiHighestLabel control)

High: $50.00

Figure 10-12: uiHighestButton's Click event procedure

The uiHighestButton's Click event procedure declares a Decimal array named dollars, and it initializes the array to the amounts that Sharon earned during the last five weeks. The procedure also declares an Integer variable named x and a Decimal variable named high. The high variable is used to keep track of the highest value stored in the dollars array, and is initialized using the value stored in the first array element. The x variable is used to keep track of the array subscripts. Notice that the procedure initializes the x variable to the number one, which is the subscript corresponding to the second element in the dollars array.

> **Notice that the loop shown in Figure 10-12 searches the second through the last element in the array. The first element is not included in the search because it is already stored in the high variable.**

The first time the loop in the uiHighestButton's Click event procedure is processed, the selection structure within the loop compares the value stored in the second array element—`dollars(1)`—with the value stored in the `high` variable. (Recall that the `high` variable contains the same value as the first array element at this point.) If the value stored in the second array element is greater than the value stored in the `high` variable, then the statement `high = dollars(x)` assigns the array element value to the `high` variable. The statement `x = x + 1` then adds the number one to the `x` variable, giving 2. The next time the loop is processed, the selection structure compares the value stored in the third array element—`dollars(2)`—with the value stored in the `high` variable, and so on. When the loop ends, which is when the `x` variable contains the number five, the procedure displays the contents of the `high` variable in the uiHighestLabel control. As Figure 10-12 indicates, the procedure displays $50.00.

Next, you learn how to update the values stored in a one-dimensional array.

Updating the Values Stored in a One-Dimensional Array

The sales manager at Jillian Company wants a procedure that allows her to increase the price of each item the company sells. She also wants the procedure to display each item's new price in the uiNewPricesLabel control. The uiUpdateButton's Click event procedure shown in Figure 10-13 will perform these tasks.

Pseudocode

1. declare a Decimal array named prices
2. declare two Decimal variables named element and increase
3. assign the increase amount in the uiIncreaseTextBox control to the increase variable
4. display the heading "New Prices" in the uiNewPricesLabel control
5. repeat for each element in the prices array
        add the increase amount to the value stored in the current array element
        display the contents of the current array element in the uiNewPricesLabel control
   end repeat

Visual Basic .NET code

```
Dim prices() As Decimal = {150.35D, 35.60D, 75.75D, 25.30D}
Dim element As Decimal        'represents an array element
Dim increase As Decimal       'stores increase amount

increase = Decimal.Parse(Me.uiIncreaseTextBox.Text)
Me.uiNewPricesLabel.Text = "New Prices" & ControlChars.NewLine
For Each element in prices
        element = element + increase
        Me.uiNewPricesLabel.Text = Me.uiNewPricesLabel.Text _
             & element.ToString("C2") & ControlChars.NewLine
Next element
```

Results (displayed in the uiNewPricesLabel control)

New Prices (assuming the user enters the number 5)
$155.35
$40.60
$80.75
$30.30

Figure 10-13: uiUpdateButton's Click event procedure

The procedure shown in Figure 10-13 declares a Decimal array named `prices`, using four values to initialize the array. The procedure also declares two Decimal variables named `element` and `increase`. The procedure stores the contents of the uiIncreaseTextBox control, converted to Decimal, in the `increase` variable. It then assigns the string "New Prices" and the newline character to the uiNewPricesLabel control.

The loop in the procedure repeats its instructions for each element in the array. Notice that the procedure uses the `element` variable to represent each array element. The first instruction in the loop, `element = element + increase`, updates the contents of the current array element by adding the increase amount to it. The second instruction in the loop then displays the updated contents in the uiNewPricesLabel control. The loop ends when all of the array elements have been updated. Figure 10-13 shows the results of the procedure when the user enters the number five as the increase amount. Notice that each new price is five dollars more than the corresponding original price.

Next, you learn how to sort the data stored in a one-dimensional array.

Sorting the Data Stored in a One-Dimensional Array

At times, a procedure might need to arrange the contents of an array in either ascending or descending order. Arranging data in a specific order is called **sorting**. When an array is sorted in ascending order, the first element in the array contains the smallest value, and the last element contains the largest value. When an array is sorted in descending order, on the other hand, the first element contains the largest value, and the last element contains the smallest value.

You use the **Array.Sort method** to sort the elements in a one-dimensional array in ascending order. The method's syntax is **Array.Sort(*arrayname*)**, where *arrayname* is the name of the one-dimensional array to be sorted. The uiSortButton's Click event procedure shown in Figure 10-14 uses the Array.Sort method to sort the `numbers` array in ascending order.

Pseudocode

1. declare an Integer array named numbers
2. declare an Integer variable named x
3. declare a StreamReader variable named sortStreamReader
4. if the numbers.txt sequential access file exists
    open the file for input
    repeat until the array is filled or there are no more numbers to read
        read a number from the file and assign it to the current array element
        add 1 to the contents of the x variable
    end repeat
    close the numbers.txt file
    sort the numbers array in ascending order
    repeat for each element in the numbers array
        display the contents of the current array element in the uiSortedLabel control
    end repeat
  else
    display an appropriate message
  end if

Figure 10-14: uiSortButton's Click event procedure

Visual Basic .NET code

```
Dim numbers(5) As Integer
Dim x As Integer    'keeps track of subscripts
Dim sortStreamReader As IO.StreamReader

'use the numbers.txt file to fill the array
If IO.File.Exists("numbers.txt") Then
      'open the file
        sortStreamReader = IO.File.OpenText("numbers.txt")
        'read each number in the file until the array is filled
        'or there are no more numbers to read
        Do Until x > numbers.Length - 1 _
            OrElse sortStreamReader.Peek() = -1
                numbers(x) = _
                    Integer.Parse(sortStreamReader.ReadLine())
                x = x + 1
      Loop
      'close the file
      sortStreamReader.Close()

        'sort the array in ascending order
        Array.Sort(numbers)

        'display the contents of the array
        For x = 0 To numbers.Length - 1
            Me.uiSortedLabel.Text = Me.uiSortedLabel.Text _
                    & Convert.ToString(numbers(x)) _
                    & ControlChars.NewLine
      Next x
Else
      'display an appropriate message
      MessageBox.Show("The numbers.txt file does not exist.", _
            "Numbers", MessageBoxButtons.OK, _
            MessageBoxIcon.Information)
End If
```

Results (displayed in the uiSortedLabel control

```
1         (assuming the numbers.txt file contains the numbers 75, 3, 400, 1, 16, and 7)
3
7
16
75
400
```

Figure 10-14: uiSortButton's Click event procedure (continued)

The procedure shown in Figure 10-14 declares an Integer array named numbers, as well as an Integer variable named x and a StreamReader variable named sortStreamReader. The selection structure in the procedure verifies the existence of a sequential access file named numbers.txt. If the numbers.txt file does not exist, the computer processes the instruction in the selection structure's false path, which displays an appropriate message in a message box. However, if the numbers.txt file does exist, the computer processes the instructions in the selection structure's true path.

The first instruction in the selection structure's true path opens the numbers.txt file for input. Next, the computer processes the Do...Loop statement, which repeats its instructions until one (or both) of the following is encountered: the end of the

• • • • • • • • • • • • • • • •

Recall that an array's Length property stores the number of elements in the array and is always one number more than the highest subscript.

array or the end of the numbers.txt file. The first instruction in the loop reads a number from the numbers.txt file and stores the number in the current element in the `numbers` array. The second instruction in the loop increases by one the value stored in the `x` variable, which keeps track of the array subscripts. When the loop stops, which is when the value in the `x` variable is six or when there are no more numbers to read in the numbers.txt file, the procedure closes the numbers.txt file.

The `Array.Sort(numbers)` statement in the procedure sorts the numbers in the `numbers` array in ascending order. The For...Next statement then displays the contents of the `numbers` array in the uiSortedLabel control. As Figure 10-14 indicates, the For...Next statement displays the numbers 1, 3, 7, 16, 75, and 400. Notice that the numbers appear in ascending numerical order.

To sort a one-dimensional array in descending order, you first use the Array.Sort method to sort the array in ascending order, and then use the **Array.Reverse method** to reverse the array elements. The syntax of the Array.Reverse method is **Array.Reverse(*arrayname*)**, where *arrayname* is the name of the one-dimensional array whose elements you want reversed. The uiSortDescButton's Click event procedure shown in Figure 10-15 sorts the contents of the `states` array in descending order, and then displays the contents of the array in the uiSortedLabel control.

Pseudocode

1. declare a String array named states
2. declare a String variable named element
3. sort the states array in descending order
4. repeat for each element in the states array
        display the contents of the current array element in the uiSortedLabel control
    end repeat

Visual Basic .NET code

``
Dim states() As String = _
    {"Colorado", "Hawaii", "Alaska", "Florida"}
Dim element As String
 	
Array.Sort(states)   'sort the array in ascending order,
Array.Reverse(states)   'then reverse the array elements
 	
For Each element in states
    Me.uiSortedLabel.Text = Me.uiSortedLabel.Text _
            & element & ControlChars.NewLine
Next element
``

Results (displayed in the uiSortedLabel control)
Hawaii Florida Colorado Alaska

Figure 10-15: uiSortDescButton's Click event procedure

The procedure shown in Figure 10-15 declares a String array named `states` and a String variable named `element`. It then uses the Array.Sort and Array.Reverse methods to sort the array elements in descending order. The loop in the procedure displays the contents of the `states` array in the uiSortedLabel control. As Figure 10-15 indicates, the loop displays Hawaii, Florida, Colorado, and Alaska. Notice that the state names appear in descending alphabetical order.

You learned about scope in Chapter 3.

In all of the procedures you viewed so far in this lesson, the arrays were declared in a procedure and, therefore, had procedure scope. Arrays also can be declared in the form's Declarations section, which gives them module scope. An array with module scope can be used by all of the procedures in the form, including the procedures associated with the controls contained on the form.

Using a Module-Level One-Dimensional Array

Assume that an application needs to display the names contained in a sequential access file. The application should give the user the choice of displaying the names in either ascending or descending order. Figure 10-16 shows the code for an application that performs this task, and Figure 10-17 shows a sample run of the application. Notice that the names appear in ascending alphabetical order in Figure 10-17.

```
'Project name:          Names Project
'Project purpose:       The project sorts names in ascending and descending order.
'Created/revised by:    <enter your name here> on <enter date here>

Option Explicit On
Option Strict On

Public Class NamesForm
    Inherits System.Windows.Forms.Form

[Windows Form Designer generated code]

    'declare module-level array
    Dim names(9) As String

    Private Sub NamesForm_Load(ByVal sender As Object, ByVal e As System.EventArgs) _
        Handles MyBase.Load
        'fills the names array with data from a sequential access file

        'declare variables
        Dim x As Integer      'keeps track of subscripts
        Dim sortStreamReader As IO.StreamReader

        'use the names.txt file to fill the array
        If IO.File.Exists("names.txt") Then
            'open the file
            sortStreamReader = IO.File.OpenText("names.txt")

            'read each name in the file until the array is filled
            'or there are no more names to read
            Do Until x > names.Length - 1 OrElse sortStreamReader.Peek() = -1
                names(x) = sortStreamReader.ReadLine()
                x = x + 1
            Loop
            'close the file
            sortStreamReader.Close()
        Else
            'display an appropriate message
            MessageBox.Show("The names.txt file does not exist.", _
            "Names", MessageBoxButtons.OK, MessageBoxIcon.Information)
        End If
    End Sub
```

Figure 10-16: Code for the Names application

```
    Private Sub uiAscendingButton_Click(ByVal sender As Object, _
        ByVal e As System.EventArgs) Handles uiAscendingButton.Click
        'displays the names array in ascending order

        'declare variable
        Dim element As String

        'sort the array in ascending order
        Array.Sort(names)

        'clear the uiNamesLabel control, then display the contents of the array
        Me.uiNamesLabel.Text = ""
        For Each element In names
            Me.uiNamesLabel.Text = Me.uiNamesLabel.Text _
            & element & ControlChars.NewLine
        Next element
    End Sub

    Private Sub uiDescendingButton_Click(ByVal sender As Object, _
        ByVal e As System.EventArgs) Handles uiDescendingButton.Click
        'displays the names array in descending order

        'declare variable
        Dim element As String

        'sort the array in descending order
        Array.Sort(names)
        Array.Reverse(names)

        'clear the uiNamesLabel control, then display the contents of the array
        Me.uiNamesLabel.Text = ""
        For Each element In names
            Me.uiNamesLabel.Text = Me.uiNamesLabel.Text _
            & element & ControlChars.NewLine
        Next element
    End Sub

    Private Sub uiExitButton_Click(ByVal sender As Object, _
        ByVal e As System.EventArgs) Handles uiExitButton.Click
        'ends the application
        Me.Close()
    End Sub
End Class
```

Figure 10-16: Code for the Names application (continued)

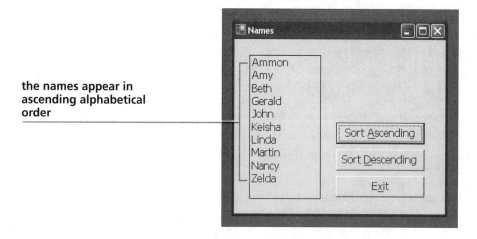

the names appear in
ascending alphabetical
order

Figure 10-17: Sample run of the Names application

When you start an application that contains more than one form, the start-up form's Load event occurs. The Load events of the other forms occur when those forms are first displayed.

In the code shown in Figure 10-16, the `names` array is declared in the form's Declarations section, making it a module-level array. The array is filled with data in the form's Load event procedure. As you learned in Chapter 3, a form's Load event occurs before the form is displayed the first time.

Notice that the module-level `names` array is used by three procedures in the application's code: the form's Load event procedure, the uiAscendingButton's Click event procedure, and the uiDescendingButton's Click event procedure.

You now have completed Lesson A. You can either take a break or complete the end-of-lesson questions and exercises before moving on to the next lesson. You learn more about one-dimensional arrays in Lesson B. In Lesson C, you learn about two-dimensional arrays, and you code the Tax Calculator application that you previewed at the beginning of the chapter.

SUMMARY

To declare a one-dimensional array:

- Use either of the following two syntax versions:
  Version 1: {**Dim** | **Private**} *arrayname(highestSubscript)* **As** *datatype*
  Version 2: {**Dim** | **Private**} *arrayname()* **As** *datatype* = {*initialValues*}
- Use the keyword Dim to declare a procedure-level array. Use the keyword Private to declare a module-level array. *Arrayname* is the name of the array, and *datatype* is the type of data the array variables will store.
- The *highestSubscript* argument, which appears in Version 1 of the syntax, is an integer that specifies the highest subscript in the array. Using Version 1's syntax, the computer automatically initializes the elements (variables) in the array.
- The *initialValues* section, which appears in Version 2 of the syntax, is a list of values separated by commas and enclosed in braces. The values are used to initialize each element in the array.

To refer to a variable included in an array:

- Use the array's name followed by the variable's subscript. Enclose the subscript in a set of parentheses following the array name.

To determine the number of elements (variables) in an array:

■ Use the array's Length property in the following syntax: *arrayname*.**Length**.

To sort the array elements in ascending order:

■ Use the Array.Sort method. The method's syntax is **Array.Sort**(*arrayname*).

To reverse the order of the elements included in an array:

■ Use the Array.Reverse method. The method's syntax is **Array.Reverse**(*arrayname*).

Q U E S T I O N S

1. Which of the following is false?
   a. The elements in an array are related in some way.
   b. All of the elements in an array have the same data type.
   c. All of the elements in an array have the same subscript.
   d. All of the elements in an array have the same name.
   e. The first element in an array has a subscript of zero.

2. Elements in an array are identified by a unique _____.
   a. data type
   b. initial value
   c. order
   d. subscript
   e. symbol

3. Which of the following statements declares a one-dimensional array named `prices` that contains five elements?
   a. `Dim prices(4) As Double`
   b. `Dim prices(5) As Double`
   c. `Dim prices(4) As Double = {3.55, 6.70, 8, 4, 2.34}`
   d. `Dim prices(5) As Double = {3.55, 6.70, 8, 4, 2.34}`
   e. Both b and d.

4. Assume that the `items` array is declared using the statement `Dim items(20) As String`. Also assume that the `x` variable, which keeps track of the array subscripts, is initialized to the number zero. Which of the following Do clauses will process the loop instructions for each element in the array?
   a. `Do While x > 20`
   b. `Do While x < 20`
   c. `Do While x >= 20`
   d. `Do While x <= 20`
   e. `Do Until x <= 20`

Use the `sales` array to answer Questions 5 through 10. The array was declared with the following statement: `Dim sales() As Integer = {10000, 12000, 900, 500, 20000}`.

5. The statement `sales(3) = sales(3) + 10` will _____.
   a. replace the 500 amount with 10
   b. replace the 500 amount with 510
   c. replace the 900 amount with 10
   d. replace the 900 amount with 910
   e. result in an error

6. The statement `sales(4) = sales(4 - 2)` will _____.
   a. replace the 20000 amount with 900
   b. replace the 20000 amount with 19998
   c. replace the 500 amount with 12000
   d. replace the 500 amount with 498
   e. result in an error

7. The statement `Me.uiTotalLabel.Text = Convert.ToString(sales(0) + sales(1))` will _____.
   a. display 0
   b. display 22000
   c. display 10000 + 12000
   d. display `sales(0) + sales(1)`
   e. result in an error

8. Which of the following If clauses can be used to verify that the array subscript, named x, is valid for the `sales` array?
   a. `If sales(x) >= 0 AndAlso sales(x) < 4 Then`
   b. `If sales(x) >= 0 AndAlso sales(x) <= 4 Then`
   c. `If x >= 0 AndAlso x < 4 Then`
   d. `If x >= 0 AndAlso x <= 4 Then`
   e. `If x > 0 AndAlso x < 4 Then`

9. Which of the following will correctly add 100 to each variable in the `sales` array? (You can assume that the x variable was initialized to the number zero.)
   a.
   ```
   Do While x <= 4
        x = x + 100
   Loop
   ```
   b.
   ```
   Do While x <= 4
        sales = sales + 100
   Loop
   ```
   c.
   ```
   Do While sales < 5
        sales(x) = sales(x) + 100
   Loop
   ```
   d.
   ```
   Do While x <= 4
        sales(x) = sales(x) + 100
        x = x + 1
   Loop
   ```
   e. None of the above.

10. Which of the following statements sorts the `sales` array in ascending order?
   a. `Array.Sort(sales)`
   b. `sales.Sort`
   c. `sales.Sort(Ascending)`
   d. `Sort(sales)`
   e. `SortArray(sales)`

Use the numbers array to answer Questions 11 through 16. The array was declared with the following statement: Dim numbers() As Integer = {10, 5, 7, 2}. Assume that the total and x variables are Integer variables, and the average variable is a Double variable. The variables are initialized to the number zero.

11. Which of the following will correctly calculate and display the average of the elements included in the numbers array?

a. ```
Do While x < 4
    numbers(x) = total + total
    x = x + 1
Loop
average = total / x
Me.uiAvgLabel.Text = Convert.ToString(average)
```

b. ```
Do While x < 4
    total = total + numbers(x)
    x = x + 1
Loop
average = total / x
Me.uiAvgLabel.Text = Convert.ToString(average)
```

c. ```
Do While x < 4
    total = total + numbers(x)
    x = x + 1
Loop
average = total / x - 1
Me.uiAvgLabel.Text = Convert.ToString(average)
```

d. ```
Do While x < 4
    total = total + numbers(x)
    x = x + 1
Loop
average = total / (x - 1)
Me.uiAvgLabel.Text = Convert.ToString(average)
```

e. None of the above.

12. The code in Question 11's answer a will display _____.
   a. 0
   b. 5
   c. 6
   d. 8
   e. None of the above.

13. The code in Question 11's answer b will display _____.
   a. 0
   b. 5
   c. 6
   d. 8
   e. None of the above.

14. The code in Question 11's answer c will display _____.
   a. 0
   b. 5
   c. 6
   d. 8
   e. None of the above.

15. The code in Question 11's answer d will display _____.
    a. 0
    b. 5
    c. 6
    d. 8
    e. None of the above.

16. Which of the following displays the number of elements included in the
    numbers array?
    a. `Me.uiNumLabel.Text = Convert.ToString(Len(numbers))`
    b. `Me.uiNumLabel.Text = Convert.ToString(Length(numbers))`
    c. `Me.uiNumLabel.Text = Convert.ToString(numbers.Len)`
    d. `Me.uiNumLabel.Text = Convert.ToString(numbers.Length)`
    e. None of the above.

17. Which of the following statements is false?
    a. Data stored in an array can be accessed faster than data stored in a disk file.
    b. Data stored in an array needs to be entered only once.
    c. Arrays allow the programmer to store information in internal memory.
    d. Arrays allow the programmer to use fewer variable names.
    e. Visual Basic .NET allows the programmer to create only one-dimensional and two-dimensional arrays.

18. The first subscript in a 25-element array is the number _____.

19. The last subscript in a 25-element array is the number _____.

20. quantity(7) is read _____.

EXERCISES

1. Write the statement to declare a procedure-level one-dimensional Integer array named
   `numbers`. The array should have 20 elements.

2. Write the statement to store the value 7 in the second element contained in the
   `numbers` array.

3. Write the statement to declare a module-level one-dimensional String array named
   `products`. The array should have 10 elements.

4. Write the statement to store the string "Paper" in the third element contained in the
   `products` array.

5. Write the statement to declare a procedure-level one-dimensional Double array named
   `rates` that has five elements. Use the following numbers to initialize the array: 6.5,
   8.3, 4, 2, 10.5.

6. Write the code to display the contents of a one-dimensional Double array named
   `rates`, which has five elements. Use the For...Next statement. Display each rate on a
   separate line in the uiRatesLabel control.

7. Rewrite the code from Exercise 6 using the Do...Loop statement.

8. Write the statement to sort the `rates` array in ascending order.

9. Write the statement to reverse the contents of the `rates` array.

10. Write the code to calculate the average of the elements included in a one-dimensional
    Double array named `rates`, which has five elements. Display the average in the
    uiAvgLabel control. Use the For...Next statement.

11. Rewrite the code from Exercise 10 using the Do...Loop statement.

12. Write the code to display the largest number stored in a one-dimensional Double array named `rates` array, which has five elements. Use the Do...Loop statement. Display the highest number in the uiHighLabel control.

13. Rewrite the code from Exercise 12 using the For...Next statement.

14. Write the code to subtract the number one from each element in a one-dimensional Double array named `rates`, which has five elements. Use the Do...Loop statement.

15. Rewrite the code from Exercise 14 using the For...Next statement.

16. Write the code to multiply by two the number stored in the first element of a one-dimensional Integer array named `numbers`. Store the result in the `doubleNum` variable.

17. Write the code to add together the numbers stored in the first and second elements of a one-dimensional Integer array named `numbers`. Display the sum in the uiSumLabel control.

18. In this exercise, you code an application that displays the number of days in a month.
    a. If necessary, start Visual Studio .NET. Open the Month Solution (Month Solution.sln) file, which is contained in the VBNET\Chap10\Month Solution folder. If necessary, open the designer window.
    b. Open the Display Days button's Click event procedure. Declare a 12-element, one-dimensional Integer array named `days`. Use the number of days in each month to initialize the array. (Use 28 for February.)
    c. Code the uiDisplayButton's Click event procedure so that it displays (in a message box) the number of days in the month corresponding to the number entered by the user in the uiMonthTextBox control. For example, if the uiMonthTextBox control contains the number one, the procedure should display 31 in a message box. The procedure should display an appropriate message in a message box if the user enters an invalid number in the uiMonthTextBox control.
    d. Save the solution, then start the application. Enter the number 20 in the uiMonthTextBox, then click the Display Days button. An appropriate message should appear in a message box. Close the message box.
    e. Now test the application by entering numbers from 1 through 12 in the uiMonthTextBox. Click the Display Days button after entering each number.
    f. Click the Exit button to end the application.
    g. Close the Output window, then close the solution.

19. In this exercise, you code an application that displays the lowest value stored in an array.
    a. If necessary, start Visual Studio .NET. Open the Lowest Solution (Lowest Solution.sln) file, which is contained in the VBNET\Chap10\Lowest Solution folder. If necessary, open the designer window.
    b. Open the Display Lowest button's Click event procedure. Declare a 20-element, one-dimensional Integer array named `scores`. Assign the 20 numbers contained in the scores.txt file to the array. The scores.txt file is a sequential access file located in the VBNET\Chap10\Lowest Solution\Lowest Project\bin folder.
    c. Code the uiDisplayButton's Click event procedure so that it displays (in a message box) the lowest score stored in the array.
    d. Save the solution, then start the application. Click the Display Lowest button. A message containing the lowest score (13) should appear in a message box. Close the message box.
    e. Click the Exit button to end the application.
    f. Close the Output window, then close the solution.

20. In this exercise, you code an application that updates each value stored in an array.

   a. If necessary, start Visual Studio .NET. Open the Prices Solution (Prices Solution.sln) file, which is contained in the VBNET\Chap10\Prices Solution folder. If necessary, open the designer window.

   b. In the form's Declarations section, declare a 10-element, one-dimensional Double array named prices.

   c. In the form's Load event procedure, assign the 10 prices stored in the prices.txt file to the prices array. The prices.txt file is a sequential access file located in the VBNET\Chap10\Prices Solution\Prices Project\bin folder.

   d. Open the Increase button's Click event procedure. The procedure should ask the user for a percentage amount by which each price should be increased. It then should increase each price by that amount, and then save the increased prices to a sequential access file named newprices.txt.

   e. Save the solution, then start the application. Click the Increase button. Increase each price by 5%.

   f. Click the Exit button to end the application.

   g. Open the prices.txt and newprices.txt files. The prices contained in the newprices.txt file should be 5% more than the prices in the prices.txt file.

   h. Close the prices.txt and newprices.txt windows. Close the Output window, then close the solution.

21. In this exercise, you modify the application from Exercise 20. The modified application allows the user to update a specific price.

   a. Use Windows to make a copy of the Prices Solution folder, which is contained in the VBNET\Chap10 folder. Change the name of the folder to Prices2 Solution.

   b. If necessary, start Visual Studio .NET. Open the Prices Solution (Prices Solution.sln) file, which is contained in the VBNET\Chap10\Prices2 Solution folder. Open the designer window.

   c. Open the Increase button's Click event procedure. Modify the procedure so that it also asks the user to enter a number from one through 10. If the user enters the number one, the procedure should update the first price in the array. If the user enters the number two, the procedure should update the second price in the array, and so on.

   d. Save the solution, then start the application. Click the Increase button. Increase the second price by 10%. Click the Increase button again. This time, increase the tenth price by 2%.

   e. Click the Exit button to end the application.

   f. Open the prices.txt and newprices.txt files. The second price contained in the newprices.txt file should be 10% more than the second price in the prices.txt file. The tenth price in the newprices.txt file should be 2% more than the tenth price in the prices.txt file.

   g. Close the prices.txt and newprices.txt windows. Close the Output window, then close the solution.

22. In this exercise, you code an application that displays the number of students earning a specific score.

   a. If necessary, start Visual Studio .NET. Open the Scores Solution (Scores Solution.sln) file, which is contained in the VBNET\Chap10\Scores Solution folder. If necessary, open the designer window.

   b. Open the Display button's Click event procedure. Declare a 20-element, one-dimensional Integer array named scores. Assign the 20 numbers contained in the scores.txt file to the array. The scores.txt file is a sequential access file located in the VBNET\Chap10\Scores Solution\Scores Project\bin folder.

   c. Code the uiDisplayButton's Click event procedure so that it prompts the user to enter a score from zero through 100. The procedure then should display (in a message box) the number of students who earned that score.

d. Save the solution, then start the application. Use the application to answer the following questions.

- How many students earned a score of 72?
- How many students earned a score of 88?
- How many students earned a score of 20?
- How many students earned a score of 99?

e. Click the Exit button to end the application.

f. Close the Output window, then close the solution.

23. In this exercise, you modify the application that you coded in Exercise 22. The modified application allows the user to display the number of students earning a score in a specific range.

a. Use Windows to make a copy of the Scores Solution folder, which is contained in the VBNET\Chap10 folder. Change the name of the folder to Scores2 Solution.

b. If necessary, start Visual Studio .NET. Open the Scores Solution (Scores Solution.sln) file, which is contained in the VBNET\Chap10\Scores2 Solution folder. Open the designer window.

c. Open the Display button's Click event procedure. Modify the procedure so that it prompts the user to enter a minimum score and a maximum score. The procedure then should display (in a message box) the number of students who earned a score within that range.

d. Save the solution, then start the application. Use the application to answer the following questions.

- How many students earned a score between 70 and 79, including 70 and 79?
- How many students earned a score between 65 and 85, including 65 and 85?
- How many students earned a score between 0 and 50, including 0 and 50?

e. Click the Exit button to end the application.

f. Close the Output window, then close the solution.

24. Jacques Cousard has been playing the lottery for four years and has yet to win any money. He wants an application that will select the six lottery numbers for him. Each lottery number can range from 1 through 54 only.

a. If necessary, start Visual Studio .NET. Open the Lottery Solution (Lottery Solution.sln) file, which is contained in the VBNET\Chap10\Lottery Solution folder. If necessary, open the designer window.

b. Open the Display Numbers button's Click event procedure. Code the procedure so that it displays six unique random numbers in the interface. (*Hint*: Store the numbers in a one-dimensional array.)

c. Save the solution, then start the application. Click the Display Numbers button several times. Each time you click the button, six unique random numbers between 1 and 54 (inclusive) should appear in the interface.

d. Click the Exit button to end the application.

e. Close the Output window, then close the solution.

25. In this exercise, you code an application that sorts (in ascending order) the values stored in a sequential access file.

a. If necessary, start Visual Studio .NET. Open the Sort Solution (Sort Solution.sln) file, which is contained in the VBNET\Chap10\Sort Solution folder. If necessary, open the designer window.

b. Open the Sort button's Click event procedure. Code the procedure so that it stores the 10 integers contained in the unsorted.txt file in an array. The unsorted.txt file is a sequential access file contained in the VBNET\Chap10\Sort Solution\Sort Project\bin folder. The procedure should sort the numbers in ascending order, and then save the sorted numbers to a sequential access file named sorted.txt.

    c. Code the Print button's Click event procedure so that it prints the contents of the unsorted.txt file followed by a blank line, and the contents of the sorted.txt file on the printer.

    d. Save the solution, then start the application. Click the Sort button, then click the Print button.

    e. Click the Exit button to end the application.

    f. Close the Output window, then close the solution.

26. In this exercise, you modify the application that you coded in Exercise 25. This modified application sorts (in descending order) the values stored in a sequential access file.

    a. Use Windows to make a copy of the Sort Solution folder, which is contained in the VBNET\Chap10 folder. Change the name of the folder to Sort2 Solution.

    b. If necessary, start Visual Studio .NET. Open the Sort Solution (Sort Solution.sln) file, which is contained in the VBNET\Chap10\Sort2 Solution folder. If necessary, open the designer window.

    c. Open the Sort button's Click event procedure. Modify the procedure so that it sorts the numbers in descending order.

    d. Save the solution, then start the application. Click the Sort button, then click the Print button.

    e. Click the Exit button to end the application.

    f. Close the Output window, then close the solution.

discovery ▶ **27.** In this exercise, you learn about the Array.GetUpperBound method.

    a. Display the Help screen for the Array.GetUpperBound method. What is the purpose of the method?

    b. Write the statement to display (in the uiHighLabel control) the highest subscript included in a one-dimensional array named `items`.

LESSON B
o b j e c t i v e s

After completing this lesson, you will be able to:

- Create and manipulate parallel one-dimensional arrays
- Create a structure
- Declare a structure variable
- Create and manipulate a one-dimensional array of structures

More on One-Dimensional Arrays

Parallel One-Dimensional Arrays

Takoda Tapahe owns a small gift shop named Treasures. She wants an application that allows her to display the price of the item whose product ID she enters. Figure 10-18 shows a portion of the gift shop's price list.

Product ID	Price
BX35	13
CR20	10
FE15	12
KW10	24
MM67	4

Figure 10-18: A portion of the gift shop's price list

Recall that all of the variables in an array have the same data type. So how can you store a price list, which includes a string (the product ID) and a number (the price), in an array? One way is to use two one-dimensional arrays: a String array to store the product IDs and an Integer array to store the prices. Both arrays are illustrated in Figure 10-19.

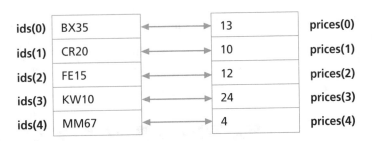

Figure 10-19: Illustration of a price list stored in two one-dimensional arrays

The arrays shown in Figure 10-19 are referred to as parallel arrays. **Parallel arrays** are two or more arrays whose elements are related by their position—in other words, by their subscript—in the arrays. The ids and prices arrays shown in Figure 10-19 are parallel because each element in the ids array corresponds to the element located in the same position in the prices array. For example, the first element in the ids array corresponds to the first element in the prices array. In other words, the item whose product ID is BX35 [ids(0)] has a price of $13 [prices(0)]. Likewise, the second elements in both arrays—the elements with a subscript of 1—also are related; the item whose product ID is CR20 has a price of $10. The same relationship is true for the remaining elements in both arrays. If you want to know an item's price, you simply locate the item's ID in the ids array and then view its corresponding element in the prices array. Figure 10-20 shows the uiDisplayPriceButton's Click event procedure, which displays the item's price based on the ID entered by the user.

Pseudocode

1. declare a String array named ids
2. declare an Integer array named prices
3. declare an Integer variable named x
4. declare a String variable named searchFor
5. assign the product ID entered in the uiIdTextBox control, converted to uppercase, to the searchFor variable
6. repeat while x is less than the number of elements in the ids array and, at the same time, the value stored in the searchFor variable is not equal to the value stored in the current element in the ids array
       add 1 to x
   end repeat
7. if the x variable contains a number that is less than the number of elements in the ids array
           display, in the uiPriceLabel control, the appropriate price from the prices array
   else
           display the message "Product ID is not valid" in the uiPriceLabel control
   end if

Visual Basic .NET code

parallel arrays

```vb
Dim ids() As String = {"BX35", "CR20", "FE15", "KW10", "MM67"}
Dim prices() As Integer = {13, 10, 12, 24, 4}
Dim x As Integer
Dim searchFor As String
searchFor = Me.uiIdTextBox.Text.ToUpper()

'search the array
Do While x < ids.Length AndAlso searchFor <> ids(x)
     x = x + 1
Loop

'determine whether the ID was located in the ids array
If x < ids.Length Then
     Me.uiPriceLabel.Text = "Price: $" _
          & Convert.ToString(prices(x))
Else
     Me.uiPriceLabel.Text = "Product ID is not valid"
End If
```

Results (displayed in the uiPriceLabel control)

Price: $12   (assuming the user enters FE15 as the product ID)
Product ID is not valid   (assuming the user enters XX90 as the product ID)

Figure 10-20: uiDisplayPriceButton's Click event procedure

The procedure shown in Figure 10-20 declares and initializes two parallel one-dimensional arrays: a five-element String array named `ids` and a five-element Integer array named `prices`. Notice that each item's ID is stored in the `ids` array, and each item's price is stored in the corresponding location in the `prices` array. The procedure also declares an Integer variable named `x` and a String variable named `searchFor`. After declaring the arrays and variables, the procedure assigns the contents of the uiIdTextBox control, converted to uppercase, to the searchFor variable.

The loop in the procedure continues to add the number one to the `x` variable as long as the `x` variable contains a value that is less than the number of elements in the `ids` array and, at the same time, the product ID has not been located in the array. The loop stops when either of the following conditions is true: the `x` variable contains the number five (which indicates that the loop reached the end of the array without finding the product ID) or the product ID is located in the array.

After the loop completes its processing, the selection structure in the procedure compares the number stored in the `x` variable with the value stored in the array's Length property, which is 5. If the `x` variable contains a number that is less than five, it indicates that the loop stopped processing because the product ID was located in the `ids` array. In that case, the procedure displays (in the uiPriceLabel control) the corresponding price from the `prices` array. However, if the `x` variable's value is not less than five, it indicates that the loop stopped processing because it reached the end of the array without finding the product ID. In that case, the message "Product ID is not valid" is displayed in the uiPriceLabel control. As Figure 10-20 indicates, the procedure displays a price of $12 if the user enters FE15 as the product ID, and the message "Product ID is not valid" if the user enters XX90 as the product ID.

Using two parallel one-dimensional arrays is only one way of solving the price list problem. You also can use a one-dimensional array of structures.

Structures

In previous chapters, you used only the data types built into Visual Basic .NET, such as the Integer, Decimal, and String data types. You also can create your own data types in Visual Basic .NET using the **Structure statement**. Data types created using the Structure statement are referred to as **user-defined data types** or **structures**. Figure 10-21 shows the syntax of the Structure statement and includes an example of using the statement to create a structure (user-defined data type) named Employee.

Syntax

Structure *structureName*
    Public *memberVariable1* **As** *datatype*
    [**Public** *memberVariableN* **As** *datatype*]
End Structure

Example
| ```
Structure Employee
     Public number As String
     Public firstName As String
     Public lastName As String
     Public salary As Decimal
End Structure
``` |

Figure 10-21: Syntax and an example of the Structure statement
```

The Structure statement begins with the Structure clause, which contains the keyword `Structure` followed by the name of the structure. In the example shown in Figure 10-21, the name of the structure is Employee. The Structure statement ends with the End Structure clause, which contains the keywords `End Structure`. Between the Structure and End Structure clauses, you define the members included in the structure. The members can be variables, constants, or procedures. However, in most cases, the members will be variables; such variables are referred to as **member variables**. In this book, you learn how to include only member variables in a structure.

As the syntax shown in Figure 10-21 indicates, each member variable's definition contains the keyword `Public` followed by the name of the variable, the keyword `As`, and the variable's *datatype*. The *datatype* identifies the type of data that the member variable will store and can be any of the standard data types available in Visual Basic .NET; it also can be another structure (user-defined data type). The Employee structure shown in Figure 10-21 contains four member variables: three are String variables and one is a Decimal variable.

In most applications, you enter the Structure statement in the form's Declarations section, typically below the `Windows Form Designer generated code` entry in the Code Editor window. After entering the Structure statement, you then can use the structure to declare a variable.

Using a Structure to Declare a Variable

As you can with the standard data types built into Visual Basic .NET, you can use a structure (user-defined data type) to declare a variable. Variables declared using a structure are often referred to as **structure variables**. Figure 10-22 shows the syntax for creating a structure variable. The figure also includes examples of declaring structure variables using the Employee structure from Figure 10-21.

Syntax
**{Dim	Private}** *structureVariableName* **As** *structureName*

Examples
`Dim manager As Employee` declares a procedure-level Employee variable named `manager`
`Private salaried As Employee` declares a module-level Employee variable named `salaried`

Figure 10-22: Syntax and an example of declaring a structure variable

You use the keyword `Dim` to create a procedure-level structure variable, and the keyword `Private` to create a module-level structure variable. In the syntax, *structureVariableName* is the name of the structure variable you are declaring and *structureName* is the name of the structure (user-defined data type).

Similar to the way the `Dim age As Integer` instruction declares an Integer variable named `age`, the `Dim manager As Employee` instruction, which is shown in the first example in Figure 10-22, declares an Employee structure variable named `manager`. However, unlike the `age` variable, the `manager` variable itself contains four member variables. In code, you refer to the entire structure variable by its name—in this case, manager. To refer to an individual member variable within a structure variable, however, you precede the member variable's name with the name of the structure variable in which it is defined. You use the dot member access operator (a period) to separate the structure variable's name from the member variable's name. For instance, the names of the member variables within the manager structure variable are manager.number, manager.firstName, manager.lastName, and manager.salary.

The Private salaried As Employee instruction shown in the second example in Figure 10-22 declares a module-level Employee structure variable named salaried. The names of the members within the salaried variable are salaried.number, salaried.firstName, salaried.lastName, and salaried.salary.

You can use an assignment statement to enter data into the member variables contained in a structure variable. Figure 10-23 shows the syntax of such an assignment statement and includes several examples of using the syntax to enter data into the member variables created by the statements shown in Figure 10-22.

Syntax
structureVariableName.memberVariableName = *value*

Examples
manager.number = "0477" manager.firstName = "Janice" manager.lastName = "Lopenski" manager.salary = 34500D
assigns data to the member variables contained in the manager variable
manager.number = empStreamReader.ReadLine()
assigns the line read from a sequential access file to the manager.number member variable
salaried.salary = salaried.salary * 1.05D
multiplies the contents of the salaried.salary member variable by 1.05, and then assigns the result to the member variable
salaried.firstName = Me.uiFirstTextBox.Text
assigns the value entered in the uiFirstTextBox control to the salaried.firstName member variable

Figure 10-23: Syntax and examples of storing data in a member variable

In the syntax, *structureVariableName* is the name of a structure variable, and *memberVariableName* is the name of a member variable within the structure variable. *Value* is the data you want assigned to the member variable. The data type of the *value* must match the data type of the member variable.

In the first example shown in Figure 10-23, the first three assignment statements assign the strings "0477", "Janice", and "Lopenski" to the String members of the manager variable. The fourth assignment statement in the example assigns a Decimal number to the Decimal member of the manager variable.

The second example in Figure 10-23 reads a line of data from a sequential access file and stores the data in the `number` member of the `manager` variable. The third example multiplies the contents of the `salaried.salary` member variable by 1.05, and then assigns the result to the member variable. The last example assigns the value entered in the uiFirstTextBox control to the `salaried.firstName` member variable.

Programmers use structures (user-defined data types) to group related items into one unit. The advantages of doing so will become more apparent as you read through the next two sections.

Passing a Structure Variable to a Procedure

The personnel manager at Johnsons Lumber wants an application that he can use to save each manager's employee number, name, and salary in a sequential access file. Figure 10-24 shows a sample run of the Johnsons Lumber application, and Figure 10-25 shows how you can code the application without using a structure.

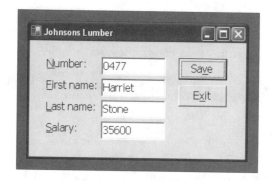

Figure 10-24: Sample run of the Johnsons Lumber application

```
'Project name:          Johnsons Project
'Project purpose:       The project writes employee information to
'                       a sequential access file.
'Created/revised by:    <enter your name here> on <enter the date here>

Option Explicit On
Option Strict On

Public Class JohnsonsForm
    Inherits System.Windows.Forms.Form

[Windows Form Designer generated code]
```

Figure 10-25: Code for the Johnsons Lumber application (without a structure)

```
Private Function GetData(ByRef num As String, _
                         ByRef first As String, _
                         ByRef last As String, _
                         ByRef pay As Decimal) As Boolean
    'gets the employee data and returns a Boolean value
    'indicating whether the data is OK

    'declare variable
    Dim dataOK As Boolean = True

    'assign input to variables
    num = Me.uiNumberTextBox.Text
    first = Me.uiFirstTextBox.Text
    last = Me.uiLastTextBox.Text
    'remove any dollar signs from the salary
    Me.uiSalaryTextBox.Text = _
        Me.uiSalaryTextBox.Text.Replace("$", "")

    Try
        pay = Decimal.Parse(Me.uiSalaryTextBox.Text)

    Catch exFormat As FormatException
        dataOK = False
        MessageBox.Show("The salary must be numeric.", _
            "Johnsons Lumber", MessageBoxButtons.OK, _
            MessageBoxIcon.Information)
    End Try

    Return dataOK
End Function

Private Sub uiSaveButton_Click(ByVal sender As Object, _
    ByVal e As System.EventArgs) Handles uiSaveButton.Click
    'save the employee information to a sequential access file

    'declare variables
    Dim number As String
    Dim firstName As String
    Dim lastName As String
    Dim salary As Decimal
    Dim goodData As Boolean
    Dim saveStreamWriter As IO.StreamWriter

    'call a function to get the data and return a Boolean
    'value indicating whether the data is OK
    goodData = GetData(number, firstName, _
        lastName, salary)

    If goodData Then
        Try
            'open the file for append
            saveStreamWriter = IO.File.AppendText("employees.txt")

            'write the employee information
            saveStreamWriter.WriteLine(number _
                & "#" & firstName & "#" _
                & lastName & "#" _
                & Convert.ToString(salary))
```

receives four variables *by reference*, and assigns data to the variables

declare four variables to store the input data

passes four variables to the GetData function

writes the information stored in each variable to the file

Figure 10-25: Code for the Johnsons Lumber application (without a structure) (continued)

```
                          'clear the text boxes
                          'then send the focus to the Number text box
                          Me.uiNumberTextBox.Text = ""
                          Me.uiFirstTextBox.Text = ""
                          Me.uiLastTextBox.Text = ""
                          Me.uiSalaryTextBox.Text = ""
                          Me.uiNumberTextBox.Focus()

                          'close the file
                          saveStreamWriter.Close()

                 Catch ex As Exception
                     MessageBox.Show(ex.Message, "Johnsons Lumber", _
                         MessageBoxButtons.OK, MessageBoxIcon.Information)
                 End Try
             End If
        End Sub

        Private Sub uiExitButton_Click(ByVal sender As Object, _
            ByVal e As System.EventArgs) Handles uiExitButton.Click
            'ends the application
            Me.Close()
        End Sub
End Class
```

Figure 10-25: Code for the Johnsons Lumber application (without a structure) (continued)

When the user clicks the Save button in the interface, the uiSaveButton's Click event procedure shown in Figure 10-25 declares the necessary variables. It then calls the GetData function, passing it four variables *by reference*. The GetData function is responsible for assigning to the variables the employee data entered by the user. Notice that the function also verifies that the salary entry can be converted to the Decimal data type. The function returns the Boolean value True if it does not find a problem with the conversion; otherwise, it returns the Boolean value False.

If the GetData function did not encounter a problem when assigning the employee data to the variables, the uiSaveButton's Click event procedure writes the contents of the variables to a sequential access file; otherwise, the uiSaveButton's Click event procedure ends.

Figure 10-26 shows a more convenient way of writing the code for the Johnsons Lumber application. In this version of the code, the Employee structure from Figure 10-21 is used to group together the employee data.

```
'Project name:         Johnsons Project
'Project purpose:      The project writes employee information to
'                      a sequential access file.
'Created/revised by:   <enter your name here> on <enter the date here>

Option Explicit On
Option Strict On

Public Class JohnsonsForm
    Inherits System.Windows.Forms.Form
```

Figure 10-26: Code for the Johnsons Lumber application (with a structure)

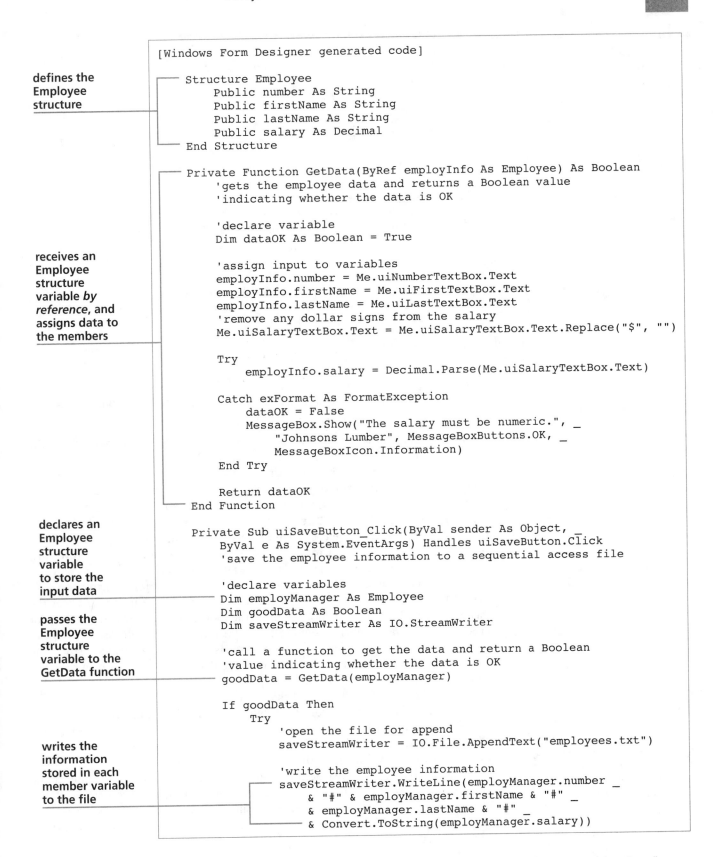

defines the
Employee
structure

receives an
Employee
structure
variable *by
reference*, and
assigns data to
the members

declares an
Employee
structure
variable
to store the
input data

passes the
Employee
structure
variable to the
GetData function

writes the
information
stored in each
member variable
to the file

```
[Windows Form Designer generated code]

Structure Employee
    Public number As String
    Public firstName As String
    Public lastName As String
    Public salary As Decimal
End Structure

Private Function GetData(ByRef employInfo As Employee) As Boolean
    'gets the employee data and returns a Boolean value
    'indicating whether the data is OK

    'declare variable
    Dim dataOK As Boolean = True

    'assign input to variables
    employInfo.number = Me.uiNumberTextBox.Text
    employInfo.firstName = Me.uiFirstTextBox.Text
    employInfo.lastName = Me.uiLastTextBox.Text
    'remove any dollar signs from the salary
    Me.uiSalaryTextBox.Text = Me.uiSalaryTextBox.Text.Replace("$", "")

    Try
        employInfo.salary = Decimal.Parse(Me.uiSalaryTextBox.Text)

    Catch exFormat As FormatException
        dataOK = False
        MessageBox.Show("The salary must be numeric.", _
            "Johnsons Lumber", MessageBoxButtons.OK, _
            MessageBoxIcon.Information)
    End Try

    Return dataOK
End Function

Private Sub uiSaveButton_Click(ByVal sender As Object, _
    ByVal e As System.EventArgs) Handles uiSaveButton.Click
    'save the employee information to a sequential access file

    'declare variables
    Dim employManager As Employee
    Dim goodData As Boolean
    Dim saveStreamWriter As IO.StreamWriter

    'call a function to get the data and return a Boolean
    'value indicating whether the data is OK
    goodData = GetData(employManager)

    If goodData Then
        Try
            'open the file for append
            saveStreamWriter = IO.File.AppendText("employees.txt")

            'write the employee information
            saveStreamWriter.WriteLine(employManager.number _
                & "#" & employManager.firstName & "#" _
                & employManager.lastName & "#" _
                & Convert.ToString(employManager.salary))
```

Figure 10-26: Code for the Johnsons Lumber application (with a structure) (continued)

```
                    'clear the text boxes
                    'then send the focus to the Number text box
                    Me.uiNumberTextBox.Text = ""
                    Me.uiFirstTextBox.Text = ""
                    Me.uiLastTextBox.Text = ""
                    Me.uiSalaryTextBox.Text = ""
                    Me.uiNumberTextBox.Focus()

                    'close the file
                    saveStreamWriter.Close()

                Catch ex As Exception
                    MessageBox.Show(ex.Message, "Johnsons Lumber", _
                        MessageBoxButtons.OK, MessageBoxIcon.Information)
                End Try
            End If
        End Sub

        Private Sub uiExitButton_Click(ByVal sender As Object, _
            ByVal e As System.EventArgs) Handles uiExitButton.Click
            'ends the application
            Me.Close()
        End Sub
    End Class
```

Figure 10-26: Code for the Johnsons Lumber application (with a structure) (continued)

In the code shown in Figure 10-26, the Structure statement that defines the Employee structure is entered in the form's Declarations section, immediately below the `Windows Form Designer generated code` entry. The `Dim employManager As Employee` statement in the uiSaveButton's Click event procedure uses the Employee structure to declare a structure variable named `employManager`. The `goodData = GetData(employManager)` statement in the uiSaveButton's Click event procedure calls the GetData function, passing it the `employManager` structure variable *by reference*. When you pass a structure variable, all of the member variables are automatically passed.

The GetData function receives the address of the Employee structure variable passed to it, and it assigns the employee data entered by the user to each of the member variables. The function returns the Boolean value True if it did not encounter a problem when assigning the data; otherwise, it returns the Boolean value False. If the GetData function returns the Boolean value True, the uiSaveButton's Click event procedure writes the data stored in each member variable to a sequential access file; otherwise, the procedure ends.

Notice that the uiSaveButton's Click event procedure shown earlier in Figure 10-25 uses four scalar variables to store the input data; however, in Figure 10-26's code, the procedure uses only one structure variable for this purpose. The uiSaveButton's Click event procedure in Figure 10-25 also must pass four scalar variables (rather than one structure variable) to the GetData function, which must use four scalar variables (rather than one structure variable) to accept the data. Imagine if the employee data consisted of 20 items rather than just four items! Passing a structure variable would be much less work than passing 20 individual scalar variables.

Another advantage of grouping related data into one unit is that the unit then can be stored in an array.

tip

As you learned in Lesson A, a scalar variable is one that is unrelated to any other variable in memory.

Creating an Array of Structure Variables

Earlier in this lesson, you learned how to use two parallel one-dimensional arrays to store a price list for Takoda Tapahe, the owner of a small gift shop named Treasures. (The code is shown in Figure 10-20.) As you may remember, you stored each product's ID in a one-dimensional String array, and stored each product's price in the corresponding location in a one-dimensional Integer array. In addition to using parallel one-dimensional arrays, you also can use a one-dimensional array of structure variables.

Figure 10-27 shows a sample run of the Treasures application, and Figure 10-28 shows the Treasures application's code using an array of structure variables.

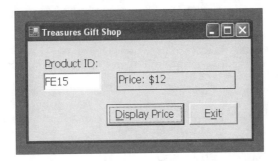

Figure 10-27: Sample run of the Treasures application

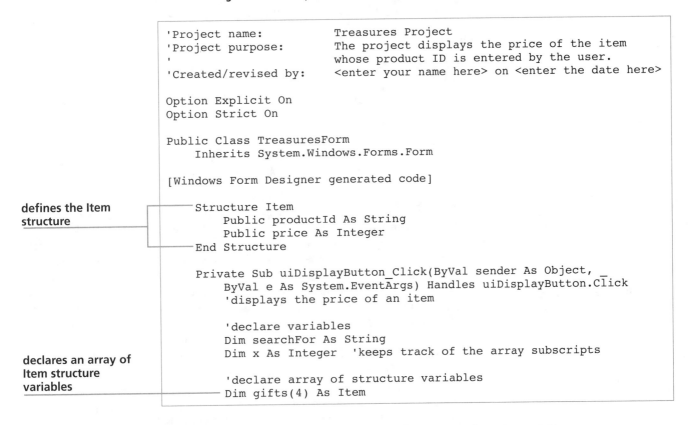

```
'Project name:          Treasures Project
'Project purpose:       The project displays the price of the item
'                       whose product ID is entered by the user.
'Created/revised by:    <enter your name here> on <enter the date here>

Option Explicit On
Option Strict On

Public Class TreasuresForm
    Inherits System.Windows.Forms.Form

[Windows Form Designer generated code]

    Structure Item
        Public productId As String
        Public price As Integer
    End Structure

    Private Sub uiDisplayButton_Click(ByVal sender As Object, _
        ByVal e As System.EventArgs) Handles uiDisplayButton.Click
        'displays the price of an item

        'declare variables
        Dim searchFor As String
        Dim x As Integer  'keeps track of the array subscripts

        'declare array of structure variables
        Dim gifts(4) As Item
```

defines the Item structure

declares an array of Item structure variables

Figure 10-28: Treasures application using an array of structure variables

```
                         'assign product IDs and prices to the array
                         gifts(0).productId = "BX35"
                         gifts(0).price = 13
                         gifts(1).productId = "CR20"
fills the structure      gifts(1).price = 10
variables with data      gifts(2).productId = "FE15"
                         gifts(2).price = 12
                         gifts(3).productId = "KW10"
                         gifts(3).price = 24
                         gifts(4).productId = "MM67"
                         gifts(4).price = 4

                         'assign input to variable
                         searchFor = uiProductTextBox.Text.ToUpper()

                         'search the array for the product ID
                         Do While x < gifts.Length _
                             AndAlso searchFor <> gifts(x).productId
                             x = x + 1
                         Loop

                         'determine whether the ID was located in the productId array
                         If x < gifts.Length Then
                             'display the price
                             Me.uiPriceLabel.Text = _
                                 "Price: $" & Convert.ToString(gifts(x).price)
                         Else
                             Me.uiPriceLabel.Text = "Product ID is not valid"
                         End If
                     End Sub

                     Private Sub uiExitButton_Click(ByVal sender As Object, _
                         ByVal e As System.EventArgs) Handles uiExitButton.Click
                         'ends the application
                         Me.Close()
                     End Sub
                 End Class
```

accesses the length of the array and the contents of the productId member variable contained in the current array element

accesses the contents of the price member variable contained in the current array element

Figure 10-28: Treasures application using an array of structure variables (continued)

Recall that in most applications, the values stored in an array come from a file on the computer's disk.

The uiDisplayButton's Click event procedure declares a String variable named searchFor and an Integer variable named x. The searchFor variable will store the product ID entered by the user, and the x variable will keep track of the array subscripts. The procedure uses the Item structure, which is defined in the form's Declarations section, to declare a five-element, one-dimensional array named gifts. Each element in the gifts array is a structure variable that contains two member variables: a String variable named productId and an Integer variable named price. After declaring the array, the procedure assigns the appropriate IDs and prices to the array. Assigning initial values to an array is often referred to as **populating the array**. Notice that you refer to a member variable in an array element using the syntax *arrayname*(*subscript*).*memberVariableName*. For example, you use gifts(0).productId to refer to the productId member contained in the first element in the gifts array. Likewise, you use gifts(4).price to refer to the price member contained in the last element in the gifts array.

After populating the gifts array, the uiDisplayButton's Click event procedure assigns the contents of the uiProductTextBox control, converted to uppercase, to the searchFor variable. The loop in the procedure then continues to add the number one to the x variable as long as the x variable contains a value that is less than the number

Recall that the value stored in an array's Length property is always one number more than the highest subscript in the array.

of elements in the `gifts` array (in this case, 5) and, at the same time, the product ID has not been located in the `productId` member in the array. The loop stops when either of the following conditions is true: the x variable contains the number five (which indicates that the loop reached the end of the array without finding the product ID) or the product ID is located in a `productId` member in the array.

After the loop completes its processing, the selection structure in the procedure compares the number stored in the x variable with the value stored in the `gifts` array's Length property, which is 5. If the x variable contains a number that is less than five, it indicates that the loop stopped processing because the product ID was located in a `productId` member in the array. In that case, the procedure displays (in the uiPriceLabel control) the price from the corresponding `price` member in the array. However, if the x variable's value is not less than five, it indicates that the loop stopped processing because it reached the end of the array without finding the product ID. In that case, the message "Product ID is not valid" is displayed in the uiPriceLabel control. As Figure 10-27 indicates, the procedure displays a price of $12 if the user enters FE15 as the product ID.

You now have completed Lesson B. You can either take a break or complete the end-of-lesson questions and exercises before moving on to the next lesson. In Lesson C, you learn about two-dimensional arrays, and you code the Tax Calculator application that you previewed at the beginning of the chapter.

SUMMARY

To create parallel one-dimensional arrays:

■ Create two one-dimensional arrays. When assigning values to both arrays, be sure that the value stored in each element in one array corresponds to the value stored in the same element in the other array.

To create an array of structures:

■ Use the Structure statement to create a record structure (user-defined data type). Then use the record structure to declare the array.

To refer to a member variable in an array:

■ Use the syntax *arrayname*(*subscript*).*memberVariableName*.

QUESTIONS

1. If the `state` and `capital` arrays are parallel arrays, the capital of the state stored in the `state(0)` variable is contained in the _____ variable.

2. Parallel arrays are related by their subscripts.
   a. True
   b. False

3. You use the _____ statement to create a user-defined data type.
   a. Datatype
   b. Define
   c. Record
   d. Structure
   e. UserType

4. Assume that each record in the `inventory` array contains two fields: a String field named `number` and an Integer field named `quantity`. Which of the following assigns the inventory number "123XY" to the first element in the array?
   a. `number(0).inventory = "123XY"`
   b. `inventory(0).number = "123XY"`
   c. `inventory(1).number = "123XY"`
   d. `inventory.number(0) = "123XY"`
   e. `inventory.number(1) = "123XY"`

EXERCISES

1. In this exercise, you code an application that allows Professor Carver to display a grade based on the number of points he enters. The grading scale is shown in Figure 10-29.

Minimum points	Maximum points	Grade
0	299	F
300	349	D
350	399	C
400	449	B
450	500	A

Figure 10-29

   a. If necessary, start Visual Studio .NET. Open the Carver Solution (Carver Solution.sln) file, which is contained in the VBNET\Chap10\Carver Solution folder. If necessary, open the designer window.
   b. Store the minimum points in a five-element, one-dimensional Integer array named `points`. Store the grades in a five-element, one-dimensional String array named `grades`. The arrays should be parallel arrays.
   c. Code the Display Grade button's Click event procedure so that it searches the `points` array for the number of points entered by the user, and then displays the corresponding grade from the `grade` array.
   d. Save the solution, and then start the application. Enter 455 in the Points text box, then click the Display Grade button. A grade of A appears in the interface.
   e. Enter 210 in the Points text box, then click the Display Grade button. A grade of F appears in the interface.
   f. Click the Exit button to end the application.
   g. Close the Output window, and then close the solution.

2. In this exercise, you modify the application that you coded in Exercise 1. The modified application allows the user to change the grading scale when the application is started.

    a. Use Windows to make a copy of the Carver Solution folder, which is contained in the VBNET\Chap10 folder. Change the name of the folder to Carver2 Solution.

    b. If necessary, start Visual Studio .NET. Open the Carver Solution (Carver Solution.sln) file, which is contained in the VBNET\Chap10\Carver2 Solution folder. Open the designer window.

    c. When the form is loaded into the computer's memory, the application should use the InputBox function to prompt the user to enter the total number of possible points—in other words, the total number of points a student can earn in the course. Modify the application's code to perform this task.

    d. Modify the application's code so that it uses the grading scale shown in Figure 10-30. For example, if the user enters the number 500 in response to the InputBox function, the code should enter 450, which is 90% of 500, as the minimum number of points for an A. If the user enters the number 300, the code should enter 270, which is 90% of 300, as the minimum number of points for an A.

Minimum points	Grade
Less than 60% of the possible points	F
60% of the possible points	D
70% of the possible points	C
80% of the possible points	B
90% of the possible points	A

Figure 10-30

    e. Save the solution, and then start the application. Enter 300 as the number of possible points, then enter 185 in the Points text box. Click the Display Grade button. A grade of D appears in the interface.

    f. Click the Exit button to end the application.

    g. Start the application again. Enter 500 as the number of possible points, then enter 363 in the Points text box. Click the Display Grade button. A grade of C appears in the interface.

    h. Click the Exit button to end the application.

    i. Close the Output window, and then close the solution.

3. In this exercise, you code an application that allows Ms. Laury to display a shipping charge based on the number of items ordered by a customer. The shipping charge scale is shown in Figure 10-31.

Minimum order	Maximum order	Shipping charge
1	10	15
11	50	10
51	100	5
101	99999	0

Figure 10-31

a. If necessary, start Visual Studio .NET. Open the Laury Solution (Laury Solution.sln) file, which is contained in the VBNET\Chap10\Laury Solution folder. If necessary, open the designer window.

b. Store the maximum order amounts in a four-element, one-dimensional Integer array named `order`. Store the shipping charge amounts in a four-element, one-dimensional Integer array named `ship`. The arrays should be parallel arrays.

c. Code the Display Shipping Charge button's Click event procedure so that it searches the `order` array for the number of items ordered by the user, and then displays the corresponding shipping charge from the `ship` array. Display the shipping charge with a dollar sign and two decimal places.

d. Save the solution, and then start the application. Enter 65 in the Quantity ordered text box, then click the Display Shipping button. A shipping charge of $5.00 appears in the interface.

e. Enter 500 in the Quantity ordered text box, then click the Display Shipping button. A shipping charge of $0.00 appears in the interface.

f. Click the Exit button to end the application.

g. Close the Output window, and then close the solution.

4. Write a Structure statement that defines a structure named Book. The structure contains three member variables: `title`, `author`, and `cost`.

5. Write a Structure statement that defines a structure named Tape. The structure contains four member variables: `name`, `artist`, `song`, and `length`.

6. Write a Private statement that declares a Book variable named `fiction`.

7. Write a Dim statement that declares a Tape variable named `blues`.

8. Assume that an application contains the following structure:

```
Structure Computer
        Public model As String
        Public cost As Decimal
End Structure
```

a. Write a Dim statement that declares a Computer variable named `homeUse`.

b. Write an assignment statement that assigns the string "IB-50" to the `model` member variable.

c. Write an assignment statement that assigns the number 2400 to the `cost` member variable.

9. Assume that an application contains the following structure:

```
Structure Friend
        Public last As String
        Public first As String
End Structure
```

a. Write a Dim statement that declares a Friend variable named `school`.

b. Write an assignment statement that assigns the value in the uiFirstTextBox control to the `first` member variable.

c. Write an assignment statement that assigns the value in the uiLastTextBox control to the `last` member variable.

d. Write an assignment statement that assigns the value in the `last` member variable to the uiLastLabel control.

e. Write an assignment statement that assigns the value in the `first` member variable to the uiFirstLabel control.

10. Assume that an application contains the following structure:

```
Structure Computer
        Public model As String
        Public cost As Decimal
End Structure
```

a. Write a Private statement that declares a 10-element, one-dimensional array of Computer variables. Name the array business.

b. Write an assignment statement that assigns the string "HPP405" to the model member variable contained in the first array element.

c. Write an assignment statement that assigns the number 3600 to the cost member variable contained in the first array element.

11. Assume that an application contains the following structure:

```
Structure Friend
        Public last As String
        Public first As String
End Structure
```

a. Write a Private statement that declares a 5-element, one-dimensional array of Friend variables. Name the array home.

b. Write an assignment statement that assigns the value in the uiFirstTextBox control to the first member variable contained in the last array element.

c. Write an assignment statement that assigns the value in the uiLastTextBox control to the last member variable contained in the last array element.

12. In this exercise, you modify the application that you coded in Exercise 1. The modified application uses a one-dimensional array of structures, rather than two parallel one-dimensional arrays.

a. Use Windows to make a copy of the Carver Solution folder, which is contained in the VBNET\Chap10 folder. Change the name of the folder to Carver3 Solution.

b. If necessary, start Visual Studio .NET. Open the Carver Solution (Carver Solution.sln) file, which is contained in the VBNET\Chap10\Carver3 Solution folder. Open the designer window.

c. Create a record structure that contains two fields: an Integer field for the minimum points and a String field for the grades.

d. Use the record structure to declare a five-element, one-dimensional array named gradeScale. Modify the application's code so that it stores the grading scale in the gradeScale array.

e. Modify the application's code so that it searches the gradeScale array for the number of points earned, and then displays the appropriate grade from the array.

f. Save the solution, and then start the application. Enter 455 in the Points text box, then click the Display Grade button. A grade of A appears in the interface.

g. Enter 210 in the Points text box, then click the Display Grade button. A grade of F appears in the interface.

h. Click the Exit button to end the application.

i. Close the Output window, and then close the solution.

13. In this exercise, you modify the application you coded in Exercise 3. The modified application uses a one-dimensional array of structures, rather than two one-dimensional parallel arrays.

a. Use Windows to make a copy of the Laury Solution folder, which is contained in the VBNET\Chap10 folder. Change the name of the folder to Laury2 Solution.

b. If necessary, start Visual Studio .NET. Open the Laury Solution (Laury Solution.sln) file, which is contained in the VBNET\Chap10\Laury2 Solution folder. Open the designer window.

c. Create a record structure that contains two Integer fields: one for the maximum order amounts and the other for the shipping charge amounts.

d. Use the record structure to declare a four-element, one-dimensional array named shipScale. Modify the application's code so that it stores the shipping charge scale in the shipScale array.

e. Modify the application's code so that it searches the shipScale array for the number of items ordered, and then displays the appropriate shipping charge from the array.

f. Save the solution, and then start the application. Enter 65 in the Quantity ordered text box, then click the Display Shipping button. A shipping charge of $5.00 appears in the interface.

g. Enter 500 in the Quantity ordered text box, then click the Display Shipping button. A shipping charge of $0.00 appears in the interface.

h. Click the Exit button to end the application.

i. Close the Output window, and then close the solution.

discovery ▶ **14.** In this exercise, you learn about the ReDim statement.

a. Display the Help screen for the ReDim statement. What is the purpose of the statement?

b. What is the purpose of the keyword Preserve?

c. If necessary, start Visual Studio .NET. Open the ReDim Solution (ReDim Solution.sln) file, which is contained in the VBNET\Chap10\ReDim Solution folder. If necessary, open the designer window.

d. Open the Code Editor window and view the uiDisplayButton Click event procedure. Study the existing code, then modify the procedure so that it stores any number of sales amounts in the sales array.

e. Save the solution, then start the application. Click the Display Sales button, then enter the following sales amounts: 700, 550, 800, and then click the Cancel button. The button's Click event procedure should display each sales amount in a separate message box.

f. Click the Display Sales button again, then enter the following sales amounts: 5, 9, 45, 67, 8, and then click the Cancel button. The button's Click event procedure should display each sales amount in a separate message box.

g. Click the Exit button to end the application.

h. Close the Output window, and then close the solution.

After completing this lesson, you will be able to:

- Create and initialize a two-dimensional array
- Store data in a two-dimensional array
- Search a two-dimensional array

Using a Two-Dimensional Array

Two-Dimensional Arrays

As you learned in Lesson A, the most commonly used arrays are one-dimensional and two-dimensional. You learned about one-dimensional arrays in Lessons A and B. In this lesson, you learn about two-dimensional arrays.

Recall that you can visualize a one-dimensional array as a column of variables. A **two-dimensional array**, however, resembles a table in that the variables are in rows and columns. Figure 10-32 illustrates a two-dimensional array.

AC34	Shirt	Red
BD12	Coat	Blue
CP14	Blouse	White

Figure 10-32: Illustration of a two-dimensional array

Each variable (element) in a two-dimensional array is identified by a unique combination of two subscripts, which the computer assigns to the variable when the array is created. The subscripts specify the variable's row and column position in the array. Variables located in the first row in a two-dimensional array are assigned a row subscript of 0 (zero). Variables located in the second row are assigned a row subscript of 1 (one), and so on. Similarly, variables located in the first column in a two-dimensional array are assigned a column subscript of 0 (zero). Variables located in the second column are assigned a column subscript of 1 (one), and so on. You refer to each variable in a two-dimensional array by the array's name and the variable's row and column subscripts, which are separated by a comma and specified in a set of parentheses immediately following the array name. For example, to refer to the variable located in the first row, first column in a two-dimensional array named `products`, you use `products(0, 0)`—read "`products` sub zero comma zero." Similarly, to refer to the variable located in the second row, third column in the `products` array, you use `products(1, 2)`. Figure 10-33 illustrates this naming convention. Notice that the row subscript is listed first in the parentheses.

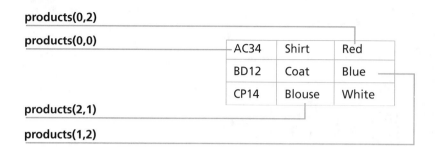

products(0,2)

products(0,0)

AC34	Shirt	Red
BD12	Coat	Blue
CP14	Blouse	White

products(2,1)

products(1,2)

Figure 10-33: Names of some of the variables contained in the `products` array

Recall that, before you can use an array, you first must declare (create) it. Figure 10-34 shows two versions of the syntax you use to declare a two-dimensional array in Visual Basic .NET. The figure also includes an example of using each syntax.

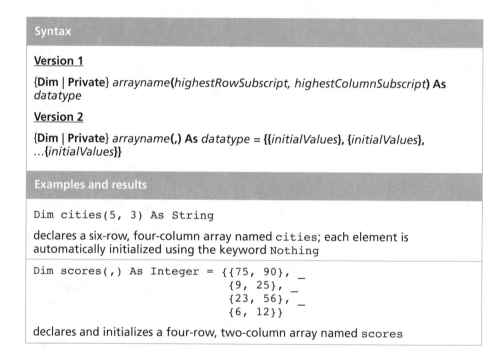

Syntax

Version 1

{**Dim** | **Private**} *arrayname*(*highestRowSubscript*, *highestColumnSubscript*) **As** *datatype*

Version 2

{**Dim** | **Private**} *arrayname*(,) **As** *datatype* = {{*initialValues*}, {*initialValues*}, ...{*initialValues*}}

Examples and results

```
Dim cities(5, 3) As String
```

declares a six-row, four-column array named `cities`; each element is automatically initialized using the keyword `Nothing`

```
Dim scores(,) As Integer = {{75, 90}, _
                            {9, 25}, _
                            {23, 56}, _
                            {6, 12}}
```

declares and initializes a four-row, two-column array named `scores`

Figure 10-34: Syntax versions and examples of declaring a two-dimensional array

You use the keyword `Dim` to declare a procedure-level array, and the keyword `Private` to declare a module-level array. *Arrayname* is the name of the array, and *datatype* is the type of data the array variables (elements) will store. Recall that each of the elements in an array has the same data type.

In Version 1 of the syntax, *highestRowSubscript* and *highestColumnSubscript* are integers that specify the highest row and column subscripts, respectively, in the array. When the array is created, it will contain one row more than the number specified in the *highestRowSubscript* argument, and one column more than the number specified in the *highestColumnSubscript* argument. This is because the first row subscript in a two-dimensional array is zero, and the first column subscript also is zero. When you use the syntax shown in Version 1 to declare a two-dimensional array, the computer automatically initializes each element in the array when the array is created.

You use the syntax shown in Version 2 in Figure 10-34 to declare a two-dimensional array and, at the same time, specify each element's initial value. Using Version 2's syntax, you include a separate *initialValues* section, enclosed in braces, for each row in the array. If the array has two rows, then the statement that declares and initializes the array should have two *initialValues* sections. If the array has five rows, then the declaration statement should have five *initialValues* sections.

Within the individual *initialValues* sections, you enter one or more values separated by commas. The number of values to enter corresponds to the number of columns in the array. If the array contains 10 columns, then each individual *initialValues* section should contain 10 values.

In addition to the set of braces that surrounds each individual *initialValues* section, notice in the syntax that a set of braces also surrounds all of the *initialValues* sections. Also notice that a comma appears within the parentheses that follow the array name. The comma indicates that the array is a two-dimensional array. (Recall that a comma is used to separate the row subscript from the column subscript in a two-dimensional array.)

Study closely the two examples shown in Figure 10-34. The statement shown in the first example creates a two-dimensional String array named `cities`; the array has six rows and four columns. The computer automatically initializes each element in the `cities` array using the keyword `Nothing`. The statement shown in the second example creates a two-dimensional Integer array named `scores`; the array has four rows and two columns. The statement initializes the `scores(0, 0)` variable to the number 75, and initializes the `scores(0, 1)` variable to the number 90. The `scores(1, 0)` and `scores(1, 1)` variables are initialized to the numbers 9 and 25, respectively. The `scores(2, 0)` and `scores(2, 1)` variables are initialized to the numbers 23 and 56, respectively, and the `scores(3, 0)` and `scores(3, 1)` variables are initialized to the numbers 6 and 12, respectively.

After declaring the array, you can use various methods to store data in the array.

Storing Data in a Two-Dimensional Array

As with one-dimensional arrays, you generally use an assignment statement to enter data into a two-dimensional array. Figure 10-35 shows the syntax of such an assignment statement and includes several examples of using the syntax to enter data into the arrays declared in Figure 10-34. In the syntax, *arrayname(rowSubscript, columnSubscript)* is the name and subscripts of the array variable to which you want the *value* (data) assigned.

Syntax
arrayname(*rowSubscript*, *columnSubscript*) = *value*

Examples
| ```
cities(0, 0) = "Madrid"
cities(0, 1) = "Paris"
cities(0, 2) = "Rome"
cities(0, 3) = "London"
``` |
| assigns the strings "Madrid", "Paris", "Rome", and "London" to the elements contained in the first row in the `cities` array |
| ```
For row = 0 To 3
      For column = 0 To 1
            scores(row, column) = 0
      Next column
Next row
``` |
| assigns the number zero to each element in the `scores` array |
| ```
For Each num In scores
      num = 0
Next num
``` |
| assigns the number zero to each element in the `scores` array |

Figure 10-35: Syntax and examples of entering data into a two-dimensional array

The code shown in the first example in Figure 10-35 uses four assignment statements to assign values to the elements contained in the first row in the `cities` array. The code shown in the second and third examples assigns the number zero to each element contained in the `scores` array. The second example uses a nested For...Next loop to make the assignments, while the third example uses a For Each...Next statement.

Next, you view a procedure that searches a two-dimensional array.

Searching a Two-Dimensional Array

In Lesson B, you viewed a procedure created for Takoda Tapahe, the owner of a small gift shop named Treasures. As you may remember, the procedure allows Takoda to display the price of the item whose product ID she enters. In that procedure, shown in Figure 10-20 in Lesson B, you used two parallel one-dimensional arrays to store the gift shop's price list. In the procedure shown in Figure 10-36, you use a two-dimensional array. To do so, you will need to treat the price as a string rather than as an integer, because all of the elements in an array must be of the same data type.
```

Pseudocode

1. declare a String array named items
2. declare an Integer variable named row
3. declare a String variable named searchFor
4. assign the product ID entered in the uiIdTextBox control, converted to uppercase, to the searchFor variable
5. repeat while row is less than the number of rows in the items array and, at the same time, the value stored in the searchFor variable is not equal to the value stored in the first column of the current element in the items array
       add 1 to row
   end repeat
6. if the row variable contains a number that is less than the number of rows in the items array
       display, in the uiPriceLabel control, the appropriate price from the second column of the current element in the items array
   else
       display the message "Product ID is not valid" in the uiPriceLabel control
   end if

Visual Basic .NET code

two-dimensional array ——

```
Dim items(,) As String = {{"BX35", "13"}, _
                          {"CR20", "10"}, _
                          {"FE15", "12"}, _
                          {"KW10", "24"}, _
                          {"MM67", "4"}}

Dim row As Integer
Dim searchFor As String
searchFor = uiIdTextBox.Text.ToUpper()

'search the array
Do While row < 5 AndAlso searchFor <> items(row, 0)
        row = row + 1
Loop

'determine whether the ID was located in the items array
If row < 5 Then
        Me.uiPriceLabel.Text = "Price: $" & items(row, 1)
Else
        Me.uiPriceLabel.Text = "Product ID is not valid"
End If
```

Results (displayed in the uiPriceLabel control)

Price: $12   (assuming the user enters FE15 as the product ID)
Product ID is not valid (assuming the user enters XX90 as the product ID)

Figure 10-36: uiDisplayPriceButton's Click event procedure using a two-dimensional array

The procedure shown in Figure 10-36 declares and initializes a two-dimensional array named items; the array has five rows and two columns. Notice that each item's ID is stored in the first column of the items array, and each item's price is stored in the corresponding row in the second column. The procedure also declares an Integer variable named row and a String variable named searchFor. After declaring the array and variables, the procedure assigns the contents of the uiIdTextBox control, converted to uppercase, to the searchFor variable.

The loop in the procedure continues to add the number one to the row variable as long as the row variable contains a value that is less than the number five (which is the number of rows in the items array) and, at the same time, the product ID has not been located in the first column of the array. The loop stops when either of the following conditions is true: the row variable contains the number five (which indicates that the loop reached the end of the array without finding the product ID) or the product ID is located in the array.

After the loop completes its processing, the selection structure in the procedure compares the number stored in the row variable with the number five. If the row variable contains a number that is less than five, it indicates that the loop stopped processing because the product ID was located in the first column of the items array. In that case, the procedure displays (in the uiPriceLabel control) the corresponding price from the second column in the array. However, if the row variable's value is not less than five, it indicates that the loop stopped processing because it reached the end of the array without finding the product ID; in that case, the message "Product ID is not valid" is displayed in the uiPriceLabel control. As Figure 10-36 indicates, the procedure displays a price of $12 if the user enters FE15 as the product ID, and the message "Product ID is not valid" if the user enters XX90 as the product ID.

Now that you know how to use a two-dimensional array, you can begin coding the Tax Calculator application that you previewed at the beginning of this chapter.

The Tax Calculator Application

Recall that your task in this chapter is to create an application that John Blackfeather, the owner and manager of the Perrytown Gift Shop, can use to calculate the weekly federal withholding tax for his employees. On your computer's hard disk is a partially completed Tax Calculator application.

To open the Tax Calculator application:

1   Start Microsoft Visual Studio .NET, if necessary.

2   If necessary, close the Start Page window.

3   Open the **Perrytown Solution** (Perrytown Solution.sln) file, which is contained in the VBNET\Chap10\ Perrytown Solution folder.

4   Auto-hide the Toolbox, Solution Explorer, and Properties windows, if necessary. Figure 10-37 shows the user interface for the Tax Calculator application.

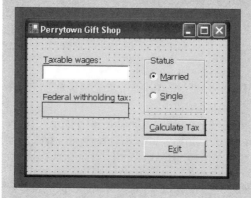

Figure 10-37: Interface for the Tax Calculator application

To calculate the federal withholding tax, the user needs simply to enter the taxable wages in the Taxable wages text box and then click the Calculate Tax button. The Tax Calculator application will use the tax tables shown in Figure 10-38 to calculate the appropriate federal withholding tax (FWT). Notice that the tax amount is based on an employee's taxable wages and his or her marital status.

FWT Tables – Weekly Payroll Period

Single person (including head of household)

If the taxable wages are:	The amount of income tax to withhold is			
Over	But not over	Base amount	Percentage	Of excess over
	$ 51	0		
$ 51	$ 187	0	10%	$ 51
$ 187	$ 592	$ 13.60 plus	15%	$ 187
$ 592	$1,317	$ 74.35 plus	25%	$ 592
$1,317	$2,880	$ 255.60 plus	28%	$1,317
$2,880	$6,177	$ 887.64 plus	33%	$2,860
$6,177		$1,782.25 plus	35%	$6,177

Married person

If the taxable wages are:	The amount of income tax to withhold is			
Over	But not over	Base amount	Percentage	Of excess over
	$ 154	0		
$ 154	$ 429	0	10%	$ 154
$ 429	$1,245	$ 27.50 plus	15%	$ 429
$1,245	$2,270	$ 149.90 plus	25%	$1,245
$2,270	$3,568	$ 406.15 plus	28%	$2,270
$3,568	$6,271	$ 769.59 plus	33%	$3,568
$6,271		$1,661.58 plus	35%	$6,271

Figure 10-38: Weekly FWT tables for 2003

Both tables shown in Figure 10-38 contain five columns of information. The first two columns list various ranges, also called brackets, of taxable wage amounts. The first column—the Over column—lists the amount that a taxable wage in that range must be over, and the second column—the But not over column—lists the maximum amount included in the range. The remaining three columns (Base amount, Percentage, and Of excess over) tell you how to calculate the tax for each range. For example, assume that you are married and your weekly taxable wages are $288.46. Before you can calculate the amount of your tax, you need to locate your taxable wages in the first two columns of the Married table. In this case, your taxable wages fall within the $154 through $429 range. After locating the range that contains your taxable wages, you then use the remaining three columns in the table to calculate your tax. According to the Married table, taxable wages in the $154 through $429 bracket have a tax of 10% of the amount over $154; therefore, your tax is $13.45.

You can use the weekly 2003 tax tables in the Tax Calculator application by simply storing each table in a separate two-dimensional array. To save you time, the application already contains the code to declare and initialize the arrays.

To view the code that declares and initializes the two-dimensional arrays:

1 Open the Code Editor window. Replace the `<enter your name here>` and `<enter the date here>` text with your name and the current date.

The code to declare and initialize the arrays is located in the form's Declarations section, as shown in Figure 10-39. Notice that each array contains seven rows and four columns. The four columns in each array correspond to the "But not over", "Base amount", "Percentage", and "Of excess over" columns in each table.

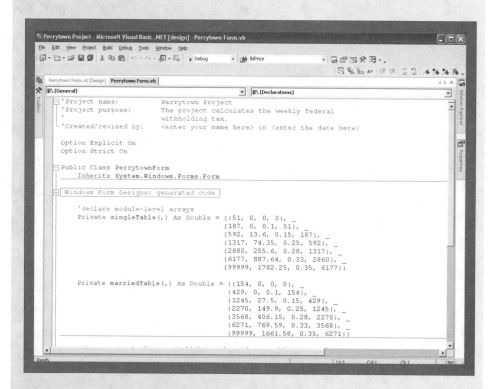

Figure 10-39: Code to declare and initialize the two-dimensional arrays

The last two zeroes in the first row in each array correspond to the empty blocks in the "Percentage" and "Of excess over" columns in the tax tables. The 99999 in the last row in each array represents the empty block in the "But not over" column in the tax tables. You can use any large number to represent the empty block in the "But not over" column, as long as the number is greater than the largest weekly taxable wage you expect the user to enter.

Figure 10-40 shows the TOE chart for the Tax Calculator application.

Task	Object	Event
1. Calculate the federal withholding tax 2. Display the federal withholding tax in the uiFwtLabel	uiCalculateButton	Click
End the application	uiExitButton	Click
Display the federal withholding tax (from uiCalculateButton)	uiFwtLabel	None
Get and display the taxable wages	uiTaxableTextBox	None
Select the existing text		Enter
Clear the contents of the uiFwtLabel		TextChanged
Get the marital status	uiMarriedRadioButton, uiSingleRadioButton	None
Clear the contents of the uiFwtLabel		Click

Figure 10-40: TOE chart for the Tax Calculator application

Almost all of the event procedures listed in Figure 10-40 have already been coded for you. You just need to code the uiCalculateButton's Click event procedure.

Coding the uiCalculateButton Click Event Procedure

According to the TOE chart, the uiCalculateButton's Click event procedure is responsible for calculating the federal withholding tax (FWT) and displaying the calculated amount in the uiFwtLabel control. Figure 10-41 shows the pseudocode for the procedure.

---

uiCalculateButton

1. declare a Double array named taxTable
2. declare two Double variables named taxable and fwt, an Integer variable named row, and a Boolean variable named found

include the following in the Try section of a Try/Catch block:

3. remove any dollar signs and spaces from the uiTaxableTextBox
4. assign the taxable wages stored in the uiTaxableTextBox to a variable
5. if the Single radio button is selected
       assign the module-level singleTable array to the taxTable array
     else
       assign the module-level marriedTable array to the taxTable array
     end if
6. repeat while there are still rows in the tax table to search and the taxable wages have not been found
       if the taxable wages are less than or equal to the value stored in the first column of the current row in the tax table
         use the information stored in the second, third, and fourth columns in the tax table to calculate the federal withholding tax

         indicate that the taxable wages were found by assigning the value True to the found variable
       else
         add 1 to the contents of the row variable to continue the search in the next row in the tax table
       end if
     end repeat
7. display the federal withholding tax in the uiFwtLabel
8. send the focus to the uiTaxableTextBox

include the following in the Catch section of a Try/Catch block:

1. use a general Catch statement to handle any errors
     if an error occurs, display a description of the error in a message box

---

Figure 10-41: Pseudocode for the uiCalculateButton's Click event procedure

---

To code the uiCalculateButton's Click event procedure:

1   Open the code template for the uiCalculateButton's Click event procedure. Type '**calculates the FWT** and press **Enter** twice.

The first step in the pseudocode is to declare an array and four variables.

2   Type the following five Dim statements, and then press **Enter** twice.

```
dim taxTable(5, 3) as double
dim taxable as double
dim fwt as double
dim row as integer
dim found as boolean
```

Next, begin entering a Try/Catch block.

3   Type **try** and press **Enter**.

Now remove any dollar signs and spaces from the uiTaxableTextBox control.

4   In the Try section of the Try/Catch block, type '**remove any dollar signs and spaces from the taxable wages** and press **Enter**.

5   Type **me.uitaxabletextbox.text = me.uitaxabletextbox.text.replace("$", "")** and press **Enter**.

6 Type **me.uitaxabletextbox.text = me.uitaxabletextbox.text.replace(" ", "")** and press **Enter**.

Now assign the taxable wages to the `taxable` variable.

7 Type '**assign taxable wages to a variable** and press **Enter**, then type **taxable = double.parse(me.uitaxabletextbox.text)** and press **Enter** twice.

Now determine whether the tax should be calculated using the information stored in the `singleTable` or `marriedTable` array.

8 Type the comment and selection structure shown in Figure 10-42, then position the insertion point as shown in the figure.

enter this comment and
selection structure

position the insertion
point here

```vbnet
uiCalculateButton                                    Click

    Private Sub uiCalculateButton_Click(ByVal sender As Object, ByVal e As System.EventArgs)
        'calculates the FWT

        Dim taxTable(5, 3) As Double
        Dim taxable As Double
        Dim fwt As Double
        Dim row As Integer
        Dim found As Boolean

        Try
            'remove any dollar signs and spaces from the taxable wages
            Me.uiTaxableTextBox.Text = Me.uiTaxableTextBox.Text.Replace("$", "")
            Me.uiTaxableTextBox.Text = Me.uiTaxableTextBox.Text.Replace(" ", "")
            'assign taxable wages to a variable
            taxable = Double.Parse(Me.uiTaxableTextBox.Text)

            'determine appropriate array
            If Me.uiSingleRadioButton.Checked Then
                taxTable = singleTable
            Else
                taxTable = marriedTable
            End If


        Catch ex As Exception

        End Try
    End Sub
```

Figure 10-42: Comment and selection structure entered in the procedure

Now begin a loop that repeats its instructions while the `row` variable contains a value that is less than six (which indicates that there are more array elements to search) and, at the same time, the `found` variable contains the value False (which indicates that the appropriate wage bracket has not yet been located).

9 Type '**search for the taxable wages in the first column in the array** and press **Enter**. Type **do while row < 6 andalso not found** and press **Enter**.

If the taxable wages are less than or equal to the value stored in the first column in the current row in the `taxTable` array, then use the information stored in the array's second, third, and fourth columns to calculate the federal withholding tax. Also, assign the value True to the `found` variable to indicate that the appropriate wage bracket was located.

10 Type the comment and additional lines of code indicated in Figure 10-43, then position the insertion point as shown in the figure.

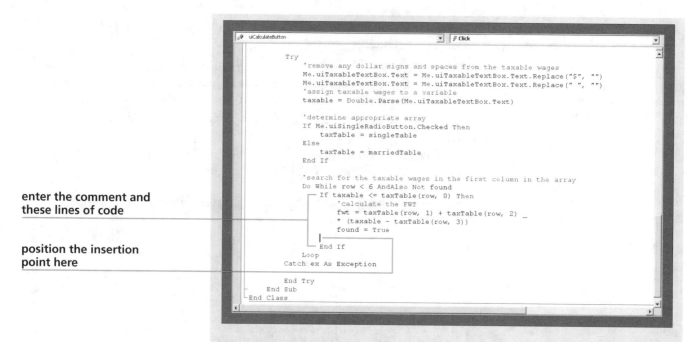

Figure 10-43: Additional code entered in the procedure

enter the comment and these lines of code

position the insertion point here

If the correct wage bracket was not found in the current row in the `taxTable` array, then the procedure should search the next row in the array. To do so, you need to add the number one to the contents of the `row` variable.

11 Type **else** and press **Enter**, then type **row = row + 1**.

Finally, display the federal withholding tax in the uiFwtLabel control, and also send the focus to the uiTaxableTextBox control. Additionally, complete the Catch section of the Try/Catch block.

12 Type the additional code shaded in Figure 10-44, which shows the completed uiCalculateButton's Click event procedure.

```
Private Sub uiCalculateButton_Click(ByVal sender As Object, ByVal e As System.EventArgs)
Handles uiCalculateButton.Click
        'calculates the FWT

        Dim taxTable(5, 3) As Double
        Dim taxable As Double
        Dim fwt As Double
        Dim row As Integer
        Dim found As Boolean

        Try
            'remove any dollar signs and spaces from the taxable wages
            Me.uiTaxableTextBox.Text = Me.uiTaxableTextBox.Text.Replace("$", "")
            Me.uiTaxableTextBox.Text = Me.uiTaxableTextBox.Text.Replace(" ", "")
            'assign taxable wages to a variable
            taxable = Double.Parse(Me.uiTaxableTextBox.Text)

            'determine appropriate array
            If Me.uiSingleRadioButton.Checked Then
                taxTable = singleTable
```

Figure 10-44: Completed uiCalculateButton's Click event procedure

```
        Else
            taxTable = marriedTable
        End If

        'search for the taxable wages in the first column in the array
        Do While row < 6 AndAlso Not found
            If taxable <= taxTable(row, 0) Then
                'calculate the FWT
                fwt = taxTable(row, 1) + taxTable(row, 2) _
                * (taxable - taxTable(row, 3))
                found = True
            Else
                row = row + 1
            End If
        Loop

        'display the FWT
        Me.uiFwtLabel.Text = fwt.ToString("C2")

        'set the focus
        Me.uiTaxableTextBox.Focus()

    Catch ex As Exception
        MessageBox.Show(ex.Message, "Perrytown Gift Shop", _
            MessageBoxButtons.OK, MessageBoxIcon.Information)
    End Try
End Sub
```

Figure 10-44: Completed uiCalculateButton's Click event procedure (continued)

Now test the uiCalculateButton's Click event procedure to verify that it is working correctly.

To test the uiCalculateButton's Click event procedure:

1 Save the solution, then start the application.

First, calculate the FWT for a married taxpayer with taxable wages of $288.46.

2 Type **288.46** in the Taxable wages text box, then click the **Calculate Tax** button. The application calculates and displays a tax of $13.45, as shown in Figure 10-45.

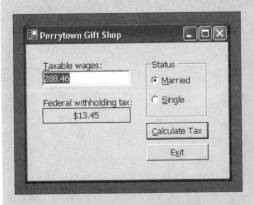

Figure 10-45: FWT displayed in the interface

Now calculate the FWT for a single taxpayer with taxable wages of $600.

3   Type **600** in the Taxable wages text box, then click the **Single** radio button. Press **Enter** to select the Calculate Tax button, which is the default button in the interface. The application calculates and displays a tax of $76.35.

4   Click the **Exit** button to end the application. When you return to the Code Editor window, close the Output window, then close the Code Editor window.

5   Click **File** on the menu bar, and then click **Close Solution**.

You now have completed Chapter 10. You can either take a break or complete the end-of lesson questions and exercises.

SUMMARY

To declare a two-dimensional array:

■   Use either of the following two syntax versions:
Version 1: {**Dim** | **Private**} *arrayname*(*highestRowSubscript*, *highestColumnSubscript*) **As** *datatype*
Version 2: {**Dim** | **Private**} *arrayname*(,) **As** *datatype* = {{*initialValues*}, {*initialValues*}, ...{*initialValues*}}

■   *Arrayname* is the name of the array, and *datatype* is the type of data the array variables will store.

■   The *highestRowSubscript* and *highestColumnSubscript* arguments, which appear in Version 1 of the syntax, are integers that specify the highest row and column subscripts, respectively, in the array. Using Version 1's syntax, the computer automatically initializes the elements (variables) in the array.

■   The *initialValues* section in Version 2 of the syntax allows you to specify the initial values for the array. You include a separate *initialValues* section for each row in the array. Each *initialValues* section should contain the same number of values as there are columns in the array.

To refer to a variable included in a two-dimensional array:

■   Use the syntax *arrayname*(*rowSubscript*, *columnSubscript*).

QUESTIONS

1.   The individual elements in a two-dimensional array are identified by a unique _____.

   a.   combination of two subscripts
   b.   data type
   c.   order
   d.   subscript
   e.   Both a and b.

2. Which of the following statements creates a two-dimensional Single array named `temps` that contains three rows and four columns?
   a. `Dim temps(2, 3) As Single`
   b. `Dim temps(3, 4) As Single`
   c. `Dim temps(3, 2) As Single`
   d. `Dim temps(4, 3) As Single`
   e. `Dim temps(3)(4) As Single`

Use the sales array to answer Questions 3 through 6. The array was declared with the following statement:

```
Dim sales(,) As Decimal = {{1000, 1200, 900, 500, 20000}, _
                           {350, 600, 700, 800, 100}}
```

3. The statement `sales(1, 3) = sales(1, 3) + 10` will _____.
   a. replace the 900 amount with 910
   b. replace the 500 amount with 510
   c. replace the 700 amount with 710
   d. replace the 800 amount with 810
   e. result in an error

4. The statement `sales(0, 4) = sales(0, 4 - 2)` will _____.
   a. have no effect on the array
   b. replace the 20000 amount with 900
   c. replace the 20000 amount with 19998
   d. replace the 20000 amount with 19100
   e. result in an error

5. The statement `sum = sales(0, 3) + sales(1, 3)` will _____.
   a. assign 1300 to the `sum` variable
   b. assign 1600 to the `sum` variable
   c. assign `sales(0, 3) + sales(1, 3)` to the `sum` variable
   d. assign 0 to the `sum` variable
   e. result in an error

6. Which of the following If clauses can be used to verify that the array subscripts named `row` and `column` are valid for the `sales` array?
   a. `If sales(row, column) >= 0 AndAlso sales(row, column) < 5 Then`
   b. `If sales(row, column) >= 0 AndAlso sales(row, column) <= 5 Then`
   c. `If row >= 0 AndAlso row < 3 AndAlso column >= 0 AndAlso column < 6 Then`
   d. `If row >= 0 AndAlso row < 2 AndAlso column >= 0 AndAlso column < 5 Then`
   e. None of the above.

7. Which of the following statements assigns the string "California" to the variable located in the third column, fifth row of a two-dimensional array named `states`?
   a. `states(3, 5) = "California"`
   b. `states(5, 3) = "California"`
   c. `states(2, 4) = "California"`
   d. `states(4, 2) = "California"`
   e. None of the above.

8. Which of the following assigns the number zero to each element in a two-dimensional Integer array named sums? The sums array contains two rows and four columns. You can assume that the row and column variables were declared using the statement Dim row, column As Integer. You also can assume that the element variable was declared using the statement Dim element As Integer.

```
a. For row = 0 To 1
        For column = 0 To 3
                sums(row, column) = 0
        Next column
   Next row
b. Do While row < 2
        column = 0
        Do While column < 4
                sums(row, column) = 0
                column = column + 1
        Loop
        row = row + 1
   Loop
c. For Each element In sums
        element = 0
   Next element
```

d. All of the above.

e. None of the above.

E X E R C I S E S

1. Write the statement to declare a procedure-level two-dimensional Decimal array named balances. The array should have four rows and six columns.

2. Write a loop that stores the number 10 in the balances array declared in Exercise 1. Use the For...Next statement.

3. Rewrite the loop from Exercise 2 using a Do...Loop statement.

4. Write the statement to assign the Boolean value True to the variable located in the third row, first column of a Boolean array named answers.

5. In this exercise, you code an application that sums the values contained in a two-dimensional array.

   a. If necessary, start Visual Studio .NET. Open the Inventory Solution (Inventory Solution.sln) file, which is contained in the VBNET\Chap10\Inventory Solution folder. If necessary, open the designer window.

   b. Code the Display Total button's Click event procedure so that it adds together the values stored in the inventory array. Display the sum in the uiTotalLabel control.

   c. Save the solution, and then start the application. Click the Display Total button to display the sum of the array values.

   d. Click the Exit button to end the application.

   e. Close the Output window, and then close the solution.

6. In this exercise, you code an application that sums the values stored in a two-dimensional array.

   a. If necessary, start Visual Studio .NET. Open the Conway Solution (Conway Solution.sln) file, which is contained in the VBNET\Chap10\Conway Solution folder. If necessary, open the designer window.

   b. Code the Display Totals button's Click event procedure so that it displays the total domestic sales, total international sales, and total company sales in the appropriate label controls.

   c. Save the solution, and then start the application. Click the Display Totals button. The button's Click event procedure should display domestic sales of $235,000, international sales of $177,000, and company sales of $412,000.

   d. Click the Exit button to end the application.

   e. Close the Output window, and then close the solution.

7. In this exercise, you code an application that displays the number of times a value appears in a two-dimensional array.

   a. If necessary, start Visual Studio .NET. Open the Count Solution (Count Solution.sln) file, which is contained in the VBNET\Chap10\Count Solution folder. If necessary, open the designer window.

   b. Code the Display Count button's Click event procedure so that it displays the number of times each of the numbers from one through nine appears in the numbers array. (*Hint*: Store the counts in a one-dimensional array.)

   c. Save the solution, and then start the application. Click the Display Count button to display the nine counts.

   d. Click the Exit button to end the application.

   e. Close the Output window, and then close the solution.

8. In this exercise, you code an application that displays the highest score earned on the midterm exam and the highest score earned on the final exam.

   a. If necessary, start Visual Studio .NET. Open the Highest Solution (Highest Solution.sln) file, which is contained in the VBNET\Chap10\Highest Solution folder. If necessary, open the designer window.

   b. Code the Display Highest button's Click event procedure so that it displays (in the appropriate label controls) the highest score earned on the midterm exam and the highest score earned on the final exam.

   c. Save the solution, and then start the application. Click the Display Highest button to display the highest scores earned on the midterm and final exams.

   d. Click the Exit button to end the application.

   e. Close the Output window, and then close the solution.

discovery ▶ 9. In this exercise, you code an application that sorts the contents of a two-dimensional array.

   a. If necessary, start Visual Studio .NET. Open the Names Solution (Names Solution.sln) file, which is contained in the VBNET\Chap10\Names Solution folder. If necessary, open the designer window.

   b. Code the Sort button's Click event procedure so that it sorts the contents of the two-dimensional `unsorted` array. The procedure should store the sorted values in a one-dimensional array named `sorted`.

   c. Code the Print button's Click event procedure so that it prints the contents of the `sorted` array on the printer.

   d. Save the solution, and then start the application. Click the Sort button, then click the Print button.

   e. Click the Exit button to end the application.

   f. Close the Output window, and then close the solution.

discovery ▶ **10.** In this exercise, you modify the Tax Calculator application that you coded in Lesson C. The modified application passes the appropriate array to a function.

    a. Use Windows to make a copy of the Perrytown Solution folder, which is contained in the VBNET\Chap10 folder. Change the name of the folder to Modified Perrytown Solution.

    b. If necessary, start Visual Studio .NET. Open the Perrytown Solution (Perrytown Solution.sln) file, which is contained in the VBNET\Chap10\Modified Perrytown Solution folder. Open the designer window.

    c. Open the Code Editor window. Remove any reference to the `taxTable` array from the uiCalculateButton's Click event procedure. Modify the selection structure so that it passes the taxable wages and the appropriate array—either `singleTable` or `marriedTable`—to a user-defined function named CalcFwt.

    d. Create a user-defined function named CalcFwt. The function will need to accept the taxable wages and the array passed to it. Move the code that calculates the federal withholding tax from the uiCalculateButton's Click event procedure to the CalcFwt function.

    e. Save the solution, then start the application. Use the application to display the tax for a married employee with taxable wages of $288.46. The application should display $13.45 as the tax. Now use the application to display the tax for a single employee with taxable wages of $600. The application should display $76.35 as the tax.

    f. Click the Exit button to end the application.

    g. Close the Output window, and then close the solution.

debugging ▶ **11.** In this exercise, you debug an existing application.

    a. If necessary, start Visual Studio .NET. Open the Debug Solution (Debug Solution.sln) file, which is contained in the VBNET\Chap10\Debug Solution folder. If necessary, open the designer window.

    b. View the application's code. The `names` array contains five rows and two columns. Column one contains five first names, and column two contains five last names. The uiDisplayButton's Click event procedure should display the first and last names in the uiFirstListBox and uiLastListBox controls, respectively.

    c. Notice that a jagged line appears below some of the lines of code in the Code Editor window. Correct the code to remove the jagged lines.

    d. Save the solution, then start the application. If an error message appears in a dialog box, click the Break button. Click Debug, then click Stop Debugging.

    e. Correct the errors in the application's code, then save the solution and start the application. Click the Display button to display the first and last names in the uiFirstListBox and uiLastListBox controls, respectively.

    f. Click the Exit button to end the application.

    g. Close the Output window, then close the solution.

Classes and Objects

Creating the Cornwall Calendars Application

case ▶ Jesse Washington, the manager of the Accounts Payable department at Cornwall Calendars, wants an application that he can use to keep track of the checks written by his department. More specifically, he wants to record (in a sequential access file) the check number, date, payee, and amount of each check.

Previewing the Cornwall Calendars Application

Before creating the Cornwall Calendars application, you first preview the completed application.

To preview the completed application:

1 Use the Run command on the Windows Start menu to run the **Cornwall** (Cornwall.exe) file, which is contained in the VBNET\Chap11 folder on your computer's hard disk. The Cornwall Calendars application's user interface appears on the screen, as shown in Figure 11-1.

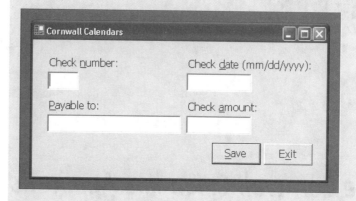

Figure 11-1: User interface for the Cornwall Calendars application

First, enter the information for check number 1001.

2 Type **1001** in the Check number text box, then press **Tab**.

3 Type **10/09/2006** in the Check date text box, then press **Tab**.

4 Type **North Central Electric** in the Payable to text box, then press **Tab**.

5 Type **56.89** in the Check amount text box, then click the **Save** button. The application writes the check information to a sequential access file.

6 Click the **Exit** button to end the application.

7 Start a text editor, such as Notepad. Open the checks.txt file, which is contained in the VBNET\Chap11 folder on your computer's hard disk. Figure 11-2 shows the contents of the checks.txt file.

check information written to the file

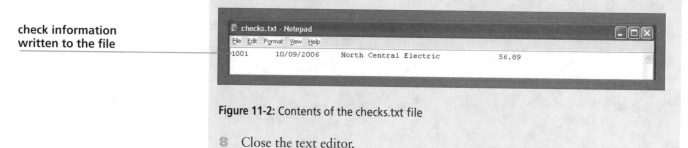

Figure 11-2: Contents of the checks.txt file

8 Close the text editor.

In this chapter, you learn how to create a class and then instantiate objects from the class. You use a class to code the Cornwall Calendars application in Lesson C.

LESSON A

objectives

After completing this lesson, you will be able to:

- Define a class
- Add properties to a class
- Instantiate an object from a class that you define

Classes and Objects

As you learned in the Overview, object-oriented programs are based on objects, which are created, or instantiated, from classes. A text box, for example, is created from the TextBox class. Similarly, buttons and label controls are created from the Button class and Label class, respectively.

Recall that a class contains (encapsulates) the properties (attributes) that describe the object it creates, and the methods (behaviors) that allow the object to perform tasks. The TextBox class, for instance, contains the Name, CharacterCasing, and Text properties. Examples of methods contained in the TextBox class include Focus (which allows a text box to send the focus to itself) and SelectAll (which allows a text box to select its existing text).

In previous chapters, you created objects using classes that are built into Visual Basic .NET, such as the TextBox and Label classes. The objects created from the classes were used in a variety of ways in many different applications. For example, in some applications a text box was used to enter a name, while in other applications it was used to enter a sales tax rate. Similarly, label controls were used to identify text boxes and also display the result of calculations. The ability to use an object for more than one purpose saves programming time and money—an advantage that contributes to the popularity of object-oriented programming.

In addition to using the Visual Basic .NET classes, you also can define your own classes, and then create objects from the classes. The classes that you define can represent something encountered in real life—such as a credit card receipt, a check, and an employee.

Defining a Class

Like the Visual Basic .NET classes, your classes must specify the properties and methods of the objects they create. The properties describe the characteristics of the objects, and the methods specify the tasks that the objects can perform.

You use the **Class statement** to define a class in Visual Basic .NET. Figure 11-3 shows the syntax of the Class statement and includes an example of using the statement to create a class named TimeCard.

tip

Recall from Chapter 1 that each tool in the toolbox represents a class. When you drag a tool from the toolbox to the form, Visual Basic .NET uses the class to instantiate the appropriate object.

tip

Although you can code a class in just a matter of minutes, the objects produced by such a class probably will not be of much use. The creation of a good class—one whose objects can be used in a variety of ways by many different applications—requires a lot of time, patience, and planning.

Syntax

Public Class *classname*
    properties section
    methods section
End Class

Example

```
Public Class TimeCard
```
    variables and Property procedures appear in the properties section

    Sub and Function procedures appear in the methods section
```
End Class
```

Figure 11-3: Syntax and an example of the Class statement

The Class statement begins with the keywords `Public Class`, followed by the name of the class; it ends with the keywords `End Class`. Although it is not required by the syntax, the convention is to capitalize the first letter in a class name, as well as the first letter in any subsequent words in the name. The names of Visual Basic .NET classes—such as String and TextBox—also follow this naming convention.

Within the Class statement, you define the properties and methods of the class. The properties are represented by variables and Property procedures, and the methods are represented by Sub and Function procedures. You learn various ways of defining the properties and methods later in this chapter.

You enter the Class statement in a class file. Figure 11-4 shows how to add a class file to a project, and Figure 11-5 shows an example of a completed Add New Item – *projectname* dialog box.

Adding a class file to a project

1. Click Project on the menu bar.
2. Click Add Class. The Add New Item – *projectname* dialog box opens with Class selected in the Templates list box.
3. Type the name of the class followed by a period and the letters vb in the Name box.
4. Click the Open button.

Figure 11-4: Procedure for adding a class file to a project

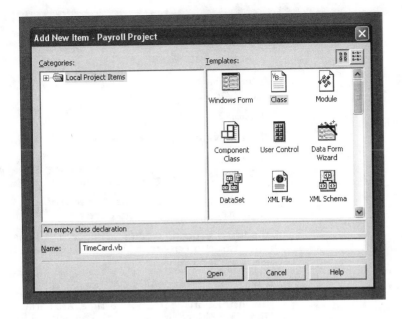

Figure 11-5: Completed Add New Item – *projectname* dialog box

When you click the Open button in the Add New Item – Payroll Project dialog box shown in Figure 11-5, the computer adds a file named TimeCard.vb to the current project. It also opens the file in the Code Editor window, as shown in Figure 11-6.

form file

class file

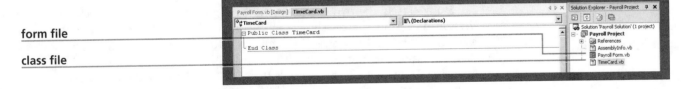

Figure 11-6: TimeCard.vb file opened in the Code Editor window

As you learned in Chapter 1, the .vb on a filename indicates that the file is a "Visual Basic" source file. Recall that a source file is a file that contains program instructions.

Notice that Visual Basic .NET automatically enters the Class statement in the TimeCard.vb file. You complete the Class statement by entering the properties and methods of the class. (Recall that you learn how to enter the properties and methods later in this chapter.)

After you define a class, you then can use the class to create objects. Figure 11-7 shows two versions of the syntax you use to create objects from a class. It also includes an example of using each syntax.

Syntax
Version 1
{**Dim** | **Private**} *objectVariable* **As** *class* *objectVariable* = **New** *class*
Version 2
{**Dim** | **Private**} *objectVariable* **As New** *class*

Examples
```Private empTimeCard As TimeCard``` ```empTimeCard = New TimeCard```
the first instruction creates a TimeCard variable named `empTimeCard`; the second instruction creates a TimeCard object and assigns its address to the `empTimeCard` variable
```Dim empTimeCard As New TimeCard```
the instruction creates both a TimeCard variable named `empTimeCard` and a TimeCard object, and assigns the object's address to the variable

Figure 11-7: Syntax and examples of creating an object from a class

In both versions of the syntax for creating an object, *class* is the name of the class the computer will use to create the object, and *objectVariable* is the name of a variable that will store the object's address.

Study closely the two examples shown in Figure 11-7. The first example uses Version 1 of the syntax shown in the figure. In the example, the `Private empTimeCard As TimeCard` statement creates a variable named `empTimeCard` that can store the address of a TimeCard object. The `empTimeCard = New TimeCard` statement in the example then creates a TimeCard object and assigns its address to the `empTimeCard` variable.

The second example shown in Figure 11-7 uses Version 2 of the syntax. In the example, the `Dim empTimeCard As New TimeCard` statement creates both a variable named `empTimeCard` and a TimeCard object, and it assigns the object's address to the variable. Notice that the difference between both versions of the syntax used to create an object relates to when the object is actually created. In Visual Basic .NET, the statement that contains the `New` keyword creates the object.

The easiest way to learn how to define classes and create objects is to view a few examples. In this lesson, you view a simple example that uses a class containing properties only. You will view additional examples in Lessons B and C.

Using a Class That Contains Properties Only

In Chapter 10, you learned that you can use the Structure statement to group together related data; you also can use the Class statement. For example, assume that the sales manager at Sweets Unlimited wants an application that allows him to save each salesperson's name, quarterly sales amount, and quarterly bonus amount in a sequential access file. The bonus amount is calculated by multiplying the sales amount by 5%. Figure 11-8 shows a sample run of the Sweets Unlimited application, and Figure 11-9 shows the Salesperson class defined in the Salesperson.vb file.

Notice that the Salesperson.vb file contains the `Option Explicit On` and `Option Strict On` statements. As is true when coding a form, it's a good programming practice to enter both statements when coding a class.

Figure 11-8: Sample run of the Sweets Unlimited application

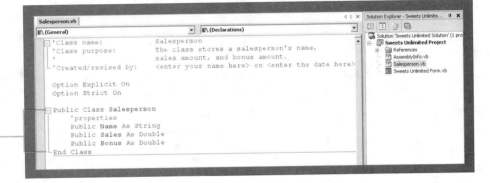

defines the Salesperson class

Figure 11-9: Salesperson class defined in the Salesperson.vb file

tip

The `Option Explicit On` and `Option Strict On` statements have the same meaning in a class file as they do in a form file.

The Salesperson class contains three properties; each property is represented by a variable. Notice that the property names (Name, Sales, and Bonus) do not begin with a lowercase letter. This is because the rules for naming properties differ slightly from the rules for naming variables. Properties should be assigned a name composed of one or more words, with the first letter of each word being capitalized. You should use nouns and adjectives to name a property, as in Bonus, TotalIncome, and FirstQuarterEarnings.

Notice that each property declaration in the Salesperson class begins with the keyword `Public`. When a property is declared using the `Public` keyword, it can be accessed by any application that uses an object created from the class. Figure 11-10 shows how you use the Salesperson class to code the Sweets Unlimited application.

```
'Project name:          Sweets Unlimited Project
'Project purpose:       The project writes the salesperson's name,
'                       quarterly sales amount, and a 5% quarterly bonus
'                       amount to a sequential access file.
'Created/revised by:    <enter your name here> on <enter the date here>

Option Explicit On
Option Strict On

Public Class SweetsForm
    Inherits System.Windows.Forms.Form

[Windows Form Designer generated code]

    Private Sub uiSaveButton_Click(ByVal sender As Object, ByVal e As System.EventArgs) _
        Handles uiSaveButton.Click
        'saves the sales information to a sequential access file

        'declare variables
        Dim sweetsSalesperson As New Salesperson
        Dim saveStreamWriter As IO.StreamWriter

        Try
            'assign values to properties
            sweetsSalesperson.Name = Me.uiNameTextBox.Text
            sweetsSalesperson.Sales = Decimal.Parse(Me.uiSalesTextBox.Text)
            sweetsSalesperson.Bonus = sweetsSalesperson.Sales * 0.05

            'open the file for append
            saveStreamWriter = IO.File.AppendText("sales.txt")

            'write the sales information
            saveStreamWriter.WriteLine(sweetsSalesperson.Name _
                & "#" & sweetsSalesperson.Sales.ToString("F2") & "#" _
                & sweetsSalesperson.Bonus.ToString("F2"))

            'inform user that the record was written
            MessageBox.Show("The record was written.", _
                "Sweets Unlimited", MessageBoxButtons.OK, _
                MessageBoxIcon.Information)

            'clear the text boxes
            'then send the focus to the Name text box
            Me.uiNameTextBox.Text = ""
            Me.uiSalesTextBox.Text = ""
            Me.uiNameTextBox.Focus()
```

writes the contents of the object's properties to a sequential access file

assigns values to the object's properties

creates a Salesperson object and assigns its address to the sweetsSalesperson **variable**

Figure 11-10: Code for the Sweets Unlimited application

```
            'close the file
            saveStreamWriter.Close()

    Catch exFormat As FormatException
        MessageBox.Show("The sales amount must be numeric.", _
            "Sweets Unlimited", MessageBoxButtons.OK, _
            MessageBoxIcon.Information)
    Catch ex As Exception
        MessageBox.Show(ex.Message, "Sweets Unlimited", _
            MessageBoxButtons.OK, MessageBoxIcon.Information)
    End Try
End Sub

Private Sub uiExitButton_Click(ByVal sender As Object, ByVal e As System.EventArgs) _
    Handles uiExitButton.Click
    'ends the application
    Me.Close()
End Sub
End Class
```

Figure 11-10: Code for the Sweets Unlimited application (continued)

When you type sweetsSalesperson. in the Code Editor window, the properties of a Salesperson object appear in a list. You then can select the appropriate property from the list.

In the uiSaveButton's Click event procedure shown in Figure 11-10, the Dim sweetsSalesperson As New Salesperson statement uses the Salesperson class to create a Salesperson object; the statement assigns the object's address to the sweetsSalesperson variable. After the object is created and its address assigned to a variable, you can access its properties using the syntax *objectVariable.property*, where *objectVariable* is the name of the variable that stores the object's address, and *property* is the name of the property you want to access. For example, you use sweetsSalesperson.Name to access the Name property of the Salesperson object created in Figure 11-10. Likewise, you use sweetsSalesperson.Sales and sweetsSalesperson.Bonus to access the Sales and Bonus properties, respectively.

Notice that the uiSaveButton's Click event procedure shown in Figure 11-10 uses three assignment statements to assign values to the properties of the Salesperson object. The sweetsSalesperson.Name = Me.uiNameTextBox.Text statement assigns the contents of the uiNameTextBox control to the object's Name property. Similarly, the sweetsSalesperson.Sales = Decimal.Parse(Me.uiSalesTextBox.Text) statement assigns the contents of the uiSalesTextBox control, converted to Decimal, to the Sales property. Finally, the sweetsSalesperson.Bonus = sweetsSalesperson.Sales * 0.05 statement multiplies the contents of the Sales property by 5%, and then stores the result in the Bonus property. The procedure uses the WriteLine method to write the contents of the Name, Sales, and Bonus properties to a sequential access file named sales.txt.

You now have completed Lesson A. You can either take a break or complete the end-of-lesson questions and exercises before moving on to the next lesson. You learn more about classes and objects in Lessons B and C. In Lesson C, you code the Cornwall Calendars application that you previewed at the beginning of the chapter.

SUMMARY

To create a class:

- Use the syntax shown in Figure 11-3.

To add a class file to a project:

- Click Project on the menu bar, and then click Add Class. In the Add New Item – *projectname* dialog box, type the name of the class followed by .vb in the Name box, then click the Open button.

To create (instantiate) an object from a class:

- Use either of the following syntax versions:
- Version 1:
  {**Dim** | **Private**} *objectVariable* **As** *class*
  objectVariable = **New** *class*
  Version 2:
  {**Dim** | **Private**} *objectVariable* **As New** *class*

To access the properties of an object:

- Use the syntax *objectVariable.property*, where *objectVariable* is the name of the variable that stores the object's address, and *property* is the name of the property you want to access.

QUESTIONS

1. Which of the following statements is false?
   a. An example of an attribute is the Minutes property in a Time class.
   b. An example of a behavior is the SetTime method in a Time class.
   c. An object created from a class is referred to as an instance of the class.
   d. A class is considered an object.
   e. You can use a class to create procedure-level and module-level objects.

2. In Visual Basic .NET, you enter the Class statement in _____.
   a. a class file that has a .vb extension on its filename
   b. a class file that has a .cls extension on its filename
   c. a form file that has a .cla extension on its filename
   d. a form file that has a .cls extension on its filename
   e. a form file that has a .frm extension on its filename

3. The properties of an object are represented by _____ in a class.
   a. constants
   b. functions
   c. methods
   d. procedures
   e. variables

4. The name of an object's property should begin with a lowercase letter.
   a. True
   b. False

5. Which of the following declares a Pet object named `myDog`?
   a. `Dim myDog As Pet`
   b. `Dim myDog As New Pet`
   c. `Dim myDog As New Pet()`
   d. `Dim Pet As myDog`
   e. `Dim Pet As New myDog`

6. The `Option Explicit On` and `Option Strict On` statements can be entered in a form file only; they cannot be entered in a class file.
   a. True
   b. False

EXERCISES

1. Write a Class statement that defines a class named Book. The class contains three Public properties named Title, Author, and Cost.

2. Write a Class statement that defines a class named Tape. The class contains four Public properties named Name, Artist, SongNumber, and TapeLength.

3. Use the syntax shown in Version 1 in Figure 11-7 to declare a variable named `fiction` that can store the address of a Book object. Create the Book object and assign its address to the `fiction` variable.

4. Use the syntax shown in Version 2 in Figure 11-7 to declare a Tape object and assign its address to a variable named `blues`.

5. In this exercise, you create an application that uses a class.
   a. If necessary, start Visual Studio .NET. Create the Sweets Unlimited interface shown in Figure 11-8. Name the solution Sweets Unlimited Solution. Name the project Sweets Unlimited Project. Save the application in the VBNET\Chap11 folder.
   b. Add a class file to the project. Name the class file Salesperson.vb. Use the code shown in Figure 11-9 to define the class.
   c. Use the code shown in Figure 11-10 to code the Sweets Unlimited application.
   d. Save the solution, and then start and test the application.
   e. Click the Exit button to end the application, then close the solution.

After completing this lesson, you will be able to:

- Add Property procedures to a class
- Create constructors
- Add methods to a class

More on Classes and Objects

tip

Recall that "OOP" stands for "object-oriented programming."

Using a Class That Contains Properties and Methods

Although you can define a class that contains properties only—like the Salesperson class shown in Figure 11-9 in Lesson A—that is rarely done. This is because the purpose of a class in OOP is to encapsulate both the properties that describe an object and the methods that allow the object to perform tasks. In this lesson, you learn how to create a class named Square and use the class in the Area application. The Square class, which contains one property and two methods, creates an object that calculates and returns the area of a square, using the side measurement provided by the application. Figure 11-11 shows a sample run of the Area application, and Figure 11-12 shows the Square class defined in the Square.vb file.

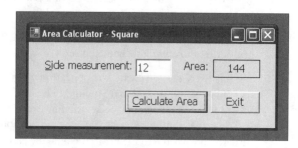

Figure 11-11: Sample run of the Area application

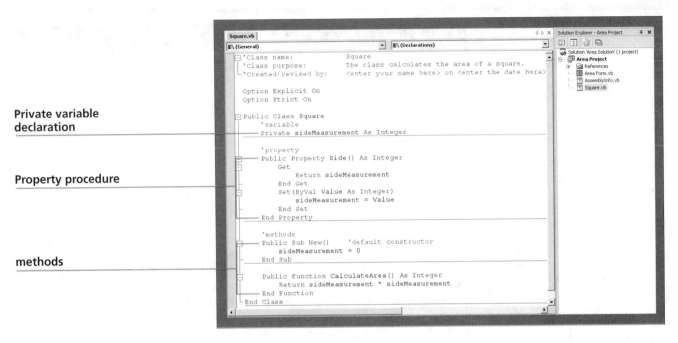

Figure 11-12: Square class defined in the Square.vb file

The Square class contains the `Private sideMeasurement As Integer` statement, which declares a Private variable named `sideMeasurement`. The class will use the `sideMeasurement` variable to store the side measurement of the square whose area is to be calculated. The `Private` keyword indicates that the variable can be used only by the class in which it is defined. In this case, the `sideMeasurement` variable can be used only by the code entered in the Square class.

When you use a class to create an object in an application, only the variables and procedures declared using the `Public` keyword are exposed (made available) to the application; the variables and procedures declared using the `Private` keyword are hidden. When an application needs to assign data to or retrieve data from a Private variable in a class, it must use a Public property to do so. In other words, an application cannot refer, directly, to a Private variable in a class. Rather, it must refer to the variable indirectly, through the use of a Public property. You create a Public property using a **Property procedure**. Figure 11-13 shows the syntax of a Property procedure. The figure also includes the Property procedure entered in the Square class.

Syntax

Public Property *propertyName*() **As** *datatype*
   Get
      [*instructions*]
      instruction to return the contents of the Private variable
   End Get
   Set(ByVal Value As *datatype*)
      [*instructions*]
      instruction to assign, to the Private variable, either the contents of the Value parameter or a default value
   End Set
End Property

Figure 11-13: Syntax and an example of creating a Property procedure

Example

```
Public Property Side() As Integer
    Get
        Return sideMeasurement
    End Get
    Set(ByVal Value As Integer)
        sideMeasurement = Value
    End Set
End Property
```

Figure 11-13: Syntax and an example of creating a Property procedure (continued)

tip

As you learned earlier, properties should be assigned a name composed of one or more words, with the first letter of each word being capitalized. You should use nouns and adjectives to name a property.

A Property procedure begins with the keywords `Public Property`, followed by the name of the property, a set of parentheses, the keyword `As`, and the property's *datatype*. The data type of the property must match the data type of the Private variable associated with the Property procedure. A Public Property procedure creates a property that is visible to any application that creates an object from the class.

A Property procedure ends with the keywords `End Property`. Within the Property procedure you define a Get block of code and a Set block of code. The code contained in the **Get block** allows an application to retrieve the contents of the Private variable associated with the property. The code in the **Set block**, on the other hand, allows the application to assign a value to the Private variable.

The Get block uses the **Get statement**, which begins with the keyword `Get` and ends with the keywords `End Get`. Most times, you will enter only one instruction in the Get statement. The instruction—typically, **Return** *privateVariable*—directs the computer to return the contents of the Private variable.

The Set block uses the **Set statement**, which begins with the keyword `Set` and ends with the keywords `End Set`. As shown in Figure 11-13, the `Set` keyword is followed by a parameter enclosed in parentheses. The parameter begins with the keywords `ByVal Value As`, followed by a *datatype*, which must match the data type of the Private variable associated with the Property procedure. The Value parameter temporarily stores the value that the application wants assigned to the Private variable.

You can enter one or more instructions within the Set statement. For example, you can enter the code to validate the value received from the application before assigning it to the Private variable. If the value is valid, the last instruction in the Set statement should assign the contents of the Value parameter to the Private variable; you can use the *privateVariable* = `Value` statement to do so. However, if the value received from the application is not valid, the last instruction in the Set statement should assign a default value—for example, the number zero—to the Private variable.

In the example shown in Figure 11-13, the property's name is Side, and its data type is Integer to agree with the Private variable, named `sideMeasurement`, associated with the Property procedure. The Get block in the Side property tells the computer to return the contents of the `sideMeasurement` variable. The Set block, on the other hand, tells the computer to assign the contents of the Value parameter to the `sideMeasurement` variable. An application that uses a Square object uses the Side property to assign values to and retrieve values from the `sideMeasurement` variable.

As shown earlier in Figure 11-12, the Square class also contains two methods named New and CalculateArea. The New method is the default constructor for the class.

Constructors

A **constructor** is a method whose instructions the computer processes, automatically, each time an object is created (instantiated) from the class. The sole purpose of a constructor is to initialize the class's variables. Figure 11-14 shows the syntax of a constructor; it also includes the constructor entered in the Square class.

Syntax
Public Sub New([*parameterlist*]**)** *instructions to initialize the class's variables* **End Sub**
Example

`Public Sub New()`
`     sideMeasurement = 0`
`End Sub`

Figure 11-14: Syntax and an example of creating a constructor

A constructor begins with the keywords `Public Sub New`, followed by a set of parentheses that contains an optional *parameterlist*. A constructor ends with the keywords `End Sub`. Within the constructor you enter the code to initialize the class's variables.

Every class should have at least one constructor. Each constructor included in a class has the same name, New, but its parameters (if any) must be different from any other constructor in the class. If a constructor contains one or more parameters, the values of the parameters are used to initialize the class's variables. A constructor that has no parameters is called the **default constructor**. (In Lesson C, you learn how to create a class that has more than one constructor.)

The Square class contains one constructor, which is shown in the example in Figure 11-14. The constructor is the default constructor because it has no parameters. When you use the Square class to create a Square object, the computer automatically processes the class's default constructor, which, in this case, initializes the `sideMeasurement` variable to the number zero.

A class also can contain methods other than constructors. The Square class, for example, contains a method named CalculateArea.

Methods Other Than Constructors

Except for constructors, which must be Sub procedures, the methods included in a class can be either Sub procedures or Function procedures. As you learned in Chapter 7, the difference between both types of procedures is that a Function procedure returns a value after performing its assigned task, whereas a Sub procedure does not return a value.

Figure 11-15 shows the syntax of a method that is not a constructor. The figure also includes the CalculateArea method entered in the Square class.

Syntax

Public {Sub | Function} *methodname*(**[***parameterlist***]**) **As** *datatype*
    instructions
End {Sub | Function}

Example

```
Public Function CalculateArea() As Integer
    Return sideMeasurement * sideMeasurement
End Function
```

Figure 11-15: Syntax and an example of creating a method that is not a constructor

The {**Sub** | **Function**} in the syntax shown in Figure 11-15 indicates that you can select only one of the keywords appearing within the braces. In this case, you can choose either the keyword `Sub` or the keyword `Function`.

The rules for naming methods are similar to the rules for naming properties. Like property names, method names should be composed of one or more words, with the first letter of each word being capitalized. However, unlike property names, the first word in a method name should be a verb; any subsequent words in the name should be nouns and adjectives. The name CalculateArea follows this naming convention.

The CalculateArea method in the Square class is represented by a Function procedure. The `Return sideMeasurement * sideMeasurement` statement within the procedure uses the contents of the class's Private variable, `sideMeasurement`, to calculate the area of a square. The statement then returns the area to the application that called the procedure.

Figure 11-16 shows how you can use the Square class to code the Area application.

```
'Project name:          Area Project
'Project purpose:       The project calculates the area of a square.
'Created/revised by:    <enter your name here> on <enter the date here>

Option Explicit On
Option Strict On

Public Class AreaForm
    Inherits System.Windows.Forms.Form

[Windows Form Designer generated code]

    Private Sub uiCalcButton_Click(ByVal sender As Object, ByVal e As System.EventArgs) _
        Handles uiCalcButton.Click
        'calculates the area of a square

        'declare variables
        Dim squareObject As New Square
        Dim area As Integer
```

> creates a Square object and assigns its address to the `squareObject` **variable**

Figure 11-16: Code for the Area application

```
        'assign input value to the property
        squareObject.Side = Integer.Parse(Me.uiSideTextBox.Text)

        'call method to calculate and return the area
        area = squareObject.CalculateArea()

        'display the area
        Me.uiAreaLabel.Text = Convert.ToString(area)
    End Sub

    Private Sub uiExitButton_Click(ByVal sender As Object, ByVal e As System.EventArgs) _
        Handles uiExitButton.Click
        'ends the application
        Me.Close()
    End Sub
End Class
```

uses the CalculateArea
method to calculate the area
of the square object

assigns a value to the
Side property

Figure 11-16: Code for the Area application (continued)

The `Dim squareObject As New Square` statement shown in Figure 11-16 tells the computer to create a Square object, and then assign the object's address to a variable named `squareObject`. When creating the Square object, the computer uses the class's default constructor to initialize the Private variable (named `sideMeasurement`) contained in the class.

The `squareObject.Side = Integer.Parse(Me.uiSideTextBox.Text)` statement shown in Figure 11-16 assigns the user's input to the Square object's Side property. The `area = squareObject.CalculateArea()` statement tells the computer to use the Square object's CalculateArea method to calculate and return the area of the object. The statement assigns the result to the `area` variable.

You now have completed Lesson B. You can either take a break or complete the end-of-lesson questions and exercises before moving on to the next lesson. In Lesson C, you learn more about classes and objects, and you also code the Cornwall Calendars application that you previewed at the beginning of the chapter.

S U M M A R Y

To create a Public property:

■ Use a Property procedure. The syntax of a Property procedure is shown in Figure 11-13.

■ The Get block allows an application to retrieve the contents of the Private variable associated with the property.

■ The Set block allows an application to assign a value to the Private variable associated with the property.

To create a constructor:

■ Use the syntax shown in Figure 11-14.

■ A constructor that has no parameters is called the default constructor.

To create a method other than a constructor:

■ Use the syntax shown in Figure 11-15.

QUESTIONS

1. A Private variable in a class can be accessed directly by a Public method in the same class.
   a. True
   b. False

2. If a variable in a class is declared using the `Public` keyword, the variable can be accessed by any application that uses an object created from the class.
   a. True
   b. False

3. An application can access the Private variables in a class _____.
   a. directly
   b. using properties created by Property procedures
   c. through Private procedures contained in the class
   d. using methods created by Property procedures
   e. None of the above.

4. To expose a variable or method contained in class, you declare the variable or method using the keyword _____.
   a. `Exposed`
   b. `Private`
   c. `Public`
   d. `Viewable`
   e. `Viewed`

5. The name of the default constructor for a class named Animal is _____.
   a. Animal
   b. AnimalConstructor
   c. Constructor
   d. DefaultConstructor
   e. None of the above.

6. A constructor can return a value.
   a. True
   b. False

7. A constructor _____.
   a. is a Function procedure
   b. is a Property procedure
   c. is a Sub procedure
   d. can be either a Function procedure or a Sub procedure
   e. None of the above.

8. Which of the following creates an Animal object and assigns the object's address to the dog variable?

   a. `Dim dog As Animal`

   b. `Dim dog As New Animal`

   c. `Dim dog As Animal`
      `dog = New Animal`

   d. Both b and c.

   e. None of the above.

9. Assume an application creates an Animal object and assigns its address to the dog variable. Which of the following calls the DisplayBreed method, which is contained in the Animal class?

   a. `Animal.DisplayBreed()`

   b. `DisplayBreed.Animal()`

   c. `DisplayBreed().dog`

   d. `dog.DisplayBreed()`

   e. None of the above.

10. Most classes contain only properties.

    a. True

    b. False

11. Assume an application creates a Date object and assigns its address to the payDate variable. Also assume that the Date class contains a Month property, which is associated with a String variable named monthNumber. Which of the following assigns the number 12 to the Month property?

    a. `payDate.Month = "12"`

    b. `payDate.Month.monthNumber = "12"`

    c. `payDate.monthNumber = "12"`

    d. `Date.monthNumber = "12"`

    e. None of the above.

12. In a Property procedure, the Return statement is entered in the _____.

    a. Get block

    b. Set block

EXERCISES

1. Assume that an application contains the class definition shown in Figure 11-17.

```
Public Class Computer
     'variables
     Private modelNumber As String
     Private modelCost As Decimal

     'properties
     Public Property Model() As String
          Get
                    Return modelNumber
          End Get
          Set(ByVal Value As String)
                    modelNumber = Value
```

Figure 11-17

```
            End Set
       End Property

    Public Property Cost() As Decimal
         Get
                Return modelCost
         End Get
         Set(ByVal Value As String)
                modelCost = Value
         End Set
    End Property

    'methods
    Public Sub New()
         modelNumber = ""
         modelCost = 0D
    End Sub

    Public Function IncreasePrice() As Decimal
         Return modelCost * 1.2D
    End Function
End Class
```

Figure 11-17 (continued)

a. Write a Dim statement that creates a Computer object and assigns its address to a variable named homeUse.

b. Write an assignment statement that uses the Computer object created in Step a to assign the string "IB-50" to the modelNumber variable.

c. Write an assignment statement that uses the Computer object created in Step a to assign the number 2400 to the modelCost variable.

d. Write an assignment statement that uses the Computer object created in Step a to call the IncreasePrice method. Assign the method's return value to a variable named newPrice.

2. In this exercise, you create an application that uses a class.

a. If necessary, start Visual Studio .NET. Create the Area application's interface, which is shown in Figure 11-11. Name the solution Area Solution. Name the project Area Project. Save the application in the VBNET\Chap11 folder.

b. Add a class file to the project. Name the class file Square.vb. Use the code shown in Figure 11-12 to define the class.

c. Use the code shown in Figure 11-16 to code the Area application.

d. Save the solution, and then start and test the application.

e. Click the Exit button to end the application, then close the solution.

Coding the Cornwall Calendars Application

Using a Class That Contains Two Constructors and Data Validation

Before coding the Cornwall Calendars application, you view an example of a class that contains more than one constructor; it also performs some data validation. The class, named MyDate, creates an object that returns a month number, followed by a slash, and a day number. You then use the class in the Personnel application. Figure 11-18 shows a sample run of the Personnel application, and Figure 11-19 shows the MyDate class defined in the MyDate.vb file.

Figure 11-18: Sample run of the Personnel application

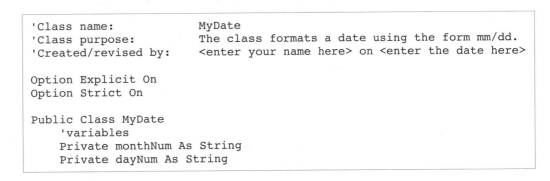

```
'Class name:          MyDate
'Class purpose:       The class formats a date using the form mm/dd.
'Created/revised by:  <enter your name here> on <enter the date here>

Option Explicit On
Option Strict On

Public Class MyDate
    'variables
    Private monthNum As String
    Private dayNum As String
```

Figure 11-19: MyDate class defined in the MyDate.vb file

```
            'properties
            Public Property Month() As String
                Get
                    Return monthNum
                End Get
                Set(ByVal Value As String)
                    'verify that the Value parameter contains
                    'a number from 1 through 12

                    Try
                        'declare variable
                        Dim number As Integer
                        'assign value to variable
                        number = Integer.Parse(Value)
                        'validate month number
                        If number >= 1 AndAlso number <= 12 Then
                            'assign Value to variable
                            monthNum = Value
                        Else  'assign empty string to variable
                            monthNum = ""
                        End If

                        Catch ex As Exception
                            MessageBox.Show("The Month must be numeric.", _
                                "Month", MessageBoxButtons.OK, _
                                MessageBoxIcon.Information)
                    End Try
                End Set
            End Property

            Public Property Day() As String
                Get
                    Return dayNum
                End Get
                Set(ByVal Value As String)
                    dayNum = Value
                End Set
            End Property

            'methods
            Public Sub New()        'default constructor
                monthNum = ""
                dayNum = ""
            End Sub

            Public Sub New(ByVal m As String, ByVal d As String)
                'assign month number to property
                Month = m
                'assign day number to property
                Day = d
            End Sub

            Public Function GetNewDate() As String
                'declare variable
                Dim newDate As String
                'format the date
                newDate = monthNum & "/" & dayNum
                'return the formatted date
                Return newDate
            End Function
        End Class
```

the Set block in the Month Property procedure validates the month number

Figure 11-19: MyDate class defined in the MyDate.vb file (continued)

The MyDate class contains two Private variables named `monthNum` and `dayNum`. It also contains two Property procedures named Month and Day. The Month Property procedure is associated with the `monthNum` variable, and the Day Property procedure is associated with the `dayNum` variable.

Notice that the Set block in the Month Property procedure checks whether the Value parameter contains a number in the range of one through 12. If the month number is within the range, the Set block assigns the contents of the Value parameter to the `monthNum` variable; otherwise, it assigns the empty string to the variable.

In addition to the Private variables and Property procedures, the MyDate class also contains three methods: two named New and one named GetNewDate. Both New methods are constructors. The first constructor is the default constructor, because it does not have any parameters. The computer processes the default constructor when you use a statement such as `Dim payDate As New MyDate` to create a MyDate object. Notice that, in the default constructor shown in Figure 11-19, two assignment statements initialize the two Private variables to the empty string.

The second constructor in the MyDate class allows you to specify the initial values for a newly created MyDate object. In this case, the initial values must be strings, because the constructor's *parameterlist* contains two String variables. You enter the initial values in the statement that creates the object. You enclose the initial values in parentheses because they are arguments. For example, the statement `Dim payDate As New MyDate(numMonth, numDay)` creates a MyDate object and passes two String variables (arguments) to the MyDate class. The computer determines which class constructor to use by matching the number and data type of the arguments with the number and data type of the parameters listed in each constructor's *parameterlist*. In this case, the computer uses the constructor that contains two String variables in its *parameterlist*.

The GetNewDate method in the MyDate class is a Function procedure. Its purpose is to return the month and day numbers, separated by a slash. The month and day numbers are stored in the class's Private variables.

The methods in a class can reference the class's Private variables either directly (by name) or indirectly (through the Public properties). For example, in the MyDate class shown in Figure 11-19, both the default constructor and the GetNewDate method use the names of the Private variables to reference the variables directly. The second New constructor, on the other hand, uses the Public properties to reference the Private variables indirectly. You should always use a Public property to assign a value received from a program, because doing so ensures that the Set block, which typically contains validation code, is processed.

Figure 11-20 shows how you can use the Date class to code the Personnel application.

tip

· · · · · · · · · · · · · · · ·

When two or more methods have the same name but different parameters, the methods are said to be overloaded. You can overload any methods contained in a class. However, if the methods are not constructors, you must use the keyword `Overloads` after the `Public` keyword in the first line of the method. The `Overloads` keyword is not used when overloading constructors.

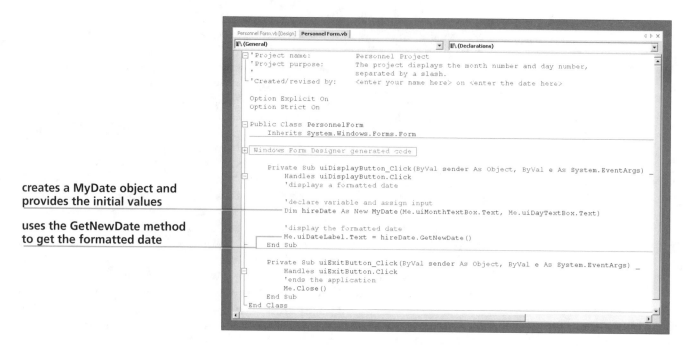

creates a MyDate object and
provides the initial values

uses the GetNewDate method
to get the formatted date

Figure 11-20: Code for the Personnel application

The `Dim hireDate As New MyDate(Me.uiMonthTextBox.Text,` `Me.uiDayTextBox.Text)` statement creates a MyDate object, using the contents of the text boxes in the interface to initialize the Private variables in the class. The statement assigns the MyDate object's address to the `hireDate` variable. The statement is equivalent to the following three lines of code:

```
Dim hireDate As New MyDate
hireDate.Month = Me.uiMonthTextBox.Text
hireDate.Day = Me.uiDayTextBox.Text
```

The `Me.uiDateLabel.Text = hireDate.GetNewDate()` statement uses the MyDate object's GetNewDate method to return the month and day numbers, separated by a slash. The statement displays the formatted date in the uiDateLabel control.

In the remainder of this lesson, you code the Cornwall Calendars application.

Coding the Cornwall Calendars Application

Recall that your task in this chapter is to create an application that Jesse Washington, the manager of the Accounts Payable department at Cornwall Calendars, can use to record (in a sequential access file) the check number, date, payee, and amount of each check written by his department. On your computer's hard disk is a partially completed Cornwall Calendars application.

To open the Cornwall Calendars application:

1 Start Microsoft Visual Studio .NET, if necessary.

2 If necessary, close the Start Page window.

3 Open the **Cornwall Calendars Solution** (Cornwall Calendars Solution.sln) file, which is contained in the VBNET\Chap11\Cornwall Calendars Solution folder.

4   Auto-hide the Toolbox, Solution Explorer, and Properties windows, if necessary. Figure 11-21 shows the user interface for the Cornwall Calendars application.

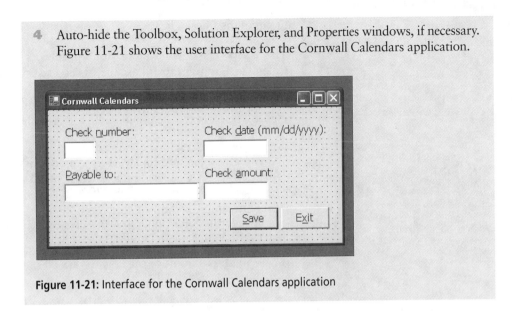

Figure 11-21: Interface for the Cornwall Calendars application

Figure 11-22 shows the TOE chart for the Cornwall Calendars application.

Task	Object	Event
Get and display the check amount	uiAmountTextBox	None
Select the existing text		Enter
Allow the text box to accept numbers, the period, and the Backspace key		KeyPress
Get and display the check date	uiDateTextBox	None
Select the existing text		Enter
Allow the text box to accept numbers, the slash, and the Backspace key		KeyPress
Get and display the check number	uiNumberTextBox	None
Select the existing text		Enter
Allow the text box to accept numbers and the Backspace key		KeyPress
Get and display the payee	uiPayeeTextBox	None
Select the existing text		Enter
End the application	uiExitButton	Click
Save the check information to a sequential access file	uiSaveButton	Click

Figure 11-22: TOE chart for the Cornwall Calendars application

First you will create a class named Check that the Cornwall Calendars application can use to create a Check object.

Creating the Check Class

The Check class will contain four properties and two methods. The Cornwall Calendars application will use the Check class to create a Check object. It will store the user input in the object's properties, and use the object's methods to initialize the Private variables and save the check information to a sequential access file. Figure 11-23 shows the pseudocode for the Check class.

New method (default constructor) – Check class
1. initialize the number, dateWritten, and payee variables to the empty string
2. initialize the amount variable to zero

SaveCheckInfo method – Check class
include the following in the Try section of a Try/Catch block:
1. open for append the sequential access file whose name is passed to the procedure
2. write the contents of the Private variables to the sequential access file
3. close the sequential access file

include the following in the Catch section of a Try/Catch block:
use a general Catch statement to handle any errors
  if an error occurs, display a description of the error in a message box

---

Figure 11-23: Pseudocode for the Check class

To create the Check class:

1 Click **Project** on the menu bar, and then click **Add Class**. The Add New Item – Cornwall Calendars Project dialog box opens with Class selected in the Templates list box.

2 Type **Check.vb** in the Name box, as shown in Figure 11-24.

class filename

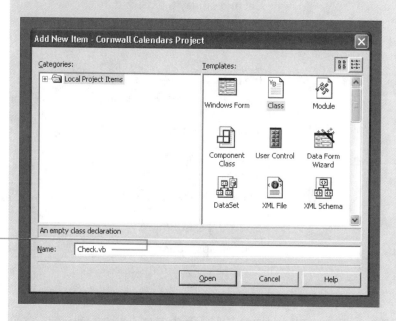

Figure 11-24: Add New Item – Cornwall Calendars Project dialog box

3   Click the **Open** button. The computer adds a file named Check.vb to the current project and also opens the file in the Code Editor window.

4   Temporarily display the Solution Explorer window. See Figure 11-25.

class filename

Figure 11-25: Check.vb file added to the project and opened in the Code Editor window

5   Insert a blank line above the `Public Class Check` clause.

6   Type the following comments, replacing the *<enter your name here>* and *<enter the date here>* text with your name and the current date, then press Enter twice.

   'Class name: Check
   'Class purpose: The class saves the check information to a sequential
   '   access file.
   'Created/revised by: *<enter your name here>* on *<enter the date here>*

7   Type **option explicit on** and press **Enter**, then type **option strict on** and press **Enter** twice.

First declare the class's Private variables. The class will use four Private variables to store the check number, check date, payee, and check amount.

8   Type the comment and additional lines of code shown in Figure 11-26, and then position the insertion point as shown in the figure.

enter this comment and these lines of code

position the insertion point here

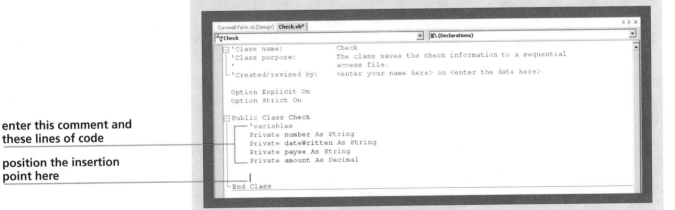

Figure 11-26: Private variables entered in the procedure

Recall that when an application needs to assign data to or retrieve data from a Private variable in a class, it must use a Public property to do so. In other words, an application cannot refer, directly, to a Private variable in a class. Rather, it must refer to the variable indirectly, through the use of a Public property. Recall that you create a Public property using a Property procedure.

9   Type **public property CheckNumber as string** and press **Enter**. The property procedure's template appears in the Code Editor window, as shown in Figure 11-27.

The data type of the Property procedure must be the same as the data type of the Private variable associated with the Property procedure.

Get block

Set block

You can enter one or more instructions within the Set block. For example, you can enter the code to validate the value received from the application before assigning it to the Private variable. If the value is valid, the last instruction in the Set block should assign the content of the Value parameter to the Private variable. However, if the value received from the application is not valid, the last instruction in the Set block should assign a default value to the Private variable.

enter this line of code

position the insertion point here

```
Cornwall Form.vb [Design]  Check.vb*
Check                                                    CheckNumber
'Class name:              Check
'Class purpose:          The class saves the check information to a sequential
'                        access file.
'Created/revised by:     <enter your name here> on <enter the date here>

Option Explicit On
Option Strict On

Public Class Check
    'variables
    Private number As String
    Private dateWritten As String
    Private payee As String
    Private amount As Decimal

    Public Property CheckNumber() As String
        Get
            |
        End Get
        Set(ByVal Value As String)

        End Set
    End Property
End Class
```

Figure 11-27: Template for the CheckNumber property procedure

The code in the Get block allows an application to retrieve the contents of the Private variable associated with the property. Most times, you will enter only one instruction in the Get block. The instruction—typically Return *privateVariable*—directs the computer to return the contents of the Private variable.

10 Type **return number**.

The code in the Set block, on the other hand, allows the application to assign a value to the Private variable associated with the property.

11 Type the additional statement shown in Figure 11-28, and then position the insertion point as shown in the figure.

```
    Public Property CheckNumber() As String
        Get
            Return number
        End Get
        Set(ByVal Value As String)
            number = Value
        End Set
    End Property

    |
End Class
```

Figure 11-28: Property procedure associated with the number variable

12 Create a Property procedure for the dateWritten variable. Name the property **CheckDate**. Complete the Get and Set blocks appropriately.

13 Create a Property procedure for the payee variable. Name the property **CheckPayee**. Complete the Get and Set blocks appropriately.

14 Create a Property procedure for the amount variable. Name the property **CheckAmount**. Complete the Get and Set blocks appropriately.

15 Position the insertion point two lines below the last End Property clause, but above the End Class clause.

Every class should have at least one constructor. As you learned in Lesson B, a constructor is a method whose instructions the computer processes, automatically, each time an object is created (instantiated) from the class. The sole purpose of a constructor is to initialize the class's variables. Each constructor included in a class has the same name (New), but its parameters (if any) must be different from any other constructor in the class. A constructor that has no parameters is called the default constructor. According to the pseudocode shown earlier in Figure 11-23, the Check class will use only one constructor: the default constructor. In this case, the default constructor will initialize the number, dateWritten, and payee variables to the empty string, and initialize the amount variable to the number zero.

16 Type the comments and additional lines of code shown in Figure 11-29, and then position the insertion point as shown in the figure.

enter these comments and lines of code

position the insertion point here

```
    Public Property CheckAmount() As Decimal
        Get
            Return amount
        End Get
        Set(ByVal Value As Decimal)
            amount = Value
        End Set
    End Property

    'methods
    Public Sub New() 'default constructor
        number = ""
        dateWritten = ""
        payee = ""
        amount = 0
    End Sub

    |
End Class
```

Figure 11-29: Default constructor entered in the procedure

The Check class will also contain a method named SaveCheckInfo that saves the contents of the Private variables to a sequential access file. The SaveCheckInfo method will receive the name of the file from the procedure that invokes it.

17 Type **public sub SaveCheckInfo(byval nameOfFile as string)** and press **Enter**.

18 Type **'saves the contents of the Private variables to a sequential access file** and press **Enter** twice.

First, declare a StreamWriter variable that the method will use to store the address of a StreamWriter object.

19 Type **'declare variables** and press **Enter**.

20 Type **dim saveStreamWriter as io.streamwriter** and press **Enter** twice.

According to the pseudocode, the SaveCheckInfo method uses a Try/Catch block.

21 Type **try** and press **Enter**.

The first instruction in the Try section should open a sequential access file for append. The name of the file to be opened is passed to the SaveCheckInfo method by the procedure that invokes the method. When the method receives the filename, it stores the name in the nameOfFile variable.

22 Type **'open the file for append** and press **Enter**.

23 Type **savestreamwriter = io.file.appendtext(nameoffile)** and press **Enter**.

The next instruction should write the contents of the Private variables to the sequential access file. You will write the contents of the variables in four columns.

24 Type '**write the contents of the Private variables** and press **Enter**.

25 Type **savestreamwriter.writeline(number.padright(10)** _ and press **Enter**. Press **Tab**, then type **& datewritten.padright(15)** _ and press **Enter**.

26 Type **& payee.padright(25) & amount.tostring("N2").padleft(15))** and press **Enter**.

The last instruction in the SaveCheckInfo method should close the sequential access file.

27 Type '**close the file** and press **Enter**.

28 Type **savestreamwriter.close()** and press **Enter**.

You have finished coding the Try section. Next, you code the Catch section.

29 Enter the MessageBox.Show method shown in Figure 11-30.

```
'Class name:          Check
'Class purpose:       The class saves the check information to a sequential
'                     access file.
'Created/revised by:  <enter your name here> on <enter the date here>

Option Explicit On
Option Strict On

Public Class Check
    'variables
    Private number As String
    Private dateWritten As String
    Private payee As String
    Private amount As Decimal

    Public Property CheckNumber() As String
        Get
            Return number
        End Get
        Set(ByVal Value As String)
            number = Value
        End Set
    End Property

    Public Property CheckDate() As String
        Get
            Return dateWritten
        End Get
        Set(ByVal Value As String)
            dateWritten = Value
        End Set
    End Property
```

Figure 11-30: Completed Check class

```
    Public Property CheckPayee() As String
        Get
            Return payee
        End Get
        Set(ByVal Value As String)
            payee = Value
        End Set
    End Property

    Public Property CheckAmount() As Decimal
        Get
            Return amount
        End Get
        Set(ByVal Value As Decimal)
            amount = Value
        End Set
    End Property

    'methods
    Public Sub New() 'default constructor
        number = ""
        dateWritten = ""
        payee = ""
        amount = 0
    End Sub

    Public Sub SaveCheckInfo(ByVal nameOfFile As String)
        'saves the contents of the Private variables to a sequential access file

        'declare variables
        Dim saveStreamWriter As IO.StreamWriter

        Try
            'open the file for append
            saveStreamWriter = IO.File.AppendText(nameOfFile)
            'write the contents of the Private variables
            saveStreamWriter.WriteLine(number.PadRight(10) _
                & dateWritten.PadRight(15) _
                & payee.PadRight(25) & amount.ToString("N2").PadLeft(15))
            'close the file
            saveStreamWriter.Close()

        Catch ex As Exception
            MessageBox.Show(ex.Message, "File Error", _
                MessageBoxButtons.OK, MessageBoxIcon.Information)
        End Try
    End Sub
End Class
```

enter these lines of code

Figure 11-30: Completed Check class (continued)

30 Click **File** on the menu bar, and then click **Save All** to save the solution.

Now that you have finished coding the Check class, you can code the uiSaveButton's Click event procedure.

Coding the uiSaveButton Click Event Procedure

Figure 11-31 shows the pseudocode for the uiSaveButton's Click event procedure.

```
uiSaveButton
1.  use the Check class to create a Check object
2.  if the user entered the check number, date, payee, and amount
       assign the check number to the CheckNumber property of the Check object
       assign the date to the CheckDate property of the Check object
       assign the payee to the CheckPayee property of the Check object
       assign the amount to the CheckAmount property of the Check object
       call the Check object's SaveCheckInfo method to write the check information to a
       sequential access file named checks.txt
    else
       display an appropriate message in a message box
    end if
3.  send the focus to the uiNumberTextBox control
```

Figure 11-31: Pseudocode for the uiSaveButton's Click event procedure

To code the uiSaveButton's Click event procedure:

1   Click the **Cornwall Form.vb [Design]** tab, then open the Code Editor window.

2   Replace the `<enter your name here>` and `<enter the date here>` text with your name and the current date, respectively.

3   Open the code template for the uiSaveButton's Click event procedure.

4   Type **'saves the check information to a sequential access file** and press **Enter** twice.

According to the pseudocode shown in Figure 11-31, the first step in the uiSaveButton's Click procedure is to create a Check object using the Check class.

5   Type **'create Check object** and press **Enter**, then type **dim checkObject as new check** and press **Enter** twice.

The next step in the pseudocode is a selection structure that determines whether the user entered the check information—in this case, the check number, date, payee, and amount. If the user neglected to enter one or more of the items, the selection structure's false path should display an appropriate message.

6   Type the comment and additional lines of code shown in Figure 11-32, and then position the insertion point as shown in the figure.

position the insertion point here

enter these comments and lines of code

```
Private Sub uiSaveButton_Click(ByVal sender As Object, ByVal e As System.EventArgs) Hand
    'saves the check information to a sequential access file

    'create Check object
    Dim checkObject As New Check

    'assign input to object's properties, but only if each text box
    'contains data
    If Me.uiNumberTextBox.Text <> "" AndAlso Me.uiDateTextBox.Text <> "" _
        AndAlso Me.uiPayeeTextBox.Text <> "" _
        AndAlso Me.uiAmountTextBox.Text <> "" Then

    Else
        MessageBox.Show("Please enter a check number, date, payee, and amount.", _
            "Cornwall Calendars", MessageBoxButtons.OK, _
            MessageBoxIcon.Information)
    End If
End Sub
```

Figure 11-32: Comments and additional lines of code shown in the procedure

However, if the user entered all of the check information, the selection structure's true path should assign each item of information to a property of the Check object.

7 Type **checkobject.checknumber = me.uinumbertextbox.text** and press **Enter**. This statement assigns the check number to the CheckNumber property of the Check object.

8 Type **checkobject.checkdate = me.uidatetextbox.text** and press **Enter**.

9 Type **checkobject.checkpayee = me.uipayeetextbox.text** and press **Enter**.

10 Type **checkobject.checkamount = decimal.parse(me.uiamounttextbox.text)** and then press **Enter** twice.

After assigning the check information to the Check object's properties, the selection structure's true path should call the Check object's SaveCheckInfo method to write the check information to a sequential access file named checks.txt.

11 Type **'call object's method to write information to the checks.txt** and press **Enter**, then type **'sequential access file** and press **Enter**.

12 Type **checkobject.savecheckinfo("checks.txt")**.

The last step in the pseudocode is to send the focus to the uiNumberTextBox.

13 Position the insertion point two lines below the `End If` clause, but above the `End Sub` clause.

14 Type **'set the focus** and press **Enter**, then type **me.uinumbertextbox.focus()**. Figure 11-33 shows the code for the uiSaveButton's Click event procedure.

```
Private Sub uiSaveButton_Click(ByVal sender As Object, ByVal e As System.EventArgs) Hand
    'saves the check information to a sequential access file

    'create Check object
    Dim checkObject As New Check

    'assign input to object's properties, but only if each text box
    'contains data
    If Me.uiNumberTextBox.Text <> "" AndAlso Me.uiDateTextBox.Text <> "" _
        AndAlso Me.uiPayeeTextBox.Text <> "" _
        AndAlso Me.uiAmountTextBox.Text <> "" Then
        checkObject.CheckNumber = Me.uiNumberTextBox.Text
        checkObject.CheckDate = Me.uiDateTextBox.Text
        checkObject.CheckPayee = Me.uiPayeeTextBox.Text
        checkObject.CheckAmount = Decimal.Parse(Me.uiAmountTextBox.Text)

        'call object's method to write information to the checks.txt
        'sequential access file
        checkObject.SaveCheckInfo("checks.txt")
    Else
        MessageBox.Show("Please enter a check number, date, payee, and amount.", _
            "Cornwall Calendars", MessageBoxButtons.OK, _
            MessageBoxIcon.Information)
    End If

    'set the focus
    Me.uiNumberTextBox.Focus()
End Sub
```

Figure 11-33: Code for the uiSaveButton's Click event procedure

Now that you have finished coding the application, you can test the application to verify that the code is working correctly.

To test the application:

1 Save the solution, then start the application.

First, observe what happens when you click the Save button without entering the check information.

2   Click the **Save** button. The message box shown in Figure 11-34 appears on the screen.

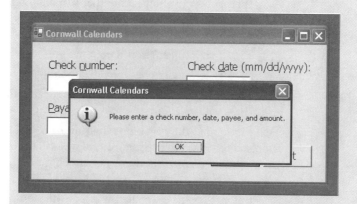

Figure 11-34: Message box that appears when the user does not enter all of the check information

3   Click the **OK** button to close the message box.

4   On your own, verify that the message box shown in Figure 11-34 appears when you enter one item, two items, or three items of check information.

Next, you will enter all of the required check information.

5   Enter **104** in the Check number box, **10/25/2006** in the Check date box, **Tri-County Electric** in the Payable to box, and **125.67** in the Check amount box. Click the **Save** button. The uiSaveButton's Click procedure uses the properties and methods of the Check object to save the check information to the checks.txt file. It then sends the focus to the uiNumberTextBox, as shown in Figure 11-35.

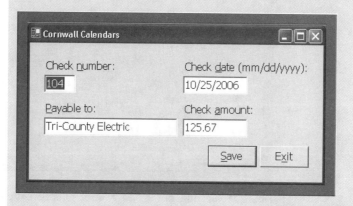

Figure 11-35: Cornwall Calendars application

6   Use the application to save the information for the following two checks:

Check number:	105
Check date:	10/30/2006
Payable to:	Henson Grocery
Check amount:	45.89

Check number: 106
Check date: 11/01/2006
Payable to: Jacob Hardware
Check amount: 6.78

7   Click the **Exit** button to end the application.

Now open the checks.txt file to verify its contents.

8   Click **File** on the menu bar. Point to **Open,** and then click **File.** The Open File dialog box opens.

9   Open the bin folder contained in the VBNET\Chap11\Cornwall Calendars Solution\Cornwall Calendars Project folder. The checks.txt filename should be selected in the list of filenames.

10 Click the **Open** button to open the checks.txt file. Figure 11-36 shows the contents of the file.

Close button

Figure 11-36: Contents of the checks.txt file

11 Close the checks.txt window by clicking its **Close** button.

12 Close the Output window, and then close the Cornwall Form.vb window and the Check.vb window.

You are finished with the solution, so you can close it.

13 Click **File** on the menu bar, and then click **Close Solution.**

You now have completed Chapter 11. You can either take a break or complete the end-of lesson questions and exercises.

S U M M A R Y

To include more than one constructor in a class:

▪ Each constructor's parameters (if any) must be different from any other constructor in the class.

To include data validation in a class:

▪ Place the data validation in the Set block of a Property procedure.

QUESTIONS

1. Before a class assigns values to its Private variables, it should validate the values. You enter the validation code in the _____ block in a Property procedure.
   a. Assign
   b. Get
   c. Set
   d. Validate
   e. Validation

2. Following the naming convention discussed in the chapter, which of the following would be considered a good name for a method contained in a class?
   a. Bonus
   b. SalesIncome
   c. SetDate
   d. Width
   e. None of the above.

3. Following the naming convention discussed in the chapter, which of the following would be considered a good name for a property contained in a class?
   a. CalculateBonus
   b. salesAmount
   c. FirstName
   d. Validate
   e. Both b and c.

4. A class cannot contain more than one constructor.
   a. True
   b. False

EXERCISES

1. Write the class definition for a class named Employee. The class should include Private variables and Property procedures for an Employee object's name and salary. (The salary may contain a decimal place.) The class also should contain two constructors: the default constructor and a constructor that allows an application to assign values to the Private variables.

2. Add another method to the Employee class you defined in Exercise 1. The method should calculate an Employee object's new salary, based on a raise percentage provided by the application using the object. Before calculating the new salary, the method should verify that the raise percentage is greater than or equal to zero. If the raise percentage is less than zero, the method should assign the number 0 as the new salary.

3. In this exercise, you use the Employee class from Exercise 2 to create an object in an application.
   a. If necessary, start Visual Studio .NET. Open the Salary Solution (Salary Solution.sln) file, which is contained in the VBNET\Chap11\Salary Solution folder. If necessary, open the designer window.
   b. Open the Employee.vb class file in the Code Editor window, then enter the class definition from Exercise 2.

    c. View the Salary Form.vb file in the Code Editor window. Use the comments that appear in the code to enter the missing instructions.

    d. Save the solution, and then start the application.

    e. Test the application by entering your name, a current salary amount of 54000, and a raise percentage of 10 (for 10%). The application should display the number $59,400.

    f. Click the Exit button to end the application, then close the solution.

4. In this exercise, you create an application that uses a class.

    a. If necessary, start Visual Studio .NET. Create the Personnel application's interface, which is shown in Figure 11-18. Name the solution Personnel Solution. Name the project Personnel Project. Save the application in the VBNET\Chap11 folder.

    b. Add a class file to the project. Name the class file MyDate.vb. Use the code shown in Figure 11-19 to define the class.

    c. Use the code shown in Figure 11-20 to code the Personnel application.

    d. Save the solution, and then start and test the application.

    e. Click the Exit button to end the application, then close the solution.

5. In this exercise, you modify the application that you created in Exercise 4.

    a. Use Windows to make a copy of the Personnel Solution folder, which is contained in the VBNET\Chap11 folder. Rename the folder Modified Personnel Solution.

    b. If necessary, start Visual Studio .NET. Open the Personnel Solution (Personnel Solution.sln) file contained in the Modified Personnel Solution folder. Open the designer window.

    c. Modify the interface to allow the user to enter the year number.

    d. The MyDate class should create an object that returns a month number, followed by a slash, a day number, a slash, and a year number. Modify the class appropriately.

    e. Modify the MyDate class to validate the day number, which should be from 1 through 31.

    f. Make the necessary modifications to the Personnel application's code.

    g. Save the solution, and then start and test the application.

    h. Click the Exit button to end the application, then close the solution.

6. Monica Kessler, the owner of Kessler Landscaping, wants an application that she can use to estimate the cost of laying sod.

    a. If necessary, start Visual Studio .NET. Open the Kessler Solution (Kessler Solution.sln) file, which is contained in the VBNET\Chap11\Kessler Solution folder. If necessary, open the designer window.

    b. Add a class file to the project. Name the class file MyRectangle.vb. Create a MyRectangle class that contains two Property procedures named Length and Width, a default constructor, and a method named CalculateArea. The CalculateArea method should calculate and return the area of a rectangle. Additionally, the MyRectangle class should verify that the length and width entries are valid. To be valid, the entries must be greater than zero. If an entry is not valid, assign the number zero to the corresponding Private variable, and display an appropriate message.

    c. Code the Kessler application so that it calculates the total price of the sod. Be sure to verify that the Sod price text box has been completed. If it hasn't been completed, assign the number zero to the `sodPrice` variable.

    d. Save the solution, then start and test the application.

    e. Click the Exit button to end the application, then close the solution.

7. In this exercise, you modify the MyRectangle class that you created in Exercise 6, and then use the class in a different application.

   a. Assume that Jack Sysmanski, the owner of All-Around Fence Company, wants a program that he can use to calculate the cost of installing a fence. If necessary, start Visual Studio .NET. Create an interface that allows the user to enter the length and width (both in feet) of a rectangle, as well as the fence cost per linear foot. Name the solution Fence Solution. Name the project Fence Project. Save the application in the VBNET\Chap11 folder.

   b. Use Windows to copy the MyRectangle.vb file from the VBNET\Chap11\ Kessler Solution\Kessler Project folder to the VBNET\Chap11\Fence Solution\Fence Project folder.

   c. Use the Project menu to add the existing MyRectangle.vb class file to the Fence project.

   d. Modify the MyRectangle class so that it calculates the perimeter of a rectangle. To calculate the perimeter, the class will need to add together the length and width measurements, and then multiply the sum by two.

   e. Code the Fence application so that it displays the cost of installing the fence.

   f. Save the solution, and then start the application. Test the application using 120 as the length, 75 as the width, and 10 as the cost per linear foot. The application should display $3,900.00 as the installation cost.

   g. End the application, then close the solution.

8. In this exercise, you modify the MyRectangle class that you created in Exercise 6, and then use the class in a different application.

   a. The manager of Pool-Time, which sells in-ground pools, wants an application that the salespeople can use to determine the number of gallons of water required to fill an in-ground pool—a question commonly asked by customers. (*Hint*: To calculate the number of gallons, you need to find the volume of the pool. You can do so using the formula length * width * depth.) If necessary, start Visual Studio .NET. Create an appropriate interface. Name the solution Pool Solution. Name the project Pool Project. Save the application in the VBNET\Chap11 folder.

   b. Use Windows to copy the MyRectangle.vb file from the VBNET\Chap11\ Kessler Solution\Kessler Project folder to the VBNET\Chap11\Pool Solution\Pool Project folder.

   c. Use the Project menu to add the existing MyRectangle.vb class file to the Pool project.

   d. Modify the MyRectangle class appropriately.

   e. Code the Pool application so that it displays the number of gallons. To calculate the number of gallons, you divide the volume by .13368.

   f. Save the solution, and then start the application. Test the application using 25 feet as the length, 15 as the width, and 6.5 feet as the depth. The application should display 18,233.84 as the number of gallons.

   g. Click the Exit button to end the application, then close the solution

9. In this exercise, you define a Triangle class. You also create an application that uses the Triangle class to create a Triangle object.

   a. If necessary, start Visual Studio .NET. Create an interface that allows the user to display either the area of a triangle or the perimeter of a triangle. (*Hint*: The formula for calculating the area of a triangle is ½ * base * height. The formula for calculating the perimeter of a triangle is a + b + c, where a, b, and c are the lengths of the sides.) Name the solution Math Solution. Name the project Math Project. Save the application in the VBNET\Chap11 folder.

    b. Add a class file to the project. Name the class file Triangle.vb. The Triangle class should verify that the dimensions are greater than zero before assigning the values to the Private variables. The class also should include a method to calculate the area of a triangle and a method to calculate the perimeter of a triangle.

    c. Save the solution, and then start and test the application.

    d. Stop the application, then close the solution.

10. Maria Jacobsen, a professor at Mayflower College, wants an application that allows her to enter each student's name and three test scores. The application should calculate and display each student's average test score.

    a. If necessary, start Visual Studio .NET. Open the Mayflower Solution (Mayflower Solution.sln) file, which is contained in the VBNET\Chap11\Mayflower Solution folder. If necessary, open the designer window.

    b. Add a class file to the project. Name the class file Student.vb. The Student class should contain four properties and two methods. The Mayflower application will use the class to create a Student object. It will store the user input in the object's properties, and use the object's methods to initialize the Private variables and calculate and return the average test score.

    c. Save the solution, and then start and test the application.

    d. Stop the application, then close the solution.

11. In this exercise, you modify the Student class you created in Exercise 10. The modified class will include an additional method named ValidateScores. The ValidateScores method will verify that each test score is greater than or equal to a minimum value, but less than or equal to a maximum value. The minimum and maximum values will be passed to the method by the procedure that invokes the method.

    a. Use Windows to make a copy of the Mayflower Solution folder, which is contained in the VBNET\Chap11 folder. Rename the folder Modified Mayflower Solution.

    b. If necessary, start Visual Studio .NET. Open the Mayflower Solution (Mayflower Solution.sln) file, which is contained in the VBNET\Chap11\Modified Mayflower Solution folder. Open the designer window.

    c. Make the appropriate modifications to the Student class.

    d. Modify the uiCalcButton's Click event procedure so that it invokes the ValidateScores method, passing it the minimum and maximum values for a test score. In this case, the minimum value will be zero and the maximum value will be 100.

    e. Save the solution, and then start and test the application.

    f. Stop the application, then close the solution.

discovery ▷ 12. In this exercise, you learn how to create a region of code. The Code Editor window uses a region to hide the code generated by the Windows Form Designer. You also can create a region to hide sections of your code.

    a. Use Windows to make a copy of the Cornwall Calendars Solution folder, which you created in this chapter. Rename the copy Cornwall Region Solution.

    b. If necessary, start Visual Studio .NET. Open the Cornwall Calendars Solution (Cornwall Calendars Solution.sln) file, which is contained in the VBNET\Chap11\ Cornwall Region Solution folder. Open the designer window.

    c. Use the Help menu to research the #Region statement.

    d. Modify the application so that it uses a region to hide the properties contained in the Check class, and a region to hide the methods contained in the class.

    e. Save the solution. Practice collapsing and expanding each region.

    f. Close the solution.

debugging 13. Open the Code Editor window. In this exercise, you find and correct an error in an application. The process of finding and correcting errors is called debugging.

   a. If necessary, start Visual Studio .NET. Open the Debug Solution (Debug Solution.sln) file, which is contained in the VBNET\Chap11\Debug Solution folder. If necessary, open the designer window.

   b. Open the Code Editor window. Review the existing code in the Debug Form.vb and Address.vb files.

   c. Notice that a jagged line appears below some of the lines of code in the Code Editor window. Correct the code to remove the jagged lines.

   d. Save the solution, then start the application.

   e. Correct the errors in the application's code, then save the solution and start the application. Test the application.

   f. Click the Exit button to end the application, then close the solution.

ADO.NET and ASP.NET

Creating the Cartwright Industries Application

case ▶ Carl Simons, the sales manager at Cartwright Industries, records the item number, name, and price of each product the company sells in a Microsoft Access database named Items.mdb. Mr. Simons wants an application that the sales clerks can use to enter an item number and then display the item's price.

Previewing the Cartwright Industries Application

Before creating the Cartwright Industries application, you first preview the completed application.

To preview the completed application:

1 Use the Run command on the Windows Start menu to run the **Cartwright** (Cartwright.exe) file, which is contained in the VBNET\Chap12 folder on your computer's hard disk. The user interface for the Cartwright Industries application appears on the screen.

Use the application to display the price of item number PRT45.

2 Click **PRT45** in the Item number list box. The item's price appears in the Price label control, as shown in Figure 12-1.

Figure 12-1: Price displayed in the Cartwright Industries user interface

3 Click the **Exit** button to end the application.

In this chapter, you learn how to use ADO.NET to access the data stored in a Microsoft Access database. You also learn how to use ASP.NET to create a Web application. You code the Cartwright Industries application in Lesson B.

After completing this lesson, you
will be able to:

■ Define the terms used when talking
about databases

■ Explain the purpose of the
DataAdapter, Connection, and
DataSet objects

■ Explain the role of the provider

■ Create and configure an
OleDbDataAdapter object

■ Write SQL SELECT statements

■ Create a dataset

■ Display a dataset in a DataGrid
control

Database Terminology

In order to maintain accurate records, most businesses store information about their employees, customers, and inventory in files called databases. In general, a **database** is simply an organized collection of related information stored in a file on a disk. Many computer products exist for creating databases; some of the most popular are Microsoft Access, Oracle, and SQL Server. You can use Visual Basic .NET to access the data stored in databases created by these products. This allows a company to create a standard interface in Visual Basic .NET that employees can use to access database information stored in a variety of formats. Instead of learning each product's user interface, the employee needs to know only one interface. The actual format the database is in is unimportant and will be transparent to the user.

In this lesson, you learn how to access the data stored in a Microsoft Access database. Databases created by Microsoft Access are relational databases. A **relational database** is one that stores information in tables, which are composed of columns and rows. Each column in a table represents a field, and each row represents a record. As you learned in Chapter 9, a field is a single item of information about a person, place, or thing—such as a name, address, or phone number—and a record is a group of related fields that contain all of the necessary data about a specific person, place, or thing. A **table** is a group of related records. Each record in the group pertains to the same topic, and each contains the same type of information—in other words, the same fields.

A relational database can contain one or more tables. A one-table database would be a good choice for storing the information regarding the college courses you have taken. An example of such a table is shown in Figure 12-2.

ID	Title	Hours	Grade
CIS100	Intro to Computers	5	A
Eng100	English Composition	3	B
Phil105	Philosophy	5	C
CIS203	Visual Basic .NET	5	A

Figure 12-2: Example of a one-table relational database

Notice that each record in the table contains four fields: an ID field that indicates the department name and course number, a course title field, a number of credit hours field, and a grade field. In most tables, one of the fields uniquely identifies each record and is called the **primary key**. In the table shown in Figure 12-2, you could use either the ID field or the Title field as the primary key, because the data in those fields will be unique for each record.

If you were storing information about your CD (compact disc) collection, you typically would use a two-table database: one table to store the general information about each CD (such as the CD's name and the artist's name) and the other table to store the information about the songs on each CD (such as their title and track number). You then would use a common field—for example, a CD number—to relate the records contained in both tables. Figure 12-3 shows an example of a two-table database that stores CD information.

the two tables are related by the Number field

Number	Name	Artist
01	Western Way	Dolly Draton
02	Midnight Blue	Paul Elliot

Number	Song title	Track
01	Country	1
01	Night on the Road	2
01	Old Times	3
02	Lovely Nights	1
02	Colors	2
02	Heavens	3

Figure 12-3: Example of a two-table relational database

The first table shown in Figure 12-3 is often referred to as the **parent table**, and the second table as the **child table**. In the parent table, the Number field is the primary key, because it uniquely identifies each record in that table. In the child table, the Number field is used solely to link the song title and track information to the appropriate CD in the parent table. In the child table, the Number field is called the **foreign key**.

Storing data in a relational database offers many advantages. The computer can retrieve data stored in that format both quickly and easily, and the data can be displayed in any order. For example, the information in the CD database shown in Figure 12-3 can be arranged by artist name, song title, and so on. A relational database also allows you to control how much information you want to view at a time. You can view all of the information in the CD database, or you can view only the information pertaining to a certain artist, or only the names of the songs contained on a specific CD.

In Visual Basic .NET, you use ADO.NET to access the data stored in a database.

ADO.NET

The previous version of Visual Basic (Version 6.0) used a technology called **ADO (ActiveX Data Objects)** to connect an application to a database. The connection allows the application to read information from and write information to the database. The technology used in Visual Basic .NET to perform the same task is called **ADO.NET**.

ADO.NET works differently from its predecessor, ADO. Using ADO, the connection between an application and a database remains open the entire time the application is running. This does not pose a problem when only a few applications are connected to the database. However, when many applications are connected, at some point the demands on the database will exceed its ability to respond in a timely fashion.

With ADO.NET, the connection between an application and a database is only a temporary one. When an application first connects to a database, it makes a copy of the records and fields it wants to access; the copy, called a **dataset**, is stored in the computer's internal memory. The application then closes both the database and the connection to the database. The application reconnects to the database when any changes made to the dataset (which is in internal memory) need to be saved. After saving the changes, the application again closes the database and the connection to the database. Unlike ADO, ADO.NET allows multiple users to access the same database without tying up limited resources. ADO.NET also was designed to better operate with the Web.

You use three ADO.NET objects (DataAdapter, Connection, and DataSet), as well as a provider, to access a database from a Visual Basic .NET application. Figure 12-4 illustrates the relationships among an application, the ADO.NET objects, a provider, and a database.

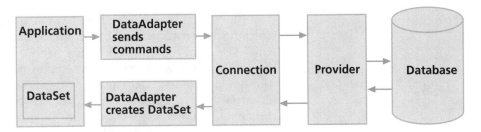

Figure 12-4: Illustration of the relationships among an application, the ADO.NET objects, a provider, and a database

When an application needs to access the data stored in a database, it submits the appropriate request using a **DataAdapter object**. The DataAdapter object, in turn, contacts the **Connection object**, which is responsible for establishing the connection to the database, and then submitting the request for data. The Connection object communicates with the database using one of several different providers, depending on the type of database. For example, the Connection object uses a provider named Microsoft Jet 4.0 OLE DB Provider to communicate with a Microsoft Access database. However, it uses a provider named Microsoft OLE DB Provider for Oracle to communicate with an Oracle database. A provider is like a translator in that it allows communication between two entities that do not speak the same language. In this case, the **provider** translates the Connection object's request for data into a language that the database can understand.

The database sends the requested data back to the provider, which translates the data into a language that the Connection object can understand. The Connection object sends the data to the DataAdapter object, which stores the data in a DataSet object. The data in the DataSet object is then made available to the application.

In the remainder of this lesson, you learn how to access the data stored in a Microsoft Access database named Employees.mdb. Figure 12-5 shows the database opened in Microsoft Access.

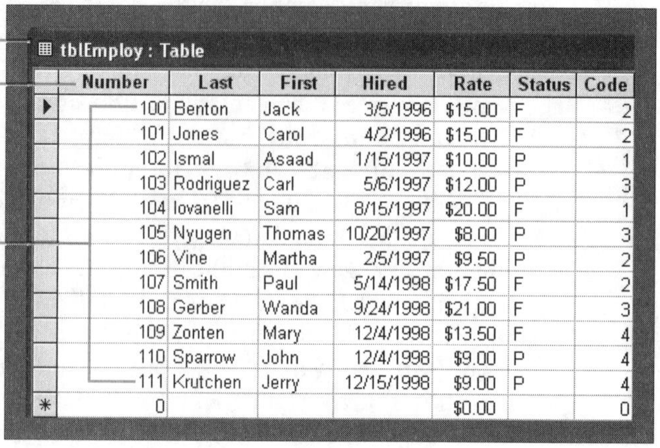

table name

field names

records

	Number	Last	First	Hired	Rate	Status	Code
▶	100	Benton	Jack	3/5/1996	$15.00	F	2
	101	Jones	Carol	4/2/1996	$15.00	F	2
	102	Ismal	Asaad	1/15/1997	$10.00	P	1
	103	Rodriguez	Carl	5/6/1997	$12.00	P	3
	104	Iovanelli	Sam	8/15/1997	$20.00	F	1
	105	Nyugen	Thomas	10/20/1997	$8.00	P	3
	106	Vine	Martha	2/5/1997	$9.50	P	2
	107	Smith	Paul	5/14/1998	$17.50	F	2
	108	Gerber	Wanda	9/24/1998	$21.00	F	3
	109	Zonten	Mary	12/4/1998	$13.50	F	4
	110	Sparrow	John	12/4/1998	$9.00	P	4
	111	Krutchen	Jerry	12/15/1998	$9.00	P	4
✳	0				$0.00		0

tblEmploy : Table

Figure 12-5: Employees.mdb database opened in Microsoft Access

The Employees.mdb database has one table, named tblEmploy, that contains seven fields and 12 records. The Number, Last, First, Hired, and Rate fields store employee numbers, last names, first names, hire dates, and rates of pay, respectively. The Status field contains the employment status, which is either the letter F (for full-time) or the letter P (for part-time). The Code field identifies the employee's department: 1 for Accounting, 2 for Advertising, 3 for Personnel, and 4 for Inventory. In the tblEmploy table, the Number field is the primary key, because it uniquely identifies each record.

Recall that the DataAdapter object is one of the three ADO.NET objects you use to connect an application to a database. In the next section, you learn how to create a DataAdapter object, and then configure the object.

Creating and Configuring a DataAdapter Object

As illustrated earlier in Figure 12-4, the DataAdapter object is the link between the application and the Connection object. Its purpose is to contact the Connection object whenever the application needs to read data from or write data to a database. Figure 12-6 shows the procedure you follow to create and configure a DataAdapter object for an application that connects to a Microsoft Access database.

The procedure shown in Figure 12-6 is only one way of creating and configuring a DataAdapter object; there are other ways.

"OleDb" stands for "Object Linking and Embedding for Databases."

The Data tab on the Toolbox window contains four tools that you can use to create DataAdapter objects. The appropriate tool depends on the type of database used by the application.

Creating and configuring a DataAdapter object for a Microsoft Access database

1. Drag the OleDbDataAdapter tool from the Data tab on the Toolbox window to the form. This adds an OleDbDataAdapter object to the component tray and also displays a Welcome screen. (See Figure 12-7.)

2. Click the Next > button on the Welcome screen to display the Choose Your Data Connection screen. (See Figure 12-8.)

3. Click the New Connection button on the Choose Your Data Connection screen.

4. Click the Provider tab on the Data Link Properties dialog box, then click Microsoft Jet 4.0 OLE DB Provider in the OLE DB Provider(s) list box. (See Figure 12-9.)

5. Click the Connection tab on the Data Link Properties dialog box, then click the ... (ellipsis) button that appears next to the "Select or enter a database name" text box.

6. Locate and then click the name of the database in the Select Access Database dialog box.

7. Click the Open button, and then click the Test Connection button. (See Figure 12-10.)

8. Click the OK button to close the Microsoft Data Link dialog box, and then click the OK button to close the Data Link Properties dialog box; this displays the Choose Your Data Connection screen. (See Figure 12-11.)

9. Click the Next > button on the Choose Your Data Connection screen; this displays the Choose a Query Type screen. (See Figure 12-12.)

10. Verify that the Use SQL statements radio button is selected on the Choose a Query Type screen, and then click the Next > button; this displays the Generate the SQL statements screen. (See Figure 12-14.)

11. Click the Query Builder button on the Generate the SQL statements screen; this displays the Query Builder and Add Table dialog boxes. (See Figure 12-15.)

12. Click the name of the table on the Tables tab in the Add Table dialog box. Click the Add button, and then click the Close button; this displays the Query Builder dialog box. (See Figure 12-16.)

13. Select the check boxes next to the desired fields. (See Figure 12-17.)

14. Click the OK button in the Query Builder dialog box; this displays the Generate the SQL statements screen. (See Figure 12-18.)

15. Click the Next > button on the Generate the SQL statements screen to display the View Wizard Results screen. (See Figure 12-19.)

16. Click the Finish button on the View Wizard Results screen. If the "Do you want to include the password in the connection string?" dialog box opens, click the Don't include password button. Visual Basic .NET adds an OleDbConnection object to the component tray.

Figure 12-6: Procedure for creating and configuring a DataAdapter object for a Microsoft Access database

When you drag the OleDbDataAdapter tool to the form, which is the first step in the procedure shown in Figure 12-6, Visual Basic .NET creates a DataAdapter object; more specifically, it creates an OleDbDataAdapter object named OleDbDataAdapter1. It places the object in the component tray in the Form Designer window, as shown in Figure 12-7. As you learned in Chapter 1, the component tray stores the objects that do not appear in the interface when an application is running. Additionally, the Welcome screen for the Data Adapter Configuration Wizard appears. As the Welcome screen shown in Figure 12-7 indicates, the wizard helps you specify the connection and commands that will be used to access the data in the database.

this tool creates a DataAdapter object for a Microsoft Access database

DataAdapter object

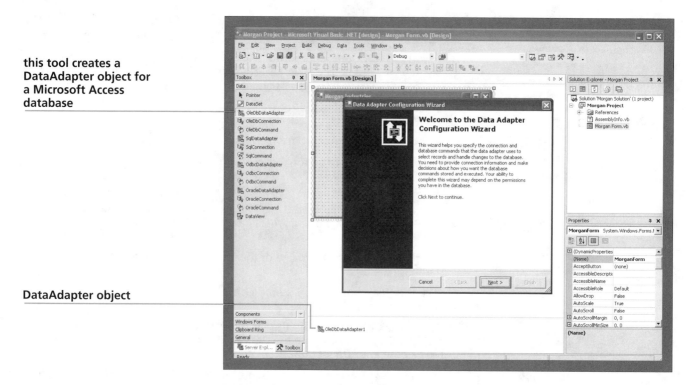

Figure 12-7: Result of dragging the OleDbDataAdapter tool to the form

When you click the Next > button on the Welcome screen, the Choose Your Data Connection screen appears, as shown in Figure 12-8. You can use this screen to create a new connection to a database, or to select an existing connection.

use this button to create a new connection

use this list box to select an existing connection

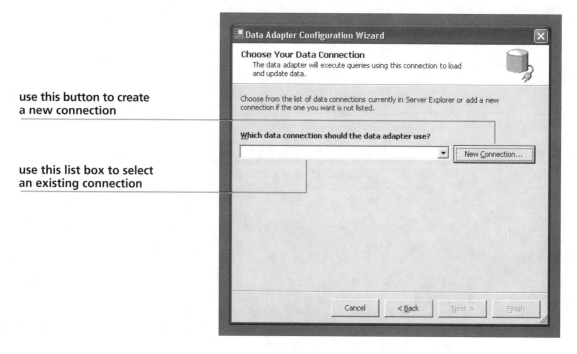

Figure 12-8: Choose Your Data Connection screen

Clicking the New Connection button on the Choose Your Data Connection screen opens the Data Link Properties dialog box. You use the Provider tab on the dialog box to specify the name of the provider. Recall that the provider facilitates the communication between the Connection object and the database. The provider for all Microsoft Access databases is named Microsoft Jet 4.0 OLE DB Provider. Figure 12-9 shows an example of a completed Provider tab. (Your list of providers may differ from the list shown in Figure 12-9.)

provider for Microsoft Access databases

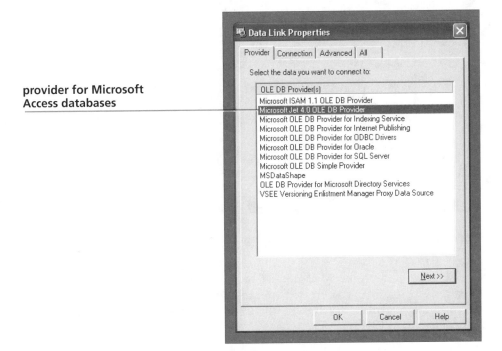

Figure 12-9: Provider tab

You use the Connection tab on the Data Link Properties dialog box to specify the name of the database to which you want to connect. The tab also contains the Test Connection button, which allows you to test the connection to the database. If the connection is successful, the message "Test connection succeeded." appears in the Microsoft Data Link dialog box; otherwise, the dialog box displays an error message. Figure 12-10 shows an example of a completed Connection tab. The figure also shows the Microsoft Data Link dialog box that appears when the connection is successful.

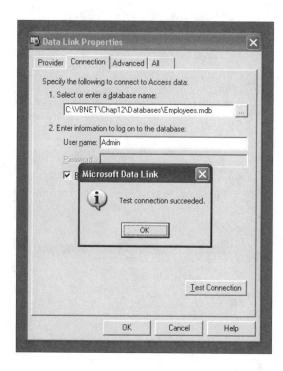

Figure 12-10: Connection tab and Microsoft Data Link dialog box

When you close the Microsoft Data Link and Data Link Properties dialog boxes, the connection you created appears in the "Which data connection should the data adapter use?" list box on the Choose Your Data Connection screen, as shown in Figure 12-11.

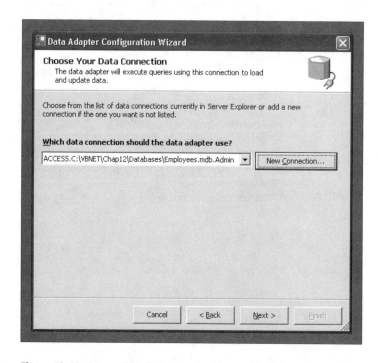

Figure 12-11: Connection shown on the Choose Your Data Connection screen

Clicking the Next > button on the Choose Your Data Connection screen displays the Choose a Query Type screen, as shown in Figure 12-12.

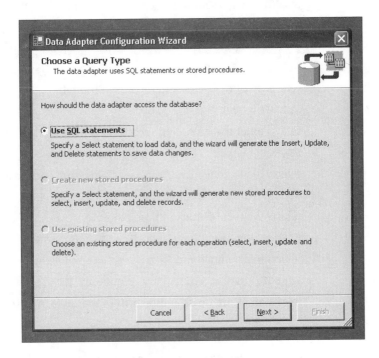

Figure 12-12: Choose a Query Type screen

You use the Choose a Query Type screen to specify how the DataAdapter object should access the database. Notice that the Use SQL statements radio button is selected in Figure 12-12. You learn about SQL in the next section.

SQL

SQL, pronounced like the word *sequel*, stands for **Structured Query Language**. SQL is a set of commands that allows you to access and manipulate the data stored in many database management systems on computers of all sizes, from large mainframes to small microcomputers. You can use SQL commands to perform database tasks such as storing, retrieving, updating, deleting, and sorting data.

The SELECT statement is the most commonly used command in SQL. The **SELECT statement** allows you to specify the fields and records you want to view, as well as control the order in which the fields and records appear when displayed. Figure 12-13 shows the basic syntax of the SELECT statement and includes several examples of using the statement to access the data stored in the Employees.mdb database (shown earlier in Figure 12-5). As you may remember, the database contains one table (named tblEmploy) and seven fields. The Number, Rate, and Code fields contain numeric data. The Last, First, and Status fields contain text data, and the Hired field contains dates.

The SQL syntax, which refers to the rules you must follow to use the language, was accepted by the American National Standards Institute (ANSI) in 1986. You can use SQL in many database management systems and programming languages.

The full syntax of the Select statement contains other clauses and options that are beyond the scope of this book.

Syntax
SELECT *fields* **FROM** *table* [**WHERE** *condition*] [**ORDER BY** *field*]

Examples and results
SELECT Code, First, Hired, Last, Number, Rate, Status FROM tblEmploy selects all of the fields and records in the table
SELECT * FROM tblEmploy selects all of the fields and records in the table
SELECT Number, First, Last FROM tblEmploy selects the Number, First, and Last fields from each record in the table
SELECT * FROM tblEmploy WHERE Status = 'F' selects the records for full-time employees
SELECT Number, Rate FROM tblEmploy WHERE Code = 3 selects the Number and Rate fields for employees in the Personnel department
SELECT * FROM tblEmploy ORDER BY Hired selects all of the fields and records in the table, and sorts the records in ascending order by the Hired field
SELECT * FROM tblEmploy WHERE Status = 'p' ORDER BY Code selects the records for part-time employees, and sorts the records in ascending order by the Code field

Figure 12-13: Syntax and examples of the SELECT statement

tip

You do not have to capitalize the keywords SELECT, FROM, WHERE, and ORDER BY in a SELECT statement; however, many programmers do so for clarity.

In the SELECT statement's syntax, *fields* is one or more field names (separated by commas), and *table* is the name of the table containing the fields. Notice that the syntax contains two clauses that are optional: the WHERE clause and the ORDER BY clause. The **WHERE clause** allows you to limit the records that will be selected, and the **ORDER BY clause** allows you to control the order in which the records appear when displayed.

Study closely the examples shown in Figure 12-13. The SELECT Code, First, Hired, Last, Number, Rate, Status FROM tblEmploy statement in the first example selects all of the fields and records from the tblEmploy table. The SELECT * FROM tblEmploy statement in the second example produces the same result and shows you a simpler way of selecting all of the fields in a table. Rather than entering each field name in the *fields* portion of the SELECT statement, you simply enter an asterisk (*). When the computer processes the SELECT statement, it replaces the asterisk with the names of the fields in the table; the field names appear in alphabetical order.

The SELECT Number, First, Last FROM tblEmploy statement in the third example selects only three of the fields from each record in the tblEmploy table. The SELECT * FROM tblEmploy WHERE Status = 'F' statement in the fourth example uses the WHERE clause to limit the records that will be selected. In this case, the statement indicates that only records for full-time employees should be selected. Notice that, when comparing the contents of the Status field (which contains text) with a string, you enclose the string in single quotation marks rather than in double quotation marks.

The SELECT Number, Rate FROM tblEmploy WHERE Code = 3 statement in the fifth example in Figure 12-13 selects only the Number and Rate fields for employees working in the Personnel department. The SELECT * FROM tblEmploy ORDER BY Hired statement in the sixth example selects all of the fields and records from the tblEmploy table, and then uses the ORDER BY clause to sort the records in ascending order by the Hired field. To sort the records in descending order, you use SELECT * FROM tblEmploy ORDER BY Hired DESC. The "DESC" stands for "descending".

The SELECT * FROM tblEmploy WHERE Status = 'p' ORDER BY Code statement shown in the last example in Figure 12-13 selects the records for part-time employees, and it sorts the records in ascending order by the Code field. Notice that the statement compares the contents of the Status field (which contains uppercase letters) with a lowercase 'p'. The statement works correctly because SQL commands are not case-sensitive.

Now that you know how to write SELECT statements, you can continue learning how to configure the DataAdapter object.

Using the Query Builder to Enter a SELECT Statement

When you click the Next > button on the Choose a Query Type screen (shown earlier in Figure 12-12), the Generate the SQL statements screen appears, as shown in Figure 12-14.

Figure 12-14: Generate the SQL statements screen

You enter the appropriate SELECT statement in the "What data should the data adapter load into the dataset?" box. You can enter the SELECT statement yourself, or you can have the Query Builder enter it for you. To use the Query Builder, you click the Query Builder button. After doing so, the Query Builder and Add Table dialog boxes open, as shown in Figure 12-15.

Tables tab

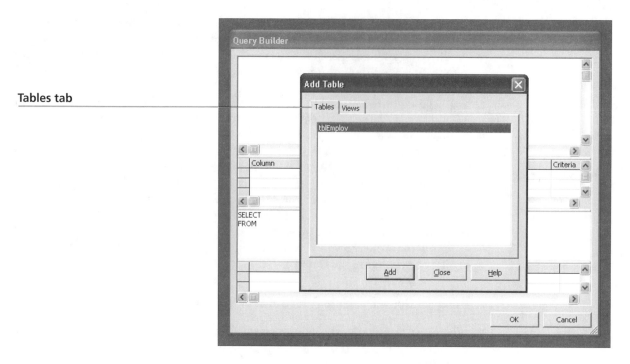

Figure 12-15: Query Builder and Add Table dialog boxes

Notice that tblEmploy, which is the name of the table contained in the Employees.mdb database, appears on the Tables tab in the Add Table dialog box. The tblEmploy table contains the employee information that you want to access. You add the tblEmploy table to the Query Builder dialog box by clicking the Add button. You then click the Close button to close the Add Table dialog box.

When you close the Add Table dialog box, the names of the seven fields contained in the tblEmploy table appear in a list box in the Query Builder dialog box, as shown in Figure 12-16. Notice that the field names are listed in ascending alphabetical order (which is not the order in which the fields appear in the table). Additionally, the Query Builder begins entering a SELECT statement for you.

scroll the list box to
view the remaining field
names

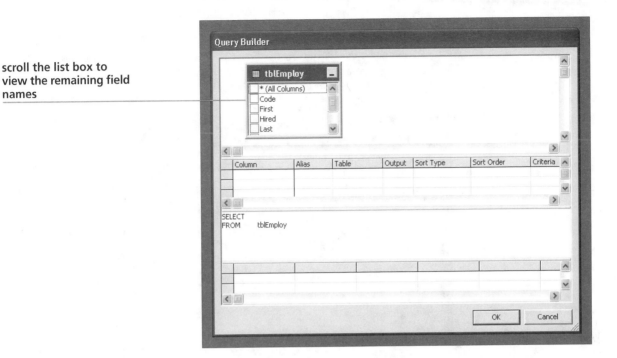

Figure 12-16: Query Builder dialog box showing the fields and SELECT statement

Assume you want to display each employee's number, name, and rate of pay. To do so, you select the check boxes next to the Number, First, Last, and Rate fields, as shown in Figure 12-17. When you select a check box, the corresponding field name appears in the SELECT statement. Notice that the Number field, which is the primary key, appears in brackets in the SELECT statement; it also appears in bold text in the listing of field names.

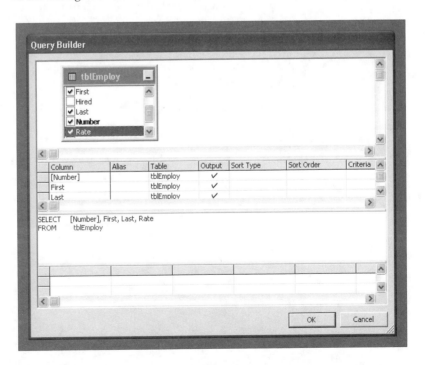

Figure 12-17: Completed SELECT statement in the Query Builder dialog box

The SELECT statement shown in Figure 12-17 tells the DataAdapter object to select only four of the seven fields from all of the records in the tblEmploy table. When you click the OK button to close the Query Builder dialog box, the Generate the SQL statements screen appears and displays the SELECT statement created by the Query Builder, as shown in Figure 12-18.

Figure 12-18: SELECT statement entered in the Generate the SQL statements screen

When you click the Next > button in the Generate the SQL statements screen, the View Wizard Results screen appears, as shown in Figure 12-19. The screen indicates that the "OleDbDataAdapter1" object was configured successfully.

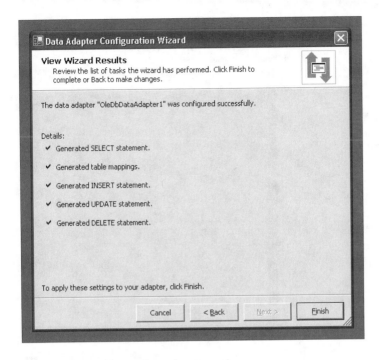

Figure 12-19: View Wizard Results screen

Finally, you click the Finish button in the View Wizard Results screen to close the Data Adapter Configuration Wizard dialog box. If the "Do you want to include the password in the connection string?" dialog box opens, you click the Don't include password button. At this point, Visual Basic .NET creates a Connection object; more specifically, it creates an OleDbConnection object named OleDbConnection1. It places the object in the component tray in the Form Designer window, as shown in Figure 12-20.

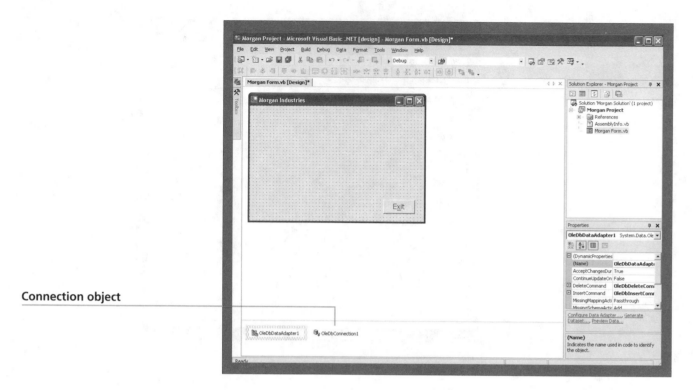

Connection object

Figure 12-20: OleDbConnection1 object added to the component tray

You have now finished creating and configuring the DataAdapter object. The next step in accessing the data stored in a Microsoft Access database is to create a dataset.

Creating a Dataset

A dataset contains the data you want to access from the database, as specified in the SELECT statement associated with the DataAdapter object. In this case, the dataset will contain each employee's number, name, and rate of pay. Figure 12-21 shows the procedure you follow to create a dataset, and Figure 12-22 shows a completed Generate Dataset dialog box.

Creating a dataset

1. Right-click the DataAdapter object in the component tray, then click Generate Dataset.

2. Verify that the New radio button is selected in the Generate Dataset dialog box.

3. Assign a meaningful name to the dataset.

4. Select the appropriate table(s) from the Choose which table(s) to add to the dataset list box.

5. Verify that the Add this dataset to the designer check box is selected. (See Figure 12-22.)

6. Click the OK button to close the Generate Dataset dialog box. (See Figure 12-23.)

7. To preview the contents of the dataset, right-click the DataAdapter object in the component tray. Click Preview Data, and then click the Fill Dataset button in the Data Adapter Preview dialog box. (See Figure 12-24.)

8. Click the Close button to close the Data Adapter Preview dialog box.

Figure 12-21: Procedure for creating a dataset

name assigned
to the dataset

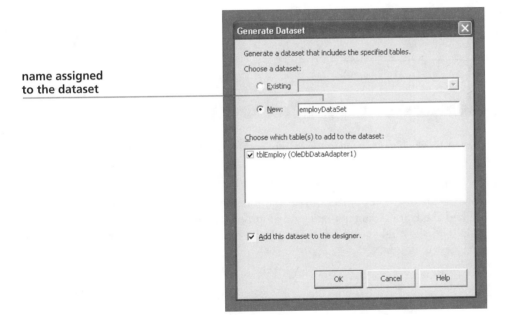

Figure 12-22: Generate Dataset dialog box

When you close the Generate Dataset dialog box in Step 6, a DataSet object appears in the component tray, as shown in Figure 12-23. Notice that Visual Basic .NET names the object using the dataset's name (with the first letter capitalized) followed by the number one. The number one indicates that the EmployDataSet1 object is the first DataSet object created using the EmployDataSet dataset. Also notice that the Solution Explorer window contains a new file named employDataSet.xsd. The .xsd extension on the filename indicates that the file is an

XML schema definition file. **XML**, which stands for **Extensible Markup Language**, is a text-based language used to store and share data between applications and across networks and the Internet. An **XML schema definition file** defines the tables and fields that make up the dataset. (You view the contents of an .xsd file in Lesson B's Exercise 6.)

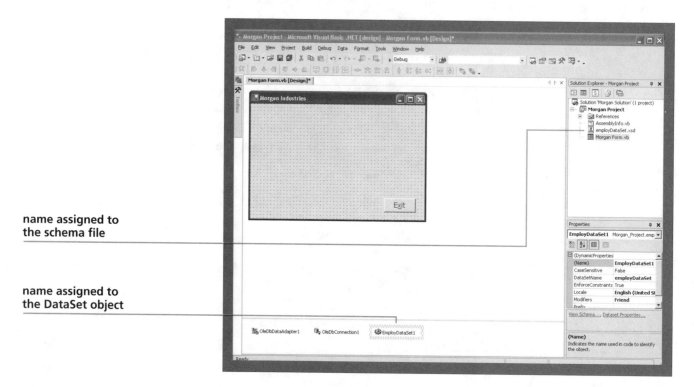

name assigned to
the schema file

name assigned to
the DataSet object

Figure 12-23: Changes made to the component tray and Solution Explorer window

Once you have created the dataset, you can preview its contents by right-clicking the DataAdapter object in the component tray, and then clicking Preview Data. When the Data Adapter Preview dialog box opens, you click the Fill Dataset button. Figure 12-24 shows the EmployDataSet dataset displayed in the Data Adapter Preview dialog box.

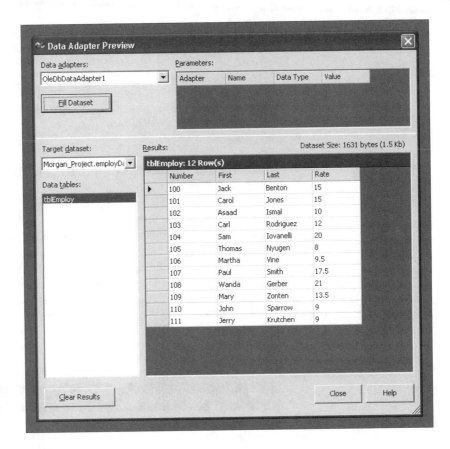

Figure 12-24: Data Adapter Preview dialog box

The Data Adapter Preview dialog box allows you to preview the dataset while you are designing the application. To fill the dataset with data when the application is running, you use the DataAdapter object's Fill method.

Using the Fill Method

You use the DataAdapter object's **Fill method** to fill a dataset with data while an application is running. The SELECT statement you entered when configuring the DataAdapter object determines the appropriate data. Figure 12-25 shows the syntax of the Fill method and includes an example of using the method.

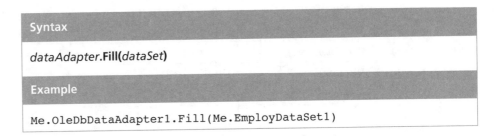

Syntax

dataAdapter.**Fill**(*dataSet*)

Example

```
Me.OleDbDataAdapter1.Fill(Me.EmployDataSet1)
```

Figure 12-25: Syntax and an example of the Fill method

In the Fill method's syntax, *dataAdapter* is the name of a DataAdapter object, and *dataSet* is the name of a DataSet object. The example shown in Figure 12-25 will fill the dataset associated with the EmployDataSet1 object with the data specified in the OleDbDataAdapter1 object's SELECT statement. In most cases, you enter the Fill method in the form's Load event procedure, because you typically want to fill the dataset when the application first starts.

For the user to view the dataset in an application, you need to bind the DataSet object to one or more controls in the interface. In this lesson, you learn how to bind the DataSet object to a DataGrid control.

Binding the DataSet Object to a DataGrid Control

You view the data contained in a dataset by connecting its DataSet object to one or more controls in the interface. Connecting a DataSet object to a control is called **binding**, and the connected controls are referred to as **bound controls**. You bind a control using one or more properties listed in the Properties window. The appropriate property (or properties) to use depends on the control you are binding. For example, you use the DataSource and DataMember properties to bind a DataGrid control. However, you use the DataSource and DisplayMember properties to bind a ListBox control. To bind label and text box controls, you use the DataBindings/Text property. Figure 12-26 shows the procedure you follow to bind a DataSet object to a DataGrid control.

Binding a DataSet object to a DataGrid control
1. Set the DataGrid control's DataSource property to the name of the DataSet object.
2. Set the DataGrid control's DataMember property to the name of a table.

Figure 12-26: Procedure for binding a DataSet object to a DataGrid control

When bound to a DataSet object, the **DataGrid control** displays the data from the dataset in a row and column format, similar to a spreadsheet. Each field in the dataset appears in a column in the DataGrid control, and each record appears in a row. The intersection of a row and a column in the DataGrid control is called a cell. Figure 12-27 lists the names and uses of several properties of a DataGrid control.

Property	Use to
CaptionText	specify the caption that appears at the top of the control
ColumnHeadersVisible	control the display of the column headings
DataMember	specify the table to associate with the control
DataSource	specify the DataSet object to associate with the control
Name	give the DataGrid control a meaningful name
ReadOnly	specify whether changes can be made to the data displayed in the control
RowHeadersVisible	control the display of the row headings
Note: The DataGrid control also has an Auto Format link that appears in the Properties window when the control is selected. You can use the link to display a dialog box that allows you to select from a list of predefined formats for displaying data.	

Figure 12-27: Properties of a DataGrid control

Figure 12-28 shows a sample run of an application that contains a DataGrid control, and Figure 12-29 shows the code entered in the form's Load event procedure. In the application, the DataGrid control's Name property is set to uiEmployDataGrid, its CaptionText property to "Employee Records", its ReadOnly property to True, and its RowHeadersVisible property to False. Additionally, the control's DataSource and DataMember properties are set to EmployDataSet1 (the name of the DataSet object) and tblEmploy (the name of the table within the DataSet object), respectively.

tip

You also could have set the DataGrid control's DataSource property to EmployDataSet1.tblEmploy, and then left the Data-Member property empty.

Figure 12-28: Sample run of an application that contains a DataGrid control

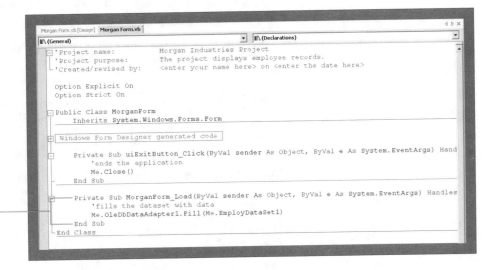

load event procedure

Figure 12-29: Form's Load event procedure shown in the Code Editor window

When you start the application, the Fill method in the form's Load event procedure fills the dataset associated with the EmployDataSet1 object with data. Because the EmployDataSet1 object is bound to the DataGrid control, the records from the dataset appear in the control, as shown in Figure 12-28. You can use the arrow keys on your keyboard to access a different field and/or record in the DataGrid control. Notice that scroll bars appear when there is more data than will fit into the control.

Now assume that you want to display (in the DataGrid control) the number, name, pay rate, and department code of employees working in the Personnel department. Additionally, you want the records displayed in ascending last name order. To accomplish this task, you need to reconfigure the DataAdapter object.

Reconfiguring the DataAdapter Object

Figure 12-30 shows the procedure you follow to reconfigure an existing DataAdapter object.

Reconfiguring an existing DataAdapter object

1. Right-click the DataAdapter object in the component tray, and then click Configure Data Adapter.

2. Click the Next > button on the Welcome to the Data Adapter Configuration Wizard screen.

3. Click the Next > button on the Choose Your Data Connection screen.

4. Click the Next > button on the Choose a Query Type screen.

5. Click the Query Builder button on the Generate the SQL statements screen.

6. Make the desired modifications to the SELECT statement in the Query Builder dialog box.

7. Click the OK button to close the Query Builder dialog box.

8. Click the Next > button on the Generate the SQL statements screen.

9. Click the Finish button on the View Wizard Results screen.

10. Right-click the DataAdapter object in the component tray, then click Generate Dataset.

11. Click the OK button in the Generate Dataset dialog box.

12. To preview the contents of the dataset, right-click the DataAdapter object in the component tray. Click Preview Data, and then click the Fill Dataset button in the Data Adapter Preview dialog box. Click the Close button to close the Data Adapter Preview dialog box.

Figure 12-30: Procedure for reconfiguring an existing DataAdapter object

Figure 12-31 shows the modifications made to the SELECT statement in the Query Builder dialog box, and Figure 12-32 shows the new dataset displayed in the DataGrid control.

the funnel symbol
indicates that the Code
field is used in the
WHERE clause

this symbol indicates
that the dataset is
sorted in ascending
alphabetical order by
the Last name field

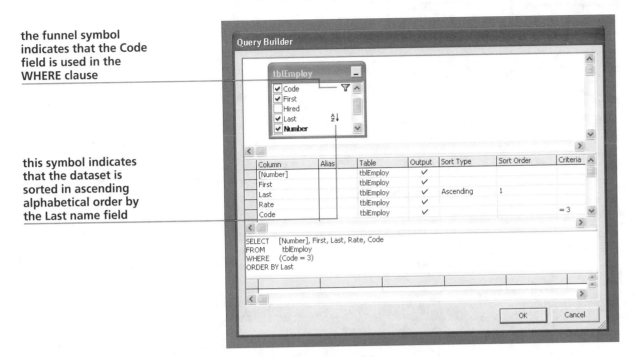

Figure 12-31: Modifications made to the SELECT statement in the Query Builder dialog box

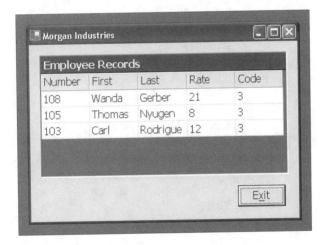

Figure 12-32: New dataset displayed in the DataGrid control

You now have completed Lesson A. You can either take a break or complete the end-of-lesson questions and exercises before moving on to the next lesson. In Lesson B, you learn how to bind label, text box, and list box controls to a DataSet object. You also code the Cartwright Industries application that you previewed at the beginning of the chapter. In Lesson C, you learn how to use ASP.NET to create a Web application.

SUMMARY

To access a database from a Visual Basic .NET application:

■ Use the DataAdapter, Connection, and DataSet objects.

To create and configure a DataAdapter object for a Microsoft Access database:

■ Use the procedure shown in Figure 12-6.

To specify the fields and records you want to view, as well as control the order in which the fields and records appear when displayed:

■ Use the SQL SELECT statement. The syntax of the SELECT statement is **SELECT** *fields* **FROM** *table* [**WHERE** *condition*][**ORDER BY** *field*].

To create a dataset:

■ Use the procedure shown in Figure 12-21.

To fill a dataset with data while an application is running:

■ Use the Fill method. The syntax of the Fill method is *dataAdapter*.**Fill**(*dataSet*).

To bind a DataSet object to a DataGrid control:

■ First set the DataGrid control's DataSource property to the name of the DataSet object, then set its DataMember property to the name of a table.

To reconfigure a DataAdapter object:

■ Use the procedure shown in Figure 12-30.

QUESTIONS

1. A(n) _____ is an organized collection of related information stored in a file on a disk.
    a. database
    b. field
    c. object
    d. record
    e. structure

2. A _____ database is one that stores information in tables.
    a. columnar
    b. relational
    c. sorted
    d. tabular
    e. vertical

3. A group of related records in a database is called a _____.
    a. column
    b. field
    c. row
    d. table
    e. None of the above.

4. Which of the following statements are true about a relational database?
   a. Data stored in a relational database can be retrieved both quickly and easily by the computer.
   b. Data stored in a relational database can be displayed in any order.
   c. A relational database stores data in a column and row format.
   d. All of the above are true.
   e. None of the above is true.

5. When binding a DataSet object to a control, you set the control's _____ property to the name of the DataSet object.
   a. Data
   b. Dataset
   c. DataMember
   d. DataSource
   e. Source

6. _____ is a set of commands that allow you to access the data stored in many databases.
   a. ADO.NET
   b. DB.NET
   c. OLE.NET
   d. SQL
   e. QUERY

Use the following database table, named tblState, to answer Questions 7 through 9.

Field name	Data type
State	Text
Capital	Text
Population	Numeric

7. Which of the following statements allows you to view all of the records in the table?
   a. `SELECT ALL records FROM tblState`
   b. `SELECT * FROM tblState`
   c. `VIEW ALL records FROM tblState`
   d. `VIEW * FROM tblState`
   e. None of the above.

8. Which of the following statements allows you to retrieve only the record whose State field contains the two letters "NY"?
   a. `SELECT * FROM tblState FOR "NY"`
   b. `SELECT * FROM tblState WHERE State = "NY"`
   c. `SELECT * FROM tblState WHERE State = 'ny'`
   d. `SELECT "NY" FROM tblState`
   e. None of the above.

9. Which of the following statements allows you to retrieve all records having a population that exceeds 5,000,000?
   a. `SELECT ALL FROM tblState FOR Population > 5000000`
   b. `SELECT ALL FROM tblState FOR Population > "5000000"`
   c. `SELECT * FROM tblState WHERE Population > "5000000"`
   d. `SELECT * FROM tblState WHERE Population > '5000000'`
   e. None of the above.

10. A field that uniquely identifies each record in a table is called a _____.
    a. foreign field
    b. foreign key
    c. primary field
    d. primary key
    e. None of the above.

11. The _____ contains the SELECT statement, which specifies the data the application wants to access.
    a. DataAdapter object
    b. Connection object
    c. DataSet object
    d. Provider
    e. None of the above.

12. A _____ allows the database to communicate with the Connection object.
    a. DataAdapter object
    b. DataSet object
    c. Provider
    d. Translator object
    e. None of the above.

13. In a SELECT statement, the _____ clause is used to limit the records that will be selected.
    a. LIMIT
    b. ORDER BY
    c. SELECT
    d. SET
    e. None of the above.

14. Controls connected to a DataSet object are called _____ controls.
    a. bound
    b. connected
    c. data
    d. dataset
    e. None of the above.

15. You can use the _____ to build a SELECT statement.
    a. Query Builder
    b. Select Builder
    c. SQL Builder
    d. SQL Helper
    e. None of the above.

16. If a funnel symbol appears next to a field's name in the Query Builder, it indicates that the field is _____.
    a. used in an ORDER BY clause in a SELECT statement
    b. used in a WHERE clause in a SELECT statement
    c. the primary key
    d. the foreign key
    e. None of the above.

17. Objects that do not appear in the interface when an application is running are stored in the _____.
   a. component tray
   b. control tray
   c. object tray
   d. system tray
   e. None of the above.

18. You use the _____ tool to create a DataAdapter object for a Microsoft Access database.
   a. OleDataAdapter
   b. OleDbAdapter
   c. OleDbDataAdapter
   d. OleDataDbAdapter
   e. None of the above.

19. Which of the following tells the DataAdapter object to load the StateDataSet dataset with data? The dataset is associated with the StateDataSet1 object.
   a. `Me.OleDbDataAdapter1(Me.StateDataSet)`
   b. `Me.OleDbDataAdapter1.Fill(Me.StateDataSet)`
   c. `Me.OleDbDataAdapter1.Fill(Me.StateDataSet1)`
   d. `Me.OleDbDataAdapter1.Load(Me.StateDataSet1)`

20. The SQL SELECT statement is case-sensitive.
   a. True
   b. False

E X E R C I S E S

1. In this exercise, you create an application that accesses the data stored in a database.
   a. If necessary, start Visual Studio .NET. Create the Morgan Industries interface shown in Figure 12-23. Name the solution Morgan Solution. Name the project Morgan Project. Save the solution in the VBNET\Chap12 folder.
   b. Add the DataAdapter, Connection, and DataSet objects shown in Figure 12-23 to the application. The Employees.mdb database is contained in the VBNET\Chap12\Databases folder.
   c. Use the application to test each of the SELECT statements shown in Figure 12-13. Enter each SELECT statement, one at a time, on the Generate the SQL statements screen (see Figure 12-14). After entering each statement, regenerate the dataset and then preview the data to verify that the statement selects the appropriate records.
   d. Write the SELECT statement to select only records with a hire date of 12/4/1998.
   e. Save the solution.

2. In this exercise, you create an application that displays a dataset in a DataGrid control.
   a. Use Windows to make a copy of the Morgan Solution folder, which you created in Exercise 1. Rename the folder Morgan DataGrid Solution.
   b. If necessary, start Visual Studio .NET. Open the Morgan Solution (Morgan Solution.sln) file contained in the Morgan DataGrid Solution folder.
   c. Add a DataGrid control to the interface. The control should display each employee's number, name, and pay rate, as shown in Figure 12-28. Use the code shown in Figure 12-29 to code the form's Load event procedure.
   d. Save the solution, and then start and test the application.
   e. Click the Exit button to end the application.
   f. Modify the application so that it displays the fields and records shown in Figure 12-32.
   g. Save the solution, and then start and test the application.
   h. Click the Exit button to end the application, then close the solution.

More on Binding Controls

Binding the DataSet Object to a Label Control or a Text Box

Figure 12-33 shows the procedure you follow to bind a DataSet object to a label control or text box, and Figure 12-34 shows an example of setting the DataBindings/Text property in the Properties window.

Binding a DataSet object to a label control or text box
1. Select the label control or text box.
2. Click (DataBindings) in the Properties list.
3. Click the plus box that appears to the left of (DataBindings).
4. Click Text in the properties list.
5. Click the list arrow in the Settings box, and then click the plus box that appears next to the name of the DataSet object.
6. Click the plus box that appears next to the table name, and then click the name of the field. (See Figure 12-34.)

Figure 12-33: Procedure for binding a DataSet object to a label control or text box

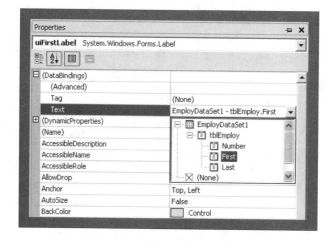

Figure 12-34: DataBindings/Text property shown in the Properties window

Figure 12-35 shows a sample run of an application that uses label controls to display the data contained in the dataset, and Figure 12-36 shows the application's code.

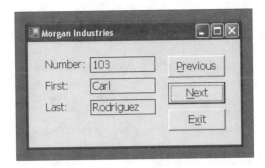

Figure 12-35: Sample run of an application that uses label controls to display the dataset

```
'Project name:           Morgan Labels Project
'Project purpose:        The project displays information from the
'                        Employees.mdb database.
'Created/revised by:     <enter your name here> on <enter the date here>

Option Explicit On
Option Strict On

Public Class MorganForm
    Inherits System.Windows.Forms.Form

[Windows Form Designer generated code]

    Private Sub uiExitButton_Click(ByVal sender As Object, _
        ByVal e As System.EventArgs) Handles uiExitButton.Click
        'ends the application
        Me.Close()
    End Sub

    Private Sub MorganForm_Load(ByVal sender As Object, _
        ByVal e As System.EventArgs) Handles MyBase.Load
        'fills the dataset with data
        Me.OleDbDataAdapter1.Fill(Me.EmployDataSet1)
    End Sub

    Private Sub uiNextButton_Click(ByVal sender As Object, _
        ByVal e As System.EventArgs) Handles uiNextButton.Click
        'moves the record pointer to the next record in the dataset
        Me.BindingContext(Me.EmployDataSet1, "tblEmploy").Position = _
            Me.BindingContext(Me.EmployDataSet1, "tblEmploy").Position + 1
    End Sub

    Private Sub uiPreviousButton_Click(ByVal sender As Object, _
        ByVal e As System.EventArgs) Handles uiPreviousButton.Click
        'moves the record pointer to the previous record in the dataset
        Me.BindingContext(Me.EmployDataSet1, "tblEmploy").Position = _
            Me.BindingContext(Me.EmployDataSet1, "tblEmploy").Position - 1
    End Sub
```

Figure 12-36: Code for the application shown in Figure 12-35

Notice that the interface shown in Figure 12-35 contains two buttons labeled "Previous" and "Next". You use the Previous and Next buttons to display the previous and next records, respectively, from the dataset.

To display the next record, you need to move the record pointer, which keeps track of the current record, to the next position in the dataset. You can move the record pointer using the syntax **Me.BindingContext**(*datasetObject*, *tablename*).**Position** = *value*. In the syntax, *datasetObject* is the name of the DataSet object associated with the dataset, and *tablename* (which must be enclosed in quotation marks) is the name of the table within the dataset. *Value* is the value you want assigned to the BindingContext.Position property. For example, to move the record pointer to the next record in the database, you use the statement `Me.BindingContext(Me.EmployDataSet1,  "tblEmploy").Position  =  Me .BindingContext(Me.EmployDataSet1, "tblEmploy").Position + 1`, as shown in the uiNextButton's Click procedure in Figure 12-36. Similarly, to move the record pointer to the previous record in the database, you use the statement `Me.BindingContext(Me.EmployDataSet1,  "tblEmploy").Position  =  Me .BindingContext(Me.EmployDataSet1, "tblEmploy").Position - 1`, as shown in the uiPreviousButton's Click procedure in Figure 12-36. To move the record pointer to the first record in the dataset, you use the number 0 as the *value*, because the first record is in position 0 (zero). To move the record pointer to the last record in the dataset, you use `Me.EmployDataSet1.tblEmploy.Rows.Count` - 1 as the *value*.

Now you can begin coding the Cartwright Industries application.

Coding the Cartwright Industries Application

Recall that Carl Simons, the sales manager at Cartwright Industries, records the item number, name, and price of each product the company sells in a database named Items.mdb. Figure 12-37 shows the Items.mdb database opened in Microsoft Access. The database contains one table named tblItems. The Number and Name fields contain text, and the Price field contains numbers.

Number	Name	Price
ABX12	Chair	$45.00
CSR14	Desk	$175.00
JTR23	Table	$65.00
NRE09	End Table	$46.00
OOE68	Bookcase	$300.00
PPR00	Coffee Table	$190.00
PRT45	Lamp	$30.00
REZ04	Love Seat	$700.00
THR98	Side Chair	$33.00
WKP10	Sofa	$873.00
		$0.00

tblItems : Table

Figure 12-37: Items.mdb database opened in Microsoft Access

On your computer's hard disk is a partially completed Cartwright Industries application.

To open the Cartwright Industries application:

1 Start Microsoft Visual Studio .NET, if necessary.

2 If necessary, close the Start Page window.

3 Open the **Cartwright Solution** (Cartwright Solution.sln) file, which is contained in the VBNET\Chap12\Cartwright Solution folder.

4 Auto-hide the Toolbox, Solution Explorer, and Properties windows, if necessary. Figure 12-38 shows the user interface for the Cartwright application.

Figure 12-38: Interface for the Cartwright application

Figure 12-39 shows the TOE chart for the Cartwright Industries application.

Task	Object	Event
End the application	uiExitButton	Click
Display the price from the dataset	uiPriceLabel	None
Get the item number	uiItemNumListBox	None
Fill the dataset with the item numbers and prices from the Items.mdb database	CartwrightForm	Load
Access the data in the Items.mdb database	OleDbDataAdapter1, OleDbConnection1, ItemsDataSet1	None

Figure 12-39: TOE chart for the Cartwright Industries application

Recall that you use three ADO.NET objects (DataAdapter, Connection, and DataSet) and a provider to access a database from a Visual Basic .NET application.

To access the Items.mdb database:

1 Click the **Data** tab on the Toolbox window.

2 Click the **OleDbDataAdapter tool** in the toolbox, and then drag an OleDbDataAdapter control to the form. When you release the mouse button, the control appears in the component tray, and a Welcome screen appears on the screen.

3 Click the **Next >** button to display the Choose Your Data Connection screen.

4 Click the **New Connection** button on the Choose Your Data Connection screen. The Data Link Properties dialog box opens.

5 Click the **Provider** tab on the Data Link Properties dialog box, then click **Microsoft Jet 4.0 OLE DB Provider** in the OLE DB Provider(s) list box.

6 Click the **Connection** tab on the Data Link Properties dialog box, then click the **...** (ellipsis) button that appears next to the "Select or enter a database name" text box. The Select Access Database dialog box opens.

7 Open the VBNET\Chap12\Databases folder. If necessary, click **Items.mdb** in the list of filenames.

8 Click the **Open** button, and then click the **Test Connection** button. The "Test connection succeeded." message appears in the Microsoft Data Link dialog box, as shown in Figure 12-40.

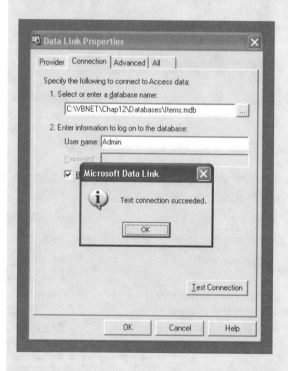

Figure 12-40: Message displayed in the Microsoft Data Link dialog box

9 Click the **OK** button to close the Microsoft Data Link dialog box.

10 Click the **OK** button to close the Data Link Properties dialog box. The Choose Your Data Connection screen appears, as shown in Figure 12-41.

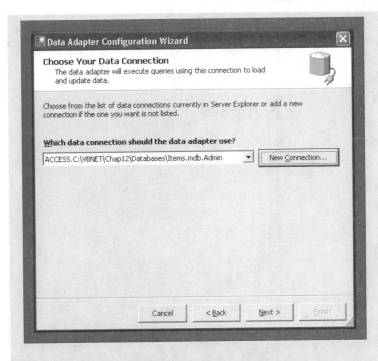

Figure 12-41: Choose Your Data Connection screen

11 Click the **Next >** button to display the Choose a Query Type screen.

12 Verify that the Use SQL statements radio button is selected on the Choose a Query Type screen, and then click the **Next >** button. The Generate the SQL statements screen appears.

13 Click the **Query Builder** button to display the Query Builder and Add Table dialog boxes.

14 Click the **Add** button to add the tblItems table to the Query Builder dialog box.

15 Click the **Close** button to close the Add Table dialog box. The names of the fields contained in the tblItems table appear in the Query Builder dialog box.

16 Click the *** (All Columns)** check box to select it, then click the **OK** button to close the Query Builder dialog box. The Generate the SQL statements screen appears, as shown in Figure 12-42.

selects all of the fields
in the table

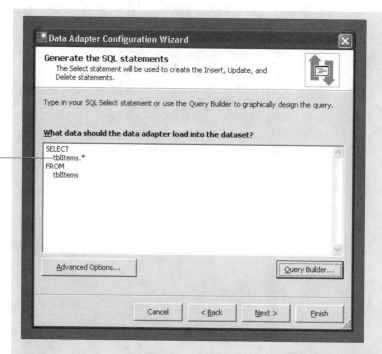

Figure 12-42: Completed Generate the SQL statements screen

17 Click the **Next >** button to display the View Wizard Results screen shown in Figure 12-43.

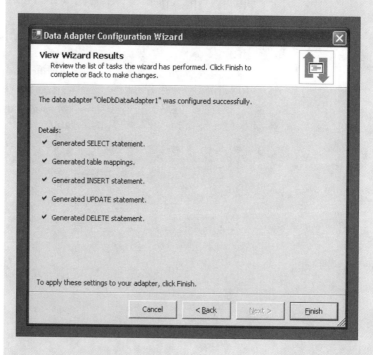

Figure 12-43: View Wizard Results screen

18 Click the **Finish** button. If the "Do you want to include the password in the connection string?" dialog box opens, click the **Don't include password**

button. Visual Basic .NET adds an OleDbConnection object to the component tray.

Now you can generate the dataset.

19 Right-click the **OleDbDataAdapter1** object in the component tray, then click **Generate Dataset**. The Generate Dataset dialog box opens.

20 Verify that the New radio button is selected in the Generate Dataset dialog box. Also verify that the tblItems (OleDbDataAdapter1) and Add this dataset to the designer check boxes are selected.

21 In the text box that appears to the right of the New radio button, replace DataSet1 with **itemsDataSet**. Figure 12-44 shows the completed Generate Dataset dialog box.

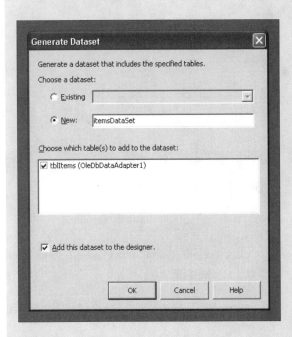

Figure 12-44: Completed Generate Dataset dialog box

22 Click the **OK** button to close the Generate Dataset dialog box. Visual Basic .NET adds a DataSet object to the component tray and adds an XML schema definition file to the Solution Explorer window.

23 Temporarily display the Solution Explorer window. See Figure 12-45.

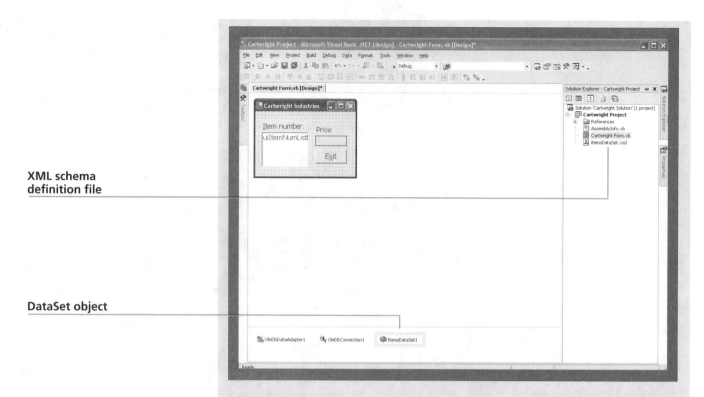

XML schema definition file

DataSet object

Figure 12-45: Screen showing the DataSet object and XML schema definition file

Now preview the contents of the dataset.

24 Right-click the **OleDbDataAdapter1** object in the component tray, and then click **Preview Data**. The Data Adapter Preview dialog box opens.

25 Click the **Fill Dataset** button in the Data Adapter Preview dialog box. The records stored in the Items.mdb database file appear in the dialog box, as shown in Figure 12-46.

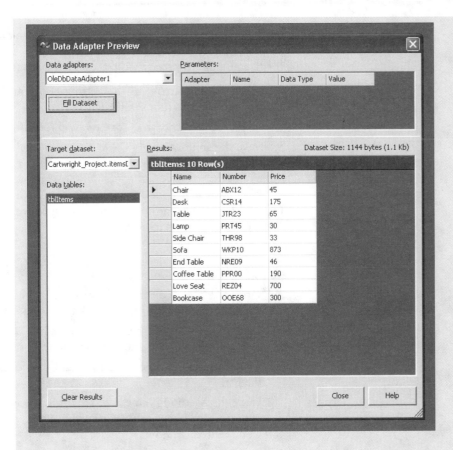

Figure 12-46: Data Adapter Preview dialog box

26 Click the **Close** button to close the Data Adapter Preview dialog box.

Next, you will bind the uiItemNumListBox and uiPriceLabel controls to the dataset. As you learned earlier, you bind a label control using the control's DataBindings/Text property. You bind a ListBox control using the control's DataSource and DisplayMember properties.

To bind the list box and label control to the dataset:

1 Click the **uiItemNumListBox** control in the interface. Set the control's DataSource property to **ItemsDataSet1**, and set its DisplayMember property to **tblItems.Number**.

2 Click the **uiPriceLabel** control in the interface. Click the **plus box** that appears next to the (DataBindings) property in the properties list, then click **Text**.

HELP? When the properties list is arranged alphabetically, the (DataBindings) property is at the top of the list. When the properties list is arranged by category, the (DataBindings) property is listed in the Data section.

3   Click the **list arrow** in the Settings box, and then click the **plus box** that appears next to ItemsDataSet1.

4   Click the **plus box** that appears next to tblItems, and then click **Price**.

5   Save the solution.

Now you can code the application. According to the TOE chart shown in Figure 12-39, only the uiExitButton's Click event procedure and the form's Load event procedure need to code.

To code the application, and then test it:

1   Open the Code Editor window. Notice that the window already contains the code for the uiExitButton's Click event procedure.

2   Replace the `<enter your name here>` and `<enter the date here>` text with your name and the current date.

3   Click the **Class Name** list arrow, and then click (**CartwrightForm Events**) in the list.

4   Click the **Method Name** list arrow, and then click **Load** in the list. The code template for the CartwrightForm's Load event procedure appears in the Code Editor window.

According to the TOE chart, the Load event procedure is responsible for filling the dataset with the item numbers and prices stored in the Items.mdb database.

5   Type **'fills the dataset with data** and press **Enter**.

As you learned in Lesson A, you use the DataAdapter object's Fill method to fill a dataset with data while an application is running. The SELECT statement you entered when configuring the DataAdapter object determines the appropriate data. Recall that the syntax of the Fill method is *dataAdapter*.**Fill**(*dataSet*), where *dataAdapter* is the name of a DataAdapter object and *dataSet* is the name of a DataSet object.

6   Type **me.oledbdataadapter1.fill(me.itemsdataset1)** and press **Enter**. The application's code is shown in Figure 12-47.

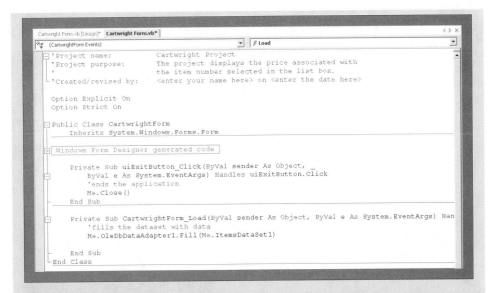

Figure 12-47: Code for the Cartwright Industries application

7 Save the solution, then start the application. The form's Load event procedure fills the dataset with data, and the interface appears on the screen, as shown in Figure 12-48.

Figure 12-48: Result of running the Cartwright Industries application

Notice that the item numbers appear in the list box control; this is because the control is bound to the Number field in the dataset. The price of the first item in the dataset appears in the label control because the control is bound to the Price field in the dataset.

8 Click **PRT45** in the list box. The label control displays 30 as the price of item number PRT45.

9 Click the **Exit** button to end the application.

10 Close the Output window, and then close the Code Editor window.

You are finished with the solution, so you can close it.

11 Click **File** on the menu bar, and then click **Close Solution**.

You now have completed Lesson B. You can either take a break or complete the end-of-lesson questions and exercises before moving on to the next lesson. In Lesson C, you learn how to use ASP.NET to create a Web application.

SUMMARY

To bind a DataSet object to a label control or text box:

■ Use the procedure shown in Figure 12-33.

To bind a DataSet object to a list box:

■ Set the list box's DataSource property to the name of the DataSet object, and set its DisplayMember property to the name of the table and field.

QUESTIONS

1. To bind a text box to a dataset, you set the text box's DataBindings/Value property.
   a. True
   b. False

2. To bind a list box to a dataset, you set the list box's _____ property to the name of the DataSet object.
   a. Binding
   b. DataBindings
   c. DataMember
   d. DataSource
   e. DisplayMember

3. Which of the following moves the record pointer to the first record in the dataset? The name of the DataSet object is EmployDataSet1. The name of the table is tblEmploy.
   a. `Me.BindingContext(Me.EmployDataSet1, "tblEmploy").Position = 0`
   b. `Me.BindingContext(Me.EmployDataSet1, "tblEmploy").Position = 1`
   c. `Me.BindingContext(Me.EmployDataSet1, "tblEmploy").Record = 0`
   d. `Me.BindingContext(Me.EmployDataSet1, "tblEmploy").Record = 1`
   e. None of the above.

EXERCISES

1. In this exercise, you modify the Cartwright Industries application you completed in the lesson.
   a. Use Windows to make a copy of the Cartwright Solution folder, which is contained in the VBNET\Chap12 folder. Rename the folder Modified Cartwright Solution.
   b. If necessary, start Visual Studio .NET. Open the Cartwright Solution (Cartwright Solution.sln) file contained in the Modified Cartwright Solution folder. Open the designer window.

c. Modify the application so that it also displays the name of the item associated with the item number selected in the list box.

d. Save the solution, then start and test the application.

e. Click the Exit button to end the application, then close the solution.

2. In this exercise, you create an application that displays a dataset in label controls.

a. If necessary, start Visual Studio .NET. Create the interface shown in Figure 12-35. Name the solution Morgan Labels Solution. Name the project Morgan Labels Project. Save the application in the VBNET\Chap12 folder.

b. Add DataAdapter, Connection, and DataSet objects to the application. The Employees.mdb database is contained in the VBNET\Chap12\Databases folder.

c. Use the code shown in Figure 12-36 to code the application.

d. Save the solution, and then start and test the application.

e. Click the Exit button to end the application.

f. Add two buttons to the interface. One of the buttons should display the first record in the dataset, and the other should display the last record. Code the buttons appropriately.

g. Save the solution, and then start and test the application.

h. Click the Exit button to end the application, then close the solution.

3. In this exercise, you create an application that displays a dataset in label controls.

a. Create a Microsoft Access database named Friends.mdb that keeps track of the names and addresses of your friends. (Or, use the Friends.mdb database contained in the VBNET\Chap12\Databases folder.)

b. If necessary, start Visual Studio .NET. Create an application that allows you to display (in label controls) the records contained in the Friends.mdb database. Name the solution Friends Solution. Name the project Friends Project. Save the application in the VBNET\Chap12 folder.

c. Save the solution, and then start and test the application.

d. End the application, then close the solution.

4. In this exercise, you create an application that allows the user to enter a seat number in a playhouse, and then displays the name and phone number of the person who reserved the seat. The seat numbers and patron names and phone numbers are stored in the Play.mdb database, which is contained in the VBNET\Chap12\Databases folder.

a. If necessary, start Visual Studio .NET. Create an appropriate interface. Name the solution Addison Solution. Name the project Addison Project. Save the application in the VBNET\Chap12 folder.

c. Code the application.

d. Save the solution, and then start and test the application.

e. End the application, then close the solution.

5. In this exercise, you create an application that allows the user to display the course title, credit hours, and grade associated with a course ID. The course IDs, course titles, credit hours, and grades are stored in the Courses.mdb database, which is contained in the VBNET\Chap12\Databases folder.

a. If necessary, start Visual Studio .NET. Create an appropriate interface. Name the solution College Solution. Name the project College Project. Save the application in the VBNET\Chap12 folder.

b. Code the application.

c. Save the solution, and then start and test the application.

d. End the application, then close the solution.

discovery ▶ 6. In this exercise, you learn about the XML schema definition file.

a. If necessary, start Visual Studio .NET. Open the Cartwright Solution (Cartwright Solution.sln) file contained in the VBNET\Chap12\Cartwright Solution folder.

b. Right-click the name of the XML schema definition file in the Solution Explorer window, and then click Open. What information appears in the window?

c. Click the XML tab at the bottom of the window. Explain the following line:
`<xs:element name="Number" type="xs:string" />`.

d. Close the itemsDataSet.xsd window. Close the solution.

debugging 7. In this exercise, you find and correct an error in an application. The process of finding and correcting errors is called debugging.

a. If necessary, start Visual Studio .NET. Open the Debug Solution (Debug Solution.sln) file, which is contained in the VBNET\Chap12\Debug Solution folder.

b. Open the Code Editor window. Review the existing code.

c. Notice that a jagged line appears below one of the lines of code in the Code Editor window. Correct the code to remove the jagged line.

d. Save the solution, then start and test the application. Notice that the application is not working correctly. Click the Exit button to end the application.

e. Correct the errors in the application's code, then save the solution and start the application. Test the application.

f. Click the Exit button to end the application, then close the solution.

After completing this lesson, you will be able to:

- Define the terms used when talking about the Web
- Create a Web application
- Add controls to a Web form
- Start a Web application
- Use the validator controls
- Include a list box on a Web form
- Determine whether a postback has occurred
- Include a DataGrid control on a Web form

Creating Web Applications Using ASP.NET

Web Terminology

The **Internet** is the world's largest computer network, connecting millions of computers located all around the world. One of the most popular features of the Internet is the **World Wide Web**, often referred to simply as **WWW** or the **Web**. The Web consists of documents called **Web pages** that are stored on Web servers. A **Web server** is a computer that contains special software that "serves up" Web pages in response to requests from clients. A **client** is a computer that requests information from a Web server. The information is requested and subsequently viewed through the use of a program called a **Web browser** or, more simply, a **browser**. Currently, the two most popular browsers are Microsoft Internet Explorer and Netscape Communicator. Figure 12-49 illustrates the relationship between a client, a browser, and a Web server.

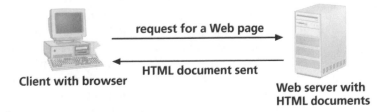

Client with browser → request for a Web page → **Web server with HTML documents**

← HTML document sent

Figure 12-49: Illustration of the relationship between a client, a browser, and a Web server

Many Web pages are static. A **static Web page** is a document whose purpose is merely to display information to the viewer. You can create a static Web page by opening a document in a text editor (such as Notepad) and then saving the document using a filename extension of .htm or .html. Within the document you enter the information you want displayed on the Web page. You then use **HTML (Hypertext Markup Language)** tags to tell the browser how to display the information. Figure 12-50 shows a static Web page created for the Greenview toy store. Displayed on the Web page shown in Figure 12-50 are the toy store's name, address, telephone number, and business hours.

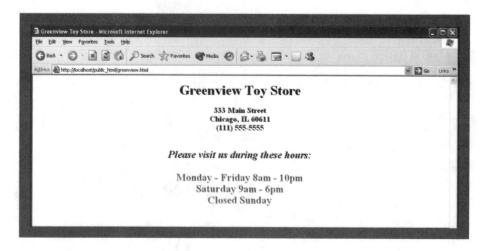

Figure 12-50: Example of a static Web page

Every Web page has a unique address that indicates its location on the Web. The address is called a **URL**—an acronym for **Uniform Resource Locator**. To view a Web page, you simply enter the page's URL in the appropriate box of a Web browser. As the Address box shown in Figure 12-50 indicates, the URL for the Greenview toy store's Web page is http://localhost/public_html/greenview.html.

A URL consists of four parts. The first part of the URL shown in Figure 12-50, http://, refers to the **HTTP communication protocol**, which is the protocol used to transmit Web pages on the Web. A **protocol** is simply an agreement between a sender and a receiver regarding how data are sent and interpreted. If you do not enter the communication protocol in a URL, Web browsers assume the HTTP protocol.

The second part of the URL is the name of the Web server where the document resides; the Web server is also referred to as the **host**. A Web server can be a remote computer, or you can make your local machine a Web server by installing and configuring Microsoft IIS (Internet Information Services). In the URL shown in Figure 12-50, the Web server's name is localhost and refers to your local machine.

The third part of the URL is the **path**, which specifies the location of the document on the Web server. The URL shown in Figure 12-50 indicates that the document is located in the public_html folder on the localhost server. It is important that the path you enter in the URL is exact; otherwise, the browser will not be able to locate the document. If you do not specify a path, the Web server assumes that the document is contained in a default location on the server. The network administrator defines the default location when the Web server is configured.

The last part of the URL specifies the name of the document—in this case, greenview.html. If you do not specify the name, most Web servers send a default home page to the Web browser.

When you type a URL in the Address box and then press the Enter key, the browser looks for the Web server specified in the URL. If the browser is able to locate the Web server, it submits your request. When the Web server receives a request for a static Web page, it locates the file, opens it, and then transfers its contents to the browser. The browser interprets the HTML instructions it receives and renders the Web page on the client's screen.

One drawback of static Web pages is that they are not interactive. The only interaction that can occur between a static Web page and the user is through links that allow the user to "jump" from one Web page to another.

To do business on the Web, a company must be able to do more than just list information on static Web pages. Rather, the company needs to be able to interact with customers through its Web site. The Web site should allow customers to submit inquiries, select items for purchase, provide shipping information, and submit payment information. It also should allow the company to track customer inquiries and process customer orders. Tasks such as this can be accomplished using dynamic Web pages.

Unlike a static Web page, a **dynamic Web page** is interactive; it can accept information from the user and also retrieve information for the user. If you have ever completed an online form—for example, to purchase merchandise or submit a resume—then you have used a dynamic Web page. Figure 12-51 shows an example of a dynamic Web page that converts American dollars to British pounds. To use the Web page, you enter the number of American dollars in the American dollars box and then click the Convert button. The button displays the corresponding number of British pounds on the Web page.

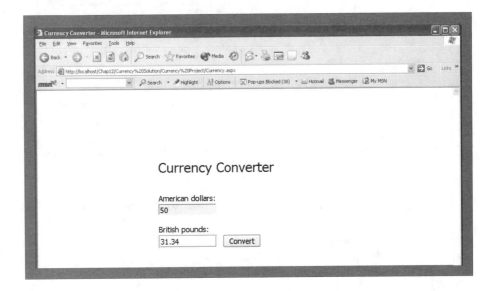

Figure 12-51: Example of a dynamic Web page

In the remainder of this lesson, you learn how to create Web applications that contain dynamic Web pages.

Creating Web Applications

You use a Web form, rather than a Windows form, to create a Web page in Visual Basic .NET. You create (or design) the Web page in the **Web Form Designer window**. (Recall that Windows forms are created in the Windows Form Designer window.) Figure 12-52 shows the procedure you follow to create a Web application.

Creating a Web application

1. Click File on the menu bar, point to New, and then click Blank Solution. The New Project dialog box opens with Visual Studio Solutions selected in the Project Types box, and Blank Solution selected in the Templates box.

2. Enter an appropriate name in the Name box.

3. In the Location box, enter the path to the folder that stores your Web applications. (See Figure 12-53.)

4. Click the OK button to close the New Project dialog box.

5. Click File on the menu bar, point to Add Project, and then click New Project. The Add New Project dialog box opens.

6. Verify that Visual Basic Projects is selected in the Project Types list box, then click ASP.NET Web Application in the Templates list box.

7. In the Location text box, enter the URL of the Web server and folder where you want to create your project, followed by the project name. (See Figure 12-54.)

8. Click the OK button to close the Add New Project dialog box. (See Figure 12-55.)

9. Assign a more meaningful name to the Web form file; however, be sure to keep the .aspx extension on the name.

10. Click the Design tab on the Web Form Designer window, then use the Properties window to assign a more meaningful value to the DOCUMENT object's title property. (See Figure 12-56.)

Figure 12-52: Procedure for creating a Web application

You will use the procedure shown in Figure 12-52 to create the Currency Converter application shown in Figure 12-51.

To create the Currency Converter application:

1   Start Visual Studio .NET, if necessary.

First, create a new, blank solution.

2   Click **File** on the menu bar, point to **New**, and then click **Blank Solution**. The New Project dialog box opens with Visual Studio Solutions selected in the Project Types box, and Blank Solution selected in the Templates box.

2   Type **Currency Solution** in the Name box.

4   In the Location box, type the path to the folder that stores your Web applications. In Figure 12-53, the path is C:\Inetpub\wwwroot\Chap12.

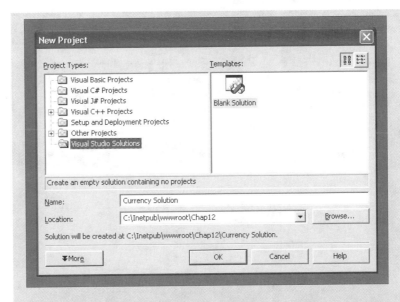

Figure 12-53: Completed New Project dialog box

5   Click the **OK** button to close the New Project dialog box.

Now add a Web project to the solution.

6   Click **File** on the menu bar, point to **Add Project**, and then click **New Project**. The Add New Project dialog box opens.

7   Verify that Visual Basic Projects is selected in the Project Types box, then click **ASP.NET Web Application** in the Templates box.

8   In the Location box, type the URL of the Web server and folder where you want to create your project, followed by the project name. In Figure 12-54, the URL and project name are http://localhost/Chap12/Currency Solution/ Currency Project.

**use this template
to create a Web
application**

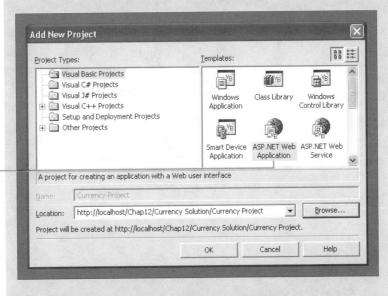

Figure 12-54: Completed Add New Project dialog box

9 Click the **OK** button to close the Add New Project dialog box. The Create New Web message box appears momentarily, and then a new Web application appears on the screen.

10 Permanently display the Solution Explorer and Properties windows, as shown in Figure 12-55. Notice that the default name for the Web form file in the application is WebForm1.aspx.

default name for the Web form file

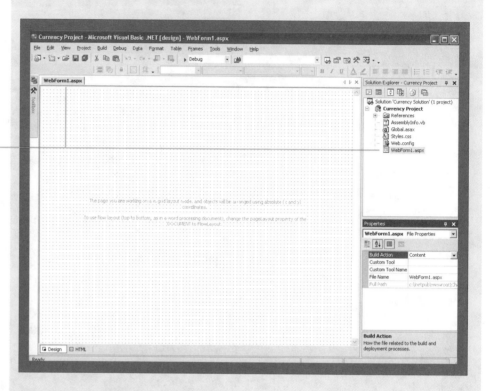

Figure 12-55: New Web application

Next, assign a more meaningful name to the Web form file.

11 Right-click **WebForm1.aspx** in the Solution Explorer window, and then click **Rename**. Type **Currency.aspx** and press **Enter**.

Now assign a more meaningful value to the title property of the DOCUMENT object, which is the Web form itself. When the Web form is displayed in a browser, the content of its title property appears in the browser's title bar.

12 Click the **Currency.aspx** * tab in the Web Form Designer window, then click **title** in the Properties list. Type **Currency Converter** and press **Enter**. Figure 12-56 shows the changes made to the form file's name and the DOCUMENT object's title property.

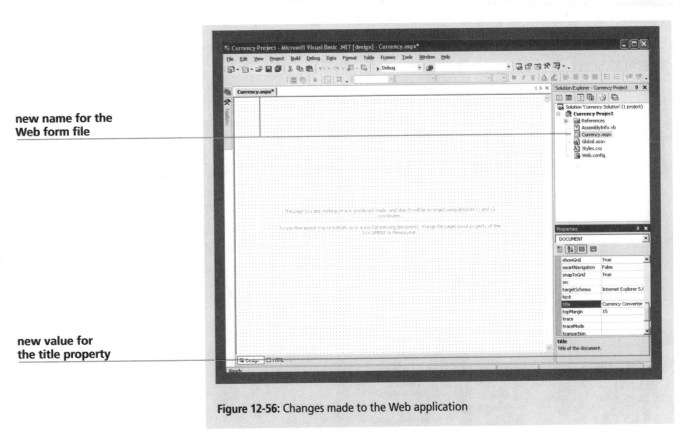

new name for the Web form file

new value for the title property

Figure 12-56: Changes made to the Web application

Next, you learn how to add controls to a Web form.

Adding Controls to a Web Form

Similar to the way you add controls to a Windows form, you use the tools contained in the Toolbox window to add controls to a Web form. However, the tools for a Web form are located on the Web Forms tab in the toolbox rather than on the Windows Forms tab. The Web Forms tab is shown in Figure 12-57. You can add a control to a Web form by simply dragging the corresponding tool from the Web Forms tab to the form.

Web Forms tab

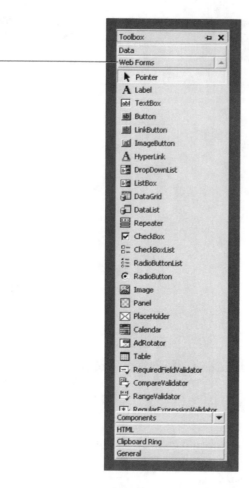

Figure 12-57: Web Forms tab in the toolbox

Notice that the Web Forms tab contains many of the same tools found on the Windows Forms tab—such as the Label, TextBox, and Button tools. You can use these tools to create label, text box, and button controls for your Web applications. Although Web controls operate in a manner similar to their Windows counterparts, they are not identical to the Windows controls. For example, Web controls have an ID property rather than a Name property.

In the next set of steps, you add the appropriate controls to the interface, and then set the values of some of their properties.

To add the appropriate controls, then set the values of some of their properties:

1   Use the Label tool to add four label controls to the Web form.

2   Use the TextBox tool to add a text box to the Web form.

3   Use the Button tool to add a button to the Web form.

4   Use the information shown in Figure 12-58 to set the properties of each control.

Object	Property	Setting
Label1	ID Font/Name Font/Size Text	uiIdAmericanLabel Tahoma Medium American dollars:
Label2	ID Font/Name Font/Size Text	uiIdBritLabel Tahoma Medium British pounds:
Label3	ID Font/Name Font/Size Text	uiHeadingLabel Tahoma X-Large Currency Converter
Label4	ID BorderStyle Font/Name Font/Size Height Text Width	uiBritishLabel Groove Tahoma Medium 30px (empty) 138px
TextBox1	ID BackColor BorderStyle Font/Name Font/Size Height Text Width	uiAmericanTextBox Beige (on the Web tab) Inset Tahoma Medium 26px (empty) 137px
Button1	ID Font/Name Font/Size Height Text	uiConvertButton Tahoma Medium 30px Convert

Figure 12-58: Property settings for the controls in the Currency Converter application

5   Position the controls as shown in Figure 12-59.

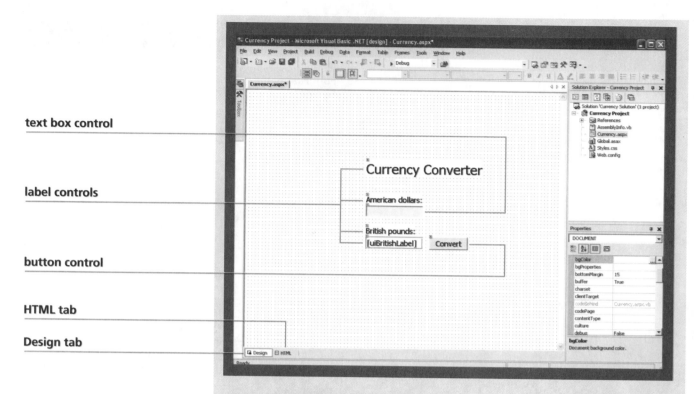

text box control

label controls

button control

HTML tab

Design tab

Figure 12-59: Controls positioned in the interface

Notice that two tabs—labeled Design and HTML—appear at the bottom of the Web Form Designer window. The Design tab shows the controls included on the Web page. The HTML tab, on the other hand, contains the HTML tags that tell the browser how to render the Web page.

6   Click the **HTML** tab. See Figure 12-60. (The font used to display the text in the Code Editor window shown in Figure 12-60 was changed to 10-point so that you could view more of the code in the figure. It is not necessary for you to change the font.)

indicates the location of the Visual Basic .NET code

this file contains the information shown on the Design and HTML tabs

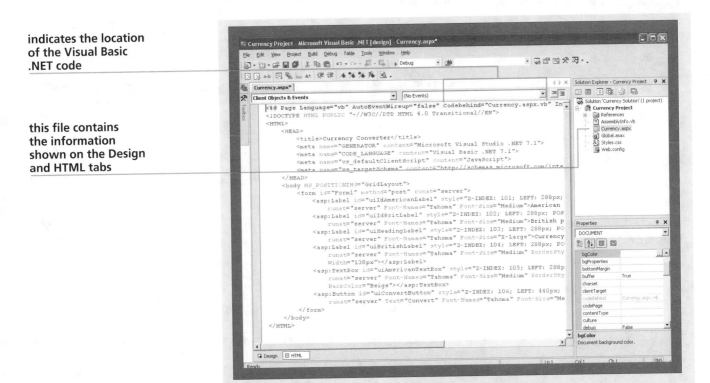

Figure 12-60: HTML tab for the Currency Converter Web page

Notice the `Codebehind="Currency.aspx.vb"` text that appears in the first line of code in Figure 12-60. Whereas a static Web page is simply an HTML file, a dynamic Web page usually requires two files: one of the files has an .aspx extension on its filename, while the other has an .aspx.vb extension. The .aspx file contains the controls and HTML that define the Web page's interface. In other words, it contains the information shown on the Design and HTML tabs on the Web Form Designer window. As indicated in Figure 12-60, the controls and HTML for the Currency Converter Web page are stored in a file named Currency.aspx. The .aspx.vb file, on the other hand, contains program code. The code tells the computer how to process the data submitted by or retrieved for the user, and is referred to as the "code behind the Web page." The `Codebehind="Currency.aspx.vb"` text indicates that the code behind the Currency Converter Web page is contained in a file named Currency.aspx.vb.

7   Click the **Design** tab.

8   Auto-hide the Solution Explorer and Properties windows.

9   Click **File** on the menu bar, and then click **Save All** to save the solution.

Now that the interface is complete, you can code the application.

To code the application:

1   Right-click the **Web form**, and then click **View Code** to open the Code Editor window.

2   Type the comments shown in Figure 12-61, replacing the `<enter your name here>` and `<enter the date here>` text with your name and

the current date. Also type the Option statements shown in the figure, and change the name of the class from WebForm1 to **CurrencyConverter**.

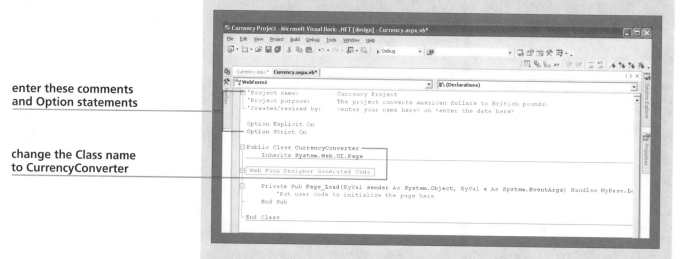

enter these comments and Option statements

change the Class name to CurrencyConverter

Figure 12-61: Code Editor window showing comments, Option statements, and new class name

3   Click the **Class Name** list arrow, and then click **uiConvertButton** in the list.

4   Click the **Method Name** list arrow, and then click **Click** in the list. The code template for the uiConvertButton's Click event procedure appears in the Code Editor window.

5   Type the code shown in Figure 12-62.

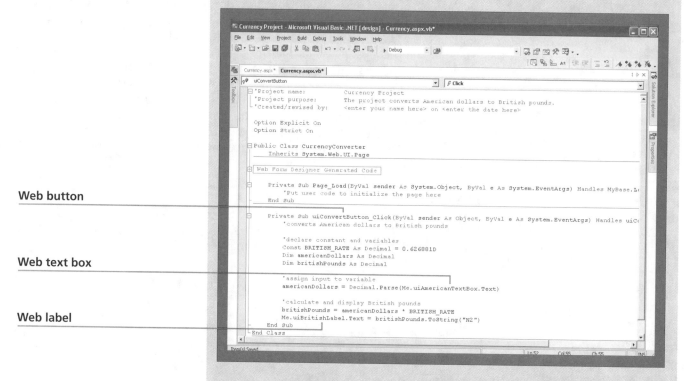

Web button

Web text box

Web label

Figure 12-62: Code for the Currency Converter Web application

tip

> If an application contains more than one Web form, the Web form designated as the start page appears in the browser window when the application is started. You designate the start page by right-clicking the name of the Web form file in the Solution Explorer window, and then clicking Set As Start Page. Recall that Web form files have an .aspx extension on their filenames.

use the Close button to close the Microsoft Internet Explorer browser window

tip

> To set the default browser, click File on the menu bar, and then click Browse With. Select the name of the browser in the Browser list, and then click the Set as Default button. Click the Close button to close the Browse With dialog box.

Now that you have finished coding the application, you can test the application to verify that the code is working correctly.

To test the application:

1   Save the solution.

You can display the Web form in your default browser or in the internal Web browser built into Visual Studio .NET. First you will display the Web form in your default browser.

2   Click **Debug** on the menu bar, and then click **Start** to display the Web form in your default browser.

3   Click the **American dollars** text box. Type 50 and then click the **Convert** button. The Convert button's Click event procedure calculates and displays the number of British pounds, as shown in Figure 12-63.

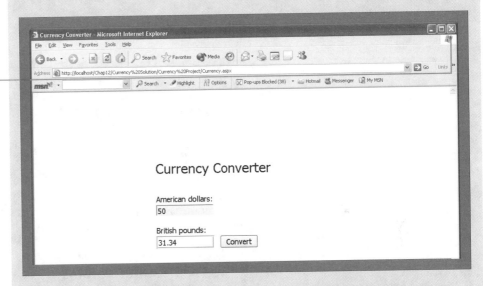

Figure 12-63: Currency Converter Web form displayed in Microsoft Internet Explorer

4   Close the Currency Converter application by clicking its **Close** button.

5   Close the Output window.

Now display the Web form in the internal Web browser built into Visual Studio .NET.

6   Click **File** on the menu bar, and then click **View in Browser** to display the Web form in the Visual Studio .NET internal Web browser.

7   Click the **American dollars** text box. Type 50 and then click the **Convert** button. The Convert button's Click event procedure calculates and displays the number of British pounds, as shown in Figure 12-64.

use this Close button to close the internal browser window

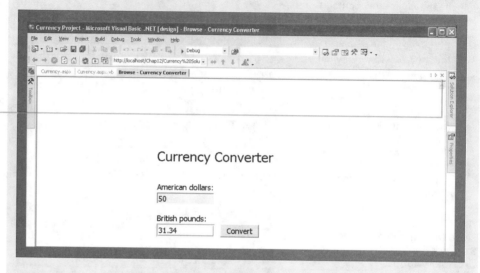

Figure 12-64:   Currency Converter Web form displayed in the internal browser built into Visual Studio .NET

8   Close the Browse - Currency Converter window by clicking its **Close** button.

9   Close the Code Editor window.

The Web Forms tab in the toolbox contains five tools that allow you to validate user input. These tools are referred to as the validator tools.

Using the Web Validator Tools

Figure 12-65 lists the names, uses, and several properties of the validator tools found on the Web Forms tab in the toolbox.

Name	Use to	Properties
RequiredFieldValidator	verify that a control contains data	ControlToValidate ErrorMessage
RangeValidator	verify that an entry is within the specified minimum and maximum values	ControlToValidate ErrorMessage MinimumValue MaximumValue Type
RegularExpressionValidator	verify that an entry matches a specific pattern	ControlToValidate ErrorMessage ValidationExpression
CompareValidator	compare an entry with a constant value or the property value stored in a control	ControlToValidate ControlToCompare ErrorMessage Type ValueToCompare
CustomValidator	verify that an entry passes the specified validation logic	ControlToValidate ErrorMessage ClientValidationFunction

Figure 12-65: The Web validator tools

In the next set of steps, you add a RequiredFieldValidator control and a RangeValidator control to the Currency Converter Web form. The RequiredFieldValidator control will verify that the uiAmericanTextBox control contains data. The RangeValidator control will determine whether the data is a number within the 1 through 100,000 range.

To add two validator controls to the Currency Converter Web form, then test the application:

1 Click the **RequiredFieldValidator** tool in the toolbox, then drag a RequiredFieldValidator control to the form. Position the control as shown in Figure 12-66.

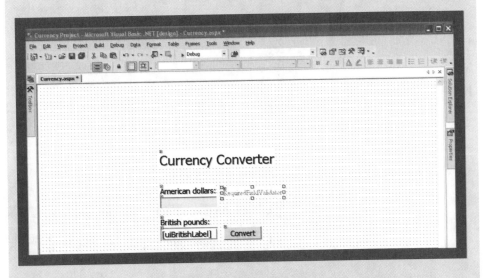

Figure 12-66: RequiredFieldValidator control added to the form

2 Set the following properties of the RequiredFieldValidator control. The "Please enter the number of American dollars." message will appear on the Web page only if the user clicks the Convert button before entering any data in the uiAmericanTextBox control.

ControlToValidate	**uiAmericanTextBox**
ErrorMessage	**Please enter the number of American dollars.**
Font/Name	**Tahoma**
Font/Size	**Small**

3 Click the **RangeValidator** tool in the toolbox, then drag a RangeValidator control to the form. Position the control immediately below the RequiredFieldValidator control.

4 Set the following properties of the RangeValidator control. The "Please enter a number from 1 through 100,000." message will appear on the Web page only if the user clicks the Convert button after entering (in the uiAmericanTextBox control) a value that is not within the 1 through 100,000 range.

ControlToValidate	**uiAmericanTextBox**
ErrorMessage	**Please enter a number from 1 through 100,000.**
Font/Name	**Tahoma**
Font/Size	**Small**
MaximumValue	**100000**
MinimumValue	**1**
Type	**Currency**

Figure 12-67 shows both validator controls in the interface.

RequiredFieldValidator control

RangeValidator control

Figure 12-67: Validator controls shown on the Currency Converter Web form

5   Save the solution.

6   Click **File** on the menu bar, and then click **View in Browser** to display the Web form in the Visual Studio .NET internal Web browser.

7   Click the **Convert** button. The "Please enter the number of American dollars." message appears in the RequiredFieldValidator control, as shown in Figure 12-68.

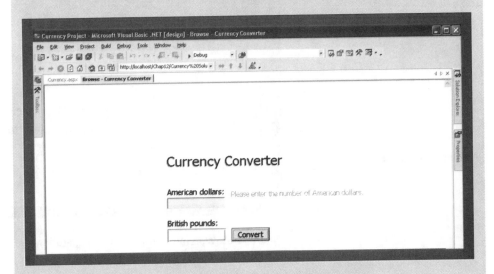

Figure 12-68: Message displayed in the RequiredFieldValidator control

8   Click the **American dollars** text box. Type 0 and then click the **Convert** button. The application removes the message from the RequiredFieldValidator control. However, the "Please enter a number from 1 through 100,000." message appears in the RangeValidator control.

9   Type **100** in the American dollars text box, then click the **Convert** button. The application removes the message from the RangeValidator control, and displays the number of British pounds (62.69) in the interface.

10 Close the Browse - Currency Converter window by clicking its **Close** button.

You are finished with the solution, so you can close it.

11 Click **File** on the menu bar, and then click **Close Solution**.

In applications where the user is expected to enter one or more specific values, it is better to use controls such as list boxes, radio buttons, or check boxes to display the values. Then, rather than typing the desired value in a text box, the user can select the appropriate value from one of these other controls. In the next section, you learn how to include a list box on a Web form.

Including a List Box on a Web Form

You use the ListBox tool on the Web Forms tab to add a list box to a Web form. As you can with a list box on a Windows form, you can use a list box on a Web form to display a list of choices from which the user can select one or more choices.

For this next example, assume that Stovall Pharmacies is located in five stores in southern Florida. The pharmacists have asked for an application that allows them to display the names of the manager and assistant manager at each of the stores. You will use a list box to display the store numbers, and label controls to display the names of the manager and assistant manager. Figure 12-69 shows the Web form for the Stovall application.

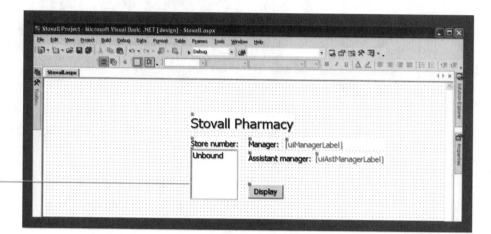

Web list box control

Figure 12-69: Web form for the Stovall application

The Stovall Web form contains six labels, one button, and one list box. The list box's ID property is set to uiNumberListBox, its Rows property to 5, and its Width property to 112px. Additionally, its Font/Name and Font/Size properties are set to Tahoma and Medium, respectively. Figure 12-70 shows the Stovall application's code.

the Page_Load procedure is processed only when the Web form is first displayed in the browser window

```
'Project name:          Stovall Project
'Project purpose:       The project displays the names of a store's manager
'                       and assistant manager.
'Created/revised by:    <enter your name here> on <enter the date here>

Option Explicit On
Option Strict On

Public Class Stovall
    Inherits System.Web.UI.Page

[Web Form Designer Generated Code]
    Private Sub Page_Load(ByVal sender As System.Object, _
        ByVal e As System.EventArgs) Handles MyBase.Load
        'Put user code to initialize the page here
        'fills the list box with data
        'then selects the first item

        If Not Me.IsPostBack Then
            Me.uiNumberListBox.Items.Add("1001")
            Me.uiNumberListBox.Items.Add("1002")
            Me.uiNumberListBox.Items.Add("1005")
            Me.uiNumberListBox.Items.Add("1007")
            Me.uiNumberListBox.Items.Add("1010")
            Me.uiNumberListBox.SelectedIndex = 0
        End If
    End Sub
```

Figure 12-70: Stovall application's code

```
Private Sub uiDisplayButton_Click(ByVal sender As Object, _
    ByVal e As System.EventArgs) Handles uiDisplayButton.Click
    'displays the names of the manager and assistant manager

    'declare variable
    Dim number As String

    'assign input to variable
    number = Me.uiNumberListBox.SelectedValue

    'display names
    Select Case number
        Case "1001"
            Me.uiManagerLabel.Text = "Jeffrey Jefferson"
            Me.uiAstManagerLabel.Text = "Paula Hendricks"
        Case "1002"
            Me.uiManagerLabel.Text = "Barbara Millerton"
            Me.uiAstManagerLabel.Text = "Sung Lee"
        Case "1005"
            Me.uiManagerLabel.Text = "Inez Baily"
            Me.uiAstManagerLabel.Text = "Homer Gomez"
        Case "1007"
            Me.uiManagerLabel.Text = "Lou Chan"
            Me.uiAstManagerLabel.Text = "Jake Johansen"
        Case "1010"
            Me.uiManagerLabel.Text = "Henry Abernathy"
            Me.uiAstManagerLabel.Text = "Ingrid Nadkarni"
    End Select
End Sub
End Class
```

Figure 12-70: Stovall application's code (continued)

The Page_Load procedure in the code fills the uiNumberListBox control with the five store numbers, and then selects the first store number in the list. The Page_Load event occurs the first time the Web form is displayed, as well as each time the user clicks the Display button. This is because those actions cause a postback to occur. A **postback** refers to the client requesting data from the server, and the server responding. Each time a postback occurs, the Web page is redisplayed on the client's screen. You can use the Web form's **IsPostBack property** to determine whether the Web form is being displayed for the first time or as a result of a postback. The property contains the Boolean value False the first time the form is displayed; otherwise, it contains the Boolean value True. The `If Not Me.IsPostBack Then` clause in the Page_Load procedure tells the computer to process the six instructions contained in the selection structure's True path only the first time the Web form is displayed, and to ignore the instructions when it is a postback.

When the user clicks a store number in the uiNumberListBox control and then clicks the Display button, the uiDisplayButton's Click event procedure displays the names of the store's manager and assistant manager in the uiManagerLabel and uiAstManager controls. Figure 12-71 shows a sample run of the Stovall application.

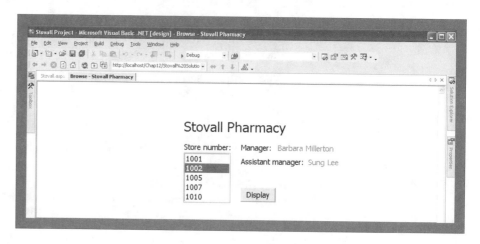

Figure 12-71: Sample run of the Stovall application

In Lesson A, you learned how to display information in a DataGrid control on a Windows form. You also can display information in a DataGrid control on a Web form.

Including a DataGrid Control on a Web Form

Recall that a DataGrid control displays the data from a dataset in a row and column format, similar to a spreadsheet. Each field in the dataset appears in a column in the DataGrid control, and each record appears in a row.

For this example, assume that Jack Benton, the Personnel Manager at Fairview Industries, has asked you to create a Web application that displays the names of the company's 12 employees, as well as their employee numbers, hourly pay rates, and status (either F for full-time or P for part-time). The employee information is stored in a Microsoft Access database named Employees.mdb. The Employees.mdb file is contained in the inetpub\wwwroot\Chap12\Databases folder. Figure 12-72 shows the Web form for the Fairview application.

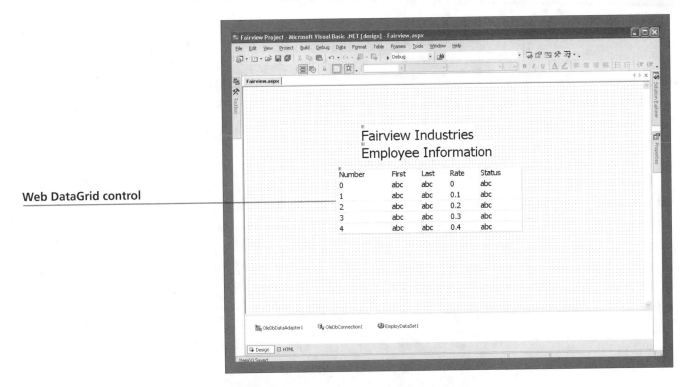

Web DataGrid control

Figure 12-72: Web form for the Fairview application

The Fairview Web form contains an OleDbDataAdapter object, an OleDbConnection object, and a DataSet object; you learned how to use these objects in Lesson A. The Web form also contains two labels and a DataGrid control. The DataGrid control's ID property is set to uiEmployDataGrid, its DataSource property to EmployDataSet, its DataMember property to tblEmploy, and its Width property to 440px. Additionally, its Font/Name and Font/Size properties are set to Tahoma and Medium, respectively. Figure 12-73 shows the Fairview application's code.

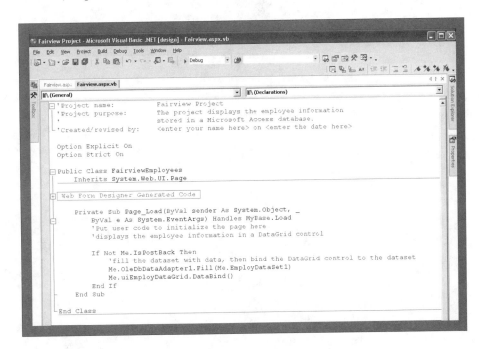

Figure 12-73: Fairview application's code

tip

The DataBind method is necessary to bind a Web DataGrid control to a dataset. However, it is not used when binding a Windows DataGrid control to a dataset.

In the Page_Load procedure, the two instructions in the selection structure's True path will be processed only once, which is when the Web form first appears in the browser. The first instruction fills the dataset with the employee data. The second instruction uses the DataGrid control's **DataBind method** to bind the control to the dataset.

Finally, you learn how to customize the appearance of the data displayed in a Web DataGrid control.

Customizing the Appearance of the Web DataGrid Control's Data

The DataGrid control provides many properties that you can use to control the appearance of its output. For example, the ShowHeader property allows you to specify whether the column headings should be shown or hidden. The BackColor property allows you to select the background color for the control. The DataGrid control also provides an Auto Format dialog box that allows you to select from a list of predefined formats, or schemes, for displaying data. You can open the dialog box by right-clicking the DataGrid control and then clicking Auto Format. Or, you can click the DataGrid control and then click the Auto Format link that appears below the Properties list in the Properties window. The Auto Format dialog box is shown in Figure 12-74.

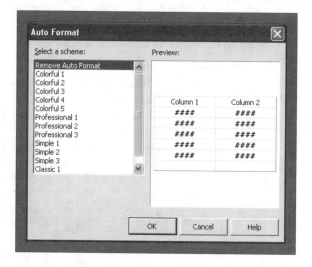

Figure 12-74: Auto Format dialog box

Figure 12-75 shows a sample run of the Fairview application with the DataGrid control formatted using the Professional 2 scheme.

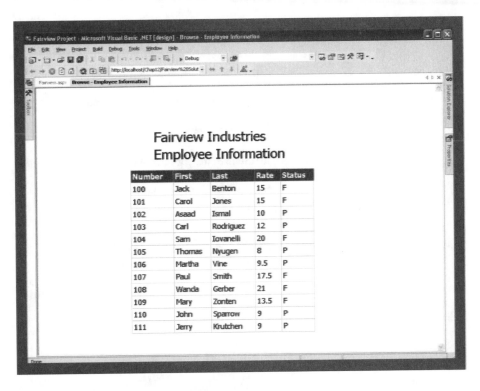

Figure 12-75: Sample run of the Fairview application

You now have completed Chapter 12. You can either take a break or complete the end-of lesson questions and exercises.

S U M M A R Y

To create a Web application:

🔲   Follow the procedure shown in Figure 12-52.

To add a control to a Web form:

🔲   Use the tools on the Web Forms tab in the toolbox.

To view a Web page in a browser:

🔲   Click File, then click View in Browser to display the Web page in the internal Web browser built into Visual Studio .NET.

🔲   Click Debug, then click Start to display the Web page in your default browser.

To validate user input on a Web page:

🔲   Use one or more Web validator tools, which are listed in Figure 12-65.

To determine whether a postback has occurred:

■ Use the Web form's IsPostBack property. The property contains the Boolean value False the first time the form is displayed; otherwise, it contains the Boolean value True.

To bind a Web DataGrid control to a dataset:

■ Use the DataBind method.

To customize the appearance of a Web DataGrid control:

■ Use the Auto Format dialog box.

QUESTIONS

1. Every Web page is identified by a unique address called _____.
    a. an AP
    b. an ASP
    c. a ULR
    d. a URL
    e. None of the above.

2. A computer that requests information from a Web server is called a client.
    a. True
    b. False

3. A _____ is a program that requests and then displays a Web page.
    a. browser
    b. client
    c. server
    d. requester
    e. None of the above.

4. An online form that you use to purchase a product is an example of a _____.
    a. dynamic Web page
    b. static Web page

5. When using ASP.NET to create a dynamic Web page, the _____ file contains the controls and HTML that define the interface.
    a. .asp
    b. .aspx
    c. .aspx.vb
    d. .vb
    e. None of the above.

6. When using ASP.NET to create a dynamic Web page, the _____ file contains the program code.
    a. .asp
    b. .aspx
    c. .aspx.vb
    d. .vb
    e. None of the above.

7. Which of the following Web validator controls allows you to verify that a text box contains data?
   a. DataValidator
   b. RangeValidator
   c. TextValidator
   d. ValidateControl
   e. None of the above.

8. Which of the following Web validator controls allows you to verify that the data entered in a text box is between 1 and 5?
   a. DataValidator
   b. RangeValidator
   c. TextValidator
   d. ValidateControl
   e. None of the above.

9. _____ occurs when a server responds to a request from a client.
   a. An AnswerBack
   b. A CallBack
   c. A ReturnBack
   d. A ServerResponse
   e. None of the above.

10. You use the DataBind method to bind Web DataGrid controls and Windows DataGrid controls to a dataset.
    a. True
    b. False

11. The first time a Web form is displayed in a browser, its _____ property contains the Boolean value False.
    a. IsBack
    b. IsBackPost
    c. IsPostBack
    d. PostBack
    e. None of the above.

12. The _____ event occurs each time a Web form is displayed in the browser window.
    a. Load_Page
    b. Page_Load
    c. Web_Page_Load
    d. Validate
    e. None of the above.

13. "URL" is an acronym for "Universal Resource Locator".
    a. True
    b. False

14. "ASP" is an acronym for "Active Server Pages".
    a. True
    b. False

15. "HTML" is an acronym for "Hypertext Markup Language".
    a. True
    b. False

16. _____ is the communication protocol used to transmit Web pages on the Web.
    a. ASP
    b. HTML
    c. HTTP
    d. URL
    e. None of the above.

17. You can use a _____ to display a list of choices from which the user can select one or more choices.
    a. DataGrid
    b. Data
    c. List
    d. ListBox
    e. None of the above.

18. A client computer is also referred to as a host.
    a. True
    b. False

19. You test a Web application using a browser.
    a. True
    b. False

20. A URL contains the communication protocol, the name of the Web server, the path to the Web page, and the name of the Web page.
    a. True
    b. False

EXERCISES

1. In this exercise, you modify the Currency Converter application you created in the lesson.
    a. Start Visual Studio .NET, if necessary. Open the Currency Solution (Currency Solution.sln) file, which is contained in the Inetpub\wwwroot\Chap12\Currency Solution folder.
    b. Modify the application so that it also displays the number of Canadian dollars and the number of Japanese yen. Use the following conversion rates:
    1 American dollar = 1.3874 Canadian dollar
    1 American dollar = 118.24 Japanese yen
    c. Save the solution, then start and test the application.
    d. Close your browser and the solution.

2. In this exercise, you create a Web application that allows the user to select a store number from a list box. The application then displays the names of the store's manager and assistant manager.
    a. Start Visual Studio .NET, if necessary. Use Figures 12-69 and 12-70 to create the Stovall Pharmacy application. Name the solution Stovall Solution. Name the project Stovall Project. Name the Web form file Stovall.aspx. Save the application in the Inetpub\wwwroot\Chap12 folder.
    b. Save the solution, then start and test the application.
    c. Close your browser and the solution.

3. In this exercise, you create a Web application that displays employee information stored in a Microsoft Access database named Employees.mdb. The database is contained in the Inetpub\wwwroot\Chap12\Databases folder.
    a. Start Visual Studio .NET, if necessary. Use Figures 12-72 and 12-73 to create the Fairview Industries application. Name the solution Fairview Solution. Name the project Fairview Project. Name the Web form file Fairview.aspx. Save the application in the Inetpub\wwwroot\Chap12 folder.
    b. Use the Auto Format dialog box to format the DataGrid control.
    c. Save the solution, then start and test the application.
    d. Close your browser and the solution.

4. In this exercise, you create a Web application that calculates and displays a bonus amount.
    a. Start Visual Studio .NET, if necessary. Create a Web application that allows the user to enter a sales amount and a bonus rate. The user must enter the sales amount, which should be from $1 through $100,000. Use a list box to display bonus rates of 2% through 10%. The application should calculate and display the bonus amount. Name the solution Bonus Solution. Name the project Bonus Project. Name the Web form file Bonus.aspx. Save the application in the Inetpub\wwwroot\Chap12 folder.
    b. Save the solution, then start and test the application.
    c. Close your browser and the solution.

5. In this exercise, you create a Web application that allows the user to enter a voter's political party, and also save the information to a sequential access file. The application also calculates and displays the number of voters in each political party.
    a. Start Visual Studio .NET, if necessary. Create a Web application that uses a list box for entering a voter's political party—Democrat, Republican, or Independent. The application should save the information to a sequential access file named pao.txt. It also should display the number of voters in each political party. Name the solution PAO Solution. Name the project PAO Project. Name the Web form file PAO.aspx. Save the application in the Inetpub\wwwroot\Chap12 folder. Save the pao.txt file in the Inetpub\wwwroot\Chap12\PAO Solution\PAO Project folder.
    b. Save the solution, then start and test the application.
    c. Close your browser and the solution.

6. In this exercise, you create a Web application that allows the user to convert a temperature from Fahrenheit to Celsius, and from Celsius to Fahrenheit.
    a. Start Visual Studio .NET, if necessary. Create an appropriate Web application. Name the solution Temperature Solution. Name the project Temperature Project. Name the Web form file Temperature.aspx. Save the application in the Inetpub\wwwroot\Chap12 folder.
    b. Save the solution, then start and test the application.
    c. Close your browser and the solution.

discovery ▶ 7. In this exercise, you create a Web application that allows the user to enter an item number and then display the item's name and price. The item numbers, names, and prices are stored in a Microsoft Access database named Items.mdb. The database is contained in the Inetpub\wwwroot\Chap12\Databases folder. Figure 12-76 shows the Items.mdb database opened in Microsoft Access. The database contains one table named tblItems. The Number and Name fields contain text, and the Price field contains numbers.

tblItems : Table		
Number	**Name**	**Price**
ABX12	Chair	$45.00
CSR14	Desk	$175.00
JTR23	Table	$65.00
NRE09	End Table	$46.00
OOE68	Bookcase	$300.00
PPR00	Coffee Table	$190.00
PRT45	Lamp	$30.00
REZ04	Love Seat	$700.00
THR98	Side Chair	$33.00
WKP10	Sofa	$873.00
		$0.00

Figure 12-76

a. Start Visual Studio .NET, if necessary. Create an appropriate Web application. Name the solution Item Solution. Name the project Item Project. Name the Web form file Item.aspx. Save the application in the Inetpub\wwwroot\Chap12 folder.

b. Save the solution, then start and test the application.

c. Close your browser and the solution.

Basic Tools Included in the Windows Form Designer Toolbox

Tool icon	Tool name	Purpose
	Pointer	allows you to move and size forms and controls
	Button	displays a standard button that the user can click to perform actions
	CheckBox	displays a box that indicates whether an option is selected or deselected
	CheckedListBox	displays a scrollable list of items, each accompanied by a check box
	ColorDialog	displays the standard Windows Color dialog box
	ComboBox	displays a drop-down list of items
	ContextMenu	implements a menu that appears when the user right-clicks an object
	CrystalReport Viewer	allows a Crystal Report to be viewed in an application
	DataGrid	displays data in a series of rows and columns
	DateTimePicker	allows the user to select a single item from a list of dates or times
	DomainUpDown	displays a list of text items that users can scroll through using the up and down arrow buttons

Tool icon	Tool name	Purpose
	ErrorProvider	displays error information to the user in a non-intrusive way
	FontDialog	displays the standard Windows Font dialog box
	GroupBox	provides a visual and functional container for controls; similar to the Panel control, but can display a caption but no scroll bars
	HelpProvider	associates an HTML Help file with a Windows application
	HScrollBar	displays a horizontal scroll bar
	ImageList	stores images
	Label	displays text that the user cannot edit
	LinkLabel	adds a Web style link to a Windows Forms application
	ListBox	displays a list from which a user can select one or more items
	ListView	displays items in one of four views (text only, text with small icons, text with large icons, or report view)
	MainMenu	displays a menu while an application is running
	MonthCalendar	displays an intuitive graphical interface for users to view and set date information
	NotifyIcon	displays an icon for a process that runs in the background and would not otherwise have a user interface
	NumericUpDown	displays a list of numerals through which users can scroll with up and down arrow buttons
	OpenFileDialog	displays the standard Windows Open File dialog box
	PageSetupDialog	displays the standard Windows Page Setup dialog box
	Panel	provides a visual and functional container for controls; similar to a GroupBox control, but can display scroll bars but no caption
	PictureBox	displays graphics in bitmap, GIF, JPEG, metafile, or icon format
	PrintDialog	displays the standard Windows Print dialog box
	PrintDocument	prints a document within a Windows application
	PrintPreview Control	allows you to create your own Print Preview dialog box
	PrintPreviewDialog	displays the standard Windows Print Preview dialog box
	ProgressBar	indicates the progress of an action by displaying an appropriate number of rectangles arranged in a horizontal bar

Tool icon	Tool name	Purpose
	RadioButton	displays a button that indicates whether an option is selected or deselected
	RichTextBox	allows users to enter, display, and manipulate text with formatting
	SaveFileDialog	displays the standard Windows Save As dialog box
	Splitter	allows the user to resize a docked control while an application is running
	StatusBar	displays status information related to the object that has the focus
	TabControl	displays multiple tabs
	TextBox	accepts and displays text that the user can edit
	Timer	performs actions at specified time intervals
	ToolBar	displays menus and bitmapped buttons that activate commands
	ToolTip	displays text when the user points at an object
	TrackBar	allows a user to navigate through a large amount of information, or to visually adjust a numeric setting
	TreeView	displays a hierarchy of nodes that can be expanded or collapsed
	VScrollBar	displays a vertical scroll bar

GUI Design Guidelines

Chapter 1 – Lesson C

■ Set the form's FormBorderStyle, ControlBox, MaximizeBox, MinimizeBox, and StartPosition properties appropriately:

■ A splash screen should not have a Minimize, Maximize, or Close button, and its borders should not be sizable.

■ A form that is not a splash screen should always have a Minimize button and a Close button, but you can choose to disable the Maximize button. Typically, the FormBorderStyle property is set to Sizable, but also can be set to FixedSingle.

Chapter 2 – Lesson A

■ The information in an interface should flow either vertically or horizontally, with the most important information always located in the upper-left corner of the screen.

■ You can use a text box control to give the user an area in which to enter data.

■ Related controls should be grouped together using white space, a group box control, or a panel control.

■ Buttons are typically positioned either in a row along the bottom of the screen, or stacked in either the upper-right or lower-right corner. Use no more than six buttons on a screen. The most commonly used button should be placed first.

■ Button captions should be meaningful. They should be from one to three words and appear on one line. Additionally, they should be entered using book title capitalization.

■ Labels that identify text boxes should be left-aligned and positioned either above or to the left of the text box.

■ The text in an identifying label should be from one to three words and appear on one line. It should be left-justified, end with a colon (:), and be entered using sentence capitalization.

■ You should align the borders of controls wherever possible to minimize the number of different margins used in the interface.

Chapter 2 – Lesson B

■ When positioning the controls on a form, you should maintain a consistent margin from the edge of the form; two or three dots are recommended.

■ Related controls typically are placed on succeeding dots. Controls that are not part of any logical grouping may be positioned from two to four dots away from other controls.

■ When buttons are positioned horizontally on the screen, all the buttons should be the same height; their widths, however, may vary if necessary. When buttons are stacked vertically on the screen, all the buttons should be the same height and the same width.

■ Try to create a user interface that no one notices.

■ Include a graphic only if it is necessary to do so. If the graphic is used solely for aesthetics, use a small graphic and place it in a location that will not distract the user.

■ Use only one font for all of the text in the interface. Use a sans serif font— preferably the Tahoma font. If the Tahoma font is not available, use either Microsoft Sans Serif or Arial.

■ Use 8-, 9-, 10-, 11-, or 12-point fonts for the text in an interface.

■ Limit the number of font sizes used to either one or two.

■ Avoid using italics and underlining, because both make text difficult to read.

■ Limit the use of bold text to titles, headings, and key items that you want to emphasize.

■ Build the interface using black, white, and gray first, then add color only if you have a good reason to do so.

■ Use white, off-white, or light gray for an application's background, and black for the text.

■ Never use a dark color for the background or a light color for the text. A dark background is hard on the eyes, and light-colored text can appear blurry.

■ Limit the number of colors in an interface to three, not including white, black, and gray. The colors you choose should complement each other.

■ Never use color as the only means of identification for an element in the user interface.

■ Leave the BorderStyle property of text boxes at the default value, Fixed3D.

■ Leave the BorderStyle property of labels that identify other controls at the default value, None.

■ Set to FixedSingle the BorderStyle property of labels that display program output, such as those that display the result of a calculation.

■ In Windows applications, a control that contains data that the user is not allowed to edit does not usually appear three-dimensional. Therefore, you should avoid setting a label control's BorderStyle property to Fixed3D.

■ Lock the controls in place on the form.

- Assign a unique access key to each control (in the interface) that can receive user input (for example, text boxes, buttons, and so on).
- When assigning an access key to a control, use the first letter of the caption or identifying label, unless another letter provides a more meaningful association. If you can't use the first letter and no other letter provides a more meaningful association, then use a distinctive consonant. Lastly, use a vowel or a number.
- Assign a TabIndex value (begin with 0) to each control in the interface, except for controls that do not have a TabIndex property. The TabIndex values should reflect the order in which the user will want to access the controls.
- To give users keyboard access to text boxes, assign an access key to the text box control's identifying label. Set the TabIndex property of the label control so that its value is one number less than the value in the TabIndex property of the corresponding text box. (In other words, the TabIndex value of the text box should be one number greater than the TabIndex value of its identifying label control.)

Chapter 3 – Lesson B

- In the InputBox function, use sentence capitalization for the *prompt*, and book title capitalization for the *title*.
- You can use a form's AcceptButton property to designate an optional default button. The default button should be the button that is most often selected by the user, except in cases where the tasks performed by the button are both destructive and irreversible. The default button typically is the first button.

Chapter 4 – Lesson B

- In a group box control, use sentence capitalization for the optional identifying label, which is entered in the control's Text property.
- When using the MessageBox.Show method to display a message box:
  - Use sentence capitalization for the *text* argument, but book title capitalization for the *caption* argument. The name of the application typically appears in the *caption* argument.
  - Avoid using the words "error," "warning," or "mistake" in the message, as these words imply that the user has done something wrong.
  - Display the Warning Message icon ⚠ in a message box that alerts the user that he or she must make a decision before the application can continue. You can phrase the message as a question.
  - Display the Information Message icon ⓘ in a message box that displays an informational message along with an OK button only.
  - Display the Stop Message icon ⊗ when you want to alert the user of a serious problem that must be corrected before the application can continue.
  - The default button in the dialog box should be the one that represents the user's most likely action, as long as that action is not destructive.

Chapter 5 – Lesson B

- Use radio buttons when you want to limit the user to one of two or more related and mutually exclusive choices.
- The minimum number of radio buttons in a group is two, and the recommended maximum is seven.
- The label in the radio button's Text property should be entered using sentence capitalization.

- Assign a unique access key to each radio button in an interface.
- Use a group box control (or a panel control) to create separate groups of radio buttons. Only one button in each group can be selected at any one time.
- Designate a default radio button in each group of radio buttons.
- Use check boxes when you want to allow the user to select any number of choices from a group of one or more independent and nonexclusive choices.
- The label in the check box's Text property should be entered using sentence capitalization.
- Assign a unique access key to each check box in an interface.

Chapter 6 – Lesson C

- It is customary in Windows applications to highlight (select) the existing text in a text box when the text box receives the focus.

Chapter 7 – Lesson B

- A list box should contain a minimum of three selections.
- A list box should display a minimum of three selections and a maximum of eight selections at a time.
- Use a label control to provide keyboard access to a list box. Set the label control's TabIndex property to a value that is one number less than the list box's TabIndex value.
- List box items are either arranged by use, with the most used entries appearing first in the list, or sorted in ascending order.
- If a list box allows the user to make only one selection at a time, then a default item should be selected in the list box when the interface first appears. The default item should be either the most used selection or the first selection in the list. However, if a list box allows more than one selection at a time, you do not select a default item.

Chapter 8 – Lesson B

- Menu title captions, which appear on the menu bar, should be one word, with the first letter capitalized. Each menu title should have a unique access key.
- Menu item captions, which appear on a menu, can be from one to three words. Use book title capitalization and assign a unique access key to each menu item. Assign shortcut keys to commonly used menu items.
- If a menu item requires additional information from the user, place an ellipsis (...) at the end of the item's caption, which is entered in the item's Text property.
- Follow the Windows standards for the placement of menu titles and items.
- Use a separator bar to separate groups of related menu items.

Creating Reports Using Crystal Reports

Creating a Crystal Report

Assume that Mike Warren, the owner of Warren Sporting Goods, uses a Microsoft Access database to store each salesperson's name and annual sales amount. The database contains one table, which is named tblSales. It also contains two fields: Name and Sales. Figure C-1 shows the tblSales table opened in Microsoft Access.

tblSales : Table	
Name	**Sales**
Carol Abdul	$14,300.00
Hilda Johnson	$4,675.00
Inez Williams	$14,250.00
Jake Hendrick	$35,000.00
John Materson	$13,400.00
Kate Baland	$40,000.00
Ned Iber	$25,000.00
Opal Smith	$23,000.00
Paula Smith	$40,000.00
Phil Jones	$36,000.00
	$0.00

Figure C-1: tblSales table opened in Microsoft Access

Mike would like a report that lists each salesperson's name and sales amount. You can create the report using the Crystal Reports designer, which is built into Visual Studio .NET. However, before you can create the report, you need to open the Warren Sporting Goods application.

To open the Warren Sporting Goods application:

1 If necessary, start Visual Studio .NET.

2 Open the Warren Solution (Warren Solution.sln) file, which is contained in the VBNET\AppC\Warren Solution folder. The user interface is shown in Figure C-2.

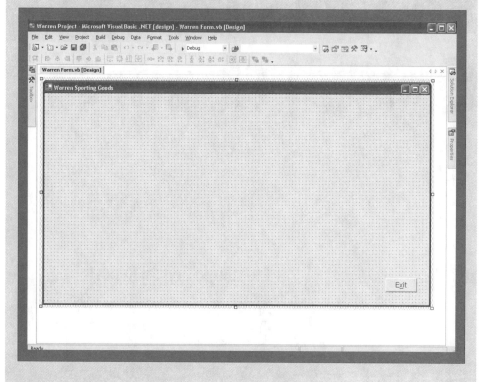

Figure C-2: Interface for the Warren Sporting Goods application

In the next set of steps, you learn how to open the Crystal Reports designer and create a report.

To open the Crystal Reports designer and create a report:

1 Click **File** on the menu bar, and then click **Add New Item**. The Add New Item – Warren Project dialog box opens.

2 The Local Project Items folder should be selected in the Categories box. Scroll the Templates box until you see Crystal Report, then click **Crystal Report**.

3 Type **SalesReport.rpt** in the Name box. (Be sure to include the .rpt extension on the filename. The .rpt stands for "report".) See Figure C-3.

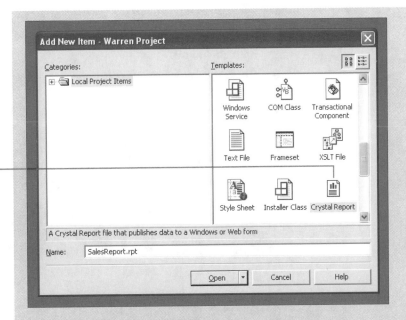

Figure C-3: Completed Add New Item – Warren Project dialog box

select Crystal Report in the Templates list

4 Click the **Open** button to close the dialog box. The Crystal Report Gallery dialog box opens. Notice that the Using the Report Expert radio button is selected, and so is the Standard entry. See Figure C-4.

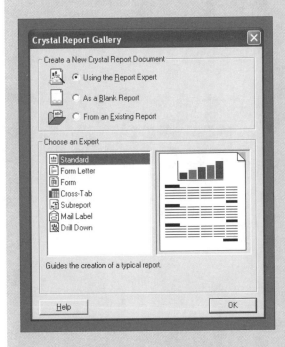

Figure C-4: Crystal Report Gallery dialog box

HELP? If the Crystal Decisions Registration Wizard dialog box opens, click the Register Later button.

5 Click the **OK** button to use the Report Expert to create a Standard report. The Standard Report Expert dialog box opens and displays the information on the Data tab.

6 Click the **plus box** next to the Database Files folder. The Open dialog box opens.

7 Open the VBNET\AppC\Warren Solution\Warren Project folder, then click **Sales.mdb** in the list of filenames.

8 Click the **Open** button to close the Open dialog box. The Data tab on the Standard Report Expert dialog box appears.

9 Click **tblSales** in the Available data sources list, and then click the **Insert Table** button. See Figure C-5.

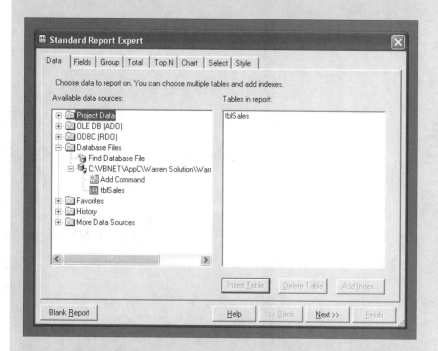

Figure C-5: Completed Data tab

10 Click the **Fields** tab, and then click the **Add All ->** button to display the Name and Sales fields in the report. See Figure C-6.

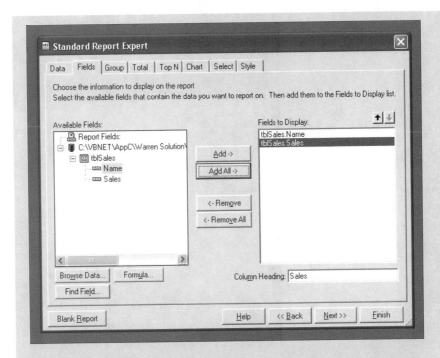

Figure C-6: Completed Fields tab

You can use the remaining tabs on the Standard Report Expert dialog box to create sophisticated, presentation-quality reports. In this case, however, the Warren application requires only a simple report.

11 Click the **Style** tab. Standard should be selected in the Style box. Type **Sales Report** in the Title box. See Figure C-7.

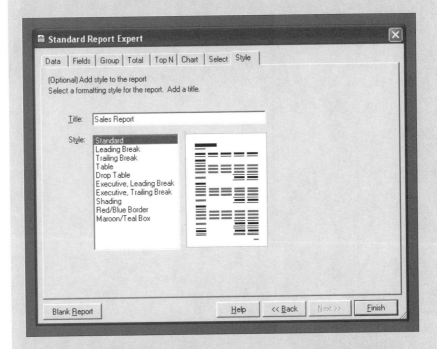

Figure C-7: Completed Style tab

12 Click the **Finish** button. The Crystal Reports designer appears in the IDE. Temporarily display the Solution Explorer window. See Figure C-8.

PrintDate element

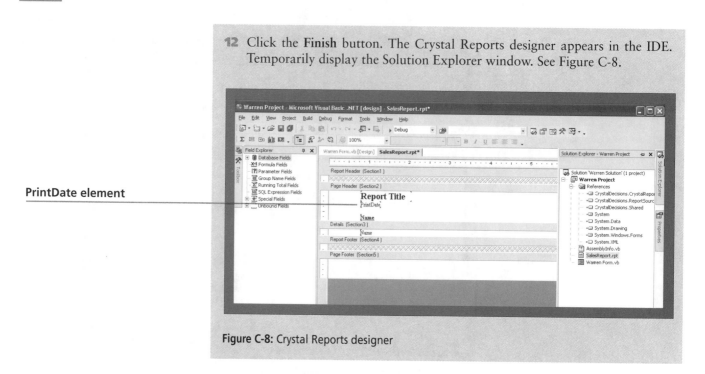

Figure C-8: Crystal Reports designer

The Crystal Reports designer contains five sections: Report Header, Page Header, Details, Report Footer, and Page Footer. You can add, edit, or delete information from these sections. For example, in the next set of steps, you format the PrintDate element in the Page Header section so that it displays the month number, followed by a slash and the day number.

To format the PrintDate element:

1 Right-click **PrintDate** in the Page Header section, then click **Format.** The Format Editor dialog box opens and displays the Date tab.

2 Click **3/1** in the Style list. See Figure C-9.

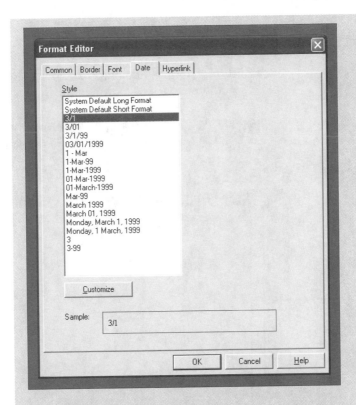

Figure C-9: Completed Date tab

3 Click the **OK** button to close the Format Editor dialog box.

4 Click **File** on the menu bar, and then click **Save All** to save the solution.

5 Close the Crystal Reports designer by clicking its **Close** button.

You use the CrystalReportViewer tool to view a Crystal Report while a Visual Basic .NET application is running. Usually, the CrystalReportViewer tool is the last tool on the Windows Forms tab in the toolbox.

To add a CrystalReportViewer tool to the current form:

1 Drag the **CrystalReportViewer** tool to the form. When you release the mouse button, a CrystalReportViewer control appears on the form.

Now set the CrystalReportViewer control's ReportSource property to the name of the Crystal Report—in this case, SalesReport.rpt.

2 Click **ReportSource** in the Properties window. Click the **list arrow** in the Settings box, and then click **Browse** in the list. The Open an Existing Crystal Report dialog box opens.

3 Open the VBNET\AppC\Warren Solution\Warren Project folder, then click **SalesReport.rpt** in the list of filenames.

4 Click the **Open** button to close the Open an Existing Crystal Report dialog box.

Now set the CrystalReportViewer control's DisplayGroupTree, Location, and Size properties.

5 Set the **DisplayGroupTree** property to **False**.

6   Set the **Location** property to **24, 24**.

7   Set the **Size** property to **872, 392**.

8   Click the **form's title bar** to select the form. Figure C-10 shows the CrystalReportViewer control in the form.

CrystalReportViewer control

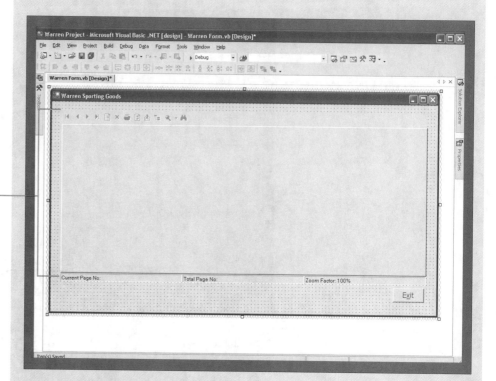

Figure C-10: CrystalReportViewer control shown in the form

Next, save the solution and then start and test the application.

To save the solution, and then start and test the application:

1   Click **File** on the menu bar, and then click **Save All**.

2   Click **Debug** on the menu bar, and then click **Start**. The Sales Report appears on the form, as shown in Figure C-11. (The date in your report may be different from the one shown in the figure.)

Print button

Figure C-11: Sales Report displayed on the form

You can use the Print button that appears on the CrystalReportViewer control to print the report.

3   If your computer is connected to a printer, click the **Print** button.

4   Click the **Exit** button to end the application.

5   Close the solution, then exit Visual Studio .NET.

Index

Symbols

& (ampersand), 105, 179
' (apostrophe), 122
* (asterisk), 30, 31, 305–307, 476, 683
\ (backslash), 29
: (colon), 92
, (comma), 132, 540, 541
{} (curly braces), 152, 366, 571
. (decimal point), 230–233
$ (dollar sign), 125, 132, 525
" (double quotes), 154, 183
... (ellipsis), 32, 47, 493
= (equal sign), 118, 153
! (exclamation point), 307
> (greater-than sign), 364
- (hyphen), 306
< (less-than sign), 364
() (parentheses), 57, 124, 129, 325, 330
% (percent sign), 125, 131
. (period), 156, 186, 267
| (pipe symbol), 366
+ (plus sign), 128, 179
# (pound sign), 305–307, 540–542
? (question mark), 305–307
[] (square brackets), 118, 161, 306

A

abstraction, 4–5
AcceptButton property, 188
Access (Microsoft), 673, 675–681
access keys
    assigning, 104–106
    described, 83
    menu titles and, 490
    Order screen and, 83, 104–106, 110
    rules for, 110

accumulators, 371–375
Add method, 427, 428
ADD mnemonic, 2
Add New Project dialog box, 19
Add Project command, 18
addition (+) operator, 124, 125, 227
ADO (Microsoft ActiveX Data Objects), 674–675
ADO.NET (Microsoft), 671–742
age variable, 180, 415
algorithms, 291–296
Align command, 48, 98, 103
Alphabetic button, 20, 26, 28
And operator, 224–230
AndAlso operator, 224–230, 233, 293
APIE (Abstraction, Polymorphism, Inheritance, and Encapsulation) acronym, 5
apostrophe ('), 122
Appearance and Themes category (Control Panel), 105
AppendText method, 521, 532
application(s). *See also* projects; *specific applications*
    creating, 13–39, 84–85
    ending, 50–53
    planning, 84–96
    previewing, 146–147
    starting, 50–53
    tasks, identifying, 85–97
    use of the term, 13
Area application, 642–644
argumentlist, 411–412
arithmetic operators, 124–125, 217–218, 227
ArithmeticException, 272
array(s)
    described, 567–630
    displaying the contents of, 573–574

highest value stored in, determining, 579–580
manipulating, 373–384
module-level, 584–586
one-dimensional, 469–586, 595–612
parallel, 595–612
populating, 606
searching, 576, 616–618
sorting data in, 581–584
storing data in, 571–572, 615–616
structures and, 597–607
two-dimensional, 613–730
updating values in, 580–581
Array.Reverse method, 584
Array.Sort method, 581–582
As keyword, 644
ASCII (American Standard Code for Information Interchange), 234, 306, 428
ASP.NET (Microsoft), 671–742
assemblers, 2
assembly languages, 2–3
AssemblyInfo.vb, 24
Assign Grade button, 387–389
assignment operator, 154
assignment statements, 55, 118, 122, 181, 184–188
    described, 153–158
    Math Practice application and, 345
    Monthly Payment Calculator application and, 250
asterisk (*), 30, 31, 305–307, 476, 683
At Startup list box, 14
attributes. *See also* properties
    described, 4
    exposed, 4
    hidden, 4
Auto Hide button, 19, 20–21, 25
AutoSize property, 44–45, 55